WHAT ARE
THE SEVEN WONDERS
OF THE WORLD?

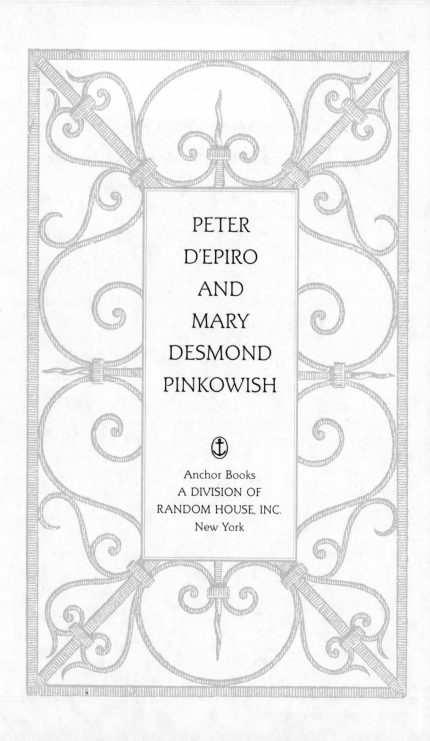

PETER
D'EPIRO
AND
MARY
DESMOND
PINKOWISH

Anchor Books
A DIVISION OF
RANDOM HOUSE, INC.
New York

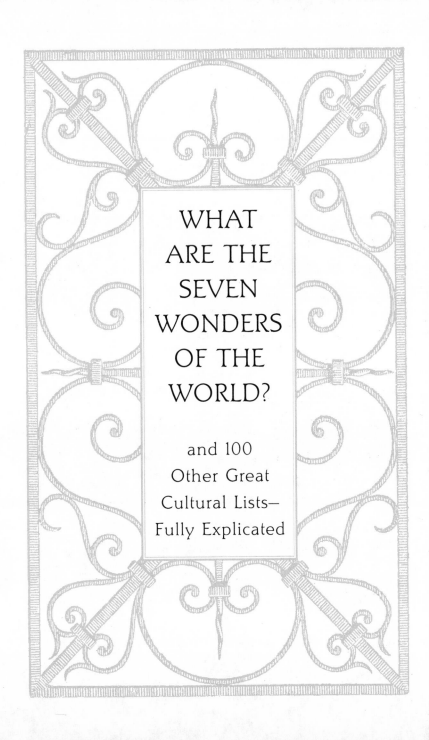

WHAT ARE THE SEVEN WONDERS OF THE WORLD?

and 100 Other Great Cultural Lists— Fully Explicated

First Anchor Books Edition, December 1998

Illustrated by Joel and Sharon Harris, Articulate Graphics, St. Louis, Missouri.

Library of Congress Cataloging-in-Publication Data
D'Epiro, Peter.
What are the seven wonders of the world? and 100 other great cultural lists—fully explicated /
Peter D'Epiro and Mary Desmond Pinkowish. — 1st Anchor Books ed.
p.   cm.
Includes bibliographical references and index.
1. Curiosities and wonders.   2. Questions and answers.
I. Pinkowish, Mary Desmond.   II. Title.
AG243.D55   1998
031—dc21   98-23377
CIP

ISBN 0-385-49062-3

Book design by Ellen Cipriano

www.anchorbooks.com

Printed in the United States of America
14   13   12

*To study with the white wings of time passing
is not that our delight?*

—Ezra Pound,
The Pisan Cantos

CONTENTS

SEVEN

EIGHT

For our fathers

ANTHONY D'EPIRO
and

JOHN F. DESMOND

How many loved your moments of glad grace.

—William Butler Yeats

 QUESTION 00

Which 17 people would the authors like to thank for their gracious help?

Dante D'Epiro, who wrote the essays for Questions 22, 37, and 47
Nancy Walsh D'Epiro, who contributed the essays for 31, 39, 43, 48, and 85; made cogent criticisms throughout; and coped with it all
Edward W. Desmond, who wrote the essays for 50, 58, and 92
Joan Frawley Desmond, who collaborated with us on the essays for 7, 52, and 69
Tom Matrullo, *bos amic,* who wrote the essays for 51 and 62, and subjected a goodly number of others to his learned scrutiny
William A. Walsh, Ph.D., the author of essay 28.

The commentators on large chunks of manuscript: **Vladimir Babadzhan, Ph.D., Vivian Dudro, Richard Jackson, Ph.D., George Johnson-Orban, Bobby Kuruvilla,** and **Morgan Ryan.**

Michael Pinkowish, who provided his mother with invaluable late-night commentary on essays 33 and 80 (although he should have been in bed); and **Peter Pinkowish,** for red sauce, black coffee, and lots of patience.

Our agent, **Raphael Sagalyn,** who believed in us from the start, and **Neil Howe,** who introduced us to Rafe.

And our editor, **Tina Pohlman,** who was always in our corner.

PREFACE

A flock of sheep that leisurely pass by,
One after one. . . .
I have thought of all by turns and yet do lie
Sleepless!

> —William Wordsworth,
> "To Sleep. II, A Flock of Sheep"

Wordsworth . . . was a silly old sheep.
> —Ezra Pound

If Wordsworth could have read this book, he would have counted other things besides sheep. His mind would have been so well stocked with great cultural lists that he could at least have amused and edified himself by recalling the Seven Wonders of the Ancient World (Question 51) or the names and associated arts of the Nine Muses (Question 75), even if he didn't sleep a wink all night. The next day he could have had some fun using these lists to quiz Coleridge and his other Lake District pals.

What Are the Seven Wonders of the World? presents a fund of information that even people who aren't famed poets will enjoy becoming acquainted with, or meeting again after a long estrangement. The book contains 101 of the most culturally significant lists that we could devise over several pensive years—our own personal omnium gatherum of high culture as embodied in various canonical listings and numeric groupings.

Each question with its accompanying list is followed by an essay that identifies all the items of the answer and places the list in its larger historical or cultural context. Many readers will heartily disagree with our inclusions and omissions, but our guiding principle has been to choose materials we considered to be fundamental components of educated Western awareness. We have excluded pop culture, sports, and celebrity trivia, since information in these areas is not lacking elsewhere and only somewhat enhances our ability to lead a more satisfying intellectual life.

While focusing on Western culture, we've included some non-Western items that have entered educated Western consciousness. Because we wanted to include only lists that could plausibly be memorized, we reluctantly excluded Luther's ninety-five theses, the catalogue of Popes, and the nine hundred theological and philosophical propositions that twenty-three-year-old Pico della Mirandola offered to defend in debate against all comers in 1486. Maybe next time.

The attribution of mystical and sacred properties to numbers and numbered lists has a long history. In early Christianity, the numbers three, seven, ten, and twelve were especially venerated because of their association with the Persons of the Trinity, days of Creation, Commandments, and Apostles, respectively (Questions 7, 52, 82, and 91). In Jewish tradition, *gematria* was the numerologic interpretation of words and phrases in Scripture. And in the ancient Greek world, the Pythagoreans claimed that the entire cosmos was made of numbers. They practically worshiped the *tetractys*, a triangle envisioned with one point at its apex, two beneath it, three beneath those, and four at the base, which embraced unity, duality, the mystical number three, and four, the number of justice and of the elements (Question 20)—all adding up to ten, the perfect and sacred number.

Though neither of us is a practicing Pythagorean, we thought it would be fun and instructive to compose a challenging question-and-answer book organized around numbered lists that have become "standard" (the 12 Tribes of Israel, the 12 Labors of Heracles) or that otherwise convey significant cultural data via numeric groupings. Whether you read, browse, test yourself, or quiz your family and friends, we hope you enjoy this attempt to convey some of the Western world's age-old fascination with hierarchies and discernments, which is still apparent in all our Top 10s, Top 40s, and Fortune 500s—not to mention the spate of Top 100 Film lists, Novel lists, and so on.

Peter D'Epiro
Mary Desmond Pinkowish

WHAT ARE
THE SEVEN WONDERS
OF THE WORLD?

✢ QUESTION 1

Who were the 3 sons of Adam and Eve?

> Cain
> Abel
> Seth

Sure, you got Cain and Abel, but what about Seth? If not, consider the fact that the Bible strongly implies that Seth, and not his more illustrious siblings, was the ancestor of us all.

Let's start with **Cain** and **Abel**. In the book of Genesis, Cain is a tiller of the soil whose offering of the fruits of the earth is deemed unacceptable by God. His brother Abel, a keeper of flocks, makes an offering of one of his best firstlings, on which God looks favorably. In a pique of jealousy, Cain lures his brother into a field and kills him. When God asks him the whereabouts of Abel, Cain counters with his famous rhetorical question: "Am I my brother's keeper?"

Since Cain has desecrated the soil with Abel's blood, which cries out to God for vengeance, the ground will no longer bear fruit for him. When God condemns him to a nomadic existence, Cain fears that his wandering life will make him an easy target for xenophobes: "Anyone may kill me at sight." God thus puts a mark on Cain— probably a tattoo—to warn off any potential assailants. And so Cain goes off and settles to the east of Eden in the land of Nod, which merely means "the land of the nomads" but has given rise to countless jokes about boring sermons and their somnolent effect on church-goers.

Note that "the mark of Cain" was not originally meant to brand him as a murderer, as in our usage, but to *protect* him from other murderers. Yet several questions suggest themselves. If the only people in the world at this time are Adam, Eve, and Cain, whom is Cain so afraid of? And when he becomes the father of Enoch (not the better-known Enoch who was the father of Methuselah and was taken up alive into heaven)—where had Cain found a wife? She must have been one of the unnamed daughters of Adam and Eve who, along with other unnamed sons, are mentioned in Genesis 5:4. But what was she doing in the land of Nod? In any event, among Cain's descendants we meet the world's first bigamist, Lamech; the first musician, Jubal; and the first metalworker, Tubalcain.

Why does God reject Cain's offering? There must be something missing in our biblical text: Cain must have sacrificed in a way that was alien to the ancient Hebrews. Later assertions in the New Testament try to posit a reason: "By faith Abel offered unto God a more excellent sacrifice than Cain" (Hebrews 11:4). In 1 John 3:12 we read that Cain killed Abel "because his own works were evil, and his brother's righteous." Or was it simply a case of God's "election" of Abel—that is, an instance of Calvinist predestination, which assumes that God chooses certain individuals for salvation and condemns others to damnation only because it is his own inscrutable will?

But what about **Seth** (or Sheth)? Adam sires him, at the age of 130, to take the place of Abel. And although Abel was later viewed as a foreshadowing (or "type") of Christ (because both were good shepherds whose blood was shed unjustly), the genealogy of Christ is nonetheless traced back to Adam and God through *Seth* (Luke 3:38). Presumably Abel is killed before he has a chance to propagate—the Bible mentions no descendants—and to trace Christ's descent through the fratricidal Cain (or one of his anonymous brothers) would have been inconceivable. In fact, in one of the authorial strands in Genesis, that of the so-called priestly tradition, Seth is considered the firstborn of Adam and Eve, and Adam's line is followed forward to Noah and the Flood (and presumably to all of us) through Seth (Genesis 5).

It's ironic that, unlike Cain the brother-slayer or Abel the original victim of violent crime, Seth remains a colorless figure, a man without a story, almost a nonentity. His name seems to mean "granted," because God granted him to Adam and Eve after Abel's death—and we tend to take him a bit for granted, too. Like all the patriarchs, Seth was blessed with great genes: He had a son Enosh (or Enos) at age 105 and lived a total of 912 years (just 18 fewer than Adam). That's it, though. We don't even know what line of work old Seth was in. It's probably enough to have the entire human race trace its descent through him.

✢ QUESTION 2

Who are the 3 gods of the Hindu Trinity (the Trimurti)?

Brahma
Vishnu
Shiva

The three gods of the Trimurti (Sanskrit, "three forms") are really more of a chief triad of Hindu deities (in a pantheon of about thirty million) than a Trinity in the Christian sense (see Question 7). They embody the supreme, impersonal, eternal, universal Spirit or World-Soul, Brahman, in its threefold aspect as creator, preserver, and destroyer.

But the creator god **Brahma** must not be confused with Brahman (the absolute World-Spirit mentioned above) or with Brahmans (or Brahmins), the members of the highest Hindu caste. Born from the lotus in Vishnu's navel, Brahma is often portrayed as a four-faced god sitting on a lotus flower. With his own hand, on leaves of gold, he is said to have written the *Rig-Veda,* a collection of 1,028 ancient Sanskrit hymns to the gods.

Worship of Brahma petered out because once his main job of creating the universe was done, the ball was in Vishnu's and Shiva's court. Or perhaps we should say the egg, since some Hindu writings speculate that Brahma laid and hatched the egg of the universe. Hindu tradition also asserts that a day in the life of Brahma lasts one *kalpa,* or 4,320,000,000 years. After each "day of Brahma," all that exists is destroyed, only to be reborn in the eternal cycle of death and creation.

Vishnu, the preserver god, has had nine major avatars (incarnations), and the tenth and last will be Kalki, the rider on a white horse who, sword blazing in hand, will put an end to all sin and sinners. Among Vishnu's avatars were his seventh, as Ramachandra or Rama, his eighth as Krishna, and his ninth as Buddha (see Question 26).

Rama is the hero of the Sanskrit epic, the *Ramayana,* in which the young protagonist regains his kingdom and his bride in a mere fifty thousand lines of verse. Later, when a tyrannical demon-king was wreaking havoc in India, Krishna descended to earth after Vishnu plucked a black hair from himself—which became Krishna ("black"), who's often represented in art as black or dark blue. Krishna appears as a mighty warrior in the other great Sanskrit epic, the *Mahabharata,* which, at more than two hundred thousand lines, is the undisputed heavyweight champion of the poetic world.

Vishnu is probably the most popular Hindu god, willingly incarnating himself to save the world and mankind from various giants, demons, tyrants, and other calamities. "When order, justice, and mortals are in danger," said Vishnu, "I come down to earth." Many Hindus worship him as the supreme deity. Early in this century, Indian Christians feared that Christ would also be assimilated into the figure of Vishnu by being considered just one more of his avatars. Vishnu is a god of love through and through, and his greatest avatar, Krishna, is often shown playing a flute to attract the *gopis* (milkmaids he has seduced) to dance with him in the moonlight.

The destroyer god **Shiva** is a composite figure. His fierceness is counterbalanced by kinder, gentler qualities that make him a favorite deity of ascetics and a patron of arts, letters, music, and dancing. His most famous representations show him as a white, four-armed figure performing his cosmic dance on the body of a nasty little demon whose back he has broken. The dance of Shiva symbolizes the eternal alternation of destruction and creation in the universe since, in Hindu thought, destruction always implies a subsequent restoration.

This idea is responsible for another major aspect of Shiva: his lordship over the powers of fertility and reproduction. As such, his symbol is the lingam, or phallus (as his consort's emblem is the yoni, or vulva). Shiva's phallus is said to be so enormous that even with Brahma traveling up as far as he could and Vishnu journeying down as far as *he* could, neither of them managed to discover where that epic phallus began or ended. Shiva is certainly a god of contradictions: He drinks a narcotic potion made of hemp (and some of his statues show him with "stoned" eyes), but he also practices yoga. He protects cattle, but he's also the source of the fire that destroys the universe at the appointed end of its eons. And he has an evil third eye in his forehead that he usually keeps closed because, when he doesn't, it acts much like a flamethrower.

Unlike Vishnu, Shiva is more esteemed for his consorts than for his avatars. His principal consort Kali ("The Black One") is a bloodthirsty goddess indeed. Our word *thugs* originally referred to her worshipers in northern India who ritually strangled human victims to propitiate her. Kali is usually portrayed as a naked black woman with four arms, a protruding tongue dripping blood, fanglike teeth, and red eyes. She wears earrings of corpses and a necklace of skulls and is girdled with snakes. Her face and breasts are smeared with blood. Yet Kali is the goddess of motherhood, too.

The Trimurti, represented in art as a male figure with three heads, is still at least theoretically a feature of contemporary Hinduism, although the worship of the second and third deities of the triad, along with their avatars and consorts, has left the cult of Brahma out in the cold.

⚜ QUESTION 3

What are Kepler's 3 Laws of Planetary Motion?

1. Each planet in the solar system has an elliptical orbit, with the sun at one of the two foci of the ellipse.
2. A line from the center of the sun to the center of a planet sweeps across equal areas in equal amounts of time. This means that the closer a planet is to the sun, the faster it travels.
3. The cube of every planet's mean distance from the sun equals the square of the time it takes to revolve around the sun.

German astronomer Johannes Kepler (1571–1630) was the man who dared to put the ellipse in the solar system, and some consider him, rather than Copernicus, Galileo, or Newton, the father of modern astronomy. Copernicus, a Polish priest, had elaborated a heliocentric (sun-centered) theory of the universe in *On the Revolutions of the Heavenly Spheres* in 1543. But it was Kepler who concluded that planetary orbits around the sun must be elliptical, shattering the hoary belief that orbits were round—and therefore perfect (as befitting God's handiwork).

Kepler derived his laws from the meticulous planetary observations of his mentor, the Danish astronomer Tycho Brahe (1546–1601), a brilliant but mercurial gentleman who lost part of his nose in a duel and made himself a gold-and-silver prosthesis. In Brahe's rather cumbersome picture of the universe, the unmoving earth, at the center of it all, was orbited by the sun, around which all the other planets revolved. Like Copernicus, however, Kepler found he had to abandon any model that retained earth at the center of the universe.

Kepler became a mathematician, and later an astronomer, because he couldn't afford a career as a theologian. At one point he cast horoscopes to support himself. It's not surprising that he brought a strong streak of mysticism to his astronomical studies, which he was sure would, in his words, celebrate God more fully. In this vein, he drew analogies between various heavenly bodies and the Persons of the Trinity (see Question 7). And his momentous realization that **planetary orbits are elliptical,** enshrined in his first law of planetary motion, saddened him because ellipses were only the poor cousins of theologically respectable circles (see the figure).

Kepler's second law, positing that **the velocity of a planet is greater when closer to the sun in its orbit, and less when farther away,** is also illustrated in the figure. His third law means that **if you know a planet's distance from the sun (D), you can calculate how long it takes to go around the sun (its period, or P)—and vice versa.** For these purposes, D is usually expressed in astronomical units and P in years. (One astronomical unit is 92.9 million miles, or the approximate distance between the center of the earth and the center of the sun.) Here is an example of Kepler's third law, or $D^3 = P^2$:

✦ Mercury is 36 million miles from the sun, or 0.388 astronomical units. If we cube 0.388, we get 0.058. Speedy Mercury takes just 88 days to journey around the sun, so its period of revolution is 0.241 years. If we square 0.241, we get 0.058 again. Not bad for a man who never laid hands on a telescope.

Does this work even for planets that Kepler had never heard of? Here are the same calculations for Uranus, first discovered in 1781, more than 150 years after Kepler's death:

Kepler's First Two Laws

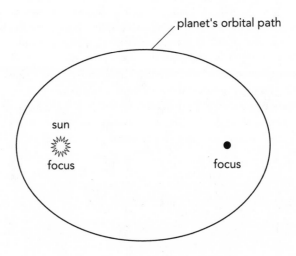

planet's orbital path

sun

focus

focus

The sun is at one of the ellipse's two foci.

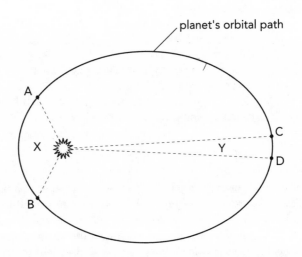

planet's orbital path

A

X

Y

C

D

B

If it takes as long for a planet to move between A and B
as it does between C and D, then the area X is equal to the area Y.
Also, the planet is moving faster when it travels
between A and B than between C and D.

✦ Uranus is 1,784 million miles, or 19.2 astronomical units, from the sun. The cube of 19.2 is 7,078. It takes Uranus a long human lifetime—a little more than 84 years—to revolve around the sun, and the square of 84.01 is 7,058. Awfully close.

At a time when the ancient geocentric view of the universe still largely prevailed—with the earth ensconced at the center of things—Kepler defended Copernicus's radical heliocentric model. He also said his aim was "to show that the celestial machine is to be likened not to a divine organism but rather to a clockwork." A half century later, Sir Isaac Newton (1642–1727) built on Kepler's laws of planetary motion to develop his law of universal gravitation (see Question 17).

✣ QUESTION 4

Who are the 3 daughters of King Lear?

    Goneril
    Regan
    Cordelia

FOOL: . . . I can tell why a snail has a house.
LEAR: Why?
FOOL: Why, to put 's head in, not to give it away to his
      daughters and leave his horns without a case.
                —Shakespeare, *King Lear*
                  (1.5.28–32)

William Shakespeare wrote his tragic masterpiece *King Lear* in about 1605, but the story that begins with a bad daughters/good daughter fairy-tale motif and ends in horror was first recorded in England in the twelfth century by Geoffrey of Monmouth in his unhistorical *History of the Kings of Britain*. It also appeared in various guises in the second edition of Raphael Holinshed's *Chronicles of England, Scotlande, and Irelande* (1587) and Edmund Spenser's *The Faerie Queen* (1590).

Shakespeare's major source, however, was an anonymous play called *The True Chronicle History of King Leir,* written about 1590 and published in 1605.

Shakespeare's version of the familiar tale is darker than those he encountered in his sources. In choosing a story set in pagan Celtic times, as many as eight centuries before the birth of Christ, he avoided the thematic limitations that a Christian framework might have imposed. He was thus able to probe more deeply and freely the cosmic questions on Providence, Nature, and the meaning (or meaninglessness) of life that so intrigued him.

At the beginning of Shakespeare's play, we meet a vain, self-righteous octogenarian, King Lear, who has decided to divide his kingdom among his three daughters. The portion each receives will be commensurate with the love she expresses for him in a public display of affection. Lear expects each to fawn over him and vie with the others in making the most toadying speech.

The elder sisters don't disappoint. Goneril professes to love her father more than "eyesight, space, and liberty." Regan claims her sister's sentiments are but a pale shadow of her own and that she abjures all joys except that of basking in her father's love. In reward for their fulsome tributes, Lear bestows choice portions of his kingdom on his two worldly-wise daughters.

Cordelia, the youngest, dumbstruck by the simpering hypocrisy of her sisters, and despite her deep love for her foolish old father, can't bring herself to make a beau geste. To her father's request of what she can say to earn an even richer share, she replies, "Nothing, my lord," explaining that she loves him according to her "bond" (filial obligation). The enraged king disinherits and banishes his favorite child, dividing her portion between his other two daughters. The King of France, however, more perspicacious than Lear, takes the dowerless Cordelia as his wife: "She is herself a dowry," he recognizes.

As soon as Goneril and Regan have effective power in the kingdom, they turn on their father, mocking him and stripping him of his retinue of knights. Lear soon learns "How sharper than a serpent's tooth it is / To have a thankless child." The two sisters eventually turn him out of doors on a tempestuous night, in which Lear—now attaining the tragic stature of a Sophoclean Oedipus—braves the elements and sounds the raving depths of despair, regret, and madness in the company of the faithful Earl of Kent, his Fool, and an apparent lunatic (whom we know to be the disguised Edgar).

A parallel subplot, derived from Sir Philip Sidney's *Arcadia* (1590), involves the old Earl of Gloucester, who, like Lear, tragically misjudges his children, the bastard Edmund and his legitimate son Edgar. In an attempt to inherit the earldom despite his illegitimacy, Edmund devises a treacherous scheme to disgrace Edgar in their father's eyes.

Shakespeare links this subplot to the main plot when he makes Edmund join forces with Goneril and Regan to fight the invading French Army, which Cordelia has mobilized in her father's defense. Ambitious Edmund, seeing a way to the throne, hands over his father Gloucester to Regan's husband, who gouges out the old man's eyes in retaliation for his support of Lear. Edmund then defeats Cordelia's army, capturing her and Lear.

In the meantime, Goneril and Regan, both infatuated with Edmund, spar over his attentions. Goneril eventually poisons Regan and kills herself. Edmund orders Cordelia hanged. As he lies dying after being defeated in a duel by his valiant brother Edgar, he tries, too late, to countermand the order. In the play's final scene, a broken Lear enters carrying Cordelia's body. "Thou'lt come no more," he says to her. "Never, never, never, never, never." A moment afterward, the old man dies of his accumulated griefs.

Generations of scholars have debated which of Lear's elder daughters is the more evil. **Goneril** is certainly the stronger leader. Always clear-eyed (unlike her father), she understands that Lear loves Cordelia best and that his banishment of her is a sign of his deteriorating judgment. She suggests to Regan that they may have to deal harshly with him. When the old King goes to live with her, she gives her servant permission to treat him rudely. On her demand that Lear discharge half of his one hundred knights, Lear angrily departs in expectation of better treatment at Regan's hands. Although Goneril has been compared with Lady Macbeth, she is a less complex character, much too consistently hard-hearted ever to succumb to physical or emotional illness as a result of a guilty conscience.

When Lear flees to his second oldest, **Regan,** she greets him with "O, sir, you are old," and continues thus:

> . . . *You should be ruled, and led*
> *By some discretion that discerns your state*
> *Better than you yourself. Therefore I pray you*

That to our sister you do make return,
Say you have wronged her (2.4.147–51).

Regan is typically described as a pale version of her older sister, a woman easily led by both Goneril and her own husband, the monstrous Duke of Cornwall. Actually, she is quite as fierce as her sister, a pit bull with no shortage of evil designs of her own:

CORNWALL: The army of France is landed. *[To servants]* Seek out the traitor Gloucester.
REGAN: Hang him instantly.

When her husband, in one of the most horrific scenes ever staged, scoops out one of Gloucester's eyes (rather than hanging him), Regan urges him to take both: "One side will mock another. Th' other too." When an appalled servant tries to stop Cornwall, she kills him herself, but not before he mortally wounds her husband. Widowed, Regan now plans to make Edmund her husband.

This makes the still-wed Goneril so fiercely jealous that she claims she'd rather lose the battle against Cordelia and the French than lose Edmund to her sister. Already teeming with hate, Goneril becomes even more vicious when her husband, the Duke of Albany, expresses remorse over Lear's plight and his intention to make amends. "O Goneril!" he says. "You are not worth the dust which the rude wind / Blows in your face." Albany eventually discovers that scheming Goneril has written to Edmund, declaring her love and begging him to kill her husband. That's when this fine flower of womanhood decides to rid the world of her pestilential self.

The two wicked sisters are variously likened, mostly by Lear, to serpents, sea-monsters, wolves, vultures, foxes, dogs, lionesses, tigresses, degenerate bastards, unnatural hags, hogs, boils, plague-sores, and embossèd carbuncles (swollen tumors). Goneril is said to have a boar's fangs, and she is ultimately the more thoroughly depraved of the two. As the renowned Shakespearean critic A. C. Bradley noted, our disgusted reaction to Regan is somewhat mitigated because, unlike Goneril, she *didn't* commit adultery, plot to murder her husband, cosign the order for the death of Lear and Cordelia, or poison her sister.

But who is **Cordelia**? Is she a paragon of virtue whose refusal to stoop to glibness unleashes a tragic chain reaction? Is her murder in prison a Christ-like redemptive act linked to the achievement of greater wisdom and insight on the part of Lear, Edgar, Kent, Albany—and perhaps even Edmund? Or do the tragic life and death of this saintly woman express a nihilistic view of human existence?

Shakespeare probably intended Cordelia to symbolize untainted virtue. She is distant, even from the other decent characters. An unidentified gentleman describes her as one "who redeems nature from the general curse" (4.6.209). Her tears are "holy water from her heavenly eyes" (4.3.31).

In an aside, during the public flattery contest in the first scene of the play, Cordelia leaves no doubt of her own sincerity: "I am sure my love's / More ponderous than my tongue." When her turn comes, she declares plainly, "Unhappy that I am, I cannot heave / My heart into my mouth. I love your Majesty / According to my bond, no more nor less." The stunned Lear exhorts her, "Mend your speech a little, / Lest you may mar your fortunes." Cordelia responds to Lear's attempt to extort love (via an economic threat) with a reminder that she must save half her love for a future husband. She finds it odd that her sisters have husbands, yet have given all their love to their father. When Cordelia emphasizes her truthfulness, Lear's rejoinder is "Thy truth then be thy dower!," once again linking her deficient profession of love to financial loss. Is Cordelia just being stiff-necked? The King of France, who has witnessed the scene, doesn't think so. Interpreting her behavior as the mark of a sterling character, he takes the disinherited Cordelia as his wife.

Shakespeare's refusal to give his play a poetically just or melodramatic ending, with the innocent Cordelia surviving, was considered so unbearable that for about 150 years English audiences could see only a 1681 version of *King Lear* by Nahum Tate, who rewrote about half of the play. In this version, Lear, Cordelia, and Gloucester survive, and Cordelia marries Edgar. In 1823, the legendary British actor Edmund Kean finally restored Shakespeare's ending, and by the end of the 1830s the original version of the play was again the standard.

In Tate's happy-ending reworking, the play ends with Edgar's line, "Truth and Vertue shall at last succeed." The stern moralist and Shakespearean editor and critic Samuel Johnson (1709–84) preferred Tate's version because Cordelia "retired with victory and felicity." This is a far cry indeed from the prevailing tone of the play and from the sentiment Shakespeare put into blind old Gloucester's mouth: "As flies to wanton boys, are we to th' gods, / They kill us for their sport."

✦ QUESTION 5

What are the 3 stages of Hegel's dialectic?

> Thesis
> Antithesis
> Synthesis

The Greek Presocratic philosopher Heraclitus (c. 540–c. 480 B.C.) maintained that "all is flux" *(panta rhei),* that Becoming, rather than Being, is the law of the evolving cosmos. His dynamic idea that progress and movement occur through the strife of contradictory forces was the ultimate root of the dialectic (literally, the art of logical debate), as worked out by the German philosopher Georg Wilhelm Friedrich Hegel (1770–1831).

Hegel's monstrous, monumental, omnivorous system of philosophy, including his masterpiece, *The Phenomenology of Spirit* (1807), is strewn with triads. Only some of these triads are "dialectical" ones, that is, groups of three concepts related in the following way. The very existence of a **thesis,** A, calls into being its opposite or contradiction or **antithesis,** B (because if A can be conceived, so can the negation of A). These two forces clash, thus giving rise to a **synthesis,** C, which preserves the best of A and B while shedding much of their dreck in a reconciling process called sublation *(Aufhebung).* But this higher stage, C, now becomes the thesis A′ in a new series of three dialectical, sonata-form-like steps, and the resultant A″ initiates yet another advance in the inexorable progression of the *Geist* (the personified World Spirit or Soul, Absolute Mind, or Reason), which drives the whole dialectical process toward greater human freedom, rationality, and self-fulfillment, and toward the ever-increasing manifestation of the Mind of God in the world.

For Hegel, History has moved from the idea that One can be

free (in Oriental despotisms), to the idea that Some can be free (in aristocratic Greco-Roman civilization), to the idea that All can be free (in Christian or Germanic culture). Exceptional geniuses who embody the World Spirit can sometimes give the historical process a shove forward. When Hegel saw Napoleon riding through Jena in 1806, just before creaming the Prussians, the philosopher gushed to a friend, "I saw the Emperor—the *Weltgeist*—riding out to reconnoiter the city. It is a truly wonderful sensation to see such an individual, . . . sitting on a horse, yet reaching across the world and mastering it." For the *Geist* was a juggernaut, you see.

But after Napoleon's fall, the *Weltgeist* apparently passed from the French to the Germans. This meant that a German state (Prussia, perhaps) would now presumably be free—indeed, morally constrained—to achieve its *Geist*-enhancing aims by any means, including war, "which protects the people from the corruption that an everlasting peace would bring upon it." The highest form of government is constitutional monarchy, which is the synthesis of Despotism and its antithesis, Revolt against Despotism. We finally learn, in *The Philosophy of Right* (1821), our proper attitude toward the supreme earthly embodiment of Hegel's Absolute Idea: "We must therefore worship the State as the manifestation of the divine on earth." Since "what is real is rational, and what is rational is real," we must also apparently accept things as they are (or become, through the dialectic), because they could not be otherwise. *Ipse dixit.*

As Hegel supposedly said, "Only one man has understood me, and even *he* has not." In alluding to this sole semilucid personage, Hegel certainly was not thinking of the German crown prince of pessimism, Arthur Schopenhauer (1788–1860). Aside from theoretical differences between Hegel's absolute idealism and Schopenhauer's subjective idealism (which we won't get into), the latter thinker took much umbrage when, deliberately scheduling his philosophy lectures to coincide with those of Hegel at the University of Berlin in 1822, he ended up talking to the walls.

In his twelve-hundred-page masterpiece of gloom, *The World as Will and Representation (Die Welt als Wille und Vorstellung,* 1818, 1844, 1859), Schopenhauer calls Hegel "that intellectual Caliban," "ponderous and witless," "a repulsive and dull charlatan and an unparalleled scribbler of nonsense," "this repulsive philosophaster," "that coarse and clumsy charlatan," and, perhaps most damning of all, "a man with a common mind." Hegel's philosophic work is likened to the jabbering heard in madhouses and is predicted to remain "a lasting monument of German stupidity."

If Hegel is the thesis, and Schopenhauer his vitriolic antithesis, would the synthesis be Karl Marx? In his philosophy of dialectical materialism, Marx (1818–83) used Hegel's dialectic to parse out his own notions of a deterministic progression of history. Thus, bourgeois capitalism, in giving rise to an antithetical proletariat, would necessarily find a higher synthesis in communism.

Marx and his collaborator Friedrich Engels (1820–95) thought they had found Hegel standing on his head and proposed to set him right side up. Forget all that stuff about the ethereal *Geist:* Marx lived in a solidly material world, in which the economic relations of production were the driving forces of history. All the rest of society's clatter—religion, politics, laws, art, philosophy, morals—constituted a superstructure spawned by the economic base to justify and perpetuate the exploitation of the workers by the drones. History was mainly a series of violent revolutions and class wars that expropriated the expropriators—whether slaveholders in the ancient world, feudal lords, or bourgeois capitalists—and replaced them with the next set of exploiters, until the workers seize power and (after a regrettably unavoidable dictatorship of the proletariat) establish a classless, fulfilled, nonalienated, nonexploitative society in which everybody shares everything while enjoying socialist-realist art. The family, government, and religion will then wither away for lack of any further need to prop up the ideology of a decadent bourgeoisie.

Such hookah visions come of spending too much time doing research in the British Museum and none actually dealing with workers in mills, factories, mines, or other industrial worksites. Nonetheless, Marx's secular religion became, for countless millions, a substitute for the traditional variety, which he considered "the sigh of the oppressed creature, . . . the opium of the people."

✦ QUESTION 6

What are the 3 Laws of Thermodynamics?

1. In any process, energy can be changed from one form to another, but it is never created or destroyed.
2. All natural processes tend to proceed toward increased entropy (that is, greater disorder).
3. The change in entropy associated with any reversible process approaches zero as the temperature approaches absolute zero. (Or: All perfect crystals at absolute zero have the same—that is, zero—entropy.)

Thermodynamics examines the complex interrelationships among heat, work, and energy. If at least *some* people didn't understand thermodynamics, we'd be without air-conditioning, refrigerators, furnaces, chemical or petroleum manufacturing, steam power plants, and gas turbines.

Mass and energy are considered equivalent. Think of mass as an inherent property that does not depend on an object's surroundings or the forces acting on it. The more mass an object has, the more inertia. A chunk of granite four feet in diameter has more mass than a four-foot helium balloon, and it certainly exhibits more inertia. Mass is not to be confused with weight, however. Weight is a function of gravity and thus varies accordingly. But mass is independent of such variables, so the four-foot granite block would weigh considerably more than it does on earth wherever gravity is stronger, such as on Jupiter, but it has the same mass wherever it is.

The more mass an object has, the more energy it has, too. Energy is the ability to do work, and work is force applied over a given distance. All objects contain two kinds of energy: potential and kinetic. Consider a pair of acrobats: One of these fearless souls is standing on the end of a seesaw, and the other is perched on a platform high above the floor, ready to jump on the "up" end of the seesaw. This second fellow's potential energy, the work he's capable of, is equal to the product of his mass, his height above the floor, and the acceleration of gravity. When he jumps, his potential energy will be converted to kinetic energy, and the guy on the other end of the seesaw, if he doesn't chicken out, will be propelled somewhere high and far away, like onto the shoulders of yet another intrepid acrobat.

The first law of thermodynamics is usually referred to as the law of conservation of energy (or mass-energy, since the two are equivalent). Energy cannot be created or destroyed, but it can be changed into other forms. In an isolated system, the sum of the energy changes must total zero. Consider the acrobat: In theory, no energy is lost in the performance. Most is transferred to the human catapulter, but some is also absorbed, painfully, by the jumper's legs and lower back, as well as the floor and the seesaw. The jumper's total energy is equal to the sum of his potential and kinetic energy, which is all there somewhere.

The first law of thermodynamics was formulated by several nineteenth-century scientists, including Julius Mayer, James Joule, Rudolf Clausius, and Hermann von Helmholtz. Mayer and Joule came to the same conclusion almost simultaneously by different routes: Heat and work are different manifestations of energy. In Joule's 1847 experiment, the work performed by falling weights that turned paddles in a tank of water was shown to heat the water by friction. Furthermore, Joule demonstrated that the temperature of the water increased as a function of how far the weights dropped. The potential energy lost by the weights as they dropped was transformed into the increased heat of the water.

Some energy is always lost in these transactions, however. The outside of a refrigerator, for example, is a bit warm to the touch. The heat you feel is wasted; a thermodynamically perfect refrigerator would expend all of its energy on cooling its interior. Furthermore, a machine cannot produce more energy than it uses, which means that a perpetual-motion machine will never exist. The heat generated by any form of friction is also wasted energy.

But is it possible to build another kind of perpetual-motion machine, not one that produces more energy than it uses, but one that powers itself by recycling its output to run the engine? For example, could a steam engine be designed so that the steam was converted back into heat, again fueling the engine? For that to happen, the cold water produced when the steam condenses would have to be able to reheat the boiler, thus producing more steam to power the engine.

As first enunciated by Lord Kelvin in 1851 (based in part on work by Sadi Carnot in 1824), the rather disconcerting **second law of thermodynamics** rules out that possibility. This law states that all physical events in a closed system progress toward greater disorder, or entropy. The classic example of the second law is the observation that heat (energy) always flows from a high-temperature substance or body to a low-temperature one. Ice floating in a gin and tonic melts. The drink doesn't freeze, at least not in the average bar. And cold water won't heat a boiler. Sure, liquids can be frozen or heated, but work must be done in each system. Ice cubes are created when energy (work) is used to lower the temperature of the freezer to the point at which water hardens. Coal is burned to heat the boiler in the steam engine.

According to the second law, these processes in closed systems are irreversible—that is, the heat lost by a steam engine during its operation cannot be recaptured. It's wasted, and the entropy of the system has increased. A perpetual-motion machine that can refuel itself will never be built. In fact, the second law suggests that the future can be defined as the direction of time in which entropy increases. It thus predicts the gradual winding down of the universe, like a top slowly flopping to a standstill or a clock unwinding. In the nastiest-case scenario, everything in the universe will eventually be transformed into wasted heat energy within a few hundred billion years. This assumes, though, that the laws of thermodynamics apply everywhere in the universe.

The third law of thermodynamics, as formulated by German theoretical physicist Max Planck in 1911 (based on earlier work by Walter H. Nernst), states that the entropy of a pure, crystalline element or compound is zero at a temperature of absolute zero. This is the coldest theoretical temperature, −273.15°C. or −459.67°F., and as a substance approaches it, all molecular jangling and buzzing slow to a near-standstill.

The third law has a wide application in chemistry and makes it possible to determine the entropy of specific compounds. Chemists have used it to construct tables that list these data at a standard temperature, for example, 25°C. With this information, and knowledge of other parameters such as pressure, it's possible to calculate whether or not a given chemical reaction will occur.

 QUESTION 7

Who are the 3 Persons of the Christian Trinity?

The Father
The Son (Jesus Christ)
The Holy Spirit

At the core of Christian belief is the mystery of the Holy Trinity. In this conception, God is viewed as three distinct, coequal, coeternal Persons—the Father, the Son, and the Holy Spirit (or Holy Ghost). Although the orthodox view of the Trinity was encapsulated in Thomas Aquinas's dictum, "The whole perfection of the Divine nature is in each of the Persons," the difficulty of expounding the doctrine of the Trinity has taxed some of the sharpest minds of the Christian world for the last two millennia.

Judaism, the parent religion of Christianity, represented a decisive repudiation of the ancient world's polytheism. The Ten Commandments God gave to Moses begin with the admonition, "I am the Lord thy God. . . . Thou shalt have no other gods before me" (see Question 82). How could the severely monotheistic faith of Abraham and Moses have led to the Christian notion of three Persons in one God?

The God of the Jews, often called **God the Father** by Christians, is not a remote figure, but a being who visits the Garden of Eden, speaks to Moses, and defends the nation he has chosen against its enemies. Yet Yahweh, the Creator of the world, remains an inscrutable God—"I am who am" (Exodus 3:14)—whose furious wrath flares out against all who transgress his laws. Shortly after confirming

Moses in his mission to deliver Israel from Egypt, "the Lord came upon Moses and would have killed him" (Exodus 4:24–26). For one shortcoming, he doesn't permit Moses to enter the Holy Land (Deuteronomy 32:50–52). Among the laws he gives Moses is the *lex talionis,* or law of retribution: "Limb for limb, eye for eye, tooth for tooth!" (Leviticus 24:20). When the Ark of the Covenant is being transported by oxcart, he strikes Uzzah dead for having dared reach out his hand to steady it (2 Samuel 6:1–10).

Christians claim that, in the New Testament, man's understanding of God is deepened through the ministry of **God the Son, Jesus Christ,** the divine and eternal Logos, or Word, of the Father, through whom all things were created: "In the beginning was the Word, and the Word was with God, and the Word was God. . . . All things came to be through him, and without him nothing came to be" (John 1:1–3). To reconcile God and man, "the Word became flesh and dwelt among us."

Thus viewed, Jesus, the Christian Messiah and Son of God, is both true God and true man, the Second Person of the Trinity who came into the world and assumed a human nature. His teachings and actions—culminating in his laying down his life for the eternal salvation of sinful humanity—emphasize God's mercy, as opposed to the Old Testament's emphasis on his power. Christ's Sermon on the Mount (Matthew 5–7) may be seen as the revelation of a Christian ethic highlighting qualities such as charity, kindness, meekness, deference, altruism, and absolute renunciation of revenge: "You have heard that it was said, 'An eye for an eye and a tooth for a tooth.' But I say to you, offer no resistance to one who is evil. When someone strikes you on your right cheek, turn the other one to him as well" (Matthew 5:38–39).

Despite Christ's claim that he did not come to abolish the Law and the prophets, but to fulfill them, his actions challenged the faith of his first followers, who were devout Jews. Like their forefathers, they believed in only one God, infinitely transcendent, who had nonetheless entered into the history of the Jewish people. They then discovered that, with God-like power, Jesus healed the sick, raised the dead, and forgave sins. Although Jesus sometimes subordinated his power and knowledge to God the Father's—stating, for example, that the time of the end of the world is known to "neither the angels of heaven, nor the Son, but the Father alone" (Matthew 24:36) and that "the Father is greater than I" (John 14:28)—he also closely associated himself with the Father: "The Father and I are one" (John 10:30) and "Whoever has seen me has seen the Father" (John 14:9). Thus, according to the evidence of the Gospels, Jesus is not God the Father, but he, too, must be God.

The Third Person of the Trinity is **God the Holy Spirit,** whom Christians consider to have inspired and spoken through the prophets of the Old Testament. In art, the Holy Spirit is represented as the dove that descended from heaven at the time of Christ's baptism (Matthew 3:13–17). In fact, this scriptural event brings together all three Persons of the Trinity: the Holy Spirit descending on Christ, who is in the waters of the Jordan, while God the Father says of him: "This is my beloved Son, in whom I am well pleased." The Holy Spirit figures in key episodes in the New Testament at the beginning and toward the end of Christ's life. He miraculously causes Mary to become pregnant with Jesus in the Annunciation delivered by the Angel Gabriel (Luke 1:26–38). At the Last Supper, Jesus promises his Apostles to send the Holy Spirit—the Paraclete (an advocate, comforter, consoler)—to guide the new Church and infuse it with grace (John 14:15–31).

After Christ's Ascension into heaven, the Holy Spirit descended to the disciples on Pentecost with the sound of a rushing wind and in the form of tongues of flame, infusing them with his power and endowing them with the courage and zeal to preach the Gospel to a hostile world (Acts of the Apostles 2:1–13). Surely this mysterious Spirit must be divine. Once again, the same perplexing problem arose for the early Church: How can the Holy Spirit, the Son, and the Father all be God—who yet remains *one*?

Christian theologians often cite two scriptural passages in support of the Trinitarian dogma. After the Resurrection, Jesus commissions his Apostles to preach the Gospel with these words: "Go, therefore, and make disciples of all nations, baptizing them in the name of the Father, and of the Son, and of the Holy Spirit" (Matthew 28:19). At the end of his second epistle to the Corinthians, St. Paul invokes the blessings of the Trinity: "The grace of the Lord Jesus Christ and the love of God and the fellowship of the Holy Spirit be with all of you."

In the early Church, the great conciliar debates settled the basic outlines of the Trinitarian doctrine by the end of the fourth century. The endlessly speculative minds of early churchmen, especially those weaned on the subtleties and sophistries of Greek philosophy, had spawned heresy after heresy on the more obscure "inner relations" of the Three Persons of the Trinity and on the nature of Christ. As St. Augustine wrote, "No error is more dangerous than any regarding the Trinity."

Here are just a few of them: Was there only one Person in God, with three successive manifestations, as Sabellius thought? Was Christ actually only God and not man, as the Docetists and some Monophysites believed, and thus did only a "phantasm" of him die on the cross? Was Jesus actually only the highest created being, and not God, as the Arians claimed? In other words, was his substance identical with the Father's (consubstantial, Greek *homoousios*), as the Council of Nicaea declared in A.D. 325, or was it only similar (*homoiousios*), as Arius claimed? Was Mary the mother only of Christ's human nature, as the Nestorians insisted, or, as the mother of both his divine and human natures, was she entitled to be called "the mother of God" (*Theotokos*)? Did the Holy Spirit "proceed" from the Father only—as in John 15:26 and the teachings of the Nestorians—or from both the Father and the Son, as St. Athanasius asserted in the fourth century and Aquinas affirmed in the thirteenth?

Augustine and Aquinas both taught, more than eight centuries apart, that the Son was begotten by the Father—from all eternity, not at any time—as an emanation of the Father's intellect, his Word or Wisdom. Similarly, God the Holy Spirit proceeded, from all eternity, from an act of the divine will—the infinite love between God the Father and God the Son. Although these abstruse speculations are far removed from St. Patrick's simple analogy between the Persons of the Trinity and the three leaves of a shamrock, they may not bring us much closer to the heart of this most profound and seemingly paradoxical Christian mystery.

✣ QUESTION 8

Who are the 3 Musketeers?

> Athos
> Porthos
> Aramis

"All for one, one for all!" You know it even if you haven't read the book—the rallying cry of the Three Musketeers and their protégé, D'Artagnan, as they swashbuckle their way through seventeenth-century France during the reign of Louis XIII.

The plot of *Les Trois Mousquetaires,* by Alexandre Dumas, goes something like this. In 1625, a poor young man from the countryside, D'Artagnan, arrives in Paris after several adventures along the way, including a scuffle with a scar-faced man who had mocked his yellow pony. Determined to join the Musketeers (who served the King of France as guards), D'Artagnan soon duels with Athos, Porthos, and Aramis, the cream of the Musketeers, but wins their admiration when he helps them drive off the guard of the King's scheming enemy, Cardinal Richelieu. Soon admitted to the Musketeers as an apprentice, D'Artagnan learns that **Athos** is gallant, of noble bearing, and a bit mysterious about his background and love life. Not so **Porthos,** who is strong, less intellectually inclined, and given to bragging about his female conquests. **Aramis** views his tenure in the Guard as just a stop on the way to the cloister.

Bankruptcy looms for the Musketeers, who've spent all the gold given them by the King for their help against the Cardinal. An apparent solution presents itself when D'Artagnan's landlord, Bonacieux, says he'll forgive the overdue rent if D'Artagnan and his friends find his wife Constance, who has been abducted by a man whose description reminds D'Artagnan of the man with the scar.

As the Queen's dressmaker and go-between, Constance knows

much of her romantic involvement with the English Duke of Buckingham. This information is irresistibly tempting to the Cardinal in his quest to destabilize the royal household and further his own power. Constance frees herself from her abductors and, in the ensuing chase and scuffle, meets D'Artagnan, who falls in love with her on the spot. Constance is too busy to discuss the situation, however, since she must take the disguised Buckingham to meet the Queen, who gives him twelve diamond studs as a token of her love. The ubiquitous Cardinal learns of this gift and, knowing that the diamonds were a present from the King to the Queen, decides to enlighten the monarch as to their current whereabouts.

How lucky the Cardinal is! His good friend, the beautiful and clever Lady de Winter, or simply Milady, happens to be in London at the same time as Buckingham. At his bidding, she clips two of the diamond studs from Buckingham's evening clothes, which the Cardinal can now present to the King as evidence of the Queen's unfaithfulness. D'Artagnan, however, finds out about the plot from Constance and thwarts it.

Soon afterward, D'Artagnan spots the woman who was with the scar-faced man. What a small world! She is chatting with his friend, Lord de Winter, whose life he had spared in a duel. The lady is Lord de Winter's sister-in-law, and the hormonally enhanced D'Artagnan (probably a self-portrait by Dumas) promptly falls in love with Lady de Winter. She doesn't reciprocate, however, since she is in love with a Monsieur de Wardes, whose recent death has not yet come to her notice. When D'Artagnan disguises himself one night as de Wardes, Milady gives him a substantial sapphire. D'Artagnan shows it to Athos, who recognizes it as the one he had given his wife, a beautiful but wicked woman on whose shoulder he noticed a fleur-de-lis criminal brand only after the honeymoon—and whom he thought he had hanged until she was dead.

D'Artagnan learns that when he saved Lord de Winter's life in the duel, he unwittingly derailed a scheme by Milady to have de Winter killed so that she could inherit his money. He also finds out that she is Richelieu's spy and the mastermind behind Constance's second abduction and imprisonment. In a climactic altercation, Milady's dress gets pulled from her shoulder to reveal the telltale fleur-de-lis. She's Athos's undead wife!

In the midst of these events, the war between England and France is coming to a head at the siege of La Rochelle, a French town that was allied with the English. The Cardinal tries unsuccessfully to enlist D'Artagnan on his side. Lady de Winter fails in her attempt to have him killed at La Rochelle but succeeds in having hapless Buckingham stabbed to death and Constance poisoned. She is eventually captured and executed. With her death and the fall of La Rochelle to the French, we experience the happy conjuncture of the main strands of the plot. The Cardinal, impressed by D'Artagnan's ability to outwit him, offers him a commission in the Musketeers. Athos returns to his estate, Porthos marries well, and Aramis finds his cloister. D'Artagnan is eventually reconciled even to old Scarface, who turns out to be a nobleman.

The Three Musketeers has been enormously popular since its 1844 publication. It's been translated into countless languages and cinematized at least five times. The creator of this melodramatic concoction has been called the French Sir Walter Scott—and even more unflattering names.

Alexandre Dumas *père* (1802–70) was the grandson of a French nobleman who had settled in Hispaniola and a black woman who was a native of the island. His father was a general in Napoleon's army, and Alexandre himself had a flashy military career that included participation in Garibaldi's Sicilian campaign of 1860. Dumas called history "the nail on which I hang my novels," and he and his collaborator, Auguste Maquet, found many of their characters and plots in historical sources. Charles de Baatz D'Artagnan was a historical figure, and Dumas says in his preface to the *Musketeers* that D'Artagnan's memoirs (which were actually written years later by someone else) contain a reference to three characters named Athos, Porthos, and Aramis. And apparently Louis XIII's queen really *did* have an affair with the Duke of Buckingham.

Among the 300 volumes attributed to the prolific Dumas are *The Count of Monte Cristo* and *The Viscount of Bragelonne*—the latter the source of the tragic tale of "The Man in the Iron Mask."

QUESTION 9

Who were the 3 sons of Noah?

Shem
Japheth
Ham

The Hebrew deluge story is one of many. The Babylonian flood myth, glimpsed in *The Epic of Gilgamesh*, features a Noah-figure named Utnapishtim. The Greek version involves Prometheus's son, Deucalion, and the latter's wife, Pyrrha, who repopulate the world after the flood by throwing stones behind their backs. The stones Deucalion threw became men, while Pyrrha's popped up from the ground as women. In ancient India's flood myth, Manu, the son of the sun, is warned to build an ark by the god Vishnu (or Brahma) in the form of a fish (see Question 2). After the deluge, Manu becomes the progenitor of the human race through his daughter.

In the Genesis account, Noah, ninth in descent from Adam (see Question 1), lived in a time when the whole world had become ineffably wicked, corrupt, and violent. At age 600, Noah is ordered by God to build an ark with his three 100-year-old sons, bring male and female of each animal aboard, and embark with his wife, sons, and daughters-in-law to escape the universal flood in which all other humans and animals drown. In this story, the dove, olive leaf, and rainbow first assume their symbolic meanings of peace and the covenant established between humanity and the incensed deity. After the waters recede and the ark comes to rest in the Ararat mountains in eastern Turkey, Noah disembarks and lives another 350 years, dying at age 950.

If you work out the numbers in Genesis, you'll find that Methuselah, who was Noah's grandfather and survived to be 969 years old, died in the year of the flood. He's unlikely to have drowned in it, since, as part of Noah's extended family and as the record-holder for human longevity, he probably was favored by God and wasn't one of the wicked. Let's say he succumbed to natural causes just before the deluge. And when was that? In 2348 B.C., if you count the years from Adam to the flood in Genesis *and* accept the chronology of the seventeenth-century Irish Anglican archbishop James Ussher, who pinpointed the day of the world's creation as Sunday, October 23, 4004 B.C.

But let's get to Noah's sons, whom the biblical narrative identifies as the ancestors of all the main ethnic groups known to the ancient Jews. **Shem,** the eldest son, is the eponymous ancestor of the Semites, including the Jews, Arabs, Assyrians, Elamites, and Aramaeans—but not the Canaanites. His great-grandson, Eber, is the eponymous ancestor of the Hebrews. Abram (later Abraham), ninth in descent from Shem, was born 291 years after the flood. Shem himself lived to be 600.

One of the narrative strands in Genesis makes **Japheth** (JAY-futh) the second son of Noah, while another considers him the youngest. As the father of Javan, who was associated with the Ionian Greeks, Japheth was seen as the ancestor of all the Greek tribes in general. In later antiquity he himself was sometimes identified with the Greek Titan Iapetos, the father of Prometheus. In addition to the Greeks, Japheth's descendants included other Mediterranean and island peoples, the Armenians, the Medes, and the inhabitants of Asia Minor (now Turkey).

Ham is said to have been the father of four sons, including Cush (ancestor of the Ethiopians), Mizraim (progenitor of the Egyptians), and Canaan (eponymous ancestor of the original Semitic inhabitants of Palestine). Cush was the father of Nimrod, that "mighty hunter before the Lord" who was sometimes identified as the frustrated builder of the Tower of Babel (Babylon), where the Confusion of Tongues occurred.

But Ham's story turns tragic, with implications reaching almost to our own times. We are told that Noah was the first to cultivate the fruit of the vine and get drunk on it. When Ham stumbles upon Noah, dead drunk and buck naked in his tent, he goes to call his brothers. The more pious (or merely craftier) Shem and Japheth clothe their substance-abusing father without peeking at his nakedness. When Noah comes to his senses, he curses Ham's son, Canaan, and destines him to be the slave of Shem and Japheth.

We can understand why the Hebrew author of this passage makes

Noah curse Canaan, since the Hebrews were fierce enemies of the Canaanites and supplanted them in Palestine. But here's the ironic part: Ham's putative connection with Egypt and Ethiopia caused a stigma to attach itself to his African "descendants." This means that a biblical passage intended to explain Hebrew animosity against the Canaanites—and indeed the original drunken-Noah episode probably specified Canaan, not Ham, as the unwilling voyeur—was later misinterpreted as a universal condemnation of Africans. The story of Ham the accursed was used by some to justify African slavery well into the period of the American Civil War.

Noah was often a figure of fun in medieval mystery plays, which tended to portray him as an uxorious man driven to drink by a shrewish wife who at first refuses to board the ark. In a more somber vein is Michelangelo's depiction of the deluge among his frescoes on the ceiling of the Sistine Chapel in Rome (1508–12). His handling of Noah's drunkenness points a moral about the submission of human reason to enslavement by the body. James Joyce, on the other hand, always maintained a healthy respect for the body's demands. In his *Ulysses* (1922), the interior monologue of the book's hero, Leopold Bloom, who is scanning the shelves of a pub trying to decide what to have for lunch, contains a bit of nonsense involving multiple culinary puns: "Ham and his descendants mustered and bred there."

❧ QUESTION 10

What are the 3 ages of Vico's historical cycle?

> Theocratic (The Age of Gods)
> Aristocratic (The Age of Heroes)
> Democratic (The Age of Men)

When Giambattista Vico (1668–1744) was seven years old, he took a nasty fall from the top of a ladder, fracturing his skull. He was unconscious for five hours, and his surgeon prognosticated that he would either die of his injury or grow up to be an idiot. Instead, he became the greatest Italian philosopher.

Vico's importance rests on his cyclical theory of history, enunciated in *Principles of New Science . . . Concerning the Common Nature of the Nations,* usually referred to as *The New Science,* first published in 1725 and revised for the third and last time in 1744. This immensely pedantic tome, described by nineteenth-century American historian John Fiske as "the driest, obscurest, metaphysicalest book I ever got hold of," is a seminal work of historical theory. Ignored in its own time, and despite Fiske and Vico's surgeon, it went on to influence writers like Goethe, Hegel, Herder, Michelet, Coleridge, Comte, Marx, Carlyle, Croce, and Joyce.

The product of a Jesuit education and the early Enlightenment, Vico mingled with the best minds in his native Naples, where he was professor of Rhetoric (Latin Eloquence) at the university. After the Newtonian revolution in physics and astronomy, some scholars began applying scientific methods—regular laws, constant conjunctions, predictability—to the study of mankind. Vico chose human history as his field of investigation, and his "New Science" claimed an authority that had hitherto been accorded only to the exact sciences. So, what are the laws of history?

This first modern historian begins his quest just after the universal flood has wiped out all but eight humans (see Question 9). A devout (and prudent) Catholic, Vico confines his historical speculations to the postdiluvian gentile nations—the descendants of Ham, Japheth, and the non-Hebraic scions of Shem, who, within two hundred years of the deluge, have degenerated into speechless savages roaming the jungles and forests, copulating promiscuously in the open, and preying on each other in a Hobbesian state of nature. Vico's theories thus do not apply to Judeo-Christian sacred history, which he claimed was under the direct influence of Providence.

With the drying out of the sodden earth, the first thunderclap rings out. Picture the terror of these savages, who interpret this as the storm god bellowing down at them: "Stop copulating like dogs where I can see you! And do something with those dead bodies so I don't have to smell them or watch them rot!" The men flee into caves, each dragging a woman with him. Thus begins **the age of gods,** with the foundation of primitive religion, marriage (and the family), and burial of the dead (which holds out the promise that, if properly done, human souls can attain immortal life). These are the three basic institutions of society, according to Vico. The form of government is a theocracy based on auspices, auguries, and divine revelations. The rulers are the patriarchs, who combine the powers of kings, priests, prophets, and judges. The form of wisdom is oracular and theological, and all physical things are thought to be animated by gods (animism).

In **the age of heroes,** some of the remaining wandering savages weary of fighting off fierce marauders and appeal for protection to the patriarchs, who have made clearings in the forest. The patriarchs kill off as many marauders as they can and, as villages evolve, make agricultural serfs of the helpless suppliants, who lack all rights. Uniting against the serfs, the patriarchs form feudal aristocratic commonwealths in which the serfs are severely oppressed. Gradually, when the serfs begin to rebel, the first agrarian laws are passed. This warlike, valiant, and barbaric age is poetic, mythic, and imaginative, as in the Homeric poems.

The age of men begins when the serfs become plebeians in newly emerging city-states. They assert their right to the privileges formerly denied them not only by social and political tradition but also by religious taboo—the right to own land, marry according to religious ritual, bequeath property, become citizens, hold political office, and even take the auspices. The ethos of this age is rational; legal codes are drawn up, and scientific and philosophical thought emerges. This is a more benign and humane age, in which reason applies itself to bettering the lot of all citizens. First, popular republics are established under leaders like Pericles, but soon the mad rush toward equality leads to civil wars, such as those of Rome. More or less enlightened monarchs, such as Alexander the Great or Julius Caesar, assume power to keep order while still loosely preserving the concept of civil rights for all citizens before the law.

But the ease and luxury of the democratic age lead to egoism, bread and circuses, decadence, political corruption à la Caligula and Nero, cynicism, religious skepticism—in short, to the much later Italian concept of *menefreghismo* ("I-don't-give-a-damn-ism"). The society either implodes through internal strife or is conquered by a more vigorous people: "He who cannot govern himself must let himself be governed by another who can. . . . The world is always governed by those who are naturally fittest"—Vico's latter assertion anticipating social Darwinism by a century and a half.

Barbarism now descends on Europe again, and the whole cycle recurs (Vico's law of eternal *ricorso*), but on a higher level this time, for the cycles proceed in an upward spiral. Improvement and progress in human dignity and rationality occur because the race retains what it has learned in previous cycles. So, after the Germanic barbarians conquer the Roman Empire, a new theocratic age results, in which the early God-fearing Christians revert to prophecies, miracles, irrationality, revelations, and signs and portents. The crusading and chivalric age is next, the new age of knightly heroes, with its feudalism and martial epics—think of *Beowulf, The Song of Roland, El Cid*. Dante is the new Homer of this aristocratic age. Finally, Vico recognizes the return of the new age of men in the natural-law philosophy and age of reason of the seventeenth century. He predicts the rise of democratic republics within a half century of his time—and is vindicated in 1776.

An important point of Vico's thought is that human nature is not static, but develops in step with changes in religion, law, politics, economic relationships, and the arts. The cycles of history represent individual psychological development writ large: Nations think childishly at first, then like adolescents, and then mature adults, before lapsing into senility. Societies also mirror the stages of biologic development. They are born, mature, decline, and die—only to be replaced by their offspring, in which the cycle begins again. This organic theory of historical development is driven by class struggle. People with similar rights (or lack thereof) bind together to suppress or overthrow the others.

Vico's cyclical theory supplied James Joyce with the basic organizing principle of his polyglot *Finnegans Wake* (1939), in which characters, places, and events keep recurring in multifarious guises. This mammoth epic of birth, life, death, and resurrection—this collective unconscious of the human race—is thus divided into four parts, in which theocratic, heroic, human, and *ricorso* themes predominate, respectively. Joyce's book closes with a sentence fragment ("A way a lone a last a loved a long the") that is completed by the book's opening words: "riverrun, past Eve and Adam's, from swerve of shore to bend of bay, brings us by a commodious vicus of recirculation back to Howth Castle and Environs." Who could ask for a better *ricorso* than that? (And *vicus,* which means "street" in Latin, is also the Latin form of Vico's name.) Like its hero, Humphrey Chimpden Earwicker, *Finnegans Wake* "moves in vicous cicles yet remews the same."

With New Ageism, the continuing decline of education, the increasing mistrust of science, spates of near-death-experience mem-

33

oirs, proliferating cults, and the growing influence of religious funda-
mentalism here and abroad, are we—like Yeats's rough beast—slouch-
ing toward a new theocratic age?

❧ QUESTION 11

Who were the 3 Magi, and what gifts did they bring?

Melchior (gold)
Caspar (frankincense)
Balthazar (myrrh)

Although entrenched in Christmas lore, the Magi actually appear
only in the Gospel of Matthew. Luke's Gospel, the only other with a
Nativity narrative, does not mention them. Furthermore, Matthew
specifies no number, saying only that "some wise men" come to
Jerusalem from the East, led by a new star, which traditionally signi-
fied the birth of a ruler. They seek the help of King Herod the Great,
Roman King of Judea (reigned 37–4 B.C.), in finding the "infant King
of the Jews" to whom they want to pay homage. Herod sends them
on to Bethlehem and orders them to return when they find the child,
so that he, too, can offer his respects. Continuing on their way, the
wise men eventually find the infant in a house (not a manger in
Matthew) over which the star has paused. They worship the child and
offer their gifts of gold, frankincense, and myrrh. When a dream
warns them to avoid Herod, who fears the child as a rival, they return
home by another route. In describing how Herod plotted to kill the
infant, Matthew was probably associating Christ with infant Moses,
whom Pharaoh had tried to kill (along with all other male Hebrew
infants) and who went on to deliver Israel from Egypt.

Magi were well-known figures in the ancient world. The word is
the plural of Latin *magus,* "wise man" (from Greek *magos,* from Persian *magush*), designating a member of the priestly caste of several
religions, especially the Zoroastrianism of ancient Persia. After the
conquest of Babylon by Persia in the sixth century B.C., Zoroastrianism was tainted by Babylonian religious practices. Eventually, Persian

magi came to be considered the genuine keepers of true and ancient wisdom, while the Babylonian magi—largely sorcerers, magicians, and astrologers—were widely regarded as tricksters and charlatans, as our word *magic* still attests. In fact, in the Acts of the Apostles (8:9–24), Simon Magus is a Samaritan sorcerer who tries to buy from St. Peter the gift of conferring the Holy Spirit by the laying on of hands. His sacrilegious request gave us the word *simony* for the buying or selling of church offices.

Back to the Matthew narrative. His apparently straightforward, twelve-verse account teems with Jewish and Christian symbolism and is written so that several Old Testament prophecies are fulfilled, notably Isaiah 60:6, "All they from Saba [Sheba, probably Yemen] shall come, bringing gold and frankincense, and showing forth praise to the Lord," and Psalm 72:10–11, "The kings of Tarshish and the Isles shall offer gifts; the kings of Arabia and Seba shall bring tribute. All kings shall pay him homage, all nations shall serve him." Apparently because of these passages, early Christian writers transformed the Magi into Kings.

In Jewish ritual, only three kinds of people were anointed: kings, priests, and prophets. Gold is a gift for a king, frankincense for a priest, and pungent myrrh for a sharp-tongued prophet. (Myrrh was used in embalming, and its presentation to Christ also portends his death.) The conferring of all three gifts on the infant Jesus means he is triply anointed. Now, "the anointed one" is a translation both of the Greek *christos* and the Hebrew *mashiach,* and Matthew, writing in about A.D. 85 for Jewish Christians, was trying to demonstrate that Jesus of Nazareth was the Christ, the Jewish Messiah. The Magi, of course, were gentiles, and their veneration of Christ also supports the claim that he came to save all nations.

By the eighth century the three Kings had acquired names and kingdoms: Melichior **(Melchior),** King of Persia; Gathaspa (Gaspar or **Caspar**), King of India; and Bithisarea (**Balthazar** or Baltasar), King of Arabia. Melchior means "king of light," Gaspar "the white one," and Balthazar "lord of the treasures." The English historian Bede (c. 672–735) opined that Balthazar, the youngest, was black, reemphasizing the idea that Christ had come to save all humankind.

According to a medieval tradition, the three Magi met to celebrate Christmas in Sewa, a town in Turkey, more than half a century after they followed the Star of Bethlehem to the scene of Christ's birth. Then, in early January, they all died, each well over a hundred years old. The legend adds that their bodies were taken from Sewa to Milan, from where they were filched by the German Emperor Frederick Barbarossa in the twelfth century and brought to Cologne. The Magi were renamed the Kings of Cologne, and their remains are still dubiously said to repose in the cathedral.

Marco Polo (1254–1324) probably had a better trail on the Magi. Sojourning in Saveh, southwest of present-day Tehran, he reported seeing their sepulchers in separate, ornate buildings. Their bodies, which he viewed, apparently had undergone only minor decomposition. According to legend still current in this area, the three came, respectively, from Saveh, Hawah, and Kashan (all within about a hundred miles of Tehran), and traveled west together to greet the mysterious child. Among the tales Marco heard, one contributed to the theme of "Christ came for all men": As each King entered separately the house where the infant Jesus lay in Bethlehem, he saw a Christ who bore a great resemblance to himself.

Perhaps the medieval legend places the deaths of the three Magi in early January because it was on the sixth of this month that the Western Church came to celebrate their visit to Christ. The Feast of the Epiphany, one of the Church's oldest liturgical festivals, has its roots in pre-Christian rites. In Latin America and some Mediterranean countries, January 6, called "Little Christmas," may be celebrated as lavishly as Christmas itself. In the Eastern Church, the Epiphany memorializes not only the visit of the Magi, but also Christ's baptism and the marriage feast at Cana, where Christ performed his first miracle, changing water into wine. This triple commemoration is in keeping with the Greek *epiphaneia*, meaning "manifestation"—in this case, of divine power or godhead.

The Magi story, beginning with only a dozen verses in Matthew, took on a long, varied life of its own. The Adoration (or Journey) of the Magi became a stock motif in medieval and Renaissance art, partly because it reminded earthly potentates that even they had to submit to Christ, the King of Kings. The Italian Masters Giotto, Sassetta, Gentile da Fabriano, Fra Angelico, Benozzo Gozzoli, Ghirlandaio, and Leonardo da Vinci are only a few of the myriad painters who treated this subject. Even in the skeptical twentieth century, T. S. Eliot wrote a devotional poem entitled "Journey of the Magi."

What are the 3 components of the Freudian psyche?

Id *(das Es)*
Ego *(das Ich)*
Superego *(das Über-Ich)*

Tripartite divisions of the human psyche, soul, or mind long antedate the work of Sigmund Freud (1856–1939), the Austrian psychiatrist who mapped our modern mental topography, pioneered psychoanalysis, and became one of the most revolutionary and influential thinkers of the twentieth century. Plato (c. 429–347 B.C.) had divided the individual soul into three faculties, each corresponding to a class of citizens in his ideal *Republic:*

+ Appetite, concerned with the pleasures of nutrition and generation, was characteristic of the merchant class.
+ High spirit (or angry passions and a thirst for martial glory and fame) was the distinguishing mark of the warrior class.
+ Reason, imbuing the souls of the ruling class, delighted in wisdom, learning, philosophy, and justice.

Plato's student Aristotle (384–322 B.C.), in *De Anima (On the Soul),* posited the triad of a nutritive or vegetative soul (nutrition, growth, reproduction), a sensitive soul (sensations, emotions, memory), and an intellective or rational soul (thought, judgment, reasoning, contemplation), each coexisting to varying degrees in all humans.

But a more immediate influence on Freud's three psychic faculties may be found in the nineteenth century. In *The Brothers Karamazov,* which Freud called "the most magnificent novel ever written," Fyodor Dostoyevski (1821–81) created three characters—the brothers of the title—who roughly embody Freud's id, ego, and superego: the debauched, drunken brawler Dmitri, the atheistic intellectual Ivan, and the saintly monk Alyosha.

According to Freud, the **id** (or "it") is the unconscious seat of sexual and self-preserving instincts, primitive passions, and irrational urges. It is the infant howling to be fed—and not only that. In Freud's largely discredited view, little boys develop an Oedipus complex, and girls an Electra complex—a libidinous attachment of the id to the parent of the opposite sex and a rivalry with the same-sex parent. When this is seen to be a losing game (especially for boys, with the ever-present threat of castration), the id strategically retreats by shedding the Oedipus complex and identifying with the parent of the same sex.

If allowed free rein, the id, "this great reservoir of libido," would transport us back to Thomas Hobbes's "war of all against all" and to his vision of life in a state of Nature: "solitary, poor, nasty, brutish, and short"—or to Darwin's Nature, "red in tooth and claw" (in Tennyson's phrase). This roiling, roistering, old roué of an id understands only the pleasure principle.

But the **ego** ("I"), on the other hand, is concerned with the reality principle. Out of the id's amorphous mass of instincts, a primitive ego develops through increasing contact with the environment. It begins to realize that adapting to its surroundings increases the odds of survival more effectively than the id's in-your-face style. The ego, representing reason and common sense, increasingly brings the reality principle to bear on the id's constant demands for instant gratification and uses repression (the erasing from consciousness of unacceptable impulses) in the attempt to nullify the id's clamorings. Freud once succinctly defined psychoanalysis as "an instrument to enable the ego to achieve a progressive conquest of the id." But a weak ego remains prey to anxiety not only from the environment and the id, but also from the superego.

The **superego,** incorporated into a coherent theory with the other two components of the mind in Freud's *The Ego and the Id* (1923), is an outgrowth of the ego that internalizes parental and societal values. This "super-I," or internal cop, holds the ego to strict account for not adhering to the various taboos and moral strictures of home, school, religion, society, and the law. Its cruelly punitive weapons are the guilt it induces and the conscience it wields so self-righteously. Like the id, the superego works mainly unconsciously, so that feelings of guilt are often misinterpreted by the person as neurotic or somatic symptoms. Freud believed that the superego's effects could be seen in the development of religions that feature wrathful, vengeful deities.

Freud's division of the psyche emphasizes how our thoughts and actions are determined by the unconscious interplay and conflict of our biologic drives (id), our adjustment of those drives to external reality (ego), and our reactions to the restrictions of society (superego). Though all his theoretical constructs are metaphorical and based on anecdotal evidence from the couch rather than on verifiable scientific experimentation, Freud profoundly stirred the imagination of healers, artists, writers, and thinkers throughout the twentieth century with concepts like infantile sexuality, repression, sublimation, the unconscious, and dozens more. An apt comment on Freud's epic saga of the soul may be this Italian saying, *"Se non è vero, è ben trovato"* ("It may not be true, but it's a *great* story").

⅍ QUESTION 13

What 3 beasts confront Dante in Canto 1 of the _Inferno_?

Leopard
Lion
She-wolf

Before Dante Alighieri (1265–1321) embarks on the epic journey to the otherworldly realms of the Inferno, Purgatorio, and Paradiso described in the three parts of his *Divine Comedy,* he pictures himself losing his way in a terrifying forest where he wanders throughout a "dark night of the soul." At dawn he finds himself at the foot of a hill whose sun-clad summit encourages him to leave behind the gloomy forest, which symbolizes the sin, ignorance, and spiritual death that threaten to engulf him.

Just as he starts climbing the hill, Dante sees a nimble **leopard** in his path—and then a ferocious **lion** and a famished **she-wolf.** There is a crescendo of fearsomeness in the three mysterious beasts, which seem to materialize out of thin air. After the menacing she-wolf appears, Dante turns tail and starts dashing for cover in the dark forest.

But now there's another apparition—the spirit of the long-dead Roman poet Virgil (70–19 B.C.), author of the greatest Latin epic, the *Aeneid,* and Dante's literary idol and poetic model. Virgil checks Dante's headlong retreat, explaining that he was sent by the heavenly spirit of Beatrice, Dante's dead love, to rescue him from the perils of sinfulness that might land him in Hell. But Virgil, who is a soul in Limbo, where virtuous heathens go after death, also informs Dante that he can't escape the forest by climbing the hill. He assures him that the beasts barring his path—especially the she-wolf—won't let him through alive.

Where did the beasts come from? On a literary level, from the Bible:

> *And this is why a lion from the forest strikes them down,*
> *a desert wolf makes havoc of them,*
> *a leopard lurks around their towns:*
> *whoever goes out is torn to pieces—*
> *because of their countless crimes,*
> *their ever-increasing apostasies.*

This is Jeremiah (5:6) launching a jeremiad against the corrupt kingdom of Judah. But what do the three beasts mean in Dante's poem? Most scholars agree that they represent either the sins of lust, pride, and avarice, respectively, or the three major degrees of sin: 1) incontinence (lack of self-control), resulting in sins such as lust, gluttony, and anger; 2) violence; and 3) fraud (or malice). Compare 1 John 2:16: "For all that is in the world, the lust of the flesh [the leopard], and the lust of the eyes [the she-wolf], and the pride of life [the lion], is not of the Father, but is of the world."

Because of these evil propensities of ours, we need divine grace to attain eternal salvation. Thus, in the fiction of the poem, Beatrice, symbol of divinely revealed Truth, sends Virgil to guide Dante through Hell (so that he can see firsthand the wretched effects of sin on the human soul) and Purgatory (so that he can witness the long, laborious, painful process of the soul's repentance). Beatrice herself will then appear to Dante at the summit of Mount Purgatory and lead him through the ten heavens of Paradise, so that he can experience the ineffable joy of the saints in heaven, who have managed to overcome the sinfulness of our fallen nature and achieve the goal for which humans were created: the Beatific Vision of God in a perpetual peace "which passeth all understanding."

Only after completing this cosmic journey (in 14,233 lines of sublime verse) does Dante merit the vision of God vouchsafed at the end of the *Paradiso*. There are no shortcuts to salvation. Like Dante, we all must take the long way home, through knowledge and purgation, instead of trying to sneak past the barriers symbolized by the three beasts of our evil nature.

Was Dante personally assailed by the leopard with the pretty pelt (lust), the fierce lion (pride), and the starving she-wolf (avarice)? We glean from his own poems that, after the death of his beloved Beatrice in 1290, he was attracted to various other women, and in the *Purgatorio* (Canto 27) Dante depicts himself crossing the wall of flame that is the punishment of the lustful souls he encounters there. As for pride, there never lived a prouder human being than Dante Alighieri, the embittered and scornful political exile who boasted in the *Paradiso* that he had formed a party of himself alone, since his political enemies in Florence and his fellow exiles were equally reprehensible. Avarice he would have denied—though it was precisely for the (trumped-up) charge of graft and embezzlement of government funds that Dante was exiled and, subsequently, condemned to death by burning in 1302. (He wisely never returned to face charges.)

No matter what sinful qualities the three beasts of Canto 1 of the *Inferno* symbolize, Dante receives the counterbalancing intercession of three blessed ladies in the very next canto. There, Virgil informs him of how the Virgin Mary summoned St. Lucy, who then appealed to Beatrice, who in turn descended to Limbo to send Virgil on his rescue mission for Dante's imperiled soul. This threefold chain of grace on the part of sainted women in Heaven more than tips the scale against the three beasts that bar Dante's path. In Dante's view, God gives all of us more than a fair crack at working out our salvation, if only we can get beyond the beast in us.

41

Who were the 3 Furies?

Alecto
Megaera
Tisiphone

In Canto 9 of the *Inferno*, Dante approaches the walls of lower Hell,

> *Where I beheld three hellish Furies rise*
> *Erect at once, with clotted blood embrowned:*
> *Women they seemed in body and in guise,*
> *But greenest hydras girded them around,*
> *And hornèd snakes they had instead of hair;*
> *With vipers were their savage temples bound.*

These fierce apparitions, who proceed to terrify Dante by shrieking while clawing their breasts and striking themselves with their hands, had their literary origins more than two millennia earlier in the Erinyes (uh-RIN-ee-eze) of Homer, who were as yet nameless and of undetermined number. In Homer and later Greek myth, they were the embodiments of curses—dread ministers of vengeance whose bailiwick was murder (especially of blood relatives), crimes against parents or the elderly, perjury, and violations of the customs protecting guests or beggars. The Erinyes, who sprang from the blood of Uranus when his son Cronus castrated him with a sickle (see Question 88), came to symbolize the remorse of conscience. The Furies, or *Dirae*, are their Latin equivalents.

As avenging goddesses of the underworld who pursue those guilty of heinous crimes, these snaky-haired crones with blood oozing from their eyes figure prominently in *The Eumenides* of Aeschylus (c. 525–456 B.C.). This is the concluding play of *The Oresteia*, the tragic trilogy that won first prize in the Athenian dramatic festival in

458 B.C. Aeschylus's greatest work—and the only Greek dramatic trilogy that has survived complete—*The Oresteia* also includes *Agamemnon* and *The Libation Bearers (Choephoroe)*.

In the first play of the trilogy, Clytemnestra, wife of the returning commander-in-chief of the Greek forces in the Trojan War, King Agamemnon of Argos, treacherously stabs him to death in his bath. The lonely Queen, sister to another femme fatale, Helen of Troy, had taken a lover during Agamemnon's ten-year absence—his cousin, Aegisthus. The chorus of the play provides some exposition: We are told how Agamemnon's father Atreus had been cuckolded by his brother Thyestes and thus had butchered two of Thyestes' young sons and served them up cooked to their father, who unknowingly fed on their flesh. When informed of the nature of his meal, Thyestes quite understandably cursed Atreus and his descendants. But Thyestes' son Aegisthus escaped and vowed revenge. Apart from this crime of his father's, Agamemnon had made a human sacrifice of his daughter Iphigenia to obtain a fair wind to sail to Troy. To cap things off, the proud conqueror of Troy returns home with a young mistress, the Trojan princess and prophetess Cassandra, who is also duly murdered by Clytemnestra.

At the command of Apollo, however, and with his sister Electra's enthusiastic support, Agamemnon's son Orestes avenges his father's murder by cutting his mother's throat with a sword. Of course, he also dispatches Aegisthus. For the sacrilege of matricide, Orestes is immediately haunted by the Erinyes, who, at the end of *The Libation Bearers,* chase him from Argos and hound him to the edge of insanity. Orestes flees to the oracle of Apollo at Delphi and is absolved of his crime—but the relentless Erinyes refuse to abandon their pursuit. Apollo bids him flee to Athens, where Athene will protect him.

The third play, *The Eumenides,* is the story of a clash between, on the one hand, Apollo and Athene (and the civilized, enlightened values of the Olympian gods) and, on the other, the Erinyes, who embody the primitive, barbarous, prerational *lex talionis*—the law of an eye for an eye and of "cruel and unusual punishments." The Erinyes are draconian literalists, considering neither the motivation of the accused nor any extenuating circumstances in their blind pursuit of revenge. Supposedly this play's chorus of wildly dancing Erinyes—probably twelve of them—was so horrific with their long black robes and red tongues that pregnant women in the original audience had miscarriages and children went into convulsions.

A murder trial ends the play. Athene appoints twelve Athenian jurors to try the vexed case of Orestes, who pleads the equivalent of our "guilty with an explanation"—namely, that Apollo himself had commanded him to kill Clytemnestra and that he was now cleansed of guilt through his sufferings. Apollo, Orestes' defense attorney and a formidable shyster, argues that only fathers are true parents of their children, since a mother serves only to nurture the husband's seed. Thus, he concludes, Orestes is innocent of any blood guilt. When the jury becomes deadlocked at six ballots for each side, Athene casts the deciding vote in favor of acquittal, putting an end to the three-generational curse on the House of Atreus.

The Erinyes are furious, but Athene's blandishments soon prove too much for them. They accept an honored shrine and worship at Athens as the Eumenides ("The Kindly Ones")—gentle chthonic fertility goddesses with whom they now become identified. Aeschylus thus provides a mythic explanation both for the origin of the Eumenides cult and for the divine foundation of the Athenian Court of the Areopagus, the revered council that tried cases of homicide, arson, treason, and offenses against religion. The reconciliation at the end of the play stands for the mitigation of the instinctual rights of older folk customs by the intellectual virtues of reason and moderation. As such, *The Eumenides* celebrates the establishment of the rule of law in place of the crude justice of tribal vendettas and blood feuds.

Euripides (c. 484–406 B.C.), in his play *Orestes,* is the earliest author to refer to the Erinyes as a group of three, and later Alexandrian Greek writers named them. Virgil (70–19 B.C.) used these names in his *Aeneid,* where the Furies are depicted either as monstrous dispensers of torment in the underworld or as inspirers of terror, strife, and warfare on earth. **Alecto** means "she who does not rest" (in her pursuit); **Megaera** (muh-JEER-uh) is "the envious one"; and **Tisiphone** (tiss-IFF-uh-nee) is "the avenger of murder." Greek vases often represent them as dog-headed and bat-winged.

St. Paul preached before the Council of the Areopagus, some of whom burst into incredulous laughter when he claimed that God had raised Christ from the dead (Acts 17:19–34). John Milton's impassioned plea for nonlicensing of the English press is named *Areopagitica* in honor of that ancient council, and the Erinyes make a cameo appearance in the Hell of his *Paradise Lost* as the "harpy-footed Furies."

Who were the 3 members of the First Triumvirate?

Julius Caesar
Pompey the Great
Crassus

The First Triumvirate (Latin, "group of three men") is what historians have called an informal association of the three most powerful and ambitious men in Rome at the time of the moribund Roman republic. This cabal was intended to break the power of the aristocratic oligarchy that had controlled political life for centuries through its bastion, the Roman Senate. By insulting and thwarting each of these three formidable men, the Senate cut its own throat, forcing the trio to band together for their own advancement and the destruction of the republican constitution.

Gaius Julius Caesar (100–44 B.C.), returning from victorious wars in Spain in 60 B.C., was forced by the Senate to choose between standing as a candidate for the consulship, the highest magistracy in the state, or celebrating a triumph in Rome—a spectacular procession that paraded a conquering general's captives and spoils before him and his soldiers. Caesar, choosing the reality of power rather than its shadow, forfeited his triumph and aspired to be one of the two consuls, whose term was one year.

Late in 62 B.C. Pompey the Great—**Gnaeus Pompeius Magnus** (106–48 B.C.)—had returned to Rome after conquering the redoubtable King Mithridates of Pontus in Asia Minor. But the Senate was suspicious of his intentions and jealous of his stupendous military reputation as "the new Alexander the Great." Pompey had annihilated the Mediterranean pirates, added most of Pontus to the Roman Empire, annexed Syria and Palestine, and made Armenia a client kingdom. The Senate tried to cut him down to human size by denying him two key requests: that his settlement of the newly conquered provinces be ratified and that his veterans be allotted land in Italy.

Marcus Licinius Crassus (c. 115–53 B.C.), often considered the richest man in Rome, was rebuffed by the Senate when it refused to pass legislation favorable to the financial and tax-collecting interests he represented.

Caesar was the instigator of the entente. He first approached Pompey in December of 60 B.C. and Crassus early in 59. The problem was that Crassus, whose wealth made him an attractive partner, hated Pompey. They had been openly inimical while sharing the consulship in 70 B.C., and Crassus also resented the fact that after he had suppressed the slave revolt led by Spartacus, Pompey had claimed the credit although he had only conducted the mopping-up operations. Caesar reconciled them and also tried to enlist Marcus Tullius Cicero—a senator, former consul, and the greatest orator of his time (Caesar was next greatest)—but Cicero refused to turn against the Senate. Each of the three partners agreed to support no political measure that was opposed by one of the others and to use his horde of followers to help grease their political machine and break heads as needed. To cement the alliance, Pompey took Caesar's daughter Julia as his fourth wife.

The understanding called for Caesar to be elected consul for the year 59 B.C. He proceeded to ram through all the legislation favored by his partners and opposed by the Senate and his cowed partner in the consulship, Bibulus, who stayed at home for most of his term of office. Instead of the consulship of Bibulus and Caesar, the joint tenure was jokingly referred to as the consulship of Julius and Caesar. Caesar also awarded himself the governorship of Roman Gaul and Illyricum for five years after expiration of his term as consul. This proconsulship, as it was called, included authorization to conduct operations in the vast unconquered part of Gaul.

When the triumvirate started to unravel because of quarreling between Pompey and Crassus, Caesar held a conference to patch things up with his partners at Lucca in 56 B.C. As a result, Pompey and Crassus became consuls in 55 and assigned themselves the proconsulships of Spain and Syria, respectively, for five years after their term. Caesar's commission in Gaul was also extended for another five years. Between 58 and 51 B.C., Caesar conquered most of modern-day France, Switzerland, Belgium, southern Holland, and Germany west of the Rhine, and invaded Britain twice. The military reputation he garnered, celebrated in his *Commentarii de bello Gallico* (*The Gallic Wars,* bane of Latin students everywhere), combined with political contacts, wealth, and a fiercely loyal army of battle-hardened soldiers, made Caesar an extremely dangerous man to his enemies and rivals.

Meanwhile, Julia had died in childbirth, dissolving a strong remaining bond between Caesar and Pompey. And Crassus, seeking military glory to surpass that of his partners, had embarked on a reckless invasion of Parthia on Rome's Euphrates frontier. He led his army of forty-four thousand to a stunning defeat at Carrhae in 53 B.C., where he was killed, decapitated, and made to play the severed head of King Pentheus in Euripides' tragedy *The Bacchae* for the delight of the Parthian King.

Rome now wasn't big enough for both Caesar and Pompey. When Caesar's term as proconsul ended, the Senate gave him an ultimatum: either lay down his military command or be declared an enemy of the state. Caesar tried to negotiate, but the terrified politicians at Rome refused to compromise, conferring dictatorial powers on Pompey as the lesser of two evils. Caesar then led one of his legions across the Rubicon (a small stream near Rimini) into Italy proper on January 10, 49 B.C., thereby igniting civil war—*"Alea jacta est"* ("the die is cast").

But Pompey was not so Great anymore; an early bloomer, he was now a vacillating politician and feckless general. With loyal senators and his troops, he fled from Rome to Greece, hoping eventually to crush Caesar between the pincers of his eastern army and his forces in Spain. Caesar entered Rome and seized the Treasury. First he defeated Pompey's generals in Spain, then Pompey himself at the Battle of Pharsalus in Thessaly, Greece, on August 9, 48 B.C., destroying an army more than twice the size of his own. Pompey fled to Egypt, where he was murdered by order of the Egyptian court. Finally, Caesar defeated Pompey's sons in northern Africa and Spain in 46 and 45, making himself sole master of the Roman world. His *Commentarii de bello civili (The Civil War)* is a superb account.

Caesar was made dictator for ten years in 46 B.C.; in February of 44, he became dictator for life. He undertook numerous reforms, including the Julian calendar, but could not dispel the suspicion that he was aiming at a monarchy, with Cleopatra, who had supposedly borne him a son, as his Queen. A conspiracy was formed, led by Brutus and Cassius, both of whom Caesar had pardoned for fighting against him in the civil war. Like Crassus and Pompey before him, Caesar was murdered, stabbed to death at a meeting of the Senate on the Ides (the 15th) of March, 44 B.C. He fell at the foot of a statue of Pompey the Great.

 QUESTION 16

Who were the 3 members of the Second Triumvirate?

Octavian (later Augustus)
Mark Antony
Lepidus

Unlike the First Triumvirate, which was a private agreement to control the Roman state for the benefit of three cronies (see Question 15), the Second Triumvirate was established in 43 B.C. with official autocratic powers to reestablish order after Julius Caesar's assassination in 44.

Marcus Antonius (c. 83–30 B.C.) was a trusted general of Caesar's and co-consul with him in the year of the dictator's murder. After the Ides of March, Mark Antony tried to slip into Caesar's sandals. He turned the people of Rome against the conspirators—who were forced to flee—by delivering a stirring funeral oration over the body, with its twenty-three stab wounds, and by publishing Caesar's will, which left some cash to every Roman citizen. But there was a snag: Caesar's great-nephew—and adopted son and heir—the eighteen-year-old **Gaius Octavius** (63 B.C.–A.D. 14) rushed to Rome, assumed the name Gaius Julius Caesar Octavianus, and received an enthusiastic reception from Caesar's veteran troops.

At first, this shrewdest of young men joined the Senate in trying to neutralize Antony, who had been declared a public enemy for trying to wrench a provincial command from one of the conspirators against Caesar. Octavian led an army to Mutina (Modena) and defeated Antony in April of 43 B.C., but realized that the Senate, led by Cicero, was just using him to get rid of Antony before it disposed of him, too. Octavian now marched on Rome and demanded the consulship and a death sentence against Caesar's murderers.

Antony fled beyond the Alps and joined his troops with those of **Marcus Aemilius Lepidus,** who had been consul with Caesar in 46 B.C., and was now provincial governor in Spain. Together they marched toward Rome with a formidable army. Octavian wisely decided to come to an understanding with these two most powerful Caesarian leaders at Bologna. This Second Triumvirate, sanctioned by Roman law on November 27, 43 B.C., and invested with unlimited powers for five years, was essentially a dictatorship of three for the purpose of *rei publicae constituendae* ("reorganizing the commonwealth"). A reign of terror ensued in which more than two thousand enemies of the Triumvirs were proscribed. Though many were butchered, many escaped.

But not Cicero (106–43 B.C.), who had backed Octavian as a young lad who might easily be controlled by the likes of wise old senators like himself. Cicero had inveighed against Antony in his *Philippics,* fourteen savagely vituperative speeches that he named after Demosthenes' three orations against Philip of Macedon (delivered when the father of Alexander the Great was threatening the freedom of Greece). This sarcastic genius was beheaded by Antony's order, and his head and hands were nailed to the Rostra in the Roman Forum, where he had delivered some of his diatribes against Antony.

Fresh from these massacres, the Triumvirs pounced on the army of republican resistance to their rule. Thanks to the superb generalship of Antony, he and Octavian crushed the forces of Brutus and Cassius at the two battles of Philippi in Macedonia (42 B.C.), while Lepidus was consul at Rome. The two chief assassins of Caesar committed suicide.

In the East, Antony met Cleopatra VII (60–30 B.C.), the fascinating Queen of Ptolemaic Egypt who was of Macedonian Greek descent, spoke numerous languages, wrote books on cosmetics and the Egyptian currency, and, though no great beauty, was "of infinite variety." He returned to Egypt with her, playing the role of Dionysus-Osiris to her Aphrodite-Isis (see Question 73).

Meanwhile, back in Italy, Antony's wife Fulvia and his brother began warring against Octavian. After defeating them, Octavian came to a new agreement with Antony and his followers in October of 40 B.C. Fulvia had conveniently died, leaving Antony free to marry his rival's sister, Octavia. A new distribution was made of the Roman

Empire, by which Antony received the rich eastern provinces, Octavian the core western provinces, including Rome itself, and Lepidus only northern Africa. In 37 B.C., the Triumvirate was renewed for another five years, but Antony had tired of the virtuous Octavia and returned to Cleopatra. In the following year, when the feckless Lepidus tried to acquire Sicily, Octavian stripped him of all power but allowed him to remain Roman high priest *(pontifex maximus*—still one of the Pope's titles) and kept him under strict guard in a Roman town until his death in 13 or 12 B.C.

And then there were two. Spurred by Octavian's devastating smear campaign—in which Antony and Cleopatra (now his fifth wife) were seen as planning to move the capital of the Empire to Alexandria and enslave Rome under a Greco-Egyptian-Oriental monarchy—the Senate revoked Antony's command and declared war against Cleopatra. The naval battle of Actium, September 2, 31 B.C., fought off the coast of Epirus in northwestern Greece, put an end to civil war, which had plagued Rome for much of the century, beginning with the clashes of Marius and Sulla. Antony's fleet was defeated by Octavian's admiral Agrippa, and his land forces defected or melted away. Antony himself, with forty ships, followed Cleopatra's sixty, which bolted for Egypt. Antony committed suicide in Alexandria in 30 B.C. when Octavian hunted him down there, and Cleopatra killed herself with the help of an asp (cobra) after an attempt to charm the calculating Octavian failed.

Octavian now ordered the murder of the young man whom Cleopatra claimed she had borne to Julius Caesar (Ptolemy Caesar, nicknamed Caesarion—"Little Caesar"). Her twins by Antony (Alexander Helios—the Sun—and Cleopatra Selene—the Moon) were sent to Rome to grace Octavian's triumph. The once-mighty kingdom of Egypt and its stupendous treasure fell prey to Octavian, who ended the three-hundred-year reign of the Ptolemies. Octavian was sole, undisputed ruler of Rome and its enormous empire.

In 27 B.C., Octavian received the name Augustus ("venerable, majestic, revered") from the Senate. Though he disguised his absolute power under the title of *princeps civitatis* ("first citizen") and *princeps senatus* ("leader of the Senate"), he was now actually the first Roman Emperor—the old term *imperator* (a military general or commander-in-chief) receiving a new meaning as one of the titles of Augustus and his successors. He deprived Rome of a specious liberty but inaugurated an epoch of peace, the *pax Romana,* under a facade of revived republican forms in which all the real power was his.

Augustan Rome—with its poets Virgil, Horace, Tibullus, Propertius, and Ovid, the historian Livy, and the literary patron Maecenas—fostered a glorious cultural efflorescence. Yet the untrammeled vigor of Cicero, Caesar, Lucretius, Sallust, and Catullus of the preceding age was gone. After a long reign (27 B.C.–A.D. 14), Augustus died at age seventy-six and was succeeded by his stepson Tiberius. The tenure of the Western Roman emperors lasted until 476, when the Germanic chieftain Odoacer deposed Romulus Augustulus and became the first barbarian king of Italy.

 QUESTION 17

What are Newton's 3 Laws of Motion?

1. **An object moves at a constant velocity—which may include zero velocity—unless an outside force intervenes. (Or: An object in motion tends to stay in motion, and an object at rest tends to stay at rest, unless compelled to change that state by forces impressed upon it.)**
2. **The change of motion is proportional to the motive force impressed and is made in the direction of the straight line in which that force is impressed.**
3. **For every action, there is an equal and opposite reaction.**

Referring to his predecessors, including Galileo and Kepler, English mathematician and physicist Isaac Newton (1642–1727) wrote to fellow scientist Robert Hooke, "If I have seen further it is by standing on the shoulders of Giants." Newton's graciousness did not extend to his contemporaries, however. The man who explained the rainbow, invented calculus, provided the foundation for modern optics, devised the three laws of motion, and formulated the law of universal gravitation was bellicose, absentminded, insecure, and suspicious. He was nearly constantly embroiled in rancorous disputes with some of the finest minds of his time, most notably Hooke and German philosopher and mathematician Gottfried Leibniz. Probably rivaled only by Einstein for scientific achievement, Newton wrote more about theology than about mathematics or physics, and he interpreted the Bible literally, especially the books of Daniel and Revelation. He was also devoted to the study of astrology.

Tiny, sickly Isaac Newton was born near Lincolnshire on Christmas Day in 1642, a few months after the death of his father (and Galileo). His mother married a wealthy minister two years later and moved to a nearby hamlet, leaving Isaac with his grandmother. He lived apart from his mother for nearly a decade and later wrote that the trauma of this separation made him consider burning down the house in which she lived with his stepfather.

After an unremarkable performance in grammar school, Newton entered Trinity College, Cambridge, in 1661. Although the curriculum was still Aristotelian, Newton soon immersed himself in the work of French mathematician and philosopher René Descartes and English chemist Robert Boyle. In a notebook he kept at this time he wrote, "Plato is my friend, Aristotle is my friend, but my best friend is truth." He insisted that he did not invent hypotheses, meaning that he chose to provide observations, not explanations, and strove to describe his observations mathematically.

Shortly after he received his baccalaureate in 1665, the university was closed because of the advancing plague, and Newton remained at home for the next two years—perhaps the most significant two years in the history of science. Working in solitude, Newton devised calculus, revolutionized optics, and formulated the laws of motion and of universal gravitation.

Newton returned to Cambridge in 1667, circulated his manuscript on "fluxions," or calculus, and became Lucasian Professor of Mathematics. His initial lecture series covered most of the material later included in Book One of his *Opticks*. A major contribution was his observation that white light could be separated by a prism into its rainbow components—red, orange, yellow, green, blue, indigo, and violet—and reassembled into white light when passed through another prism. This elucidation of the composition of light had vast consequences in astronomy and physical optics.

It wasn't until 1687 that Newton published *Philosophiae Naturalis*

Principia Mathematica, in which he expounded his three laws of motion and the law of universal gravitation. The *Principia,* probably the greatest scientific book ever written, brought international acclaim to its author.

The laws of motion are axiomatic, that is, they can't be proven. **The first law** seems logical enough, and Galileo had proposed it a half century earlier: An object at rest wants to stay at rest, and an object in motion wants to stay in motion, unless an outside force acts on it. A force is nothing more than a tug or push in one direction or another. Couch potatoes will understand why the first law is also called the Law of Inertia.

The trick with the first law is that it specifies a constant velocity. Velocity is not the same as speed because the velocity of an object changes if the direction of the object changes. Thus, a race car traveling around a track at a constant speed is traveling at a constantly changing velocity.

The second law implies that the force (F) of an object is the product of the object's mass (M) and its acceleration (A), often expressed as $F = MA$. The law confirms our intuition: The greater an object's mass, the more force will be required to get it moving up a ramp or across a floor. Conversely, the greater its mass and acceleration, the greater will be the force of the impact if it collides with something. Applying the second law becomes more difficult when the mass of an object changes during acceleration, an unusual complication best exemplified by the launch of a spacecraft, when boosters and rocket stages drop off as the craft accelerates spaceward.

The third law specifies that if an object acts with a given force on a second object, the second object reacts with an equal, but opposite, force. Imagine yourself standing on ice in leather-soled shoes trying to liberate your car from a snow rut. Lean over and give that bumper a push—the car goes nowhere, but you fly backward.

Just warming up, Newton applied the laws of motion to the study of circular motion, since he hoped to determine the nature and strength of a force that could persuade an object such as a planet moving in a straight line to adopt a circular course. The result was Newton's law of universal gravitation, which states that two bodies (such as the earth and sun) attract each other with a force that is proportional to their masses and inversely proportional to the square of the distance that separates them. If the mass of one object is doubled, the attractive force between the objects is also doubled. On the other hand, as the distance between the objects grows, the force between them diminishes by the inverse of the square of the distance between them. So, if the distance between two objects is quadrupled, the force between them is now only $1/16$ what it was. The law may be expressed algebraically as

$$F = \frac{G \times m_1 \times m_2}{d^2}$$

Here, F is the force of gravitational attraction between any two objects, the two m's stand for their respective masses, d is the distance between them, and G is a constant called the constant of gravitation.

When Newton proposed his law of gravitation, critics noted his failure to provide a description of the nature of gravity. Much later, Albert Einstein hypothesized that it was due to the warpage of space-time in the vicinity of massive objects. Newton himself was content to explain how gravity worked rather than what it was. And yes, he did claim that the idea of gravitation was "occasioned by the fall of an apple."

After publication of the *Principia,* Newton became the acknowledged dean of British science, and this was the peak of his career. Over the next several years he suffered at least one mental breakdown and became increasingly involved in theological and astrological studies. His quarrels with his scientific contemporaries continued. He moved to London, where he was appointed Warden of the Royal Mint. During his tenure there, he became obsessed with counterfeiting and, applying himself to that problem with the same assiduity he had shown in mathematics and physics, he sent several men to the gallows for transgressions against the Crown's coinage. Newton was appointed president of the Royal Society in 1703 (a post he held until his death), and when Queen Anne knighted him at Cambridge in 1705, he became the first person so recognized for his scientific achievements.

Throughout his later years, Sir Isaac continued to revise his major works and publish Latin and English editions of them. He sharply challenged Leibniz over which of them had first established the methods of calculus (Newton had), and he continued his vicious attacks long after his rival had gone to his grave.

It's difficult to reconcile this Newton with the man who wrote in his memoirs, "I do not know what I may appear to the world; but to myself I seem to have been only like a boy playing on the seashore, and diverting myself in now and then finding a smoother pebble or a prettier shell than ordinary, whilst the great ocean of truth lay all undiscovered before me."

✤ QUESTION 18

What were the 3 Temptations of Christ?

1. To turn stones into loaves of bread with which to feed himself
2. To throw himself down from the parapet of the Temple to prove he was the Son of God
3. To worship Satan in return for all the kingdoms of the world

In Matthew's Gospel, when Jesus is baptized by John the Baptist in the River Jordan, the voice of God proclaims Christ to be his Son. Jesus then goes into the wilderness to fast and be tempted by Satan for forty days (Matthew 4:1–11). When the Devil tempts him **to turn stones into bread,** the famished Christ replies by quoting Scripture: "Man does not live on bread alone but on every word that comes from the mouth of God" (Deuteronomy 8:3). This may be interpreted as a refusal to distrust God's providence and a rejection of a mission dedicated to satisfying merely physical and material needs.

Since "the Devil can cite Scripture for his purpose," Satan now whisks Christ away, dares him **to throw himself down from the parapet of the Temple at Jerusalem to prove he is the Son of God,** and reminds him of the words of Psalm 91 (11–12): "He will put angels in charge of you, and they will support you in their arms, for fear you should strike your foot against a stone." But Christ refuses to be the type of miracle-worker who gains converts with "magic tricks" to win over an incredulous populace. Fighting Scripture with

Scripture, Christ rejects Satan's proposal by citing Deuteronomy 6:16: "You must not put the Lord your God to the test."

In the third temptation, Christ is taken to a very high mountain and asked **to fall at Satan's feet and worship him in return for all the kingdoms of the world,** which are visible from that eminence. Christ now chases the pest away ("Get thee behind me, Satan!"), quoting Deuteronomy for the third time—"You must worship the Lord your God, and serve him alone" (6:13)—thus flatly rejecting any bargain with the Devil. After Satan's departure, angels come and minister to Christ, who, on leaving the wilderness, returns to Galilee and calls his first four disciples (see Question 91).

Matthew, writing for Jewish Christians, draws parallels between the experiences of Christ and of Moses in the wilderness. The forty days that Christ spends in the desert, subjected to Satanic temptations before embarking on his public ministry, recall the forty years that the Jews wander in the desert before their entry into the Holy Land. The temptation to turn stones into bread mirrors the Jews' longing for "the fleshpots of Egypt" and their being fed with breadlike manna (and quails) in Exodus 16. Christ's refusal to perform a miracle to prove that he is the Son of God is reminiscent of the Jews' clamoring for Moses to give them water to drink, to which he replied, "Why do you put Yahweh to the test?" (Exodus 17). And Christ's refusal to worship Satan contrasts with the Jews' idolatrous worship of the golden calf (Exodus 32).

Medieval exegetes saw an instructive contrast between the failure of the first man, Adam, to withstand Satan's temptation, and the exemplary triumph of Christ, the second Adam, over the Adversary. Thus, Adam's tasting of the forbidden fruit in the Garden of Eden was paralleled by Christ's refusal to change stones into bread and succumb to the sin of gluttony. The Devil's appeal to vainglory took the form of "You shall be as gods" in Genesis and "If you are the Son of God, throw yourself down" in the New Testament. Finally, Satan's promises that Adam and Eve will know good and evil and that Christ will receive all the kingdoms of the world were both temptations of avarice. These two sets of temptations were said to be recalled in 1 John 2:16.

John's Gospel does not mention the temptations of Christ, Mark's does so very cursorily (1:12–13), and Luke gives a version similar to Matthew's but switches the order of the second and third temptations (4:1–13). This is the order that John Milton (1608–74) followed in his brief epic, *Paradise Regained* (1671). After his full-length epic poem, *Paradise Lost* (1667), which deals with the consequences of Adam's disobedience of God, Milton decided to celebrate in verse the perfect obedience and trust in God of the second Adam at the outset of his ministry.

The climax of *Paradise Regained* occurs when Satan cruelly and cynically places Christ on the needlepoint pinnacle of the Temple, bidding him either stand there or else cast himself down and presumptuously rely on God's providence. Miraculously, Christ continues to stand, thus fully recognizing his own divinity and, at the same time, manifesting it to Satan, who falls from the heights, vanquished. Milton implies that, like Christ, each human must withstand the snares of Satan and the world to regain the paradise lost by Adam. This is not a mere place (the garden of Eden), nor only a moral state (the "paradise within . . . , happier far" of *Paradise Lost*), but eternal salvation in heaven, whose gates Christ reopened by his sacrificial death on the cross and final rout of Satan.

In 1951, the Greek writer Nikos Kazantzakis (1883–1957), author of *Zorba the Greek,* caused a furor with his novel *The Last Temptation of Christ,* mainly for a long dream sequence that takes place during a split second when Christ faints while on the cross. This last and most powerful of Satan's temptations makes Christ believe he has only dreamed that he was crucified. The vision entices him with the lure of the flesh and the delights of this world in the form of a sex scene with the prostitute Mary Magdalene in an Edenic garden and, after her death, a ménage à trois with Martha and Mary of Bethany, who bear his children. But Christ soon wakes in agony on the cross, rejects the seductive vision sent by Satan, and fulfills his redemptive mission by dying for mankind.

Martin Scorsese's 1988 film version of the novel adheres to it closely. As a result, on the day before it opened, twenty-five thousand protestors demonstrated against it at Universal Pictures in Los Angeles.

Norman Mailer's 1997 novel, *The Gospel According to the Son,* is a first-person narrative of Christ's life. The book contains an expanded version of the temptations of Christ in which Satan claims to share power with God—a tempting theodicy that absolves God of blame for the evil in the world by ascribing it to a wicked Other, as did the Albigensians, Manicheans, and Zoroastrians long before Mailer.

Who were the 3 Fates?

Clotho
Lachesis
Atropos

Daughters of the night. Weavers of destiny. Distributors of good and evil, prosperity and suffering. They are the Three Fates, or *Moirai* (MOY-rye), the awe-inspiring goddesses whom the ancient Greeks considered the dispensers of all good luck and ill fortune. Because of their prominent role at the very beginning of human life, they were sometimes viewed as goddesses of childbirth. But since the Fates dash human aspirations more often than they abet them, these three sisters were nearly always depicted as jealous, capricious, and malevolent creatures. No guardian angels or merry midwives here.

In his *Theogony,* the Greek poet Hesiod (fl. c. 800 B.C.) was apparently the first to enumerate three of these charming ladies, as opposed to the earlier abstract concept of Fate. **Clotho** (CLOE-thoe), "the spinner," is said to be the youngest of the sisters. She forms the child in the womb and, distaff in hand, spins out the thread of the newborn's life. **Lachesis** (LACK-uh-sis), "the measurer," determines the length of the thread of life spun by Clotho and assigns a destiny to the newborn. **Atropos** (AT-roe-poss), "she who cannot be avoided," is the oldest of the sisters. With her "abhorred shears" (as John Milton called them), Atropos cuts the thread of life at the point determined by Lachesis. Our word *atropine* (for a drug of the belladonna or deadly nightshade family) is derived from her name.

Greek mythology contains various accounts of the origin of the Fates and the extent of their dominion. According to Hesiod, Zeus fathered the Fates on Themis, the goddess of justice and right. Other poets identified them as the daughters of Erebus (Hell) and Nyx

(Night) or as the parthenogenous offspring of the grim goddess Ananke (Necessity).

Aeschylus insisted that not even Zeus himself stood above the Fates' decrees, "For he, too, cannot escape what is fated." Other poets claimed Zeus maintained veto power over what the Fates ordained, while some sanguine thinkers believed it was possible to lengthen Lachesis's thread by behaving judiciously—the ancient equivalent of wearing a seat belt or quitting smoking. On one occasion the god Apollo got the Fates drunk to save the life of his doomed friend Admetus. Even so, the Three Tipplers drove a hard bargain: Admetus had to find someone willing to die in his place. His young wife Alcestis agreed, but the play of Euripides named for her has a happy ending after Heracles descends into the underworld and brings the heroic woman back.

Not surprisingly, the Fates are usually represented in art as ugly, deformed old women. Occasionally they are given a statelier, more classical look, with Clotho holding a spindle, Lachesis a scroll (probably a book of fate), and Atropos a blade for cutting the thread of life.

To the Romans, the Fates were the *Parcae* (PAR-kye or PAR-see) or the *Fata*. Some say the origin of the word *parcae* is *parere,* "to bring forth," in an allusion to the Fates' connection with childbirth. Another theory maintains the root is *parcere,* "to show mercy," suggesting their name had an apotropaic function, that is, it would ward off evil by euphemism and wishful thinking, much as the Greeks sometimes called the dreaded Furies the Eumenides or "Kindly Ones" (see Question 14). The Latin word *Fata* comes from *fatum*—something spoken or decreed. At the end of a newborn's first week of life, the *Fata Scribunda* were called down to inscribe the child's fate in life. The Roman names for the individual Fates were Nona, Decuma, and Morta, which again were references to childbirth: a nine-months' birth (Nona), a ten-months' birth (Decuma), or a stillborn child (Morta).

In Norse mythology, the function of the Fates was assumed by the Norns—Urth, Verthandi, and Skuld, meaning past, present, and future, respectively. They, too, were said to haunt the cradles of newborns. The Norns also guarded the well that fed Yggdrasil, the great ash tree that supports the universe. They put in an appearance in the first scene of Richard Wagner's opera *Götterdämmerung* to determine the fate of the universe (it's bad news for everyone). The three witches or "Weird Sisters" in Shakespeare's *Macbeth* are probably British descendants of the Norns.

The Three Fates have even managed to survive in twentieth-century Greek consciousness. The *Moirai* are still said to appear on the third night after a baby's birth to lay out the course of its life.

What were the 4 elements and their associated humors?

> Earth: melancholic
> Water: phlegmatic
> Air: sanguine
> Fire: choleric

What are things made of? Various Presocratic philosophers of ancient Greece speculated about which material substance was the ultimate building block of the universe. Thales considered water the origin of all things (see Question 62). For Anaximenes, it was air. Heraclitus opted for fire, Pherecydes for earth. The Sicilian Greek philosopher Empedocles (fifth century B.C.) claimed that all four of these substances might be the primal "elements" of things. Although he considered the elements permanent and unchangeable in themselves, he thought they could be divided, combined, and rearranged in various proportions through the actions of Love and Strife, the constructive and destructive forces in the world. This perpetual intermixture generated all things in nature—including ourselves.

Aristotle (384–322 B.C.), who later articulated the theory of the four elements into an influential philosophical system, believed that the elements could even be changed into one another. For example, cold and moisture produced water, but if heat were then applied, the result would be air (steam). He also taught that each of the four elements had its proper "sphere" or habitation: earth and water here on the earth, air above us, and fire above the sphere of air, but below that of the moon. Stars were accordingly thought to be tiny holes in the sphere of air that revealed glimpses of the fire blazing in the sphere above it.

Medieval and Renaissance medicine and psychology, taking their cue from the Greek physician Galen (c. 129–c. 200), often associated the four elements with four bodily fluids and four temperaments. Imbalances of these fluids produced the temperaments (or personality types) called "humors."

Earth corresponded to black bile (or gall), and too much of this fluid, secreted from the kidneys and spleen, caused a person to be **melancholic** (Greek, "black bile"). Hamlet, "the melancholy Dane," is Shakespeare's most famous study of this temperament, which was marked by introspection, weltschmerz, depression, affectation, and reclusiveness. The melancholic intellectual, like Hamlet, was only one type. The melancholic lover, furiously scribbling love sonnets, was a staple of Elizabethan comedy. There was also the melancholic malcontent, like the spiteful and slanderous Thersites in *Troilus and Cressida* and the malicious Don John of *Much Ado About Nothing*. And nobody knows why Antonio, the merchant of Venice, was melancholic. He himself was clueless: "In sooth, I know not why I am so sad." The seventeenth-century English author Robert Burton wrote his interminable treatise *The Anatomy of Melancholy* (1621) as a therapeutic attempt to alleviate his own melancholic depression.

Water was linked to phlegm, the body's watery substances. An excess of these resulted in **phlegmatic** characters, who were cowardly, dull, sluggish, and apathetic—in short, cold fish. The puritanical killjoy Malvolio in *Twelfth Night*—who has to be reminded by Sir Toby Belch, "Dost thou think because thou art virtuous, there shall be no more cakes and ale?"—might serve as an example of the phlegmatic humor.

The element of **air** was associated with blood (Latin, *sanguis),* and too much blood produced someone like Falstaff, a larger-than-life embodiment of the **sanguine** humor—lusty, cheerful, good-natured, optimistic, carefree.

Fire corresponded to yellow bile (Greek, *chole),* secreted from the liver, and produced a **choleric** man like King Lear or the young Henry Percy (Hotspur) in *Henry the Fourth, Part I*—easily angered, stubborn, vindictive, and impatient.

Shakespeare's friend Ben Jonson elaborated his own version of these notions in his "comedies of humours," in which the main characters of plays such as *Every Man in His Humour, Every Man Out of His Humour,* and *Volpone* all have a dominant "humour"—a character trait, whim, or quirky obsession. It's a short step from this sense of "humourous" characters in comedy to our own meaning of "funny" or "amusing."

The psychology and physiology of the humors died hard. In the eighteenth century, the noted botanist and taxonomist Linnaeus (see Question 57) absurdly tried to associate the four humors with four main ethnic groups:

+ Africans: phlegmatic
+ American Indians: choleric
+ Asians: melancholic
+ Europeans: sanguine

And well into the nineteenth century, some physicians tried to restore the balance of their patients' humors by bleeding them or making them sweat, vomit, or purge their bowels.

But Aristotle had suspected that, beyond the four material (or sublunary) elements, there was the mysterious quintessence ("fifth essence or element")—the pure, immaterial, unchangeable substance of the heavenly bodies. In a different vein, Pope Boniface VIII in 1300 identified the fifth element with the wealthy and ambitious Florentines, who, like the other four elements, "seem to rule the world." And much later, Napoleon, bogged down in the nightmarish fiasco of his invasion of Russia (see Question 46), disgustedly asserted that the fifth element was none other than mud.

❧ QUESTION 21

What are the 4 voyages of Lemuel Gulliver?

1. **To Lilliput**
2. **To Brobdingnag**
3. **To Laputa, Balnibarbi, Glubbdubdrib, Luggnagg, and Japan**
4. **To the country of the Houyhnhnms**

Gulliver's Travels (1726), the masterpiece of Jonathan Swift (1667–1745), an Anglican churchman born of English parents in Dublin, was published anonymously as *Travels into Several Remote Nations of the World. In Four Parts. By Lemuel Gulliver, First a Surgeon, and then a Captain of several Ships.* The book is a satire of travel narratives, utopian literature, contemporary England and Europe—and one of the most trenchant excoriations of the vices, stupidities, and pretensions of our species.

After serving the Tory government in London as a political journalist, Swift hoped to be rewarded with an English bishopric. His satire on religious factions, however, *A Tale of a Tub* (1704), had offended the Archbishop of York by its coarseness, and his caustic wit had alienated at least one duchess, so in 1713 Queen Anne made Swift the Dean of St. Patrick's Cathedral in Dublin instead. Soured by the ingratitude of the high-and-mighty, he viewed his appointment as a sentence of exile.

Is it accidental that *Gulliver's Travels* chronicles the change of the narrator—an honest, reasonably well educated (though naive) ship's surgeon—from a kindly man into a misanthrope? The four voyages represent the successive stages of the gullible Gulliver's education on the nature of the human race: its petty political and personal malice, physical and moral grossness, intellectual aberrations, and quintessential bestiality. Gulliver becomes progressively more disgusted with humans—corrupt in soul, body, and mind—finally identifying them with the repulsive Yahoos.

Book I is mainly a satire on court life and its sycophancy, vindictiveness, treachery, and cruelty. Gulliver, shipwrecked on **Lilliput** (presumably an island southwest of Sumatra), finds himself among the six-inch Lilliputians, in whose country everything is one twelfth the size of ours. In the political allegory, the Emperor of Lilliput represents King George I (reigned 1714–27), and the Empress is based on his predecessor Queen Anne (1702–14). The neighboring island of Blefuscu (France) is also populated with tiny inhabitants, and the age-old conflict between it and Lilliput had originated in the division between Big-Endians and Little-Endians (Catholics and Protestants) over the momentous question of which end to crack their eggs on. After Gulliver ends the current war between them (the War of the Spanish Succession, 1701–14) by capturing the entire Blefuscudian fleet, he becomes the Lilliputians' man-mountain of the hour.

But when the Empress's apartments catch fire and Gulliver urinates on part of the palace to quench the flames, she conceives a deep enmity for him. Soon other court intrigues and ministerial jealousies seal his fate. When the fickle Lilliputians sentence him to be starved to death, Gulliver escapes to Blefuscu, whence he returns to England.

On his second voyage, Gulliver ends up in **Brobdingnag** (somewhere near Alaska), whose gigantic denizens enjoy an exemplary political system. Gulliver now looks out the other end of the telescope to discover that he is one tenth the size of the sixty-foot Brobdingnagians. On this voyage he realizes that concepts such as human beauty and power are highly relative. Because his senses are exquisitely acute in this gargantuan land, the body odor and skin blemishes of the saucy Maids of Honor at the royal court, who strip him naked and place him on their breasts or nipples, arouse his unspeakable disgust. But when Gulliver proudly recounts the fierce wars and political machinations of Europeans, the humane King of Brobdingnag concludes that Gulliver and his kind are "the most pernicious Race of little odious Vermin that Nature ever suffered to crawl upon the Surface of the Earth." Now it's Gulliver's turn to feel like an insectile Lilliputian as the moral and physical puniness of his species is revealed.

After returning home and embarking again, Gulliver encounters various corruptions of the intellect in Book III, which describes unknown islands located east of Japan. Swift's close friend Alexander Pope (1688–1744) wrote that "the proper study of mankind is Man," and the useless speculation and scientific research ridiculed in this book are absurdly irrelevant to human well-being and moral wisdom. In Swift's view, the adherents of abstract science, abstruse mathematics, and musical theory in **Laputa** (Spanish, *la puta,* "the whore") have prostituted their reason to the service of a barren intellectualism. They might as well live in the Cloud-Cuckoo-Land of Socrates as depicted by Aristophanes—and, indeed, their Flying Island of Laputa is literally in the clouds.

The Laputans, absentminded professors par excellence, need "flappers" to smack them with a balloonlike device on the mouth when they're expected to speak, on the ears when they should listen, and on the head before they cross the street. They're so constantly engrossed with their cogitations and calculations that their wives can cuckold them in front of their eyes, provided the husbands are furnished with pencil and paper.

Balnibarbi, the island beneath Laputa, contains the city of

Lagado, with its Grand Academy (read the Royal Society of London), where "projectors" spend years engaged in experiments such as trying to extract sunbeams from cucumbers, change human excrement back into food, develop sheep without wool, build houses from the roof downward, and write books with the aid of a protocomputer that spits out random words. Others substitute things for words in a "language" that requires people to carry huge sacks of objects for whatever they might want to say. On the neighboring island of **Glubbdubdrib,** where magicians summon up the spirits of the dead, Gulliver learns that many of the movers and shakers of the past hundred years were "bawds, whores, pimps, parasites, and buffoons." In the island of **Luggnagg,** the ghastly death-in-life of the immortal Struldbruggs conveys a warning to those who hope that science might someday conquer death. From Luggnagg, Gulliver sails to **Japan** before proceeding to Amsterdam and England.

After five months at home, Gulliver's wanderlust gets the better of him again. This time he sets out as a ship's captain, but his men mutiny and abandon him on an unknown island, **the country of the Houyhnhnms.** In Book IV, the futile attempt to transcend human limitations is portrayed in the dull, functional, sovietized, spartan, stoical, impersonal society of the equine Houyhnhnms (HWIN-ims, suggesting a horse's whinnying). These parodic equivalents of the citizens of Plato's Republic or Thomas More's Utopia lack all emotion, good or bad, and face the myriad vicissitudes of life with the sangfroid of well-programmed robots. The choice of horses as the epitome of reason is ironic: In his *Phaedrus,* Plato had used the image of a charioteer reining in his horses to represent reason controlling the excesses of passion, and the half-man, half-horse centaurs of Greek myth were, except for wise Chiron, a lusty, brawling, drunken crew.

Counterbalancing the Houyhnhnms are their slaves—the obscene, filthy, malicious Yahoos, who seem to be swinishly savage naked humans on all fours. Gulliver is astonished to learn that his beloved Houyhnhnms, with whom he has lived three years, after hearing his account of European events, consider his people to be Yahoos with "some small Pittance of Reason" that makes them even more dangerous. In the end, despite Gulliver's fervent wish to remain with them and advance in virtue, they send him away to protect themselves from his corrupting influence. Gulliver sadly reflects, "I thought it might consist with Reason to have been less rigorous."

How far does Gulliver speak for Swift in idolizing the Houy-hnhnms and equating the loathsome Yahoos with humans? This is the main scholarly crux of *Gulliver's Travels*. Let's examine the book's ending.

Gulliver relates that, after returning to England, he faints in horror when his wife kisses him on his arrival: "My Wife and Family received me with great Surprize and Joy . . . but I must freely confess, the Sight of them filled me only with Hatred, Disgust and Contempt." When he's told that he still walks and whinnies much like a horse, he takes this to be a great compliment. Finding the smell of his family intolerable, he buys a pair of stallions and talks with them for at least four hours a day in the barn.

True, the author shared Gulliver's obsession with bodily functions and human smells, which has been called Swift's "excremental vision" and is also evident in some of his humorously scatological poems, such as "The Lady's Dressing Room" and "A Beautiful Young Nymph Going to Bed." But Gulliver, who considers his wife and children to be Yahoos, is ludicrously deranged by the end of the book, his long gaze into the abyss of human nature on his four voyages having driven him hopelessly insane.

In Book IV, Swift has separated humans into two parts, rationality and bestiality. While humans are capable of subordinating their irrational passions to their reason, they cannot banish the emotions that result from their corporeality and fallen natures. Swift's deeply conservative view of the limited potential of mankind, ultimately rooted in his Christianity, led him to claim that man was not a rational animal, but an *"animal rationis capax"*—one only *capable* of reason. While habitual irrationality is self-destructive, any attempt to live unwaveringly by the dictates of reason is doomed to failure and highly presumptuous. The corollary of Gulliver's modeling himself on the prelapsarian Houyhnhnms is his ridiculous blindness to anything but bestiality in his fellow humans. A cynic is often a disillusioned idealist.

The Houyhnhnms love their species but are indifferent to individuals; Swift claimed that he loved individuals but hated the human species in the abstract. Perhaps both viewpoints are forms of misanthropy: In the Latin epitaph he wrote for himself, Swift tells us he has departed to where "fierce indignation *[saeva indignatio]* can lacerate his heart no more."

One thing is clear: *Gulliver's Travels* is anything but "a children's book." The usually astute Samuel Johnson (1709–84) was dead wrong to say of it, "When once you have thought of big men and little men, it is very easy to do all the rest."

⚛ QUESTION 22

What are the 4 conic sections?

> Circle
> Ellipse
> Parabola
> Hyperbola

A conic section is one of four possible curves that can be generated by slicing through a circular double cone with a plane (see Figure 1). This double cone comprises two "halves" or nappes, which share an axis that runs directly through the center of each and continues infinitely in both directions. It has no true top or bottom, just two open ends that extend infinitely into space. A base is created only if the cone is intersected in some way by a plane. Depending on the angle at which the cone is sliced, we end up with a different conic section.

A **circle** is formed when a plane slices a nappe perpendicularly to its axis. Tilting the intersecting plane will result in an **ellipse,** formed when the plane slices one nappe neither perpendicularly to its axis nor parallel to the axis or any generating line on the surface of the cone. Tilting the intersecting plane farther will result in a **parabola,** generated when the plane slicing a nappe is parallel to any generating line on the cone's surface. Finally, tilting the plane even farther toward the axis or vertical will result in a **hyperbola,** which comprises two curves, each called a branch of the hyperbola. The plane must slice the cone such that it is parallel to the axis of the cone and intersects both the upper and lower nappes.

Each conic section has its own graph on a Cartesian coordinate plane, as first formulated by René Descartes in his *Géométrie* (1637).

The Conic Sections and Their Graphs

Figure 1

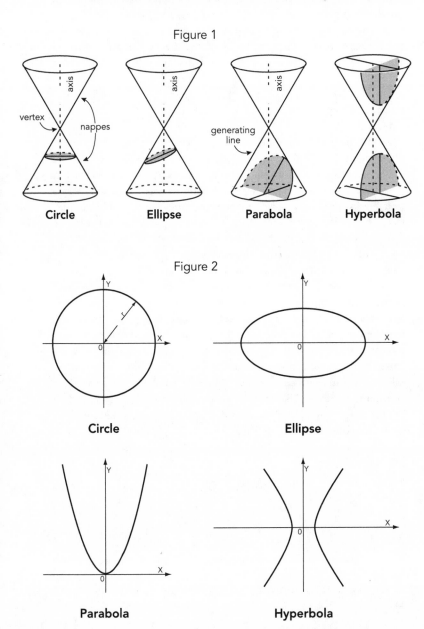

Circle   Ellipse   Parabola   Hyperbola

Figure 2

Circle   Ellipse

Parabola   Hyperbola

The graph of each section is merely a two-dimensional representation of what that particular slice of the cone looks like (see Figure 2). Each conic section also has its own characteristic equation. For example, the equation of a circle with its center at the origin (marked 0 on our graph) and radius r is $x^2 + y^2 = r^2$. This means that, for any point on a circle in this position, the square of the value of its x coordinate (along the horizontal axis), plus the square of the value of its y coordinate (along the vertical axis), equals the square of the circle's radius, r.

The ancient Greeks were originally responsible for all this slashing of perfectly good cones. The theory of conic sections probably arose in Plato's Academy, since the first to use them was Menaechmus, a pupil of Plato, in about 350 B.C. Somewhat later, Euclid wrote four books on conics that have been lost but were probably summarized in the first four books of the *Conics* of Apollonius of Perga, the first surviving treatise on the subject (c. 225 B.C.). In this work, Apollonius introduced the terms *ellipse* ("defect"), *parabola* ("equality"), and *hyperbola* ("excess," related to our word *hyperbole*).

Conic sections have scads of practical applications in fields such as mechanics, engineering, optics, astronomy, navigation, and warfare—from the elliptical paths of the planets, first postulated by Johannes Kepler (see Question 3), to the parabolic motion of projectiles such as artillery shells, to the parabolic structure of headlights, contact lenses, and satellite dishes. The design of a headlight, for example, calls for a source of light at the focus of a parabolic reflector. This allows the light to strike all parts of the reflector's surface and then bounce off in parallel beams instead of remaining a diffuse, localized glow like that of a lantern.

⚛ QUESTION 23

What are the 4 sections of a symphony orchestra?

Strings
Woodwinds
Brass
Percussion

In ancient Greek theaters, the orchestra ("dancing place") referred to a circular area in front of the stage where a chorus of about a dozen men in masks danced and sang their choral odes. A modern symphony orchestra has forgone the dancing, singing, and masks while greatly increasing the number of members to about one hundred, depending on the scheduled musical program.

The **strings** are the largest section, with about thirty-two violins, ten violas, twelve cellos, ten double basses, and often a harp. The violins are further categorized as first and second, with sixteen in each subsection. One player among the first violins, usually the most senior or proficient, is designated the concertmaster and serves as a kind of assistant conductor. The concertmaster, who may also double as a soloist if required, ensures that all the first-violin players bow their instruments in synchrony. He or she also tunes the orchestra before the conductor arrives on the podium.

First and second violins are identical instruments. Second violins, or "second fiddles," may play a countermelody or supporting harmonic passage but occasionally play the same passage as the first violins. If violins are the sopranos, the darker, richer violas are the altos. The cellos provide even richer, warmer tones, and the basses function like Atlas, supporting all that goes on above.

The **woodwinds** usually feature one piccolo, two flutes, two clarinets, two oboes, and two bassoons in their section. Depending on the musical program, a saxophone may also make an appearance. All are made of wood except for flutes, most of which are now metallic, and saxophones. Woodwinds can be classified as single-reed or double-reed. The single-reed instruments—clarinets and saxophones—produce sound when the musician blows air into the narrow gap between the mouthpiece and a reed held in place against it, causing the air inside the instrument to vibrate. The pitch is varied when holes along the side of the instrument are covered and uncovered. The double-reeds—oboes, bassoons, and English horns—have two smaller, thinner reeds at the mouthpiece and produce a nasal sound, as compared with the warm, earthy single-reeds. The flute and piccolo, which are not reed instruments, are descended from simple pipes of very ancient times. The musician blows air across the opening at the mouthpiece—a bit like making sounds by blowing across the top of a soda bottle.

The **brass** section typically includes four horns, two trumpets, three trombones, and a tuba. Rather than blowing across a hole or into a reed, brass players blow into a cupped mouthpiece, and their lips act as the reeds. Each register is produced by a different lip pressure, and individual notes are generated by the use of keys, valves, and slide positions. The trumpet is the soprano, the trombone the tenor and baritone, the tuba the bass, and the French horn (so called to distinguish it from the English horn, which is an alto oboe) defies categorization with its wide range of voice.

The **percussion** section exhibits the most diversity and may include timpani (kettledrums), snare and bass drums, a xylophone, vibraphone, glockenspiel, and a host of miscellaneous items—chimes, bells, triangles, cymbals, wood blocks, maracas, and gongs. The timpani can be tuned to a specific pitch, and most orchestras have three or four in a group.

Seating plans for orchestras vary somewhat. In 1998, the Boston Symphony Orchestra featured the first and second violins to the left of the conductor, the violas to the right, and the cellos and double basses behind the violas. The flutes, clarinets, oboes, bassoons, and French horns were seated directly in front of the conductor. At the rear, from left to right, were the harps, percussion, trumpets, trombones, and tuba.

The modern orchestra didn't assume this familiar shape until the time of Ludwig van Beethoven (1770–1827). Only in the seventeenth century were bowed and wind instruments first brought together in an organized fashion, and musicologists generally credit Claudio Monteverdi (1567–1643) with the creation of the orchestral effect.

To better appreciate Monteverdi's contribution, consider what "orchestral" music was like up to this point. What passed for an orchestra in the sixteenth century might have included viols, violins, flutes, oboes, cornets, and harps. The basso continuo part (or figured bass) was a ubiquitous feature in the music of this time. A type of musical shorthand, the basso continuo allowed composers pressed for time and printing costs to indicate a chord by writing just one note and a numeral beneath it; this part was played on a bass or cello. The musicians playing a keyboard instrument or a lute would elaborate the harmony as they saw fit during the performance. Instrument families apparently played in sequence rather than as a harmonious whole; that is, the strings would play a melody, and when they finished, the cornets and trumpets would repeat it. The musicianship wasn't always exemplary, even at Italian and French courts, with actors and dancers often doubling as instrumentalists.

For his opera *Orfeo* (1607), Monteverdi instructed that various instruments accompany the voices, doubling (imitating) them. At the opening of *Orfeo* in Mantua, the orchestra comprised two keyboard instruments, two double basses, ten arm-viols, a harp, two ordinary violins, three violas da gamba, two lutes, two pipe organs, a portable organ, four trombones, two cornets, a flute, and a trumpet—a large and diverse instrumental assemblage for the time. Most startling, the score of *Orfeo* also called for integrating instrument families by requiring, for example, the trombones to play simultaneously with the bass viols and double basses.

To Monteverdi's listeners, the drama and intensity of the vocal music, as enhanced by the instrumental color added by the orchestral ensemble, were probably astonishing. This was the effect Monteverdi intended, having written that "the end of all good music is to affect the soul."

In addition to formulating what evolved into the modern orchestra, Monteverdi also raised the stakes for musicians by composing material that was more difficult than much of the music previously written. In fact, the availability and skill of musicians were major determinants of how composers of this period orchestrated their works. Johann Sebastian Bach (1685–1750) apparently included four oboes (two oboes d'amore and two oboes da caccia) in his *Christmas*

Oratorio because the musicians were available and up to the task. Mozart was the first composer to showcase the clarinet (an improved version of the older *chalumeau),* in part because the instrument became widely available during his lifetime.

Composers were slow to follow Monteverdi's lead. It wasn't until the latter part of the seventeenth century that Jean-Baptiste Lully (1632–87), the enormously influential Italian-born French court composer, maintained a standing orchestra that also included woodwinds, flutes, and horns. In the eighteenth century, composers including Johann Wenzel Stamitz and Carl Philipp Emanuel Bach wrote orchestral works with parts for flutes, oboes, horns, bassoons, and strings, among other instruments. Stamitz and his fellow composers of the so-called Mannheim school eventually standardized an orchestra comprising the four sections we recognize today. By 1760, the basso continuo had been abandoned, as had the lute and harpsichord, and composers kept musicians on a shorter improvisational leash.

Although these large German orchestras had a modern structure, the strings still predominated. Instruments from other families were used as necessary to suggest a military theme (drums or trumpets), a grave situation (trombones), or an exotic locale (the triangle). It was Franz Joseph Haydn (1732–1809) and Wolfgang Amadeus Mozart (1756–91) who finally endowed the brass, woodwinds, and percussion instruments with independent musical identities in the orchestra. In their early works, both composers used these sections as a supporting cast to bolster the strings with color, volume, and harmonics. In his third symphony, however, Haydn charged the oboes with an essential role in the first movement. In his sixth symphony, *Le Matin* (1761), he used a kind of ensemble within the orchestra—a bassoon, two oboes, two horns, and a flute—that was on an equal footing with the strings. In addition, Haydn also stopped using the strings, especially the violins and violas, as a single unit, and gave the violas independent parts, increasing the textural complexity of this section of the orchestra.

Mozart visited Mannheim in 1777, by which time the large orchestras there were renowned for their sophistication, musical proficiency, and especially their use of crescendo and diminuendo. This visit had a profound influence on Mozart, and his *Paris Symphony* (K. 297), written the next year, was far more richly scored than his earlier works. In particular, he wrote up to five distinct parts for the various string instruments, a refinement in orchestration that peaked in Beethoven's time.

Technical improvements in the design and manufacture of musical instruments also enhanced the growth of the orchestra during the eighteenth and nineteenth centuries. Valves were added to trumpets. The volume and brilliancy of violins were enhanced by refinements in construction that allowed a higher string tension. Ultimately, composers benefited the most from the creative horizons broadened by the evolution of the orchestra, technical improvements in the design and construction of instruments, and an increasingly higher level of musicianship.

By the late nineteenth and early twentieth centuries, some composers, notably Richard Wagner, Edward Elgar, Gustav Mahler, Richard Strauss, Maurice Ravel, and Igor Stravinsky, used enlarged orchestras to accommodate their lush, grandiose works. The brass sections required for some of their compositions are triple or quadruple their customary size. Wagner in particular specified outsized string and woodwind sections for his operas to enhance tone color and volume. These orchestras simply can't be seated in some halls.

Everything seems to come full circle, and orchestra sizes are no exception. Paul Hindemith and Béla Bartók, among other twentieth-century composers, often called for more compact orchestras, partly because of budgetary constraints and partly in reaction to the perceived orchestral excesses of the previous generation.

Conductors have evolved, too. In the days of the basso continuo, the musician at the keyboard often doubled as a kind of conductor. At the same time, a leader from among the violinists—a *Konzertmeister* or *Takt-führer* (time-beater)—would keep time by foot-tapping or bow-banging. The results were comical when these two musicians couldn't coordinate their efforts.

In a modern orchestral production, the conductor directs from the podium, poring over an orchestral score that includes the parts for all the sections. It's easy to underestimate this solitary figure as a kind of musical traffic cop. In fact, the orchestra is the conductor's "instrument," and what you hear is his or her interpretation of the composer's work. A sophisticated listener can usually differentiate the work of Herbert von Karajan from that of Seiji Ozawa. No wonder Mozart wrote of wanting to rip the violin from the hands of a conductor and "conduct myself." Or that Beethoven once personally conducted his *Choral Symphony* (the Ninth) even though he couldn't hear a note of it. Blustery, self-important Lully made the ultimate (and rather undignified) sacrifice for the conductor's art, dying of an infection he acquired after stabbing his foot with his heavy conducting stick.

❧ QUESTION 24

What were the 4 Freedoms of Franklin Delano Roosevelt?

> **Freedom of speech and expression**
> **Freedom of worship**
> **Freedom from want**
> **Freedom from fear**

The occasion is the State of the Union address on January 6, 1941. Franklin D. Roosevelt has been reelected to an unprecedented third term as President. His task is to prepare Congress and the people for massively increased American aid to the nations battling the Axis powers (see Question 50), which had annexed or occupied Ethiopia, Austria, Czechoslovakia, Poland, Albania, Denmark, Norway, Belgium, the Netherlands, Luxembourg, half of France, and much of China and Indochina. It was clearly time for the United States to act.

Roosevelt did not mince words or throw sops to his isolationist opponents, some of whom called him a warmonger and dictator. He warned Americans that their security and freedom had never been so jeopardized from abroad. Like a salvo of torpedoes, Roosevelt's words to the nations at war with the Rome-Berlin-Tokyo Axis made no secret of where our national sympathies lay: "We shall send you, in ever-increasing numbers, ships, planes, tanks, guns. This is our purpose and our pledge." But Roosevelt also looked forward to a time when the Axis pestilence would be just a bad memory. Toward the end of his speech, he offered a vision of a postwar world in which all people would enjoy the freedoms he proceeded to enunciate.

Roosevelt's Four Freedoms are an amalgam of two sacrosanct American values, **freedom of speech and worship,** and two values desperately needed to counteract the totalitarianism that was swallowing up the world, **freedom from want and fear** (as opposed to the standard operating procedure of the Axis: starvation, exploitation, appropriation of resources, terror, torture, deportations, and forced-labor camps).

To move toward freedom from want, Roosevelt proposed "economic understandings which will secure to every nation a healthy peacetime life for its inhabitants," which seems to envision international economic policies saner than those that had plunged the world into the Great Depression and the war itself. An important aspect of freedom from fear was "a world-wide reduction of armaments to such a point and in such a thorough fashion that no nation will be in a position to commit an act of physical aggression against any neighbor." This was spoken shortly before the United States, "the great arsenal of democracy," began the most colossal arms buildup the world had ever seen, arming not only itself but the rest of the Allies through the Lend-Lease Act.

In the Atlantic Charter of August 14, 1941, Roosevelt and British Prime Minister Winston Churchill issued a joint declaration of principles embodying the aims of their two nations for a better postwar world, "after the final destruction of the Nazi tyranny." The guiding ideas of the Four Freedoms were largely incorporated into this brief, eight-point document that unequivocally asserted American solidarity with the Allied cause. Critics noted, however, that freedom of worship was not mentioned and freedom of speech was only implied. Some thought these omissions were made in deference to the Soviets, but the United States claimed they were an oversight.

Although the Four Freedoms have been criticized as mere wartime slogans too vague to be useful, they still embody ideals worth striving for, even if they remain chimerical in much of the world more than a half century after Roosevelt invoked them. In fact, the conquest and subsequent domination of Eastern Europe by our Soviet ally made the Four Freedoms seem moot even before the end of the war. New tyrannies have quashed freedoms quite as effectively as the old ones in many parts of the world. And though some strides have been made in arms limitation, especially regarding U.S. and Russian nuclear weapons, most nations still agree with Machiavelli that "all unarmed prophets have come to grief."

❋ QUESTION 25

What were the 4 chief winds in ancient Greece?

> Boreas: the North Wind
> Zephyrus: the West Wind
> Notus: the South Wind
> Eurus: the East Wind

The ancient Greeks saw gods and goddesses everywhere, even in the wind. Although most of their many wind-gods, including **Notus** and **Eurus,** remained mere names or abstractions, two of them—Boreas and Zephyrus—were more individualized than the rest.

Boreas, the North Wind, had two winged sons, Calais and Zetes, who accompanied Jason on his quest for the Golden Fleece. Armed with swords, they used their power of flight to drive off the bird-women Harpies, who were starving the blind old prophet King Phineus by either snatching his food or defecating on it whenever he tucked in for a meal. In historical times, the Athenians built a shrine for Boreas because a nor'easter had shattered part of King Xerxes' invading Persian fleet (480 B.C.).

Zephyrus, the West Wind (compare our word *zephyr* for a gentle breeze), once fell in love with a beautiful young Spartan prince named Hyacinthus. He became so jealous of Apollo, though, who was also courting Hyacinthus, that when the god and the boy were throwing the discus one day, Zephyrus caused Apollo's cast to come crashing down onto Hyacinthus's skull, killing him. The hyacinth sprang from the young prince's blood.

Since horses that were "as swift as the wind" were often said to be the offspring of a wind-god, the two immortal horses of Achilles in Homer's *Iliad* were thought to have been sired by Zephyrus. One of them, Xanthus, had the power of speech (several millennia before Jonathan Swift's Houyhnhnms [see Question 21] and Mr. Ed) and prophesied Achilles' death to him in one of the more moving episodes of the poem. Similarly, the twelve fillies born from the mating of Boreas with twelve Trojan mares could skim over the waves of the sea and race over the tops of standing grain without bending the crops.

The Greeks also believed that mares could conceive merely by lifting their tails and turning their hindquarters to the caresses of the lascivious winds. In more primitive times, it was believed that even women could be impregnated by gusts of wind, which represented the spirits of dead ancestors. And the Roman polymath Pliny the Elder (A.D. 23–79), who believed just about anything, assures us in his encyclopedic *Natural History* that if a menstruating woman is exposed to the wind with her belly naked, all hailstorms, whirlwinds, and lightning will be promptly scared off.

In Greco-Roman myth, the ruler of all the winds was Aeolus. When Odysseus and his men land at Aeolus' island kingdom while trying to sail to Ithaca on their way back from the Trojan War, Aeolus traps all the winds in an ox-skin bag—except the West Wind, which the wanderers will need to waft them gently home. But Odysseus' men think that the bulging bag stowed in the ship's hold contains a gift of gold and silver that their captain has neglected to share with them. Already in sight of their homeland (and with Odysseus safely asleep), they open the bag: The howling winds rush out and blow them all the way back to Aeolus' island. Convinced that the gods must be angry with a shipload of such bunglers, Aeolus sends them packing without the benefit of a new ox-skin bag. This adds years to Odysseus' odyssey and thousands of verses to Homer's *Odyssey*.

In Virgil's *Aeneid,* the goddess Juno decides to postpone Aeneas' destined founding of the Roman people, who will one day conquer her beloved Greece. As he and his men sail toward Italy, fleeing their devastated homeland after the Trojan War, the goddess bribes Aeolus with a lovely nymph to grace his marriage bed if he will unleash the fury of the winds that he normally keeps pent up in a cavern. Aeolus complies, and the shrieking winds stir up a seastorm that blows the ships of the Trojan refugees off course to Carthage on the north African coast. There Aeneas dallies with Queen Dido until the gods order him to get on with his heroic mission in Italy, and Dido is left to her suicidal rage.

Aeolus lent his name to the aeolian (or wind) harp, which produces musical chords when breezes play over its strings. The aeolian harp became a favorite Romantic image of the poet's mind, which is receptive to the "intellectual breeze" of inspiration and pours forth the music of verse in response. Famous examples of this image occur in Samuel Taylor Coleridge's lyrics "The Eolian Harp" and "Dejection: An Ode."

✦ QUESTION 26

What are the 4 Noble Truths of Buddhism?

1. Life is full of suffering.
2. The cause of suffering is craving, which leads to the cycle of rebirth (samsara).
3. Craving—and thus suffering—can be annihilated.
4. The way of escape from craving, suffering, and samsara is the Noble Eightfold Path.

"This will be my last birth," announced Siddhartha Gautama shortly after emerging from his mother's right side. The child destined to become the Buddha thus stated his early determination to escape the nightmarish cycle of rebirth into the suffering of life.

So runs the pious legend. But the historical Siddhartha (563–483 B.C.) wasn't always aware of the first Noble Truth he was later to preach—that **all existence is suffering.** His royal father had made sure that the young north Indian prince remained sheltered behind the walls of his three palaces, bathed in pleasure and luxury. But after several excursions into the outside world, Siddhartha became obsessed with the pain he had witnessed—old age, sickness, death. At age twenty-nine, he left his wife and infant son in search of the wisdom that would help him and others transcend the suffering of life. What made his goal all the more crucial was a belief he shared with his contemporaries that all living things keep being reborn into this endless cycle of misery and that nothing but "good karma" keeps humans from returning as paupers, pariahs, or even animals.

For six years he wandered, exploring yoga, theology, and asceticism as various means of escape from the horror of life. The legend records that in his ascetic phase he lived on grass, dung, and, finally, just a single grain of rice a day.

And then one evening he sat beneath a bo tree (a type of large fig), vowing to meditate there until he had discovered the answer to the riddle of salvation. After dispersing demonic temptations, he entered a trance in which he penetrated the deepest mysteries of life. At dawn he rose as the Buddha, or Enlightened One.

In his first sermon, he taught his five disciples the Four Noble Truths, which form the core of Buddhist doctrine. In brief, they embody the notion that **the suffering of life and rebirth (samsara) ends only when we renounce all desire**—even the desire for nonexistence—since desire binds us to life. Fortunately, **there is a way to annihilate all craving,** and **those who follow this Noble Eightfold Path** (see Question 70) **achieve nirvana** (release, nonattachment, utter peace) by avoiding the pain inherent in repeated births and deaths throughout countless eons.

After forty-five years of teaching and preaching, the Buddha achieved his ultimate goal of *maha-parinirvana* ("great total extinction"), but not before founding a religious system that spread to much of Central and East Asia and today claims more than 350 million adherents.

✳ QUESTION 27

Which 4 U.S. Presidents were assassinated—and who were their killers?

Abraham Lincoln: John Wilkes Booth
James Garfield: Charles J. Guiteau
William McKinley: Leon Czolgosz
John F. Kennedy: Lee Harvey Oswald

"Though I may be executed for what I have done, I do not care. I shall become the most celebrated man in modern history." Which presidential assassin said this? You're right if you guessed Charles J.

Guiteau, though he was quite wrong about his great fame. Yet the world will long remember the names of Oswald and Booth.

John Wilkes Booth (1838–65), his brother Edwin, and their father, Junius Brutus Booth, would still be recognized as eminent Shakespearean actors and the foremost theatrical family in American history even if John Wilkes had not assassinated Abraham Lincoln only five days after Robert E. Lee surrendered at Appomattox Court House, Virginia. Junius, born in London, was considered the peer of the great actor Edmund Kean before moving to America in 1821. Of his ten children, only John Wilkes and Edwin followed him into serious acting.

Despite the acclaim John Wilkes Booth garnered for his performances in the South during the Civil War, his attentions were not focused entirely on his thespian career. He was a staunch Confederate and a member of the militia that hanged John Brown. By 1864, he had conspired with a Washingtonian named John Surratt and several others to kidnap the President. When these plans failed and the Confederacy lurched to defeat, Booth and his co-conspirators decided to kill Lincoln, Vice President Andrew Johnson, and Secretary of State William H. Seward.

Booth was a familiar face at Ford's Theater in Washington, where President and Mrs. Lincoln and another couple went on April 14, 1865 (Good Friday), to see the frivolous play *Our American Cousin*. Easily gaining access to the presidential box during the third act, Booth shot Lincoln from about two feet away. He then jumped from the box to the stage, breaking his leg in the process and shouting "Sic semper tyrannis!" ("Thus always to tyrants!")—the state motto of Virginia. He escaped through an alley. Lincoln died the following morning.

Booth's accomplice, Lewis Payne, managed to wound Seward and his son at their home, but both survived. The plot against Vice President Johnson failed. Federal troops tracked Booth and a companion to a tobacco farm in Bowling Green, Virginia, where Booth was shot or shot himself, it's unclear which. Four co-conspirators, including John Surratt's mother Mary, who was probably innocent, were hanged in July after a trial by a military commission.

Charles J. Guiteau (gih-TOE) (1841–82), certainly *not* the most celebrated man in modern history, but quite probably a schizophrenic, was born in Freeport, Illinois. He was a hyperactive child, and his father beat him to help rid him of a speech impediment. As a disciple of Perfectionism and the writings of John Humphrey Noyes, the elder Guiteau believed that death could be defeated and sin was irrelevant. This last bit came in handy at the cult's community in Oneida, New York, where members lived in so-called complex marriages (use your imagination).

Young Charles Guiteau also became a follower of Noyes and moved to the Oneida compound when he was in his early twenties. There, he remained friendless—and celibate—after sharing the news that he was destined to be President of the United States and, eventually, ruler of the world. In addition to free love, the Oneida group also had frequent free-criticism sessions. Subjected to way too much free criticism, Guiteau moved to New York City, where his mental health deteriorated and his various careers flopped.

In 1880, Guiteau distributed numerous copies of a cockamamie speech he had written for the presidential campaign of liberal Republican James A. Garfield and his running mate, Chester A. Arthur. Guiteau became a joke in the campaign with his delusional beliefs that he was an intimate of Garfield and that his hard work would be rewarded with a high-level diplomatic post in Paris or Vienna. After the election, the joke became a pest, visiting the White House and State Department to demand his European appointment. Once he actually made it into Garfield's office before being whisked away.

Garfield and Arthur represented different factions of the Republican party whose major differences centered on the issue of federal patronage jobs. Once elected, Garfield ignored Arthur and other members of the so-called Stalwart faction when filling top government positions. News coverage of this political infighting inflamed Guiteau, who, frustrated with his inability to land a federal job, sided with the Stalwarts. He decided that Garfield was destroying the Republican party and must die.

Guiteau spent June of 1881 stalking the President, who walked around Washington openly and sometimes alone. On July 2, at the Baltimore & Potomac Station, as the President was preparing to go vacationing, Guiteau came up behind him and shot him twice. Garfield had been in office for only four months. When he was caught by a police officer, Guiteau explained, "I am a Stalwart. Arthur is now President of the United States."

One of the first people to arrive at the station after the shooting was a distraught Robert Todd Lincoln, Abraham Lincoln's son and a member of Garfield's cabinet. Only sixteen years had passed since his father's assassination.

Garfield lingered painfully for seventy-nine days, finally succumbing on September 19, 1881, at a seaside home in Elberon, New Jersey, where he had been moved. Guiteau was hanged in June 1882, while singing an original ditty, "I am going to the Lordy."

Some consider the assassination of President William McKinley by **Leon Czolgosz** (CHOL-gosh) (1873–1901) the last gasp of the violent anarchist movement in the United States. Czolgosz, born in Detroit to Polish parents, is said, like Guiteau, to have had a history of mental problems. As a young wire-mill worker in Cleveland, he was exposed to anarchist doctrines and came to believe that the U.S. government and economy were the natural enemies of all workers. He thus decided to make the ultimate anarchist gesture and kill McKinley, a Republican who had defeated Democrat William Jennings Bryan for the presidency in 1896 and 1900.

McKinley was a rather spineless President. Although aware that Spain was willing to make concessions after the American battleship *Maine* was blown up in Havana Harbor on February 15, 1898, he kowtowed to the warhawks in Congress, who rallied the press and spoke for big business in declaring war—"Remember the *Maine!*" As a result of the four-month Spanish-American War, the United States gained Puerto Rico, Guam, and the Philippines (see Question 83).

Early in his second term, on September 6, 1901, the President appeared at a Pan-American trade exposition in Buffalo, New York, during which he greeted the public in a receiving line at the exposition's Temple of Music. This aspect of the trip in particular worried some of his staff because the 1900 presidential campaign had been marred by anonymous threatening letters. McKinley would tolerate no increased security measures, however. While a Bach sonata was played, the President reached out to welcome Czolgosz, who fired two shots from a gun hidden in a handkerchief. McKinley collapsed, saying of the angry bystanders, "Don't let them hurt him." The President died in Buffalo on September 14, 1901, after his wound became gangrenous. Theodore Roosevelt succeeded him, the youngest man (age forty-two) to become President. Czolgosz was electrocuted in the prison at Auburn, New York, on October 29, 1901. In 1903, Congress passed laws facilitating the exclusion and deportation of foreign anarchists.

Norman Mailer asks, "Can there be an American of our century who, having failed to gain stature while he was alive, now haunts us more?" He's speaking, of course, about **Lee Harvey Oswald** (1939–63), the enigmatic figure who shot and killed President John F. Kennedy and wounded Texas Governor John B. Connally in Dallas on November 22, 1963. Two days later, while being transferred to another jail, Oswald himself was shot dead by Jack Ruby, a Dallas nightclub owner—on live, nationwide television.

That's where the facts end and conjectures begin. Did Oswald act alone, as the Warren Commission (1963–64) concluded? Or was he one of two or three gunmen involved in a conspiracy, a possibility left open by a special U.S. House of Representatives Assassinations Committee in 1979? If he acted with others, who were his co-conspirators? Cubans? Soviets? Oswald had moved to the Soviet Union in 1959, married a Russian, and tried to renounce his American citizenship. Repatriated in 1962, he then tried to travel to Cuba. Why? Did he have links to the FBI or CIA? Jack Ruby, who claimed he acted as an enraged citizen and died of cancer before his trial, had deep ties to the underworld, raising questions about possible Mob involvement. So much time has now passed that any secrets will probably remain in Oswald's Texas grave.

☀ QUESTION 28

What are the 4 fundamental forces?

Gravitation
Electromagnetism
The weak nuclear force
The strong nuclear force

These four forces appear to govern all the interactions of the physical universe. They can be distinguished by the types of bodies or particles they act on, the distances over which they exert their force, the energy levels of their interactions, and various other properties.

Gravitation is the attractive force that all material bodies, like the earth, exert on all other bodies, like our own. The universal law of gravitation, formulated by Sir Isaac Newton (1642–1727), states that the gravitational force exerted by one body on another varies directly with the product of their masses, but inversely with the square of the intervening distance (see Question 17). Phenomena like tides, the weight or fall of objects on earth, and planetary orbits around the sun are caused by gravitation, which is, however, by far the weakest fundamental force. If the strongest, the strong nuclear force, were assigned a strength of 1, that of gravitation would be about 10^{-39}. This minuscule force, negligible at the subatomic level, nonetheless operates over immense distances.

Although a quantitative description of gravity has been available for more than three centuries, its actual nature remains unclear. One hypothesis suggests that gravitation results from exchanges of massless uncharged particles between the attracting bodies, but these postulated gauge bosons (force-transmitting particles) of gravitation—called gravitons—have never been detected.

Electromagnetism, the second most powerful force, is 137 times weaker than the strong nuclear force. It governs the interactions of electrons, other charged particles, and many forms of radiation, including radio waves and microwaves; infrared, visible, and ultraviolet light; and X rays and gamma rays. It acts on all particles with electrical charge, those with opposite charges attracting and those with similar charges repelling one another. This force arises from exchanges of photons, uncharged particles with zero mass, which are the gauge bosons of the electromagnetic force. In the eighteenth century, French physicist Charles Coulomb discovered that the force between two charged particles varies in a way similar to that of the gravitational force; that is, it depends on the product of the charges divided by the square of the distance between them.

The orbiting of negatively charged electrons around the nucleus of an atom, which is positively charged because of the presence of protons, is just one example of electromagnetic attraction. In fact, all chemical, biologic, and electrical processes are governed by electromagnetism.

The weak nuclear force, about 100,000 times weaker than the strong nuclear force, is manifested by radioactive decay processes, specifically beta decay. In substances with unstable nuclei, the weak nuclear force permits subatomic interactions characterized by spontaneous emissions of energy (in the form of photons) and particles.

Depending on the element involved, beta decay causes emission of either an electron or a positron (a positively charged particle with mass equal to that of an electron), along with an antineutrino or a neutrino, respectively. (Both are uncharged subatomic particles.) The weak nuclear force is transmitted by three extremely short-lived but very massive gauge bosons, which accommodate all possible electrical charges: W^+ (positive), W^- (negative), and Z^0 (no charge).

Emission of a W^- particle (which immediately transforms into an electron and an antineutrino) signifies that a neutron in the nucleus has transmuted into a proton, with a +1 change in the atomic number. This radioactive decay or disintegration affects elements with atomic numbers above 83, whose nuclei have too many neutrons for stability. Some examples are the radioactive elements polonium, radon, radium, uranium, and plutonium. Emission of a W^+ particle (which immediately transforms into a positron and a neutrino) indicates that a proton in the nucleus has transmuted into a neutron, with a −1 change in the atomic number. Some isotopes of elements that are produced in cyclotrons, including carbon 11, oxygen 15, and iodine 124, decay by positron emission. In interactions involving no net change in charge, the Z^0 particle is emitted.

The strong nuclear force binds together quarks to form protons and neutrons, and protons and neutrons together to maintain the integrity of the nucleus (see Question 43). This force, whose massless gauge bosons are termed gluons, is of very limited range. Beyond a distance of about 10^{-15} meters, it is essentially nil. At shorter distances, however, it is more than 100 times stronger than the electromagnetic force. It is this colossal force that is unleashed when atomic nuclei are wrenched apart or fused in nuclear fission or fusion reactions. The strong nuclear force is independent of charge, causing a proton to be equally attracted to either neutrons or other protons.

Physicists ascribe tremendous significance to unification of the four fundamental forces, whose paths have diverged since gravitation separated itself from the other three at 10^{-43} seconds after the Big Bang. The others followed suit very shortly thereafter. Unification would require demonstrating that the individual forces as currently understood actually represent different forms or aspects of a single force—if they could only be raised to a sufficiently high energy state.

The greatest success to date has been achieved with the electromagnetic and weak nuclear forces, now often jointly termed the electroweak force. When the weak nuclear force's bosons, whose existence had been predicted in 1967, were detected in 1983 after the requisite energy levels had become attainable, the discovery validated a theory that had also predicted that electromagnetism's photons and the weak nuclear force's bosons would behave similarly at still-higher energies.

Current efforts center on unifying the electroweak force with the strong nuclear force via a grand unified theory (GUT). A major obstacle is the fact that the energy level at which unification would be expected to occur is vastly beyond foreseeable technical capabilities. Consequently, researchers are trying to validate components of or predictions associated with their GUTs, according to the logic that if aspects and consequences of the theory prove valid, so should the entire construct.

The ultimate goal is full unification of the four fundamental forces, including gravitation, in a so-called supersymmetry theory, or a theory of everything (TOE). If these efforts ever succeed, they would represent the most stupendous scientific achievement of all time—a system of consistent, fully inclusive explanations for the physical processes of the universe at scales ranging from the infinitesimal to the infinite.

✷ QUESTION 29

Who are the 4 Horsemen of the Apocalypse?

> War (or Conquest or Christ) on a white horse
> Slaughter (or War or Violence) on a red horse
> Famine (or Pestilence or Poverty) on a black horse
> Death on a pale horse

When the Lamb (Christ) breaks the first four of seven seals from the scroll in the sixth chapter of the book of Revelation (also called by its Greek-derived title, the Apocalypse), four horrific horsemen materialize, one for each seal, and set out on their task of destruction. The vision of which they're part bodes ill to the Romans, who at the time of this work (c. A.D. 95) were massacring Christians under the Emperor Domitian (reigned 81–96).

The Book of Revelation, written by an unknown "I, John," is traditionally ascribed to St. John the Evangelist (see Question 32) in exile on the island of Patmos. This last book of the New Testament, which had a hard time making it into the accepted scriptural canon, comprises a series of visions that Christ vouchsafed to the writer. Its purpose was to strengthen Christians in their resolve to die, if need be, rather than worship the Roman gods and deified emperors during a time of persecution.

Just before the vision of the horsemen, God is pictured on his throne holding a scroll with seven seals that contains a prophecy of what must come to pass (Revelation 4). The source of this scroll is Ezekiel 2:9–10, where "dirges and laments and words of woe" aimed at Jerusalem are written all over another scroll that Ezekiel, like the author of Revelation, is ordered to eat. God speaks of four dreadful scourges that he will send against Jerusalem as "sword and famine, wild beasts and pestilence" in Ezekiel 14:21—pretty close to what the Four Horsemen serve up. In any event, these riders stand for war and its consequences, which will precede the end of the world and destroy the rulers and the rich, while sparing God's servants and martyrs—but judge for yourself (Revelation 6:1–8):

"Then I watched as the Lamb broke the first of the seven seals. . . . **And there before my eyes was a white horse, and its rider held a bow.** He was given a crown, and he rode forth, conquering and to conquer.

"When the Lamb broke the second seal, . . . out came **another horse, all red. To its rider was given power to take peace from the earth and make men slaughter one another;** and he was given a great sword.

"When he broke the third seal, . . . there, as I looked, was **a black horse; and its rider held in his hand a pair of scales.** And I heard what sounded like a voice from the midst of the living creatures, which said, 'A whole day's wage for a quart of flour, a whole day's wage for three quarts of barley-meal! But spare the olive and vine.'

"When he broke the fourth seal, . . . there, as I looked, was **another horse, sickly pale; and its rider's name was Death,** and Hades came close behind. To him was given power over a quarter of the earth, with the right to kill by sword and by famine, by pestilence and wild beasts."

Albrecht Dürer (1471–1528), greatest of German artists, carved a series of fifteen large woodcuts illustrating the Apocalypse (1498). His depiction of the Four Horsemen is justly famous for its Gothic terror. Various well-fed figures are prostrated beneath the horses' hooves, and the riders include a grinning, emaciated Death on an emaciated, grinning horse.

In 1916, the Spanish writer Vicente Blasco Ibáñez (1867–1928) published an international-blockbuster novel entitled *The Four Horsemen of the Apocalypse (Los cuatro jinetes del Apocalipsis),* contrasting French and German attitudes toward World War I and advocating the Allied cause. In it, Tchernoff, a bearded Russian socialist revolutionary intellectual wino living in Paris at the outbreak of hostilities, conjures up for the young protagonist and another friend the four biblical horsemen, which here stand for conquest (or plague), war, famine, and death. The American edition of the 1918 English translation of the book went through fifty-six printings in six months. Film versions of the novel include a 1921 silent classic starring Rudolph Valentino and a 1962 box-office bomb featuring Glenn Ford.

The Ingmar Bergman film *The Seventh Seal (Det Sjunde Inseglet,* 1956) evokes the stark, doomsday atmosphere of Revelation, from which it derives its title. The protagonist is a knight (Max von Sydow), home from the Crusades, who plays a game of chess with the hooded figure of Death in a time of plague. At stake is the knight's life. The film is sometimes considered the Swedish director's masterpiece and firmly established his worldwide reputation.

The events foreseen in Revelation were supposed to be imminent—the end of the world, the defeat of the seven-headed dragon Satan by Michael the Archangel, the reign of the beast (thought to be Antichrist), the destruction of the Whore of Babylon (the Roman Empire), the Millennium, the battle of Armageddon, the Last Judgment, the establishment of the New Jerusalem. When these events were delayed, Christian exegetes began allegorizing them in thousands of ways, some of them dangerous.

Of the book of Revelation itself, Harold Bloom has written: "The influence of Revelation always has been out of all proportion to its literary strength or spiritual value. Though it has affected the strongest poets, from Dante and Spenser through Milton on to Blake and Shelley, it also has enthralled the quacks and cranks of all ages down to the present moment in America. A lurid and inhumane work, . . . it *is* a nightmare of a book: without wisdom, goodness, kindness, or affection of any kind. D. H. Lawrence judged it pungently: 'The Apocalypse does not worship power. It wants to murder the powerful, to seize power itself, the weakling.' "*

When will the Four Horsemen ride? The American religious leader William Miller (1782–1849) predicted the end of the world would occur "about the year 1843," and then, more precisely, on October 22, 1844. When nothing happened, the nonevent was dubbed the Great Disappointment. Nonetheless, the Millerite movement gave rise to such thriving millenarian sects as the Seventh-Day Adventists and, less directly, Jehovah's Witnesses.

Predictions of the Apocalypse abound. Some saw it in World War I, others in the Persian Gulf War. One of the more curious identifications of the beast that rises from the sea—whose number is 666—was that it stood for Ronald Wilson Reagan, each of whose names contains six letters. Biblical scholars have applied the number, somewhat more appropriately, to another chief executive, the Christian-slaughtering Emperor Nero. In the continuing saga of Revelation and its vicissitudes, the Branch Davidian cult, expecting Armageddon, instead met an apocalyptic death in 1993 at the hands of the Bureau of Alcohol, Tobacco, and Firearms at Waco, Texas. And still this 4.5-billion-year-old "pragmatical, preposterous pig of a world," as Yeats called it, just keeps schlepping along.

❧ QUESTION 30

Who were the Big Four, and what nations did they represent at the Paris Peace Conference (1919)?

Woodrow Wilson: United States
David Lloyd George: Great Britain
Georges Clemenceau: France
Vittorio Emanuele Orlando: Italy

---

* Harold Bloom, *The American Religion: The Emergence of the Post-Christian Nation,* New York, Simon & Schuster, 1992, pp. 162–63.

On January 18, 1919, the representatives of twenty-seven nations that had been the principal Allied and Associated Powers in World War I assembled at Paris to impose a peace treaty on the vanquished Central Powers. The plenary sessions, however, were just window dressing; the important decisions were made by the Big Four—or, as Orlando quickly realized, the Big Three. The American President and the three European prime ministers did not a happy mix make: Wilson was idealistic, stubborn, Calvinistically smug and dour, and lacking in diplomatic tact; Lloyd George was fickle, opportunistic, and irascible; Clemenceau, nicknamed "The Tiger" because of his ruthless toppling of French ministries, was a cynical seventy-seven-year-old fiercely nationalistic Germanophobe and duelist (with sword or pistol); and Orlando was a Sicilian law professor and feckless Italian politico.

Thomas Woodrow Wilson (1856–1924) had been president of Princeton University and governor of New Jersey before serving as Democratic President of the United States (1913–21). On January 22, 1917, before America entered the war, he gave his "Peace Without Victory" speech, which envisioned an eventual settlement that would eschew vengefulness, minimize enmity, and incorporate his idea for a League of Nations. But when Germany's unrestricted submarine warfare had exhausted his country's patience, Wilson asked Congress to declare war on April 2, 1917, claiming that "the world must be made safe for democracy."

While American doughboys and industrial wealth were helping to put an end to the Great War, Wilson urged Germany in October 1918 to accept an armistice based on the Fourteen Points he had enunciated on January 8 (see Question 96)—and which Germany now recognized as the best deal it could hope to get. The shooting stopped on November 11, and at the peace conference Wilson put his plan for a peacekeeping League of Nations ahead of all other considerations. In return for concessions to the Allies that compromised the liberal sentiments of his Fourteen Points—and enraged helpless Germany, which felt betrayed—the covenant of the League was written into the peace treaty with Germany, the Treaty of Versailles (1919). The U.S. Senate demurred at certain provisions of the League of Nations, but Wilson's stiff-necked refusal to have the treaty significantly amended inspired him to undertake a speaking tour of the nation to defend the League. The result was physical collapse, two incapacitating strokes, and a slow decline toward death. Wilson's League was established at Geneva in 1920—the year he won the Nobel Peace prize—but his country never joined it. The Senate refused to ratify the Treaty of Versailles, and separate peace treaties were negotiated with Germany, Austria, and Hungary in August 1921, under Republican President Warren G. Harding.

In Paris, Wilson had generally tried to follow criteria of language, nationality, and self-determination in reshaping the boundaries of Europe, but the mind-numbing complexities of this problem were bound to anger and "betray" some group in just about every instance. Old majorities became new minorities, and vice versa, and Wilson did not appreciate the myriad intricacies and acrimonies of European nationalistic micropolitics.

David Lloyd George (1863–1945) was the Liberal prime minister of Great Britain (1916–22) who, as chancellor of the exchequer, had presided over the introduction of old-age pensions and national health insurance. His successful political campaign in December 1918 had featured the altruistic slogans "Hang the Kaiser!" and "Make Germany pay!" At the peace conference his main goal was to preserve or, better yet, expand the British Empire—which he certainly did, in both the Middle East and Africa. He generally tried to mediate between Clemenceau's vindictiveness and Wilson's crusading idealism. Lloyd George feared, rightly, that the redistribution of 13 percent of Germany's 1914 territory and France's demand for excessive reparations could only lead to German revanchism and another European war.

Georges Clemenceau (clay-mahn-SO) (1841–1929) was a man of intellectual tastes. In his youth he had translated Goethe's *Faust* into French verse. He also founded the journal *L'Aurore,* in which he defended Alfred Dreyfus, publishing (and entitling) Émile Zola's open letter, "J'accuse," in 1899. Twice premier of France (1906–9 and 1917–20), Clemenceau headed a dictatorial "victory cabinet" during the war and rallied France to absolute victory and a fight to the death.

Clemenceau found that peacemaking was also a tough business, sitting, as he claimed, between a man who thought himself Napoleon Bonaparte (Lloyd George) and another who fancied himself the Messiah (Wilson). His main concerns at the peace conference were to provide for the security of France against another German invasion and to exact reparations from Germany for all expenses and damage incurred during the war, including the cost of war pensions. Wilson and Lloyd George thought his reparations claims much too extravagant and bitterly contested French claims on German territories. Yet the Tiger—who was shot and wounded during the conference—fell from power in 1920 for supposedly having let Germany off too lightly.

A close friend of Claude Monet, Clemenceau wrote a monograph on him, as well as a book of philosophy and one on the Greek orator Demosthenes, in his mid-eighties. He certainly made the most of his sunset years.

Vittorio Emanuele Orlando (1860–1952) wasted everybody's time at the conference by demanding Fiume (current Rijeka), a small Croatian seaport city on the Adriatic that was home to twenty-five thousand Italians. This particular bubble was burst, mostly by Woodrow Wilson. According to the secret Treaty of London (April 26, 1915), England and France pledged to award Italy substantial territories of its age-old enemy, the Austrian Empire, if Italy entered the war on the Allied side. Although Italy received Trieste and large Austrian possessions in northern Italy after the war, it didn't get the Dalmatian coast of future (now former) Yugoslavia and other cities and islands in the Adriatic—not to mention Fiume, which the Treaty of London had stipulated should remain Croatian. Orlando stomped out of the conference over the Fiume issue but returned two weeks later when he realized his tantrum hadn't changed anyone's mind. He resigned the premiership in June 1919, after serving for less than two years.

In September 1919, the flamboyant Italian poet, war hero, and protofascist Gabriele D'Annunzio (1863–1938) seized Fiume bloodlessly with about three hundred disgruntled military men and held it for fifteen months. By declaring Fiume a separate state, with himself as leader, D'Annunzio thumbed his nose at "cowardly Italy" (on which he declared "war") while retroactively bearding the detested Woodrow Wilson. Discontents—and malcontents—such as these contributed to Mussolini's accession to power in October 1922. Soon after that, Italy did get Fiume, only to lose it again permanently in the chaos of World War II.

When the two-hundred page peace treaty was presented to the Germans in May 1919, they indignantly refused to sign it. Germany was to assume responsibility for the war in the infamous "war-guilt clause." It was to hand over its fleet (which it scuttled at Scapa Flow in the Orkneys—seventy-four warships in five hours—rather than comply with this stipulation). It was to have no air force, tanks, or submarines, and an army limited to a hundred thousand men. Alsace-Lorraine, seized in the Franco-Prussian War of 1870–71, was to be returned to France. Germany was to lose all its colonies, which were assigned to various Allies as mandates under the League of Nations covenant. Poland was to be an independent state and enlarged at Germany's expense, with the "Polish corridor" splitting East Prussia from the rest of Germany. Reparations were to be paid (the amount fixed at $33 billion in 1921).

Since the Allied naval blockade would continue to starve Germany until it signed the treaty, two German nobodies were dispatched to append their signatures to the shameful document of "dictated peace" on June 28, 1919. This was the fifth anniversary of the assassination of Archduke Francis Ferdinand of Austria, and the signing took place in the Hall of Mirrors at Versailles—where Germany had proclaimed itself an empire in 1871 after thrashing France in the Franco-Prussian War.

By the Treaty of St. Germain (September 10, 1919), Austria was shorn of its empire, which became independent states such as Hungary and Czechoslovakia, part of new composite countries such as Yugoslavia and Poland, or territories ceded to Italy. By the Treaty of Sèvres (August 10, 1920), the former Middle East empire of the Ottoman Turks was distributed as mandates to Great Britain (Palestine, Jordan, and Iraq) and France (Syria, including Lebanon), while Arabia became independent.

The Treaty of Versailles that the Allies forced on Germany—which had no part in the negotiations—pleased few. The Germans saw it as so humiliating that it paved the way for Adolf Hitler's repudiation of everything it stood for. The French judged it far too lenient. The American Senate refused to ratify the treaty, mainly because of its inclusion of the League of Nations covenant. The Italians were disgusted that they got no major colonial plums (or Fiume). The Chinese walked out of the conference. The Russians, still consolidating their Bolshevik revolution, did not attend this conference of capitalistic imperialists and deplored its outcomes.

Centuries earlier, Machiavelli said of the Prince's personal enemies that they "must either be coddled or crushed." As it was, the territorial losses and reparations imposed on Germany were harsh enough to inflame but not to utterly prostrate the country. The treaty caused enormous rancor without attaining its primary objective of rendering Germany incapable of waging aggressive warfare. Worst of all, the Allies did not enforce the treaty rigorously in later years and modified it too casually.

Paris, venue of the Big Four's failure to take the long view of things, found itself in Nazi hands less than twenty-one years after the signing of the Treaty of Versailles, when, in May and June 1940, the German blitzkrieg resulted in French capitulation within five weeks.

❧ QUESTION 31

Who were the 4 Brontë siblings?

> **Charlotte**
> **Emily**
> **Anne**
> **Branwell**

The tiny village of Haworth in the West Riding district of Yorkshire was home to a remarkable and reclusive family from 1820 to the 1850s. The story of the Brontës began in September 1802, when a young Irishman named Patrick Brunty left the wild and rough Mountains of Mourne in County Down, sailed for England, and modified his surname in honor of Lord Nelson, who had been created Duke of Bronte (in Sicily) by the King of Naples in 1800. Patrick studied theology at St. John's College, Cambridge, began his Yorkshire ministry, married, and fathered six children. In 1820 the family took up residence in the Haworth Parsonage. Although Haworth was hardly a destitute village, conditions were primitive. Amenities such as sewers were lacking, and the drinking water was frequently contaminated. The average age at death was twenty-five.

Not long after the Brontë family settled in at the parsonage,

Maria, the frail mother, died and left her young brood to her dour, scholarly husband. He determined that their well-being would best be served by residence at the Clergy Daughters' School in Cowan Bridge, Lancashire. In 1824 the two eldest children, Maria and Elizabeth, departed for the boarding school that would later be immortalized as the ghastly Lowood School in Charlotte's *Jane Eyre,* where young girls had their characters improved with scant heat and food and much harshness. While their souls were carefully tended with interminable sermons, the girls themselves sat shivering in chapel in rain-soaked clothes. Both Maria and Elizabeth promptly contracted tuberculosis and died in 1825 within a month of each other at ages eleven and ten, respectively.

Charlotte and Emily also attended Cowan Bridge briefly until the elder girls became ill. The surviving children remained at the parsonage for the next five years, receiving their education from an aunt and one another, and creating the two imaginary worlds of Angria and Gondal. The hundred tiny notebooks of the chronicles of Angria (the work of Charlotte and Branwell) still survive and tell of the exotic, and often erotic, adventures of the men and women of a vast African empire. In the kingdom of Gondal (brainchild of Emily and Anne), factions of Royalists and Republicans warred and intrigued against each other. Nothing has survived of this saga except the poems Emily wrote for it.

Much of what is known about the reticent Brontës stems from **Charlotte** (1816–55), the oldest surviving sibling. More willing than the others to venture beyond the gates of the parsonage, Charlotte attended school in Roe Head, Yorkshire, and then in Brussels (1842–44) in the school of Constantine Héger. She chronicled her experiences in the Belgian capital—and disguised her frustrated love for the married Héger—in her first novel, *The Professor* (published posthumously in 1857), and in her last, *Villette* (1853), in which the imaginary city of Villette, based on Brussels, is the backdrop for the loneliness and unhappiness of Lucy Snowe. Charlotte's extensive correspondence provided much of the information for her friend Elizabeth Gaskell's *Life of Charlotte Brontë* (1857), a detailed depiction of the Brontë world.

Charlotte's masterpiece, *Jane Eyre,* was published in October 1847. The novel follows the orphaned heroine as she endures years of misery at Lowood School and the death by consumption of her childhood friend. Jane later accepts a post as governess at Thornfield Hall, where she meets and falls in love with her Byronic employer, Edward Rochester. After considerable effort, he persuades her to marry him, but we and Jane learn just before the wedding that he is already married—to Bertha, a mad Creole woman who has long been kept in the attic. Jane and Rochester are unhappily separated for many years and through numerous vicissitudes. Only toward the end of the novel are they reunited, Rochester now blind and maimed from an unsuccessful attempt to save his wife from a fire that ravaged Thornfield Hall. *Jane Eyre* was an immediate popular and critical success, and such it remains both in print and on film.

Charlotte's novel *Shirley* (1849), set in the latter part of the Napoleonic Wars, features an independent-minded heroine, Shirley Keeldar (based on her sister Emily). At this time the mill towns in northern England were suffering because of war restrictions and the agitation of the Luddites, who expressed their reservations about the mechanization of the textile industry by smashing machinery. In part a plea for greater freedom of employment choices for women, the book was intended by its author to be "as unromantic as Monday morning."

Charlotte, the only Brontë sibling to marry, was wed to Arthur Bell Nicholls, her father's curate, in 1854. She died the following year, of pregnancy toxemia complicated by tuberculosis, a few weeks before her thirty-ninth birthday.

Her sister **Emily** (1818–48) remains a more evasive and enigmatic figure. The obsessive intensity, darkness, and flouting of convention in *Wuthering Heights* (1847) caused the novel to be greeted with considerable incomprehension and disapprobation. Today it stands as the greatest of the Brontë achievements. The tragedy of Heathcliff and Catherine Earnshaw—their shared wild childhood contrasting with their misery-plagued, "civilized" adult existences lived out in separation—is the romantic story of two characters so intimately fused ("I *am* Heathcliff," Cathy realizes) that their being kept apart, by circumstance and convention, destroys them. Without the primeval, demonic life force of Heathcliff, Cathy is as shallow, foolish, and banal as Emily considered society to be. But without Cathy's civilizing influence, tempestuous Heathcliff devolves into a monster of icy cruelty and violence. (The Earnshaw home into which he was adopted becomes truly *wuthering,* a Yorkshire term for "tempest-tossed.") Their tragedy is resolved only when order is restored to the universe of their bleak Yorkshire moors by the union of their children.

Before dying of tuberculosis in 1848 at age 30, Emily also composed an impressive body of poetry. Charlotte described her younger sister's verse as "wild, melancholy, and elevating."

Anne (1820–49) briefly attended school with Emily at Roe Head but was educated largely at home. She worked in two households as governess of spoiled, ill-behaved children and recorded her experiences in her first novel, *Agnes Grey* (1847).

Anne's better-known work is *The Tenant of Wildfell Hall* (1848), the story of a mysterious widow, Helen Graham, who, with her small son, moves into a large, dilapidated house near the residence of Gilbert Markham, the book's narrator. Gilbert falls in love with Helen, defending her against the vicious gossip of neighbors who believe she is sexually involved with the owner of Wildfell Hall. In fact, the owner is her brother, who has provided her with a refuge from her violent, debauched husband, Arthur Huntingdon. Helen returns to him, however, on learning of his protracted fatal illness, which he exacerbates by ongoing dissipation. After his death, the two principals are united.

In a biographical notice about Anne after her death from tuberculosis at age twenty-nine, Charlotte suggested that the awful Huntingdon was modeled on none other than brother **Branwell** (1817–48), whose childhood promise in the arts remained unfulfilled. He failed as a portrait painter and as a tutor (after a romantic involvement with his employer's wife), and he got fired from a railway job. He spent his last years at Haworth solacing himself with alcohol and opium, much to the grief of his sisters. He died at age thirty-one.

Biographers and critics continue to be fascinated with all the Brontës, and periodic attempts are made at rehabilitating poor Branwell. These foredoomed efforts are hilariously satirized in a subplot of Stella Gibbons's 1932 novel, *Cold Comfort Farm,* in which the ludicrous Mr. Mybug is busy writing a "Life of Branwell Brontë," setting forth the hypothesis that the latter actually wrote all the Brontë books. (After all, the sisters had published their poems and novels under the male pseudonyms of Currer Bell, Ellis Bell, and Acton Bell. Startled disbelief ensued when the sex of the authors was revealed.) In Mr. Mybug's view, the sisters, "devoured by jealousy of their brilliant brother," engaged in the game of "passing his manuscripts off as their own. . . . They wanted to have him under their noses so that they could steal his work and sell it to buy more drink . . . for themselves. They were all drunkards, but Anne was the worst of the lot."

A minority view, to be sure. Today the Brontë reputation rests solidly on Charlotte, Emily, and Anne, and the astonishing novels and poems they created out of a cloistered world but a seemingly boundless imaginative faculty. In Branwell's haunting oil portrait of them, the Brontë sisters still gaze into mystery like three doomed young Fates.

✳ QUESTION 32

Who were the 4 Evangelists, and what were their symbols?

> Matthew: a man (or angel)
> Mark: a lion
> Luke: an ox
> John: an eagle

The Evangelists are the traditional authors of the four canonical Gospels (*godspel* means "good news" in Anglo-Saxon, a literal translation of the Latin *evangelium* and Greek *euangelion*—the opening word of Mark). These accounts of the life, sayings, and teachings of Jesus, proclaiming the good news that the Messiah had come and the kingdom of God was at hand, were written in Koine ("common") Greek, the lingua franca of the eastern Mediterranean at the time of Christ. In Gothic and later art, Matthew was often depicted as writing his Gospel while looking over his shoulder at an angel; Mark while in the company of a reclining winged lion; Luke while an ox placidly chews the cud of rumination; and John the Divine as an epicene young man with an eagle in the background. Sometimes, especially in earlier art of the Romanesque period, an angel (or man), winged lion, winged ox, and eagle were used to represent the Evangelists themselves.

These icons all derive from the four "living creatures," or angels, in Revelation 4:7 and, ultimately, from the four-faced cherubim of

Ezekiel 1 and 10. The second-century Church Father Irenaeus first used the creatures of Revelation to symbolize the four Evangelists, claiming that the man's face stands for Christ's Incarnation, the lion for his royalty, the ox (or calf) for his priestly (sacrificial) office, and the eagle for the grace of the Holy Spirit. Other interpretations based on the characteristics of the four Gospels are mentioned below.

Matthew was one of the twelve Apostles (see Question 91), but the attribution to him of the first Gospel, written c. A.D. 85, after the fall of Jerusalem, is traditional rather than historical. This Gospel, which may have been composed in Antioch, Syria, is addressed to Jewish Christians and often quotes from the Old Testament to prove that Christ is the Messiah and that his life fulfilled many prophecies of the Hebrew scriptures. Matthew accordingly begins with the genealogy of Jesus, a descendant of David and Abraham (but only through his foster father, St. Joseph). This emphasis on Christ's humanity helps explain Matthew's symbol in art as a man. The stories of Christ's infancy in Matthew are meant to draw parallels between him and Moses, just as the Sermon on the Mount is the "New Law" of perfection that transcends the Mosaic Law.

The Gospel of **Mark** is the shortest and most primitive of the four canonical Gospels, and also the earliest (c. A.D. 65–70), though orthodox tradition placed it second. It was probably composed at Rome and addressed to Christians who were suffering persecution there. Its author was said to have been an associate of St. Peter or the John Mark who traveled with St. Paul and St. Barnabas.

Mark's symbol of the lion is sometimes explained by his beginning his Gospel with John the Baptist and Jesus in the wilderness. Since the lion was supposed to sleep with its eyes open, and its cubs were thought to be born dead until their sire roared three days later, it also symbolized Christ's Resurrection after three days in the tomb.

In the ninth century, some Venetian merchants smuggled Mark's body out of Alexandria, Egypt—assuring the Moslem customs inspector that their casket was full of pork—and brought it to Venice. Thus, Mark became Venice's patron saint, and the magnificent cathedral and square dedicated to him are the pride of "La Serenissima," the city of lagoons, the serene queen of the Adriatic.

The third Gospel, of **Luke,** probably written between A.D. 80 and 90, and its sequel, the Acts of the Apostles (the fifth book of the New Testament), may be the work of a non-Jewish Christian. The author was traditionally identified with the Luke who was a companion of St. Paul—"the beloved physician" of Colossians 4:14. In some works of art, Luke is shown painting a picture because of the legend that he once painted a portrait of the Virgin Mary. In medieval guilds, both painters and apothecaries belonged to the guild of St. Luke.

The Gospel begins with the Jewish priest Zechariah, soon to be the father of John the Baptist, sacrificing in the Temple at Jerusalem. The ox, symbol of sacrifice, was thus seen to be a fitting emblem of Luke and of Christ's Passion. Luke's is the only Gospel that contains the parables of the Good Samaritan and the Prodigal Son. Like Matthew's, Luke's Gospel provides an account of the birth of Jesus. The splendid hymns usually referred to as the "Magnificat" (of Mary) and the "Nunc Dimittis" (of Simeon) also have their origin in Luke. This Gospel is notable for its humane concern with the poor, the oppressed, the outcast. Ernest Renan, the French author of a highly controversial and rationalistic *Life of Jesus* (1863), considered Luke's Gospel the most beautiful book ever written.

Matthew and Luke both used the Gospel of Mark as a source. They also relied heavily on a hypothetical Greek document called "Q" (for German *Quelle,* "source"), which apparently consisted mostly of Christ's sayings, such as the Lord's Prayer, the Sermon on the Mount, and the eight Beatitudes (see Question 72), but also contained some narratives such as the preaching of John the Baptist and the temptation of Christ (see Question 18). The text of Q has been reconstructed by biblical scholars.

The first three Gospels are called synoptic (Greek, "viewed together") because they have many parallel passages (including much exact wording) that can be compared side by side. The relationship among them seems to be roughly as follows: Both Matthew and Luke used Mark and Q as sources; in addition, Matthew used a separate hypothetical source (referred to as "M"), whereas Luke used another ("L")—both of which may have been oral traditions. Of the 661 verses in the Gospel of Mark, only 31 are totally unrepresented in either Matthew or Luke. Because Matthew reproduces more than 600 of Mark's verses, his Gospel has been referred to as "the second edition of Mark, revised and expanded." In addition, the Gospels of Matthew and Luke have about 235 verses that are parallel and seem to derive from the Q source. And did Matthew or Luke know the other's Gospel? Hard to say.

The soaring eagle, symbol of **John,** denotes the sublimity of his Gospel, which begins with a prologue identifying Christ with both God and the Logos (Divine Reason or Wisdom, the Word) of Greek philosophy. St. John, the Galilean fisherman who was one of the twelve Apostles, was *not* the author of the fourth Gospel, the three epistles of John, and Revelation (see Question 29). A disciple of John at Ephesus, John the Elder, may have been the author of the Gospel.

Throughout, John's highly spiritual Gospel stresses the mystery of the Incarnation—"the Word became flesh and dwelt among us"— and the divinity of Jesus much more insistently than the synoptic Gospels. The eagle was supposed to be the only creature capable of gazing directly at the sun, which was a symbol of divinity. Christ's Ascension into heaven is also figured forth by the lofty flight of John's eagle.

John's Gospel, the latest, while having some affinities with the three synoptics, is largely an independent text probably written in Asia Minor between A.D. 95 and 100. It describes Christ's ministry as taking place mostly in Judea and mentions three Passovers, whereas the synoptics concentrate on Christ's teaching in Galilee and on only one Passover. From John's Gospel we thus deduce that Christ's ministry lasted three years. Unlike the synoptics, this Gospel is characterized by long discourses, few parables, and no exorcisms. Its tone is austere, august, and majestic; knowledge of God and Christ is emphasized over good works.

The influence the Gospels have exerted on Western theology, philosophy, literature, art, music, and everyday life is incalculable. As the authorized "biographies" of Christ, providing accounts of his words and teachings, they were regarded with infinite awe and veneration. Here, from four different angles, Christian readers could ponder the earthly existence and cosmic significance of their God and Redeemer. In the eighteenth century, however, a few scholars began pointing out irreconcilable contradictions among the four Gospels and expressing some doubt about the authenticity of the miracles recounted therein. By the twentieth century, skepticism regarding the Gospels had become the norm for much of the intelligentsia.

The Evangelists are recalled in Samuel Beckett's play *Waiting for Godot* (1952) by Vladimir ("Didi") for the unwilling edification of Estragon ("Gogo"). Didi's point is that only one of the Evangelists (Luke) assures us that one of the thieves crucified with Christ was saved ("Today shalt thou be with me in paradise"; see Question 69). "One out of four" is Didi's somber comment on the thief's chances of attaining salvation—and maybe ours.

✦ QUESTION 33

What are the 4 properties of a musical tone?

> **Pitch**
> **Duration**
> **Intensity**
> **Timbre (tone color)**

How is middle C different from middle A? Why does middle C sound different when it's played on a violin and on a piano? At a much more basic level, what's the difference between a musical tone and noise?

Music is organized sound, and tones are its building blocks. Musical instruments produce sounds that have regular, periodic vibrations. Most people, even those with no formal musical education, tend to think of random, chaotic vibrations as noise—especially when emanating from a leafblower, a phone-addicted colleague, or a whining generator (*pace* John Cage)—and regular vibrations as musical tones. The purposeful manipulation of pitch, duration, intensity, and timbre allows composers and performers to marshal individual tones into the patterns of musical compositions.

Pitch refers to the height of a tone, as in a high or low note. It is determined by the frequency of the vibrations producing the sound. Low notes result from slow vibrations, high notes from rapid ones, whether the sources are the reeds on oboes and other woodwinds, the calfskin heads of timpani, or even the lips of trumpeters and trombonists (see Question 23). The strings in the bass of a piano (left-hand end) are thick and produce low notes when struck by the hammer or plucked with a finger. It's possible to see them vibrate. Moving up the keyboard to the higher notes, we see the strings that produce them become increasingly fine. Their rapid vibration can't be seen—only heard.

Most music of the Western world is based on the pitch scale of the octave, as in the keys running from middle C to the next C on a piano keyboard, or from the A above middle C to the next A, and so forth. By convention, the A note above middle C is tuned to 440 cycles per second on all instruments. Because the next A above middle A is tuned to 880 cycles per second, it sounds like a duplicate tone. (Pitch audible to human ears falls in the range of 15 to 18,000 cycles per second.)

The octave includes twelve keys—seven white and five black on a keyboard—and their corresponding pitches. The interval between C and C# (the adjoining black key) is a half-tone. The interval between C and D, the adjoining white key, is a whole tone. The diatonic scale includes only eight notes, as in do, re, mi, etc., and can be major or minor. The chromatic scale—C#, D, D#, E, F, F#, etc.—includes all twelve tones in the octave. Chords composed of chromatic tones tend to stir the emotions and were widely used in music written late in the nineteenth century.

Whenever musicians play together, standardization of pitch becomes crucial. Regardless of how well the musicians have rehearsed, Schubert's piano trio in E flat will fail miserably if the pianist, violinist, and cellist neglect to tune their instruments to the same pitch. In an orchestra, the task falls to the concertmaster, who ensures conformity by playing a perfectly tuned middle A (or using an electronically generated tone of 440 cycles/second) while the other musicians tune their instruments to it.

This standardization of middle A is a rather recent development: Its pitch had been rising for at least two centuries. If modern listeners could be transported back a century or two, a familiar piece of music written in the key of D, for example, would probably sound as if it were being played in the key of C, a full tone lower.

Duration is the length of time a tone persists. When a piano key is struck and held down, a tone is audible until the string stops vibrating because of air friction and its own inertia. Letting go of the piano key, though, causes a damper to rest against the string, stopping its vibration. Musical tones are rarely given the luxury of persisting as long as they please, since the composer decides how long a note will be sustained. If a piano piece, for example, is written in 4/4 time, a whole note is held for four beats, a half note for two, and a quarter note for just one beat.

Intensity is the loudness of a tone. Musical scores are marked with derivations of the Italian words for loud, *forte,* and soft, *piano.* These include fortississimo, fff (extremely loud); fortissimo, ff (very loud); forte, f (loud); mezzo forte, mf (medium loud); forte-piano, f p (loud, then soft); piano-forte, pf (soft, then loud); mezzo piano, mp (medium soft); piano, p (soft); pianissimo, pp (very soft); and pianississimo, ppp (extremely soft). Musicians can also be instructed to increase the intensity gradually by the marking *crescendo* or to decrease it by *decrescendo* or *diminuendo.*

Timbre (TAM-bur), more often called tone color, is what differentiates the sound of a cello from that of a clarinet. These differences are caused by overtones. Only a flute—not much more than a simple metal pipe—has a nearly pure tone; other instruments produce a variety of them. This occurs because the vibrating portion, such as a reed, vibrates not only as a whole but also in its individual parts. An A played on a clarinet is really a composite of pure tones produced by the various parts of the reed. We are aware only of the lowest of these tones, the fundamental. We can't consciously discern the rest, called overtones or harmonics, because the fundamental's intensity is so much greater.

The character of the overtones is determined by an instrument's shape and range of tone, among other features of the vibrations it produces. We obviously sense the presence of overtones at some level, since we are able to distinguish tones produced by different instruments, even when the tones have the same pitch, duration, and intensity. Instrumentalists can also modify overtones. That's why a piano has pedals and why string players spend years learning to create a tremolo effect by quivering the bow over the strings or a vibrato effect by vibrating the fingers of the left hand on the strings, thus subtly raising and lowering the pitch. When a violinist puts the bow aside and plucks the strings to create a pizzicato effect, the violin's timbre changes again. So does the timbre of a trumpet when a mute is held over the bell.

Timbre is the most subjective property of musical tones. Depending on the instrument that produces the tone, timbre can be described as woody, nasal, shrill, brilliant, warm, earthy, comical, or colorless, and different listeners discern different characteristics.

✦ QUESTION 34

What are the 4 parts of T. S. Eliot's *Four Quartets* and their associated elements?

> "Burnt Norton": air
> "East Coker": earth
> "The Dry Salvages": water
> "Little Gidding": fire

The *Four Quartets* (1943) of the Anglo-American poet, dramatist, and critic T. S. Eliot (1888–1965) is often considered his poetic masterpiece. Each of the four parts, originally published separately, is loosely structured around one of the four elements of the ancient world (see Question 20). Each "quartet" has five sections differing in format—from rhymed, metered verse to free verse—which may be seen as the equivalent of movements in a musical work. Eliot also named each poem for a place that had personal significance for him. The overall title invites comparison with Beethoven's later quartets. Eliot considered calling the poem *Kensington Quartets,* after the London neighborhood where he had lived.

Each of the five sections of each poem has its own distinct tonality or timbre. Poetic themes are stated, developed, and recapitulated, as in the musical themes of the classical sonata. The first section or "movement" of each poem states the theme in the context of a landscape. The second section begins with a formal lyric, which is followed by a piece in free verse (or a formal narrative piece in the case of the last quartet). The third section is in a colloquial style. The fourth is a short lyric, usually rhymed. The fifth is a meditative resolution of the quartet's theme that includes thoughts on the difficult task of writing poetry.

The dominant themes of *Four Quartets* are the human struggle with time, the meaning of history, and the poet's struggle with the recalcitrance of language. The poem is a tour de force in the homiletic, philosophical, and lyrical modes—a profoundly religious and a deeply personal work. Eliot's reliance on paradoxes throughout the poem hints at the ineffable truths that he senses but cannot verbalize because they deal with matters outside of time and the realm of rational discourse. His search for the flickering moment of joyous illumination recalls Proust's epic quest in search of lost time. Ultimately, he sees the Incarnation of Christ, the intersection of time and eternity, as the most meaning-endowing event in world history, far surpassing all other Proustian moments, Joycean epiphanies, and Wordsworthian "spots of time."

"Burnt Norton" (1936) was named after a manor house and garden in the Cotswolds of Gloucestershire, built on the site of a house that had burned down in the seventeenth century. In the summer of 1934 Eliot stayed with a close American friend of his, Emily Hale, at the house of her relatives in a nearby village. The poet was still legally married to his mentally disturbed first wife, Vivien, and "Burnt Norton" hints at chances not taken, opportunities missed, paradises lost. The first word of the poem is "Time," and the speaker tries to determine how inexorable time can be redeemed. The opening section leads up to a timeless moment in a rose garden, in the autumn **air,** in which children are playing and laughing—but the door to the garden was never opened. Although a potentially transcendent experience was refused, a moment of insight was nonetheless vouchsafed. The last section of the poem brings us around again to the laughter of children in the garden and the moment of illumination it represents.

"East Coker" (1940) derives its title from a Somerset village, home of Eliot's ancestors, which he had visited in 1937. In the first section of the poem he describes the return of all things to the **earth** in death. Eliot quotes from *The Book of the Governor* (1531) by his ancestor Sir Thomas Elyot to introduce a vision of the long-dead rustics of East Coker dancing around a fire—symbols of the futility of coupling and of life. The second section takes issue with Wordsworth's notion that the years "bring the philosophic mind": Since increasing age doesn't bring wisdom, we need humility in the face of death and transience. In such straits, we must shed our desires and wait in patience for illumination from God. There is a Buddhistic emphasis on the need to empty ourselves not only of desire but also of knowledge, ownership, and even our own identity. In a lyric on Christ's Passion—another intersection of time and eternity—Eliot emphasizes the possibility of salvation through suffering with Christ. The poem ends with a meditation on poetry and on how Eliot's life was largely wasted in the period between the two world wars. This section deals with the disappointments of middle age and the poet's continuing struggle to master his medium—words. The quest for meaning must continue, no matter what impediments the years and the formidable difficulties of verbal communication throw in our way.

"The Dry Salvages" (sal-VAY-jez) (1941) takes its name from a group of rocks with a beacon that served as a seamark off Cape Ann on the Massachusetts coast, where Eliot went sailing as a boy out of Gloucester Harbor. **Water** figures prominently in this poem: The opening depicts the Mississippi River—Eliot was born and spent his childhood years in St. Louis—as a Yahweh-like god that punishes those who forget him. The lyric of the second section is in the form of a Provençal *canso,* or song, about Massachusetts fishermen risking death *(Moby-Dick* hovers in the background of this poem). Yet the third section jumps all the way back to ancient India in evoking the *Bhagavad Gita,* which tells of the god Krishna's injunction to the warrior Arjuna to fare forward boldly (see Question 2). In the fourth section, the lyric on the death of seamen recalls that of Phlebas the Phoenician in the fourth section of Eliot's modernist masterpiece, *The Waste Land* (1922). This lyric is a prayer to Mary who, as *Stella Maris,* Star of the Sea, was traditionally invoked by sailors. The poem ends with a scornful reference to all those who want to know the future by any means possible and an assertion that a more proper object of our knowledge is the intersection of the timeless with time—the Incarnation of Christ.

"Little Gidding" (1942) is entitled for a Huntingdonshire manor that was the seat of a seventeenth-century Anglican religious community. Raided in 1646 by Cromwell's Puritans during the English Civil War, it was rebuilt in the nineteenth century as an Anglican shrine. Eliot had gone there on a midwinter afternoon to pray and meditate on those who had prayed there three centuries earlier. The poet reflects on England's bloody Civil War and its present trial by **fire** during the German blitz of World War II. This contemplative war poem, which explicitly mentions the four ancient elements as symbols of decay and impermanence, is the finest of the four quartets.

The high point of the poem is a Dantesque passage in modified terza rima that Eliot called the closest equivalent to a canto of *The Divine Comedy* that he could achieve. At dawn after a German attack—Eliot was an air-raid warden in London during the war—a dead poetic master appears to him, in a scene reminiscent of Dante's meeting with his old master, Brunetto Latini, in Canto 15 of the *Inferno*. There's more than a bit of William Butler Yeats, who had died in 1939, in this spirit, but also something of Mallarmé, Swift, and Poe. The spirit talks of the craft of writing, of the physical, spiritual, and moral disappointments of old age, and the slow and difficult process of purgation, in which only a refining fire can save us. This last notion alludes to Dante's having to pass through a wall of fire in the *Purgatorio*, the last step in his active purgation. The spirit disappears when the horn of the all-clear sounds, much as the ghost of Hamlet's father "faded on the crowing of the cock."

In the third section, Eliot recalls that the fierce enemies in the English Civil War of the mid-seventeenth century are now reconciled in death because it's impossible to think of one without remembering the other, whether it's the doomed King Charles I and his Royalist supporters or the blind poet John Milton on the Puritan side. He suggests that in philosophic detachment, and in the view of past suffering as purgation, a sense of peace and renewal might be achieved. The implication is that time will heal the devastating wounds of World War II, as it has done with those of the English Civil War.

The rhymed lyric of the fourth section juxtaposes the dove of peace—as when the Holy Spirit descended in tongues of flame on Pentecost—with a German bomber in the blitz over London. The fire of war destroys, but it is also a refining fire that cleanses and purifies. Which fire are we to choose—the fire of purgation or that of sin and the senses? A moment of timeless insight is achieved when the poet realizes that suffering is part of God's plan for rendering humanity fit to transcend its bounds and aspire to eternal life.

Four Quartets closes, as it opens, in a transcendent garden, but now known for the first time. Although the poem dwells on journeys, both inner and outer, the state at the end is one of stillness, simplicity, and resolution of opposites. The image of children in an apple tree recalls the Edenic garden of childhood—a sudden moment of insight harking back to the opening of *Four Quartets*. The last line of the poem—"And the fire and the rose are one"—unites the fire of suffering with Dante's rose of love in the *Paradiso*, where the souls of the blessed appear as points of fire in a celestial white rose, a symbol of perfect heavenly love.

In Poets' Corner of London's Westminster Abbey, Eliot's cenotaph is graced by a line from "Little Gidding" that expresses his belief in the ultimate inability of all merely human discourse to convey what's most important: "The communication of the dead is tongued with fire beyond the language of the living." Perhaps, but Eliot's living language still speaks eloquently to those who want to think about life instead of just live it.

☀ QUESTION 35

What are the 4 Last Things?

> Death
> Judgment
> Heaven
> Hell

In Christian eschatology (Greek, "study of last things")—not to be confused with scatology—the focus is on the ultimate destiny of humanity. Far from viewing **death** as the last thing, Christian thought posits a particular **judgment** of the soul immediately after death, and a universal or general judgment, which will take place at the end of the world. After its acquittal or conviction, the individual soul will partake of the bliss of **heaven** or the pain of **hell** for all eternity.

Let's backtrack a bit. Someone dies. In the Christian schema, that person's soul, a completely spiritual entity, appears before Christ, the judge of all Creation. The soul's merits and demerits are weighed, and a judgment is delivered. The options are

- ✦ Heaven: Very few make it here straight from earth. These instant saints have led lives of devotion, asceticism, service, self-sacrifice—forget it.
- ✦ Hell: Those who die in a state of mortal (serious) sin proceed directly to hell. Whether hell is a state of physical suffering, or solely the deprivation of the vision of God, will remain unknown until we get there.
- ✦ Purgatory: This is a purely Catholic compromise between

heaven and hell. Those who die with only venial (less serious) sins on their soul are sent to purge away the dross of their lives in purgatory, a state of temporary—as opposed to eternal—suffering.

Meanwhile, time goes by on earth. Then it stops altogether. The end of the world takes place. Everybody on earth dies. The Last Judgment, the Second Coming of Christ, Doomsday, the Parousia, painted by Michelangelo and countless others, and regarded with trepidation in the medieval hymn "Dies Irae" (Day of Wrath), is envisioned as Christ's judgment of all angels (whether good or bad) and all humans in the valley of Jehoshaphat, east of Jerusalem.

Those still alive when the world ended now have their particular and general judgment all rolled into one—except that purgatory is not an option: The possibilities are only heaven and hell. Those who were expiating their guilt in purgatory are now joyously received into heaven. Those who were already in hell or heaven stay there; their second judgment is merely pro forma, a public confirmation of Christ's earlier verdict in which the private sins and virtues of each are now made manifest to all. Now the earthly bodies of all the people who ever lived are resurrected from the dead and rejoined to their souls to suffer or feel bliss with them. Now the good sheep are separated from the wicked goats, who are told to depart into everlasting fire. (For James Joyce's hilariously terrifying treatment of the Four Last Things, read Chapter 3 of *A Portrait of the Artist as a Young Man.*)

In Christian thought, the two last things will be heaven and hell. All that is not heaven will be hell, where Satan, his fellow devils, and all the wicked of the earth—whether three or three trillion—will be punished eternally, and all that is not hell will be heaven, where the angels and the saints—all the saved—will rejoice forever in the immediate presence of the Trinity (see Question 7).

✧ QUESTION 36

What are the 5 Pillars of Islam?

1. Witnessing that God is one and Mohammed is his prophet
2. Praying five times daily
3. Giving a portion of one's wealth to charity yearly
4. Fasting during daylight hours in the holy month of Ramadan
5. Making the pilgrimage to Mecca at least once

Islam was founded in Arabia between 610 and 632 by Mohammed (570–632), an inhabitant of Mecca. Derived from the Arabic root *salaama* ("peace," "purity"), *Islam* means "submission" to the will of God; one who has made this submission is called by the related word *Muslim*.

It's said that while meditating in the desert, Mohammed (or Muhammad) received a number of revelations enjoining him to lead the idolatrous Arabs to a knowledge of the one true God, Allah. The angel Gabriel brought down to him the Koran *(Qur'an)*, the eternal, uncreated Word of Allah. The 114 suras (chapters) of this sacred book of Islam and the *sunna,* made up of collections of traditions *(hadith)* of the deeds and sayings of Mohammed, are the sources of the Islamic creed.

Mohammed saw himself as the culminating prophet in a series of at least twenty-five Old and New Testament figures, including Adam, Noah, Abraham, Ishmael, Isaac, Moses, David, and Jesus. He was the Seal of the Prophets, that is, the last and most important. Mohammed had to flee from Mecca to Medina, where his prophetic mission was well received. This event, which occurred on Friday, July 16, A.D. 622, is known as the hegira *(hijrah,* "migration") and marks the beginning of the Muslim era—Anno Hegirae (or AH) 1. In 630 Mohammed entered Mecca as a conqueror, and he died two years later at

Medina, where his tomb is the object of religious pilgrimage. From Arabia, his followers propagated their faith by the sword in a wide swath stretching from Morocco and Spain in the West to Indonesia in the East.

The edifice of Islam is supported by five pillars that represent the basic duties of those who wish to be considered part of the Islamic community. The first is a statement of faith, and the other four are manifestations of it. **Witnessing** (*shahada*) **that Allah is one and Mohammed is his prophet** must be done publicly at least once in a lifetime. It involves a fervent recitation of the following words, with full acceptance and understanding of all the main articles of Islamic belief: *Ashhadu alla ilaha illa Allah wa ashhadu anna Muhammad rasulu Allah* ("I bear witness that there is no God but Allah, and I bear witness that Muhammad is His messenger"). Here the uncompromising monotheism of Islam and its teaching that Mohammed is the final fulfillment of all prophecy are affirmed.

Praying (*salat*) **five times daily** is incumbent on every Muslim past puberty who is sane and, in the case of women, free from menstruation and the confinement of childbirth. These prayers, prefaced by ablution (*wudu*) of face, hands (to the elbow), and feet, are always the same, containing verses from the Koran recited in Arabic while the Muslim faces in the direction of Mecca. Muslims say these prayers while bowing and prostrating themselves on a carpet with shoes removed and head covered. At the following times each day a *muezzin,* or crier, calls Muslims to their five obligatory prayers from the minaret of a mosque:

- Early morning: after dawn and before sunrise
- Noon: after the sun begins to decline until it is about midway on its course to set
- Midafternoon: between the expiration of the noon prayer-time and sunset
- Sunset: immediately after sunset until the red glow in the western horizon disappears
- Evening: between the expiration of the sunset prayer-time and dawn.

Any delayed obligatory prayers must be made up. While these daily prayers can be said almost anywhere, Muslims are required to offer their Friday noon prayer in a mosque together with its congregation. The prayers, led by an imam, are supplemented by readings from the Koran and a sermon.

Obligatory almsgiving *(zakat)* involves a donation of 2.5 percent that Muslims must pay each year on their net assets, given in kind or coin, if their net worth is above a certain level. The recipients are mainly the poor, needy, wayfaring, and debt-ridden. Any voluntary charity over and above the *zakat* is called *sadaqat.*

Fasting *(sawm)* **between dawn and sunset during Ramadan,** the Islamic year's ninth month (which migrates throughout the seasons because of the Muslims' uncorrected lunar calendar), involves complete abstinence from eating, drinking, sexual relations, and smoking. It was during this month that the Koran was sent down by Allah from the seventh heaven (see Question 61) to Gabriel in the first heaven that it might be revealed to Mohammed. Every adult Muslim is required to keep the fast, except those who are mentally or physically unfit, elderly, on a journey, serving in the armed forces, working as manual laborers, or, in the case of women, menstruating, pregnant, or nursing a child. The end of Ramadan is celebrated with a festival called *Id al-Fitr.*

The pilgrimage *(hajj)* **to the holy Arabian city of Mecca at least once in a lifetime** is required of all Muslims who are mentally, physically, and financially sound. Each year, several million Muslims journey from all quarters of the globe during the twelfth month of the Islamic year to take part in the world's largest religious convention. Pilgrims, wearing simple garments, commemorate the rituals observed by Abraham and his son Ishmael, father of the Arabs. These two were believed to have built the Kaaba *(ka'bah,* "square building"), a small stone edifice located in the court of the Great Mosque *(al-Haram)* at Mecca. The Kaaba is considered the house of Allah on earth, although it had earlier contained the idols of the pagan Meccans. It enshrines a sacred black stone, apparently of volcanic or meteoric origin, thought by Muslims to be one of the stones of paradise given by the angel Gabriel to Abraham. Pilgrims circle the Kaaba seven times (three times running, four times slowly, in memory of Adam's imitation of the circling of the angels around the throne of Allah), kiss the black stone, run seven times between the hills of Safa and Marwa, as Hagar did during her frantic search for water for her son Ishmael, and stand together and pray in the broad plain of Mount Arafat in anticipation of the Day of Judgment.

An important duty during the *hajj* is that of sacrificing a ram in the valley of Mina on the tenth day of the pilgrimage month. A visit to the tomb of Mohammed in Medina is recommended but not obligatory. The close of the annual period of the *hajj* is marked by the great festival of *Id al-Adha,* celebrated with prayers and the exchange of gifts in Muslim communities all over the world.

Jihad ("striving") is sometimes seen as an additional duty imposed on Muslims, but interpretations of it range from "holy war" to a personal striving for adherence to the ethical norms of the Koran.

✦ QUESTION 37

What were the 5 events of the ancient Olympic pentathlon?

Footrace
Discus throw
Javelin throw
Long jump
Wrestling

The first Olympian Games, held in Olympia in western Greece, are said to have been celebrated in 776 B.C., the year when the first champion was listed in their records. They were inaugurated as a religious festival—some said by Heracles—in honor of the chief god, Zeus. But to the Greeks, the games were not only a religious ceremony and a sporting event but an art form in which the beauty, gracefulness, and strength of the human body were displayed to full advantage in the context of friendly competition. So important were these games to the Greeks that the four-year intervals between them were called Olympiads. Not only were the dates of events kept with reference to Olympiads, but the Greek calendar itself began in 776 B.C.

The games were held during the second or third full moon after the summer solstice, usually between August 6 and September 19. Foreigners and married women were not allowed to compete. (Young and unmarried girls, however, had their own games, the Heraia, in honor of Zeus's queen, Hera, which took place at Olympia, probably just before the men's games, and consisted only of a footrace.) Any man could compete in the Olympian Games, provided he was of pure Hellenic blood, free of any legal infraction, and clear of any penalty owed to Zeus.

Although these were the only requirements, the standard training procedure for the games usually necessitated some funding. Despite the existence of government-subsidized gymnasiums in the city-states of ancient Greece, proper training could involve considerable time, money, and instruction. By the sixth century B.C., athletes began training in specialized areas under expert coaches. Many subjected themselves to regimens regarding diet, exercise, and sex, although some of these were idiosyncratic by modern standards. For example, Milo of Croton in southern Italy (late sixth century B.C.), the greatest Olympian wrestler, allegedly consumed forty pounds of meat and bread at one sitting, washing it down with two gallons of wine. Families usually absorbed the bulk of the expenses, although at least one trainer requested government subsidies by about 300 B.C. Two centuries later, professional athletes with memberships in young men's organizations began to surface.

Athletes trained for ten months before the games with great intensity and focus. Their last month of training, the most strenuous, was spent under the guidance of Olympian judges called Hellanodicae, who had completed ten months of training themselves. During this last harrowing month, these judges weeded out the weaker competitors.

The remaining qualifiers had to take an oath administered by the Hellanodicae and attesting to their worthiness: "If you have exercised yourself in a manner worthy of the Olympian Games, if you have been guilty of no slothful or ignoble act, go on with a good courage. You who have not so practiced, go wherever you wish." After swearing this oath, the athletes formed a religious procession. Before a statue of Zeus, the contestants offered a boar as sacrifice. They then placed their hands on the beast's entrails and swore they had trained faithfully for ten months and would treat the other competitors fairly and honestly. The judges swore they would render fair and honest decisions without accepting any bribes.

Because the ancient Greeks considered the human body to be pure and beautiful, male athletes competed naked. (In fact, it is from the Greek *gymnos,* "naked," that we derive *gymnast* and *gymnasium.*) In the *Republic,* Plato claims that one of the differences between barbarians and Greeks was that the latter weren't ashamed to compete in the nude.

Admission to the games was free. Except for the judges and officials, most spectators sat on the ground. A capacity crowd may have been about ten thousand. The only married woman allowed to attend was the priestess of Demeter, all others being barred on pain of being hurled off a nearby mountain. Unmarried girls were free to come and watch, presumably in lieu of anatomy class.

The only known attempt of an adult woman to circumvent the rules occurred when the aristocratic Callipatira disguised herself in a unisex robe as the trainer of her son, who was competing in the boys' boxing match. When he won, she was so excited that she leaped over the barricade to congratulate him—and her robe flew open. The Hellanodicae pardoned her but ruled that, in the future, trainers had to appear naked.

Initially, there was only one Olympian event, a **footrace** that covered one length of track. This measured about two hundred meters, a distance referred to as a stade, which gave rise to our word *stadium.* More events were gradually added, including the two-stade race in 724 B.C. and the long-distance race (probably about three miles) in 720 B.C. By 708 B.C., the complete pentathlon ("five contests") was in place.

The **discus throw** involved hurling a flat piece of stone or metal that was hardly standardized. The few discuses that have been dug up range in weight (three to twelve pounds), diameter (seven to thirteen inches), and material. By comparison, the modern discus weighs a bit less than four and a half pounds. Although the exact ancient method of throwing the discus remains unknown, Roman copies of the *Discus Thrower (Discobolus)* of the Greek sculptor Myron (fifth century B.C.) suggest it did not differ significantly from modern techniques. In the only surviving description of the distance of a toss, the great athlete Phayllus of Croton managed one of about one hundred feet.

The **javelin throw** was judged for distance or, in later times, accuracy. The javelin itself was a light, six-foot wooden pole that was blunt at both ends. Ancient Greeks threw it in much the same way that modern athletes do, with a running start to the throwing line. By the end of the fifth century B.C., the goal of the event shifted from the distance to the accuracy of the toss. The pole was replaced by a spear that was hurled toward a target both from on foot and from horse-back.

The **long jump** involved getting a running start, jumping as far as possible, and landing with the feet together. The Greeks also used two jumping weights (something like dumbbells) to help them put greater momentum behind their leaps. The distance of the jump seems to have included the hop and skip, too, as opposed to only the jump itself. This helps explain the fifty-five-foot jump recorded of Phayllus of Croton.

The final event of the pentathlon was **wrestling,** in which the two top overall competitors from the previous events battled each other. Ancient Greek wrestlers took certain liberties—choking, shoving, finger-twisting—that are now frowned upon. The winner was the first to bring his opponent down with three separate clean throws.

Historians still debate how the pentathlon was scored. Some form of progressive elimination, down to the final wrestling event, must have been used. Although victors in the Olympian Games received only a wreath of wild olive, this was only the beginning. On returning to their hometowns, they were often honored with statues bearing their likeness, as well as significant monetary awards—none more generous than the equivalent of $300,000 that Athens granted its Olympian winners in the time of Solon (early sixth century B.C.). A few lucky winners in the first half of the fifth century B.C. were presented with splendid epinician ("victory") odes by the Greek lyric poet Pindar (see Question 79). Although most of his odes were written for victories in chariot racing, Pindar celebrates one winner of a pentathlon at the Olympian Games of 464 B.C., Xenophon of Corinth *(Odes,* "Olympian 13"). It's far from his best poem.

After Rome had consolidated its conquest of Greece in 146 B.C., participation in the games at Olympia (and the rest of Greece) dwindled as the city of Rome gradually became the center of athletic competition in the empire. The Olympian Games continued, however, until growing Christian influence on the government prompted Emperor Theodosius I to abolish them as pagan practices in A.D. 393.

It was only in 1896 that these games were revived in Athens as the Olympics. Since then, they have been held in different venues every four years, except for 1916, 1940, and 1944, when they were suspended for the grimmer competition of war. (In ancient times, it was often the other way around, wars being suspended because of the games.) The chasm dividing the original five competitions of the pentathlon and the constantly proliferating summer and winter Olympic events is just one indication of the vastly broadened conception of "athletics" over the past twenty-eight centuries.

❧ QUESTION 38

What are the 5 basic positions of the feet in classical ballet?

On your feet! You've got to act this answer out.

First

Second

Third

Fourth

Fifth

Figure 1

Arabesque   Attitude

According to the formalized rules of classical ballet, every move-ment—*jeté, entrechat, pirouette, tour en l'air, glissade*—must begin and end with one of the five basic positions of the feet, or *cinq positions des pieds.* In all the positions and their variations, the legs are turned sideways so that the toes point at a 180-degree angle and the dancer's weight is distributed evenly over both feet. Pierre Beauchamp (1636–1705), the first choreographer of the Paris Opéra and a dancer noted for his pirouettes, is credited with defining the five basic positions. It was Beauchamp's rigorous attention to technical standards that ele-vated the ballet beyond the realm of the talented amateur—and en-sured that French would henceforth be the language of ballet. His career included momentous collaborations with Molière and Jean-Baptiste Lully.

The five positions of the feet are sometimes paired with the five positions of the arms, or *positions des bras,* of the French School (as they have been in the illustration on the previous page). The two major body positions in classical ballet are the *arabesque* and the *attitude* (see Figure 1). In the *arabesque,* the dancer stands on one leg, which may be straight or bent, with the other leg extended behind, knee unbent. An *arabesque* can be varied by changing the carriage of the head, angle of the torso, placement of the arms, or height of the extended leg. The body weight is supported on a flat foot, the ball of the foot, or the toe *(pointe).*

In an *attitude,* the extended leg is always bent and maintained at a ninety-degree angle to the torso. As in an *arabesque,* variations are obtained by subtle changes in the positions of the head, arms, torso, and the foot that remains on the floor. According to ballet lore, the *attitude* was inspired by a statue of the god Mercury in flight.

✣ QUESTION 39

Which were the 5 Civilized Tribes?

Cherokee
Creek
Seminole
Chickasaw
Choctaw

These five Native American tribes of the Southeast were labeled the Civilized Tribes by European settlers because of the ease and rapidity with which they adopted the settlers' ways. The Cherokee were of Iroquoian descent; the other four tribes were Muskogee. The most powerful Muskogee tribe was the **Creek,** which had established its own loose confederacy of some fifty villages during the eighteenth century. The Creek were friendly toward the British, fighting against the Americans in the War of 1812 only to be defeated by General Andrew Jackson. The **Seminole** were originally members of the Creek tribe but broke away during the eighteenth century, settling in northern Florida. Mississippi was the home of the other two tribes of Muskogee descent, the **Chickasaw** in the northern part of the state and the **Choctaw** in the southern. Like the other Muskogee tribes, they were agricultural. In the conflicts of the eighteenth and early nineteenth centuries the Chickasaw sided with the British and the Choctaw with the French.

The dominant group of the Civilized Tribes was the **Cherokee,** who had been in contact with European explorers as early as 1710. During the eighteenth century they gradually adopted European-style laws and representative government, and cultivated skills such as spinning. Many children from these tribes attended missionary schools. A written version of the Cherokee language was developed by the Cherokee warrior Sequoyah. The first Native American newspaper, the *Cherokee Phoenix,* was published at the Cherokee capital of New Echota, Georgia, from February 21, 1828, until May 31, 1834.

The early years of the United States saw a tremendous increase in the white population and its domination of the Southeast. Georgia alone saw a sixfold population increase between 1790 and 1830. While the white settlers may have considered their predecessors civilized, that didn't stop them from appropriating Native American lands. The first two decades of the nineteenth century were a chronicle of broken treaties and forceful destruction of some tribes.

The independence of the Cherokee had been ensured by the federal government in a treaty of 1791. But in 1828 gold was discovered on Cherokee lands in northern Georgia. A rush ensued, and the state of Georgia evinced little interest in defending federally protected lands where fortunes were to be made. In 1830 President Andrew Jackson signed the Indian Removal Act, which mandated the displacement of all the Eastern tribes from their homes to the Indian territories west of the Mississippi River. In return for leaving their homes, the Five Tribes were deeded territory from the area acquired by the United States in the Louisiana Purchase, which was already occupied by other tribes. The federal government authorized $500,000 for the removal program to cover the expenses of the move and provide a year's subsistence for the deportees.

Unwilling to leave, the Cherokee sought to defend their lands through the U.S. court system. In 1832 the Reverend Samuel Worcester, missionary to the Cherokee Nation, successfully argued the unconstitutionality of the Indian Removal Act, and the Supreme Court under Chief Justice John Marshall decided that the state of Georgia had no authority within federally mandated Cherokee territory. The struggle for states' rights was well under way, however, and state authorities in Georgia refused to accept the verdict. Siding with the states and against the Supreme Court, President Jackson remarked that "John Marshall has made his decision. Now let him enforce it." Jackson subsequently sent federal troops to assist the settlers, and the state of Georgia held a lottery to determine the disposition of what had once been the home of the Cherokee Nation. Self-determination for indigenous peoples was not of particular concern to Jacksonian lawmakers, nor was the harshness of the fate to which they were dooming them.

A protest signed by more than fifteen thousand Cherokee and whites had no effect. Tennessee Senator Davy Crockett's political career ended abruptly when he spoke out in support of the rights of the Five Tribes. The removal began. From a grim encampment at Rattlesnake Springs, Tennessee, where they were being held prior to their journey west, the Cherokee promulgated their "Last Resolution" in August 1838. This document claimed a perpetual right to the territories granted them by treaties with the federal government, asserting that "the free consent of the Cherokee people is indispensable to a valid transfer of the Cherokee title, and . . . the said Cherokee people have, neither by themselves nor their representatives, given such consent." Beginning that same month, some twelve thousand Cherokee were forced to set out for their new lands in the western Indian territories. As many as four thousand died during the thousand-mile journey that became known as the Trail of Tears. Starvation, exposure, and diseases such as cholera and measles took their dreadful toll.

The survivors set about rebuilding their farms and society west of the Mississippi, and the Five Tribes remained independent until 1907, when the federal government opened the Indian territories to white settlement. The state of Oklahoma was admitted to the Union in the same year.

Oklahoma, the forty-sixth state, today celebrates its heritage as the adopted home of the descendants of the Five Civilized Tribes. The state seal features a large five-pointed star on a blue background surrounded by forty-five smaller stars. Each arm of the central star represents one of the Five Tribes; in the center a Native American is depicted shaking hands with a white man as Themis, Greek goddess of justice, looks on. Incidentally, the opposite number of Themis in the Greek pantheon was Hybris, whose name meant "insolent encroachment on the rights of others."

What are the 5 classical architectural orders?

Doric
Ionic
Corinthian
Composite
Tuscan

The monumental achievements of Greco-Roman architecture are epitomized in their architectural orders. An order is a discrete, standard style unit consisting of a column, base, and entablature. Three orders—the Doric, Ionic, and Corinthian—were Greek creations; the Composite and Tuscan were Roman derivatives. The orders are perhaps the best-known elements of the Western architectural vocabulary—consider the columns of the Parthenon and (to compare great things with small) those of the White House or even a Depression-era U.S. post-office building.

The earliest Greek temples were built of wood. Eventually, limestone was used and, when funds were available, marble. Regardless of the order used or the temple's size, the basic plan and function remained the same. In the center of these open, usually rectangular structures was the *cella,* or *naos.* Here was kept an image of the deity to whom the temple was dedicated. In the simplest temples, only a porch with two columns was added, whereas larger, grander temples had a second porch or even a colonnade (peristyle). All were constructed with lintels (rarely, if ever, an arch) and sloping roofs. The temple was meant to be admired from the outside, since access to the interior was somewhat restricted, and public religious ceremonies were conducted just outside the temple.

The orders share several features. Starting at the bottom, the unit rests on the stereobate and stylobate. Except for Doric constructions,

The Elements of Classical Architecture

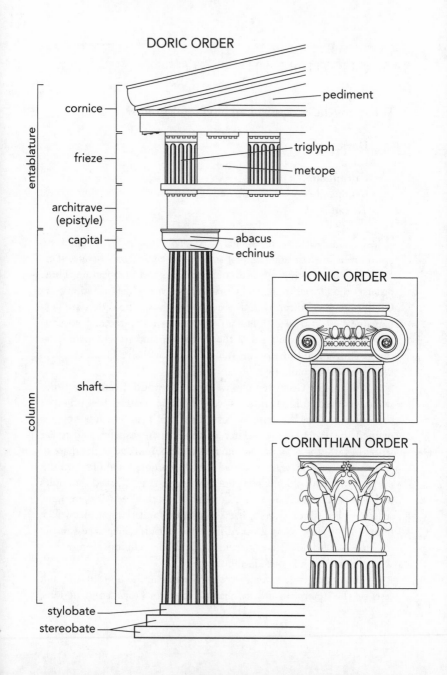

DORIC ORDER

entablature
- cornice — pediment
- frieze — triglyph
- metope
- architrave (epistyle)

column
- capital — abacus
- echinus
- shaft

IONIC ORDER

CORINTHIAN ORDER

stylobate
stereobate

the column itself rests on a base, which is more or less decorative depending on the order. The column shaft is composed of a series of drums stacked on one another and secured with bronze or wooden pivots running through the center of each. No mortar was used, attesting to the Greeks' skill and precision in cutting stone. The flutes, which were incised into the stone after the column had been assembled, contribute a visual dynamism while disguising the drum joints. The height of a column was defined in terms of its diameter at the base. For example, builders were given directions to make the columns eight or nine diameters high.

At the top of the column shaft, the neck marks the transition to the capital, comprising the echinus and abacus. The capital most readily displays the distinguishing characteristics of each order. The section above the capital, the entablature, includes in ascending order the architrave (which bears and distributes the weight above), the frieze, pediment, and cornice. The architrave, often left unadorned, might also contain panels called fasciae. Above this, the frieze might be bare or decorated with triglyphs and metopes, carvings in relief, or other elements. The remainder consists of the cornice and the pediment (which might also have been decorated). The cornice encloses the triangular form of the pediment.

The **Doric,** the oldest order, was developed in mainland Greece. What is known of one of the most ancient examples of a Doric edifice, the temple of Artemis at Corcyra (modern Corfu), suggests that the order had been codified by about 600 B.C. Although the source of their inspiration remains unclear, the architects were no doubt influenced by Greek pre-Archaic wood-and-mud-based structures, as well as by Mycenaean and Egyptian models. Compared with the other orders, the Doric seems plain, massive, and stolid, an impression confirmed by its ancient designation as a "masculine order."

Doric columns rested directly on the stylobate without a base. They tapered toward the top in a slight curve, or entasis, creating a feeling of lightness to offset the order's solidity. Conventional Doric columns contain exactly twenty flutes, which usually meet in a sharp junction. In the most ancient examples, like the so-called Basilica at Paestum in southern Italy (c. 530 B.C.), the echinus portion of the Doric capital resembles a pillow or giant marshmallow bulging from beneath the weight of an even massier abacus.

In these old exemplars, the columns were placed quite close together, prompting the Roman architect Vitruvius (first century

B.C.) to comment that their narrow spaces created problems for groups of matrons who wished to enter the temple with their arms around each other but who instead had to form a single file. In fact, these squat, closely set columns suggest that early architects were a bit unsure about how their designs would hold up—literally. Over time, the proportions of the Doric order became more visually pleasing, as the architects became more confident of the structural integrity of their design. The capitals, in particular, assumed a more refined look, and the narrower, more graceful columns were spaced more widely. This transition occurred on the Greek mainland by about 500 B.C. The outstanding example of the Doric is the Parthenon on the Athenian Acropolis, the most revered of surviving Greek temples.

The **Ionic** order was developed in Asia Minor and the Aegean Islands only shortly after the Doric, probably by about 560 B.C. Designated a "feminine order" by the manly Greeks, the Ionic features a column that is more slender and less tapering than the Doric, has a decorated base and twenty-four flutes, and is eight diameters high. Its most distinguishing feature is the scroll, or volute, that subsumes the echinus and is typically carved with a motif termed "egg and dart." As with the Doric Parthenon, the finest examples of the Ionic order are also on the Athenian Acropolis: the Erechtheum and the Temple of Athene Nike.

The highly decorative **Corinthian** order evolved by about 425 B.C. Vitruvius repeats a fanciful tale about the origins of this order, which he compares to the figure of a young girl, "for the outlines and limbs of maidens, being more slender on account of their tender years, admit of prettier effects in the way of adornment."

The story goes that the Athenian sculptor Callimachus passed by the tomb of a recently deceased Corinthian girl. Her nurse had placed a basket of her favorite possessions on top of the tomb and covered it with a tile. Beneath the basket was an acanthus plant, which sent its shoots up and through the sides of the basket. According to Vitruvius, Callimachus was so smitten with the sight of the interwoven basket and tendrils that he was inspired to design the Corinthian capital.

Unlike the Ionic capital, meant to be viewed from only two sides, the Corinthian, usually perched atop a column ten diameters high, may be admired from all four angles. At first, Corinthian capitals, which include staggered rows of elaborately carved acanthus leaves below the abacus, were used only in the interior of edifices. After a century of indoor use, they began to be erected on the exteriors of structures. The oldest surviving example is the Monument of Lysicrates in Athens (334 B.C.). Later, the Romans used the elegant, sumptuous Corinthian more widely than any other order.

Favoring more elaborate decoration than the Greeks, the Romans were somewhat less concerned with geometric perfection. They felt free to replace lintels with arches, and their entablatures were often more highly decorated. In their **Composite** order, they combined the scroll of the Ionic capital with the acanthus leaves of the Corinthian. The columns were often ten diameters in height.

The Romans also devised the **Tuscan** order, a simplification of the Doric. Tuscan columns have the characteristic Doric capital but, unlike Doric columns, rest on a base. They also lack fluting and are typically only seven diameters high.

Further variations on these themes include the Superposed and Colossal orders. The Superposed, a Roman invention, was used when columns were erected on several stories of a building. By convention, Doric columns adorned the first story, Ionic the second, and Corinthian the third, resulting in a visual epitome of the three ancient Greek orders, as in Rome's Colosseum. During the Renaissance, architects sometimes worked two- or three-story columns (or half-pillars) of a single order into their edifices—examples of the aptly named Colossal order.

❧ QUESTION 41

Who were the Russian composers known as the Mighty Five?

> **Mili Balakirev**
> **Nikolai Rimsky-Korsakov**
> **Aleksandr Borodin**
> **Modest Mussorgsky**
> **César Cui**

The history of distinctly Russian music—other than folk tunes—has been said to date from the first performance, in 1836, of the opera *A*

Life for the Czar (also called *Ivan Susanin* by the Soviets) by Mikhail Glinka (1804–57). Glinka followed with another opera, *Russlan and Ludmilla* in 1842, and portions of both were performed in Paris under the direction of Hector Berlioz—the first time that Russian orchestral music was played outside of Russia. Glinka's importance lies not only in the merits of his work but also in his role as father of the Russian nationalist movement in music. This movement peaked with the accomplishments of the Mighty Five, or Mighty Handful *(Moguchaya Kuchka),* as music critic Vladimir Stassov, later a close friend and promoter of the group, dubbed them in 1857.

Until the mid-nineteenth century, the composers most influential in Russia, as throughout Europe, were German, Italian, and French. The establishment of a consciously Russian nationalist movement in music by Glinka and his followers was a reaction to this foreign influence. Because the German musical orthodoxy was considered the most overbearing, the Mighty Five were dedicated to founding a native Russian school of music to rival Germany's.

Although the Five were near-amateurs, some music critics have asserted that this lack of formal training in theory and composition worked to their advantage. Had they been more familiar with conventional harmony and counterpoint, they might not have sought inspiration in Russian folk-song idioms.

Mili Balakirev (bah-LAH-kee-ref) (1837–1910) spent most of his early life in the company of eminent musicians. He studied mathematics and musical composition at the University of Kazan and by the mid-1850s had become a prominent concert pianist. He eventually became the concert conductor at the St. Petersburg Conservatory. During his early years in St. Petersburg, Balakirev met Glinka, who bestowed the nationalist mantle on him, modestly calling him "a second Glinka." The state of Russian musical sophistication at this time may be gauged from the fact that there were no Russian-language textbooks on composition, and since Balakirev could read little German, Glinka tutored him privately.

In 1866, Balakirev published an authoritative collection of Russian folk tunes. Traces of them are heard in his best-known compositions, *Islamey* (one of the most difficult piano pieces ever written) and the symphonic poem *Tamara.* He also became the musical mentor of Borodin and Rimsky-Korsakov.

Balakirev's later life was plagued by mental illness. Although his pupils recognized the privilege of studying with him, he apparently had always been unpleasant and almost unbearably rigid and dogmatic. Rimsky-Korsakov wrote that Balakirev the teacher was "so despotic that he insisted we remodel our music exactly according to his prescriptions." He added that entire segments of compositions ostensibly written by younger students were actually composed by Balakirev. Several bouts with severe depression took their toll on Balakirev's art. He is now remembered more for his influence on the rest of the Five and later composers than for his own compositions.

While studying at the naval academy of St. Petersburg, **Nikolai Rimsky-Korsakov** (1844–1908) met Balakirev, who urged him to broaden his earlier training in music and composition and write a symphony. His association with Balakirev was interrupted when he sailed to America after graduating, spending time in several East Coast ports during the Civil War. Reminiscences of his long sea voyages reappear throughout his works. On returning to Russia, he finished his first symphony, performed in 1865 when he was only twenty-one. This was the first "real" symphony composed by a Russian. Shortly afterward, Rimsky-Korsakov wrote *Fantasy on Serbian Themes*. His fame and reputation grew, and he found himself teaching composition at the St. Petersburg Conservatory despite his scanty musical education, limited primarily to some work with Balakirev.

His debut as a conductor took place at the first performance of his third symphony in 1874, at the start of a successful conducting career that continued into the early years of the twentieth century. He also was editor of a publishing company dedicated to the publication and preservation of Russian music.

Rimsky-Korsakov wrote quite a few operas, but the one performed most often in the West is *Le Coq d'or (The Golden Cockerel)* (1909), which was banned in Russia during his lifetime because the court of its King Dodon bore too close a resemblance to that of Czar Nicholas II. His most widely known orchestral works are *Capriccio espagnol* (1887), *Scheherazade* (1888), and *The Flight of the Bumble Bee*, from the opera *The Tale of Czar Saltan* (1900).

Rimsky-Korsakov's long career as a teacher spanned two generations of Russian composers. His students included Igor Stravinsky, Sergei Prokofiev, and Aleksandr Glazunov, as well as Italian composer Ottorino Respighi, and his influence lives on in the music of Debussy and Ravel, among others.

The charming and urbane **Aleksandr Borodin** (bore-uh-DEEN) (1833–87) was the illegitimate son of an elderly Georgian prince and a twenty-four-year-old woman who later married a doctor. Although his musical talent surfaced early in his privileged childhood, he became a surgeon and later a professor of chemistry and was known in scientific circles for his work on aldehydes. Also gifted in languages, Borodin wrote some of his scientific papers in Italian. Music never left him, however, and he wrote his first symphony soon after meeting Balakirev, who conducted at its premiere in 1869. His most celebrated work is the opera *Prince Igor,* first performed in an unfinished version in 1879 and conducted by Rimsky-Korsakov. This masterpiece, which Rimsky-Korsakov and Glazunov completed after Borodin's sudden death, includes the familiar *Polovtsian Dances.* (Parts of *Prince Igor* were also reworked decades later for the Broadway play *Kismet.*) Borodin's other important works include the symphonic sketch *In the Steppes of Central Asia* (1880), the Second Symphony in B minor (1885), and many well-regarded songs.

Because Borodin's instrument was the cello, he was inspired to compose several chamber works, an endeavor that his friend Mussorgsky initially discouraged for being overly German and therefore politically incorrect. His second string quartet, his best-known chamber work, evokes his courtship and marriage on the Italian Riviera.

Borodin is still regarded as an outstanding Russian composer. He is particularly renowned for his dual facility with lyrical and heroic subjects—and especially for exotic harmonies derived partly from Russian folk tunes that set them distinctly apart from European music of the time. In fact, his works incorporate many Russian musical elements, including abundant syncopation and dissonance. Yet he considered himself primarily a scientist and was a pioneer in organizing a medical-school curriculum for women. In view of his musical achievements, it is astounding that composition was relegated to his spare time.

Modest Mussorgsky (1839–81) is acknowledged as the most naturally gifted of the Mighty Five, although his deficiencies in musical education were the most glaring. In his autobiography, Mussorgsky credited his nurse for his early exposure to Russian fairy tales. This gave him a "familiarity with the spirit of the people . . . [and] lent the first and greatest impetus to my musical improvisations."

Although his mother taught him to play the piano at an early age, his musical studies were postponed when his father enrolled him in a military academy. Mussorgsky eventually became a member of an elite guard unit, all the while composing music. During this period he met fellow Five members Borodin and Balakirev and first heard the music of Glinka. Galvanized by the nationalist movement, he quit the military to pursue music full-time—a decision that had serious financial consequences when the serfs were freed in 1861 and he lost his inheritance.

Balakirev taught Mussorgsky most of what he knew about composition. Mussorgsky's early success with songs began in the 1860s. His most familiar work may be *A Night on Bald Mountain* (1867), which is included in the soundtrack of Walt Disney's 1937 animated feature, *Fantasia.* In 1869, he completed his masterpiece, the frenzied, brooding, somber, and flamboyant opera *Boris Godunov,* based on the play by Aleksandr Pushkin. The opera did not debut until 1874, however, because it lacked a romantic subplot, which Mussorgsky went on to provide. Since there were rumors that the imperial family resented the opera's revolutionary themes, *Boris* was soon pulled from the Imperial Opera's repertoire.

This unfortunate event was compounded by what Mussorgsky considered César Cui's betrayal in panning *Boris.* Mussorgsky tired of Balakirev, and he believed Rimsky-Korsakov and Borodin had lost their artistic identities by writing overly polished music and indulging in art for art's sake. Adding to Mussorgsky's social isolation was Rimsky-Korsakov's moving out of the apartment they shared to get married while *Boris* was being revised.

Mussorgsky's piano suite *Pictures at an Exhibition* (1874), later orchestrated by Ravel, was inspired by the death of a painter friend at age thirty-nine. During this time he worked on his opera *Khovanshchina,* which the ever-helpful Rimsky-Korsakov finished after Mussorgsky's death. Near the end of his short life, his friends spent little time with him, and Mussorgsky succumbed to alcohol-related illness at age forty-two.

If Mussorgsky was one of the least productive of the Five, he was certainly the boldest and most original, especially in his use of harmony and unconventional tonalities. His works were so idiosyncratic that Rimsky-Korsakov decided to edit nearly all of them after his friend's death to rid them of what he considered eccentricities. Fortunately, the original versions of many of his works, including *Boris,* were restored in the first half of the twentieth century. For Mussorgsky, music was a path to truth—in his case, to a full revelation of the character of the Russian people. Some of his pieces actually seem to imitate Russian speech.

César Cui (cue-EE) (1835–1918) was the son of a Lithuanian woman and a French naval officer under Napoleon's command who remained in Russia after his capture in the campaign of 1812. Although his childhood training in music and composition seemed to be directing Cui to a musical career, he took a university degree in military engineering instead. He became a professor of this discipline, and Czar Nicholas II was one of his students. Cui's friendship with Balakirev eventually led him back to music, and he wrote ten operas, including *The Prisoner of the Caucasus* (1883), *Feast in the Time of the Plague* (1901), and *The Captain's Daughter* (1911), which were based on works by Pushkin. His orchestration, however, was glaringly weak, and Balakirev and Rimsky-Korsakov rewrote much of these works. His songs and piano pieces are more highly regarded.

Cui was probably more important in his roles as music critic and journalist, which he used to boost the Russian nationalist movement in music. His extreme devotion to the nationalist cause apparently blinded him to the merits of composers outside the circle of the Mighty Five. Yet, maybe because of his non-Russian lineage, Cui's works have little of the Russian flavor so characteristic of the Five, and he himself turned to French and German sources for the majority of his operas.

 QUESTION 42

What were the 5 rivers of the classical underworld?

Acheron
Styx
Phlegethon
Cocytus
Lethe

We blasé postmodernists don't think about hell much, but when we do, we tend to associate it with fire. For the ancient Greeks, who lived when bodies of water were much more formidable obstacles than now, rivers were the most salient features of the underworld, specifically the five rivers separating the land of the living from the dead.

In Homer's *Odyssey,* the goddess Circe informs Odysseus that he must sail to the land of the dead to consult with the shade of the Theban prophet Tiresias. In the process, she reveals that four of the infernal rivers are geographically linked: "There Pyriphlegethon and Cocytus, a branch of the waters of Styx, flow into Acheron."

Issuing from a gloomy gorge, the **Acheron** (AK-ur-ahn, "river of woe") in Epirus in northwestern Greece was thought to be the entrance to the underworld realm of Hades, god of the dead, and his queen Persephone. The kingdom of Hades, guarded by the three-headed watchdog Cerberus, was imagined to be in the far west and, later, underground. Three judges decided the soul's fate (Minos, Rhadamanthys, and Aeacus); heroes and virtuous souls went to the Elysian Fields, a place of bliss, but the wicked were condemned to Tartarus, where they paid the penalty for their offenses. Those neither particularly good nor bad went to the shadowy Meadows of Asphodel.

The waters of the **Styx** (STICKS, "hated"), a small stream in Arcadia in the Peloponnese that fell from a cliff six hundred feet sheer down into a ravine, were said to be highly toxic. The nymph of the River Styx had four children—Zeal, Victory, Force, and Strength—who came to the help of the Olympian gods when they were fighting against the Titans (see Question 88). In recognition of this assistance, Zeus decreed that the gods must swear their sacred oaths by the Styx—"the fearful oath-river" in Homer's *Iliad.* When a god wished to make a solemn vow, Iris, the messenger of the gods, brought back water in a golden cup from the Styx, which the god then poured out while reciting the words of the oath. Any god who swore falsely by the Styx had to lie speechless and breathless for a year and endure banishment from the banqueting of the gods for nine years. The great majority kept their word.

The irascible and squalid old boatman Charon ferried the souls of the dead across the Styx, but only if they had been properly buried. To be left exposed without burial was a cruel fate because the soul of such a corpse could not cross the Styx to join the rest of the dead. Instead, according to Virgil (70–19 B.C.), the piteous soul was forced to wander on the near shore of that Stygian stream for a hundred years.

In Book 6 of Virgil's *Aeneid,* Charon at first demurs from conveying the living Aeneas across the Styx but immediately changes his tune when Aeneas' guide through the underworld, the Cumaean Sibyl, Deiphobe, draws a golden bough from beneath her robe. In *The Golden Bough*, the Scottish anthropologist Sir James George Frazer claimed that Aeneas' talisman was really mistletoe, considered to be protective against witches and trolls. (Remember that next Christmastime.)

Less prominent in myth than Acheron or Styx were Phlegethon and Cocytus. **Phlegethon** (FLEG-uh-thon), or Pyriphlegethon ("flaming"), was thought to be a river of liquid fire, and **Cocytus** (ko-SY-tus) was "the river of lamentation." The **Lethe** (LEE-thee; "oblivion") became popular in Roman literature. Virgil, imitating in the *Aeneid* what Plato had written in "The Myth of Er" at the end of the *Republic,* claims that the souls of the dead who are about to be reincarnated drink of the Lethean waters to forget their previous existence.

Entire books have been written on the complex "hydraulic system" of Dante's *Inferno.* All four rivers of his Hell—which are actually huge pools of still water—are interconnected. They all arise from the tears, stained with blood, of a mysteriously symbolical Old Man of Crete, a colossal statue that represents all the woes of the human race.

In Canto 3 of the *Inferno,* the souls of the recently dead Hellbound gather on the shores of Acheron. This river separates the incontinent sinners of upper Hell from the scorned fence-sitters, who weren't even committed enough to evil to be allowed into Hell proper after death (see Question 81). Charon is here the foul-tempered boatman of the Acheron rather than of the Styx. When he tries to prevent Dante—a living man destined for Purgatory—from climbing aboard, Dante's guide Virgil silences Charon's opposition by citing heavenly sanction for the epic journey to Hell and parts beyond. Charon has no choice but acquiesce and redirect his anger toward some of the terrified newly dead:

> Charon the demon, with eyes like glowing coal,
> Beckons the souls to board from all around,
> Striking whoever lingers with his pole (Inferno 3.109–11).

Farther down the slopes of Dante's Hell, those who were wrathful beat and tear one another apart in the muddy waters of the Styx, river of hate. In addition, the shades of the sullen are totally submerged in the ooze, which they choke on, as in life they choked on their own venom. Here Dante again lets Virgil pacify Phlegyas, the furious boatman of the Styx, which is imagined as a swampy circular moat around the walled city of Dis (lower Hell). While in the boat, Dante has a run-in with the muddy shade of an arrogant Florentine knight, Filippo Argenti, who hopes Dante doesn't recognize him. They exchange some verbal rapiers, culminating in Dante's nasty rejoinder, "though you're filthy, I still know your face":

> *At that, he grabbed the skiff; without delay,*
> *My wary master pushed him off and cried:*
> *"Get down there with the other dogs! Away!"*
> (Inferno 8.40–42)

Virgil then congratulates Dante on being so righteously indignant by kissing his cheek. Dante expresses the wish to see Argenti "dunked into this soup," and soon afterward the other shades of the wrathful attack Argenti while he turns his own teeth against himself in impotent rage.

All those who were violent against others—tyrants, murderers, highwaymen—are punished in Dante's Phlegethon, the river of boiling blood, guarded by centaurs armed with bows and arrows. The depth to which the sinners are immersed in the searing blood varies with the gravity of their crimes. Tyrants like Attila are sunk in the blood up to their brows, whereas the least violent of those violent souls have only their feet scorched in the liquid they loved to spill. Virgil tells Dante of the centaurs' role in making sure the sinners remain at their allotted depth:

> *In troops of many thousands they invest*
> *The moat, and shoot whichever souls withdraw*
> *More of themselves than is their guilt's bequest*
> (Inferno 12.73–75).

Dante crosses the boiling Phlegethon by riding on the back of a centaur.

At the bottom of Dante's Hell, four kinds of traitors (to kin, country, guests or friends, and benefactors) are imprisoned in the frozen pool of Cocytus, some with their heads sticking out of the ice, others entirely submerged in it, like flies inside an ice cube. The

Cocytus is frozen by the flapping wings of gigantic Lucifer, who is punished in the deepest pit of Hell. (For Dante, the sin of treachery is cold, not fiery.)

Dante does not situate Lethe in his underworld but at the summit of Mount Purgatory, in what used to be the Garden of Eden. The Lethe is a blessed river that, when tasted by souls bound for Paradise, washes away all memory of their sins. Drinking from the nearby river Eunoe (you-NO-ee; Greek, "well-minded"; Dante's own invention) restores the memory of all their good deeds to these same Heaven-aspiring souls who have completed their purgation.

In John Milton's epic, *Paradise Lost* (1667), we find the same five serviceable infernal rivers. After the devils fall into Hell, they fly off to explore their prison. They come upon the "baleful streams" of

> *Abhorred* Styx *the flood of deadly hate,*
> *Sad* Acheron *of sorrow, black and deep;*
> Cocytus, *nam'd of lamentation loud*
> *Heard on the rueful stream; fierce* Phlegethon
> *Whose waves of torrent fire inflame with rage*
> (2.577–81).

Far from these four is "Lethe the River of Oblivion," which the souls of the damned are prevented from ever tasting.

❧ QUESTION 43

What are the 6 flavors of quarks?

Up
Down
Strange
Charmed
Bottom (or Beauty)
Top (or Truth)

Atoms are composed of protons, neutrons, and electrons. For a long time, these subatomic particles were considered the irreducible building blocks of all matter. And then came quarks.

Apparently at first just a nonsense word coined at their discovery, *quarks* was later found in James Joyce's *Finnegans Wake*—"Three quarks for Muster Mark!" Usually pronounced to rhyme with corks, quarks differ from previously known particles in that each has only a partial (1/3 or 2/3) positive or negative electrical charge (see table below). Quarks are bound in families of three to form protons and neutrons; these triplets are called hadrons. The pairing of a quark with its antiquark of the same "color" is known as a meson.

The indivisible constituents of matter now appear to be the six flavors of quarks and six other kinds of particles known as leptons: the electron, muon, and tau particle, each with its own neutrino. Furthermore, according to quantum field theory, all the forces *between* particles of matter are mediated by force-carrying particles called gauge bosons. One of these, the gluon—as in glue—is responsible for holding quarks together. Other gauge bosons include the photon, associated with electromagnetic forces such as light, and the graviton, the postulated messenger particle of gravity.

Quarks are part of an evolving system known as the Standard

Model that has been proposed as an explanation of the fundamental forces of nature (see Question 28). Their existence was first postulated in 1963 by Murray Gell-Mann, a physicist at the California Institute of Technology whose work on these subatomic particles secured him the Nobel Prize in Physics in 1969. Besides naming the particles, Gell-Mann whimsically described them as coming in flavors and colors, but these reflect his imaginativeness rather than any actual physical properties. Quarks are far smaller than any particle that can be detected with visible light and have no empiric, sensory-derived qualities.

Each flavor of quark comes in three colors (red, green, and blue); each hadron, or grouping of three quarks, has one of each color. The flavors were originally classified as up, down, and strange; subsequent work established the existence of others, dubbed charmed, bottom, and top. Only the **up** and **down** flavors are believed to exist in nature today.

Protons, for example, have two up quarks and one down quark, whose electrical charges combine as follows: $2/3 + 2/3 - 1/3 = 1$. Thus, protons end up with a +1 charge. Neutrons are made of one up quark and two down quarks. The electrical charge is thus $2/3 - 1/3 - 1/3 = 0$, which accords with the neutral charge of the neutron.

The other four flavors of quarks—**strange, charmed, bottom, and top**—were theoretically present only for an infinitesimal fraction of a second during the Big Bang about thirteen to fifteen billion years ago and can now be "observed" only from the self-annihilating collisions that occur when protons and antiprotons are accelerated at speeds approaching that of light in particle accelerators. The particles that result from these high-speed collisions exist for too short a time to actually be seen—roughly a hundredth of a billionth of a billionth of a second—before starting to decay into other types of particles. But since these decay products leave "footprints" that can be detected and measured, the existence of the original particle can be inferred and its mass determined.

Only in March 1995 was the top quark finally identified amid intense rivalry between two groups of physicists at the Fermi National Accelerator Laboratory (Fermilab) in Batavia, Illinois. The top quark turns out to be a real heavyweight. Compare its mass with that of its fellows:

FLAVOR	CHARGE	MASS *(billions of electron volts)*
Up	+2/3	0.38
Down	−1/3	0.34
Strange	−1/3	0.54
Charmed	+2/3	1.50
Bottom	−1/3	4.72
Top	+2/3	175.60

The mass of the top quark is about the same as that of an atom of gold—which has a total of nearly 200 protons and neutrons.

QUESTION 44

Who were the 6 wives of Henry VIII?

> Catherine of Aragon
> Anne Boleyn
> Jane Seymour
> Anne of Cleves
> Catherine Howard
> Catherine Parr

The marital history of King Henry VIII (1491–1547) makes more sense if you consider that his father, Henry Tudor, Earl of Richmond, who wrenched the English crown from Richard III at the Battle of Bosworth Field in 1485, had only a weak claim to the throne (see Question 74). Thus, as King Henry VII, he wisely negotiated an excellent match between his elder son, Arthur, and the infanta **Catherine of Aragon** (1485–1536), daughter of Columbus's powerful patrons, Ferdinand and Isabella of Spain. The ultimate goal of this union, as in royal marriages down to our day, was a male heir.

Catherine arrived in England in 1501, after marrying Prince

Arthur twice by proxy, with the Spanish ambassador standing in for her. She and Arthur wed a third time, in person, in November of 1501 in St. Paul's Cathedral, London. Until the day she died, Catherine insisted this marriage was never consummated. In fact, Arthur, who was fifteen and ill, died four months after the wedding.

Catherine remained in England and became a wretched pawn of power politics. Although young Prince Henry obtained a papal dispensation to marry his dead brother's wife, negotiations with Spain got bogged down in wrangling over the dowry and various dynastic machinations. Seven years after she was widowed, Catherine married Henry on June 11, 1509, seven weeks after his succession to the throne.

During her marriage to Henry VIII, Catherine gave birth to six children. A daughter, Mary, went on to become Queen (1553–58). The rest died young. Henry was genuinely fond of his wife, but her failure to produce a male heir who survived infancy was a potentially lethal blow to the House of Tudor.

Henry now claimed he was troubled by his marriage to his brother's widow, despite the Pope's dispensation. By February of 1526, it became clear to members of court that the King was smitten with **Anne Boleyn** (1500/01–36), a maid of honor to Catherine and sister of the notorious Mary Boleyn, who had had a four-year affair with Henry. In 1527, Henry announced plans to seek an annulment of his marriage to Catherine, but the Pope, largely at the behest of the Queen's nephew, all-powerful Holy Roman Emperor Charles V, deferred his decision for years. By 1531, Henry had pressed the English bishops to recognize him as "Protector and Supreme Head of the Church of England," a title confirmed in 1534 by Parliament's passage of the Act of Supremacy. All ties with Rome were severed.

Henry and Anne Boleyn were secretly married on January 25, 1533, several months before the King's appointee, Thomas Cranmer, Archbishop of Canterbury, annulled his marriage with Catherine on May 23. In the same year, a baby girl, destined to reign from 1558 to 1603 as the incomparable Elizabeth I, was born to Henry and Anne, but she was followed by three stillborn infants. Again, Henry saw the House of Tudor threatened by a Queen's inability to bear a healthy son. In addition, Anne turned out to be a highly unpopular Queen who had proposed murdering Catherine and her daughter Mary at a time when they were being particularly vexatious. And Henry had a chance of gaining a much-needed alliance with Charles V—but only without Anne. Chancellor Thomas Cromwell charged her with adultery, incest with her brother George, and high treason—fabrications all. Anne Boleyn was beheaded on May 19, 1536. Just for good measure, Henry had had their marriage annulled a few days earlier.

Wasting no time, the King was betrothed to **Jane Seymour** (1507/8–37) the next day, marrying her ten days later. Jane had been lady-in-waiting to both Catherine and Anne, and Henry had courted her for at least six months before Anne's death. Throughout his life Henry claimed he loved her best of all his wives. His feelings for her were undoubtedly enhanced by the birth of a male heir, Edward (1537–53), a sickly boy who succeeded Henry in 1547 but died in his teens. Jane died twelve days after Edward's birth.

Two years passed before Henry, increasingly portly and plagued by a chronically infected, foul-smelling leg, married the German princess **Anne of Cleves** (1515–57). This political marriage, engineered by Cromwell, took place on January 6, 1540. Henry, however, found Anne so repugnant—he'd only seen a Holbein portrait of her—that they never bedded down. But Anne of Cleves was the most fortunate of Henry's wives. The marriage was annulled after seven months, and Henry paid Anne four thousand pounds a year, gave her two manors and Anne Boleyn's castle, and made her his honorary sister. Matchmaker Cromwell was executed nine days after the annulment.

On the day Cromwell died in 1540, Henry married Anne Boleyn's fifteen-year-old cousin, **Catherine Howard** (c. 1525–42), a favorite of the Catholic faction. Four months later, the Archbishop of Canterbury informed Henry that Catherine had had several lovers before her marriage, as well as an engagement that might invalidate the royal union. Serious allegations of adultery also emerged. Henry, who was probably impotent by this time, was regarded as a cuckold, and Francis I of France said of Catherine, "She hath done wondrous naughty!" Catherine got the ax, literally, on February 13, 1542—a low blow, since even her cousin Anne had merited a more refined decapitation by sword.

Twice-widowed **Catherine Parr** (1512–48) was in love with Thomas Seymour, Jane Seymour's brother, when Henry set his sights on her and had his rival posted overseas. The King married his last wife on July 12, 1543, with Anne of Cleves as a witness. This third Catherine, warm, amiable, and acutely intelligent, was a caring stepmother to Henry's daughters and young son, and an effective regent while Henry campaigned. She was renowned for her learning, and her home was a haven for young female scholars.

Henry died on January 28, 1547. And, in a finale worthy of daytime TV, Catherine Parr died the next year, after giving birth to a daughter by her new husband, Thomas Seymour.

❧ QUESTION 45

Who were the 6 French composers known as *Les Six?*

Darius Milhaud
Francis Poulenc
Arthur Honegger
Louis Durey
Georges Auric
Germaine Tailleferre

> *Wagner . . . was an idiot* [for claiming all
> art springs from suffering].
> —Darius Milhaud

The designation *Les Six* (lay CEASE) was coined in 1920 by a French music critic, Henri Collet, when he compared this group of six neoclassical musicians living in France with the Russian Mighty Five composers (see Question 41). Profoundly influenced by composer and eccentric Erik Satie (1866–1925) and by poet, essayist, and dramatist Jean Cocteau (1889–1963), the Six reacted against the Romantic excesses of Richard Wagner and Richard Strauss and the Impressionism of Claude Debussy and Maurice Ravel. That's about where their similarities end. *Les Six,* who rarely met, composed in quite distinct styles, making their grouping somewhat artificial.

The music of *Les Six* has been called *une musique de tous les jours,* everyday music. This was the legacy of Satie, who eschewed musical heroics in favor of small, precise, almost surreal pieces spiced with humor and parody. The Six felt that sentimentalism and romanticism had gone too far in the music of the nineteenth century and that, in the works of the Impressionists, the intensely personal had been allowed to outweigh clarity, precision, objectivity, and crispness. As Milhaud (mee-YO) said, "I am left helpless in the presence of rhapsodic works devoid of structure or overladen with endless developments of unnecessary complexity." Like their great contemporary Igor Stravinsky (1882–1971), they sought to balance emotion with form and order.

Darius Milhaud (1892–1974) was born into a Jewish family in Aix-en-Provence in southern France. As a student in Paris, he met the poet and dramatist Paul Claudel (1868–1955), with whom he went to Brazil when Claudel was appointed ambassador in 1917. At the end of World War I, they spent time in New York City before returning to France. During this brief period of travel, Milhaud was deeply influenced by American jazz and Brazilian music, especially samba and tango, as witnessed by the twelve dance tunes for piano he composed under the title of *Saudades do Brasil (Souvenirs of Brazil,* 1921).

Milhaud championed polytonality (the use of two or three musical keys simultaneously), a technique pioneered by Stravinsky. In some of Milhaud's pieces, such as *Les Choéphores,* the men and women of a chorus sing in different keys. (The resulting dissonance is, admittedly, an acquired taste.) Milhaud was also one of the first composers to use whips, hammers, and other noisemakers in his music.

In the early part of the twentieth century, these musical innovations shocked some of Milhaud's listeners. This, coupled with his reputation as one of the most radical and antagonistic of Cocteau's circle, ensured that his music received mixed or hostile reviews. Several decades passed before he was recognized as one of the foremost composers of the century. His musical moods vary from highly dramatic and austere to folklike and charming. In keeping with neoclassical restraint, his musical ideas are expressed succinctly and in a disciplined, logical fashion—characteristics generally revered by *Les Six.*

Milhaud's early compositions were based on texts by Claudel. During the 1920s and '30s, he traveled in Russia, Spain, and the Middle East. When France fell to the Nazis in 1940, Milhaud fled Europe, taking a position on the faculty of Mills College in Oakland, California. After the war, he continued his association with Mills and the Aspen Music School, splitting his time among Europe, California, and Colorado. His affection for America and other places he visited is reflected in the number of pieces he wrote in honor of various cities, including Boston, San Francisco, Lisbon, and Prague, and in his send-up of George Gershwin—*A Frenchman in New York*.

In fact, Milhaud and Gershwin were introducing jazz idioms into concert-hall music at roughly the same time, Milhaud with the ballet *La Création du monde* (1923), music laced with French elegance, yet deeply influenced by his 1922 visit to Harlem and the jazz he heard there. "An authentic small masterpiece," Aaron Copland called this work, which evokes the creation of the world according to African folklore. Milhaud also wrote the music for *Le Boeuf sur le toit (The Bull on the Roof,* 1919), sometimes translated as *The Do-Nothing Bar,* a comically bizarre pantomime-cum-ballet choreographed by Cocteau and set in a bar in Prohibition-era America.

Milhaud's operas include *Christophe Colomb* (1930), with libretto by Claudel, *Médée* (1939), *Bolivar* (1943), and *David* (1954). He also wrote three miniature operas based on classical myths dealing with Theseus, Ariadne, and Europa that take less than ten minutes to perform. Some critics consider his opera *Les Euménides,* the last in a trilogy based on Aeschylus as translated by Claudel, one of the finest musical works of the century, on a par with Stravinsky's *Le Sacre du printemps*.

With more than four hundred works to his credit, including eighteen string quartets, Milhaud was one of the most prolific twentieth-century composers, and he was considered France's most eminent living composer after the death of Ravel in 1937. In addition to his work in opera, ballet, and chamber music—indeed, in every branch of composition—Milhaud also wrote thirteen symphonies.

Of all the Six, the music of self-taught **Francis Poulenc** (1899–1963) is most like that of Satie, with influences from Stravinsky and even Ravel. The musical idiom of Poulenc (poo-LANK) is often marked by warmth, lucidity, and a personal quality. A master of twentieth-century song, he wrote more than a hundred polished, melodic songs based on poems by Guillaume Apollinaire and Paul Éluard, among others. His early experience as a piano accompanist enhanced his proficiency in this musical form. His best-known piano music, *Trois mouvements perpetuels,* was composed when he was nineteen, about the time he was linked with *Les Six*. His chamber music, heavily influenced by jazz during the 1920s, became somewhat more somber during the war years. His later chamber pieces included two written as memorials to Arthur Honegger and Sergei Prokofiev.

By the 1930s, Poulenc was writing chiefly religious works marked by fervor, simplicity, and serenity, including *Litanies à la Vierge Noire de Racamadour* (1936) for women's voices and organ, the *Mass in G major* (1937), and *Stabat Mater* (1951). Other prominent works are *Les Biches (The House Party,* 1923), a ballet produced by the great impresario Sergei Diaghilev; *La Voix humaine,* a one-act, forty-minute opera with libretto by Cocteau; and *Concerto in G minor* for organ, strings, and percussion.

Poulenc served in the French underground during World War II, and one of his cantatas, the subversive *Figure humaine,* was printed under the noses of the Nazis. Poulenc's masterpiece, *Les dialogues des Carmélites,* set in the French Revolution and first performed at Milan's La Scala in 1957, is considered one of the outstanding operas of the twentieth century.

Poulenc's serious, sensitive side was complemented by a witty, surreal, good-humored, and ironic one. His burlesque opera *Les Mamelles de Tirésias (The Breasts of Tiresias,* 1947), based on a 1903 play by Apollinaire, features a woman who becomes a man when her breasts (balloons) explode, while her husband becomes a woman and spawns forty thousand babies. In 1945, Poulenc wrote incidental music for *Babar the Elephant,* in part to amuse some young relatives.

Of the Six, the music of Swiss-French composer **Arthur Honegger** (1892–1955), who studied in Zurich, was the least like Satie's. With time, some listeners have come to call his music conventional. Honegger (aw-nay-GARE) couldn't quite separate himself from grandiose musical ideas, especially in his operas. His first and perhaps most lasting success was an oratorio, *Le Roi David (King David,* 1921), which was followed by the operas *Judith* (1926) and *Antigone* (1927), the latter with libretto by Cocteau. Like Milhaud, he set texts by Paul Claudel, including the oratorios *Jeanne d'Arc au bûcher (Joan of Arc at the Stake)* and *La Danse des morts (The Dance of Death).*

When *Pacific 231* was first performed in 1924, the cacophony of this orchestral tone poem imitating a locomotive stunned and amused audiences. Another program piece, *Rugby* (1928), called to mind rough-and-tumble sports. Honegger was now far removed in many ways from the ideals of Satie and Stravinsky. He also wrote music for movies and radio plays. Other works include the *Piano Concertino, Concerto da camera* for flute and strings, and the chamber orchestra piece *Pastorale d'été (Summer Pastoral).*

The music of Milhaud, Poulenc, and Honegger still lives, long after the heady, avant-garde days of the early twentieth century. The other three of the original Six are all but forgotten as serious composers.

Louis Durey (1888–1979), though he lived long, had an abbreviated musical career, apparently preferring politics. He joined the French Communist Party in 1936 and, like Poulenc, was a member of the Resistance during World War II, composing songs for the movement. In deference to Communist thought, Durey (dyoo-REE) wrote music that was supposed to appeal to "the people." Beginning in 1950, he was music critic for the Communist newspaper, *Humanité.* Nonetheless, his musical achievements were sufficiently impressive to garner the Grand Prix de la Musique in 1961.

Georges Auric (1899–1983) was best known as a composer of scores for stage productions and ballets. Three of his ballets, *Les Fâcheux* (1924), *Les Matelots* (1925), and *La Pastorale* (1926), were produced by Diaghilev. Auric (oh-REEK) wrote music for more than sixty movies, including *Moulin Rouge* (1952). In the early 1960s, he was appointed general manager of both the Paris Opéra and the Opéra-Comique. For more than twenty years, until 1977, Auric was president of the French Union of Composers and Authors.

Germaine Tailleferre (1892–1983), the only woman in the group, understandably changed her name from the more colorful Taillefesse, which can mean "ass-cutter" in French. She studied briefly with Ravel, and some critics claim she ended up as an Impressionist after all. Cocteau likened her compositions to pastels for the ears. Tailleferre (tie-FAIR) was married briefly to an American writer and subsequently to a French lawyer, both of whom discouraged her from composing.

What were the 6 major European invasions of Russia
since the days of Peter the Great?

> Invasion of Charles XII of Sweden
> Napoleonic invasion
> British and French invasion during the Crimean War
> German and Austrian invasion during World War I
> British and French (and American) invasion after the
>   Russian Revolution
> German invasion during World War II

Peter I (1672–1725), later Peter the Great, became joint czar of Russia with Ivan V in 1682 and sole ruler in 1689. A six-foot-seven giant
of a man, Peter traveled in Western Europe in 1697–98, working in
and learning about various industries, and then returned to still-medi-
eval Russia to wrench it into the modern world. To cite only one
trivial but revealing example among many, Peter outlawed all beards
in his dominions, except those of the clergy and peasantry, and personally shaved his nobles—and a painful shave it was, in most in-
stances—to imprint on their very skin his disgust with the retro ways
of his courtiers and nation.

At the beginning of the eighteenth century, Sweden was a major
European power, with extensive holdings on the mainland and control of the Baltic. Russia, Poland, and Denmark formed an aggressive
coalition against it, which led to the Great Northern War (1700–21).
Sweden's eighteen-year-old **King Charles XII** (1682–1718), an outstanding military genius, quickly invaded Denmark and subtracted it
from the coalition in 1700. Toward the end of that year, with his
weary Swedish army of only 8,000, he inflicted a severe defeat on
40,000 Russians who were besieging his stronghold in Narva, Estonia.
After that, Charles turned against Poland, taking Warsaw and Cracow

in 1702, but while engaged in subduing the country over the next several years, Peter occupied the mainland Baltic coasts.

By January 1, 1708, Charles had crossed the frozen Vistula with 44,000 men, leaving Poland behind to begin his invasion of Russia. Peter's strategy, to be repeated by the Russians several times in the face of future European invasions, was to retreat to the interior and burn or hide the crops and scatter the cattle that might feed the enemy. Charles spent two hideous winters in Russia, defeating armies but losing many thousands of men to the cold, starvation, and plague. He then turned south in search of provisions, abandoning his advance on Moscow.

While Charles was moving against Poltava in the Ukraine with the aid of the Cossack hetman (leader) Ivan Mazeppa, Peter's main Russian army approached. On June 28, 1709, with Charles incapacitated by a bullet wound in the foot, the outnumbered Swedes attacked and were trounced (see Question 97). This momentous battle of Poltava heralded the rise of Russia as a great European power and the end of Sweden in that role. In 1721, after the death of Charles, Russia acquired from Sweden Livonia, Estonia, and other strategic sites on the Baltic by the treaties of Nystadt and Stockholm. Peter built St. Petersburg (founded 1703) on the Neva River on land ceded by Sweden. This city at the head of the Gulf of Finland, which replaced inland Moscow as the capital, was to serve as Russia's main "Window on the West."

An even greater general than Charles XII invaded Russia from Europe just over one century later. It is curious that **Napoleon,** Emperor of the French, moved against Russia as a way of defeating England. On May 29, 1812, Russia formally renounced Napoleon's Continental System, which forbade all trade between England and the European continent he dominated. England was being slowly bankrupted and, if Czar Alexander I could be made to comply with his policies, the formidable island nation with the invincible navy might be forced to sue for peace.

Napoleon crossed into Russia in late June of 1812 with a multinational *Grande Armée* of 600,000—mainly French, Germans, Italians, and Poles—and the goal of having himself crowned Emperor of Europe. After capturing Smolensk and winning a grueling victory at Borodino against Marshal Mikhail Kutuzov, in which Napoleon lost 30,000 men killed or disabled, the Emperor and his typhus- and dysentery-wracked army entered Moscow on September 14. It did him no good, however, because most of the population had fled, and two thirds of the city was soon burned by prison inmates whom the Russians had freed and by others acting under the departing governor's orders, making it unfit to serve as Napoleon's winter quarters.

When the uncooperative Czar refused to talk peace, the hungry and shelterless French had no choice but to retreat, beginning on October 19. The horrendous toll exacted from Napoleon's retreating army by the winter, starvation, disease, Russian flank attacks by Kutuzov's Cossack cavalry, and the embattled crossing of the Berezina has become the stuff of legends of disaster. Napoleon himself left the army behind on December 5, heading for Paris, in disguise, in a horse-drawn carriage mounted on a sleigh. By December 8, when his army reached Vilnius in Lithuania, the *Grande Armée* had shrunk to 20,000 desperately ill and starving men. While stopping in Warsaw on his way back, Napoleon made his famous remark: "From the sublime to the ridiculous is but a step."

In 1783, well before Napoleon's invasion, Czarina Catherine the Great had annexed the Crimea. In 1787–92, in her second war with Turkey, she seized additional land along the northern shore of the Black Sea. Russia was aggressively pushing south, seeking an outlet into the Mediterranean. In 1854–56, the British and French joined Turkey in the **Crimean War** to prevent Russian expansion into the decaying empire of the Ottoman Turks, especially Constantinople (now Istanbul), the Straits, and the Balkans. The two European nations saw these Russian moves as threats to their own interests in the Middle East.

Turkey had declared war against Russia on October 4, 1853, after Czar Nicholas I's troops occupied Walachia and Moldavia, principalities of the Ottomans' Balkan empire that were united as Romania in 1858 after the war. The British under Lord Palmerston and the French under the great Napoleon's nephew, Napoleon III, declared war in March 1854, and were joined in 1855 by the proto-Italian kingdom of Piedmont-Sardinia, under Prime Minister Camillo di Cavour. This tiny country went to war against Russia hoping to have its grievances aired at the peace conference at the expense of the Austrian rulers of northern Italy.

In September 1854, the allies invaded the Crimea and began the siege of Sebastopol, headquarters of the Russian Black Sea fleet. The city was evacuated by the Russians after eleven long months. Tennyson's "The Charge of the Light Brigade" was written to commemorate an incident during the allied victory at Balaklava in October, in which 673 hapless British cavalrymen rode into surrounding cannon fire, though knowing "someone had blundered."

After further Russian defeats and Austrian threats to enter the war, the new Czar, Alexander II, sued for peace. By the Treaty of Paris (March 30, 1856), Russia ceded territories to the Turks, renounced its claims in the Balkans, and scrapped its Black Sea navy. It was in this war that Florence Nightingale became a nursing heroine for tending to the sick and wounded allies. Outbreaks of cholera, typhus, and dysentery killed more men than the battles did: The English lost almost 5,000 to wounds and more than 17,000 to disease; the French, over 20,000 to war and almost 50,000 to sickness; and the Russians, almost 38,000 to each.

The next European invasion of the Russian Empire was the massive German and Austrian assault during **World War I.** The Germans, knowing they would have to fight a two-front war, developed a strategy (the Schlieffen Plan) of holding their eastern borders while knocking France out with a lightning strike and then dispatching the lumbering Russian Bear without an enemy at their back. But after being stopped at the first Battle of the Marne in September and the first Battle of Ypres in October–November, the German invasion of France got bogged down in interminable trench warfare.

In 1914, the Russians advanced against Germany and Austria, but the Germans, after their victory at Tannenberg, came to their beleaguered ally's rescue. In May 1915, the Germans and Austrians launched an offensive they hoped would knock Russia out of the war. Breaking through the Russian lines, they poured into Lithuania and White Russia (now Belarus) and, by September, had established themselves at a vertical line two hundred miles east of Warsaw, running from Dvinsk in the north to south of the River Dniester. Russian Poland was entirely under German control. Although two million Russian soldiers were killed, wounded, or captured in 1915, the stricken nation kept fighting. During the next year, while the Germans and Austrians lost almost 400,000 men, the Russians lost another million.

The war was bleeding and starving Russia to death. In March 1917 (February in the Russian calendar of the time), the first Russian

Revolution began. After Czar Nicholas II abdicated, the provisional government continued prosecuting the war. Germany decided to use a special train to take Lenin and thirty-two other Bolsheviks from exile in Zurich to the Finland Station in Petrograd (St. Petersburg), rightly expecting that he and his fellow revolutionaries would act, in Churchill's phrase, "like a typhoid bacillus."

Immediately after the Bolsheviks seized power in November (October, Old Style), Russia, with its army falling apart from desertion and insubordination, sued for peace and was granted an armistice. Nonetheless, the Germans continued to drive ahead in the east against practically no resistance, even long after Russia signed the harsh Treaty of Brest-Litovsk in March 1918. The additional captured or ceded territory stretched from the Baltic to the northern Black Sea coast and the Crimea, including the Ukraine and the important cities of Minsk, Kiev, Odessa, Kharkov, and Sebastopol. By the treaty, the Bolsheviks renounced all claims to the Baltic provinces, Finland, Poland, White Russia, the Ukraine, Bessarabia (modern Moldova), and the Caucasus—in short, to almost all the territory the Russians had seized since the times of Peter the Great. The invaders never got near Moscow, however, which the Bolsheviks now made the Russian capital, since the Germans were only eighty-five miles from Petrograd.

Although many subjects of the Russian Empire initially welcomed the Germans as liberators, the wanton butchery of their new masters turned them into conspirators and saboteurs, thus requiring many extra soldiers to maintain German rule. And after the balance in the west was tipped by the entry of the United States into the war, Germany's power was broken, and an armistice was granted on November 11, 1918. By the terms of the Treaty of Versailles (1919), Germany had to withdraw all its troops in Russia behind its 1914 borders and evacuate all captured Black Sea ports (see Question 30). But Russia's war dead alone amounted to 1.7 million.

Meanwhile, the Western allies were not at all impressed with Russia's new system of government and its withdrawal from the war. In 1918, before the end of World War I, the **British and French invasion** of Russia began in the extreme northwest, and Murmansk and Archangel were seized. The pretext was to prevent huge caches of British military supplies in Russia from falling into German hands. President Woodrow Wilson sent 4,500 American troops to Archangel—the only time in history that U.S. soldiers fought against Russians. For a projected Allied invasion of Siberia, 72,000 Japanese, 8,000 Americans, and 1,000 French colonial troops landed in August 1918 at Vladivostok.

This Pacific port had recently been captured by a contingent of the so-called Czech Legion, a force of 60,000 released prisoners of war who had fought for Austria-Hungary in the east but were now indirectly fighting for a Czech homeland and very directly fighting against the Bolsheviks. In one of the more astonishing feats of the war, the Czechs held a three-thousand-mile line in Russia extending along the Trans-Siberian Railway from the Volga to the Pacific. Once the Allies joined the Czechs in Vladivostok, they were to proceed west through Siberia, overthrow Bolshevism, bring Russia back into the war, and attack the Germans from the east.

Then the armistice was signed. Although by the end of the year there were 180,000 Allied troops in Russian territory (including Italians, Romanians, Serbs, Latvians, and Finns), the British and Americans, after the end of the European war, generally preferred to leave Russia to its own civil war (1918–21), which was raging between the White Russian forces and Trotsky's Red Army. The French, still surprisingly hot for battle, occupied Odessa and fought in the Ukraine. And the new republic of Poland, jumping at the opportunity offered by Russia's internal chaos, enlarged its eastern boundary as a result of the battle of Warsaw (August 1920), defeating a Russian army and incorporating parts of Lithuania, White Russia, and the western Ukraine. Despite all these enemies, who never coordinated their strategies, the Russian Communist government managed to survive, mainly through Western loss of resolve, the fighting mettle of the new Red Army, and ruthless suppression of all internal opposition.

But what are all these invasions compared with the titanic struggle during **World War II** between Hitler's Nazi Germany and Stalin's Soviet Russia? Operation Barbarossa, deriving its name from the great twelfth-century German emperor Frederick I Barbarossa ("Red Beard"), was the fiercest and most powerful invasion the world had seen.

The Nazi-Soviet Pact of August 1939 had allowed Hitler to invade Poland on September 1, triggering the Second World War. A few weeks later Stalin advanced into Poland from the east and went on to incorporate the Baltic republics and attack Finland. But once again, as in the Napoleonic invasion, the road to subduing Britain led through Russia. It wouldn't do to concentrate massive amounts of German troops and resources in invading the British Isles if the giant in the east, hungry for the Balkans and the Straits, hadn't first been neutralized. And as Hitler wrote in the spring of 1941, "If Russia is beaten, England's last hope is gone." His contemplated move against India also wouldn't proceed smoothly with an undefeated Russia at the German army's flank.

In addition, the Ukrainian wheat harvests and the oil fields of the Caucasus beckoned—not to speak of Germany's seven-hundred-year obsession with its *Drang nach Osten* ("the pull of the East"). Hitler had written long before in *Mein Kampf* (1924) of Germany's need for *Lebensraum* (living space) and of "an eastern policy in the sense of acquiring the necessary soil for our German people." He adds, "If we speak of soil in Europe today, we can primarily have in mind only *Russia* and her vassal border states."

The Russians forgot that threat, but Hitler never did. The Red Army was totally unprepared when the German attack began at 3:15 A.M. on June 22, 1941. The invading army, in three main groups, with contingents of Finns, Romanians, Hungarians, and Italians, totaled more than three million men, with 3,580 tanks and 2,740 aircraft. The front spanned eighteen hundred miles from the Baltic to the Black Sea. The initial progress was unstoppable: German panzers raced along parallel roads, then converged and trapped masses of Soviet troops in pockets between themselves and advancing German artillery and infantry forces behind them. Hitler's planners thought Russia could be defeated in two to four months.

By the fall, White Russia and most of the Ukraine had been conquered. The nine-hundred-day siege of Leningrad (October 1941–January 1944) had begun. The Germans were in the Crimea, besieging Sevastopol (formerly Sebastopol), which fell after nine months in 1942 with 250,000 Soviet casualties (dead, wounded, and captured). They were also within twenty miles of Moscow when a massive Russian counteroffensive led by Marshal Georgi Zhukov and his ally, "General Winter," snatched the city from them.

By now, the Germans had suffered 743,000 casualties in Russia. The four to six weeks by which Hitler had delayed the opening of Operation Barbarossa to overrun Yugoslavia and rescue his Italian allies in Greece now told against his army in terms of the vicious cold. If Moscow had been captured, Soviet resistance might have crumbled. Personally assuming military command of the Russian campaign,

Hitler redirected its main thrust south in the summer of 1942 against the Caucasus oil fields and the great industrial city of Stalingrad.

More than a thousand factories in western Russia had been dismantled, shipped east by railway, and rebuilt in the Urals, Siberia, and Central Asia within the first few months of the invasion, so that Soviet munitions production showed a huge increase over the next three years. The Germans also seriously underestimated the vast numbers of reinforcements Stalin would be able to move to the front out of the interior. And the standard Russian scorched-earth policy ensured that the Germans would not find an abundance of crops, livestock, factories, or railroad cars waiting for them. A year into the invasion, the Germans had suffered 1.3 million casualties.

By November 19, 1942, the Soviets had recaptured more than 185,000 square miles of their territory. In the German attack on Stalingrad beginning in late August 1942, the Russians fought for every pulverized street in five months of unspeakably savage fighting. The Germans at Stalingrad, who sustained 330,000 casualties and were finally encircled, surrendered on February 2, 1943.

Starving Leningrad did not capitulate, though German shellings and the ghastly siege claimed 600,000 to 1 million lives. On July 4, 1943, there was a final German initiative at Kursk, north of Kharkov. Although the Germans poured half a million men into this greatest tank battle in history, they were crushed by Zhukov. Slowly, the Soviet armies pushed the invaders out of their territory until they hounded the tattered remnant back into Berlin on April 14, 1945—in the process, replacing one form of oppression in Eastern Europe by another. The human cost of dismembering the German juggernaut in the east had been 29 million Soviet military casualties and the death—many by summary execution, starvation, or extermination—of millions of Soviet civilians.

⚞ QUESTION 47

What are the 6 trigonometric functions?

> **Sine (sin)**
> **Cosine (cos)**
> **Tangent (tan)**
> **Cotangent (cot)**
> **Secant (sec)**
> **Cosecant (csc)**

In right triangles (those that contain a 90° angle), these six functions represent the various ratios among the hypotenuse (the side of the triangle opposite the right angle) and the two shorter legs. They are constant for any right triangles with identical shapes, no matter what their size, and their values are listed in trigonometric tables. If you don't have a trig textbook handy, you can access these ratios with any scientific calculator. The top illustration on the next page shows a right triangle with its ratios. The Greek letter theta (θ) is traditionally used for one of the non-90° angles, and alpha (α) for the other.

For an easy way to remember these trigonometric (Greek, "triangle-measuring") ratios, just recall one of your mnemonics from high school: SOH-CAH-TOA (pronounced as four syllables). No, it's not the name of a volcano—it just reminds you that sin = opp/hyp (SOH), that cos = adj/hyp (CAH), and that tan = opp/adj (TOA). This alphabet soup means that, for any right triangle,

- ✦ The **sine** of an angle is defined as the ratio between the length of the side *opposite* it and that of the *hypotenuse* (SOH)
- ✦ The **cosine** of an angle is the ratio between the length of the side *adjacent* to it and the *hypotenuse* (CAH)
- ✦ The **tangent** of an angle is the ratio between the length of the side *opposite* it and the side *adjacent* to it (TOA).

163

A Right Triangle with Its Ratios

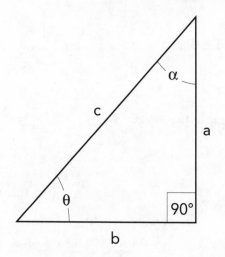

With regard to angle θ,
 a = opposite (opp)
 b = adjacent (adj)
 c = hypotenuse (hyp)

sin θ = a/c (opp/hyp)
cos θ = b/c (adj/hyp)
tan θ = a/b (opp/adj)

csc θ = c/a (hyp/opp)
sec θ = c/b (hyp/adj)
cot θ = b/a (adj/opp)

A Useful Application of Trigonometry

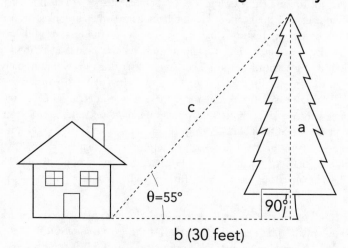

leg a = unknown height
leg b = distance from house to tree
hyp c = not applicable to this problem
angle θ = angle between ground and
       tree's apex at distance b

In addition, note that sine and **cosecant,** cosine and **secant,** and tangent and **cotangent** are reciprocals of each other (their numerators and denominators are inverted). Thus, if the sine of angle θ = a/c, then the cosecant of θ = c/a, and so on for the two other pairs. With a knowledge of these unvarying relationships (or functions), you can figure out the length of any of the sides (leg a, leg b, or hypotenuse c) or the number of degrees in angle θ or α of a right triangle by substituting known values into an equation. Which equation you use depends on which values you know and which you are trying to determine. If you know only one of the sides and one of the angles, you can figure out the other two sides and the other two angles of any right triangle. Or, if you know two of the sides, you can figure out the third side as well as all of the angles. Knowing all three angles but none of the sides will get you nowhere, however, since there are an infinite number of similar triangles possible.

What's the practical significance of the six trigonometric functions, besides serving as exquisite torture devices for high school students? In the fields of engineering, architecture, surveying, navigation, and astronomy, the trig functions prove to be very useful indeed. But what about you? Suppose you need a tree removed from your yard, and you can't wait to try out your new chainsaw. This is not at all recommended, but, if you insist, you'll need to determine how tall the tree is to make sure it doesn't come crashing down on your house.

Unless this is some celebrated tree, its height is anyone's guess. Should you want to do more than guess, all you need is trigonometry. Just imagine a right triangle between you and the tree. If you're not the imaginative type, refer to the bottom illustration.

STEP 1: Measure distance b (let's say 30 feet).

STEP 2: Measure angle θ. (For this step, you'll need to borrow some surveying equipment such as a transit.) Let's say it's 55°.

STEP 3: Choose a trig function that would help you find out what you want to know. In this case, the tangent function would work, since you know b and are trying to determine a, and tan of angle θ = a/b (opp/adj).

STEP 4: Use the tangent equation to solve for the unknown value, a:

$$\tan \theta = a/b$$
$$\tan 55° = a/b$$
$$\tan 55° = a/30 \text{ feet}$$

STEP 5: Look up the tangent of 55° in a trig table, or use a calculator. It turns out to be 1.428. So,

$$1.428 = a/30 \text{ feet}$$

Multiply both sides of the equation by 30 feet to isolate a.

$$1.428(30 \text{ feet}) = a(30 \text{ feet})/30 \text{ feet}$$

The denominator cancels out on the right side, leaving a by itself.

$$1.428(30 \text{ feet}) = a$$

Now multiply 1.428 by 30 feet:

$$42.84 \text{ feet} = a$$

We now know that the height of your tree is almost 43 feet. Since the distance from the tree to your house is 30 feet, take special care, when cutting it down, to direct it toward your neighbor's house instead.

 QUESTION 48

Which were the 6 Iroquois (or Allied) Nations?

Mohawk
Onondaga
Oneida
Cayuga
Seneca
Tuscarora

Two centuries before the foundation of the United States, a large democratic confederacy existed in eastern North America, where five Native American tribes had established an alliance centered in the state of New York. Initially known as the Five Nations, the confederacy included the Mohawk, Onondaga, Oneida, Cayuga, and Seneca tribes, which were later joined by the Tuscarora. The confederacy then became known variously as the Six Iroquois Nations, the Six Allied Nations, and the League of Six Nations. The fundamental link among the six tribes was their common language, Iroquois, but there were also cultural similarities.

The **Mohawk** inhabited the eastern limit of the Iroquois territories around the Mohawk Valley in New York State. The **Onondaga** occupied territory that extended north to Lake Ontario and south to the Susquehanna River. Their capital was the village of Onondaga in central New York State, and they were the official guardians of the council fire of all the Iroquois. The **Oneida** lived in the area stretching from Lake Oneida in the north to the Susquehanna in the south, while the **Cayuga** inhabited the lands around Cayuga Lake, also in New York State.

Farthest to the west were the **Seneca,** who initially occupied the territory between Seneca Lake and the Genesee River but later also acquired land around Lake Erie and south along the Allegheny River into Pennsylvania. The **Tuscarora** had originally lived in what is now North Carolina but migrated north to join the other Iroquois tribes in New York after being defeated by British settlers in 1713.

Most of the Iroquois tribes lived in sizable villages where life revolved around large communal houses that served both as living quarters and political gathering-places. The tribes' organizational structure was matrilineal and included numerous interconnected religious and political clans. A council of elected delegates was chosen from among all tribal chieftains to be the overall governing body. There was no single supreme authority in the confederation, and decisions were made unanimously by the league council. Delegates were responsible to their constituencies: A delegate who displeased his clan could be removed by order of the tribe's women and replaced by another of their choosing.

The Iroquois were a powerful force in precolonial America. They had a prosperous agricultural economy based on corn and supplemented by other crops, including pumpkins, beans, and tobacco. Polished shell beads known as wampum were used as currency and woven into ceremonial belts to document important tribal events and treaties. Their stable, relatively sophisticated political system, combined with fierce, highly developed skills in warfare, allowed them to expand westward, subjugating other strong tribes such as the Huron. By 1720 they controlled most of the territory from the Atlantic Ocean west to the Mississippi River, and from the St. Lawrence River south to the Tennessee River.

During colonial times the Iroquois maintained their independence, aligning themselves primarily with British interests and holding the balance of power in the area around the Canadian border. Although some of the Mohawk, Oneida, and Cayuga sided with French missionaries in the eighteenth century, the dominance of the Iroquois in the areas west of British colonization is credited with preventing further French expansion southward from Canada.

The Iroquois tribes relied on oral tradition to preserve their history. The story of the founding of the Five Nations—thought to have a basis in fact—describes the struggle of Chief Hiawatha to protect his people from the powerful Algonquin tribes. Though his name was immortalized by Henry Wadsworth Longfellow in the *Song of Hiawatha*, the historical chieftain is thought to have lived around 1570—but *not* on the shores of Gitche Gumee or the shining Big-Sea-Water (Lake Superior), as Longfellow would have it. The poet thoroughly confused him with someone else.

The years after the American Revolution saw the dispersal of most of the Iroquois tribes through Canada, Wisconsin, and western New York, where reservations were established. Their influence persists, however. Although they had no written language, the Six Nations had formalized their political system in a constitution said to have influenced the design of the U.S. Constitution, especially in its apparent provision for a separation of powers. (Of course, the Founding Fathers were already quite familiar with Greco-Roman, English, and French ruminations on this topic.)

The fate of the reservations set aside for the Iroquois tribes was similar to that of many other tribes during the nineteenth century: Territory was chipped away, conquered, and stolen through duplicitous treaties. The struggle of the former Six Nations to maintain their identities and territories continued into the twentieth century, with efforts by the Tuscarora to prevent the Niagara Power Project from taking their land in the early 1960s. The case went to the Supreme Court, which decided against the tribe.

But Justice Hugo Black wrote a dissenting opinion in which he was joined by Chief Justice Earl Warren and Justice William O. Douglas. Black said: "The record does not leave the impression that the lands of their reservation are the most fertile, the landscape the most beautiful, or their homes the most splendid specimens of architecture. But this is their home—their ancestral home. There they, their children, and their forebears were born. They, too, have their memories and their loves. Some things are worth more than money and the costs of a new enterprise. I regret that this court is the governmental agency that breaks faith with this dependent people. Great nations, like great men, should keep their word."*

What are the 6 ranges of the human voice?

> Soprano
> Mezzo-soprano
> Contralto (alto)
> Tenor
> Baritone
> Bass

Singing comes naturally to humans, and the human voice was the first musical instrument. Children sing happily with little or no instruction. For most adults, singing—or listening to fine singing—is a powerful, deeply ingrained means of stirring their emotions. Birds employ their intricate songs in courtship rituals, and many a human seduction has been hastened by the likes of "Nessun dorma," the magnificent tenor aria from Giacomo Puccini's opera *Turandot* that has become Luciano Pavarotti's signature. Because people who can't speak after a stroke often retain whatever singing abilities they used to have, speech and singing may well be under separate areas of control in the brain. In fact, the neural pathways used for singing are buried in the so-called old brain, near the areas that control emotional expression. But let's leave to poets and neurologists any further questions about *why* singing affects humans, and focus instead on the *how* of Western vocal music.

What distinguishes you from a Pavarotti or a Cecilia Bartoli? In a word, anatomy. Singers must study their art assiduously if they hope to succeed in the highly competitive opera world, but unless the physical dimensions and form of their vocal tract—the larynx, phar-

---

* *Federal Power Commission and New York Power Authority* v. *Tuscarora Indian Nation;* cited in Samuel Eliot Morison, *The Oxford History of the American People,* vol. 2, New York, Meridian, 1965, page 195.

ynx, nasopharynx, nose, and mouth—are optimal, no amount of musical training will waft them to the stage of Milan's La Scala or New York's Metropolitan Opera House. The anatomy involved in singing varies enormously from person to person, as evidenced by how well we can usually distinguish the voices of different people, even after many years. When vocal cords vibrate, the sound resonates in the upper vocal tract, and the quality of this resonance, in conjunction with vocal training, spells the difference between a prima donna of the stage and of the shower stall.

The human voice is characterized according to frequency (pitch), harmonic structure, and intensity (volume). The size of the larynx is a major determinant of a singer's range in pitch. The larger the larynx, the lower the vocal pitch. Since a woman's larynx is usually smaller than a man's, her vocal range is higher. The human voice ranges in frequency from a low of about 80 cycles per second (or hertz, Hz) to a high of about 1,050 Hz, although many singers can exceed these limits. As a point of reference, the A above middle C is standardized at 440 Hz.

The harmonic structure of a voice is somewhat analogous to the timbre of a musical tone (see Question 33). When the vocal cords vibrate, they produce a so-called fundamental tone, for example, 200 Hz. They also produce additional higher tones called harmonics. Ideally, these harmonics should be multiples of the fundamentals—in this example, 400 and 600 Hz. The more closely the harmonics match the multiples of the fundamental, the more pleasing the voice.

The intensity, or volume, of a singer's voice depends primarily on how much air pressure the singer can apply to the vocal cords. Anatomy is a factor here, and not only regarding thoracic capacity. Since the larynx is shaped a bit like the bell of a trumpet or a megaphone, the closer its resemblance to an acoustically correct horn shape, the better the voice will project.

The vocal range of a **soprano** runs from middle C to the second A above it (to about 880 Hz). Sopranos can be further classified as dramatic, lyric, and coloratura. A dramatic soprano sounds almost muscular beside a lyric soprano, who is called on to sing lighter roles demanding more vocal agility. A coloratura soprano sings the highest notes attainable by humans, sometimes hitting the second C above middle C. She gets the role of Queen of the Night in Mozart's *The*

Magic Flute if she can hit these notes confidently and accurately every time. Maria Callas and Joan Sutherland were coloraturas.

Boys with voices in the soprano range, though sometimes called sopranos, are more correctly termed trebles. Beginning in the late sixteenth century, boys with elegant soprano voices were sometimes castrated before puberty to prevent their voices from changing, hence the term *castrati* or *evirati*. As late as the seventeenth and eighteenth centuries, when much serious music was still liturgical, choirs demanded castrati because women were forbidden from performing any liturgical function, including singing. Castrati were in high demand for eighteenth-century Italian operatic productions. The most famous of the Italian opera castrati was the soprano Farinelli (Carlo Broschi) (1705–82). Farinelli, whose vocal range was an astounding 131–1,175 Hz, could hold a note for a full minute without taking a breath.

When the castrati passed into musical history at the beginning of the nineteenth century, the **mezzo-soprano** benefited tremendously. She typically has a vocal range from the A below middle C to the second F above it—midway between that of a soprano and a contralto. Dramatic mezzo-sopranos are characterized by the intensity of their voices, and lyric mezzos by an earthy suppleness. The gifts of the mezzo-soprano are well suited to the Italian art of *bel canto* ("beautiful singing"), especially as exemplified in many operas of Mozart, Bellini, and Rossini. Mezzos count among their ranks Frederica von Stade, Marilyn Horne, Cecilia Bartoli, and Anne Sofie von Otter.

Middle age takes its toll on the human voice, and many sopranos find they can no longer reach the highest notes in that range as they approach fifty. At this point, those who wish to continue singing professionally learn mezzo-soprano roles instead, with intact middle and lower vocal ranges.

A woman with a **contralto,** or alto, voice typically sings well in the range from the F below middle C to the second D above it. The rare man who can also sing in this range—without resorting to a falsetto—is called a countertenor. Most of the available music for countertenors was written during the Renaissance. If you attend a concert where a countertenor is scheduled to sing, look around at the faces of the other members of the audience. At least a few of them will appear stunned at hearing *that* voice coming out of a man.

The **tenor,** the highest conventional male voice, usually covers the tones between the second B below middle C to the G above it. Like soprano voices, tenors can be subcategorized—as dramatic, lyric, and heroic (Heldentenor). The last type was particularly favored by Richard Wagner, who used it for Siegfried in *The Ring of the Nibelung*. In medieval and Renaissance times, the tenor was perhaps the most important voice in religious music. By the late seventeenth century, castrati had stolen the limelight from the tenors, especially in Italy. Tenors in France fared better, since the French frowned on castrating boys to preserve their voices and their tenors were trained to push their voices to higher ranges. In addition to the Three Tenors—Luciano Pavarotti, Plácido Domingo, and José Carreras—other notable twentieth-century tenors include Enrico Caruso, Giovanni Martinelli, Beniamino Gigli, and Jon Vickers.

The **baritone**, intermediate between the tenor and bass, is the most common male voice, with a range from the second G below middle C to the E above it. Baritones often have a somewhat flexible range; in easier tenor roles, they might be able to sing the part comfortably, but they be less proficient in the more difficult ones. Mozart was the first important composer to write opera roles for baritones, allowing subsequent composers—no longer limited to tenors and basses—to write a wider range of male roles. Robert Merrill had an outstanding baritone singing voice.

The **bass** is the lowest male voice, with a range extending from middle C to the second E below it. Singers with a basso profundo have a rich, dark voice, whereas the basso cantante has a more lyric style. Basso buffo voices sound clear, deep, and full, and are used in comic roles. Bass voices are often reserved for heavies such as Il Commendatore in Mozart's *Don Giovanni,* the title role of Mussorgsky's *Boris Godunov* (see Question 41), Hagen in Wagner's *Götterdämmerung,* and Mephistopheles in Gounod's *Faust.*

⚜ QUESTION 50

Which were the 6 Axis Powers in World War II?

Germany
Italy
Japan
Hungary
Romania
Bulgaria

The Axis Powers comprised Adolf Hitler's Nazi Germany and the countries formally allied with it in World War II. The term was first used in this connection when Benito Mussolini claimed the Rome-Berlin alliance should be thought of as an axis around which other like-thinking nations might group themselves. This first Axis Pact between Germany and Italy was proclaimed on October 25, 1936.

Italy and Germany had in common not only fascist political systems but also expansionist ambitions rooted in rankling bitterness from the World War I peace settlement (see Question 30). **Germany** had suffered from the reparations exacted by the Allied victors, its European and overseas territorial losses, and a ruinous inflation. **Italy,** though it had sided with the Allies in the war, was aggrieved because it had received so few colonial spoils compared with Britain and France. Mussolini thus sought to enlarge Italy's foreign possessions with the conquest of Ethiopia in 1936 and the annexation of Albania in 1939. He hoped his alliance with Germany would render him more formidable to Britain and France, Italy's rivals in the Mediterranean. For Hitler, a close alliance with Italy was a vital, strategic anchor, necessary for securing the conquest of southern Europe.

On May 22, 1939, Germany and Italy signed a sweeping military and political alliance called the Pact of Steel, which bound them to fight side by side in Europe and North Africa. On September 27, 1940, a little more than a year after the outbreak of World War II,

Japan joined the two countries in the Tripartite Pact (see Question 83), which obligated its members to mutual defense. Japan entered the pact to strengthen its diplomatic hand against the United States, but neither Germany nor Italy was able to provide any meaningful military aid to Japan during the war, nor was Japan able to help its partners in the Rome-Berlin-Tokyo Axis.

Hitler now assiduously pursued Hungary, Romania, and Bulgaria, which were potentially useful allies. All three had assets or frontiers that meshed with Germany's war plans, and to varying degrees they endorsed aspects of Hitler's politics, especially his anti-Bolshevism. **Hungary** shared a militarily important frontier with the Soviet Union, which Hitler was planning to attack, and its dictator, Admiral Miklós Horthy, was grateful to Germany and Italy because in August 1940 they had transferred to Hungary northern Transylvania, which had been lost to Romania after the First World War. Hungary signed the Tripartite Pact on November 20, 1940.

In the case of **Romania,** Germany needed its oil fields at Ploesti, and its frontier with the Soviet Union would provide a valuable launching point for invading that country (see Question 46). Marshal Ion Antonescu, Romania's military dictator, believed that Hitler was bound to dominate Europe and might eventually restore lost territories to Romania. Antonescu signed the Tripartite Pact on November 23, 1940, and eagerly joined in Hitler's 1941 invasion of the Soviet Union in the hope of reclaiming Bessarabia and northern Bukovina from the Soviets.

The last to sign the Tripartite Pact, on March 1, 1941, was **Bulgaria,** which Germany desired in part as a base from which to launch the invasions of Yugoslavia and Greece. Hitler offered territorial concessions to Bulgaria's Czar Boris III to pave the way for an alliance: the restoration of southern Dobruja (from Romania) and the transfer of parts of Yugoslavia and Greece after Germany occupied those countries. Unlike Hungary and Romania, however, Bulgaria never declared war on the Soviet Union.

It was Italy, Germany's earliest ally in the Axis, that was the first to withdraw from the pact. Reversals in North Africa and the destruction of a 220,000-man Italian army at the disastrous Axis defeat at Stalingrad in January 1943 undermined Mussolini's authority at home. Italy's high command and King Victor Emmanuel III combined to depose and arrest Mussolini in July 1943. Rome began secret talks with the Allies the next month, all the while assuring Germany that the Rome-Berlin Axis was intact. On September 3, Italy secretly concluded an armistice with the Allies, but Hitler was not taken by surprise. German divisions moved in quickly to occupy Italy and hold it against the imminent Allied invasion. After German commandos, led by SS officer Otto Skorzeny, rescued Mussolini from his mountaintop confinement, Hitler installed him as a puppet leader at Salò on Lake Garda in northern Italy.

The defeat at Stalingrad also alarmed Hungary, Romania, and Bulgaria, especially after Soviet troops began moving west. When Romanian armies reeled under the onslaught of a Soviet offensive in the Ukraine in August 1944, Romania's King Michael led a coup that deposed Antonescu (who was shot as a war criminal in 1946). The King tried to make peace with the Allies before the country was overrun by Soviet forces, but the move came too late and Soviet forces soon seized Bucharest.

Bulgaria, whose Czar Boris died in August 1943, went through a series of short-lived governments that tried to position it as a neutral country, but the Allies refused to let it off the hook. As a last-ditch effort, Bulgaria declared war on Germany on September 8, 1944, but Soviet troops had already occupied the country.

In Hungary, Horthy also tried to distance himself from the disaster to come by cutting a peace deal with the United States. American diplomats, however, steered Horty toward Moscow, where Hungarian-Soviet talks were under way when Hitler learned of Horthy's duplicity. German troops, again led by Skorzeny, abducted Horthy on October 15, 1944, and the next day a pro-German successor was appointed. Germany occupied Hungary for the remainder of the war.

German troops in Italy, fighting fiercely, were slowly shoved out of the peninsula by Allied advances from the south. Mussolini was captured by Italian partisans and shot on April 28, 1945. The next morning, his body and that of his mistress, Clara Petacci, who was also shot, were taken to Milan and suspended by the feet from the girders of a bombed-out gas station. That same day saw the surrender of all German troops in Italy.

The collapse of Germany occurred after furious aerial bombardments and a two-pronged invasion by the Soviets from the east and the Americans and other Allies from the west. Hitler apparently shot himself, and his newlywed mistress Eva Braun took poison in his *Führerbunker* beneath a devastated Berlin on April 30, 1945, two days after Mussolini's death. Germany surrendered unconditionally on

May 7, and the fighting stopped the next day. In August, the American atomic bombing of Hiroshima and Nagasaki led to Japan's unconditional surrender, signed aboard the battleship *Missouri* on September 2, 1945.

Others beside the six countries listed above were allied with the Axis Powers in some capacity. For example, Prince Paul, the Regent of Yugoslavia, was behind his country's joining the Axis Pact on March 25, 1941, but his government was overthrown only two days later and the treaty was repudiated. The Nazis, taking a savage revenge, especially in the merciless bombing of Belgrade, occupied Yugoslavia on April 6. Nonetheless, they had to fight against two main insurgent groups, including Tito's, for the remainder of the war. The Finns, seeking to liberate territory seized by the Soviets, participated in the German invasion of the Soviet Union. Both Croatia and Slovakia signed the Berlin Pact, but these were only puppet-state portions of dismembered, German-occupied Yugoslavia and Czechoslovakia, respectively. Nanking China, a puppet state created by the Japanese, was another signatory.

What are the 7 Wonders of the Ancient World?

    The Great Pyramid of Cheops at Giza
    The Hanging Gardens of Babylon
    The Statue of Zeus at Olympia
    The Temple of Artemis at Ephesus
    The Mausoleum at Halicarnassus
    The Colossus of Rhodes
    The Pharos (Lighthouse) of Alexandria

In his *Natural History,* Pliny the Elder tells of encountering the shattered fragments of the Colossus of Rhodes in the first century A.D.: "Few men can clasp the thumb in their arms, and its fingers are larger than most statues. As for its broken limbs, their insides look like vast caves."

In Pliny's time, the Colossus lay where it had fallen, toppled by an earthquake. Yet that didn't diminish the Roman's awe. The Wonders tend to do strange things to people: About eighteen hundred years after Pliny penned his description, a decade-long obsessive quest to find traces of the Temple of Artemis at Ephesus drove the English archaeologist J. T. Wood to physical and emotional collapse. The pyramids, of course, have spawned overheated quests for gold, gods, and cosmic enlightenment. And shards of the great lighthouse at Alexandria are even now being uncovered by deep-sea divers on the Mediterranean floor.

Each of the Seven Wonders of the ancient world was the product of singular architectural, engineering, and artistic hubris. The sheer size of the Wonders suggests that their makers had it in for Protagoras's anthropocentric notion that "man is the measure of all things."

In about 130 B.C., the Greek poet Antipater of Sidon compiled a list of Wonders very similar to our own. But as far back as the Greek historian Herodotus in the fifth century B.C., legends abounded of magnificent sights that travelers had seen, sights *(theamata)* so arresting in their size and splendor that they were eventually called wonders *(thaumata)*.

The Great Pyramid of Cheops at Giza. Until the nineteenth century, no one ever again built anything as tall as the tomb created by the Fourth-Dynasty Pharaoh Khufu, or Cheops, around 2560 B.C. To Herodotus, the pyramids were almost as ancient as he is to us. The largest, the Great Pyramid, is by far the earliest of the Seven Wonders and also the only one still very much intact. For almost forty-four hundred years, the Great Pyramid, at 481 feet (now about 450), was the tallest edifice in the world—only 24 feet shorter than the United Nations Building in New York. What work of the twentieth century will be standing in the year 6560?

Construction began with a series of stepped layers of stone. Then the spaces between the layers were filled in with gleaming white limestone from the hills east of what is now Cairo. The pyramid's sloping sides, intended to evoke the rays of the sun god Ra emanating from the apex to the ground, were set at an angle slightly less than 55°. The sides at the base are 756 feet long. Despite the ancient builders' lack of accurate surveying equipment, there's less than eight inches of variance between the shortest and longest sides. The base covers 13.1 acres, a space that can comfortably contain St. Peter's in Rome, the cathedrals of Florence and Milan, Westminster Abbey, and St. Paul's of London.

The Great Pyramid required about 2.3 million granite blocks, each weighing an average of 2.5 tons. The blocks had to be moved on log rollers and sledges and then ramped into place, since neither the pulley nor the block and tackle would be invented for another twenty-five hundred years.

The historian Diodorus Siculus (fl. 60–30 B.C.) claimed 360,000 men worked on the pyramid, which took twenty years to complete. Herodotus had estimated that 100,000 workers were needed and even recorded the vast sum it must have cost to feed them with radishes, onions, and leeks. Modern scholars think the pyramids were built by a group of 500 to 1,000 craftsmen, assisted by 5,000 to 7,000 workmen who came to labor on the monuments in shifts from all over Egypt. Contrary to earlier belief, these workers were not slaves. Their houses, recently unearthed, resemble the pyramids in miniature, complete with little false doors.

The entrance to the Great Pyramid was concealed on the north side, facing the polestar. Several corridors branched out inside the tomb. The largest, the Grand Gallery, angled upward into the heart of the pyramid. The gallery, 153 feet long and 28 feet high, was a corbeled vault, unlike anything else in Old Kingdom architecture. It was up this ascending corridor that the funeral cortege moved, bearing the body of Cheops to its resting place in the King's Chamber. Over their heads, giant blocks of granite perched on wooden beams.

The King's Chamber was designed in a 2:1 ratio—34 feet, 4 inches long, by 17 feet, 2 inches wide. It was 19 feet, 1 inch high, and its flat roof comprised nine huge blocks that together weighed 400 tons. After the funeral procession had descended, a team remained behind to dislodge the beams holding up the gallery's blocks of granite, thus plugging up access to the King's Chamber. The workmen then escaped through a narrow shaft hidden beneath a stone at the top of the Grand Gallery, which snaked down under the pyramid.

Despite these precautions, thieves plundered the pyramid within two hundred and fifty years of its completion. They didn't find everything, however. In 1954, the solar boat of Cheops was discovered in an airtight pit beneath forty-one large blocks of limestone on the south side of the pyramid. Over a hundred feet long, it was made from 1,274 pieces of wood fit together without a single metal nail. The vessel, which may have borne Cheops on the Nile to his entombment, enabled him to sail with the sun god beyond the grave.

The Hanging Gardens of Babylon. Relying on earlier sources, the Roman historian Quintus Curtius Rufus (fl. mid-first century A.D.) claimed the trees of the Gardens were twelve feet in circumference and fifty feet tall. The tale of this forest of towering trees and tiered roof gardens rising high into the sky had already been told by the Greek poets, who embroidered it with the love of a king for his homesick lover.

The Hanging Gardens were said to be the work of Nebuchadrezzar II (reigned c. 605–562 B.C.), King of Babylonia, whose mighty capital of Babylon was located on the Euphrates in what is now Iraq. This was the king who destroyed Jerusalem in 586 B.C. and led the Jews off into captivity. He apparently had a sentimental strain, though, for he was said to have built the gargantuan Gardens of trees, flowers, and shrubs for his wife (or concubine), Amytis, who longed for the mountainous greenery of her homeland in Media (northwestern Iran).

To Philo of Byzantium (late third century B.C.), the most fascinating feature of the Gardens built within the walls of the royal palace was their resting on stone columns so that people could stroll beneath the structure while workers plowed and tended the fields overhead. He and a few other writers left circumstantial accounts of the Hanging Gardens (which seemed to "hang in air"), touching on everything from the soil and root systems to the method of irrigation of the five landscaped brick terraces, each rising fifty feet above the other and connected by marble stairways. Modern scholars of hydraulics claim that a wooden piston pump run by a waterwheel would have had to raise the water of the Euphrates to a height of about three hundred feet to cisterns in the topmost terrace of the structure.

Despite the vividness of some ancient accounts, they are second-hand at best. No cuneiform inscription from Babylon even hints at the existence of such a garden, let alone offers an eyewitness description. Herodotus, who lived in the century after the Gardens were built, describes the city of Babylon without ever mentioning this Wonder.

Of the Seven, in fact, the Hanging Gardens alone are likely to be the stuff of legend. But the detailed descriptions still tantalize. "The park extended 400 feet on each side, and since the approach to the Garden sloped like a hillside and the several parts of the structure rose from one another tier on tier, the appearance of the whole resembled that of a theater," wrote Diodorus Siculus in about 50 B.C.

The Statue of Zeus at Olympia. "Although the temple itself is very large, the sculptor is criticized for not having appreciated the correct proportions. He has shown Zeus seated, but with the head almost touching the ceiling, so that we have the impression that if Zeus moved to stand up he would unroof the temple." The Greek geographer Strabo (c. 63 B.C.–c. A.D. 24) put his finger on the strongest impression made on visitors by the statue of Zeus at the site of the sacred Olympian games, which celebrated the lord of thunder: massive, irrepressible power.

The Doric temple of Zeus at Olympia, in western Greece, was completed around 460 B.C. by the architect Libon. It was not designed to house a congregation. Instead, on the middle day of the games (see Question 37), throngs would gather before a great altar outside the temple where one hundred oxen would be slaughtered and burned as a hecatomb offering to Zeus.

The people of Olympia turned to the Athenian sculptor Phidias to forge the image of the god. This designer of the sublime sculptures of the metopes, frieze, and pediments of the Parthenon had been banished from Athens on a trumped-up charge of having stolen gold intended for the famous statue of Athene he had made for that temple. In Olympia, the chryselephantine (gold-and-ivory) statue of Zeus he completed in about 430 B.C. was built on a wood or stone core and rose to a height of forty feet, as tall as a four-story building. Bare-chested, the god sat on a high cedarwood throne whose legs were decorated with images of Theban children seized by the Sphinx and with back-to-back winged figures of Victory (Nike). Seated figures of the Sphinx—a monster with a woman's head, a lion's body, and an eagle's wings—supported the throne's armrests. Other images included those of Apollo, Artemis, and Niobe and her slain children.

The Greek traveler Pausanias (fl. A.D. 150) wrote of the statue: "On his head is a sculpted wreath of olive sprays. In his right hand he holds a figure of Victory made from ivory and gold. . . . In his left, he holds a scepter inlaid with every kind of metal, with an eagle perched on it. His sandals and robe are made of gold, and his garments are carved with animals and lilies. The throne is decorated with gold, precious stones, ebony, and ivory." The Christian writer Clement of Alexandria (c. 150–c. 220) mentions that on the finger of Zeus were etched the words, "Pantarkes is beautiful." Pantarkes won the boys' wrestling contest at the 86th Olympiad (436 B.C.), and tradition has it that this was Phidias's tribute to his beloved. Another legend tells how after the image of the god was finished, Phidias asked Zeus for a sign of approval for his masterpiece. Immediately, a lightning bolt struck the black marble floor.

Zeus sat enthroned at Olympia for more than eight centuries. In A.D. 393 the Christian clergy persuaded Roman Emperor Theodosius I to close the temple and ban the pagan games. The statue was borne off to a palace in Constantinople where, in 462, a fire destroyed both palace and statue. The great temple itself at Olympia, bereft of its cult, succumbed to fire, flood, landslides, and earthquakes.

The Temple of Artemis at Ephesus. There were actually two altars and one temple, and later two great marble temples, that rose and fell successively on the same site in Ephesus, a thriving Greek port in Ionia on the west coast of modern-day Turkey. The fourth edifice (called "D" by archaeologists) was begun in the mid-sixth century B.C., partly subsidized by fabulously wealthy King Croesus of Lydia. The architects were Chersiphron and his son Metagenes of Crete, and some of the greatest artists of antiquity, including Phidias and Polyclitus, worked on adorning the temple. This building was burned to the ground by Herostratus, a nobody whose successful claim to fame was his destruction of the temple so that posterity would remember his name. The fire occurred on July 21, 356 B.C., supposedly the same night Alexander the Great was born. The legend arose that Artemis wasn't in Ephesus to protect her dwelling-place because she was assisting at the birth of the future mighty conqueror of Asia.

The late-classical temple (called "E") was probably begun about 350 B.C. and incorporated many details of the style and design of its predecessor. Before approaching the temple, visitors stood far back in the outer courtyard to admire the decorated pediment high above. Sculpted Amazons framed the entranceway, which revealed a forest of gleaming marble columns.

Marble steps surrounded the building, the uppermost ending in a terrace 260 feet wide and 430 feet long. The temple itself was 180 by 350 feet. It's unclear whether the temple was completely roofed with tiled wood or if the inner sanctuary lay open to the sky. Inside, visitors walked amid 127 Ionic marble columns, 60 feet high and resting on sculpted rectangular bases. Each column was said to have been the gift of a different king.

In the center of the colonnade, the *cella* of the temple most likely contained a cult statue of Artemis, who, at Ephesus, was actually an Asian mother goddess attended by eunuch priests, rather than the virgin goddess and huntress of Greece. The goddess was pictured with several rows of pendulous breasts—more than forty in all—amply deserving St. Jerome's epithet for her, *Multimammia*.

"Great is Artemis of the Ephesians!" shouted the furious silversmiths of the city when St. Paul's evangelizing mission threatened their livelihood as makers of miniature silver shrines dedicated to their goddess (Acts 19:23–40). Yet the Temple of Artemis survived until A.D. 262, when it was ravaged by Ostrogoths. In 401, what remained of the once-lovely structure, with its slender, elegantly fluted columns, was destroyed by order of St. John Chrysostom.

The Mausoleum at Halicarnassus. This massive edifice of white marble, which gave its name to all subsequent large tombs, was the one Wonder known to be built by a woman, Artemisia, the wife and sister of Mausolus, satrap of Caria (reigned 377–353 B.C.). Such love did she bear her brother-husband that she reportedly mixed his ashes with water and drank him down before raising the Mausoleum in Halicarnassus, now part of southwest Turkey.

The architect was thought to be Pythius of Priene, perhaps with Satyrus of Paros. The tomb's peculiar form may have resulted from an attempt to amalgamate the architectural features of three different civilizations—Lycian, Greek, and Egyptian—in a trilayered rectangular structure. At its base, the Mausoleum measured about 127 by 100 feet. It was 140 feet high (about ten to thirteen stories) and had three main parts: the base, a stepped podium 60 feet high; the middle layer, a colonnade of thirty-six Ionic columns, 37.5 feet tall; and, over this, a stepped, pyramidal roof. The roof's twenty-four steps rose 22.5 feet to a flat surface, on which, surmounting the entire tomb, stood a 20-foot marble four-horse chariot—perhaps with statues of Mausolus and Artemisia in it. The burial chamber, with its sarcophagus of white alabaster decorated with gold, is believed to have been ensconced amid the columns on the podium.

The exterior of the Mausoleum was adorned with many friezes and freestanding statues, life-size or larger, of people, lions, horses, and other animals. The embellishment of each of the tomb's sides was said to have been assigned to one of four Greek sculptors: Scopas, Bryaxis, Timotheus, and Leochares.

The tomb stood relatively intact until the thirteenth century, when portions of it collapsed in an earthquake. Ironically, it is these fragments, deeply buried, that constitute most of the remnants of the structure we have today. In the fifteenth century, what was left of the Mausoleum was used by the Knights of St. John to erect and later fortify a massive castle. They quarried the tomb for stone and pulverized the sculptures for lime. A dozen slabs of a frieze vividly depicting the battle between the Greeks and Amazons were, with other elements such as statues of lions, built into the castle walls for decoration.

The frieze was extracted from the walls in 1846 and shipped to London's British Museum, where it is one of the glories of ancient Greek sculpture. In 1857, the British antiquarian Sir Charles T. Newton pinpointed the site of the Mausoleum and subsequently unearthed a hoard of architectural stones and statues (including those he claimed were of Mausolus and Artemisia). These priceless objects, too, followed the Amazon frieze to the British Museum.

The Colossus of Rhodes. In 305 B.C., seventy thousand Macedonians led by Demetrius Poliorcetes ("Besieger of Cities") descended on the thriving island city of Rhodes. When an agreement was reached the next year, the attackers lifted the siege. Demetrius had been so impressed with the Rhodians' fortitude that he left behind his catapults, armored towers, and other siege engines.

The people of Rhodes sold the equipment and used the money to erect an enormous statue of their patron deity, the sun god Helios. They chose Chares of Lindus (a Rhodian city) for the task, and he and his bronze-casters worked for a dozen years (c. 292–280 B.C.). The bronze was fortified from within by giant blocks of stone and iron tiebars, and the image was built upon itself: When the feet were completed, mounds of earth were piled around them so that the workers could move up to construct the ankles. As the statue rose, the completed parts lay buried.

The finished work stood 110 feet tall—easily the largest statue of antiquity. By comparison, the Statue of Liberty, "The New Colossus," rises to a height of 152 feet. Little more is known for certain about either the appearance or location of the Colossus, other than that it never bestrode the entrance to any of the harbors of Rhodes.

The best guess is that the Colossus was a naked statue of the sun god, lifting a torch in one hand while the other held a spear at his side. His legs were placed close together to provide him with columnar stability.

The Colossus stood for little more than a half century. A powerful earthquake hit Rhodes in about 224 B.C., damaging the city and breaking the statue at its weakest point—the knees. The Rhodians received an offer from Ptolemy III of Egypt to cover all restoration costs for the toppled monument. However, an oracle forbade them to rebuild the statue, which lay where it fell for nearly nine hundred years, much as Pliny the Elder experienced it.

In A.D. 653, the Arabs invaded Rhodes. They disassembled the remains of the broken Colossus, shipped them to Asia Minor, and sold them as scrap metal to a Jewish merchant from Emesa in Syria. All traces of the Colossus vanish behind the nine hundred camels that, legend has it, bore away the fragments.

The Lighthouse of Alexandria. The last of the Seven Wonders to be built was the first architecturally designed lighthouse in history. It took its name **Pharos** from the small island near the mouth of the Nile on which it was built—and gave its name to the French, Italian, and Spanish words for lighthouse: *phare, faro,* and *faro.*

Pharos lay before the harbor of Alexandria, the city founded in 332 B.C. by Alexander the Great immediately after his conquest of Egypt. The city grew rapidly and, since the Egyptian coastline offered few landmarks, the need soon arose to guide ships safely into harbor. Work on the lighthouse began under King Ptolemy I Soter, Alexander's boyhood friend who ruled Egypt from 305 to 282 B.C. It was completed in about 280 B.C. under his son and successor, Ptolemy II Philadelphus (284–246 B.C.), and was designed (or perhaps paid for) by Sostratus of Cnidus.

Ancient coins show a three-tiered tower with rectangular windows on all sides. The lighthouse had three sections: The lowest was square, 183.4 feet high with a cylindrical core; the middle was octagonal with a height of 90.1 feet; and the third, 24 feet high, was cylindrical and encircled with a broad spiral ramp. A 16-foot statue stood at the top, perhaps of Alexander the Great or King Ptolemy I in the trappings of the sun god Helios.

The total height, including the foundation base, was about 384 feet, equivalent to a thirty-five-story building. At night, a fire of resinous wood in the base of the Pharos was reflected by enormous mirrors, possibly of burnished bronze, at its top. Its beacon was said to be visible across the Mediterranean for thirty to forty miles. During the day, its mirrors reflected the sunlight, marking the port for sailors.

The Pharos was damaged in an earthquake in A.D. 956 and fell into ruin during other quakes in 1303 and 1323. An archaeological team of divers has recently uncovered more than twenty-five hundred architectural pieces beneath the waters around Pharos, including fifteen enormous granite blocks thought to be from the lighthouse, each weighing more than thirty tons. The discovery of many statues, sphinxes, obelisks, and columns nearby could lead to a new understanding of the Pharos and the role it may have played as part of a civic or religious architectural complex.

The Seven Wonders of the World arrested onlookers like Pliny with their size and majesty and by the sublime ease with which they dismissed mundane notions of what human imagination and engineering could do. A Wonder shocked by violating the continuity of scale between observer and observed.

187

How some of these artifacts were built remains a matter of intense debate. With others, we know how they were constructed and that they taxed the ingenuity of some of the most brilliant architects, engineers, and sculptors the world has seen. Their ruin—except for the eternal pyramids—complicates our awe by confronting us with forces even more titanic than the Wonders themselves.

✳ QUESTION 52

What were the works of the 7 days of Creation?

1. Light
2. Heaven
3. Earth, seas, and plant life
4. Sun, moon, and stars
5. Sea life and birds
6. Land animals and mankind
7. Rest

The seven days of Creation are described at the beginning of Genesis, the first book of the Bible. Although tradition attributes the authorship of Genesis to Moses, the leader and lawgiver of the Jews during their exodus from slavery in Egypt, it is actually a composite work.

The Genesis story of Creation is neither a historical account nor a scientific explanation of the origins of the world, a fact recognized even in the fifth century by St. Augustine, who noted that some of the descriptions in Genesis diverged from the scientific knowledge of his day. Nonetheless, many Jews and Christians still find profound truths about God, the material world, and man in the biblical story of the seven days of Creation.

Genesis contains two Creation narratives. The first, which begins in Chapter 1 and describes the works of the seven days, is a much later text than the version of the so-called Yahwist (J) that begins in Chapter 2, verse 4b. The J text appears to contradict Chapter 1 in its claim that plant life, land animals, and birds were created *after* Adam.

In Genesis 1, when God creates the heavens and the earth, the latter is at first "a formless wasteland" in which "darkness covered the abyss" of waters. This seems to refer to a kind of Ur-matter, chaotically undifferentiated, to which God subsequently brings cosmic order. His first work, then, is to create **light** (the ordering principle par excellence), separate it from darkness, and call the light *day* and the darkness *night:* Thus, "evening came, and morning followed—the first day." A refrain now begins to punctuate the story, "God saw that it was good," referring to his various creations—until a cumulative statement, at the end of his labor, proclaims them in their totality to be "very good."

On the second day, order comes to **heaven:** "Then God said, 'Let there be a dome in the middle of the waters, to separate one body of water from the other.' God called the dome *heaven.*" The ancient author was here expressing his belief that God set a dome or vault between the primordial waters now forming part of the sky (which supply rain to the earth) and the various waters remaining on earth itself.

Next, the **earth, seas, and plant life:** "Then God said, 'Let the water under the sky be gathered into a single basin, so that the dry land may appear.' God called the dry land *the earth*, and the basin of the water he called *the sea.* Then God said, 'Let the earth bring forth vegetation: every kind of plant that bears seed and every kind of fruit tree on earth that bears fruit with its seed in it.' " On the third day, dry land is created and separated from the waters under the dome. With light, water, and earth now available, plant life appears.

Only on the fourth day did God populate the sky with the **sun, moon, and stars:** "God made the two great lights, the greater one to govern the day, and the lesser one to govern the night; and he made the stars." Note that the sun and moon are not named in the biblical text, since they were worshiped by neighboring peoples as gods. Many skeptics have asked how light could have been created three days before the sun. John Milton tries to address the difficulty in *Paradise Lost* (7.245–49), where he claims that light

> . . . *from her Native East*
> *To journey through the airy gloom began,*
> *Spher'd in a radiant Cloud, for yet the Sun*
> *Was not; shee in a cloudy Tabernacle*
> *Sojourn'd the while.*

The creation of **sea life and birds** followed on the fifth day: "Then God said, 'Let the water teem with an abundance of living creatures, and on the earth let birds fly beneath the dome of the sky. . . . And God blessed them, saying, 'Be fertile, multiply, and fill the water of the seas; and let the birds multiply on the earth.' "

Finally came **land animals and mankind:** "God made all kinds of wild animals, all kinds of cattle, and all kinds of creeping things of the earth. . . . Then God said, 'Let us make man in our image, after our likeness. Let them have dominion over the fish of the sea, the birds of the air, and the cattle, and over all the wild animals and all the creatures that crawl on the ground.' "

In this first account in Genesis, God created humans last—"male and female he created them"—to imply they are the culmination of all his creatures. He endows them with a special dignity in making them overlords of the earth and all that lives on it and also directs them, as he did the animals, to be fruitful and multiply. But what does it mean to say that man was created in God's image and likeness? Does it refer to man's possession of a soul, reason, and free will, all denied to brute beasts, or was the ancient author merely imagining God anthropomorphically in his own image?

Rest is the theme of the seventh day: "So God blessed the seventh day and made it holy, because on it he rested from all the work he had done in creation." God thus sets the example for the seven-day week of the Jews, whose Law requires six days of work followed by a holy Sabbath of rest, worship, prayer, and religious study.

The entrance of evil, sin, and death into God's "very good" creation is explained in the story of the Fall of Man in the Yahwist account in Genesis 2–3. In this version, which predates Chapter 1 by many centuries, God creates a man, Adam, from the dust of the ground and places him in the Garden of Eden with instructions to cultivate it.

Eden is full of different kinds of succulent fruit trees, including the Tree of the Knowledge of Good and Evil, which Adam is forbidden to taste of or even touch. After the wild beasts and birds are created by God and named by Adam, God forms a woman, Eve, from the man's rib. She promptly succumbs to a beguiling serpent, who tricks her into eating "the Fruit / Of that forbidden Tree, whose mortal taste / Brought Death into the World, and all our woe, / With loss of Eden. . . ." (*Paradise Lost,* 1.1–4). Uxorious

Adam eats some of it, too. The knowledge they gain results only in shame at their nakedness, causing them to sew themselves pathetic fig-leaf loincloths. God sentences the woman to pain in childbirth and lust for her husband, who now becomes her master. "The master" must henceforth earn his bread with the sweat of his brow. He is informed that he will suffer death, and his sin of disobedience has shorn him of much of his former dignity: "For dust you are, and unto dust shall you return."

Christians who try to harmonize the seven days of Genesis too precisely with the eons of evolutionary time sometimes cite 2 Peter 3:8: "One day is with the Lord as a thousand years." But all attempts to calibrate biblical with scientific time are foredoomed by St. Paul's admonition that "the letter killeth, but the spirit giveth life."

✴ QUESTION 53

What were the 7 Hills of Rome?

> Palatine
> Capitoline
> Quirinal
> Viminal
> Esquiline
> Caelian
> Aventine

To settlers in the second millennium B.C., some of these seven hills, 100 to 150 feet high and just east of the Tiber, offered easily defended sites overlooking a valley with access to the river trade. Much later, the hills of the Eternal City were enclosed by the Servian Wall (378 B.C.), mistakenly ascribed to Servius Tullius, Rome's sixth king (sixth century B.C.).

All palaces are named for the **Palatine,** hub of the seven hills, which probably took its name from Pales, a deity of uncertain sex who presided over shepherds and herds. It's traditionally the site of the oldest Roman settlement. The legend says that the twins Romulus and Remus resorted to augury to decide which of them should be king of a new city and give it his name. Remus, from the Aventine, first saw a sign from heaven—six vultures—but, immediately afterward, Romulus saw twelve birds from his vantage point on the Palatine. In the ensuing discussion of the respective claims of priority or quantity, Remus was slain, and Romulus went on to found his city and name it Roma on April 21, 753 B.C., according to unreliable sources.

Many centuries later, after Augustus's house on the Palatine was enlarged, it became the first palace *(palatium)* of the emperors to be located there. Other rich and famous residents of the Palatine included Crassus, Cicero, and Mark Antony (see Questions 15 and 16).

All capitols are named for the **Capitoline** *(caput,* "head" or "top"), the religious center and citadel of ancient Rome. On one of its peaks rose the stupendous temple of Jupiter Optimus Maximus ("Jupiter Best and Greatest"), supposedly dedicated in the first year of the Roman republic (509 B.C.), with side chapels for the goddesses Juno and Minerva. The temple was roughly two hundred feet on each side, and one hundred steps led up to its bronze gates. Roman magistrates offered sacrifice here upon entering office. Victorious generals who were awarded triumphs also sacrificed to Jupiter in this temple, which was destroyed by fire and rebuilt several times.

On another peak of the Capitoline was the *Arx* or stronghold of the city (the Roman "Acropolis"). On yet a third stood the temple of Juno Moneta, which housed the mint of Rome. *Moneta,* which merely means "admonisher," thus gave rise to our word *money.* On a more somber note, traitors and murderers were flung from a cliff of the Capitoline, the Tarpeian Rock.

Petrarch was crowned Poet Laureate on the Capitoline in 1341. Here, in 1536, Michelangelo designed the superb square of the Campidoglio, flanked by three *palazzi,* one of which, the Capitoline Museum, is a treasury of ancient art. Here Edward Gibbon, in 1764, meditating on the ruins on the Capitoline and the vicissitudes of history, supposedly received the initial impetus for *The Decline and Fall of the Roman Empire.* On the Capitoline now stands the elaborately squat Monument to Victor Emmanuel II, the first King of Italy, completed in 1911. In precomputer days, facetious Romans referred to the edifice as "The Typewriter."

The **Quirinal** (QUIR-in-ul), the northernmost hill of ancient

Rome, was traditionally occupied by Sabines and named for Cures, the town from which the Sabines were supposed to have migrated to Rome. Or was the hill named for Quirinus, the Sabine god of war, who was eventually identified with the deified Romulus? Whatever the etymology, the Roman people were referred to in speeches and formal addresses as "Quirites," apparently to commemorate their ancient assimilation with the Sabines, which occurred after the end of the strife occasioned by the abduction ("rape") of the Sabine women. In the late sixteenth century Pope Gregory XIII began building the Quirinal Palace on this hill as a papal summer home, which in 1870 became the residence of the King of Italy. The Italian President now lives there.

The **Viminal** (VIM-in-ul) was named after a copse of willow trees, *vimina,* that grew there. As far as the hills of Rome go, it wasn't very important.

The name **Esquiline** (ESS-kwi-line) apparently stems from *ex-colere,* "to cultivate." It was the site of the villa and gardens of the archetypal literary patron Maecenas, who cultivated poets like Virgil, Horace, and Propertius. Nero's monstrously huge and ornate Domus Aurea (Golden House) was later built on the Esquiline and sprawled over adjoining areas—one hundred twenty-five acres' worth of palatial pleasure domes. "Now I can live like a human being," he commented.

The **Caelian** (SEEL-ee-un) was named for Caelius Vibenna, an Etruscan who came to the assistance of a Roman king. His picturesque name in Etruscan was Kaile Fipne. The Caelian is now called the Lateran Hill.

The **Aventine** (AV-in-tine), home to a temple of Diana, was named for Aventinus, a Latin king buried there. This most southerly of the seven hills was given to the Roman plebeians to settle in 456 B.C. and remained a stronghold of the proletariat, though it's a fancy residential neighborhood now.

❧ QUESTION 54

What were the 7 Liberal Arts of the medieval curriculum?

> Grammar
> Rhetoric
> Logic (these first three forming the trivium)
> Arithmetic
> Geometry
> Music
> Astronomy (these last four forming the quadrivium)

The Seven Liberal Arts were branches of learning considered appropriate for *liberi,* "free men." These arts—sometimes called the Seven Sciences—were the basis of education in the cathedral and monastic schools and, later, the universities of the Middle Ages. The Church long remained divided on whether the "pagan learning" embodied in the seven arts should be embraced or rejected. Eventually, the consensus was for "despoiling the Egyptians of their gold," that is, using the knowledge of the ancient Greeks and Romans for the Church's own purposes, much as the Jews in Exodus (12:35–36) departed from Egypt with the gold of their former heathen masters.

In the late twelfth and thirteenth centuries, someone who had studied the trivium of Latin grammar, rhetoric (Latin literature), and Aristotelian logic at a university received a baccalaureate or Bachelor of Arts degree. Those who then plowed through the quadrivium received their master's degree *(Magister Artium,* "Master of Arts"), allowing them to teach. (A *magister* was a schoolteacher.) Hardy souls who continued their studies could choose to specialize in theology at a university such as that of Paris, civil or canon law at Bologna, or medicine at Salerno. Graduates would receive a doctorate in their field of study. Some of these men would choose to teach at a university *(doctor* meant professor), whereas others pursued careers as prelates, ecclesiastical or civil lawyers, or physicians.

How did this grouping of the arts originate? In Book 7 of the *Republic,* Plato (c. 429–347 B.C.) includes in the education of his ruling elite the studies that came to be called the seven liberal arts. Several centuries later, the Roman encyclopedist Varro (116–27 B.C.) dealt with them systematically (plus architecture and medicine) in his *Disciplines.* St. Augustine (354–430), a professor of rhetoric before his conversion, wrote works on grammar, rhetoric, logic, and music—parts of an encyclopedic work on the liberal arts modeled on Varro's book.

Yet another writer influenced by Varro, the fifth-century Neoplatonist Martianus Capella, composed *The Marriage of Mercury and Philology,* a long, allegorical farrago of Latin prose and verse in which Mercury, god of eloquence, marries the learned maiden Philologia ("the science of words"). Each of the seven handmaidens of Philologia corresponds to one of the liberal arts and delivers an interminable harangue on her particular excellencies. Later writers who composed influential works on the seven arts were Cassiodorus (c. 490–c. 583) and Isidore of Seville (c. 570–636).

What was so special about these seven arts? Let's start with the **trivium.** In the Middle Ages, it served as the "threefold way" for mastering the verbal skills and reasoning tools needed to delve into study of the Bible, theology, and the Latin classics—or to preach an effective sermon. It thoroughly grounded students in

- ✦ Reading, writing, and speaking Latin
- ✦ Using figures of speech and narrative strategies to make their use of language esthetically pleasing ("the sugar-coated pill")
- ✦ Thinking logically, so that they could state an argument clearly, develop it, sustain it with proofs or examples, and refute counterarguments.

Sure, the trivium didn't have much relevance to "the real world" and so became an easy target of ridicule for the likes of Rabelais in a later age. But without the verbal and reasoning skills so obsessively, even lunatically, cultivated by medieval scholars, the achievements of the scientific revolution beginning in the mid-seventeenth century might have been postponed or stillborn.

In the Middle Ages, students usually learned the rudiments of Latin **grammar** from the fourth-century text of Donatus. Advanced students moved on to the bulkier grammar of Priscian (fl. c. A.D. 500), which incorporated a copious anthology of Roman authors. This book became synonymous with Latin grammar, so that "to crack Priscian's pate" meant to make an egregious mistake in Latin. Dante puts Donatus in his *Paradiso* and Priscian in his *Inferno,* reflecting an ambivalence about grammarians that many of us still share.

Rhetoric didn't always have pejorative connotations. What Cicero called "The Queen of the Arts" was an invaluable tool for presenting ideas effectively and elegantly in public speaking, verse, and prose. The goals of rhetoric were to teach, delight, and, above all, persuade an audience to adopt or shun a course of action. Its three main divisions were (1) arrangement or organization, (2) amplification or abbreviation of classical passages on a particular subject to suit one's own purposes, and (3) style and its ornaments, such as figures of speech.

In the ancient world, Aristotle's *Rhetoric* was a classic exposition, along with the *Institutes of Oratory* (c. A.D. 95) of the Roman rhetorician Quintilian, who also wrote on the six other liberal arts. Medieval students of rhetoric were particularly fond of Cicero's *On Invention,* the *Rhetorica ad Herennium* (misattributed to Cicero), and Horace's *Art of Poetry.* Rhetoric, "the most precious gift of the gods" (Quintilian), remained a required course at Jesuit colleges well into the twentieth century.

The names of rhetorical figures still offer incomparable means of displaying one's erudition and tony classical education:

- ✦ Aposiopesis, a sudden breaking off of speech: "Of all the dirty—I'll rip your lungs out, Jack!"
- ✦ Catachresis, a mixed metaphor: "The very heart of the central nervous system is, of course, the brain."
- ✦ Litotes, understatement expressed by negation of what is meant: "Not bad at all, that Sistine Chapel."
- ✦ Paronomasia, a sesquipedalian word for a pun.
- ✦ Synecdoche, a part for the whole or the whole for a part: "Jennifer memorized all 101 lists—what a brain she is!"

Among the debating tricks developed by rhetoricians over the ages is this neat example from the Greek Sophist Gorgias (c. 483–c. 376 B.C.): "You should kill your opponents' earnestness with jesting and their jesting with earnestness." Note that this infuriating trait didn't shorten his life span any.

While rhetoric persuades via the emotions, **logic** persuades by reason. Thousands of medieval thinkers learned how to split hairs from Latin translations of Aristotle's impenetrable works on logic—bleakest of all, the *Posterior Analytics*—collectively known as the *Organon* ("tool" or "instrument" of investigation). The author of *The Consolation of Philosophy,* Boethius (c. 480–524), "the last of the Romans and the first of the Scholastics," translated into Latin Aristotle's works on logic and composed his own works in the field. These, with other Latin translations of Aristotle's logical treatises and of countless Arabic commentaries on them, became grist for the ever-grinding mills of the Scholastic philosophers.

The self-appointed task of these "Schoolmen" was to reconcile the revealed truths of Christianity with Aristotelian logic and science, often by using acrobatically creative reasoning to prove that yes was no. (In fact, one of Peter Abelard's most important works bears the title *Sic et Non*—"Yes and No.") This tendency wasn't restricted to Christianity: Avid medieval Aristotelians included the Jewish scholar Moses Maimonides and, among many Islamic thinkers, Avicenna and Averroës (see Question 95).

The aim was a noble one: If the main tenets of a religious creed could be shown to accord with "science" (then represented by the philosophy of Aristotle), religion was not merely a belief or opinion, but a demonstrable system of truths. Thus, only a dunce could doubt its claims, since they were as self-evident as the theorems of geometry—to those who knew how to "do the proofs." By the thirteenth century, the intellectual obsession with Aristotelian logic almost drove the study of Latin humanistic literature from the universities.

The **quadrivium** was the "fourfold way" to knowledge—largely mathematical knowledge, since music and astronomy were considered applied math. Boethius wrote textbooks on the arts of the quadrivium, a word he apparently coined. His basic text on **arithmetic** became a manual for medieval schools. Although it was more Pythagorean/Platonic (dealing with the philosophy of numbers) than computational, it did include practical knowledge relating to the calendar. Since clumsy Roman numerals were still used for computing, the Venerable Bede (673–735) wrote a handy work on how to do sums on one's fingers. Only in 1202 did Leonardo Fibonacci introduce Arabic numerals (ultimately of Indian origin) into Europe.

Over the doors of Plato's Academy was the inscription "Let no one ignorant of geometry enter." Plato didn't consider **geometry** one of the practical arts—which he scorned—but an abstract study that allowed students to understand relations among ideal forms. The immutable entities of geometry permitted a glimpse into the perfect world of essences and eternal Ideas—the Good, True, Beautiful, and Just. But by far the most influential writer in the field of geometry was Euclid (fl. c. 300 B.C.). The complete text of his *Elements* first became accessible to the Scholastics when it was translated into Latin in the early twelfth century.

Boethius (or a later writer) composed an elementary treatise on **music** that long remained a standard text at Oxford and Cambridge. The study of music included practical instruction in the Church's plainsong and other liturgical applications, as well as theoretical work on the mathematical basis of music, ultimately harking back to Pythagoreanism. In the eleventh century, the Italian monk Guido d'Arezzo worked out a protomodern system of musical notation. We also owe to Guido the names of *re, mi, fa, sol,* and *la,* which, along with the precursor of *do (ut),* were taken from the first syllables of six half-lines of a Latin hymn to St. John the Baptist.

The indefatigable Boethius also compiled a Latin work based on Greek **astronomy,** mainly on Ptolemy's *Almagest* (second century A.D.). The *Almagest,* completely translated into Latin only in the twelfth century, was used to track the course of the heavenly bodies and determine the positions of more than a thousand stars. In the middle of the next century, John of Holywood wrote a commentary on the *Almagest* that became the basic text of elementary astronomy for almost four hundred years. Ptolemy's system of the universe, with the earth enthroned at the center of the cosmos, became *the* official version sanctioned by the Church (see Question 3).

And so the great synthesis that Thomas Aquinas had attempted in his *Summa Theologica*—the reconciliation of Greek science with Christian theology—was specifically extended to astronomy, too. Here, the integration of pagan science with Christian metaphysics involved harmonization of Aristotle's theory of the heavens, Ptolemy's hard astronomic data, and the traditional teachings of the Church. Ptolemy also wrote on astrology, which many ancient and medieval scholars considered to be applied astronomy.

Our word *trivial,* first attested in 1589, originally meant "commonplace, the kind of thing likely to be encountered on the street"—

more precisely, at a *trivium* or crossroad. But by that time, most humanist thinkers regarded the old educational system of the seven arts, with its emphasis on Aristotelian logic, as essentially trivial.

✳ QUESTION 55

Where do the English names of the 7 days of the week come from?

> Sunday (Old English, sunnandaeg): Sun's day
> Monday (monandaeg): Moon's day
> Tuesday (tiwesdaeg): Tiw's day
> Wednesday (wodnesdaeg): Woden's day
> Thursday (thursdaeg): Thor's day
> Friday (frigedaeg): Frigg's day
> Saturday (saeterndaeg): Saturn's day

Our 7-day week harks back to the Sumerians and Babylonians, who even designated one as a day of leisure. It's not clear why these peoples divided the year into 7-day units. Although astronomy dictates that we have a 365-day year and a 24-hour day, there's no scientific reason for a 7-day week. Nonetheless, the Babylonians named the days of their week for the sun, moon, and five planets they knew.

The Romans adopted this system of naming the days after these same heavenly bodies, which had already been named for gods, except for a period when they had an 8-day week (and a time when their calendar had only ten months, omitting 61 days during the winter—not a bad idea). In addition to **Sun's day** and **Moon's day,** the Romans had Mars's day, Mercury's day, Jove's (Jupiter's) day, Venus's day, and **Saturn's day.** The Latin names of the five weekdays are still ensconced in the French, Italian, and Spanish words for those days.

While English has kept the days named in honor of the sun, moon, and Saturn (Roman god of agriculture and father of Jupiter), the names of the remaining four are based on the Anglo-Saxon names for various Norse gods. Tuesday—**tiwesdaeg**—memorializes Tiw (or

Tiu), the Saxon version of the Norse god of war, Tyr. The son of Odin (Woden), Tyr was also a protector of justice and peace treaties.

On one occasion his fellow gods rather unkindly took advantage of Tyr's reputation as a guardian of good faith when they used the magic thread *gleipnir* (spun from the footfalls of cats, beards of women, spit of birds, breath of fish, and roots of stones) to bind the fierce wolf-monster Fenrir (sometimes called Fenris-wolf), sired by Loki. All in jest, the gods explained to Fenrir. Despite the thread's insubstantial appearance, cagey Fenrir would play the game only if Tyr placed his forearm in the wolf's mouth. When Fenrir realized he'd been tricked and was firmly bound, he bit off Tyr's right hand. Fenrir remained captive until the apocalyptic battle—Ragnarok—between the gods (called the Aesir) and, on the other side, the giants and forces of Hel, Queen of the Underworld, led by mischievously malicious Loki. The war god Tyr corresponds to the Roman god Mars, and thus Mars's day *(dies Martis)* became our Tuesday.

The chief Norse god Odin was the ultimate source of **wodnesdaeg.** Known as the All-Father, the cultured, refined, but promise-breaking Odin has only one eye, having traded the other for a drink at the Well of Wisdom in an effort to postpone the day of doom, Ragnarok. Each evening, two ravens perch on his shoulders and whisper hoarsely in his ears. The birds, named Hugin and Munin ("thought" and "memory"), fly all over the earth during the day, observing humans, and then report back to him on what they've observed. By hanging on a tree for nine agonizing days and nights, wounded by a spear, Odin earned the knowledge of runes, and by stealing the skaldic mead of the Giants he became the patron of poets. Odin also feasts all brave dead warriors brought to him at Valhalla by the Valkyries, "choosers of the slain." Because Odin/Woden was a match for the Romans' shrewdest god, Mercury, their *dies Mercurii* became our wodnesdaeg.

The strongest of the Aesir was the thunder god, Thor, from whom **thursdaeg** takes its name. The son of Odin, Thor is often depicted as the antithesis of his father—coarse, uncouth, and endowed with huge appetites. His massive belt is the source of his power, and he is invincible because of his iron gloves. Thor's hammer, Mjöllnir, which he throws to create thunderbolts, returns to him every time he hurls it, much like a boomerang. Jove's day *(dies Jovis)* became thursdaeg because the Saxons considered Thor analogous to the Roman thunderer god Jupiter.

Frigg (or Frigga), who gave her name to **frigedaeg,** was Odin's wife, Queen of the Aesir, goddess of fertility, and, by most accounts, a good mom, forever mourning Loki's treacherous murder of her son Balder. In fact, Frigg means "the one who loves." She is described as wise and silent, sitting for hours on end spinning gold thread.

Frigg is a somewhat nebulous figure whose identity may have fused with that of Freya, the Norse Venus. Freya is by most accounts far less virtuous than Frigg and considerably more colorful—driving a wagon pulled by lynxes and refusing to settle down with any of her numerous gentlemen friends. Is Friday—*dies Veneris*—named after model-wife Frigg or promiscuous Freya? Scholars disagree, although most believe the two goddesses gradually coalesced in the minds of the Teutonic peoples who worshiped both of them.

❧ QUESTION 56

What are the 7 kinds of plane triangles?

> Equilateral
> Isosceles
> Scalene
> Right
> Acute
> Obtuse
> Oblique

Triangles are categorized in terms of the relative lengths of their sides and the measurement of their angles. These two criteria produce some overlap in the seven kinds of triangles listed above.

First, let's consider triangles named for the lengths of their sides. An **equilateral** triangle has three sides of the same length, as its name suggests. The angles opposite these sides are also equal. Equilateral triangles are also known as regular triangles. An **isosceles** (eye-SOSS-uh-leez) triangle has at least two equal sides. (The equilateral, with three, is a special kind of isosceles.) The name comes from the Greek

Plane Triangles at a Glance

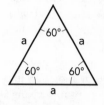

An **equilateral** triangle.
All sides are the same length,
and all angles = 60°.

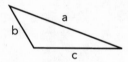

An **isosceles** triangle.
At least two sides are congruent
(have the same measure).
The base angles are also congruent.

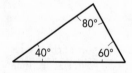

A **scalene** triangle.
No two sides are of equal length.

A **right** triangle.
It has one right (90°) angle. The
other two angles are complementary,
that is, the sum of their measures
is 90°. According to the
Pythagorean theorem, $a^2+b^2=c^2$.

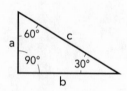

An **acute** triangle.
All angles are less than 90°.

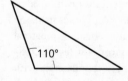

An **obtuse** triangle.
One of its angles is greater than 90°.

All but the fourth of these triangles are **oblique**
triangles because they lack a 90° angle.

isos ("equal") and *skelos* ("leg"). The two angles opposite the two equal sides are also equal. A **scalene** (SKAY-leen) triangle has three unequal sides—and thus three unequal angles. This word comes from the Greek for uneven, *skalenos,* and possibly *skolios* ("crooked"), the root of our word *scoliosis* (curvature of the spine).

When considering triangles named for their angles, keep in mind that the angles of a triangle always add up to 180°. A **right** triangle has a right angle (an angle of 90°) and two angles of less than 90°. It's "right" because the word comes from the Latin *rectus* ("straight"). The side of the triangle opposite the 90° angle is called the hypotenuse, from the Greek *hypo* ("under") and *teinein* ("to stretch"). Look at a right triangle—the hypotenuse does look stretched. (Recall that classic Pythagorean theorem, $a^2 + b^2 = c^2$, where a and b are the lengths of the legs of a right triangle, and c is the length of the hypotenuse.) An **acute** triangle has three acute angles. An acute angle (think sharp or pointed—like Latin *acus,* "needle") is less than 90° but greater than 0°. An **obtuse** triangle contains an obtuse angle (think blunt)—one greater than 90° but less than 180°. An **oblique** triangle simply has no right angles. Oblique can be another way of saying slanting. Because this triangle has no right angles, it has no straight up-and-down sides—they all look slanty.

As noted, triangles fall into more than one category. The most obvious example is the oblique, which is any triangle that is not a right triangle. If you look at the triangles in the illustration, you'll see some other overlaps. The equilateral triangle is always also an acute triangle because all its angles are less than 90°. The isosceles triangle shown here is also an acute triangle because it contains three angles of less than 90°. This particular obtuse triangle is also a scalene triangle because it has three unequal sides (this isn't always the case).

Much of what we know about triangles is based on the work of the Greek mathematician Euclid (fl. c. 300 B.C.). Educated in Athens, probably by Plato's pupils at the Academy, Euclid spent most of his life in Alexandria, Egypt, teaching at a school founded by King Ptolemy I. His most important work was the *Elements,* a treatise in thirteen books (chapters) on geometry and number theory that systematized the work of earlier Greek mathematicians. Although the *Elements* was used as a school text until the early twentieth century, you can be sure Euclid never got a drachma in royalties.

If you have less-than-fond memories of all those theorems you had to "prove" in high school, you have mainly Euclid to thank for it.

You're in good company, though. Even King Ptolemy is said to have groused about having to slog his way through them. When he asked Euclid if there was a shortcut, the master replied, "There is no royal road to geometry." This may be a recycled story, though: It had already been told of the mathematician Menaechmus (a pupil of Plato) and Alexander the Great.

 QUESTION 57

What are the 7 main levels of taxonomic classification?

Kingdom
Phylum
Class
Order
Family
Genus
Species

"Kiss, please, come on, for God's sake!" is one of several time-honored mnemonics that biology students use to remember the taxa, or levels, by which all life is classified. (*Taxonomy* comes from Greek *taxis*, "arrangement," and *nomos*, "law.") Although recent progress in molecular biology has modified the old classification, biosystematics has operated under essentially the same set of rules and with the same nomenclature since the mid-eighteenth century, when it was devised by Swedish botanist Carolus Linnaeus (1707–78).

Linnaeus, also a physician, was a founder and first president of the Swedish Royal Academy of Sciences and a professor of botany. He endeavored to classify all plants, assigning each to a class, order, genus, and species. He accomplished this, as many professors do, by dispatching his more ambitious students on prolonged, often dangerous, natural-history expeditions to collect plant specimens for him. In developing the binomial naming system of genus and species (e.g., *Homo sapiens*), he owed a debt to English systematizer John Ray (1627–

1705), who defined a species as a group of individuals who breed, producing offspring like themselves.

The more closely related two species are, the later they diverge on the taxonomic path. Consider the close relatives *Canis familiaris,* the domestic dog, and *Canis latrans,* the coyote, which diverge at the genus level. Humans and apes, which are more distant relations, split at the family level. Humans and elephants diverge at the order level, where elephants fit in among the Proboscidea (snouted ones). Octopuses *(Octopus vulgaris)* and humans diverge at the phylum level, where the octopods slither among the other Mollusca.

As criteria for classification, Linnaeus depended heavily on reproductive capacities, a reliance that made some people shun his system, lest so much emphasis on fertility inflame the minds of the young. To mollify these critics, many of whom considered his writings obscene, Linnaeus referred in an early essay to the "betrothal of plants." He published many books on classification, the most influential being *Species Plantarum* (1753) and the fifth edition of *Genera Plantarum* (1754). In 1758–59 he finally applied his nomenclature to animals in the tenth edition of *Systema Naturae.*

To see how the classification system works, let's take a relatively simple example—you.

+ At the broadest level of classification, you, *Homo sapiens,* are a member of the **kingdom** Animalia. Most biologists now recognize five kingdoms: Animalia, Plantae, Monera (including bacteria and viruses), Protista (single-celled organisms such as protozoa), and Fungi (which had been part of the plant kingdom until they were recognized to bear a resemblance to both animals and plants—without fitting in either kingdom). An alternative system recognizes just three so-called domains: Eucarya, which, among other life forms, includes plants, animals, and fungi; Bacteria; and Archaea, which includes heat-, salt-, and acid-loving bacteria.
+ Your spinal cord, brain, and internal skeleton qualify you as a member of the **phylum** Chordata. Other chordates include tadpoles and sea squirts. Your vertebral column also makes you a member of the subphylum Vertebrata.
+ You were born live (not laid in an egg), have (or had) hair, your mother produced breast milk for you, you have three bones in your middle ear, and you are warm-blooded, main-

taining a near-constant body temperature regardless of the ambient temperature—all of which places you in the **class** Mammalia. (Note that fully half of the five thousand mammalian species are rodents.) Developmental biologists note that only mammals have the ability to modify their behavior based on knowledge they acquire from their elders. You are also a member of the mammalian subclass Eutheria, whose members are distinguished according to their reproductive strategy as placentals. Members of another mammalian subclass, the Prototheria, provide just a few of the difficulties faced by taxonomists. The duck-billed platypus is one of only two members of this subclass. The platypus lays eggs and has no nipples (milk is delivered via a slightly different apparatus on the abdomen). In place of teeth it has a beak. Still, it clearly resembles other mammals far more closely than it does birds (class Aves).

+ You belong to the **order** of Primates, which includes two suborders, the prosimians (lemurs) and the anthropoids (monkeys, apes, and humans). Characteristics of primates include opposable thumbs and great toes, nails instead of claws, binocular vision, a large brain, a relatively poor sense of smell, and a prolonged childhood and adolescence. Not all primates exhibit all of these characteristics, however. You, for example, lack an opposable great toe. Primates are distinguished from other orders by an apparent evolution from species like tree shrews to humans, a progression notable for an increasingly complex brain.

+ The primates are divided into eleven **families.** You are a member of the Hominidae family, which is distinguished by erect posture. And you're it: All other members of Hominidae are extinct.

+ Homo is your **genus.** Again, your relations in this genus are extinct.

+ *Sapiens* (wise) is your **species.** Your closest relative, *Homo erectus,* who probably appeared about 1.6 million years ago, shared upright posture with *Homo sapiens* but his brain was somewhat smaller. The first *Homo sapiens* appeared in Africa about five hundred thousand years ago.

Beyond Linnaeus's wildest dreams, molecular taxonomists can fine-tune these notions by comparing the composition of the same protein in different species—a concept sometimes called a molecular clock. If the composition of a particular protein differs only slightly in humans and rhesus monkeys but extensively between humans and certain species of fish, this confirms evolutionary data suggesting that human and fish lineages split hundreds of millions of years ago. In contrast, we parted company with monkeys much more recently.

In some cases, this type of analysis has refined fossil-based evolutionary theories. Based on fossil evidence, scientists believed until fairly recently that human and ape lines split about fifteen million years ago, but analysis of proteins from humans and African apes suggests that the divergence occurred only about five million years ago.

✳ QUESTION 58

Which 7 European nations were the main colonizers of Africa in 1914?

> Great Britain
> France
> Belgium
> Portugal
> Germany
> Italy
> Spain

In postclassical times, European nations first established rudimentary outposts on the African continent in the fifteenth century, mostly for the purpose of trade, especially in slaves. Portugal led the way. Not until the nineteenth century, however, did Europeans regard Africa with colonial ambitions in mind. Several events precipitated what one British newspaper called "the scramble for Africa" late in the century.

One was the sharpening rivalry in North Africa between **Great Britain** and **France.** The French invaded Algeria in 1830 and spent the next half century subduing resistance and expanding their control.

Africa: 1914

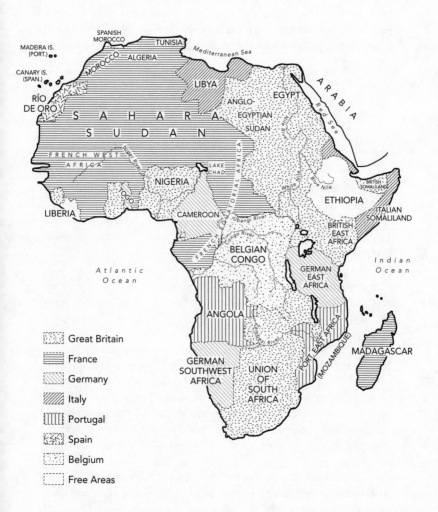

Great Britain

France

Germany

Italy

Portugal

Spain

Belgium

Free Areas

In 1882, while France was occupied with war in Tunisia, British forces seized Egypt, largely to ensure the security of the Suez Canal—which France had built, though Britain had become principal stockholder—and thereby of the sea lanes to British India. With Britain and France wrangling over territories, the rest of Western Europe took stock of its own political and financial interests in colonization. The steadily expanding European industrial output led to a growing need for raw materials and export markets. A new, chauvinistic nationalism was in the air, causing European countries to be more competitive with each other, to formulate notions of their expansionist destiny, and to view colonial empires as necessary concomitants of political and military prestige. The "scramble" to grab chunks of technologically backward Africa was inevitable.

Another development closely watched in Europe was the partnership of Leopold II, King of the Belgians, and H. M. Stanley, the reporter from the *New York Herald* who had trekked across Africa to find the celebrated Scottish medical missionary David Livingstone in 1871. After their famous encounter ("Doctor Livingstone, I presume?"), Stanley's reports on the potential wealth of the little-known African interior persuaded King Leopold to send him back to Africa in 1882 in an entirely private, nongovernmental venture to claim vast tracts of land in the Congo. Stanley was able to get more than five hundred unwitting local chieftains to sign over their land to King Leopold's International Congo Association (later called the Congo Free State). Leopold's agents, like the colonial administrators who followed them in subsequent years, brutally exploited the Africans who worked on the Congo's rubber plantations. Nonetheless, King Leopold's private empire turned out to be so economically unviable and debt-ridden that he transferred it to **Belgium** in 1908.

The King's move into the Congo, combined with enticing reports of explorers, missionaries, and traders returning from the African interior, created a vast appetite for territorial possessions. With the help of modern armaments, railroads, and steamships, European nations believed they could rapidly take charge and develop the resources of the sprawling continent. In addition, many Europeans believed they had a duty to "civilize" the Africans via "Christianity and Commerce."

In 1885, Germany sponsored the Berlin Conference, which laid down some ground rules for the great African land rush. The European nations with possessions on the coasts of East and West Africa—notably Britain, France, and Portugal—would have certain rights to interior regions. Countries claiming African territories would have to demonstrate actual control of those areas, through administrators or troops, rather than a merely nominal assertion of rule. Moreover, all the powers involved in African colonization had to keep each other apprised of their claims.

European advances into Africa meant breaking the resistance of the many African peoples who would fight before surrendering. But advanced European weaponry, like the British rapid-fire Maxim gun, gave the typically small European military detachments a decisive advantage in the dozens of bloody engagements, large and small, over the next fifteen years. In fact, the only major, lasting defeat of a European force was the rout of 20,000 Italian troops by 80,000 Ethiopians at Adowa in 1896, an event that secured the independence of Ethiopia until Italy returned and conquered it forty years later. Meanwhile, with Britain's encouragement and protection, **Portugal** moved inland from its ancient enclaves on the east and west coasts to carve out the huge colonies of Angola and Mozambique.

France, in addition to Algeria, controlled nearly all of West Africa as far east as the British territory encompassing Egypt, the Anglo-Egyptian Sudan, and the future Kenya. By 1896 it had conquered Madagascar, and it swallowed up Morocco in the first decade of the twentieth century. Great Britain, in addition to its north African holdings, ruled much of the southeast, and it fought the Boer War (1899–1902) in South Africa to establish its primacy over the independent, rebellious Dutch settlers who had first moved into the region in 1652. Britain's swath of eastern Africa, extending from Egypt to the Cape of Good Hope, was broken only by the Belgian Congo and Germany's East African colony.

This territory, sitting atop Britain's southern possessions, was Tanganyika (current-day Tanzania). **Germany,** an aggressive newcomer to the colonial game and reputedly the most brutal of the European powers in Africa, also claimed a large desert area in the southwest known today as Namibia and, farther north, Cameroon and Togo.

Initially, **Italy** had only modest holdings: Italian Somaliland, on the eastern shore of the Horn of Africa, and arid Eritrea on the Red Sea, adjoining Ethiopia. But in 1911, Italy wrested Libya from the

Turks and, in a prelude to World War II, it conquered Ethiopia in 1935–36.

The least ambitious of the European colonizers of Africa was **Spain,** which held only a sparsely populated area of the western Sahara southwest of Morocco and a slice of land on the African coast opposite the Straits of Gibraltar.

By 1914, when World War I began (at least partly as a result of German ambitions in Africa), the only African nations free of European control were Ethiopia and Liberia, the latter of which had been founded by former American slaves and was viewed as an American protectorate. It would take yet another world war to set in movement the forces that would coalesce in independence for the nations of Africa.

The colonial experience is sometimes defended as a harsh but valuable crash course in modern nation-building for backward African societies. The truth is more complex. Traditional cultures were destroyed by various schemes to coerce able-bodied men to work, often far from their homes and families. By the 1930s, 90 percent of all cultivable land had been expropriated for European use. The effects of war and dislocation were even more shattering than the slave trade of earlier centuries. An official Belgian report in 1919 concluded that the population of the Congo had been reduced by one half since King Leopold's intervention in the 1880s. For all their talk of a civilizing mission, Europeans often did more damage than good.

Beginning in the 1950s, African nations won independence from their colonial masters, sometimes, as in Algeria, after years of bloody strife. Yet the only major changes in the original colonial boundaries occurred after World War I, when Germany's African territories were divided between France and Britain. Although colonial boundaries were arbitrary and made little sense in terms of African nations, trade routes, languages, or geography, they have endured in many cases to become the boundaries—and bane—of modern-day independent African states.

✦ QUESTION 59

What are the 7 sacraments?

    Baptism
    Penance
    Holy Eucharist
    Confirmation
    Holy Orders
    Matrimony
    Extreme Unction

The word *sacramentum* originally referred to a military oath of allegiance taken by Roman soldiers at the start of a new campaign. In Roman Catholic tradition, however, a sacrament is a sacred mystery, or, in the words of the catechism, an "outward sign instituted by Christ by which invisible grace and inward sanctification are communicated to our souls."

Catholics believe that the priest who administers a sacrament acts only as an instrument of Christ. The Church's commitment to this belief is exemplified by its rejection of Donatism, a fourth-century heresy according to which a sacrament is void if administered by a "bad" priest.

Baptism (or christening) is the first and most necessary sacrament. In John (3:5), Christ says, "In all truth I tell you, no one can enter the kingdom of God without being born through water and the spirit." Indeed, he himself insisted that his cousin, John the Baptist, baptize him in the River Jordan. Baptism cleanses from the soul all taint of original sin—the legacy of Adam and Eve's disobedience of God. When those who are baptized have water poured over their head, or are fully immersed, they are said to be reborn into the life of Christ so as to share in his Resurrection. This rite of purification is also a rite of initiation into the Church for newborns as well as for older converts, whose personal sins are forgiven as well. In early

Christianity, baptism was probably reserved for adult converts. After the third century, however, a newborn Christian was assigned spiritual parents—godparents—who accepted baptism in the child's name. Baptism, confirmation, and Holy Orders can be received only once because their imprint on the soul is said to be indelible.

Christians derive their authority to baptize from the words of Christ before his ascension: "Go, therefore, make disciples of all nations; baptize them in the name of the Father and of the Son and of the Holy Spirit" (Matthew 28:19). This sacrament can be administered by a layperson in an emergency.

The rite of **penance** or confession, now often called reconciliation, is the sacrament by which Christ, through his priestly representative, forgives the sins of the contrite. In early Christian times, persons deemed to be sinners were assigned notoriously humiliating reparations, including fasting and public denouncement. These were replaced in later centuries by auricular confession, the private admission of sins to a priest (hence the confessional booths in Catholic churches).

Mortal sins, like murder, blasphemy, adultery, and theft, are so serious that, unless forgiven in the sacrament of penance, the sinner has no chance of attaining heaven. Venial sins are less heinous—fibbing, backbiting, quarreling, a raunchy thought here and there—and do not bar heaven, but the Church urges that they, too, be confessed. The process begins with an examination of conscience, in which the penitent reviews recent life events in light of the Ten Commandments (see Question 82) and the teachings of the Church, developing contrition for any sins committed. The penitent then approaches the confessional (or, more likely today, a reconciliation room) and confesses the sins to a priest, who may discuss ways to avoid these transgressions and then offers absolution with the words, "I absolve you from your sins in the Name of the Father, and of the Son, and of the Holy Spirit." A similar rite is practiced in the Eastern Orthodox Churches, but the formula of absolution is more humbly phrased: "May God, through me, a sinner, forgive thee."

Most other Christian churches offer public prayers for the forgiveness of sins, but not private confession as in the Catholic Church, claiming that only God has the power to forgive sins. Catholics counter that the priest is merely Christ's representative and cite the words of Christ to his apostles: "If you forgive anyone's sins, they are forgiven; if you retain anyone's sins, they are retained" (John 20:22–

23). And the epistle of James (5:16) says, "So confess your sins to one another, and pray for one another to be cured."

Christians believe that the following gospel passage describes Christ's institution of the **Holy Eucharist,** also known as Holy Communion or the Lord's Supper: "This is my body given for you; do this in remembrance of me" and "This cup is the new covenant in my blood poured out for you" (Luke 22:19–20). Christ seems to be asking his followers to commemorate and reenact the Last Supper by sharing bread and wine. Most Christians believe that reception of the Eucharist (Greek, *eucharistos*, "grateful" or "good grace") unites them more fully with Christ and each other. A rite of praise and thanksgiving, the Eucharist is, with baptism, one of only two sacraments recognized by nearly all Christians as established by Christ.

That's where the agreement ends. Catholics believe that in each celebration of the Eucharist, Christ, joined by the congregation, again offers himself to God the Father, as he did in the sacrifice of the Cross. According to the doctrine of impanation, the Church teaches that, with the priest's words "This is My body . . . this is My blood," the bread and wine on the altar literally become the body and blood of Christ. In this miracle of transubstantiation, all that remain of the bread and wine are their physical appearances. For centuries, only the clergy received Communion under "both species" of bread and wine; the laity received only the bread. This was somewhat amended by the Second Vatican Council. Communion in both species is not the norm at most Sunday Masses (probably because of logistical concerns) but may be reserved for special occasions such as weddings and First Communions. According to Church law, Catholics must receive the Eucharist at least once a year, during the Easter season.

The dogma of the Real Presence is also maintained by the Eastern Orthodox Churches, and the Anglican and Lutheran traditions have similar beliefs. Martin Luther (1483–1546) preached the doctrine of consubstantiation—that Christ is truly present "in, with, and under the bread and wine," which coexist with but are not transformed into his body. John Calvin (1509–64) taught that the Eucharist is a spiritually charged metaphor symbolizing unity with God but that it does not represent the actual physical body of Christ. This is the view of most Protestants today.

Confirmation involves the laying on of a bishop's hands and anointment with chrism, a mixture of consecrated olive oil and fragrant balsam. The Holy Spirit, the third person of the Holy Trinity (see Question 7), is said to descend, strengthening the soul and conferring additional grace beyond that received at baptism. The sacrament is usually administered in early adolescence, marking the beginning of adult Christian life, when one is "sealed with the Holy Spirit" and becomes obliged to witness and spread the faith. As a reminder of the possibility of persecution for the faith, the bishop may also administer a slight tap on the cheek.

The twelve Apostles (see Question 91) were the first to receive what is now called confirmation. Just before his ascension, Christ told them, "You will receive the power of the Holy Spirit which will come on you, and then you will be my witnesses" (Acts 1:8). About ten days later (or about fifty days after Christ's Resurrection—on Pentecost, from the Greek for "fiftieth day"), the Apostles were meeting when the sound of a mighty wind filled the room, "and there appeared to them tongues as of fire; these separated and came to rest on the head of each of them. They were all filled with the Holy Spirit and began to speak different languages" (Acts 2:3–4). In Acts 8, the Apostles Peter and John pray that the Holy Spirit may descend on some converts in Samaria who had only been baptized. Since Catholics consider bishops to be the successors of the Apostles, only bishops can administer confirmation.

Holy Orders confers the powers of the Catholic priesthood: to change bread and wine into the body and blood of Christ, administer baptism, grant absolution, witness marriages, and anoint the sick. A new priest is thought to receive a permanent charism (grace from the Holy Spirit). Although this charism can never be revoked, a priest can be suspended and forbidden from administering the sacraments if, for example, he breaks his vow of celibacy and marries. Like confirmation, Holy Orders can be conferred only by a bishop. During the rite, the candidate lies prone before the altar while the bishop imposes his hands and anoints him. The Church teaches that Christ made the Apostles priests when he gave them the power to change bread and wine into his body and blood at the Last Supper and to forgive sins after he rose from the dead.

Priests don't perform the sacrament of **matrimony.** In the exchange of mutual promises, the wife administers God's grace to her husband, and the husband does the same for her, while the priest acts only as the Church's witness. The Catholic Church considers marriage indissoluble, citing Christ's words in Matthew 19: "What God has joined together, man must not separate" and "If a man divorces his wife for any cause other than unchastity, and marries another, he commits adultery." Although the Church does not recognize divorce, a marriage can be declared null and void if certain conditions are met. Today, psychological problems that keep a person from making a valid marriage contract are probably cited most often in declarations of annulment, at least in the United States. Conservative Catholics believe that annulment has become too easy, while those whose marriage has been annulled at the request of their partner may feel demeaned by the Church's declaration that their marriage never existed.

The Church takes James 5:14–15 as the basis for **Extreme Unction,** now called the Anointing of the Sick: "Any one of you who is ill should send for the elders of the church, and they must anoint the sick person with oil in the name of the Lord and pray over him. The prayer of faith will save the sick person and the Lord will raise him up again; and if he has committed any sins, he will be forgiven." Anyone in danger of death because of an accident, illness, or old age is eligible for this sacrament, which can be received as often as necessary. The purposes of the anointing are to console the dying person, instill the patience to bear suffering, and prepare the soul to meet its Maker.

❧ QUESTION 60

Who were the 7 against Thebes?

Polynices
Adrastus
Capaneus
Tydeus
Parthenopaeus
Hippomedon
Amphiaraus

The twin sons of the incestuous King Oedipus and Queen Jocasta of Thebes, **Polynices** and Eteocles, agreed to share the crown in alternate years after their father's banishment. But when Eteocles refused to resign the kingship at the appointed time and expelled his brother, Polynices (polly-NICE-eez) raised an army with the help of his father-in-law, King **Adrastus** of Argos. Adrastus also enlisted five other captains who agreed to help place the exiled Polynices on the Theban throne. These chiefs became known in Greek myth as the Seven against Thebes. When they arrived at the city, each of the leaders stationed himself and his troops at one of its seven gates.

It was a smashing defeat for Greece's Magnificent Seven. **Capaneus** (CAP-uh-noose) boasted that he would scale the walls of Thebes in spite of Zeus, who promptly killed the blaspheming braggadocio with a lightning bolt. (His fierce hubris later earned him a place in Dante's *Inferno.)* King Adrastus's other son-in-law **Tydeus** (TIE-deuce; the father of Homer's Diomedes) was fatally wounded, but before dying he had the grim satisfaction of eating the brains of his killer Melanippus, who had been beheaded in the meantime. The goddess Athene was bringing a salve to cure Tydeus but was so disgusted by his savagely vengeful meal that she let him die.

Parthenopaeus (parth-en-oh-PEE-us) was the son of the Greek hero Meleager and the virgin huntress Atalanta, who had a fling after meeting at the famous Calydonian Boar Hunt, in which many mythic dignitaries came to Meleager's aid when a fierce boar was ravaging his kingdom of Calydon. Parthenopaeus, whose name means, according to Robert Graves, "son of a pierced maidenhead," was a handsome blond much loved by women and men alike, but he died at Thebes when a flung boulder smashed his proud head. And **Hippomedon** (hip-AH-mi-don), despite his huge stature, also found a bloody death beneath the walls of the besieged city.

To avert further bloodshed, the feuding brothers Polynices and Eteocles agreed to resolve the war by single combat—and proceeded to kill each other in a furious battle. King Adrastus's brother-in-law, the prophet and ex-Argonaut **Amphiaraus** (AM-fee-uh-RAY-us), foreseeing his own death at Thebes, had tried to dodge the draft, but his wife Eriphyle was bribed by Polynices with a magical necklace to persuade her doomed husband to join the expedition. As he fled in a chariot from his Theban foes, Amphiaraus was swallowed up in a chasm that Zeus mercifully opened up in his path. King Adrastus, the only one of the Seven to survive, was spirited away on his flying white horse Arion.

One of the seven extant plays of the Greek tragedian Aeschylus

(525–456 B.C.), *Seven against Thebes,* is a curiously static, undramatic treatment of the legend, first performed in 467 B.C. With its accompanying (now lost) tragedies of *Laius* and *Oedipus,* it won first prize that year at the Greater Dionysia, the Athenian spring festival at which plays were presented. Like his masterpiece, the three plays of the *Oresteia,* which deal with the curse on the House of Atreus through the three generations of Atreus, Agamemnon, and Orestes (see Question 14), Aeschylus's Theban trilogy explored the curse on the House of Thebes in the three generations of Laius (murdered by his son), Oedipus (an unwitting incestuous patricide), and Eteocles and Polynices (mutual murderers in fulfillment of Oedipus's curse on them for exiling him after his disgrace and self-blinding).

Seven against Thebes consists mainly of descriptions of the heraldic devices on the shields of the seven champions, of their impious boasts against Thebes, and of Eteocles' assignment of a Theban champion (including himself) to confront each of them. The play may have been in part a plea to strengthen the Acropolis of Athens against attack.

The tragedy closes with the dirge of a chorus of Theban women and of Antigone and Ismene over the corpses of their brothers Eteocles and Polynices. At the very end of the play, the Theban state decrees that Eteocles will be granted solemn burial with all honors, whereas the body of Polynices will be cast out unburied to glut the dogs and birds. This is too much for Antigone, who asserts that she will disobey the decree and bury her brother, traitor or not. Her defiance later provides the impetus for Sophocles' complex exploration of the relationship between the laws of the state and the rights of the individual conscience in *Antigone* (c. 442 B.C.).

In his epic poem, the *Thebaid,* the Latin poet Statius (c. A.D. 45–96) describes how, when Eteocles and Polynices are burned on the same funeral pyre, the flame enveloping their corpses rises double-crested at its peak—a final index of their undying mutual hatred.

There's a sequel, too. The sons of the Seven, called the Epigoni (the "after-born" or "successors"), had better luck against Thebes when they sacked it ten years later in a sort of copycat war. Our word *epigone* means a follower or inferior imitator, but usually of a thinker or creative artist rather than a warrior.

✿ QUESTION 61

What are the 7 Heavens of the Muslims made of—and who presides over each?

1. Pure silver: Adam and Eve
2. Pure gold: John the Baptist and Jesus
3. Pearl: Joseph
4. White gold: Enoch
5. Silver: Aaron
6. Ruby and garnet: Moses
7. Divine light: Abraham

"To be in seventh heaven" means to enjoy a bliss comparable to that of the beatific vision of God. Why seventh? Ancient Babylonian astrologers identified the five planets visible to the naked eye (Mercury, Venus, Mars, Jupiter, and Saturn) with five of their chief gods. These, with the gods of the sun and moon, were seen as inhabiting seven heavens. (The ancient Greeks and medieval Christians added several heavens more—see Question 76.)

The seven heavens of later Judaism were probably derived from Babylonian astrology. The Jewish seventh heaven, also called "the heaven of heavens," was farthest from earth and considered to be the abode of God and the loftiest angels. Islamic thought adopted this notion and filled in the details of what the various heavens were made of and which prophets and angels presided over each. Mohammed himself visited the seven heavens in his night journey *(miraj)*, briefly alluded to in the Koran and elaborated in the traditions of Mohammed's life *(hadith)*.

In the opening verses of sura 17 of the Koran, Allah tells of Mohammed's being transported from the Sacred Mosque (in this context, the Kaaba in Mecca; see Question 36) to the "Farthest Mosque" in one night. During this time he was shown "some of our signs" while being wafted through the seven heavens up to the very throne of Allah. The traditional explanation sees in the "Farthest Mosque" the holy site of Solomon's temple in Jerusalem, but some have taken it to mean the seventh heaven itself.

Mohammed's *miraj* ("ladder," later "ascent") is often thought to have taken place in the year before the hegira (622) from Mecca to Medina, though certain details argue for a time shortly after Mohammed's call as a prophet. Tradition describes how the angel Gabriel (Jibril) guided Mohammed upward through the various heavens. Some versions assert that a splendid ladder was used for the ascent, probably the one on which Jacob saw angels ascending to and descending from heaven in Genesis 28:12. In each of the seven heavens, Gabriel and Mohammed meet one of the prophets.

In **the first heaven of pure silver,** presided over by **Adam** (with **Eve),** the stars, each with its own angel, appear like lamps on chains of gold. **John the Baptist** (Yahya) and **Jesus** (Isa) are the wardens of **the second heaven of pure gold. The third heaven of pearl,** that of **Joseph** (Yusuf), is also the abode of Azrael (Izra'il), the angel of death who severs the soul from the body and writes in a book the names of all the newborn and erases those of the newly dead. **The fourth heaven of white gold** is that of **Enoch** (called Idris, "the learned") and of the enormous Angel of Tears, who never stops weeping for the uncountable sins of humans. **Aaron** (Harun) presides over **the fifth heaven of silver,** dwelling-place of the Avenging Angel. **Moses** (Musa), the prophet of **the sixth heaven of ruby and garnet,** admits that Mohammed is higher than he in Allah's esteem and has more followers. This is the abode of the Guardian Angel of heaven and earth, made of fire and snow. **Abraham** (Ibrahim) rules over **the seventh heaven of divine light** where, at the right hand of Allah, a lotus tree grows. The dwellers of this heaven are larger than the earth and have seventy thousand heads, each of which has seventy thousand faces, each of which has seventy thousand mouths, each of which seventy thousand tongues, each of which sings the praises of Allah in seventy thousand languages.

Mohammed also visits paradise and hell on his night journey. The Islamic paradise *(al-janna,* "the garden") was often thought to be in the seventh heaven, sometimes in the first. It is a paradise of carnal as well as spiritual delights, complete with fine clothes, rich gems, servants, and rivers of milk, honey, and wine. As his reward, each male Muslim will receive seventy-two houris, lovely virgins with bodies made of musk who never grow old. Some Muslim thinkers, however, consider these physical blisses to be mere allegories of the ineffable joy of beholding Allah face to face.

Did the *miraj* literature influence the cosmic journeys to hell, purgatory, and paradise of Dante's *Divine Comedy*? In about 1270, Latin and French translations were made of a *Book of the Ladder,* a now-lost work in Arabic dealing with Mohammed's night journey that had been translated into Castilian in about 1264. While Dante, born in 1265, may well have known one of these translations and borrowed some details from it, he already had precedents in Greco-Roman, biblical, and Christian traditions for just about everything he dealt with in his epic poem. Besides, he added three more heavens— that of the fixed stars, the crystalline sphere (or primum mobile), and the empyrean of God's immediate presence—to the seven heavens recognized by the Muslims.

✥ QUESTION 62

Who were the 7 Sages of Greece?

> Solon of Athens
> Pittacus of Mytilene
> Bias of Priene
> Cleobulus of Lindus
> Periander of Corinth
> Chilon of Sparta
> Thales of Miletus

Lore, history, and legend agree there were Seven Sages of Greece but differ on the exact roster. Plato's list in the *Protagoras* has been followed here, except that his Myson of Chen—about whom little is known—has been bumped by Periander, a colorful tyrant with a spectacularly awful personal life who was often considered one of the Seven.

Wait a second, you say. Who are these guys? Where are Socrates, Plato, Aristotle, and a host of others? They're not here because this group consists of seven men who all lived about 600 B.C., more than

150 years before Socrates flourished. Second, at the time their "wisdom" was celebrated, this word had more to do with mastery of the busy world of law and commerce than with contemplative profundity. The Sages were all eminent public personages in their time. Four of them—Pittacus, Cleobulus, Periander, and Chilon—were tyrants (legitimate rulers with far-reaching powers) or magistrates. Solon was an innovative lawgiver, Bias seems to have been a pleader of just causes, and Thales was a renowned scientist, philosopher, and mathematician.

The Seven were also refreshingly free of hubris. The story goes that some young men found a golden tripod in a catch of fish. They consulted Apollo's oracle, who said it should be given to "whoever is wisest." They gave it to Thales, who declined the honor. Each of the other Sages followed suit. When it finally came to Thales again, he declared that Apollo was wisest and sent the prize to the god's sanctuary at Delphi.

Another quality the Seven shared was a quick-witted penchant for shrewd one-liners that got repeated all over the Mediterranean. Plato observed that the style of the ancient Sages tended to be brief but pungent, in the laconic mode of the Spartans. As we listen to their quips and pithy wisdom, bear in mind that the Sages weren't Monday-morning quarterbacks or talk-show pundits. All, even the theoretical scientist Thales, were men of action. Some, like Solon, lived with a brilliance and vibrancy undimmed twenty-six hundred years after their time. Indeed, Solon didn't just endow his people with a new legal order, he also had the wit to survive the political turbulence his laws provoked.

"No great statesman has ever risen higher above the mere lust for power than Solon," wrote historian Werner Jaeger. It wasn't always easy, however, for **Solon of Athens** (c. 630–c. 560 B.C.) to steer clear of the fray: "I put myself on guard at every side, and turned among them like a wolf inside a pack of dogs." That's Solon in one of his few surviving poems, describing how he managed to avoid being murdered by either of the warring Athenian factions. He had failed to satisfy both the wealthy and the poor, who were threatening to destroy each other and Athens itself.

The Athenians had turned to Solon when the city was being torn apart by a political, economic, and social crisis. The rich owned most of the land, and the poor owed them money. When the poor had no more land to sell for paying their debts, and could produce no more food to bring to market, they sold themselves into slavery. Athens was on the brink of becoming a city of nothing but masters and slaves.

Solon owed his prestige to the often fickle goodwill of the people, who respected him for spurring the city to reconquer from the Megarians the nearby island of Salamis, Solon's birthplace. According to the ancient biographer Diogenes Laertius, the people sought to make Solon tyrant of Athens, but he refused, saying that tyranny was "a very fair spot, but it had no way down from it."

He also realized that, "acting where issues are great, it is hard to please all." His ultimate success was at least partly due to his mastery of double-talk. Plutarch credits him with inventing the political euphemism. For example, he called canceling the debts of the poor *seisachtheia*—a "relief" or "disencumbrance." Solon again relied on verbal legerdemain in attempting to appease the warring Athenian classes by telling them there could never be strife when things were "even." The wealthy thought he meant "in fair proportion," but the poor took him to mean "absolutely equal." Into a single word Solon packed two mutually incompatible political solutions: the promise of perpetuating hierarchic order and the commitment to eliminate class distinctions.

In the end, Solon freed people from monetary debt but did not redistribute land, as his poor supporters expected of him. His compromise set him smack in the middle of the pack of wolves, but eventually both factions went along with him.

Solon's laws defy facile categorization. For example, he ordained that

- A magistrate found intoxicated should be put to death
- Prostitution be legalized and taxed
- Anyone catching an adulterer in the act could kill him on the spot
- It was a crime to speak evil of the dead
- Dowries for women other than heiresses were banned because marriage was for love, not gain
- Women who went out were allowed no more than three articles of dress and no more than an obol's worth of food and drink.

Solon also introduced the use of wills to control inheritance. Before, everything had reverted to the family, but Solon prized friendship above family and affection above the arbitrary dictates of kinship. By making every man's estate truly his own, he broadened the individual's scope of choice, expanding the notion of individuality itself.

Solon gave Athens more than just a law code to replace that of Draco, whose draconian enactments prescribed the death penalty for most offenses. He gave the city a vision of the body politic as a whole that was dependent on the integrated functioning of all its members. All citizens had to be involved, if in nothing else, as jurors. The best city, he said, was one "where those not injured try and punish the unjust as much as those that are." For this reason, neutrals in a time of sedition were disenfranchised. Citizens no longer had the option to sit on the fence when the survival of their country was at stake.

Asked what made an orderly state, Solon replied, "When the people obey the rulers, and the rulers obey the laws." But Solon was always anchored in the all-too-human world of realpolitik. Unlike Minos, Hammurabi, and Numa, Solon made no claim that his laws were delivered to him by a god. He remained plainspoken to the end. Asked if he had given the Athenians the best laws he could give, Solon said, "The best they could receive."

When Solon finished hammering out his laws, he sailed from Athens, having demanded of the city a commitment to abide by them for ten years. He then traveled the world. A famous, and no doubt apocryphal, anecdote tells of his coming to the resplendent court of King Croesus of Lydia. As the Greek historian Herodotus tells the story, Croesus asked, "Who is the happiest man you have ever seen?"

Solon named an obscure Athenian who had had an honorable death. Croesus then inquired, "Who is the second happiest?" Solon named Cleobis and Biton, two brothers who died in their sleep in the prime of their youth just after drawing the cart of the goddess Hera. Croesus then angrily demanded, "What about me?" Noting that victory is not awarded to a wrestler still in the ring, Solon replied, "We call happy only a person to whom God has given happiness right up to the end."

His words proved prophetic years later, when Croesus had been crushed in battle by Cyrus the Great. As the Persian conqueror was preparing to burn him alive on a pyre, Croesus, in his anguish, called out Solon's name three times. Cyrus stopped the proceedings and, on hearing the story from Croesus and reflecting on how it could someday apply to himself, spared the broken King's life.

Solon's innate skepticism about the ephemeral perks of life allowed him to see through the vain pretense of politics. After he refused to become tyrant of Athens, the city came under the spell of Pisistratus, who feigned being wounded to drum up support for his tyranny. Solon called his bluff, saying, "This is a bad copy of Homer's Ulysses; you do to trick your countrymen, what he did to deceive his enemies." When the people put Pisistratus in charge, Solon wrote poems castigating them for their folly. For his part, Pisistratus courted Solon assiduously and retained many of his laws. This may or may not have had anything to do with the story that, long before, Solon had been Pisistratus's lover.

Though he refused the reins of power, Solon exerted an influence that outlived that of his contemporaries. The city whose laws he shaped has shaped Western culture more than any other. In a phrase whose terse audacity might have pleased Solon himself, Werner Jaeger calls him "the first Athenian." But Solon himself should have the last word, this time on successful aging: "As I grow old, I keep learning so many new things."

Like Solon, **Pittacus of Mytilene** (c. 650–570 B.C.) was a moderate democratic reformer. His bailiwick was Mytilene, the chief city of the island of Lesbos and home of the early Greek lyric poets Sappho and Alcaeus (see Question 79). Pittacus (PIT-uh-cus) was famed for his courage and morality. His most memorable law doubled the penalty for all offenses committed while under the influence. His sayings include the sad but true observation "Hard it is to be noble" and an early version of Horace's *carpe diem* advice: "Seize time by the forelock."

Plutarch relates how when Pittacus was entertaining some friends one evening, his wife burst in, furious about something. As he watched her overturn the dining table, Pittacus said, "No one's life is perfect. Anyone with only my troubles is very well off." Spoken like a true sage.

Little is remembered of **Bias of Priene** in Caria (fl. 570–550 B.C.). His main claim to fame seems to be how he answered a riddle. Asked which part of the sacrificial animal is best and which is worst, he cut out the tongue and sent it back as his answer to both questions. Someone else asked him which creature is the most formidable. "The tyrant is the most formidable wild creature," he replied, "and the flatterer is the domesticated creature most to be feared." A saying often attributed to him is "Most men are bad," along with the advice to live as if our life span will be both long and short. Another piece of sagacity reminds us that "the most unfortunate of men is he who has not learned how to bear misfortune." Bias also shrewdly observed that "power proves the man," and he seems to have coined an early form of the proverb "Too many cooks spoil the broth."

Another fairly obscure Sage was **Cleobulus of Lindus** on the island of Rhodes (fl. 580 B.C.). Besides being tyrant of Lindus, strong and handsome Cleobulus (clee-oh-BOO-liss) was a lyric poet and the man who foreshadowed Aristotle's golden mean and Horace's *aurea mediocritas* with his dictum "Moderation is best." He was also famed for his riddles, such as, "One father, twelve children, each of them with thirty children, partly black and partly white; and though immortal, they all die." The answer? "The year."

Periander of Corinth ruled his bustling city from about 625 to 585 B.C. in one of the longest dictatorships in the history of Greece. He was the Greek Citizen Kane—a titan of commerce who came to a tragic end.

Periander had no use for idleness in his subjects, focusing on a vigorous expansion of Corinth's economic base. His motto was "Forethought in all things." He built triremes, sailed the seas, established state coinage, and lowered taxes to promote industry. For a time, Periander's Corinth was the foremost city in Greece. But he wasn't just a Corinthian Bill Gates. He also undertook great public works, protected small business by limiting the number of slaves any one man could employ, and made the wealthy contribute to a gigantic golden statue. Yet this busiest of the Greeks also spoke for every true Mediterranean when he said, "What a beautiful thing leisure is!"

Periander's legend has a darker side. Herodotus tells of how he sent a messenger to Thrasybulus, master of Miletus, for advice on how to rule. Instead of offering precepts, Thrasybulus took Periander's messenger for a walk in a field, during which he lopped off the tallest ears of wheat and flung them away. When the messenger reported this to Periander, he at once took the meaning and went on a bloody, systematic purge of all the most powerful and prominent citizens of Corinth.

Periander is also said to have thrown his wife, Melissa, down a flight of stairs, killing her. After her death, he was unable to find something and sent envoys to the oracle of the dead to discover where he had mislaid it. The shade of Melissa rose up from Hades, refusing to answer the question and complaining she was forced to wander in the underworld naked and cold because her husband "had put his loaves in a cold oven." When he heard this, Periander knew his envoys were telling the truth because only Melissa knew that he had made love to her corpse.

Then, says Herodotus, Periander summoned the Corinthian women to what they believed was a festival and ordered them stripped of their clothing and jewels. As he burned their sumptuous silks in her honor, Periander prayed to his dead wife. Propitiated, she told him where to find what he was looking for.

Tragedy attended the relations of Periander with his son Lycophron. At a young age, when the boy learned his father had killed his mother, he refused to have any dealings with him. Periander drove him into exile, but when he was very old he sought to make peace with him and make him tyrant of Corinth. Lycophron steadfastly refused, saying he would never set foot in Corinth as long as Periander lived there. Finally, Periander offered to exchange places, making Lycophron tyrant of Corinth, while Periander himself would go into exile in Corcyra. But when the people of Corcyra learned of the plan, they put Lycophron to death, just to keep the dangerous old lion out of their country.

Herodotus called **Chilon of Sparta** (fl. c. 556 B.C.) the wisest of the Seven Sages, but little is remembered of him today. A Spartan magistrate (an ephor) and a philosopher, Chilon (KYE-lon) is credited with radically altering Spartan foreign policy, leading to the creation of the Peloponnesian League.

Chilon is known for several bits of wisdom, including "Look to the end" and "Speak no evil of the dead"—which accords with one of Solon's laws and anticipates the Roman admonition *de mortuis nil nisi bonum*. He also provides a Greek version of "Judge not, lest ye be judged," which goes, "Do not malign your neighbor if you do not want to hear distressing words in return."

Aristotle ascribed one of the two most famous Greek precepts to Chilon: *meden agan*—"nothing in excess"—a basic tenet of Aristotelian ethics. Diogenes Laertius, however, thought Solon first said it. The other fundamental tenet, "Know thyself," *gnothi sauton*, was variously attributed to Solon or Thales and was inscribed on the temple of Apollo at Delphi.

It should be clear by now that Wisdom in the sixth century B.C.

was not an ascetic clambering out of Plato's Cave to attain a vision of the timeless world of transcendental Forms. The wisdom of the time was a far more rough-and-tumble thing, often born in the heat of political action.

The seeming exception was **Thales of Miletus** (c. 624–c. 546 B.C.). Possibly of Semitic descent, Thales (THAY-leez) lived in Ionia, the west coast of what is now Turkey. He was the first of a triad of Milesian wise men (the others being Anaximander and Anaximenes) who attempted to explain the origin and composition of the universe in natural terms—the world's earliest known physicists. Plutarch made the point that Thales was different from the other Sages: "It is probable that, at that time, Thales alone had raised philosophy above mere practice into speculation; and the rest of the wise men were so-called from prudence in political concerns."

A famous anecdote about Thales offers a glimpse into how early Greeks tended to view this abstract speculation of his. When the venerable sage was taken out of doors by an old woman to observe the stars, he promptly fell into a ditch. To his cry for help, the woman responded, "How can you expect to know all about the heavens, Thales, when you can't even see what's right in front of your feet?"

Aristotle called Thales the founder of physical science, but the Ionian thinker's approach was more poetic and gnomic than systematic. Although none of his writings survive, what we know of his thought reveals a philosopher seeking the broadest truths. He was perhaps the first Western man to reduce the multiplicity of observed phenomena to a single principle.

For Thales, that principle was water, which he claimed was the origin of all things (see Question 20). In the nineteenth century, Nietzsche was still struggling with how this seemingly preposterous fancy gave rise to Greek philosophy. He concluded that "Everything is water" was actually a major step in thought for three reasons: "It enunciates something about the origin of things; it does so without figure and fable; and in it is contained, if only in chrysalis form, the idea that everything is one."

Among the Sages, Thales makes the perfect bookend to Solon. While the great Athenian enmeshed himself in the densest political thickets, producing laws of extraordinary specificity to foster individual freedom, Thales remained detached, seeking the broadest possible generalization to penetrate beneath appearances and suggest their underlying unity.

An anecdote illustrates some of the differences between Solon and Thales. Solon is urging Thales to marry, mustering all the usual arguments. One day, Thales pretends he's just learned that the Athenian's son has died. Solon collapses in grief, giving Thales his opening: Marriage binds us to the world, and thus to sorrow. Thales became a touchstone on the question of "to marry or not to marry." Montaigne, a married man, claimed Thales said it best: "When he was young and his mother urged him to marry, he answered that it was not yet time; and when advanced in years, that it was too late." Francis Bacon shortened that to "A young man, not yet; an old man, not at all."

Thales was far more than a nerdy ivory-tower intellectual. In his own day, he was celebrated as a multifaceted genius who astonished the Greeks with real-world achievements. As an engineer, he is said to have diverted the river Halys from its course so that an army could ford it. As a mathematician, he developed abstract geometry from his study of Egyptian land measurements. By measuring the length of a pyramid's shadow at a time of day when the length of a man's shadow was equal to his height, Thales was able to determine the height of the structure. As an astronomer, he predicted the year (though not the month or day) of the total solar eclipse of May 28, 585 B.C.

His versatility extended to the business world. Aristotle tells the story of how skeptics were tweaking Thales, alleging philosophy was useless because it had left him a poor man—saying, in effect, "If you're so smart, why aren't you rich?" But from his knowledge of the stars, Thales knew a bumper crop of olives was coming. He raised a little capital and put deposits on all the olive presses in Miletus and Chios. Anyone who needed them to make oil had to pay him a rental fee. By thus cornering the market, he made a killing, demonstrating that philosophers can become wealthy if they want, but that they have better things to do with their time.

Nowhere is Thales more inscrutable than when it comes to divinity. The statement that "All things are full of gods" was attributed to him. He was also reputed to maintain there was no difference between life and death. "Why, then, don't you kill yourself?" someone asked. "Because there's no difference," he replied.

However else he differed from the other Sages, Thales shared their gift for the memorable one-liner. Asked what was difficult, Thales responded, "To know oneself." What was easy? "To give advice." Why had he no children? "Because I loved children." Thales is even said to have written a song that elevates the Sages' terse style into a rule of life:

> *Many words do not declare an understanding heart.*
> *Seek one sole wisdom,*
> *Choose one sole good.*
> *Thus will you check the tongues of chatterers*
>   *prating without end.*

QUESTION 63

What are the 7 Deadly Sins?

Pride
Envy
Wrath
Sloth
Avarice
Gluttony
Lust

Pope St. Gregory the Great (reigned 590–604) distinguished these seven as capital or deadly sins. Much later, St. Thomas Aquinas (1225–74) called special attention to two of them in his *Summa Theologica:* **avarice,** or covetousness, and **pride,** or vainglory.

In elaborating on what St. Paul had said in 1 Timothy (6:10)—that the love of money is the root of all evil—Aquinas asserts that "by riches a man acquires the means of committing any sin whatever, and of sating his desire for any sin whatever, since money helps a man obtain all manner of temporal goods." It all begins with pride, though: "Now man's end in acquiring all temporal goods is that, through their means, he may have some distinctive perfection and excellence. . . . Pride, which is the desire to excel, is said to be the beginning of every sin."

For Aquinas, much of the meretricious danger of the seven deadly sins derives from their proximity to good, and he observes that many sins are committed in the pursuit of some laudable end. To strive for "excellence of honor and praise" is a fine goal, he seems to say, until sought inordinately by vainglory and expressed by boasting—when it becomes the deadly sin of pride. Similarly, avarice is an inordinate desire for satiety, and though the desire for meat and drink is natural, crossing the line to **gluttony** is sinful. Sexual intercourse preserves the species, but obsession with "the venereal pleasures" is **lust.** Both gluttony and lust aim at an overabundance of pleasure.

According to Aquinas, **sloth** is a spiritual laziness, the failure "to acquire spiritual goods because of the attendant labor." He cites an earlier theologian to the effect that sloth is an oppressive sorrow, a "sluggishness of the mind which neglects to begin good." It is evil because it "oppresses man so as to draw him away entirely from good deeds."

Of **envy** Gregory the Great says that the "self-inflicted pain wounds the pining spirit, which is racked by the prosperity of another." It was the serpent's envy of Adam and Eve in the Garden of Eden that brought sin and death into the world (Wisdom 2:24). Envy is the companion of sloth, claims Aquinas: "Sloth is grief for a Divine spiritual good, so envy is grief for our neighbor's good."

Compound envy with angry, self-righteous recrimination, and **wrath** is the result. What makes wrath so sinful, according to Aquinas, is the guise of good masking wicked intent: "The angry man desires another's evil under the aspect of just revenge."

Perhaps the most interesting aspect of Aquinas's understanding of the seven deadly sins is his observation that they are all derived from love. In his system, the soul experiences no passion that does not have its origin in some form of love, either praiseworthy or reprehensible.

Dante (1265–1321) relied heavily on this aspect of Aquinas's thought in his *Purgatorio.* He conceives of purgatory as a huge terraced mountain rising from the sea at the antipodes of Jerusalem. Souls being punished for the sinfulness they displayed during life must work their way up the seven terraces, each of which corresponds to one of the deadly sins.

Dante's guide Virgil echoes Aquinas—quite a trick for an ancient Roman born centuries earlier—when he explains that "love must be the seed in you of every virtue and of every action deserving punishment." Thus, each deadly sin in the *Purgatorio* is an example of love gone wrong. Misdirected egocentric love is exemplified by the most reprehensible of the deadly sins—pride, envy, and wrath. Sloth is defective love, a half-hearted effort to pursue good, plying "too slack an oar." Avarice, gluttony, and lust—the results of excessive love—are, in this scheme, the least blameworthy of the deadly sins. As Dante's sinners make their reparations, they climb to the top of the mountain, where the Garden of Eden is located, and from there ascend to Paradise.

Dante the literary character tells us a bit about Dante the poet in the *Purgatorio*. On three terraces, Dante joins the penitents in expiating his own sins, notably those of pride, wrath, and lust. On the last terrace, populated by the lustful, Virgil insists that Dante literally walk through fire for the sake of his beloved Beatrice.

A number of other medieval literary works deal with the seven deadly sins. *The Vision of Piers Plowman,* ascribed to William Langland, is a long allegorical English poem of the late fourteenth century containing a dream vision of the sins personified as contemporary types—Gluttony who, on his way to church, is tempted into a beer-house; Sloth as a priest who knows Robin Hood poems better than his prayers. And in the last and longest of Geoffrey Chaucer's *Canterbury Tales,* the virtuous Parson delivers a deadly prose sermon on penitence and the deadly sins, a tedious finale to a consummate masterpiece.

❧ QUESTION 64

What are the 7 Virtues?

> **Faith**
> **Hope**
> **Charity (Love)**
> **Justice**
> **Prudence**
> **Fortitude**
> **Temperance**

To combat the seven deadly sins (see Question 63), we must have recourse to the seven virtues. These are the three theological virtues of faith, hope, and charity (or love), grafted onto the four cardinal virtues of Plato—justice, prudence, fortitude, and temperance. The word *cardinal* comes from the Latin *cardo,* or hinge, and it is applied to Plato's four virtues because all moral development hinges on the possession of these qualities. The Church Fathers, steeped in the classics, couldn't resist appropriating these venerable virtues of the Greeks, but subordinated them to three new virtues of their creed.

Justice, the most important virtue for Plato (c. 429–347 B.C.), is the epic goal he sets his teacher Socrates questing for in the *Republic.* Plato believed that justice in a society results from everyone's working at the specific job for which he or she is most qualified and from the harmonious interplay among the other three cardinal virtues—each of which is crucial for one or more of the three classes of citizens in the ideal state. Thus, the prudence of the rulers, the fortitude of the warriors or soldiers, and the temperance (moderation of appetites) of the merchant and artisan class, as well as of the other two, maximize the chances that a society will be truly and fully just.

As described in Book 4 of the *Republic,* **prudence** (good counsel or wisdom) "resides in those Rulers whom we . . . call Guardians in the full sense." Plato differentiates the knowledge possessed by the ruling class from the knowledge of carpenters, farmers, and smiths. The particular knowledge of rulers—wisdom—is the defining characteristic of a specially trained and naturally qualified elite: "If a state is constituted on natural principles, the wisdom it possesses as a whole will be due to the knowledge residing in the smallest part, the one which takes the lead and governs the rest."

Plato compares the courage, or **fortitude,** instilled in the warriors to the immersion of white wool in permanent purple dye: "Their convictions about what ought to be feared and on all other subjects might be indelibly fixed, never to be washed out." During their indoctrination, says Plato, warriors should be taught that things that coarsen or debase are rightly feared and should be assiduously avoided. Suffering and death, on the other hand, confronted bravely, can ennoble the soul and help save the state and thus are not proper objects of fear.

Temperance is defined by Plato as the mastery of our better selves over the faculties inclined to indulge our pleasures and appetites. Intemperance, he says, is found "chiefly in children and women and slaves and in the base rabble of those who are free men only in name."

While Plato's cardinal virtues doubtlessly existed as pure Ideas or

Forms in some abstract world beyond the senses, their earthly counterparts were intended to guide human conduct in the here and now. In contrast, the Christian theological virtues redirect human aspirations to the metaphysical realm.

The best-known celebration of the three theological virtues, **faith, hope,** and **charity,** is found in St. Paul (1 Corinthians 13). The message is unambiguous: "If I speak in human and angelic tongues, but do not have love, I am a resounding gong or a clashing cymbal. . . . If I have all faith so as to move mountains, but do not have love, I am nothing. If I give away everything I own . . . but do not have love, I gain nothing. . . . So faith, hope, and love remain, these three; but the greatest of these is love."

St. Ambrose (339–397), Doctor of the Church and Bishop of Milan, was probably the first to incorporate the Platonic cardinal virtues into Christian thought. St. Augustine of Hippo (354–430), who was converted and baptized by Ambrose, continued the work of adapting the cardinal virtues to a Christian context in *The City of God.* Temperance—*sophrosyne* in Greek—is said to "bridle our fleshly lusts," and he cites St. Paul's war between the flesh and the spirit. Prudence, says Augustine, helps us recognize good and evil and make the correct choice between them. Justice refers to the proper hierarchical subordination of the soul to God, of the body to the soul, and of the body and soul together to God.

Augustine's explanation of fortitude, broadened from its original military focus, is the ultimate reality therapy and an odd kind of comfort. Doesn't fortitude's very function, he asks, "to bear patiently with misfortune," constitute "overwhelming evidence that human life is beset with unhappiness, however wise a man may be?" He sums up by relegating the cardinal virtues to their new subsidiary roles in the Christian schema: "No wisdom is true wisdom unless all that it decides with prudence, does with fortitude, disciplines with temperance, and distributes with justice is directed to that goal in which God is to be all in all in secure everlastingness and flawless peace." Indeed, the book of Proverbs, which is partly a paean to wisdom, proclaims that "the beginning of wisdom is the fear of the Lord."

St. Thomas Aquinas (1225–74), in his *Summa Theologica,* distinguishes the theological virtues—faith, hope, and charity—from the intellectual, or moral, virtues of Plato and of Aristotle's *Ethics.* The moral virtues pertain to our human nature, says Aquinas, and are useful for attaining human happiness by perfecting our intellect and will. They are accessible to pagans, too. In contrast, God alone infuses the theological virtues in us to perfect our souls—our supernatural selves—and to help us achieve supernatural happiness by directing us back to our source, himself.

In the *Paradiso,* Dante (1265–1321) must pass his "oral exams" on faith, hope, and charity before he can attain the Beatific Vision of God. His questioners are St. Peter on faith, St. James on hope, and St. John the Apostle on love. Why did Dante pick these examiners? The trio of Peter, James, and John were chosen by Jesus to be present at the Transfiguration and the Agony in the Garden and appear to be the leaders of the Twelve (see Question 91). Peter surely knew the pitfalls of lost faith. The first of the apostles to recognize Christ's divinity— "Thou art the Christ, the Son of the living God"—he then experienced a notorious lapse (and lack of fortitude) on the night of Jesus's arrest. James was the first apostle to be martyred, the ultimate exemplification of Christian hope in an afterlife of eternal rewards. And St. John was "the disciple whom Jesus loved." He is shown resting his head on Christ's shoulder in many depictions of the Last Supper and is also the apostle to whom Jesus entrusted his mother just before his death on the cross (see Question 69). Dante aces all three of his exams.

In about 1306, Giotto (1266?–1336) painted frescoes of the seven virtues and seven vices (see Question 63). These masterworks adorn the Arena (or Scrovegni) Chapel in the Church of the Annunziata at Padua. Giotto's patron, Enrico Scrovegni, was a Paduan moneylender whose usurious father had earned a humiliating role in Dante's *Inferno,* perhaps prompting Enrico to reach into his pockets and lavishly demonstrate his faith, hope, charity, and, most of all, prudence.

What are the 7 Ages of Man according to Shakespeare?

The infant
The whining schoolboy
The lover
The soldier
The justice
The lean and slippered Pantaloon
Second childishness and mere oblivion

The speaker is Jaques, melancholic social critic of Shakespeare's romantic comedy *As You Like It* (1599–1600), set mainly in the forest of Arden in France. Responding to the banished Duke's comment that "This wide and universal theater / Presents more woeful pageants than the scene / Wherein we play in," Jaques, a lord sharing the Duke's exile, sums up the pathetic lives of men in the play's best speech (II.vii.139–166):

> All the world's a stage,
> And all the men and women merely players.
> They have their exits and their entrances,
> And one man in his time plays many parts,
> His acts being seven ages. At first **the infant,**
> Mewling and puking in the nurse's arms.
> Then **the whining schoolboy,** with his satchel
> And shining morning face, creeping like snail
> Unwillingly to school. And then **the lover,**
> Sighing like furnace, with a woeful ballad
> Made to his mistress' eyebrow. Then **a soldier,**
> Full of strange oaths and bearded like the pard,
> Jealous in honor, sudden and quick in quarrel,
> Seeking the bubble reputation

> Even in the cannon's mouth. And then **the justice,**
> In fair round belly with good capon lined,
> With eyes severe and beard of formal cut,
> Full of wise saws and modern instances,
> And so he plays his part. The sixth age shifts
> Into **the lean and slippered Pantaloon**
> With spectacles on nose and pouch on side,
> His youthful hose, well saved, a world too wide
> For his shrunk shank, and his big manly voice,
> Turning again toward childish treble, pipes
> And whistles in his sound. Last scene of all,
> That ends this strange eventful history,
> Is **second childishness and mere oblivion,**
> Sans teeth, sans eyes, sans taste, sans everything.

This Shakespearean pessimism is counterbalanced elsewhere by the demoniacal power of his titanic heroes, the banter of his gentle clowns and wise fools, and, most of all, the floodlight beauty of his romantic heroines, the loving, long-suffering women who suffuse his stage with an incomparable humanity: "How far that little candle throws his beams!" observes Portia. "So shines a good deed in a naughty world."

As You Like It is a pastoral romance based on a novel by Thomas Lodge *(Rosalynde,* 1590). In the play, the usurping Duke Frederick has banished his elder brother, the rightful Duke, who has fled to the forest of Arden with some faithful followers. The exiled Duke's daughter Rosalind has been allowed to remain at court because she is the best friend of her cousin Celia, Duke Frederick's daughter.

Meanwhile, Orlando, the younger son of a man who had been an ardent supporter of the banished Duke, is being so mistreated by his elder brother Oliver that he decides to flee to the forest of Arden, but not before he and Rosalind fall in love. When Duke Frederick discovers Rosalind's interest in the son of his dead enemy, he banishes her, too. Celia and Touchstone, the court clown, flee with her—to the forest of Arden. Soon Frederick and Oliver also set out for the forest to finish off their enemies. After the requisite number of disguises, confusions of identity, and wooing scenes, the play's major reversals occur. Orlando saves the sleeping Oliver from a lioness, and the two brothers are reconciled. Duke Frederick, conveniently converted by an old hermit living in the forest, embraces the religious life and restores his brother to the dukedom. The world-weary Jaques announces his intention to join the reformed Frederick.

Four couples pair off at the end. Orlando wins his beloved Rosalind, having carved her name on innumerable trees and fastened countless lousy love poems on them. The new, improved Oliver marries Celia. The clown Touchstone ties the knot with the underwashed country wench Audrey. The shepherd Silvius finds nuptial bliss with the shepherdess Phebe.

Shakespeare introduces his creation of Jaques (two syllables: JAKE-iss, JACK-iss, or JAY-kweez) into his borrowed plot to deflate the excesses of romantic love and the pastoral pretensions of the banished Duke's entourage in the forest. The pastoral convention, harking back to Theocritus and Virgil, maintained that the simple ways of country folk were saner than those of their citified counterparts. (Recall the fable of the city mouse and the country mouse.) Jaques serves to remind the back-to-nature enthusiasts surrounding him, who believe that "sweet are the uses of adversity" and who find "books in the running brooks, / Sermons in stones, and good in everything," that the human condition—no matter where—is hopelessly flawed. His role is to mock the romanticization of rustic life and "the green world," which Shakespeare nonetheless presents as a corrective to the cruel, cynical, power-mad existence of urban courts.

True, Jaques is a rather absurd egoist, strutting around the forest in his affected melancholy and refusing to "adapt" (see Question 20). Rosalind ridicules him—and so does Shakespeare. Even his name may owe something to *jakes*, a coarse Elizabethan word for a privy. Yet, although the plot doesn't require him at all, Jaques remains an intriguing misanthrope who comments wryly on the goings-on around him, especially in his prolonged meditation on the banality of life and the silly parts it makes men play.

In comparing the world to a stage, Jaques makes use of a Renaissance commonplace with Hebrew, Greek, and Roman antecedents. Shakespeare's more immediate inspiration, however, may have been the motto of the new Globe Theater: *Totus mundus agit histrionem* ("All the world plays the actor"). The roles are played out in the seven ages the ancient Romans identified as infancy, childhood, adolescence, youth, manhood, old age, and decrepitude.

And so, in early life, men are helpless, whimpering, barfing burdens to their caregivers and whiny, reluctant schoolboys. Then they graduate to sighing over women and writing steamy love poems. Next they're swaggering, irascible soldiers, eager for fame though it may involve becoming cannon fodder. If they survive that stage, they settle down to paunchy, trim-bearded burgherhood, boring everyone with their proverbs and clichés. But soon they shrivel up into foolish old coots, wearing clothes that went out of style decades ago and speaking in the shrill tones of little boys again. Finally, they undergo total privation: a toothless second childhood and general system failure.

Shortly before his speech, Jaques overhears Touchstone say, "And so, from hour to hour, we ripe and ripe, / And then, from hour to hour, we rot and rot, / And thereby hangs a tale." Jaques hangs his tale of the seven ages on this theme and makes us wonder about the futility of it all.

❧ QUESTION 66

What were the 7 metals of alchemy and their associated gods and planets?

> Gold: Apollo, the sun
> Silver: Diana, the moon
> Quicksilver: Mercury
> Copper: Venus
> Iron: Mars
> Tin: Jupiter
> Lead: Saturn

> *The bodyes sevene eek, lo! hem heere anoon:*
> *Sol gold is, and Luna silver we threpe,*
> *Mars iren, Mercurie quyksilver we clepe,*
> *Saturnus leed, and Juppiter is tyn,*
> *And Venus coper, by my fader kyn!*
> —Geoffrey Chaucer, "The Canon's
> Yeoman's Tale"

The identification of the seven "planets" of medieval astronomy with the seven metals of alchemy has its roots in ancient pseudoscience and Roman mythology. The theoretical basis of alchemy was fairly consistent among the ancient civilizations that practiced it, including China, India, and Greece. It was believed that basic elements such as earth, water, air, and fire could be combined in various ways to create all material things (see Question 20). The goal of alchemy was the transmutation of base elements such as lead into precious ones like silver and gold. Alchemical beliefs usually merged with astrological ones, allowing medieval protoscientists to posit correspondences among the elements, metals, planets, and human temperaments.

The connection between **gold,** long regarded as the most precious of metals because of its beauty, durability, malleability, and purity, and **Apollo,** god of light, is relatively straightforward. Often called Phoebus ("brilliant" or "shining"), Apollo was perhaps the most revered of the Greco-Roman gods, as gold was the most cherished metal. Apollo, playing his golden lyre, was also identified with the **sun**'s disc and with Helios, the god who drove the chariot of the sun across the sky each day.

Lustrous **silver** was readily associated with the **moon**'s sheen and the Roman moon goddess, **Diana,** Apollo's twin sister (see Question 88). This was a tidy sibling arrangement, given their respective linkings with the sun and moon. Diana was also goddess of the hunt, driving her hounds to the chase from a silver chariot. The moon's inevitable associations with night, witchcraft, and magic led to the belief that those who fell under the influence of the moon—Luna in Latin—ended up as moonstruck lunatics.

The ancients believed the highly toxic metallic element **quicksilver,** or mercury, warded off evil spirits and had potent medicinal properties. It took its name from the mischievous, quick-witted god **Mercury,** heaven's speedy messenger who flew to his tasks with the aid of winged shoes. The Romans also named the planet closest to the sun, the fastest object they observed in the sky, after swift Mercury (see Question 80). Our word *mercurial,* meaning rapidly changeable or fickle, reflects the alchemical and astrological associations that accrued around the god, the planet, and the element, with its alternating liquid and solid states.

The alchemists associated **copper** with **Venus,** Roman goddess of love, because her sacred land was the island of Cyprus, Rome's source for this metal. The Romans called copper *aes Cyprium* ("metal of Cyprus") and then just *cuprum,* ancestor of our word. Venus was sometimes called "the Cyprian" because of her important shrine and cult at Paphos, on Cyprus. In its guise of the evening star (Hesperus or Vesper), the planet Venus is the brightest heavenly body, except for the sun and moon, and summons humans to love. Presumably, Venus herself was the first, but not last, to have a venereal disposition.

Iron was associated with **Mars,** god of war and protector of Rome, because of its use in weapons. The planet Mars was probably linked with the war god because of its reddish color. Wherever Mars walked on the battlefield, blood was said to ooze from the ground. People born under the influence of Mars are, of course, martial.

The association between **tin** and the god of gods, **Jupiter,** or Jove, remains obscure. Tin is a soft metal, most often used in alloys. Bronze, well known to the ancients, is an alloy of copper, Venus's metal, and tin. Perhaps the link between Jupiter and tin alludes to the god's predilection for changing himself into other beings—swans, eagles, bulls, and even mortal men—so as to escape his wife Hera's notice while he was busy seducing goddesses, nymphs, women, and handsome boys. It's easy to see why those lucky enough to be born under the sign of Jove are jovial.

The heavy metal **lead** was associated with **Saturn,** the slowest of the planets to wend its way across the heavens. Alchemists considered lead the oldest of metals and thus linked it with primeval Saturn, the dethroned old father of the chief god Jupiter. Those born under the influence of the planet Saturn are saturnine—gloomy and taciturn, true "heavies"—though Longfellow was obviously thinking only of gloomy and not of taciturn when he addressed Dante, author of the vast *Divine Comedy,* as "O poet saturnine." Even today, the term *saturnism* might be used by a pedantic, classically minded physician as a synonym for lead poisoning.

What were the 7 French dynasties?

Merovingian
Carolingian
Capetian
Valois
Bourbon
Bonapartist
Orléanist

In the beginning (58–51 B.C.), Julius Caesar conquered Gaul, which included the territory of modern-day France. The Romans ruled and Romanized Celtic Gaul for about five hundred years before it was overrun by Germanic barbarians—the Visigoths, Burgundians, and Franks. The Salian branch of the Franks was ruled by the Merovingians, who took their name from Merovech or Merowig, king of the Salian Franks (448–56; dates of rulers are of reigns).

The **Merovingian dynasty (481–751)** was inaugurated by the greatest of their kings, Clovis I (Ludwig, Louis; 481–511), the founder of the Frankish (French) monarchy. Clovis enlarged Merovech's domain enormously to contain all of northern and southwestern Gaul. This redoubtable barbarian seized Reims, had himself crowned there in 481, became a Christian with three thousand of his soldiers in 496, killed a slew of rival kings and relatives, and made Paris his capital. But his successors in the late-seventh and eighth centuries became "do-nothing kings" who were supplanted in everything but title by their Carolingian mayors of the palace (chief ministers), such as Pepin of Héristal and his son Charles Martel (see Question 97).

In 751, the last Merovingian king, Childeric III, was deposed by the son of Charles Martel, Pepin the Short (751–68). The **Carolin-**

gian dynasty (751–987) was thus formally established after many progenitors had served as de facto rulers. Pepin's son, the incomparable Charlemagne (768–814), became King of the Franks in 768 and was crowned Emperor of the reconstituted Western Roman Empire on Christmas Day of 800 by Pope Leo III in St. Peter's in Rome. Charlemagne's empire included France, Germany, northern Italy, part of northern Spain, and the Low Countries, and his main capital was at Aix-la-Chapelle (Aachen). Besides conquering, this Charles the Great, who tried hard but never learned to write, founded schools, attracted Europe's leading scholars and poets to his court, supported the arts, and presided over what has been called the Carolingian Renaissance. He was succeeded in 814 by Louis I the Pious, who ruled a united empire until 840. In 843, Louis's three sons divided the empire by the Treaty of Verdun. By 870, the Carolingian family had established separate French and German ruling lines.

The last Carolingian ruler of France, Louis V, died in 987. Hugh Capet (987–96) was offered the throne and became first king of the **Capetian dynasty (987–1328).** Although Dante claims Capet was the son of a Parisian butcher *(Purgatorio* 20.52), he was actually a descendant of the counts of Paris—and, in fact, ruled only a small kingdom around the city. The rest of France was in the possession of hundreds of feudal lords, big and small. Succeeding Capetian kings absorbed surrounding principalities and increased the power of the monarchy. Some noteworthy kings of this dynasty were Philip II, Louis IX, and Philip IV.

Philip II, called Philip Augustus (1180–1223), seized Normandy from England's pathetic King John in 1204 (see Question 74); received the submission of Maine, Anjou, and Touraine; flattened southern France in the "Albigensian Crusade"; and still found time to organize the University of Paris. Louis IX (1226–70), canonized as St. Louis in 1297, took over much of southern France for the crown (1229), was captured in Egypt by the Saracens in 1250 while on the Seventh Crusade, and died of the plague in Tunis while on another Crusade in 1270.

The ruthless Philip IV (1285–1314), called "the Fair," as in handsome, not as in fair play, took Gascony and Bordeaux from the English. In 1302, in a bid for popular support, he summoned the first Estates-General (legislative assembly), comprising members of the nobility, clergy, and bourgeoisie. Philip was termed "the new Pilate" by

Dante *(Purgatorio* 20.91) for his imprisonment and disgraceful treatment of Pope Boniface VIII. In 1305, Philip made the papacy a tool of the French monarchy, and in 1309 he instituted the so-called Babylonian Captivity of the Popes in Avignon, which lasted until 1376. The crowning achievement of his reign was his destruction of the Knights Templar, instigated by his desire to seize their immense riches and capped by his witnessing the burning at the stake of their grand master Jacques de Molay in 1313.

In 1328, Philip of Valois, grandson of an earlier Capetian King, became King of France as Philip VI, inaugurating the **Valois dynasty (1328–1589).** The first half of this dynasty's reign was plagued by the Hundred Years' War against the English (1337–1453). During the latter part of the war, in 1429, Joan of Arc helped France's irresolute Dauphin defeat his English enemies at Orléans (see Question 97) and finally get crowned at Reims as Charles VII (1422–61). The unification of France was achieved after the English were expelled from French territory (except Calais, which they held until 1558); Louis XI (1461–83) defeated Charles the Bold, Duke of Burgundy, and snatched his domains; and Charles VIII (1483–98) married Anne, Duchess of Brittany, thereby uniting her lands to the French crown.

The great Valois king Francis I (1515–47) conquered Milan in 1515 and then spent the rest of his reign waging wars against Charles I, the Habsburg King of Spain (also known after 1519 as Holy Roman Emperor Charles V). Francis found time to preside over the introduction of the Italian Renaissance into France with his patronage of artists like Leonardo da Vinci, Benvenuto Cellini, and Andrea del Sarto, and his building of Chambord and Fontainebleau. He also patronized homegrown wits like François Rabelais. Francis's son, Henry II (1547–59), the husband of Catherine de' Medici and lover of Diane de Poitiers, was killed in a jousting tournament. Henry's son, Francis II (1559–60), was briefly married to Mary, Queen of Scots, and died at age sixteen. Catherine persuaded her next son who succeeded as King, Charles IX (1560–74), to order the massacre of the French Protestant Huguenots on St. Bartholomew's Day, August 24, 1572. Catherine's third royal son, Henry III (1574–89), was stabbed to death by a Dominican monk in 1589 for having named a Protestant successor.

With the extinction of the Valois line in that year, the **Bourbon dynasty (1589–1792, 1814–30)** began with Henry of Navarre, a descendant of the French kings of the fourteenth century. This Henry IV (1589–1610), leader of the Huguenots, converted to Catholicism in 1593 to consolidate his precarious hold on the throne— "Paris is well worth a Mass," he supposedly said. Henry went on to antagonize his Catholic subjects by the Edict of Nantes (1598), guaranteeing religious freedom to the Protestants and ending the Wars of Religion, which had raged since 1562. After Henry's assassination in 1610 by the religious fanatic Francis Ravaillac, his second wife, Marie, another Medici, became Regent of France for seven years.

The absolutism of the Bourbon Kings asserted itself during the reign of Henry IV's son, Louis XIII (1610–43), who had the benefit of Cardinal Richelieu's Machiavellian statesmanship in suppressing revolts of the nobility and breaking the power of the Huguenots. Absolutist Richelieu also founded the absolutist French Academy in 1635.

Sicilian-born Cardinal Mazarin, who became chief minister after the death of Richelieu, guided the destinies of the young Louis XIV until 1661. Louis XIV, *Le Roi-Soleil* ("The Sun King") and *Le Grand Monarque,* reigned seventy-two years (1643–1715), longer than any monarch in European history. This King identified the state with himself *("L'État, c'est moi"),* revoked the Edict of Nantes in 1685 (thus exiling three hundred thousand of his most productive citizens, the French Protestants), fought four expansionist wars that prostrated his country's finances, built Versailles and made it the most magnificent (and extravagant) court of Europe, lavishly patronized all the arts in an age that produced the likes of Corneille, Racine, and Molière, and fornicated to his royal heart's content. He ruled so long he was succeeded by his great-grandson, Louis XV.

During Louis XV's reign of fifty-nine years (1715–74), this debauched King dallied with Madame de Pompadour, Madame du Barry, and a host of others; lost Louisiana to the Spanish, and Canada and possessions in India to the English; and further depleted the finances. Things got even worse during the reign of his grandson, the hapless Louis XVI.

A maladroit King who loved to tinker with locks, Louis XVI (1774–92) married Austrian archduchess and airhead extraordinaire, Marie Antoinette. He actively supported the colonists against the English in the American Revolution, but this only buried France deeper in its financial hole. On May 4, 1789, desperate for new taxes, Louis convoked the Estates-General for its first meeting since 1614—and by July 14 the royal prison of the Bastille was being stormed.

France and the morals of the royal court were bankrupt. The legitimacy of the ancien régime had been shaken by the antiabsolutist and anticlerical teachings of thinkers like Montesquieu, Voltaire, Diderot, d'Alembert, Rousseau, Baron d'Holbach, Condorcet, and scores of others. The wealthy but disfranchised bourgeoisie smoldered with resentment. The American Revolution had pointed the way. The result of this situation was the knock-your-head-off cocktail known as the French Revolution of 1789—a necessary evil that was a mishmash of idealism, sadism, hysteria, fanaticism, militarism, nationalism, propaganda, egalitarianism, science-worship, anarchy, purges, Robespierrism, and political theater that set the pattern for even more ghastly reenactments the world over, well into our times. Louis XVI and Marie Antoinette, guillotined in 1793, joined thousands who lost their heads for the sake of liberty, equality, and fraternity.

A French Republic was established in 1792, a Directory in 1795, and a Consulate in 1799. General Napoleon Bonaparte, famed for his Italian campaign of 1796–97, thought the time ripe for his seizure of absolute power as First Consul by his coup d'état of the 18th Brumaire of the Year VIII (as the French revolutionary calendar styled November 9, 1799). The attempt to found a **Bonapartist dynasty (1804–14, 1852–70)** began in earnest in May 1804 with Napoleon's crowning himself Emperor of the French. After spreading French law, civilization, and terror through most of Europe, and winning crushing victories like Austerlitz against the Austrians and Russians (1805) and Jena against the Prussians (1806), Napoleon's military machine got stuck in Spain and ruined in Russia (see Question 46). He abdicated on April 6, 1814. From his exile on the island of Elba, he returned to Paris on March 20, 1815, for his "Hundred Days" before his final defeat at Waterloo in Belgium on June 18 at the hands of the Duke of Wellington (see Question 97). This time "Boney," as the English called him, was exiled to the island of Saint Helena in the south Atlantic, where he died in 1821.

Napoleon had wanted the King of Rome, his infant son by his second wife, Marie Louise of Austria, to succeed him as Napoleon II, but this plan was thwarted by the Allies. Instead, they restored the Bourbon monarchy by trotting out Louis XVIII (1814–24), brother of the executed Louis XVI. (The son of Louis XVI and Marie Antoinette, "Louis XVII," never ruled and died at age ten.) Louis XVIII was fairly reactionary, but his brother, who succeeded him as Charles X (1824–30), wanted to roll back the clock to well before 1789 and was overthrown in the July Revolution of 1830.

The throne was now offered to the Duke of Orléans, a descendant of Louis XIII, who ruled as King Louis-Philippe, the "Citizen King" and the only **Orléanist monarch (1830–48).** Louis-Philippe, whose accession the wily politician Talleyrand supported "for want of a better and fear of a worse," was popular at the beginning of his reign. Nonetheless, economic instability, the growing power of the bourgeoisie, and Louis-Philippe's indifference to the people's clamor for universal manhood suffrage led to his overthrow in the February Revolution of 1848.

The Second Republic, established in 1848 with Napoleon's nephew, Louis Napoleon Bonaparte as president, gave way to Louis's coup d'état on December 2, 1851, and his establishment of the Second Empire, with himself as Emperor Napoleon III (1852). In comparing this Bonapartist coup with that of Napoleon I, Karl Marx commented that when history repeats itself, it does so as farce. Napoleon III sent military expeditions into Europe, Asia, and Africa, and vainly tried to obtain French control of Mexico via his puppet-emperor Maximilian. France's defeat in the Franco-Prussian War (1870–71) resulted in the loss of Alsace and Lorraine and in Napoleon III's being taken prisoner by the King of Prussia at Sedan. The Emperor was deposed in September 1870, and the Third Republic was established.

After the liberation of France from the Germans in World War II, the Fourth Republic was proclaimed (1946). This lasted until France's embroilment in a ghastly war with its Algerian colony led to the establishment of the Fifth Republic (1958–), with Charles de Gaulle as deviser of its constitution and first President.

What are the 7 voyages of Sinbad the Sailor?

1. To the Indian Ocean, where he and other crew members "go ashore" on a whale they suppose to be an island
2. To a desert island, where he sees a roc's egg, and then to the Valley of the Diamonds
3. To the land of a huge cannibal, who devours Sinbad's companions
4. To an island, where he marries a rich woman and is lowered into the Cavern of the Dead with her body after she dies
5. To a desert island, where he kills the Old Man of the Sea
6. To a rocky coast, where he sees the banks of a river glittering with precious stones
7. To an island in the China Sea, where he finds men who sprout wings and fly for one day each year

The story of Sinbad the Sailor is found in *The Arabian Nights (The Thousand and One Nights),* a large collection of stories originating mostly in Arabia, India, or Persia, and written in Arabic in the fourteenth to sixteenth centuries. The tales were introduced into Europe by the free translation (twelve volumes, 1704–17) of Antoine Galland, which was soon cast into other European languages. The best-known English translation is the unexpurgated version (fifteen volumes, 1885–86) by Sir Richard Burton. The specific tales making up the collection have been highly fluid throughout the centuries, however, and the closest approximation to a standard Arabic text was compiled only toward the end of the eighteenth century in Egypt, probably in Cairo.

The frame story, of Persian origin, tells how King Shahriyar becomes disgusted with female infidelity when he catches his Queen in the act. After putting his wife to death, he decides to marry a different virgin each night and kill her the next morning to make sure she can't cheat on him. After three years of this, when virgins are becoming extremely rare, the vizier, who is charged with procuring them, lets his daughter Shahrazad (Scheherazade) convince him that she knows how to get the better of the King. When the King marries her, Shahrazad keeps his interest piqued—and postpones her death—by telling him a long series of tales, making sure to leave him hanging by never providing the ending for any story on the same night she begins narrating it.

One of her series of tales concerns Sinbad (or Sindbad), a fictional merchant of Baghdad who went on seven marvelous sea voyages during the reign of Harun al-Rashid (caliph of Baghdad, 786–809). His adventures are probably based on tall tales brought back by Muslim seamen who traded with India, China, and the islands of the Far East in the eighth to tenth centuries. Another major influence seems to have been watered-down versions of Homer's *Odyssey* that had become part of Muslim legend. The adventures of Sinbad the Sailor, probably at first an independent work, are narrated on seven successive days by the protagonist himself to teach a poor man, Sinbad the Porter, that great wealth and fame like his are won "only after long toil, fearful ordeals, and dire peril."

First voyage. Sinbad, son of the chief merchant of Baghdad, dissipates his patrimony with riotous living like a true prodigal. Selling what remains, he buys some merchandise and decides to try his luck trading abroad. After taking a riverboat down the Tigris to Basra (as he does on all his voyages), he sets sail on the open sea in a merchant ship that puts in at numerous shores. Disembarking on a little island as lovely as the Garden of Eden, Sinbad and his companions light a fire for cooking and start exploring—when the captain screams to them from the ship that **the island they're on is really a whale!** The fire must have annoyed the leviathan, because it now submerges violently, leaving Sinbad clinging to a wooden tub while watching the ship and its crew hightail it out of there. He floats to a densely wooded island where huge mares are tethered to trees so that "sea horses" will come and mate with them and sire priceless colts and fillies. This is the native industry of the land of King Mahrajan, who soon promotes Sinbad to Comptroller of Shipping. In this capacity, Sinbad meets a sea captain who still has aboard his ship some merchandise belonging to a drowned merchant named Sinbad. After the recognition scene, a happy ending ensues when Sinbad sells his salvaged goods at a nice margin and sails home with his old mates.

Second voyage. Sinbad soon begins to experience wanderlust, so he buys some wares to trade with and sets out to sea again. After landing on an uninhabited island, Sinbad discovers on awakening from a nap that his ship has sailed off without him. While reconnoitering, he comes across a huge white dome, fifty paces in circumference, and sees an enormous bird flying above it. He realizes **the bird is a roc, which is known to feed its young on full-grown elephants, and the "dome" is the roc's egg!** Hoping to escape from the deserted island, Sinbad attaches himself to the roc by tying one end of his unwound turban to one of the bird's talons and the other around his waist. The roc flies off and soon deposits Sinbad in a valley strewn with diamonds but surrounded by insurmountably steep cliffs. When Sinbad notices a skinned sheep carcass come tumbling down the mountainside, he remembers a story about the Valley of the Diamonds and how men would fling sheep carcasses into it so that the diamonds at the bottom would stick to their soft flesh. When rocs and huge vultures swooped down on the meat to bring it to their nests, the men waiting above would make a great ruckus to frighten off the birds and make them drop the diamond-studded sheep. After unwinding his trusty turban, Sinbad uses it to tie himself to the sheep carcass—but not before having crammed his pockets with a fortune in diamonds. Sure enough, a vulture takes the bait, gets Sinbad out of the valley, and is shooed away by the diamond merchants, who eventually take the newly wealthy Sinbad home.

Third voyage. Sinbad gets bored at home again. This time, his ship is attacked by dwarf apes with gleaming yellow eyes who set him and his companions ashore on an island and make off with the ship. The stranded men enter a vast building, where soon **they see a giant come in, who proceeds to kill the three fattest men on successive nights and roast them on a spit for his supper!** This story sounds a lot like the encounter of Odysseus and his men with the cannibalistic Cyclops, except that this giant has two eyes. A curious detail is that the men are not trapped inside but actually leave the monster's "palace" for a while to build a raft for their escape. After returning to exact their vengeance, they wait until the monster falls asleep (he's not drunk on wine in this version) and then put out his eyes with the red-hot spits he's been using to barbecue their companions. As they push off on the raft, the monster and a fellow monstress hurl rocks at them, scoring direct hits on all but two of them and Sinbad, who manage to arrive at another island. There Sinbad's remaining companions are swallowed whole by a largish serpent. Next day he is rescued by the ship whose crew had inadvertently abandoned him on Roc Island on his second voyage. Since his merchandise is still on board, he trades with it, grows rich, and returns to Baghdad.

Fourth voyage. This man never learns. After setting out to sea again, Sinbad's ship is destroyed by a storm. He and some others manage to reach an island where naked savages bring them to their king. When they're offered food, Sinbad's buddies eat ravenously, but he abstains, revolted by the food's appearance. Good thing. The other men can't stop eating: Soon they're transmogrified into hoggish beasts devoid of reason that are taken out to pasture and then fed on by the King (who roasts his captives) and his followers (who prefer their meat carpaccio). Escaping from this nasty locale—which bears a resemblance to the island in the *Odyssey* where Circe changes Odysseus' men into swine—Sinbad meets some decent folk who take him to a neighboring island. There he teaches the King and all the other honchos the use of saddles for their horses, thus becoming the richest man of them all. The King is so fond of Sinbad that he wishes him to marry a beautiful young noblewoman, though Sinbad is homesick and sorely misses his first wife. (This is somewhat reminiscent of Odysseus' desperate longing for Ithaca and his wife Penelope after spending seven years as Calypso's kept man.) But when his new wife dies, Sinbad must adhere to a strict custom of the country—equal-rights suttee. **After his wife's body is thrown into a deep burial pit, Sinbad is lowered into it by a rope and provisioned with only seven loaves of bread and a pitcher of water!** But, like Odysseus, Sinbad is resourceful, a man "of many twists and turns," so when a widow is lowered down with her food and water, he bashes in her skull with the leg-bone of a skeleton and appropriates them. He does the same to other widowed unfortunates and survives for many weeks. One day he sees a wild beast in the cavern that has been attracted by the stench of carrion and tunneled through the rocky wall of the pit. Easing his way through the tunnel—after cramming his pockets with food and the jewels and pearls that have been buried with the corpses—Sinbad makes his way to a seashore, from which he is soon rescued by a ship, etc.

Fifth voyage. Was Sinbad sick and tired of all these scrapes with death? Why, he was just warming up. This time, he ends up on a deserted island, where he sees the telltale white dome that signalizes a roc's egg. Much to his horror, his companions amuse themselves by smashing the shell with rocks, dragging out the roc chick, and cooking it up. When they set out to sea, vengeful parent birds follow the ship with boulders in their talons and bomb it to pieces. Sinbad alone escapes by floating to an island on a piece of wreckage. (This episode is similar to the gods' destruction of Odysseus' ship by a lightning storm after his men have eaten the sacred oxen of the Sun.) On the island is a decrepit old man sitting by a brook who asks Sinbad to ferry him across by bearing him on his shoulders. Once in the saddle, this Old Man of the Sea (the epithet of Proteus in the *Odyssey)* refuses to dismount and torments Sinbad by clasping him about the neck and chest with his surprisingly strong legs. After many weeks of schlepping the Old Man around and doing his bidding, Sinbad manages to make some wine in a gourd and get him drunk (like Odysseus with the Cyclops). **When the monster plops to the ground, Sinbad smashes his skull to pieces with a stone, becoming the first victim of the Old Man of the Sea to escape with his life!** After being rescued by a ship, Sinbad comes to the City of the Apes. There he earns his passage money home in the following way. Like the residents, he fills up a sack with pebbles and slings it over his shoulder. Proceeding to a coconut grove far from the city, where the towering trees are impossible to climb, the men pelt the monkeys in the treetops with their pebbles. In retaliation, the monkeys bombard them with coconuts, which the crafty men gather and bring to market. On his way home to Baghdad, Sinbad trades the coconuts for spices and then pays some divers to fetch him up a fortune in pearls.

Sixth voyage. Déjà vu all over again. Sinbad's ship breaks up on a rocky coast in a fierce gale, but he manages to clamber ashore. There he finds a river that flows into a mountain gorge. **Unlike other rivers, this one's banks are covered with rubies, emeralds, and pearls!** Sinbad decides to follow the river's course into the gorge, hoping its outlet is frequented by ships. The rocky shore is also supplied with rare Chinese aloes and ambergris, so he builds a raft and piles it high with these commodities—and many sacks of jewels, too. On reemerging from the gorge, he is kindly received by some Indians and Abyssinians. They take him to their King, who makes him a trusted courtier and wants to send a magnificent gift to Harun al-

Rashid. Sinbad accordingly sails back home to Baghdad and obtains an audience with the famed caliph. Harun orders that Sinbad's adventure be inscribed on parchment in letters of gold for the edification of posterity.

Seventh voyage. Though past the prime of life, Sinbad still hasn't seen enough of the world and its ways. He sails to the China Sea, where a tempest rages near the Realm of Kings, burial place of Solomon. A whale much bigger than Moby-Dick swallows their ship, but Sinbad dives off just in time and escapes to an island. He builds a raft and sails it down a river toward the interior, where he is saved from flying off a precipice by a group of men who trap his raft in their net. A venerable old man takes him to the city and regales him with food, drink, a bath, and servants. Imagine Sinbad's surprise when, at an auction, his raft garners him eleven hundred pieces of gold—it was made of rare sandalwood, it turns out—and the buyer is the old man himself. Sinbad's generous friend wants him to marry his beautiful young daughter—his sole heir—and become in time chief merchant of the city. Sinbad joyfully accedes to the old man's wish, and he and his bride live together happily. He soon discovers, however, that **the men of this land grow wings once a year and fly around for a whole day!** Sinbad begs a friend to take him along, so on the appointed day he grabs hold of the man's waist and soars upward with him. They fly so high that Sinbad hears the angels singing hymns to Allah. He can't resist shouting out his praises, too. At that, his friend plummets from the sky and leaves Sinbad on a mountaintop, calling down curses on him as he flies away. After Sinbad meets what seem to be two angels—one of whom gives him his golden staff and points him on his way—he bumps into his winged friend who, no longer angry, explains that the mention of Allah's name always has this depressing effect on his countrymen's flying abilities. Sinbad's wife later explains that their fellow citizens—all except her deceased father—are brothers of Satan. (Now she tells him!) After selling their houses and goods, they flee to Baghdad, where Sinbad, who has been away twenty-seven years on this voyage, vows to stay put. Sinbad the Porter, who has been treated to all these inspiring tales, becomes a bosom friend of wise old Sinbad the Sailor.

After 1,001 nights of storytelling, including the tales of Aladdin and the Enchanted Lamp (did you know Aladdin was Chinese?) and Ali Baba and the Forty Thieves, Shahrazad reveals to the King the three sons she has borne him in the meantime and begs for her life for their sake. But the King has already fallen in love because he has found her to be "chaste and tender, wise and eloquent." The irresistible magic that Shahrazad weaves with her words is an apt emblem of the narrator's art.

❧ QUESTION 69

What are the 7 Last Words of Christ?

> "Father, forgive them; for they know not what they do."
> "Verily I say unto thee, Today shalt thou be with me in paradise."
> "Woman, behold thy son!" and "Behold thy mother!"
> "Eloi, Eloi, lama sabachthani?" ("My God, my God, why hast thou forsaken me?")
> "I thirst."
> "It is finished."
> "Father, into thy hands I commend my spirit."

The New Testament records that Jesus spoke seven times while he was dying on the cross. These utterances, culled from the Gospel accounts of the Crucifixion, have been formally ordered into a sequence known as the Seven Last Words, partly as an attempt to harmonize the internal chronology of the Passion narratives. Still used in liturgical worship during the commemoration of Christ's death on Good Friday, the Seven Last Words have also inspired numerous musical arrangements, including those of Franz Joseph Haydn and the nineteenth-century Italian composer Saverio Mercadante.

"Father, forgive them; for they know not what they do" (Luke 23:34). Theologians have interpreted this verse—which does not appear in the most ancient manuscripts—to mean that Jesus may have sought to protect his tormentors from God's wrath as he was being nailed to the cross at Golgotha (the "Place of the Skull," Latinized as Calvary). Forgiveness is emphasized throughout the New Testament. In the Sermon on the Mount, Jesus instructed his hearers to

254

"love your enemies, and pray for those who persecute you" (Matthew 5:44).

But whom does Jesus ask God to forgive—the Roman soldiers who crucified him? the Jewish Sanhedrin? the mob that demanded his crucifixion? lily-livered Pontius Pilate? Certainly not Judas, who knew exactly what he was doing. In any event, Christ's plea for forgiveness specifically cites the lack of knowledge of those who sought his death—the implication being they did not know he was the Messiah and were thus unaware of the enormity of their crime. Indeed, in the following verses, the leaders of the people sneer at Christ, saying "let him save himself if he is the chosen one, the Messiah of God." Luke records that "even the soldiers jeered at him."

"Verily I say unto thee, Today shalt thou be with me in paradise" (Luke 23:43). Forgiveness also figures in the second utterance from the cross, directed at the Good Thief (whom later legend named Dysmas), one of two criminals crucified on either side of Christ. When the unrepentant criminal reviles Jesus as a false Messiah unable to save himself and his two companions in agony, the other rebukes him and says to Christ, "Lord, remember me when thou comest into thy kingdom." Jesus responds to this remarkable display of faith by promising him eternal salvation, despite his deeds. In contrast, shortly before this exchange, Peter, leader of the Apostles and recently designated by Jesus as head of the nascent Church, had denied his association with him three times (see Question 91).

"Woman, behold thy son!" and **"Behold thy mother!" (John 19:26–27).** On the face of it, Jesus merely exercised his duty as a good Hebrew son in attending to the future well-being of his widowed mother by these utterances directed respectively at Mary and "the disciple whom he loved," apparently the Apostle John. Yet the term of address Christ used while establishing a family bond between the two, "woman," seems oddly distanced.

The Church Fathers later allegorized this exchange, reported only in John's Gospel, by contrasting the first woman, Eve ("the mother of all the living" whose disobedience toward the divine plan in Eden resulted in sin, death, and the need for Christ's redemptive mission), with Mary, the perfect woman, the mother of the Savior who remained fully obedient to God's plan from the moment she replied to the angel Gabriel's annunciation, "Behold the handmaid of the Lord; be it done unto me according to thy word" (Luke 1:38). Mary, the second Eve, was thus seen as having borne the new Adam, the perfect man. Together, they repaired the cosmic damage wrought by their predecessors. Thus the Church Fathers.

But on several occasions in the Gospels themselves, Christ emphasizes the importance of his God-appointed mission over the need to defer to Mary and other family members. At age twelve, when he accompanied his mother and his foster father, St. Joseph, to Jerusalem to observe Passover, he stayed behind after their departure in order to converse with some doctors of the Law in the Temple (Luke 2:41–52). After Mary and Joseph, who both thought he was with the caravan, became aware he was missing, they rushed back to the city, full of grief and anxiety. When they found him, Mary asked why he had done this to them and told him how much they had worried. "Why were you looking for me?" he replied. "Did you not know that I must be about my Father's work" (or "in my Father's house")?

In his first miracle, when he turned water into wine at the wedding at Cana, Jesus had been asked to perform the deed by Mary as a kindness to the celebrants (John 2:1–11). "They have no wine," she says to her son when the supply is running short. He answers sharply, "Woman, how does your concern affect me? My hour has not yet come." Again the word *woman* and the reference to a higher calling. Yet he accedes to his mother's will.

In Luke 8:19–21, when told his mother and brothers are waiting to see him but can't approach because of the crowd, Christ replies, "My mother and my brothers are those who hear the word of God and act on it."

"Eloi, Eloi, lama sabachthani?" ("My God, my God, why hast thou forsaken me?") (Mark 15:34). When Christ uttered these words (recorded by Mark in Aramaic, the spoken language of the Jews after their Babylonian exile), nature itself was said to be shrouded in gloom as the result of a three-hour eclipse of the sun. Some onlookers mistakenly thought Jesus was calling on the prophet Elijah, whom many Jews believed would return to earth just before the coming of the Messiah. In Matthew's version (27:46), the Hebrew for God, "Eli," is substituted, as being closer to Elijah's name.

In this lament, Christ was echoing Psalm 22, which begins with this cry of sad confusion over God's abandonment of a faithful servant. Some have questioned whether Christ succumbed to despair when he accused the Father of forsaking him. This would, of course, strike at the heart of Christian belief in Jesus as both God and man (see Question 7).

Psalm 22, however, begins with the suffering of a just man but goes on to assert that God "has not scorned the downtrodden, nor shrunk in loathing from his plight, nor hidden his face from him, but gave heed to him when he cried out." According to Christian thought, the human and divine natures of Jesus each had come to the fore during his agony in the Garden of Gethsemane. Before going off to pray, he tells Peter, James, and John, "My soul is sorrowful even to death." He then prays, "My Father, if it is possible, let this cup [his imminent death on the cross] pass from me." Immediately afterward, however, he adds, "yet, not as I will, but as you will" (Matthew 26:36–46).

"I thirst" (John 19:28). Later used as an affirmation of Christ's humanity against attacks from Docetists (heretics who denied he was truly man), these words also illustrate the fortitude of Jesus, who suffered hours of torture before expressing a physical need. A sponge soaked in sour wine (or vinegar) is raised to his lips, and he drinks before he dies. Once again, Psalm 22 (verse 16) figures in the background of this detail: "My throat is dried up like baked clay, my tongue cleaves to my jaws," as well as Psalm 69 (verse 21): "They . . . gave me vinegar when I was thirsty."

"It is finished" (John 19:30). These are Christ's words immediately after he drinks. The original Greek, the single word *tetelestai,* is related to the noun *telos* ("goal, end, purpose") and has given us our word *teleology.* Christ is not actually saying his *life* is finished (though it is) but that his mission of redemption—of dying for man's sins to effect his atonement with God—has been *accomplished.*

"Father, into thy hands I commend my spirit" (Luke 23:46). Christ again alludes to the Psalms in his final utterance as recorded by Luke. This time it is Psalm 31 (verses 4–5): "Pull me out of the net they have spread for me, for you are my refuge; into your hands I commit my spirit." Luke's Greek term translated as "spirit" is *pneuma,* "the breath of life, the soul," which Jesus here redirects to the divine fount of all life.

According to Christian belief, Christ rose from the dead on the third day, Easter Sunday, and then ascended into heaven, body and soul, after spending forty days with his followers, giving them their final instructions (Matthew 28:19–20): "Go, therefore, make disciples of all the nations . . . and teach them to observe all the commands I gave you. And know that I am with you always; yes, to the end of time."

What are the components of the Noble Eightfold Path of Buddhism?

> Right views
> Right intentions
> Right speech
> Right conduct
> Right livelihood
> Right effort
> Right mindfulness
> Right concentration

The last of the Four Noble Truths of Buddhism (see Question 26) promises a way of escape from the endless cycle of birth, suffering, death, and rebirth. This is the Noble Eightfold Path, the quintessential Buddhist guide for living. Those who follow this path assiduously achieve nirvana, the cessation of all selfish desire and thus of suffering. The ultimate goal is *maha-parinirvana*, "great total extinction," which for Buddhists is hitting the jackpot and for most Westerners is more terrifying than death itself.

How can humans empty themselves of desire? Darwinians and Nietzscheans would claim this is a contradiction in terms. Buddhists contend that desire results from misunderstanding the nature of the universe and of what is called the self or soul *(atman)* in Hinduism, the parent religion of Buddhism. Everything that seems to be is actually in a state of becoming; nothing is stable or simple in its essence, everything is impermanent and composite, subject to decay. Even the self is a delusion: We are shifting, momentary conjunctions of various substances, perceptions, memories, emotions. This self that does not have a unitary existence, which is actually a "no-self" *(anatman),* then makes the mistake of desiring other things that are no less evanescent and "unreal." The worst form of desire is sexual, since it results in bringing more suffering creatures into the cycle of reincarnation.

Along with the Four Noble Truths, Buddha revealed the Noble Eightfold Path to his five original disciples in his first sermon after attaining Enlightenment under the bo tree. The Eightfold Path divests the individual of selfish desire by its influence in three areas of human life: morality, mental discipline, and wisdom. Morality or ethics *(sila)* includes right speech, conduct, and livelihood. **Right speech** is that which avoids lies, gossip, backbiting, and verbal abuse. **Right conduct** involves following the "Five Moral Rules," which forbid killing any living thing (the law of *ahimsa),* stealing, making false statements, drinking intoxicating beverages, and indulging in unchaste behavior. **Right livelihood** means refusing to earn a living by improper means, such as murdering for hire or hoodwinking people with astrology or fortune-telling. It also enjoins the virtues of compassion (a great moral imperative in Buddhism), friendliness to all, joy in the joy of others, forgiveness of enemies, and serenity.

Mental discipline or training *(samadhi)* comprises **right effort, right mindfulness,** and **right concentration.** These require the practice of yoga, a system of mystic meditation adopted from Hinduism. By concentrating the mind on a single stable point or subject, yoga induces varying stages of trance or self-hypnosis that free the mind from the distractions of the external world and habituate it to exist without desiring the world's specious pleasures.

Wisdom *(prajna)* or intuitive insight results from right views and intentions. **Right views** imply an understanding of the Four Noble Truths, the impermanence of all things, and the doctrine of karma. **Right intentions** are crucial because the law of karma is based on the intention or motive governing deeds and not necessarily on the deeds themselves. Depending on the goodness or evil of intentions in their current life, people can be reborn as gods, humans, animals, hungry ghosts, or hell-dwellers. Of course, the ultimate goal is the total shedding of any attachment to desire and life, so that karma ceases to be generated and the Wheel of Rebirth *(samsara)* is permanently broken. This state of nirvana can occur on earth, though the individual who has attained it still lives on (like the Buddha after his Enlightenment), or it can mark the final extinction of the illusory self (as at the Buddha's death).

But if the self or soul is an illusion, what gets reborn in *samsara?* This is a weak spot in Buddhist metaphysics. Just as the ancient Greek philosopher Heraclitus said that one could never step into the same river twice because its waters are always flowing, so Buddhists claim that although the reborn soul partakes in a continuity of sorts, it is not the selfsame identical soul as before. Think of it as the flame of a candle that has been lit from that of another candle. In fact, only those who have attained Enlightenment can even remember any of their thousands of previous existences.

Strict adherence to the Noble Eightfold Path implies a rigorous discipline incompatible with the demands of everyday family life. Members of the *sangha,* the Buddhist monastic order, have always had a much better shot at it.

❧ QUESTION 71

Who were the American artists known as The Eight?

> Robert Henri
> John Sloan
> George Luks
> William Glackens
> Everett Shinn
> Ernest Lawson
> Arthur B. Davies
> Maurice Prendergast

The Eight, also called the New York Realists, represent an important turning point in American painting. True, they had only one group exhibition, in 1908, and their styles varied considerably, but their joint legacy was a forthright, unmistakable, heterogeneous representation of the American scene at the turn of the twentieth century.

Several of The Eight had worked extensively as newspaper illustrators in the years before photography dominated that industry, and this background had a pronounced influence on the subjects and techniques of their paintings. For years, Robert Henri, the leader of The Eight, was closely associated with John Sloan, William Glackens, George Luks, and Everett Shinn, and together they were known as

The Philadelphia Five. When Maurice Prendergast, Ernest Lawson, and Arthur B. Davies joined the group later in New York City, they became The Eight.

The slices of urban life served up by The Eight are reminiscent of works by painters as diverse as Frans Hals, Diego Velázquez, Francisco de Goya, James McNeill Whistler, Édouard Manet, and Edgar Degas. The homey charm, lack of vulgarity, and general avoidance of in-your-face sociopolitical statements tend to downplay the grittiness of the hard-boiled bar and tenement scenes of The Eight. These qualities also cast doubt on the validity of some epithets applied to them—the Apostles of Ugliness and, in 1934, years after their apogee, the Ashcan School (which was applied to a broader group that included George Bellows, Edward Hopper, and many others).

By the end of the nineteenth century, the Gilded Age had spawned a multitude of highly decorative, often allusive academic landscape paintings by artists unlikely ever to reemerge into prominence, primarily the members of the Society of American Artists and the National Academy. The glory days of the painters of the Hudson River School were over. Many of the most eminent American painters—including Whistler and Mary Cassatt—had moved to Europe. Winslow Homer lived in seclusion in Maine. Only Thomas Eakins remained in the spotlight, painting and teaching in Philadelphia at the Pennsylvania Academy of the Fine Arts, where he also served as director. There, he shook up the art establishment by painting surgery scenes and especially by insisting that his students learn to paint realistic human figures by sketching nude models.

Eakins's disputes with school officials led to his resignation in 1886, just as twenty-one-year-old **Robert Henri** (HEN-rye) (1865–1929) was about to enroll. Henri was born Robert Henry Cozad in Cincinnati, Ohio. When he was eight years old, his family moved to Nebraska, where his father founded the town of Cozad. After several violent confrontations with other homesteaders and cattlemen, his family was forced to flee the state and assume false identities. Hence the artist's name.

After Henri entered the Academy, he became the pupil of one of Eakins's students, Thomas Anshutz. Two years later, he traveled to Paris to study at l'Académie Julian—a disappointing experience and a step backward, since students were sheltered from what the faculty considered the baneful effects of the Impressionists. But Henri wandered in the city's Luxembourg Museum, which housed the works of many contemporary artists, and fell under the spell of Manet. He returned to Philadelphia in 1891 and, after another stint in Paris, settled in New York and started teaching at the Chase School and then the Art Students League. The philosophy he imparted to his students, which he set down in *The Art Spirit,* aimed at attaining through painting "a more than ordinary moment of existence." This state, he claimed, was the norm for children, whom he often painted.

In 1899, Henri scored a signal triumph when the government of France acquired his painting *La Neige (The Snow)* for the permanent collection of the Luxembourg, where he had been so inspired a decade earlier. Rivers were a favorite subject of Henri's, and he painted marvelous grayish scenes of the East River in New York City and the Seine and Marne in France. He was best known, though, for his full-length portraits of women that evoked comparison with those of Whistler and John Singer Sargent, including *Young Woman in Black* (1902) and *Jesseca Penn in Black* (1908). Henri's legacy as a painter is overshadowed, however, by his practical contributions as driving force of The Eight. *The Art Spirit,* first published in 1923 and widely disseminated, is still in print.

John Sloan (1871–1951), probably the most talented of The Eight, first met Robert Henri in 1892, shortly after the latter had returned from his first sojourn in Paris. Sloan, who was on the art staff of the *Philadelphia Inquirer,* was studying at the Pennsylvania Academy of Fine Arts with Henri's former teacher, Anshutz, along with future Eight member William Glackens. The dissatisfaction of Sloan and many fellow students with life at the Academy led to the growth of a Tuesday-night discussion group at Henri's studio. Sloan eventually followed Henri to New York City.

Like Henri, Sloan often imparted a dark, monochromatic cast to his canvases, but unlike his facile friend, Sloan was a methodical painter. Henri once said in frustration that "Sloan" must be the past participle of "Slow." Because of his shyness, Sloan hated to paint outdoors. Instead, with a journalist's eye for everyday detail that he had acquired in the news business, he roamed around New York in search of street scenes, which, with some help from sketch pad and pencil, he returned to his studio to paint.

Partly because of his sloanness, he sold his first painting at age forty-two. In 1928, Sloan made his first major sale of thirty-two paintings for $41,000. Among his noted works are *Wake of the Ferry* (1907), the spectral *Clown Making Up* (c. 1909), *Pigeons* (1910), *Sun-*

day, Women Drying Their Hair (1912), *McSorley's Bar* (1912), *Six O'Clock* (1912), and *Sun and Wind on the Roof* (c. 1915), which features a woman hanging up the wash on the roof of a tenement. (The pigeons and the women drying their hair are on roofs, too.) Sloan captured off-the-cuff moments in an intimate mode while managing to transcend their quotidian blahness and avoid voyeurism. He continued to give painting lessons and provide illustrations for magazines such as *Harper's Weekly* and *Collier's* until he was old. Only in his seventies was this great American master able to support himself by painting.

George Luks (LUKES) (1867–1933) studied at the Pennsylvania Academy of Fine Arts and then in Germany, England, and Paris before returning to a career as a newspaper illustrator for the *Philadelphia Press* in 1894. Two years later, the *Philadelphia Evening Bulletin* sent him to Cuba to cover the insurrection there and eventually published twenty-nine of his Cuban drawings to great acclaim. This was a noteworthy achievement, since Luks spent nearly all his time in various bars in Havana. He apparently did his drawings after listening to real reporters tell their frontline stories.

Finally, when even these seat-of-the-pants drawings stopped arriving in Philadelphia, Luks was fired. He then settled in New York, where he joined the staff of Joseph Pulitzer's newspaper, the *New York World*. One of his assignments was to draw a cartoon character called "The Yellow Kid," a direct competitor of a nearly identical character in the rival William Randolph Hearst newspaper, the *New York Herald*. The sensationalism purveyed by these papers thus eventually became known as "yellow journalism." In 1897, two other future members of The Eight, William Glackens and Everett Shinn, joined Luks on the art staff of the *World,* and the three illustrators also painted with Henri.

Luks's paintings include *The Spielers* (1905), a sentimentalized treatment of two little girls dancing together; *The Little Madonna* (1905); and the starkly posed and grotesquely foreshortened *The Wrestlers* (1905–7), his most famous work. Although Luks was often considered a jolly buffoon, a different side of him emerged in his sensitive portrayals of street people and breadlines, and he once told his students that a slum child was a fitter subject than a society matron. However, *The Sand Artist* (1905), which portrays such a child, makes us long for society matrons.

Despite a fair amount of sloppy, poorly conceived paintings,

Luks is sometimes compared with Frans Hals (1580–1666), the great Dutch comic realist of Haarlem, and he did achieve considerable public recognition during his lifetime. He sold a painting to Gertrude Vanderbilt Whitney, an early booster of The Eight who later founded the Whitney Museum of American Art in New York City, and he was awarded the William A. Clark Prize by the Corcoran Gallery in Washington, D.C.

William Glackens (1870–1938), another product of the Pennsylvania Academy, worked as an illustrator for several newspapers and magazines in Philadelphia. He was a high school friend of Sloan's and shared a studio with Henri, with whom he also traveled in France. Glackens's career was jeopardized when the editor of *McClure's Magazine* complained that his drawings were too original. Then, when the battleship *Maine* exploded in Havana Harbor, the same publication decided it needed his talents in Cuba to cover the Spanish-American War (see Question 83). Unlike Luks a few years before, Glackens risked his life at battles such as San Juan Hill to obtain material for his drawings. His most famous paintings include *Central Park—Winter* (1905), which captures the cozy human warmth of an evening landscape peopled with adults and children enjoying the snow; *Chez Mouquin* (1905), an uptown version of Degas' *Absinthe Drinkers;* and *The Boxing Match, July 4, 1906.*

Everett Shinn (1876–1953) paid the bills by working as an illustrator for Philadelphia newspapers and painted on the side. Although he espoused the Realism favored by The Eight, Shinn developed a yen for glitzy Manhattan life on moving to New York. A well-known color drawing of his, *A Winter's Night on Broadway,* depicts prosperous Gothamites scurrying into and out of hansom cabs on a snowy evening in front of the old Metropolitan Opera House. Shinn drew it overnight on demand, and it became the center spread for the *Harper's Weekly* of February 17, 1900.

That career high was immediately followed by an embarrassing low. *The Critic* soon commissioned Shinn to do a pastel drawing of Mark Twain for the magazine's inside cover. Working from photographs, he produced a fine likeness of Twain's head but perched it on top of an impossibly elongated body. Only when Shinn saw the published work before embarking for Paris did he realize the extent of his blunder. Sailing back to the United States a year later, he found himself on the same liner as Twain and spent most of the voyage assiduously avoiding him. Unfortunately, the editor of *The Critic* insisted that Shinn apologize to Twain at his Manhattan home. The great author graciously defused the situation, even agreeing to have Shinn try again, this time from life. Other works by Shinn include *Window Shopping* (1903) and *Mouquin's* (1904), a subject also painted by Glackens because it was a favorite New York restaurant of the group.

The remainder of The Eight were more or less shoehorned into the movement, since Lawson, Davies, and Prendergast had styles quite at odds with those of the other five. What they shared was a desire to buck America's provincial artistic taste.

Ernest Lawson (1873–1939), a soft-spoken man who favored river scenes, joined The Eight in New York. Influenced mainly by the Impressionists, he had been hailed as a world-class landscape painter, and it now seems ironic that he often worked in Manhattan's Washington Heights, then a rural, sparsely populated area on the banks of the Harlem River. There he produced works such as *Winter on the River* (1907) and *Spring Night, Harlem River* (1913). People made only cameo appearances in his canvases.

Arthur B. Davies (1862–1928), a native of Utica, New York, started his career painting romantic, often allegorical landscapes that usually included mythological creatures and refined nudes. He also had a personal mission to bring European art to the American public, and his detestation of American artistic backwardness apparently drew him to The Eight. Working with Sloan, Davies arranged for a two-week exhibition at New York's Macbeth Gallery in February 1908 that featured the work of The Eight. Most of the critics were severe, but the ensuing publicity was a great boost for attendance. Seven paintings were sold—four of them to Gertrude Vanderbilt Whitney—for a total of $4,000. The show subsequently moved to Philadelphia and eight other cities.

Maurice Prendergast (1859–1924) was a Canadian-born Bostonian who admired Winslow Homer and later studied in Paris, where he was influenced by the works of the Pointillists, the Postimpressionists (especially Paul Cézanne), and Whistler. Unlike other members of The Eight, Prendergast at first worked primarily in watercolors, and he is still regarded as one of the finest American artists in that medium. After 1904, though, much of his work was in oils. Significant paintings include *Revere Beach* (1896) and *May Day, Central Park* (1901). Like Davies, Prendergast was by no means an urban Realist, and his association with The Eight was a fluke. He met the group at the suggestion of the owner of the Macbeth Gallery, who apparently wanted to include Prendergast's works in the 1908 exhibition organized by Davies.

In 1913, Davies also was the chief organizer of the epochal Armory Show at the 69th Regiment Armory in New York City. Originally conceived as a showcase for American artists, the exhibit of about sixteen hundred items also featured more than five hundred European works, including paintings by the likes of Manet, Monet, Gauguin, Picasso, Matisse, and Marcel Duchamp. The fierce originality of the Europeans tended either to enrage or mesmerize the three hundred thousand spectators who flocked to the show in New York, Chicago, and Boston. Everyday Americans had discovered modern European art, American artists were enthralled—and the heyday of The Eight was over.

The leader of New York's Photo-Secessionists, photographer Alfred Stieglitz (1864–1946), judged The Eight to be "tame, prosaic, and conventional—phony modernists." In light of the revolutionary works emanating from the Cubists, Fauves, Expressionists, Futurists, Vorticists, and others, Stieglitz probably had a point. Even the social conscience of The Eight was often filtered through Manet's comforting (and outworn) Impressionism. Yet, when we look at their lamplit wintry night scenes, or Central Park vistas, or rush-hour streets beneath mammoth elevated trains, we're seduced by their magical (rather than raw) realism, their delicate, melancholy colors, and their city people going about their city lives. We're stirred emotionally, if not intellectually or spiritually.

✳ QUESTION 72

What are the 8 Beatitudes?

> Blessed are the poor in spirit: for theirs is the kingdom of heaven.
> Blessed are they that mourn: for they shall be comforted.
> Blessed are the meek: for they shall inherit the earth.
> Blessed are they which do hunger and thirst after righteousness: for they shall be filled.

Blessed are the merciful: for they shall obtain mercy.

Blessed are the pure in heart: for they shall see God.

Blessed are the peacemakers: for they shall be called the children of God.

Blessed are they which are persecuted for righteousness' sake: for theirs is the kingdom of heaven.

Jesus addresses the crowds with these words in the Sermon on the Mount in the Gospel of Matthew (5:3–10). Some have called the Beatitudes the charter of Christianity, which sets forth the essential characteristics of those who will attain salvation. Since Matthew, who wrote one of the two Gospel versions of the Beatitudes, is addressing Jewish Christians, he attempts to draw a parallel between Christ and Moses (see Question 32). He thus sets the scene on a mountain to remind his readers of God's giving the Ten Commandments (see Question 82) to Moses on Mount Sinai (according to the account in Exodus) or Mount Horeb (according to the account in Deuteronomy).

Although readers were to understand that Christ was presenting them with a new set of precepts, Christ himself insists that he came to fulfill and broaden, not abolish, the Mosaic law. In any event, the literary device of the beatitude is fairly common in the Old Testament: The first Psalm begins, "Blessed is the man that walketh not in the counsel of the ungodly."

Luke's version of the Beatitudes (6:20–23) includes only four blessings:

+ Blessed are you who are poor, for the kingdom of God is yours.
+ Blessed are you who are now hungry, for you will be satisfied.
+ Blessed are you who are now weeping, for you will laugh.
+ Blessed are you when people hate you, and when they exclude you and insult you, and denounce your name as evil on account of the Son of Man.

These are followed by four corresponding woes:

+ But woe to you who are rich, for you have received your consolation.
+ But woe to you who are filled now, for you will be hungry.

- ✦ Woe to you who laugh now, for you will grieve and weep.
- ✦ Woe to you when all speak well of you, for their ancestors treated the false prophets this way.

This version, part of what is known as the Sermon on the Plain, is addressed to the disciples only, not the multitudes. Some biblical scholars consider Luke's Sermon on the Plain the ordination sermon for the twelve Apostles (see Question 91), since Christ had just selected them from the larger group of disciples.

Note that in Matthew's text the emphasis is on the self-effacement, victimization, and benevolence of those who are blessed. Half of the Beatitudes promise purely spiritual rewards, while the rest set their more tangible consolations in an indeterminate future. Luke's version, nuanced somewhat differently, addresses itself to the poor and hungry (rather than "the poor in spirit" and those who "hunger . . . after righteousness"), while inveighing against the well-fed, self-satisfied burghers of the day.

Matthew's Beatitudes are part of the larger framework of Christ's reevaluation of acts of piety as practiced by the Pharisees—almsgiving, prayer, and fasting. In the Sermon on the Mount, Christ exhorts his disciples to perform these acts unobtrusively so that only God is aware of them. He contrasts this with the behavior of "the hypocrites," whose pious deeds are meant to elicit public admiration—the only benefit, Christ says, that they will receive, since "they have their reward already."

But the Beatitudes have failed to provide solace to many of "the wretched of the earth," and the values they embody have even been subjected to derision. The German philosopher Friedrich Nietzsche (1844–1900)—who in *The Antichrist* cast himself in the title role and claimed that the only character in the entire New Testament worthy of respect was Pontius Pilate—believed that Christian virtues such as meekness, mercifulness, and peacemaking constituted a "slave morality," the antithesis and subversion of the noble, heroic, proud, and warlike aristocratic code of ancient Rome. In his view, the Christian ethic was nothing more than a clever, resentful ploy to make the strong feel guilty about their ruthless superiority. As a consequence, natural leaders strove to become more like the helpless weak, who had everything to gain from the newly found altruism of their masters.

Who were the 9 great gods of ancient Egypt (The Great Ennead)?

Atum	Osiris
Shu	Isis
Tefnut	Seth
Geb	Nephthys
Nut	

An ennead is a Greek-derived word for a collection of nine things—in this case, gods. The ancient Egyptians used nine to indicate a great number (like the Hebrew forty), since it is the product of three (the number of plurality) multiplied by itself. They thus tended to group their gods in enneads to indicate "the totality" of their deities (more than two thousand!). The Great Ennead, the grouping of nine that arose in Heliopolis during the First Dynasty (c. 3000 B.C.), was the principal one and by no means confined to that locality alone.

In the cosmogony of Annu, the Egyptian city that the Greeks called Heliopolis ("City of the Sun"), **Atum** was the primeval earth hill, the creator of the world who rose from the waters of the god Nun ("the primordial ocean"). After lonely Atum masturbated and swallowed his own seed—an act sometimes attributed to the god Khepera—he gave rise to the god of air, **Shu,** and his twin, **Tefnut,** the goddess of moisture. These coupled and brought forth **Geb** or Seb (male, "earth") and **Nut** (female, "sky").

The goddess Nut was depicted in art as a naked woman arched across the heavens over her husband, the earth. Her fingertips and toes rested on Geb at the four cardinal points, and her torso was bordered with stars. Nut swallowed the sun each night and gave birth to it again in the morning. Because she was identified with the cosmic cow of the sky, she was sometimes represented as one. The coupling of earth and sky resulted in the birth of Osiris and Seth (males) and Isis and Nephthys (females), who paired off as married couples.

Osiris, or Ausar ("many-eyed"), the best loved of the gods and Lord of the Dead in the underworld, was identified at first with the deceased King but later with all dead Egyptians, who were referred to as "Osiris So-and-So," much as we would say "the late Mr. Jones." Osiris was a god of vegetation and agriculture who caused the fertilizing Nile to overflow each year. Although he died each winter, he was resurrected as the new crop in the following year. As such, he was one of the august company of Mediterranean "corn gods" including Tammuz, Adonis, Attis, Dionysus, Zagreus, and the goddess Persephone. Osiris was depicted as a green mummified man wearing a crown and wielding the scepter and scourge of kingship. In a related aspect of Osiris (his procreative forces), his embodiment was the sacred Goat of Mendes in the Nile delta, a beast that was allowed to indulge in ritual copulation with the most exceptionally beautiful women of the region.

In the underworld, an enthroned Osiris presided over the ceremony of the Weighing of the Heart of every dead Egyptian. Anubis, the jackal-headed god, balanced in a huge set of scales the heart (deeds) of the deceased against an ostrich feather of Maat, goddess of justice and truth. Then Thoth, the god of the moon, wisdom, and writing, usually portrayed as an ibis-headed man or a baboon, meticulously recorded the verdict. If the heart of the dead person counterbalanced Maat's feather, all was well for that soul for all eternity.

When the insane Persian King Cambyses conquered Egypt (525 B.C.), he scornfully killed the holy black bull at Memphis that represented the god Apis, a major manifestation of Osiris. Nonetheless, the cult of Isis and Osiris lived on for many centuries, not only in later Alexandrian Egypt but also in Greece and the Roman Empire until Christianity ousted it.

Isis, or Auset ("throne"), wife and sister of Osiris and mother of Horus, is often portrayed as a woman with the hieroglyph for *throne* on her head. In later Egyptian art, she merges with Hathor, or Hetheru, the goddess of love, beauty, music, and the dance, whose name means "house of Horus." Both the wet nurse and the wife of Horus, Hathor was identified by the Greeks with Aphrodite.

The Greek writer Plutarch offers a somewhat garbled version of the most important Egyptian myth in his essay "On Isis and Osiris." Here is his story as modified by other Greek and Egyptian sources.

Osiris was a wise king of Egypt who, while traveling abroad, left the state in the hands of his sister-wife Isis. His younger brother Seth fell in love with Isis and decided to make himself king. After Osiris's return, Seth and seventy-two other conspirators invited him to a banquet at which a magnificent chest was offered to whichever guest fitted in it most closely. The conspirators were all too short for it, but the chest turned out to be just right for Osiris. Suddenly the conspirators clapped the lid on the chest, nailed it down, and soldered it with lead. After they flung it into the Nile, it drifted out into the Mediterranean, landing at Byblos on the Phoenician coast (north of modern Beirut). The chest came to rest against a tamarisk tree, which gradually incorporated it into itself.

The King of Byblos had the splendid tree cut down and used for a pillar in his palace, but Isis persuaded him to surrender it to her. Once back in Egypt, she managed to get herself pregnant by the dead Osiris; the child she bore was named Horus.

Evil Seth soon discovered Osiris's corpse, which he dismembered into fourteen pieces and scattered all over Egypt. Isis recovered all of them except the penis, which had been eaten by the fish of the Nile. She made an image of that and, with the help of Nephthys, Horus, and Thoth, instructed Anubis in how to reassemble and mummify Osiris's body. Osiris revived and became the ruler of the dead in the underworld. He was thus the first mummy, and each subsequent mummified Egyptian hoped to share in his resurrection and eternal life. The Mysteries of Osiris were the greatest of all Egyptian festivals, including an eight-act drama on his life, death, mummification, and resurrection.

Meanwhile Horus had grown up, and he fought a battle with his uncle Seth that lasted many days, during which Horus lost an eye and Seth his testicles. When the earth god Geb was asked to arbitrate, he decided that Horus should succeed his father Osiris as king of both Upper (southern) and Lower (northern) Egypt, a union which took place historically in about 3200 B.C. under King Menes.

Horus was originally a falcon sun god and chief god of Lower Egypt who became identified with the Egyptian king at the very beginning of the First Dynasty. In later myth, he merged with another Horus, the son of Isis and Osiris who avenged the latter's murder. He thus became identified with the living Egyptian King, whereas the dead King became Osiris and ruled the underworld.

Horus, usually portrayed as a falcon or falcon-headed man and representing the rising sun, was identified with Apollo by the Greeks. He was also often pictured in Egyptian art as a child being suckled by Isis or held in her lap, uncannily prefiguring medieval Christian representations of the Madonna and Child. This domesticated version of Horus presented quite a contrast with jackal-headed Anubis, ibis-headed Thoth, ram-headed Khnum, crocodile-headed Sobek, the cat-headed goddess Bast, and, in the words of the Roman poet Juvenal, all the other "monsters adored by demented Egypt."

Seth or Set was the god of storms, darkness, war, confusion, and the sterile desert beyond the Nile valley. He was originally a god of Upper Egypt, and his struggle with Horus may have been based on an actual invasion of Upper by Lower Egypt in about 4245 B.C. Seth was sometimes represented as a man with a big-eared head resembling that of a donkey.

Nephthys, or Nebt-het ("lady of the house," that is, the house of Osiris), was the sister of Isis, Osiris, and Seth, and wife of the last, although she always supported Isis and Osiris against murderous Seth and helped restore Osiris to life. Plutarch claims she gave birth to Anubis by Osiris, though Egyptian texts state Anubis was the son of Ra, the god of the sun at noontime.

✣ QUESTION 74

What were the 9 royal houses of England after 1066?

Normandy	Stuart
Plantagenet	Hanover
Lancaster	Saxe-Coburg-Gotha
York	Windsor
Tudor	

A millennium ago, England was a Scandinavian outpost. Invaders from Denmark succeeded in collecting Danegeld—tribute money—from the Anglo-Saxon King Ethelred the Unready, and the Danes Canute, Harold I Harefoot, and Hardecanute actually became Kings of England. Although the Anglo-Saxon line was restored in 1042 in the weak person of Edward the Confessor, son of Ethelred, England might once again have succumbed to Viking attacks, but for Edward's Norman connection.

In 1051, the childless Edward named as his successor his second cousin, William the Bastard, Duke of Normandy, probably to gain Norman support in his quarrel with his formidable father-in-law, Earl Godwin, and the Earl's son, Harold Godwinson. By the time Edward died, however, he had reconciled with his brother-in-law Harold and apparently designated him his successor when on his deathbed in January 1066. The English Witan (council) confirmed Edward's choice as King Harold II.

Undeterred, William of Normandy crossed the English Channel on September 27, 1066, with five thousand knights while Harold was in the North deflecting an attack by the King of Norway, Harold Hardrada, yet another claimant to the throne. The English and Norman armies finally clashed on October 14 at the Battle of Hastings, in Sussex, where Harold was killed by a bowshot in the eye—as immortalized in the Bayeux Tapestry—and the English troops scattered (see Question 97). William then swept into London and was crowned king in Westminster Abbey on Christmas Day but spent the next several years quashing revolts in his new domain.

This first king of the royal house of **Normandy,** William the Conqueror (1066–87; dates of rulers are of reigns), was leader of the Normans (originally Viking "Norsemen"), who had settled in northern France in the tenth century and gradually become Christianized, feudalized, and semicivilized. They were prodigious conquerors and adventurers, eventually ruling or colonizing southern Italy, Sicily, Wales, Scotland, Ireland, and even Antioch, in addition to England.

The Norman conquest of England divorced the country from further Scandinavian influence and locked it into a closer, if fractious, relationship with France. The Normans codified a system of military feudalism by which, in return for providing William with knights, his nobles received fiefdoms. The native Anglo-Saxon aristocracy was stripped of its land and replaced by one that spoke Norman French. Similarly, as English prelates died, Norman churchmen were appointed to replace them. In 1086, William compiled the Domesday (DOOMZ-day) Book, a catalogue of all revenue sources for his barons and other landowners, who compared the visits from the King's commissioners to Judgment Day. This census of lands and assets remains an invaluable source for historians.

In true Norman style, William was a great adapter and imitator, and he maintained much of the structure of the Anglo-Saxon legal system and the modus operandi of local governments. A major change was his decision to remove ecclesiastical cases from the civil courts. The Normans were also magnificent builders, as the cathedrals of Durham and Winchester still attest, and they also constructed many splendid castles in England, which allowed them to sleep more soundly in the realm they had filched.

William I was injured in 1087 while sacking the town of Mantes in France, dying from the wound a couple of months later. He had grown so fat—like a pregnant woman, said the French King—that his corpse burst in two when attendants at a church in Caen tried to shoehorn it into a stone sarcophagus, filling the church with its stench.

The throne passed to the Conqueror's son, William II Rufus ("ruddy") (1087–1100). He taxed and plundered the Church, was ostentatiously undevout and blasphemous, persecuted St. Anselm, Archbishop of Canterbury (who likened him to a wild bull), and filled his court with harlots and pathics. William never married and was thought to be bisexual or homosexual. He was accidentally shot dead—perhaps murdered—with an arrow unleashed while he hunted with his retinue in the New Forest.

The third Norman King, the Conqueror's youngest son, Henry I Beauclerc ("good scholar") (1100–35), married a sister of the King of Scotland to keep the North friendly while he dealt with the invasion of his elder brother, Robert, Duke of Normandy, in the south. Although the ecclesiastical and legal business of the realm was conducted in Latin and Norman French, multicultural Henry decided to learn English, too. He was forced to recognize that the monarchy was a secular office, not a sacred one, and that he had no authority to invest bishops or expect them to form feudal bonds with him. This issue of so-called lay investiture had already been fought out on the continent when the Holy Roman Emperor Henry IV had been subjected to his famous penance in the snows at Canossa by Pope Gregory VII in 1077.

Henry I's reign was for the most part peaceful and orderly, although he did have to subdue his brother Robert's rebellious Normandy. Henry's sons, William and Richard, and a daughter had drowned in the *White Ship* tragedy of 1120. When Henry died, reportedly of overindulgence in lampreys, he left a score of bastards but only one legitimate child, Empress Matilda, widow of the Holy Roman Emperor Henry V. King Henry persuaded his nobles to accept Matilda as his heir, and he married her off to Geoffrey Plantagenet, Count of Anjou. But the Anglo-Norman nobles lacked enthusiasm for a female ruler and her Angevin consort. When Henry died, they gave their allegiance to Stephen of Blois, a grandson of William the Conqueror.

Amiable, weak-kneed Stephen's reign (1135–54) was said to be a time when "Christ and his saints slept." He spent most of his time on the throne sparring with the high-handed Empress Matilda for the English crown and attempting to secure it for his elder son. When the young man died, the English barons, weary after years of civil war, pressured Stephen to adopt Matilda's son, Henry Plantagenet (also called fitzEmpress—"son of the Empress"), as his heir.

This great-grandson of the Conqueror became Henry II (1154–89), the first **Plantagenet** King. The name of the dynasty means "sprig of broom"—a reference to the habit of Henry's father, Geoffrey of Anjou, of wearing a sprig of yellow broom plant tucked into his helmet. Since the Plantagenets derived from Anjou, the earlier Kings of the dynasty are sometimes called Angevins. In addition, the houses of Lancaster and York were descended from the Plantagenets. All told, fourteen Plantagenet Kings—including three Lancastrians and three Yorkists—ruled from Henry II to Richard III.

The greatest Plantagenet, Henry II, was fortunate in his inheritance and marriage. From his mother, Matilda, and Stephen he acquired England and Normandy. Through his father, Geoffrey, he held Anjou, Maine, and Touraine. He was heir to his brother, through whom he obtained Brittany. When he married Eleanor, the divorced wife of French King Louis VII, he gained Aquitaine. The English King held more of France than the French King.

Like his grandfather, Henry I, King Henry II believed in the centralization of power, and he spent much of his reign undoing the damage wrought by Stephen's time on the throne. He brought Wales and Brittany into step, and Pope Adrian IV (Nicholas Breakspear, the first and last English Pontiff) apparently conferred Ireland on him. Henry spent more than half his years as king on the Continent tending to his holdings there, which stretched from the English Channel to the Pyrenees.

Henry made major changes in the English legal system, including the introduction of juries, the diminished use of feudal courts in favor of royal ones, and the creation of roving judges, who ventured into the countryside to try cases. The bureaucracy initiated by the Normans continued to increase in complexity under Henry, who himself traveled constantly to maintain a strong presence throughout the kingdom. His contemporaries said Henry was never empty-handed, holding either a book or a bow at all times.

The notorious tragedy of Thomas Becket clouded Henry II's reign. The King made his old friend Archbishop of Canterbury with the aim of wedding the secular and spiritual powers. The plan backfired when Becket, awed by the majesty of his position, began to champion Church supremacy. After first acceding to the Constitutions of Clarendon (1164), in which Henry outlined customary relations between the Church and Crown (especially that capital crimes by priests be punished by royal courts), Becket retracted his support, was stripped of his estates, and fled to the Continent. When the Archbishop returned to England in 1170, he was murdered in his own Canterbury Cathedral by four knights who took literally the words of their raging King: "Will no one rid me of this turbulent priest?"

The latter part of Henry's reign was poisoned by family problems. His heir, Prince Henry, who had been crowned King during his father's lifetime, led an unsuccessful revolt and died in 1183, being memorably mourned in a *planh* (poetic lament) by one of his adherents, the great Provençal poet, baron, and warrior Bertran de Born. Henry then supported his youngest and least capable son, John, as the next King. Another son, Richard, joined forces with the unscrupulous King Philip II Augustus of France, and the two invaded England in July 1189. The old King, too weak to resist, gave in to their demands, only to find that his dear John had joined them against him.

King Richard I Coeur de Lion, the Lion-Heart (1189–99), lived when fierce warriors still prided themselves on writing verse (in his case, both in French and Provençal). After wresting the throne from John, Richard went on an unsuccessful crusade to the Holy Land, where he eventually made a truce with the mighty sultan Saladin. On his way home, he was captured by the Duke of Austria and spent a year in prison until the regents of England came up with the required ransom. During the next five years, he attempted to regain the castles in Touraine and Normandy that were lost while he was in prison and his perfidious brother John schemed with Philip Augustus. He spent only ten months of his ten-year reign in England, dying in France of a crossbow shot while besieging a rebellious castle.

John Lackland, aka Soft-Sword (1199–1216), ascended the throne after his brother Richard's death and promptly lost Normandy, Anjou, Maine, and Touraine to his erstwhile friend Philip II after tangling with French nobles over a disputed marriage contract. To obtain the support of Pope Innocent III in his conflict with France (after the Pope had placed England and Wales under interdict in 1208), John agreed to make England a papal fief. After John's loss of key battles against the French, his recalcitrant barons captured London and, at Runnymede on June 15, 1215, forced the King to agree to the terms of the Magna Carta, the "great charter" that, among other provisions, declared "no free man shall be imprisoned or dispossessed except by the lawful judgment of his peers or by the law of the land."

The reign of Henry III (1216–72), who succeeded his father John at age nine and ruled for fifty-six years, was marked by disputes with his nobles. The revolt of the barons had its genesis in 1259 with the Provisions of Westminster—their attempt to put the principles of the Magna Carta into practice. When Henry resisted, war broke out with his nobles, who were led by his brother-in-law, Simon de Montfort. Although de Montfort managed to imprison the King at one point, the rebel was killed at the Battle of Evesham (1265), and his cause was defeated. Among Henry III's cultural achievements were his rebuilding of Westminster Abbey with its memorial to Edward the Confessor, his patronage of Gothic art and architecture, and his openness to French cultural and artistic influences. Salisbury Cathedral was built during his reign.

Henry's son, Edward I Longshanks (1272–1307), was a renowned legal reformer and champion of the common law, an excellent administrator, and a tall, handsome, strong, redoubtable soldier who had crusaded in Egypt and Syria. At home, he defeated Llewelyn ap Gruffydd, Prince of Wales, secured control of that principality in 1284, began Anglicizing it, and made his son Edward the Prince of Wales in 1301, establishing the tradition that the male heir to the English throne receive that title.

King Edward expelled the Jews from England in 1290, partly to seize the assets they left behind. In his incessant search for funds for his military campaigns, he convened his "Model Parliament" (1295), which for the first time brought Lords and Commons together in one assembly. During his reign, Parliament was established as the fundamental body for conducting public business. In Edward's effort to extend his control over all Britain, this "Hammer of the Scots" defeated King John Balliol of Scotland in 1296 and removed the Stone of Scone to London. This was just the beginning of a savage and unsuccessful conflict against warriors like William Wallace and Robert Bruce that led to wars, skirmishing, and border raids for the next three centuries.

Many historians have used the example of Edward II (1307–27), son of Edward I, as an argument against hereditary monarchy. He resisted continued efforts by his nobles to limit the crown's control over finances, a position made worse by the debts he inherited from his father's Scottish ventures. That he apparently had male lovers—notably Piers Gaveston and Hugh le Despenser—only weakened his tenuous grasp on the throne. His momentous blunders at the Battle of Bannockburn in 1314 led to a rout by King Robert Bruce and assured Scotland's independence. His Queen, Isabella, "the she-wolf of France," mother of his four children, led an invasion against him with her lover, English baron Roger Mortimer. Disgusted with its King, England welcomed Isabella. After Edward abdicated in favor of his son, he was hideously murdered. The hapless monarch's tale is told with great oratorical verve in Christopher Marlowe's tragedy *Edward II*.

If Edward II was a low point in the Plantagenet line, the half-century reign of his son Edward III (1327–77) was among its glories. Inheriting the throne at age fourteen, Edward moved against Roger Mortimer in 1330, having him drawn and hanged after conviction of assorted treasons and felonies.

Edward struck the opening blow in what came to be known as the Hundred Years' War between England and France (1337–1453), capturing Brittany and Normandy and staking his claim to the French throne in opposition to the other claimant, the Count of Valois, who became King Philip VI (see Question 67). His other goals included gaining unfettered rights in Gascony and its prosperous Bordeaux wine trade and ensuring an open market in Flanders for English woolens. With the aid of his warrior son Edward, the Black Prince of Wales, he won important battles at Sluys in 1340, Crécy in 1346, and Poitiers in 1356, which were also notable for the crucial role played by English longbowmen. By 1360, Edward III controlled about one quarter of France. These successes mollified the nobles and helped ease the sting of soaring taxes. By the end of Edward's reign, however, only Calais and its environs remained in English hands. The fortunes of England continued to wax and wane during the rest of the Hundred Years' War, which extended into the reigns of Richard II, Henry IV, Henry V, and Henry VI.

The Black Death of bubonic plague visited England in 1348–50, claiming the lives of 30 to 50 percent of the population and hampering military operations in France. Edward's tenure was also notable for the division of Parliament into two houses, which were given responsibility for voting on the war effort, and the replacement of French by English as the official language of the courts in 1362.

While many of the British monarchy's troubles over the centuries have been caused by the absence of legitimate heirs, Edward had the opposite problem. He had eleven legitimate children, including four surviving sons, and the complicated, intertwined history of the Houses of Lancaster, York, and Tudor derives from them.

Since the Black Prince had died a year before Edward III, the prince's son Richard II (1377–99) succeeded to the throne, reigning ineffectively for twenty-two years, enduring a Peasants' Revolt (1381), and insisting on calling himself King of France, though establishing a twenty-eight-year truce with France in 1396. When Richard exiled Henry Bolingbroke, son of Edward III's third son, John of Gaunt, Duke of Lancaster, and then confiscated his inheritance, Henry returned to popular acclamation and won the support of nobles who feared for the safety of their own patrimonies.

Bolingbroke deposed his cousin Richard II, usurped the throne as Henry IV (1399–1413), the first King of the house of **Lancaster,** and probably ordered Richard's murder at Pontefract Castle in 1400. But Henry's claims were disputed. The fourth son of Edward III was Edmund of Langley, Duke of York. His son Richard, Earl of Cambridge, was married to Anne Mortimer, who was the great-great-granddaughter of Edward III and the heiress of his second son, Lionel, Duke of Clarence. Since, with the death of Richard II, the line of Edward's eldest son, the Black Prince, had died out, Richard, Earl of Cambridge, and later his son Richard, Duke of York, claimed the succession through Anne Mortimer's descent from Lionel.

From such dynastic *mishegoss* sprang the bloody Wars of the Roses involving the great nobles descended from the prolific Edward III. The feuding cousins, the red-rosed Lancastrians and white-rosed Yorkists, plotted, warred, and murdered, with the conflict really heat-ing up between 1455 and 1485. At the end, most of old England's warrior nobles were dead.

Henry IV spent most of his reign dealing with rebellions fomented by Lionel's descendants. The Welsh, led by Owen Glendower, and the Scots took advantage of this unsettled period to initiate rebellions of their own.

For much of the latter part of his reign, Henry IV's affairs were managed by his more capable and ruthless son, Henry V (1413–22), Shakespeare's Prince Hal. This young warrior renewed the conflict with France, successfully drawing attention away from continuing domestic turmoil. Henry V was an even more successful soldier than his great-grandfather, Edward III, and his military career was capped by his brilliant victory at the Battle of Agincourt (1415), establishing him as a national hero. Under the terms of the Treaty of Troyes (1420), Charles VI, King of France, passing over his own son, granted the French succession to Henry and gave his daughter in marriage to him. But Henry died of dysentery at age thirty-five in 1422. Had he lived another two months, he would indeed have acquired the French throne.

His nine-month-old son succeeded him as Henry VI (1422–61, 1470–71), the last Lancastrian King. During Henry VI's minority, two warring uncles served as his regents in England, while a third represented him in France. With the successes of the French Dauphin and Joan of Arc, this house of cards eventually collapsed (see Questions 67 and 97). England lost Normandy, and the Hundred Years' War was over, leaving the English with only Calais, as at the end of Edward III's reign, three quarters of a century earlier.

The War of the Roses flared up again. Richard, Duke of York, claimed the throne by virtue of his mother's descent from Edward III's second son, Lionel, besides his paternal descent from Edward's fourth son, Edmund. Henry VI traced his royal rights through his father back to Edward III's third son, John of Gaunt, Duke of Lancaster. The issue centered on whether a claim to the throne could be transmitted via a female. In the end, however, the question was decided by the superior soldiering of the new Duke of York, Edward, who defeated his Lancastrian cousins at the Battle of Towton (1461). Over the next decade, Henry VI and Edward played seesaw over the throne. Edward finally seized it permanently in 1471 after the Battle of Tewkesbury, and he had saintly Henry executed in the Tower of London.

By the time this warrior recovered the throne as Edward IV (1461–70, 1471–83), first King of the house of **York,** even his closest relatives didn't trust him. He had his own brother, George, Duke of Clarence, put to death in 1478 (according to tradition, by drowning in a butt of Malmsey wine). When he invaded France, the French King paid him to leave, and so he did. When Edward IV died in 1483, his twelve-year-old son, Edward V, reigned for only two months. The boy's uncle, Richard, Duke of Gloucester, claiming that the uncrowned young King and his siblings were born of an invalid marriage, had him and his only brother, nine-year-old Richard, Duke of York, placed in the Tower of London, where they were apparently murdered at his bidding.

Gloucester then succeeded as Richard III (1483–85), the last Yorkist (and Plantagenet) King. A man with many enemies, he soon had to contend with the claims of Henry of Richmond, who had become de facto head of the House of Lancaster (after Henry VI died) and had taken refuge in Brittany.

Part of his claim to the throne involved yet another complication in Edward III's family. John of Gaunt, Duke of Lancaster, had also launched the house of **Tudor** by virtue of his relationship with his mistress Catherine Swynford. Their children, surnamed Beaufort, were legitimized by Richard II after widower Gaunt married his mistress. Henry of Richmond claimed to be a descendant of the Plantagenets via his mother, Margaret Beaufort, a prominent member of the House of Lancaster, and founder of Christ's and St. John's Colleges, Cambridge. On his paternal side, Henry was grandson of the Welshman Owen Tudor, husband of Henry V's widow.

Although almost every living Yorkist had a better claim to the throne than Henry of Richmond, it was he who defeated Richard III (the last English King to die in battle) at Bosworth Field in 1485, bringing a much-needed stability to England. As King Henry VII (1485–1509), he had the good sense to marry the Yorkist heiress Elizabeth, daughter of Edward IV, thus uniting the houses of York and Lancaster. Elizabeth was the ultimate royal insider—daughter of Edward IV, sister of Edward V, niece of Richard III, wife of Henry VII, and mother of Henry VIII. To this day, the features of the queens in ordinary decks of playing cards are hers.

The son of Henry and Elizabeth, Henry VIII (1509–47), a statesman, theologian of sorts, and musician, is best known for breaking with the Pope in 1534 over his divorce from Catherine of Aragon and his marriage to Anne Boleyn. He went on to have six wives, two of whom were beheaded (see Question 44).

Henry's three children round out the list of the remaining Tudor monarchs. On his death, his only living son ascended the throne at age nine as Edward VI (1547–53). This sickly boy was the son of Henry's third wife, Jane Seymour. He reigned for only six years, during which the Church of England grew more powerful and the *Book of Common Prayer* was introduced. Just before his death from tuberculosis, he directed that his father's great-niece, Lady Jane Grey, inherit the throne. She reigned for nine days in 1553 and was beheaded at age seventeen, with her husband, in the next year by order of Mary Tudor.

The eldest child of Henry VIII and Catherine of Aragon, Mary I (1553–58) was, like her mother, a staunch Roman Catholic, and the populace, still largely loyal to Rome, supported her accession. At age thirty-seven, she was no stranger to court intrigues. She had shared the travails of her mother during the long years that Henry sought to have his first marriage annulled. In 1533, when Parliament had declared that marriage void, Mary was removed from the succession. She was restored to it in 1544 and pulled out of it again by fervently Protestant Edward.

When she became Queen, she renounced the title Henry VIII had given himself—Supreme Head of the Church—and began to restore the monasteries that had been the favorite confiscatory targets of her father and half-brother. She also restored the heresy laws, making it a criminal act to practice a religion different from that of the sovereign. About three hundred Protestants, including several of Henry's eminent bishops, paid for this crime at the stake during Bloody Mary's tenure. She made an unpopular marriage to the future Philip II of Spain and lost Calais in 1558 when, at her husband's bidding, she invaded France. The royal pair had no children.

When Mary died, the throne went to her half-sister, Elizabeth I (1558–1603), the last, and arguably the most brilliant, of the Tudor sovereigns. The daughter of Henry VIII by Anne Boleyn, Elizabeth was a fiercely intelligent, diplomatic, and pragmatic woman—qualities that account for her survival during the reigns of Edward VI and Mary I, when a political misstep could have cost her head. She grew up largely under the wing of Henry's sixth wife, the scholarly and kindly Catherine Parr, and received instruction in Greek and Latin from the most eminent humanists of the day, John Cheke and Roger

Ascham. The first act of Good Queen Bess was to reestablish Protestantism, but without the fanatical zeal of Edward VI.

Elizabeth shrewdly surrounded herself with capable advisers, enhancing popular support of her government. The war with France ended officially in 1559, and England thrived commercially and economically. Its sea power flourished under the navigators Sir Francis Drake and Sir Martin Frobisher. Standard coinage was introduced, restoring confidence in the monetary system, and foreign trade expanded. To her subjects, Elizabeth, or "Gloriana," was coextensive with England. She gave her name to one of the most exuberant literary periods in history, with the likes of Christopher Marlowe, Sir Philip Sidney, Edmund Spenser, William Shakespeare, and Francis Bacon active during her reign. Elizabeth herself wrote verse and translated Boethius's *The Consolation of Philosophy* from Latin into English.

Nonetheless, politics is politics. In 1567, Elizabeth imprisoned her second cousin and heir, Mary Queen of Scots, because she threatened rebellion, plotting with English Catholics, Spain, France, and the Pope. In Catholic circles, Elizabeth was the illegitimate child of Henry and Anne Boleyn, and Mary was thus the rightful queen. After an adviser uncovered a plot to assassinate Elizabeth and install Mary, Elizabeth reluctantly consented to Mary's beheading in 1587. War with Spain followed, but in 1588 Elizabeth's fleet defeated Philip II's Spanish Armada, setting the stage for England's naval supremacy and extensive colonization (see Question 97). England's first colony in the New World, Virginia, was named for the self-professed "Virgin Queen" (see Question 94). In her reign, Sir Francis Drake circumnavigated the globe, and the powerful East India Company was formed.

Perhaps Elizabeth understood all too well the political entanglements that marriage entailed for a female monarch. Nonetheless, she was deeply attached to, if not romantically involved with, Sir Walter Raleigh and the Earl of Leicester, among others. On her deathbed in 1603, she selected James VI of Scotland—the executed Mary's son—as her successor.

This first monarch of the house of **Stuart** had already ruled Scotland for more than thirty years. A direct descendant of Henry VII, he ruled England as James I (1603–25). Although he was first to be monarch of both countries, his efforts to join England and Scotland as "Great Britain" were unsuccessful, since the two peoples still viewed each other as foreigners.

James was a theologian, and the King James Version of the Bible was prepared under his direction. His religious tolerance was put to the test during the Gunpowder Plot of November 1605, when several Roman Catholics led by Guy Fawkes plotted to blow up Parliament with the King in attendance. As a result, stricter sanctions were imposed on English Catholics. Other religious dissidents, especially the Calvinistic Puritans, were also harassed, and some began settling in Massachusetts in 1620. Spineless James was unable to protect his own advisers; Raleigh, for example, was put to death to appease Spain.

The reign of James I was marked by his poor handling of the realm's financial affairs and weak relations with Parliament. The English Parliament was a stronger institution than its corresponding body in Scotland, and the English King was required to seek its counsel before waging war. It also voted money for the sovereign. On the other hand, the King had more power in England than in Scotland, where the monarch more closely resembled a senior partner among aristocratic families. James had trouble adjusting to these conditions, and the situation was exacerbated by his tendencies to prattle about "the divine right of kings" and to lavish gifts on handsome courtiers who struck his fancy.

Like his father, James's heir Charles I (1625–49) didn't quite see the point of Parliament, which he dissolved and ruled without for more than a decade when it refused him money for wars against France and Spain. His shortage of funds led to illegal taxation, which proved to be his undoing. He was, however, a shrewd patron of the arts, and Peter Paul Rubens, Sir Anthony Van Dyck, Inigo Jones, and Ben Jonson were among the beneficiaries.

He was married to the Catholic daughter of the French King, a fact which, along with Charles's High Church ways, disturbed some members of court. Relations with Parliament deteriorated to such a point that Charles tried to arrest five members of the House of Commons on charges of treason, igniting civil war. This was largely a struggle between the middle classes (mostly Puritan Dissenters and merchants from London and other port cities, derisively called "Roundheads"), who supported Parliament, and the aristocracy ("Cavaliers") and peasantry, who backed the King. The Royalists were disastrously defeated by Oliver Cromwell at Naseby (1645). Charles was eventually tried and beheaded (1649) for waging war against his own subjects. The poet John Milton defended the regicides in several learned treatises he composed in English and Latin for the victorious Puritans.

The King's son, Prince Charles, whom the Scots proclaimed as their King after the death of Charles I, was forced into exile by Cromwell's continuing military successes, and he stayed abroad for the duration of the Puritan republic (the Commonwealth). During this interregnum, England tried various forms of constitutional reforms, especially executive rule by a committee of Parliament called the Council of State (seven Army leaders and eight civilians). But by the time Cromwell became Lord Protector in 1653, he was virtual dictator of the country. At various times, his policies included the devastation of Ireland, the development of Baltic trade, readmission of the Jews, improvements in education, the conquest of Jamaica from Spain, and the mitigation of penalties for minor crimes. After he died in 1658, his son Richard ("Tumbledown Dick") failed to be a convincing Lord Protector. The ensuing power struggles led the Army to seek a Stuart Restoration in 1660.

The thirty-year-old Prince Charles returned to England as King Charles II (1660–85). This Merry Monarch is remembered primarily as a weak, debauched King (thirteen known mistresses, including the actress Nell Gwynne) who, perennially short of funds, sold Dunkirk to France. The Great Plague (1665) and the Great Fire (1666) rocked London during his reign. Conflicts with Holland culminated in a Dutch naval ship-burning expedition up the Thames (1667). By the end of Charles's time on the throne, the rudiments of a two-party political system—Whig and Tory—were becoming apparent.

Despite intense anti-Catholic feeling in the realm and the revelation of an improbable "Popish Plot" (1678), by which Jesuit priests and others were accused of conspiring to murder King Charles, the Catholic convert James II (1685–88) ascended the throne on the death of his elder brother, who had about fifteen bastards but no legitimate heir. James crushed the revolt of the Protestant Duke of Monmouth (one of Charles's) and promoted Catholics to important judicial positions. He and his second wife, also Catholic, had a son, James Edward, later known as the Old Pretender.

With the possibility of a reemergent Catholic dynasty at hand, Parliament invited the Dutch Protestant William of Orange, a grandson of Charles I who was married to James II's daughter Mary by his first (Protestant) wife, to initiate what came to be called the "Glorious

Revolution." James fled when Parliament deposed him, but he later attempted to regain the throne by conducting a French army to Ireland. He was defeated at the Battle of the Boyne (1690)—still a name to conjure with in clashes between Catholics and Protestants in Northern Ireland.

In 1689, Parliament declared William and his wife joint sovereigns as William III (1689–1702) and Mary II (1689–94). James II and his heirs—the Old Pretender and his son, Bonnie Prince Charlie—were excluded from the throne, along with all Catholics and persons married to Catholics. The sovereign was (and still is) required to take a vow upholding Protestantism. Parliament took the opportunity to increase its control over taxation and lawmaking and enhance its authority to maintain a standing army—safeguards against the excesses of the absolutist Stuarts. The party system grew rapidly with the power of Parliament (which now had to be summoned yearly), general elections were held, and the era of limited, constitutional monarchy was established via a bloodless revolution.

Mary remained childless and succumbed to smallpox at age thirty-two. When William died from being thrown by his horse, the crown passed to Mary's gouty younger sister Anne (1702–14). The dozen years of Anne's reign saw acrimonious conflicts between Whigs (generally, proponents of Parliamentary supremacy) and Tories (supporters of royal prerogatives and the established Church). In 1707, the Act of Union established a single Parliament and coinage for England and Scotland, now formally united as Great Britain. But the main events of Anne's reign were the spectacular victories of John Churchill, Duke of Marlborough, over the French armies of Louis XIV in the War of the Spanish Succession—Blenheim (1704), Ramillies (1706), Oudenaarde (1708)—leading to the Peace of Utrecht (1713).

Anne had sixteen children, but none survived. By the Act of Settlement (1701), Parliament had provided for the succession of the German Protestant Hanovers if Anne died childless. This meant that James I's granddaughter, Sophia, Electress of Hanover, would have ascended the British throne as the first monarch of the house of **Hanover,** but she died just before Anne. Instead, her son became King George I (1714–27), although historians believe at least fifty Catholics had stronger claims. George was a German princeling who spoke little English and spent most of his time in his beloved Hanover, setting the stage for the Whig statesman Sir Robert Walpole to become the country's first Prime Minister in 1721. Walpole's tenure continued well into the reign of the King's son George II (1727–60), who, in 1745, put down another threat from the Jacobites (supporters of the Stuarts, from Latin *Jacobus,* that is, James II) in the person of Bonnie Prince Charlie. George II's reign saw increased industrialization, particularly expansion of the coal and shipbuilding industries, and the capture of Quebec from the French (1759).

The best-known of the Hanoverian Georges is George III (1760–1820), grandson of the previous sovereign. His two immediate predecessors had ceded much authority to their prime ministers, and he tried to wrest some of it back. It was on his long watch that the remainder of French Canada was won (1763) and the thirteen American colonies lost (1783) (see Question 83). The Act of Union (1801) dissolved the Irish Parliament and joined Ireland to Britain. Toward the end of George's fifty-nine-year reign, Napoleon was finally defeated at Waterloo in 1815 (see Questions 67 and 97), but insanity induced by porphyria had already taken hold of the sovereign. Four years later, Percy Bysshe Shelley described him as "an old, mad, blind, despised, and dying king."

George IV (1820–30) had already ruled as Prince Regent for his incapacitated father since 1811. During the Regency, he had enjoyed the profligate company of Lord Byron and Beau Brummell and had the poet and essayist Leigh Hunt imprisoned for two years for referring to him in print as "a fat Adonis of fifty." (Charles Lamb had—anonymously—described him as "the Prince of Whales.") Hard-drinking George was more interested in gourmandizing, wenching, putting on witty performances, and collecting art than in being King—a job he nearly missed out on by secretly marrying a Catholic in his youth. He later wed Princess Caroline of Brunswick in what proved to be a notoriously unhappy marriage, complete with a scandalous separation, charges of adultery, and her futile attempt to be crowned Queen. Walter Savage Landor wrote of this King: "When George the Fourth from earth descended, / Thank God the line of Georges ended."

He was succeeded by his low-key younger brother William IV (1830–37), whose reign was marked by much-needed parliamentary reforms. He was gutsy enough to dissolve Parliament so that new elections could ensure passage of the Great Reform Act (1832), extending the franchise to the middle classes. Slavery was abolished in British colonies in 1833, and the Poor Law was reformed in 1834.

After William, his eighteen-year-old niece, Victoria (1837–

1901), granddaughter of George III, began her eventful sixty-three-year reign, the longest in British history. Since women could not sit on the Hanoverian throne, that German link was broken after 123 years. The British Empire, however, doubled in size during her tenure. Ten prime ministers served her, including the British bulldog, Lord Palmerston, the great Conservative Benjamin Disraeli, and the great Liberal William Ewart Gladstone.

Her first prime minister, Lord Melbourne, exerted the most important influence on Victoria during her early years as Queen. After her 1840 marriage to her first cousin, Prince Albert of Saxe-Coburg and Gotha, and the 1841 defeat of Melbourne's government, Victoria relied increasingly on her husband's guidance, although the political influence of the sovereign continued to wane. But not her symbolic role as Britannia itself: In 1877, Disraeli saw fit to have her declared Empress of India.

Albert, despite introducing the Christmas tree into England, was not regarded fondly, probably because he seemed inaccessibly Teutonic. Yet the Prince Consort and Victoria were the picture postcard of marital bliss and domestic concord, producing nine children in twenty-one years of marriage. Albert was a profoundly influential figure, credited with averting war with the United States just a few days before he died in 1861. After his death, the Queen largely withdrew from public view (although she continued to discharge her royal duties in private) until her golden jubilee in 1887.

Except for an Opium War or two against China, the Crimean War, various imperialistic ventures, and the Boer War (1899–1902), England remained free of major military entanglements for remarkably long: from 1815 to 1914. How could it be otherwise? Victoria, "the Grandmother of Europe," was related to the royal families of Greece, Russia, Sweden, Denmark, Norway, and Belgium. Her eldest grandson, German Kaiser William II, was devotedly present at her deathbed.

Victoria's son Edward VII (1901–10), or Bertie, initiated the royal house of **Saxe-Coburg-Gotha.** Victoria held Edward partly responsible for his father's death, since Albert was distraught over his son's affair with an Irish actress, Nellie Clifton, when he became ill with typhoid and died shortly afterward. A great sportsman, indefatigable gambler, and rotund bon vivant, Bertie had the longest tenure as Prince of Wales, bearing that title from a few weeks after his birth in

1841 until his coronation in 1902, after the death of his "eternal mother" when he was nearly sixty-one.

As a monarch, Edward VII was enormously popular with his subjects in the Empire, as well as with the French. This helped bring about the Anglo-French Entente Cordiale of 1904, an agreement that ended several territorial disputes between the two countries in Africa and other trouble spots and allowed them to use their combined diplomatic power against Germany in the several years before the First World War. Although his own mother had said he was stupid, Edward had the vision to surround himself with men who had the skills he lacked. He is credited with supporting the military changes that readied England—more or less—for the outbreak of World War I.

Edward was married to the Danish Princess Alexandra in 1863, and they had five children. He had numerous affairs, including a highly discreet one with Alice Keppel. Alexandra had to admit that in many ways this mistress was an asset to her husband, and she even invited her to the dying King's bedside. Mrs. Keppel's legacy lives on today: Her great-granddaughter, Camilla Parker Bowles, is the acknowledged mistress of Charles, the current Prince of Wales, who is Edward's great-great-grandson.

The house of **Windsor** was born of the Germanophobia that swept England during the First World War. Edward's son George V (1910–36) decreed on July 17, 1917, that the royal surname would henceforth be Windsor, thus ending the brief tenure of the house named for Prince Albert. (When the Kaiser heard the news, he quipped that he was going to the theater to see *The Merry Wives of Saxe-Coburg-Gotha.)* Nonetheless, George campaigned for better treatment of the German prisoners of war held by the British. Besides the catastrophic war, George V's reign also witnessed reform of the House of Lords, the 1916 Easter Rising in Ireland, the debut of the Labour government in 1924, and the General Strike of 1926.

Edward VIII succeeded his father in January 1936. His brief reign ended with his abdication in December of the same year for the sake of "the woman I love." Edward stunned the country by relinquishing the throne for Wallis Simpson, an American whose two divorces made her an unsuitable wife for the King and Head of the Church of England. During the crisis, Mrs. Keppel remarked, "Things were done much better in my day."

Edward's brother was made of far kinglier stuff. The quiet man who expected to live out his life as the Duke of York instead reigned as George VI (1936–52), a dedicated, much-loved wartime King. He and his Queen, Elizabeth, remained with their fellow Londoners during the German blitz and visited the most devastated areas of the city, especially the East End. After World War II, George presided over the granting of independence to India in 1947. A haunting photograph taken at his funeral in 1952 shows three clustered, black-gowned, grieving queens—his mother, Queen Mary of Teck; his wife, the Queen Consort Elizabeth; and the new Queen, his daughter Elizabeth.

Both Elizabeth II (1952–) and her husband, Prince Philip, are great-great-grandchildren of Queen Victoria. In place of the British Empire of 1952—not to speak of Victoria's—there is now a small nation with island dependencies and Gibraltar. The personal lives of this sovereign's family, while no more nor less virtuous than many others alluded to above, are open to ferocious public scrutiny. Will the British monarchy eventually be legislated away as an anachronistic drain on the public purse, especially if scandals continue to plague it? Or is it now in a time of transition, when the next sovereign—whether Charles III or William V—will have to seriously rethink the spirit, function, and direction of the venerable nine-hundred-year-old institution?

❧ QUESTION 75

Who were the 9 Muses, and what were their associated arts?

Calliope: epic poetry
Urania: astronomy
Clio: history
Terpsichore: dance
Melpomene: tragedy

Thalia: comedy and pastoral poetry
Euterpe: lyric poetry and flute music
Erato: love poetry
Polyhymnia: sacred songs

> *O for a Muse of fire, that would ascend*
> *The brightest heaven of invention. . . .*
> —Shakespeare,
> *Henry V,* Prologue, 1–2

It's entirely fitting that the Muses, the lovable, (usually) nurturing patronesses of the arts and goddesses of creative inspiration and intellectual activity, should be the daughters of Zeus by the Titaness Mnemosyne, the goddess of memory. From their mother, the Nine learned about all that had transpired in the world since the beginning of time, including stories of the Titans and the ascendancy of the twelve Olympians (see Question 88). The ancient lesson seems to be that an amply stocked memory is crucial for breathing life into the arts, whether one is creating or appreciating them.

The Muses were born in Pieria, sometimes thought to be on the slopes of Mount Olympus in Thessaly, home of the Greek gods. From Pieria, they migrated to the spring Aganippe and the fountain Hippocrene on Mount Helicon in Boeotia. The spring of Castalia on Mount Parnassus, site of Apollo's oracle at Delphi, was another of their haunts. Whoever drank from a sacred spring or fountain of the Muses was immediately suffused with artistic inspiration. Hippocrene ("horse fountain") was created by a hoof-stamp of the winged horse Pegasus—another potent symbol of inspiration—when he alighted on Helicon.

The Muses were not only inspirers but consummate performers, often entertaining the gods during their feasts on Olympus. Homer imagines Apollo, god of music and poetry, and sometimes called *Musagetes* ("leader of the Muses"), accompanying them on the lyre as they sing with ineffable voices.

It was on Mount Helicon that the Boeotian poet Hesiod (fl. c. 700 B.C.) claimed the Muses manifested themselves to him. Hesiod, author of the didactic agricultural poem, *The Works and Days,* was the first to reveal the names of the Muses in his long poem on the origin of the gods, the *Theogony,* which the Nine Sisters supposedly bade him compose.

Calliope (kuh-LIE-ah-pee, "beautiful voiced") was chief of the Nine—Ovid calls her *maxima*—and Muse of epic poetry. In this latter capacity, she was invoked by Virgil in the *Aeneid* and by Dante in the

Purgatorio. In late ancient sculpture, she was often depicted with a scroll, stylus, and tablet.

When Zeus asked Calliope to arbitrate in a dispute between Persephone and Aphrodite over Adonis, the wise Muse decreed that the gorgeous young man should spend four months with Persephone, four months with Aphrodite, and the remainder of the year on his own, presumably recovering. Neither goddess gave much heed to Calliope's directive.

The most famous offspring of all the Muses was Orpheus, in most accounts the son of Calliope and Oeagrus, King of Thrace. So ravishing was the music he made on the lyre presented to him by Apollo that it enchanted not only wild beasts but even trees and rocks.

His joy was complete when he took as his bride the lovely tree nymph Eurydice, but she died of a serpent bite on their wedding day. Confident of the persuasive power of his music, Orpheus descended to Tartarus, hoping to mollify Hades, god of the underworld. At the sound of his plaintive song, the three-headed guard dog Cerberus let him pass, and the savage Furies wept blood. At the behest of his Queen, Persephone, Hades allowed Eurydice to depart on one condition: that Orpheus wouldn't look back at her until they had both returned to the upper world. As they approached the land of the living, Orpheus turned to make sure Eurydice was following behind—and she was gone in an instant, with time only to say "Farewell."

After returning brokenheartedly to Thrace, Orpheus gave offense to a band of frenzied Maenads, female followers of Dionysus (Bacchus), the god of intoxication and revelry, either for speaking out against their orgiastic rites or for shunning the company of women. The fierce Maenads tore Orpheus limb from limb and flung his head into the River Hebrus. After drifting out to sea, still singing, it came to rest on the island of Lesbos, which later gave birth to Greece's first great lyric poets (see Question 79). John Milton evokes the dismemberment of Orpheus in *Paradise Lost* (7.32–38), where he speaks of

> . . . *the barbarous dissonance*
> *Of Bacchus and his Revellers, the Race*
> *Of that wild Rout that tore the Thracian Bard*
> *In Rhodope, where Woods and Rocks had Ears*
> *To rapture, till the savage clamor drown'd*

Both Harp and Voice; nor could the Muse defend
Her son.

The Muses gathered Orpheus's limbs and buried them at the foot of Mount Olympus, a favorite haunt of melodious nightingales. His lyre was placed in the heavens as a constellation. The Maenads were turned into oak trees.

Urania (you-RAIN-ee-ah, "heavenly") was sometimes depicted pointing to a globe. As the Muse of astronomy, she was able to predict the future by scanning the stars. Milton invokes her at the beginning of *Paradise Lost* as the "Heav'nly Muse," but in a Christianized guise that makes her the inspirer of Moses and other Hebrew prophets. In his invocation to Book 7 of the poem, at the midpoint of his poetic task, he calls on Urania again.

Clio (KLY-oh, "she that extols"), the Muse of history, is often pictured unfolding a scroll or holding a water clock. According to some accounts, Clio was the mother of Linus, the archetypal musician who invented rhythm and melody, sang the story of the Creation, and taught Orpheus and Thamyris their musical wizardry. Apollo himself was so jealous of Linus that he killed him. (This Linus must be distinguished from another musical Linus who was slain by Heracles—see Question 90.)

Terpsichore (turp-SICK-uh-ree, "she that rejoices in the dance") was often depicted dancing and holding a lyre. From her, we got our word *terpsichorean* ("pertaining to dancing"). In some stories she is the mother of the Sirens, the half-bird, half-women creatures who used their incomparably lovely voices to lure unwary mariners to their death. Odysseus, however, managed both to listen to their song and to evade their trap by having himself tied to the mast of his ship while his men stopped up their ears with wax.

Melpomene (mell-POM-in-ee, "she that sings"), the Muse of tragedy, is pictured holding a tragic mask and sometimes poising a dagger at her breast. She wears a vine wreath because of its association with Dionysus, god of wine, in whose honor festivals featuring tragic dramas were held. Melpomene's footgear is the cothurnus (or buskin), the thick-soled laced boot worn by tragic actors to endow them with a suitable stature. Although the tragic Muse seems to have been too depressed and introspective to take a lover, some think that she, rather than Terpsichore, was the mother of the Sirens.

Thalia (thuh-LYE-ah, "festive" or "flourishing") is usually pictured in the environs of a comic mask in artistic renditions of her. She may wear the low shoe or slipper of comic actors (called the sock) and hold a small rustic drum or shepherd's crook, indicating her dual role as Muse of both comedy and pastoral poetry. Some say she was the mother by Apollo of the Corybantes, attendants of the Phrygian nature goddess Cybele, "the Great Mother." The Corybantes accompanied Cybele over her mountain haunts with lit torches and wild, intoxicated dancing to the crashing sound of flutes, horns, drums, and cymbals. Later, the name was applied to Cybele's priests, who castrated themselves in the orgiastic frenzies of their rituals.

Euterpe (you-TURP-ee, "she that gladdens"), the Muse of lyric poetry, is often depicted with a double flute, which she is said to have invented. Unmarried like the rest of the Muses, Euterpe became yet another single mother in the family when she gave birth to Rhesus. On the very night he arrived to aid the beleaguered city of Troy in the Trojan War, the sleeping Rhesus was slain by the Greek warriors Odysseus and Diomedes, who sneaked up on his camp *(Iliad, Book 10)*. His snow-white, wind-swift horses were then driven off before they could taste the grass of Troy or drink its waters; an oracle had foretold that if they managed to do this, Troy could not be taken. But Odysseus and his partner in crime made a total monkey out of Rhesus.

Erato (AIR-a-toe, "passionate"), Muse of erotic poetry, is pictured with a lyre. You would figure the inspirer of so many amorous ditties would have some scandalous story of her own, but none has surfaced so far.

Polyhymnia (polly-HIM-nee-ah, "rich in hymns") is often depicted wearing a garland of roses and looking terribly serious. This Muse of sacred songs is, according to various accounts, the mother of Triptolemus, who invented farming; of Orpheus; or even of Eros himself, though that honor is almost always assigned to Aphrodite.

Usually benevolent and kindly, the Muses sometimes displayed the vengeful haughtiness at the heart of most creative artists who know their true worth. Ovid tells how Pierus, King of Macedonia, named his nine daughters after the Muses. When they later presumptuously challenged the real Muses to a singing contest, they of course lost. Calliope and her sisters turned the King's daughters into chattering magpies, a myth recalled by Dante at the beginning of his *Purgatorio* as an object lesson on the importance of humility.

A similar fate befell the Sirens, who also unsuccessfully challenged the Muses and had their wing feathers plucked by the victors, who used them to make crowns for themselves. Some versions of the story have the Sirens plummet into the sea and drown as a result of this incident.

Another unfortunate soul was the mythic poet Thamyris, who dared claim he was more skilled than the Muses at composing verse. He, too, lost the contest—and his vision, voice, and poetic craft as punishment. Milton, speaking of his own blindness in *Paradise Lost,* invites comparison with two famed Greek poets: "Blind Thamyris and blind Maeonides"—the last word being an epithet of Homer.

The followers of Pythagoras, as well as Plato and Aristotle, officially organized their schools as associations for the cult of the Muses *(thiasoi),* and our word *museum* comes from the Greek *Mouseion*— "home of the Muses." Today, if these mythological deities still linger in our consciousness, it is because they evoke music, poetry, knowledge, wisdom, beauty, grace, inspiration. And which of us, at some point in our life, hasn't longed, not just for any garden-variety Muse, but a Muse of fire?

 QUESTION 76

What are the 9 orders of angels (from lowest to highest)?

Angels	Dominations
Archangels	Thrones
Principalities	Cherubim
Powers	Seraphim
Virtues	

Angels date back at least to the time of Zoroaster (or Zarathustra), prophet of Zoroastrianism, which dominated the religious life of the Persian Empire from about the sixth century B.C. to the seventh century A.D. This tradition was messianic and included themes of resurrection, reward and punishment, and cosmic conflict between a benevolent god of light, Ahura Mazda (later called Ormazd), and his antithetical evil counterpart, Ahriman. The Talmud points to Babylon as the source of angels (or at least of their names), but by 539 B.C. Babylonia was already part of the Persian Empire.

In fact, angels with proper names don't enter Jewish tradition until after the return of the Jews from their Babylonian captivity in 538 B.C. The Hebrew word for angels is *malakhim,* or messengers (Greek, *angeloi),* and that is a primary role of theirs in the Old Testament. In the book of Daniel (8:17), Gabriel explicates visions and prophecies for Daniel, who faints in his presence. Michael is identified as "the Great Prince, defender of your people" in the same book (12:1). And Raphael, who appears in the apocryphal book of Tobit (chapter 5), is engaged by Tobit to be a guide and protector for his son Tobias as he journeys to Media. Raphael also acts as a matchmaker on this trip and restores old Tobit's sight. Angels in Jewish tradition were anthropomorphized, pictured as eating and drinking with Abraham, wrestling with Jacob, and even becoming objects of lust in Sodom.

In addition to these close encounters, the Old Testament also records several awesome apparitions. The **cherubim,** who wield a flashing sword to keep the banished Adam and Eve away from the Tree of Life, make up a living chariot for Yahweh called the *Merkabah* in Ezekiel 10. In this astonishing vision, God and his sapphire throne are pictured high above four winged cherubim, each covered all over with eyes and having four faces: those of a cherub (an ox in Ezekiel 1), man, lion, and eagle. Each cherub is beside a whirring topaz wheel—which is "like a wheel inside a wheel," also covered with eyes and instinct with the spirit of the angels. Hot coals lie scattered among the cherubim, and the sound made by their wings rivals the "voice of God Almighty when he speaks."

In Isaiah (6:3), the **seraphim** have six wings: two to cover their faces, two to cover their feet, and two for flying. Seraphim are "the burning ones" in Hebrew, and Isaiah is purified when one of them takes a live coal with tongs and touches it to the prophet's lips.

We read about messenger angels and archangels in the New Testament, too. Gabriel announces to Mary that she is to bear the son of God. An unnamed angel in white robes greets women mourning at Jesus's empty tomb, reassuring them that Christ has risen from the dead. St. Paul mentions principalities, powers, virtues, thrones, dominations, and archangels in Ephesians (1:21), Colossians (1:16), and 1 Thessalonians (4:15). In the book of Revelation, which contains a vision of Michael battling Satan, we encounter fantastic creatures like those described in the Old Testament.

Paul evidently acquired his knowledge of the various orders of angels when he was rapt into heaven—"whether in the flesh, I know not"—and allowed to view the full angelic panoply. St. Ambrose (339–97) was apparently the first to enunciate a nine-order schema, which was greatly elaborated by Dionysius the Areopagite, ostensibly an Athenian convert of Paul's who had imbibed detailed knowledge about the angels directly from him. His work, *On the Celestial Hierarchy,* was translated from Greek into Latin by Johannes Scotus Erigena (c. 810–c. 877), an Irish theologian and philosopher who was one of a handful of Western Europeans of the time who were fluent in Greek. Only in the mid-fifteenth century, with the development of Greek philology, did scholars examining the original text of Dionysius realize that its verbal forms were typical of Syria in about A.D. 500. The author, who could not have been a contemporary of Paul's, was probably a Syrian monk born centuries later—hence his current name, Pseudo-Dionysius.

Nonetheless, Erigena's translation made Pseudo-Dionysius's book a widely accessible authority on angels, whom it divided into three choirs, each with three orders. The Councillors of God comprised the seraphim, cherubim, and thrones. The Governors were the dominations, virtues, and powers. Principalities, archangels, and angels were the Messengers of God.

Unaware of relying on an imposter, St. Thomas Aquinas (1225–74) cited Pseudo-Dionysius hundreds of times in his *Summa Theologica*. Aquinas maintained that angels, created for God's glory, were pure spirits capable of masquerading as corporeal beings when expedient, usually to break the ice with humans. Each individual angel, he said, really represented a distinct species, and their number surpassed all reckoning. According to Aquinas, angels know neither the future nor the thoughts of humans, but they do have full knowledge of themselves, which allows them to understand and accept their limitations. As a result, lower-order angels accept their place without envying high-ranking colleagues. Aquinas also assigned a division of labor to the angelic orders: love to the seraphim, sight (or knowledge) to the cherubim, support to the **thrones,** leadership to the **dominations,** execution of commands to the **virtues,** judgment to the **powers,** guidance of nations to the **principalities,** guidance of leaders to

archangels, and guidance of other humans to **angels** ("guardian angels").

These nine orders were thought to be the Intelligences or Movers of the nine heavens or spheres, which contained, in ascending order, the orbits of the moon, Mercury, Venus, the sun, Mars, Jupiter, Saturn, the fixed stars, and the crystalline sphere (or primum mobile, "the first moving thing"). Unmoving Earth was at the center of this cosmos. The immediate dwelling of God, the unmoved Mover, was beyond the material universe of time and space in the Empyrean, the tenth heaven of pure spiritual fire and light, where the redeemed share in the Beatific Vision.

The orders of angels were delegated to the various heavens, from the lofty seraphim in charge of the primum mobile to the humble angels governing the sphere of the moon. By striving to attain to God and by fervently loving and contemplating him, the angelic orders caused their spheres to revolve in perfect circular orbits—infinitely fast in the primum mobile and more slowly in each descending sphere (the diurnal orbiting of the sun bringing night and day). In a celestial trickle-down effect, each sphere imparted God's love, as motion, to the sphere below it, along with his grace and effulgence. At the center was the ultimate recipient of these divine, angelic, and astrological influences, the earth and its inhabitants. This wheel-within-wheel effect, with each sphere revolving at a different speed and producing a different note, created the exquisitely harmonious music of the spheres, which crude human ears haven't been able to hear since the expulsion of Adam and Eve from Eden.

What else do we know about these creatures? Fully one third of the angels were said to have followed Lucifer (Satan), the most glorious seraph and victim of his own overweening pride, into hell (Revelation 12:4). Some churchmen argued that Satan's rebellion against God and his fall occurred immediately after the first instant of his creation, when he pronounced (or thought) his *"non serviam"* ("I will not serve," Jeremiah 2:20). Dominations were considered the first angels to be created, although no consensus exists on when. We know the names of seven archangels: Michael, Gabriel, Raphael, Uriel, Chamuel, Jophiel, and Zadkiel. And only angels and archangels speak to humans. In Islamic tradition, the four archangels are Gabriel (Jibril), the transmitter of divine revelations; Michael (Mikal) the warrior; Azrael (Izra'il) the angel of death; and Israfel (Israfil), who will sound the trumpet in Jerusalem on Resurrection Day.

On the Celestial Hierarchy and Aquinas's countless pronunciamentos on angels had quite an impact on subsequent literature. Dante (1265–1321) adopted the nine-order, three-choir view of the angels and heavenly spheres in his *Paradiso*. There Beatrice shows Dante the souls of the saved residing in the sphere that best corresponds to their character in life: for example, wise theologians and religious writers (including Dionysius), who shed intellectual light on God's mysteries, in the heaven of the sun; martial champions of God in that of Mars. Beatrice mentions Dionysius as the thinker who elucidated the angelic hierarchy and describes how Pope Gregory the Great had a laugh at his own expense when he got to heaven and saw firsthand the errors he had made in attempting to classify the angels in his writings. We are also told that each of the three angelic choirs contemplates a separate person of the Trinity (see Question 7).

Since medieval times, writers have felt increasingly free to tamper with the orthodox view of angels. John Milton, for example, surely made Aquinas turn over in his grave by claiming in *Paradise Lost* (1667) that angels were sexually active (even if only with other angels, and rather ethereally).

 QUESTION 77

What are the 9 Confucian Classics?

The Analects of Confucius	*The Book of Odes*
The Great Learning	*The Book of Changes*
The Doctrine of the Mean	*The Spring and Autumn Annals*
The Book of Mencius	*The Book of Rites*
The Book of History	

The first four of these nine canonical works of Confucianism are usually referred to as the Four Books (Shih Shu) and the others as the Five Classics (Wu Ching). Confucius, whose name is a Latinized form of K'ung Fu-tzu (K'ung the Master, c. 551–479 B.C.), was thought to be either the author or editor of most of them, though this theory is now discredited. Forming the core of Chinese education, these nine texts were memorized by schoolboys—the Four Books at the primary level and the Five Classics at the secondary level—until the early twentieth century. Although the complete texts of the books were literally carved in stone many times in the long history of China, today there are only about six million Confucians.

Confucius, the preeminent Chinese philosopher and teacher, was a secular moralist who stressed the crucial role of a proper education in achieving self-development, and the central importance of a strong family life as the building block of a just, humane, well-regulated, and peaceful society. Although he believed all people are born pretty much alike, they become different because of their varying environment and education. His key concepts are *li* (observance of ritual, good manners, decorum, propriety, grace, civility) and *jen* (benevolence, humaneness). He formulated versions of the Golden Rule long before Christ. Reverence for elders (especially parents, dead or alive, and older brothers) and respect for state authority were central to his hierarchical ordering of social relations. He harked back to the example and mores of the great rulers and sages of (largely mythical) antiquity to give his precepts the extra zing of "look how far we've degenerated from our ancestors!"

Confucius believed that the Emperor must, through his personal probity and the integrity of his appointees, set the supreme example of righteous living for all his people. If the Emperor thought and lived like a Confucian sage, the empire would practically govern itself, since the people would emulate their leader. On the other hand, if the Emperor oppressed the people, he had clearly lost "the mandate of Heaven"—the impersonal metaphysical sanction that a dynasty enjoyed only so long as it ruled wisely for the benefit of society as a whole.

The Analects of Confucius (Lun Yü, LWEN-YOU) received its outlandish English title because of a Grecianizing quirk of its noted translator, James Legge, who chose this fancy word for "collected fragments." The book preserves the aphoristic sayings, discourses, dialogues, and doings of the Master as compiled within several decades after his death. Although some have viewed Confucius as a stuffed shirt, he evinces in this work a shrewd, understated, worldly-wise humor. When he heard that a certain man thought three times before taking action, Confucius remarked, "Twice might be enough." When asked about how best to worship the spirits and ghosts, he answered, "We still don't know how to serve the living, how can we know how to serve the dead?" Indeed, Confucius avoided speculating about metaphysics or the supernatural realm, preferring practical and ethical teachings to theological controversy.

The Great Learning (Ta Hsüeh, DAH-SHOO-uh) was attributed to Tseng Tzu, a pupil of Confucius, or to the Master's grandson Tzu Ssu. Like *The Doctrine of the Mean,* it is but a single chapter that the famed Neo-Confucian Chu Hsi in the twelfth century extracted from *The Book of Rites* because of its singular importance. The opening of *The Great Learning,* supposedly written by Confucius himself on bo leaves, expounds the idea that peace and harmony in the empire depend on the proper functioning of all its components—from that of its constituent states, to that of families, to individual self-cultivation, to the rectification of unruly desires, to the use of precise definitions in thinking (no euphemisms, Newspeak, or "spin"), to the investigation of things as they really are.

The Doctrine of the Mean (Chung Yung, JUNG-YUNG), attributed to Tzu Ssu, grandson of Confucius, preserves many of the Master's sayings and basic moral precepts. It seeks to bring human life into a harmonious relationship with the workings of the universe and is thus more metaphysical and Taoist in its concerns than other Confucian works. A famous dictum of Confucius recorded here claims that an archer who misses the target seeks the cause of his failure in himself alone.

Mencius (Latinized form of Meng-Tzu, c. 372–c. 289 B.C.) was the most brilliant philosophical follower of Confucius. *The Book of Mencius (Meng-Tzu,* MENG-DZOO) was probably not written by Mencius himself but by the disciples of his disciples. Nonetheless, his conversations and teachings recorded therein are no doubt based on fairly accurate recollections of his words.

More idealistic than Confucius, Mencius believed that human nature was essentially good, though it enjoyed but a slim advantage over that of brute beasts. This advantage is the human heart *(hsin)*—the seat of natural compassion but also of serious reflection on the moral questions of life. Humans who "lose their heart" in the mad race of life sink to the bestial level. Rulers have to do their utmost to prevent poverty and misery in their subjects because people who are poor lose heart. When a certain King said he could not prevent famine, Mencius suggested he resign.

Mencius claimed the people had a right to overthrow—and even kill—a corrupt King because the person they would be putting to death would no longer be a King but an egregious criminal. He also opposed all wars except those fought in self-defense or to remove wicked rulers. His book—more complex, substantial, and profound than *The Analects*—is said to be one of the supreme examples of Chinese literary style.

In 142 B.C., an imperial university was established with five departments—one for each of the Five Classics. The first of these, ***The Book of History*** *(Shu Ching,* SHOO-JING), is a collection of ancient historical documents and speeches. The traditional theory that Confucius edited the book is no longer held, though he apparently believed it expounded the basic principles of government. This earliest Chinese work of history recounts many edifying events and myths from the earliest reigns of China, when the more-or-less unified empire supposedly had heroic, unselfish, larger-than-life emperors at the helm.

The Book of Odes *(Shih Ching,* SHIH-JING) comprises 305 ancient Chinese poems written in four-word, alternately rhyming lines that Confucius was traditionally thought to have selected from more than 3,000 lyrics. Scholars now believe the anthology was compiled after his time in the fourth century B.C. The poems were originally sung and accompanied by dance. Confucius may have set some of them to music or at least collected the existing settings. The anthology contains folk songs of peasant life and more formal odes and hymns used in religious rituals and court functions.

Confucius prized the words and music of the Odes above all other sources of moral education, claiming they formed character. He believed that the wholesome sentiments expressed in the Odes, the aesthetic pleasure of listening to them being performed, and the technical discipline involved in learning how to play the music while singing the words constituted a thorough grounding in the aristocratic code of "the perfect gentleman" that he sought to inculcate. He subtly urged his son to study the Odes, as well as *The Book of Rites*. When Confucius and some disciples were caught between warring armies without food for a week, the Master sang the Odes with exceptional enthusiasm while accompanying himself on the lute as his companions looked on in hungry disbelief.

The Book of Changes *(I Ching,* EE-JING), originally a divination text compiled before the eleventh century B.C., consists of sixty-four symbolic hexagrams made of broken and unbroken lines with accompanying texts, interpretations, and philosophical commentaries.

Consultation of the book involves casting lots to determine the appropriate hexagrams, which are combinations of any two trigrams named for heaven, thunder, water, mountain, earth, wind, fire, and lake. The book makes use of the metaphysical doctrines of the yin and yang (female and male) principles operating through all of nature. Some believe Confucius wrote the commentaries on the hexagrams and texts. Indeed, he claimed that if his life were to be extended by many years, he would devote fifty of them to studying *The Book of Changes,* so as to avoid colossal blunders. The book's prerational, non-Western exoticism made it a counterculture flash in the pan in the far-from-Confucian sixties.

The Spring and Autumn Annals (Ch'un Ch'iu, CHUN-CHEW), supposedly compiled by Confucius, is a dry history of his native state of Lu from 722 to 481 B.C. The title is a Chinese way of saying "historical annals."

The Book of Rites (Li Chi, LEE-JEE) is a collection of texts on music, social ceremonies, religious rites, and court etiquette. It was probably definitively compiled in the early first century B.C., long after the time of Confucius, but the Master had already said its rules of propriety were essential in the development of character and maintenance of social order. In this work we are reminded that, "barring cogent reasons, a scholar is never without his lute"—presumably for playing the Odes during wartime.

Tremendously influential as they were, the Confucian classics weren't always held in the highest esteem. In 213–212 B.C., during the Ch'in dynasty, all copies of the classics (except apparently *The Book of Changes* and *The Book of Mencius)* were ordered burned—and 460 scholars killed—by the so-called First Emperor, Shih Huang Ti, the "Tiger of Ch'in," who unified China and built the Great Wall. The Emperor was a partisan of the Legalist philosophical school, which preferred a government of strict laws to one of virtuous example and idealized tradition. He was also tired of Confucian criticism of his dictatorial regime. But during the Han dynasty (206 B.C.–A.D. 220), Confucianism recovered sufficiently to become the official state creed. The banned books were either dug up from hiding places or reconstituted from the excellent memories of Confucian scholars.

After the fall of Han, Confucian thought went into abeyance for about six hundred years but emerged again during the T'ang dynasty (618–906). The Sung dynasty (960–1279) saw the triumph of Neo-Confucianism, a movement that eclectically enriched the thought of

Confucius and Mencius with aspects of the hitherto opposing philosophical traditions of Taoism and Buddhism.

From 1313 to 1905, the Nine Classics formed the basis of civil-service examinations in China. These grueling tests lasted thirteen days, during which the aspirant to office was locked in a cell, sometimes with the assignment of writing down everything he knew. The Mandarins, the powerful civil servants of the highest nine grades in the empire, were those most thoroughly imbued with the letter and spirit of Confucianism.

In the twentieth century, the Confucian classics have exerted a seminal influence on the work of Ezra Pound (1885–1972), especially on his eight-hundred-page poem *The Cantos* (1917–69). His Canto 13 is a string of anecdotes about Confucius, drawn largely from *The Analects*. Canto 52 is partly derived from *The Book of Rites,* and Cantos 53–61 are a seventy-nine-page attempt to versify Chinese history from its mythic beginnings to the early eighteenth century from a Confucian perspective. Some of the most poignant lines in his *Pisan Cantos* (1948), comprising Cantos 74–84, were inspired by various Confucian texts. (An example is the epigraph to this book, Pound's creative translation of the opening of *The Analects.)* His Canto 85, replete with Chinese ideograms, is a verse commentary on selected passages from *The Book of History.*

In addition, Pound translated *The Great Learning* (1928), *The Doctrine of the Mean* (1947), *The Analects* (1950), and *The Book of Odes* (1954), although he had never formally studied Chinese. His method was to consult English, French, or Latin annotated translations of the Chinese texts and then closely study the original ideograms with the aid of a Chinese dictionary. The results range from passably reliable English versions to eerily imaginative poetic re-creations.

When Italian partisans arrested Pound in May 1945, he was typing out a translation of Mencius. As he left with the armed men, he crammed into his coat pockets the one-volume bilingual text of the Four Books and the compact Chinese dictionary he had been using. These books sustained and inspired the sixty-year-old poet when, after being handed over to the American Army in Italy as a Fascist traitor, he was imprisoned in an outdoor iron cage in a military prison camp near Pisa until his physical and emotional collapse three weeks later. Out of his abject misery, his well-stocked memory, and the wisdom of Confucian China, he wove *The Pisan Cantos,* his elegiac masterpiece and one of the greatest poetic sequences of the twentieth century.

✦ QUESTION 78

Who were the 9 Worthies?

Hector of Troy	Judas Maccabaeus
Alexander the Great	King Arthur
Julius Caesar	Charlemagne
Joshua	Godfrey of Bouillon
King David	

> *For it is notoirly known through the universal world that there been nine worthy and the best that ever were, that is to wit, three Paynims [pagans], three Jews, and three Christian men.*
> —William Caxton, Preface to
> Sir Thomas Malory's
> *Morte Darthur* (1485)

The Nine Worthies is a medieval list of the world's greatest warriors, composed with an eye toward the three historical groups that had contributed most to medieval culture. The ever-symmetrical medieval mind is revealed in the allocation of exactly three Worthies to each of the three groups: pagan warriors of antiquity, Old Testament warriors, and warriors of the Christian era.

Hector of Troy, a son of King Priam, is the greatest Trojan warrior in Homer's *Iliad*. Aided by conniving Aphrodite, Hector's brother Paris had eloped with Helen, most beautiful of women, who was daughter of Zeus and Leda and wife of Menelaus, King of Sparta. The Trojans refused to return Helen, and for ten years they fought off an allied Greek army for possession of her. Unlike his brother Paris, who preferred to make love, not war, Hector battled the Greeks valiantly, even though deeply torn by his devotion to his wife Andromache and infant son Astyanax. After being deserted by Apollo and betrayed by Athene, he was slain on the battlefield by Achilles, by far the greatest warrior at Troy. Bereft of its champion, Troy fell soon thereafter.

Hector is often seen as the noblest, most chivalrous warrior in the *Iliad*, fighting in what he recognized to be an unjust cause only for the sake of his honor and that of Troy. Nonetheless, his blustery, swaggering challenges to his foes gave us the verb *to hector*. But why wasn't Achilles picked as the first Worthy?

Several reasons. The brooding, wrathful, vengeful Achilles was the antithesis of the medieval knightly ideal. More important was the association between the Trojan people and the founding of Rome—as immortalized in Virgil's *Aeneid*, the Latin epic that relates how Trojan Aeneas, cousin of Hector and survivor of the destruction of Troy, arrives in Italy and founds a dynasty that leads to Romulus and Remus, the mythical founders of Rome. And Rome, in the fullness of time, became the seat of Christianity. In addition, many communities of Western Europe claimed a Trojan origin. For example, Brut (or Brutus), the fabled founder of the British race, was said to be a great-grandson of Aeneas and an ancestor of King Arthur. Layamon's *Brut*, an English late-twelfth-century long poem based on a work by the French poet Wace, recounted this myth.

Alexander the Great, born in 356 B.C. and tutored by Aristotle, was the son of King Philip II of Macedon. This kingdom controlled Greece by the time Philip was assassinated in 336 B.C. as he prepared to attack the Persian Empire. Alexander, who claimed descent from Achilles through his mother Olympias, a Queen of Epirus, carried out his father's plan, invading Asia Minor in 334 B.C., where, according to legend, he cut the Gordian knot. The knot had been fastened between the yoke of a wagon and its pole by the peasant Gordius, later King of Phrygia and father of Midas. It was said that the man who could undo the knot would rule Asia. Alexander sliced through it with a quick blow of his sword. He then trounced King Darius III and his Persians at the Battle of Issus and took, in succession, Syria, Tyre (in modern Lebanon), and Egypt, where he founded Alexandria in 332 B.C.

After decisively defeating the Persians at the Battle of Arbela in 331 B.C. (see Question 97) and Darius's subsequent death, Alexander declared himself successor to the Persian throne and spent the next seven years conquering and consolidating his claims eastward as far as northwest India—where his men refused to march any farther—and then returning westward again. He married Darius's daughter and presided over a celebration honoring nine thousand of his men who had already married women of the former Persian Empire, "the marriage of East and West." Alexander died of typhoid fever or malaria at age thirty-two in Babylon on June 10, 323 B.C., in the palace of Nebuchadrezzar II. His empire soon fragmented into separate states ruled as hereditary monarchies founded by his generals.

As the greatest conqueror and general of the ancient world, Alexander was a shoo-in for the Worthies competition. The Middle Ages teemed with freely embellished narratives about him, such as the *Roman d'Alexandre,* a long French poem of the twelfth century. Alexander was also famed as a magnanimous conqueror who was especially kind to captured Persian noblewomen.

Roman general and statesman **Julius Caesar** (100–44 B.C.) rounds out the pagan portion of the list of Worthies. A brilliant politician and orator, Caesar was elected consul and, with Pompey and Crassus, formed the cabal known as the First Triumvirate (see Question 15). As proconsul of Gaul, he conquered an area from the Rhine to the Pyrenees. The Senate, fearing his power and veteran troops, recalled him to Rome. Knowing this would involve laying aside his army command and subjecting himself to retaliatory criminal prosecutions, Caesar made the fateful decision to cross the Rubicon—at that time the border of Italy—and embroil Rome in civil war. He defeated Pompey and other enemies in a series of swift campaigns in Greece, Africa, Asia Minor, and Spain, and had himself proclaimed dictator. Detested by republican and senatorial aristocrats, Caesar was assassinated by a group of them led by Brutus and Cassius on March 15, 44 B.C.

Here was another natural to make the Worthies team. As a general and conqueror, Caesar ranks second—perhaps—only to Alexander, and he claimed descent, through the Julian clan, from Iulus, the son of Trojan Aeneas. In the Middle Ages, Caesar was also considered the first Roman Emperor (though that distinction actually belongs to his successor, Augustus), and the Emperors were thought to have bequeathed their temporal power over the empire to the Popes.

Joshua, first of the Old Testament Worthies and successor of Moses, brought the Israelites into the Holy Land. Marching behind the Ark of the Covenant, Joshua led his people across the Jordan River under miraculous circumstances, the very waters pausing in their course to allow the crossing. According to the book named for him in the Bible, Joshua conquered Jericho—where the walls came tumbling down at the blowing of rams' horns and the shouting of the Israelites—and overran Canaan, distributing the land among the twelve tribes of Israel (see Question 87). Historians and biblical scholars agree that the process was accomplished more gradually. Nonetheless, the Israelites had a solid foothold in Palestine by the thirteenth century B.C. Joshua, the warrior who conquered the Holy Land, was the ideal type of medieval hero in that he succeeded in an undertaking that successive waves of Crusaders tried to accomplish over the course of several hundred years.

King David, the second Israelite King, reigned from about 1000 B.C. until his death in 962 B.C. A musician and probably the author of some of the Psalms, David united Israel with its capital at Jerusalem. In Jewish tradition, he is the King par excellence, and the authors of the New Testament claim Jesus was his descendant. Although David started out as a shepherd, he became an aide to King Saul, married the King's daughter, and forged a classic friendship with Saul's son Jonathan.

When David slew the giant Philistine Goliath with only some stones and a slingshot, old King Saul became furiously jealous—"Saul has slain his thousands," the Israelite women sang, "and David his ten thousands"—forcing the young man to flee to the desert of Judah. There, leading a band of outcasts, David protected the locals from marauding bands and gained a reputation as a patriot. Although he was anointed by the prophet Samuel in Bethlehem while the manic-depressive Saul was still alive, David was not proclaimed King until after the deaths of Saul and Jonathan, both slain fighting the Philistines.

David conquered Jerusalem and made it the capital of his newly united kingdom. His family, however, was wormwood to his heart. His son Absalom killed David's eldest son, Amnon, after the latter had raped his half-sister Tamar. Absalom, to his father's great grief, was killed by one of David's generals after the young man had rebelled against him. This is how David mourned him, still unbearably plangent after three thousand years: "My son Absalom! My son! My son Absalom! Would I had died in your place! Absalom, my son, my son!" The adulterous relationship between David and Bathsheba led to the murder of her husband, Uriah, but also to the birth of their son Solomon, who succeeded David as King.

David is perhaps the most intriguing character in the Old Testament. In the Goliath story, he is the vulnerable but courageous young man who conquers despite overwhelming odds. He is the giant-killer who succeeds on the strength of his innate virtue. Countless Renaissance statues attest to the mighty symbol he gave to humanity, that of the brave champion, armed only with a righteous cause, defeating tyranny and oppression. To the medieval world he had been the perfect poet, musician, and king; conqueror of Jerusalem; and ancestor of the Savior.

Judas Maccabaeus, the mighty Jewish patriot, fought decisively against the Hellenistic Syrians, led by Seleucid King Antiochus IV Epiphanes, who tried to impose the pagan Greek religion and other related practices on the Jews. Maccabaeus, whose name probably means "Hammer," defeated Seleucid armies four times and, in December of 164 B.C., presided over the purification and rededication of the Temple of Jerusalem, an event commemorated by the eight-day Festival of Lights, or Hanukkah. The movement led by Maccabaeus and his brothers Jonathan and Simon eventually resulted in a short period of political and religious independence for the Jews. The resonance that Judas Maccabaeus had for the Middle Ages involved his being a brave, virtuous warrior who routed the foreign overlords of the Holy Land and rededicated its holy sites, much as the Crusading nations had attempted to do.

King Arthur was probably a historical figure, although much Arthurian lore and the stories of his Round Table are largely Welsh and medieval concoctions (see Question 92). His exploits attained legendary status partly because the times in which he lived were decisive for British history. The occupying Roman legions had pulled out by about A.D. 410, and the cultural and linguistic character of Britain was to undergo a profound change during the several hundred years that followed.

Arthur, who was most probably Welsh, gained a reputation as a magnificent warrior while fighting against the invading Saxons during the late fifth and early sixth centuries A.D. Fairly reputable historical evidence credits him with a major victory at Mount Badon in 490 (or 518) and another triumph in 511 (or 539) at the Battle of Camlann, where he reportedly died. He was probably an extremely adept general serving under British Kings, and his fame lived on as a powerful symbol of British resistance to invaders. There arose a vast literary tradition dealing with him, his knights, and the quest for the Holy Grail. In his character of Worthy, Arthur appears in an anonymous fourteenth-century English poem, *The Alliterative Morte Arthure,* where he dreams of Fortune's wheel and sees the six pagan and Jewish Worthies on it, already fallen from their high estate, and the three Christian Worthies, with himself at the very top, heading for predominance.

Besides Arthur's exploits and the renowned chivalry of at least some of his followers, his links to Christianity secured him a notch on the list of Worthies. Thus, the traditional number of his Round Table inner circle of knights, twelve, is the same as that of Christ's Apostles (see Question 91). There's even an empty chair left at the table, the Siege Perilous, which calls to mind the treachery of Judas Iscariot. In addition, the Grail was usually understood as the cup that Christ used at the Last Supper and in which Joseph of Arimathea caught some of his blood at the Crucifixion. The lance often associated with the Grail was the one that had pierced Christ's side while he was on the cross. Joseph of Arimathea is mentioned in the Gospels as having requested Christ's body from Pontius Pilate and buried it in "his new tomb that he had hewn in the rock" (Matthew 27:57–60). This is none other than the Holy Sepulcher, ultimate goal of Crusaders, which establishes a circuitous but undeniable link between Arthur and medieval Christian "Holy Wars."

Charlemagne (reigned 768–814), sometimes called *Rex pater Europae,* "the King Father of Europe," was the son of Pepin the Short, who had been anointed King of the Franks by the Pope (see Question 67). Charlemagne was unique in his time in that he considered himself to have official Christian endorsement of his role as warrior king of the Franks. In addition, he endeavored to make his court a center of Christian learning, and he generously subsidized the arts. A very tall, strong, cheerful man, he spoke Latin and read Greek, although he apparently never learned to write.

The empire Charlemagne carved out for himself was the largest in the West since the fall of Rome. He defeated the Germanic Lombards in Italy. He forcibly converted the Saxons to Christianity, thereby neutralizing them as opponents. His defeats of the Slavs and other peoples allowed him to open an important Danubian trade route to Constantinople. He conquered the Danes and Bavarians and marched into northern Spain, eventually uniting all Christian lands in

Western Europe except southern Italy, part of Spain, and Britain. Charlemagne was crowned Emperor Charles I of the Holy Roman Empire on Christmas Day of 800 by a grateful Pope Leo III, who had been reinstated in Rome by Charlemagne's forces. Charlemagne's vast empire survived as a unity for only a few decades after his death before splitting into essentially French and German components.

Like Alexander the Great and King Arthur, Charlemagne was at the core of an immense cycle of medieval legends, romances, and *chansons de geste,* most famously *La Chanson de Roland.* In most of the tales he is portrayed as the ideal Christian King who battles against pagans and, especially, Moors—coreligionists of the Saracens who held the Holy Land.

This brings us to the Worthy most directly associated with the Crusading ideal, **Godfrey of Bouillon** (1060–1100), Duke of Lower Lorraine and leader of the First Crusade. A descendant of Charlemagne, Godfrey became the first Latin ruler of Palestine when his armies captured Jerusalem from the Saracens in 1099. When offered the title King of Jerusalem, he refused it in favor of *Advocatus Sancti Sepulchri,* "Protector of the Holy Sepulcher." After taking Jerusalem, Godfrey engineered truces with the Muslim cities of Ascalon, Caesarea, and Acre, and repelled an Egyptian attack. He set a precedent by making himself a vassal of the Patriarch of Jerusalem, thereby making life difficult for subsequent civil and religious leaders who sought control in Jerusalem. Godfrey appears as the saintly hero and perfect Christian knight of Italian poet Torquato Tasso's late-Renaissance epic, *Gerusalemme Liberata (Jerusalem Delivered,* 1581).

An extended reference to the Worthies appears in Shakespeare's *Love's Labour's Lost.* In this early comedy, King Ferdinand of Navarre and three of his young nobles agree to eschew the company of women for three years to devote themselves to study. Ferdinand has forgotten, however, that he has a previous engagement with the Princess of France and her ladies-in-waiting, who prove most intriguing to the King and his friends. In the midst of the farcical goings-on, the pedantic schoolmaster Holofernes (famed for his teacherly exclamation, "O thou monster Ignorance, how deformed dost thou look!") musters a troupe of blockheads to present a pageant of the Nine Worthies in honor of the Princess and her ladies. The list of Worthies differs from the traditional one in that it includes Hercules and Pompey the Great. The pageant lays an egg immediately when the first yokel introduces his character as "Pompey the Big." It's all downhill from there—for the pageant, but also for the medieval conception of the Worthies themselves as bigger-than-life embodiments of martial valor.

For an idea of what the Worthies meant to an aristocratic medieval patron of the arts, take a look at the Nine Heroes Tapestries the next time you happen to be in the Cloisters (the branch museum of the New York Metropolitan Museum of Art that is devoted to art of the Middle Ages).

✤ QUESTION 79

Who were the 9 Lyric Poets of ancient Greece?

Sappho	Bacchylides
Alcaeus	Alcman
Anacreon	Stesichorus
Simonides	Ibycus
Pindar	

The golden age of the ancient Greek lyric—a poem sung to the accompaniment of a lyre—stretched about 150 years from the mid-seventh century to the end of the sixth century B.C. Long afterward, the scholars and critics of Alexandrian Egypt canonized a list of nine who had excelled in that genre. Like many others, these poets turned away from the stately dactylic hexameters of epic and didactic verse (Homer and Hesiod), perfecting instead the lyric forms, moods, and voices that were to dominate European poetry up to the fall of Rome and beyond.

Sappho (c. 620–c. 550 B.C.), the original "lesbian," was born on the wealthy and sophisticated island of Lesbos off the coast of Asia Minor and lived most of her life in its capital, Mytilene. She wrote exquisitely passionate poems to and about the members of a musical and poetic society for highborn girls. (Some say it was a cult—a *thiasos*—of Aphrodite and the Muses, others liken it to a finishing school, and still others speculate it was just a coterie.) No one knows whether Sappho's mad crushes resulted in physical intimacy, but it sure seems like it from her surviving poetry.

Sappho does mention a daughter, Cleis, but the traditional name of her husband, Kerkylas of Andros ("prick from the Isle of Man"), has the earmarks of Athenian wit about it. There's no truth in Ovid's story in his *Heroides* (ultimately derived from the Greek playwright Menander) that Sappho committed suicide by leaping from the Leucadian rock, off the coast of Epirus, after being abandoned by a much younger lover, the handsome boatman Phaon. Her literary remains, in the Aeolic dialect of Lesbos, consist almost entirely of fragments.

Standing at the origin of Western love poetry, Sappho is one of its most poignant exemplars—a woman mourning past loves and the devastation they have wrought in her soul and body. Many of her poems invoke Aphrodite and speak of the girls—Atthis, Anactoria, Gongula—whom she loved with a passion that makes her tremble at the mere memory of it: "I was in love with you once, Atthis, long ago." The poet whom Plato dubbed "the Tenth Muse" (see Question 75) was the first to call love "bittersweet."

Sappho's poem beginning *"Phainetai moi kenos isos theoisin"* ("He seems to me an equal of the gods") inspired one of the loveliest lyrics of the Roman poet Catullus (c. 84–c. 54 B.C.), who translated it into Latin in his poem 51 *("Ille mi par esse deo videtur")*. Sappho enviously describes a beloved girl sitting across from a man, probably her bridegroom. He must be a god, Sappho thinks, if he can enjoy the girl's presence without going to pieces, whereas the poet experiences an upheaval in all her senses if only she catches a glimpse of her. Here is John Addington Symonds's translation, which, despite the archaisms, deftly suggests the movement of the original stanzaic structure and meter, the sapphic strophe:

> *Peer of gods he seemeth to me, the blissful*
> *Man who sits and gazes at thee before him,*
> *Close beside thee sits, and in silence hears thee*
> *Silverly speaking,*
>
> *Laughing love's low laughter. Oh this, this only*
> *Stirs the troubled heart in my breast to tremble!*
> *For should I but see thee a little moment,*
> *Straight is my voice hushed;*

Yea, my tongue is broken, and through and through me
'Neath the flesh, impalpable fire runs tingling;
Nothing see mine eyes, and a noise of roaring
  Waves in my ear sounds;

Sweat runs down in rivers, a tremor seizes
All my limbs, and paler than grass in autumn,
Caught by pains of menacing death, I falter,
  Lost in the love-trance.

Sappho's repudiation of the epic ideal of life is evident in her poem beginning "Some say the fairest thing upon the dark earth is a troop of horsemen or a host of foot-soldiers, and others again a fleet of ships, but for me it is my beloved." In her invocation to the goddess of love beginning "Splendor-throned, deathless Aphrodite, child of Zeus, weaver of wiles" (*"Poikilothron' athanat' Aphrodita, / pai Dios doloploke"*), Sappho begs the goddess to appear, as in the past, and reassure her that the latest object of her affection will soon stop fleeing her and reciprocate her love. Sappho's magic touch is evident even in this simile comparing a bride to an apple, which is all that remains of one of her poems:

Like the sweet apple which reddens upon the topmost bough,
A-top on the topmost twig,—which the pluckers forgot
  somehow,—
Forgot it not, nay, but got it not, for none could
  get it till now.

                    —translated by
                    Dante Gabriel Rossetti

Her poems are perfused with the scent of flowers, especially the hyacinth and the rose. She calls women and goddesses "rosy-ankled" and "rosy-armed," and she transfers Homer's epithet, "rosy-fingered," from the dawn to the much more romantic moon. Although this brief lament is perhaps not by Sappho, it should be:

The moon has set, and the Pleiades.
It is midnight. Hour
drags on after hour.
And I lie alone.

"Raise high the roof beam, carpenters" is the beginning of a Victorian-era translation of an epithalamium (wedding song) by Sappho. (J. D. Salinger used the phrase as the title of an ironic story about a canceled wedding ceremony.) The rafters have to be hoisted higher because "Like Ares comes the bridegroom, taller far than a tall man."

Sappho is the earliest Western poet to claim that her verse will confer immortality on her: "When I die, I shall not be forgotten." As long as people love (and read), she won't be.

Invariably associated with Sappho is **Alcaeus** (al-SEE-us), a contemporary of hers who also lived in Mytilene and wrote love lyrics, among many other types of poems. From early youth, Alcaeus was a leading member of the aristocratic faction and fought with words and weapons against the popular party. Whether in or out of exile, he inveighed against Pittacus, one of the Seven Sages who was made tyrant of Mytilene (see Question 62). He wrote barbed political songs and describes in one of his fragments his delight in the gleaming weapons and war gear in an armory. Alcaeus was the first poet to use the "ship of state" metaphor in reference to the political turbulence of his time. His great Roman admirer Horace (65–8 B.C.) elaborated on it in his first book of *Odes,* poem 14.

The lighter side of Alcaeus found expression in the theme that Horace later epitomized in the words *"carpe diem"* ("seize the moment") *(Odes* 1.11). Alcaeus exhorts us to take a carefree attitude toward life—though *he* didn't—since we are all poised on the brink of an inexorable abyss. Horace was also greatly influenced by Alcaeus's drinking songs *(scolia),* such as the one beginning "Drink, Melanippus, and be drunk with me." In one poem, Alcaeus urges his readers to throw a log on the fire and drink wine as a defense against the rain and ice of winter. In another, he reminds men to drink wine in the summer as a defense against the parching heat and the excessive sexual demands of women, who grow particularly amorous at that season. In yet another, he reminds us we don't have to wait for nightfall to begin drinking. The Greek scholar Werner Jaeger wrote that Alcaeus's *scolia* call for "a Dionysiac intoxication to drown the cares of the world."

Anacreon (an-ACK-ree-on) (c. 570–c. 490 B.C.) was from Teos, an Ionian city in Asia Minor. He fled to Thrace with his fellow Greeks when the Persians conquered Teos, spent time at the court of Polycrates of Samos (where Ibycus was also a resident), and ended his days in Athens as a friend of Simonides. In his Ionic dialect, Anacreon celebrated wine, women, song, and young boys. One of his poems describes how he sets his sights on a pretty girl, only to discover she's from Lesbos and thus prefers "to make eyes at the ladies" instead. In another, he speaks of a scornful Thracian "filly" who needs a skilled horseman like him to mount her. The pathos of old age closing in on a sensualist is the theme of yet another poem. The pleasures of love are now just a memory, and mournful Anacreon can look forward only to the terrors of death, which are always present to him, and the dark pit of no return. The *Anacreontics*, sixty Greek poems in the style of Anacreon written many hundreds of years after his death, were influential in the English lyric of the seventeenth century, especially in the work of the Cavalier poets, Robert Herrick, Sir John Suckling, and Richard Lovelace.

Simonides (c. 556–468 B.C.), from the Ionian island of Ceos off the coast of Attica, was one of the first Greek poets to earn his living by writing verse. He was also one of the most versatile, composing victory odes, hymns, drinking songs, elegies, dirges, epitaphs, epigrams—even a couple of tragedies. He went to Athens in 490 B.C., where he excelled in dithyrambs (poems in honor of Dionysus), became a patriotic Pan-Hellenic spokesman during the Persian Wars, and enjoyed the friendship of the preeminent general and statesman Themistocles. In 476 B.C., at age eighty, he went to the court of Hiero I of Syracuse in Sicily, where his nephew and fellow Top Niner, Bacchylides, joined him. Simonides was renowned for the pathos and mellifluousness of his verse. In his poem 38, Catullus speaks of a poetic composition "sadder than the tears of Simonides."

Simonides was a brilliant, learned man who pulled no punches. In one of his poems, he calls Cleobulus of Lindus, one of the Seven Sages, a fool because he had claimed in an epitaph that the commemorative statue raised above a tomb would last as long as the sun, moon, and sea (see Question 62). On a different occasion, he corrects another Sage, Pittacus of Mytilene, who had written that "hard it is to be noble." Simonides' view is more pessimistic. In certain circumstances, it's not only hard, it's impossible: "Yes, every man is worthy if his luck is good, / and bad if it goes badly." Simonides will thus not throw his life away striving for perfection, since it is "beyond their power who win / the bread of life from spacious earth." The fragment ends with a reminder that not even the gods can fight against Necessity *(ananke)*. In another poem, he tells us that Virtue *(arete)* is rare. It abides with the gods but with few humans, unless "soul-torturing sweat has been wrung out of their vitals."

The most famous epitaph in history has traditionally been ascribed to Simonides. The speakers are the three hundred Spartan (Lakedaimonian) dead who fell with their leader Leonidas trying to hold the pass at Thermopylae against the invading Persians in 480 B.C. Since their entire force was wiped out, they ask the reader of the inscription to take a message home for them:

> *Tell them in Lakedaimon, passer-by,*
> *That here obedient to their word we lie.*

Pindar of Thebes (522 or 518–432 or 438 B.C.) was likened by Horace to a surging force of nature *(Odes* 4.2) and was referred to by the Roman rhetorician Quintilian (first century A.D.) as "by far the greatest of the nine lyric poets." Of the Nine, his are the largest number of complete works to survive—forty-four epinician odes written for the victors in the four major athletic games in four almost-intact books. Numerous fragments of his lost thirteen books of verse in many other forms are also extant.

Pindar's odes celebrated the winners in the Olympian games in honor of Zeus, the Pythian (Apollo), the Nemean (Zeus), and Isthmian (Poseidon) (see Question 37). He must have received handsome emoluments for these works, sometimes commissioned by rulers such as Hiero I or the King of Cyrene, at other times paid for by successful athletes themselves, their families, or their native towns. These elaborate poems were then performed for the victor and his family—or as a public spectacle at court—by a choir of men or boys who danced while singing the words.

The odes, written in a Dorian literary dialect, are notoriously difficult because of their allusiveness, abrupt transitions, long syntactic units, complex stanzaic forms, severely condensed metaphors, and oblique approach to mythic and other subject matter. Pindar usually begins his poems with the statement of his theme—the athlete and town he is to celebrate—sometimes preceded by a gnomic utterance such as "Best of all things is water" *("Ariston men hudor")*. He then connects the athlete, or his family, town, or site of victory, to a luminous moment in Greek myth, thus establishing a continuity between the present and the times when the gods manifested themselves to humans.

A deeply conservative and religious poet, Pindar seems to have had little interest in athletics, using the victories in the games as occasions for his profound probings into how the divine intersects with the human and how humans can attain something akin to godhead in their struggle to achieve. This formal, humorless, sublime, and aristocratic poet, who firmly believed in his vatic, or sacred, function, sometimes found it difficult to end his poems after weaving their great mythic cores. Thus, his returns to the athlete and the present after his lofty imaginative flights occasionally result in crash—or at least emergency—landings. Alexander the Great spared Pindar's house when he destroyed Thebes in 335 B.C., a century after the poet's death, probably because Pindar had lived at the court of Macedon's Alexander I and written an encomium of him.

Pindar's elaborate stanzas, built around strophe, antistrophe, and epode, led to the development of the Pindaric (irregular) ode, as opposed to the Horatian (regular) ode. English poets who wrote Pindaric odes include Abraham Cowley, John Dryden, Alexander Pope, Thomas Gray, William Collins, and William Wordsworth. Jonathan Swift's attempt to write one elicited his kinsman Dryden's remark, "Cousin Swift, you will never be a poet."

If we didn't have so many of Pindar's dazzling poems ("lords of the lyre," he called them), **Bacchylides** of Ceos (born c. 524 B.C.) might seem much more impressive than he does. He was Simonides' nephew and Pindar's rival in composing epinician odes for victors in the great athletic contests. Though polished and accomplished, he is conventional and predictable when compared with Pindar, the great "Eagle of Thebes" who soars above all other Greek lyric poets. Bacchylides (buh-KILL-ah-deez) was rescued from oblivion when fifteen of his epinicians and six of his dithyrambs were dug out of the sands and rubbish heaps of Oxyrhynchus in Upper Egypt a century ago.

He composed a victory ode for the same occasion Pindar had written about in his first Olympian ode, the victory of the rider and horse of Hiero I in 476 B.C. Bacchylides' "Ode 5" is pleasant and skillful but full of fawning that is directed not only at Hiero but also at his racehorse Pherenikos. (Love me, love my horse.) The mythic section tells how Heracles descends into Hades to bring back Cerberus as one of his twelve Labors (see Question 90); how he meets Meleager there, who bursts into tears and tells him about the Calydonian Boar Hunt and his cruel death at the hands of his own mother; how Heracles weeps for the only time in his life but is so impressed with

Meleager's beauty that he asks him if he has an unmarried sister at home; and how Meleager suggests that Heracles check out Deianira. Then the wow finish: further praise of the Sicilian tyrant and his horse, a quotation from Hesiod, and a closing image of Zeus as "the great gardener" preserving "excellent plants" such as Hiero. Bacchylides is long on wind and short on metaphor—a "talkative Siren," as that prolific Greek poet, Anonymous, called him.

The corresponding poem of Pindar, "Olympian 1," with its powerful opening images of water being the best of all things, gold gleaming in the night, and the glorious sun, adopts a somewhat less sycophantic posture. The central myth refutes the common tale about the founder of the Olympian games, the hero Pelops—that, as a boy, he was killed, cooked, and served up to the gods by his own father Tantalus; that Demeter unwittingly ate part of the shoulder before the horrific deed was discovered; that he thus received an ivory shoulder after being miraculously brought to life again—and substitutes for it a tale of the boy's being abducted by Poseidon to serve as his lover. In contrast to Bacchylides' treatment of myths as literary counters to be manipulated, Pindar's ode breathes an archaic fire by whose light the powerful old stories seem to unfold before our eyes as we read. Even while refuting the original myth of Pelops—with its child-murder, dismemberment, and cannibalism—as a blasphemous affront to the gods, providing instead a tale of divine love (though pederastic), Pindar imparts a numinous glow to his poem that envelops both the beauty and the horror within a sacramental vision.

Nonetheless, or perhaps for these very reasons, when Hiero finally won the prestigious chariot race at Olympia in 468 B.C., he asked Bacchylides rather than Pindar to compose the victory ode. That poem turned out to be a bland and banal composition flimsily built around the story of Croesus's last-minute rescue from the pyre (see Question 62). At its close, Bacchylides refers to himself as "the nightingale of Ceos," but Pindar, in his "Pythian 2," likens his rival to an ape that is pretty only in the eyes of children.

Alcman (flourished c. 630 B.C.), the earliest of the Nine, was a composer of choral odes at Sparta who may have been born in easy-living Lydia in Asia Minor. His longest extant fragment is a *parthenion,* or ode to be recited by a chorus of maidens. The most interesting parts are the elaborate compliments paid by the chorus to its two leaders, who are extravagantly praised for their beauty and compared to dazzling racehorses. Some scholars have speculated on the lesbic nature of all this, but the fragment remains intriguingly opaque.

Stesichorus (stez-ICK-a-rus) (c. 632–c. 552 B.C.) was probably born in southern Italy but lived at Himera in Sicily. His real name was said to be Teisias; Stesichorus, which means "arranger of chorales," seems to have been a title or family name. His choral lyrics apparently influenced Pindar. Although we have only very short fragments of his work, we know that his lyrics retold many of the old myths from the Homeric and other heroic cycles, such as the Labors of Heracles.

The most famous story associated with him tells how he lost his sight for a poem in which he badmouthed Helen of Troy, who was often regarded as a goddess, for being the cause of the Trojan War. After retracting his words in his "Palinode," he supposedly regained his sight. The palinode claimed that Helen never really abandoned her husband Menelaus and escaped to Troy with dashing Prince Paris, thus setting in motion the horrors of the war. No, it was only a very lifelike phantom of Helen created by Hera that did all this, while the real Helen was conveyed by Hermes to King Proteus of Egypt. Euripides later based his play *Helen* on this bizarre version of the events.

Ibycus (IB-i-kus) (fl. mid-sixth century B.C.) was born in Rhegium in southern Italy, across the Straits of Messina from Sicily, where he went to live. Like Stesichorus, by whom he was influenced, Ibycus was a choral poet and also wrote erotic verse about young boys. One of his poems begins with the springtime ripening of grapes and "Cydonian apples" (quinces, originally from Cydonia in Crete). In this season, he knows no respite from love as Aphrodite rocks his heart with storm blasts out of Thrace.

Ibycus supposedly died during a mugging in a grove while on his way to a musical competition. As the poet lay dying, his murderers heard him say to a flock of cranes overhead, "May you avenge my death!" Later, while the literati thugs were enjoying a play, cranes flew over the amphitheater during a scene in which the Furies were exacting their typically ghoulish vengeance (see Question 14). "Look!" cried one of the muggers, pointing to the sky. "The cranes of Ibycus!" At that, their heinous deed was discovered, and the murderers were duly executed. "The cranes of Ibycus" came to mean "unsuspected witnesses of a crime."

Corinna of Tanagra, who was said to have instructed Pindar, was sometimes added to the list of the greatest Greek lyric poets. She is remembered today, if at all, not for her few remaining fragments, but for a criticism of Pindar's overuse of myth in one of his poems: "One should sow by the handful, not by the sackful." The quip became a proverb, but the story may be apocryphal, since the language of Corinna's verse seems to place her in the third rather than the fifth century B.C.

✦ QUESTION 80

What are the 9 planets, and how long do they take to orbit the sun?

Mercury: 87.969 days
Venus: 224.701 days
Earth: 365.256 days
Mars: 686.98 days
Jupiter: 11.862 years

Saturn: 29.458 years
Uranus: 84.013 years
Neptune: 164.794 years
Pluto: 248.54 years

The word *planet,* from the Greek *planetes,* or wanderer, refers to any heavenly body, other than a comet, meteor, or asteroid, that orbits a star like our sun. The wanderers in our solar system are hardly lonely, though, since (except for solitary Mercury and Venus) they are accompanied in their travels by at least sixty-three moons. The whole system is probably the 4.5-billion-year-old progeny of a condensed nebula—a lot of dust and gas. And we now have evidence suggesting that other stars may also have planets.

The sun's gravitational pull on **Mercury** is so strong that the planet actually has "tides" of solid rock on its surface. During its 88-day revolution about the sun, Mercury rotates on its axis every 58.7 days, making its year about 1.5 of its days long. The Romans, aware of its speedy transit, named it after the messenger of the gods. Like Pluto, Mercury is smaller than several moons in our solar system. Because the negligible atmosphere can't trap heat, day-night temperature differences are huge—it's about 750°F. (400°C.) during the day and −300°F. (−180°C.) at night. Mercury's orbital motion differs a bit from that predicted by Sir Isaac Newton—an aberration that Albert Einstein used to prove the theory of relativity.

Venus is named for the Roman goddess of love and beauty. To ancient astronomers, the planet was known as the evening star (Hesperus or Vesper) and the morning star (Phosphorus or Lucifer). The romance ends there. Venus's clouds are composed of sulfuric acid. The greenhouse atmosphere is 96 percent carbon dioxide and produces daytime temperatures of close to 900°F. (482°C.). The atmospheric pressure on the surface is more than ninety times that at sea level on Earth. This combination of heat and pressure obliterated twelve sixties-era Soviet satellites within an hour of landing. Each day on Venus (243 Earth days) is longer than one of its years (225 Earth days), and the sun rises in the west and sets in the east.

Bypassing **Earth** in our journey outward from the sun, we arrive at **Mars,** the Red Planet, named for the Roman war god. Mars has two tiny moons (probably former asteroids), Phobos (Greek, "fear") and Deimos ("terror"), which are 13 and 7.5 miles across, respectively. The 1997 *Pathfinder* mission confirmed that the surface of Mars consists primarily of oxidized materials. The polar caps grow in winter and recede by summer. The thin atmosphere contains scant water, and morning clouds are typical. Rocks collected by *Pathfinder* and its rover suggest that flooding waters once ravaged at least parts of Mars.

Life on Mars has long been an Earthling preoccupation. American astronomer Percival Lowell, on seeing the surface *canali* first described by Italian astronomer Giovanni Schiaparelli, concluded that Martians had built canals to rival Venice's. Orson Welles panicked some Americans in 1938 by convincing them, during a radio performance of H. G. Wells's *The War of the Worlds,* that Martians had invaded. Laugh, but Mars is also the source of a tiny rock—ALH 84001—that fell to Earth thousands of years ago and has raised speculations anew about the possibility of life on the Red Planet—not canal builders, but microscopic organisms. Maybe.

Named for the ruler of the Roman gods, **Jupiter** is an enormous gaseous planet. Although more than a thousand Earths could fit inside it, its mean density is only 24 percent that of our planet. Scientists believe that Jupiter may be a kind of time capsule, closely reflecting the chemical composition of the nebula from which our solar system developed. It's gusty on Jupiter, with frequent cyclones and winds of up to four hundred miles per hour in various layers of the atmosphere. The Red Spot is a fifteen-thousand-mile-wide everlasting storm. Four of Jupiter's sixteen known moons were discovered in

1610 by Galileo, who named them the "Medicean Stars" after the Medici Grand Duke of Tuscany and his brothers. The moons were later renamed after four of Jupiter's lovers—Io, Europa, Ganymede, and Callisto.

Saturn, the second-largest planet, named for the Roman god of agriculture, is best known for its rings (actually a hundred thousand ringlets), which were discovered by Galileo. He thought they were attached to the planet and called them *ansae* (handles). The rings, labeled E, G, F, A, B, C, and D as you approach the planet, are composed of rock, ice, and frozen gas. The planetary probe *Voyager* showed that the Cassini division—the space between rings A and B discovered by Italian-French astronomer Giovanni Cassini in 1675— actually contains five faint rings. Saturn has a dumpy look because it rotates so fast—a day lasting only ten hours, thirty-nine minutes—that its poles have become flattened. Like Jupiter, Saturn is still contracting after its formation from the primordial nebula. It has at least eighteen moons and may have fourteen more. The *Cassini* probe, a NASA/ European Space Agency joint venture expected to arrive at Saturn in 2004, may clarify the issue.

No one knows what knocked over **Uranus.** Its poles are where its equator should be and vice versa. When he discovered it in 1781, English astronomer William Herschel thought he'd found a comet and named it "Georgium Sidus" ("Star of George," in honor of King George III). Then it was called Herschel for a while until a German astronomer, Johann Elert Bode, named it for the Greek god of the sky. Uranus has at least eleven rings and some partial rings, or arcs. The first of these weren't discovered until 1977, when *Voyager* investigated. *Voyager* also discovered ten of Uranus's seventeen moons, most of which are named for female characters in Shakespeare, such as Titania, Miranda, Rosalind, Portia, Juliet, Desdemona, Ophelia, and Cordelia.

Voyager spotted six of the eight moons of **Neptune.** French astronomer and mathematician Urbain-Jean-Joseph Le Verrier predicted the planet's existence in 1846, based on irregularities in Uranus's orbit, and his hunch was confirmed within 1° almost immediately by German astronomer Johann Gottfried Galle. Neptune's Great Dark Spot is about as large as the Earth, and winds near it gust up to 1,200 mph. Named for the Roman sea god, Neptune has four rings, and the largest moon, Triton (also a sea god), may provide

329

the fifth: It's being drawn slowly closer to the planet because of intense gravity and will fracture millions of years from now.

Percival Lowell predicted the existence of **Pluto** in 1905 because of disturbances in Uranus's orbit. It was sighted in 1930 after a meticulous visual search of the heavens by the recently deceased (1997) Clyde W. Tombaugh, who was at the time a twenty-four-year-old self-taught American astronomer and telescope maker. During about 8 percent of its orbital time (20 years of its 248.5-year orbit), eccentric Pluto dips inside Neptune's orbit. Some consider frigid Pluto (named for the god of the underworld) and its sole, slightly smaller moon, Charon (another underworld deity), to be the largest bodies in the Kuiper belt, a group of small icy objects at the very edge of the solar system. Pluto and Charon are linked gravitationally so that the same hemispheres always face one another—like two touch-dancers whose gazes never waver.

✳ QUESTION 81

What are the 9 Circles of Dante's *Inferno?*

1. Limbo: the Virtuous Heathens
2. The Lustful
3. The Gluttons
4. The Avaricious and the Prodigal
5. The Wrathful and the Sullen
6. The Heretics
7. The Violent
8. The Fraudulent
9. The Treacherous

The "Nine Circles" of the *Inferno* (the first part of Dante's epic poem, *The Divine Comedy*) is a bit misleading, since the author crammed about four times that number of different kinds of sins and sinners into his Hell, which is shaped like a vast inverted hollow cone beneath the surface of the ground, with its vertex at the center of the earth. But where did Dante get his main groupings from? In Canto 11 of the *Inferno,* Virgil explains the moral structure of Hell by referring to Aristotle's *Nicomachean Ethics,* where Dante found a threefold division of wrongful behavior that prompted his three major divisions of

Hell into regions where the sins of incontinence, violence, and fraud are punished (see Question 13).

Before visiting the First Circle, we have to mention "Circle Zero," the eternal home of souls who remained neutral in life—the fence sitters, the lukewarm, who were neither good nor bad, but looked out only for Numero Uno. Dante, the fierce political partisan and exile, heaps bitter scorn on these pathetic cover-your-ass types who aren't even worthy enough to get into Hell proper. Instead, they suffer their paltry punishments outside the boundaries of Hell in a kind of antechamber or vestibule.

Circle 1, or **Limbo,** is the habitation of all the unbaptized who either lived virtuous lives or died too young to sin. Since baptism was viewed as a prerequisite for salvation, these **Virtuous Heathens** cannot enter Heaven, but neither are they physically punished. Their only pain is their perpetual deprivation of the sight of God. In an exclusive neighborhood of Limbo, Dante has collected his heroes and heroines of the ancient and medieval world: great Greek, Roman, and even Moslem warriors, scholars, poets, and philosophers, culminating in a procession of the five greatest poets of antiquity who, naturally, invite Dante to join their select club.

In **Circle 2,** we find the first major grouping of the incontinent, the **Lustful,** including the star-crossed lovers Paolo Malatesta and Francesca da Rimini, forever thrashed about through the black sky of Hell by a tempest that represents their own tumultuous passions. It's interesting that Dante considers lust the least blameworthy sin (the sins and punishments get worse the farther down you go). Taken as a group, lust and most of the other incontinent sins of **Circles 2 to 5— gluttony, avarice, wrath,** and **sullenness** (which was often viewed as a form of sloth)—seem to suggest that Dante may have started his poem with the intention of covering only the seven deadly sins (see Question 63). If so, he changed his mind (saving the deadly sins as the organizing principle for his *Purgatorio* instead) and embarked on a much-expanded version of the *Inferno.*

The boundary between the upper Hell of incontinence and the lower Hell of violence and fraud is the wall of the City of Dis (a name for Pluto, god of the underworld). After a confrontation with demons guarding the city walls, Dante and Virgil enter the gates and survey the fiery torments of the **Heretics** in **Circle 6,** who, though in lower Hell, remain outside its threefold moral division. The two poets then move on to **Circle 7,** which punishes the **Violent,** who are subdivided into the violent against others, against self (suicides and spend-thrifts), and against God (blasphemers like Capaneus—see Question 60), nature (sodomites), and human industry (usurers).

To get to **Circle 8,** Dante and his guide have to fly down on the back of a monster named Geryon. The circle of **fraud,** named Malebolge ("evil pouches"), is shaped like a huge sloping circular arena divided into ten broad concentric trenches. In these, about fifteen kinds of fraudulent sinners are punished: pimps and seducers, flatterers, simoniacs (buyers and sellers of Church offices—we meet a few popes here), soothsayers and magicians, crooked politicians, hypocrites, thieves, false counselors (like Ulysses), sowers of scandal and schism, and falsifiers or phonies (alchemists, impersonators, counterfeiters, and liars).

Finally, to reach **Circle 9,** the abode of **treachery,** which is fraud compounded by a shattered bond of trust, Dante and Virgil need the services of the giant Antaeus, who picks them up and sets them down on the frozen lake forming the floor of Hell. This last circle comprises four zones: Caina (traitors to family), Antenora (political traitors), Ptolomea (betrayers of guests), and Judecca (traitors to benefactors). At the very center of Hell, the poets see the enormous three-faced figure of Lucifer (Satan), who chomps on Julius Caesar's assassins, Brutus and Cassius, with his side mouths, and Judas, the betrayer of Christ, with his central mouth. Lucifer is himself punished as the worst of all creatures for his revolt against the Benefactor who had made him brightest and mightiest of the angels (see Question 76).

What are the 10 Commandments?

1. "I am the Lord thy God, which have brought thee out of the land of Egypt, out of the house of bondage. Thou shalt have no other gods before me."
2. "Thou shalt not make unto thee any graven image, or any likeness of any thing that is in heaven above, or that is in the earth beneath, or that is in the water under the earth: Thou shalt not bow down thyself to them, nor serve them: for I the Lord thy God am a jealous God, visiting the iniquity of the fathers upon the children unto the third and fourth generation of them that hate me; and shewing mercy unto thousands of them that love me, and keep my commandments."
3. "Thou shalt not take the name of the Lord thy God in vain; for the Lord will not hold him guiltless that taketh his name in vain."
4. "Remember the sabbath day, to keep it holy. Six days shalt thou labour, and do all thy work: But the seventh day is the sabbath of the Lord thy God: in it thou shalt not do any work, thou, nor thy son, nor thy daughter, thy manservant, nor thy maidservant, nor thy cattle, nor thy stranger that is within thy gates: For in six days the Lord made heaven and earth, the sea, and all that in them is, and rested the seventh day: wherefore the Lord blessed the sabbath day, and hallowed it."
5. "Honor thy father and thy mother: that thy days may be long upon the land which the Lord thy God giveth thee."
6. "Thou shalt not kill."
7. "Thou shalt not commit adultery."

8. "Thou shalt not steal."
9. "Thou shalt not bear false witness against thy neighbor."
10. "Thou shalt not covet thy neighbor's house, thou shalt not covet thy neighbor's wife, nor his manservant, nor his maidservant, nor his ox, nor his ass, nor any thing that is thy neighbor's" (Exodus 20:2–17).

The Israelites cowered at the foot of Sinai as Moses and Aaron ascended to meet Yahweh, who was obscured by a thick cloud of smoke, fire, and lightning at the summit. Yahweh's voice could be heard over a din of thunder and trumpet blasts as he gave Moses his commandments, marking the establishment of the Mosaic Covenant between God and Israel.

The story of the Ten Commandments, also called the Decalogue (Greek, *deka logoi,* "ten words"), occurs in two similar accounts, in Exodus 20 and Deuteronomy 5. In Deuteronomy, however, the scene takes place on Mount Horeb rather than Sinai, and Yahweh himself inscribes the covenant with his finger on stone tablets. In Exodus, Moses is the transcriber. It's also in the Deuteronomy account that we are told of "the land of milk and honey" and are enjoined to "stray neither to right nor to left" and to "love the Lord, your God, with all your heart, and with all your soul, and with all your strength." Both versions of the Ten Commandments were probably derived from a more ancient source that was less elaborate—more along the order of "Thou shalt not kill." Thus, the proposed "date" of the Decalogue varies quite widely, from the sixteenth century B.C. to sometime after 750 B.C.

The arrangement of the Ten Commandments differs in Judaism, Protestantism, and Catholicism, partly because specific numbers are absent in both the Exodus and Deuteronomy texts. In the fifth century, St. Augustine compounded the ambiguity by folding the second commandment into the first so that it read, "I am the Lord thy God. Thou shalt not have strange gods before me; thou shalt not make to thyself any graven thing to adore it." The third commandment then became the second, the fourth the third, and so on. To end up with the requisite ten, it became necessary to cleave the last commandment in two. Thus, the ninth became "Thou shalt not covet thy neighbor's wife," and the tenth was reserved for all other situations in which endeavoring to keep up with the Joneses was deemed sinful. In the mid-sixteenth century, the Council of Trent adopted this arrangement—and also affirmed that the Ten Commandments applied to Christians, as they had to the Jews of the Old Testament.

The Roman Catholic and Lutheran churches still use Augustine's numbering system and justify it on the basis that the revi ed first commandment incorporates injunctions against false worship and the worship of false gods, which are clearly variations on the same heretical theme. This line of reasoning also facilitates the division of the original tenth commandment into two. Since the *acts* of adultery and theft are forbidden by two different commandments, it also made sense (at least in this schema) to separate the *desire* to commit these sins into two separate commandments. Nonetheless, critics have suggested that Catholicism adhered to Augustine because burying the second commandment within the first deemphasized it. This served to divert attention from the profusion of statues and religious images that—despite various iconoclastic rampages over the years—still enliven Catholic churches. Protestant denominations (other than Lutheranism), the Greek Orthodox Church, and Judaism use the more conventional system of enumerating the commandments.

Whatever the arrangement, the Ten Commandments were, until recently, indelibly etched—one might almost say "carved by the finger of God"—in the memory of most Jews, Catholics, and Protestants. But when the host of a late-night talk show took to the streets in the mid-1990s to ask people he met whether they could name any of the commandments, the response of one twenty-something was a diffident, shoulder-shrugging "Free speech?"

What were the 10 major U.S. wars and their dates?

Revolutionary War (1775–83)	World War I (1917–18)
War of 1812 (1812–15)	World War II (1941–45)
Mexican War (1846–48)	Korean War (1950–53)
Civil War (1861–65)	Vietnam War (1961–73)
Spanish-American War (1898)	Persian Gulf War (1991)

Why has the United States gone to war over the years? As with many nations, the causes have often been an inextricable tangle of altruism and self-interest, ranging from achieving independence and maintaining unity to gobbling up territory or colonies, from helping friends abroad defeat intolerable tyrannies to safeguarding the flow of inexpensive fuel oil, from preserving freedom of the seas to stopping the spread of communism.

Our survey starts before there was a United States. By 1763, after driving the French from Canada in the French and Indian War, the British apparently reigned supreme in North America. But the American colonists' rising discontent with British rule came to a head over taxes and eventually led them to engage the might of their mother country in the **Revolutionary War.**

Asserting their rights as Englishmen to pay taxes levied only by assemblies that represented them, the colonists first rejected the Stamp Act of 1765. In 1767, the Crown imposed new taxes on paint, paper, glass, and tea. Facing strident protests once again, King George III's government sent an ambiguous message in 1770 by repealing all the new levies—except the one on tea. This, coupled with the Crown's attempts to secure a monopoly on the tea trade for the East India Tea Company, induced the colonists to dump 342 chests of tea into Boston Harbor in December 1773 in the Boston Tea Party.

In response, the British upped the ante in 1774 by passing what the colonists called the Intolerable Acts. Instead of cowing the rebellious colonists, these measures, which included quartering British soldiers in private houses and closing Boston Harbor until restitution was made for the tea and other losses, drove the final wedge between Britain and her American subjects. Many colonists now felt that the sometimes blurry line between legitimate rule and tyranny had been definitively crossed.

On April 19, 1775, General Thomas Gage, governor of Massachusetts colony, ordered his troops to Concord to seize weapons the colonists had stored there. On the way, in Lexington, they exchanged fire with seventy-seven Minutemen. Although the British quashed this resistance, they were not so fortunate in Concord, where a militia of four hundred men, alerted by Paul Revere, sent them packing back to Boston under sniper fire the whole way. Ralph Waldo Emerson immortalized the action in his "Concord Hymn" of 1837:

> By the rude bridge that arched the flood,
>   Their flag to April's breeze unfurled,
> Here once the embattled farmers stood,
>   And fired the shot heard round the world.

Fighting continued sporadically during the next year, and the Continental Congress appointed George Washington commander-in-chief of the American forces, which comprised the Continental Army and the militia (civilians with guns). By this time, the movement had expanded beyond the fight against oppressive taxes to a struggle for complete independence from England, a transition fueled by a pamphlet entitled *Common Sense,* published in January 1776 by English-born Thomas Paine.

In a major victory, the Americans drove the British, under the command of General William Howe, from Boston on March 17, 1776. The colonies proclaimed their freedom from England in the Declaration of Independence, drafted by Thomas Jefferson and approved by the Continental Congress on July 4, 1776. The infant nation was now fighting for its survival.

Between August and December of 1776, General Howe managed to push General Washington out of Long Island and Manhattan, then out of New Jersey and across into Pennsylvania on the west bank of the Delaware River. In a bold move that may have saved the cause of independence, Washington gathered 4,000 men and crossed the

Delaware on Christmas night. In a dawn raid, the Americans captured 1,000 Hessians (much-hated German mercenaries) in a garrison at Trenton, New Jersey. Washington won a second battle on January 3, 1777, at Princeton.

General Howe again defeated Washington at Brandywine Creek in southeastern Pennsylvania and drove the Continental Congress from Philadelphia. British General John Burgoyne was less successful and, after a humiliating defeat, surrendered his forces to the Americans at Saratoga, New York, on October 7, 1777. The French, now realizing that the British could be defeated and eager to avenge their loss of Canada and other possessions, entered the war on the side of the Americans in 1778, dispatching a fleet and military advisers. The Battle of Saratoga is thus often called the turning point of the Revolutionary War (see Question 97).

Spain and the Netherlands entered the war against the British in 1779 and 1780, respectively, and kept the Crown's Navy busy in Europe. The Americans sorely needed this help, since the Continental Navy was tiny, unschooled, and undisciplined, although it had an exceptional officer in John Paul Jones. American privateers—pirates with licenses from Congress—were more effective, preying on the goods of British merchants, who begged their government to end the war.

Except for British raids against coastal towns such as New Bedford, Massachusetts, and New Haven, Connecticut, the military action now shifted from the Northeast to the Mid-Atlantic region and the South. The British held Georgia, and the Americans were handed a shattering defeat in South Carolina by Lord Cornwallis. But on October 19, 1781, Cornwallis found himself trapped in Yorktown, Virginia, wedged in between the Americans on land and the French on the Chesapeake. He surrendered his entire army of more than 7,000 men—this effectively ending the land war—while his military band played "The World Turned Upside Down." The Treaty of Paris (1783) recognized U.S. independence and American claims to all territory west to the Mississippi.

The **War of 1812** has been called one of the most unnecessary in history. Great Britain and Napoleonic France were at war, and neutrals like the United States were being harassed. Britain had initiated a blockade of all French ports and, in 1807, demanded that neutral vessels stop in England and pay duties before continuing on their way. In addition, British naval vessels stopped American ships on the high seas and relieved them of nearly 4,000 sailors, absurdly claiming they were deserters from the Royal Navy. Besides the economic consequences of having to pay duties to Britain, Americans resented their role as pawns in an international dispute. Some were also clamoring for the ejection of the British from Canada because of their support for the Shawnee Indian leader Tecumseh, who was trying to repel white settlers near the Canadian border. To demonstrate that the United States would not play second fiddle to Britain in international affairs, President James Madison reluctantly declared war.

This conflict lasted two and a half years and was marked by noteworthy battles on the Great Lakes and in Baltimore, where British attempts at invasion were foiled. In 1814, though, the British burned public buildings in Washington, most notably the newly completed White House. President Madison barely managed to escape capture. New England maritimers, who suffered particularly heavy losses during the war, met in Hartford, Connecticut, in 1814 to discuss secession from the Union.

The Treaty of Ghent ended the war on December 24, 1814, preserving the status quo. In a final absurdity, news of the treaty failed to reach British forces in New Orleans, who attacked the city on January 8, 1815. American troops, under the command of General Andrew Jackson, repelled the 7,500-man attack within the amazingly short time of thirty minutes, but not before about 300 British and 30 American soldiers lost their lives.

The events that led to the **Mexican War** began with the annexation of Texas by the United States in 1845, which the citizens of Texas had first voted for in 1836, shortly after Sam Houston defeated Mexican General Santa Anna and established Texas as an independent republic. The Mexican government immediately severed all diplomatic relations with the United States. A major dispute revolved around whether Mexico's northern border was the Nueces River, as Mexico claimed, or the Rio Grande, as the Americans asserted. In addition, President James K. Polk was rebuffed when he offered Mexico $30 million for what are now New Mexico and California.

In retaliation, Polk ordered General Zachary Taylor to lead his troops into the disputed area between the Rio Grande and the Nueces. On April 25, 1846, Mexican troops crossed the Rio Grande and shelled Fort Brown on May 3. On May 13, the United States declared war. Abolitionists viewed the entire campaign as an attempt to expand the number of slave states, and many others viewed it as raw greed.

High-principled Henry David Thoreau spent a night in jail because of his refusal to pay a tax he saw as contributing to the war. The result was his influential essay "On Civil Disobedience."

American incursions into New Mexico and California went nearly unopposed. General Taylor captured the city of Monterrey and won the Battle of Buena Vista in early 1847. In March, General Winfield Scott seized the port of Veracruz and marched inland to take Mexico City in a battle that ended on September 14. In February 1848, the war was concluded with the Treaty of Guadalupe Hidalgo. In exchange for $15 million, the United States acquired a vast region: besides Texas, the current states of New Mexico, Utah, Arizona, California, and Nevada, and part of western Colorado.

The **Civil War** had been actively brewing since the adoption of the Missouri Compromise (1820–21), which admitted Missouri as a slave state and Maine as a free state and banned slavery in all western territories. In the ensuing decades, the Southern states, struggling to preserve slavery, states' rights, a distinct culture, and a cotton-based economic system, were increasingly threatened by the North's opposition to slavery and its stranglehold on the Southern economy.

South Carolina seceded from the Union on December 20, 1860, in response to the election of Republican Abraham Lincoln. Lincoln was a known opponent of slavery whose primary goal was preservation of the Union. Six more states followed South Carolina's lead, and the Confederate States of America was founded in February of 1861 with Jefferson Davis as President. The Confederacy eventually included eleven states (see Question 85).

Confederate troops took Fort Sumter, in Charleston, South Carolina, from the Union on April 12, 1861. On April 15, Lincoln ordered a blockade of Southern ports and, in response, four more Southern states seceded. The first battle of the war was fought at Bull Run (called Manassas by the Southerners) in northern Virginia, with federal troops under the command of Irvin McDowell and the Confederates under Thomas "Stonewall" Jackson and P. G. T. Beauregard. While curious picnickers watched, what started as an amateurish contest ended with federal troops retreating hastily to Washington. Both sides now realized the gravity of the situation, and the likelihood of a prolonged war.

In 1862, Union General Ulysses S. Grant salvaged Tennessee by clearing the upper Mississippi and the lower Cumberland rivers and winning the battles of Shiloh and Corinth. Admiral David G. Farragut took New Orleans easily. In the East, however, the war went poorly for the Union. Confederate General Robert E. Lee crushed General George B. McClellan in the Peninsular Campaign in Virginia, a Union attempt to capture the Confederate capital of Richmond. McClellan was bested again at the Second Battle of Bull Run, and the Union suffered another defeat in Fredericksburg, Virginia.

On July 4, 1863, Grant captured Vicksburg, Mississippi, and the great Mississippi River was now entirely under Union control. At the same time, Lee's campaign in Pennsylvania ended when he was defeated at the Battle of Gettysburg (July 1–3, 1863) and forced to retreat to Virginia. Grant, now commander of the Union Army, kept Lee under siege in Petersburg, Virginia, for nearly a year. Union General William Tecumseh Sherman took Atlanta on September 2, 1864. Later that autumn, after torching Atlanta, he undertook his infamous, three-hundred-mile march to the sea, cutting a bloody and fiery swath through Georgia, culminating victoriously in Savannah, which he presented to Lincoln as a Christmas gift.

On April 9, 1865, Lee surrendered to Grant at Appomattox Courthouse, near Richmond. Lincoln was assassinated five days later (see Question 27). About 620,000 men died on the battlefield or in military hospitals during the Civil War, making it America's bloodiest conflict. The Union was preserved, and the slaves, who had been freed in the Confederacy by Lincoln's Emancipation Proclamation of January 1, 1863, and elsewhere by the Thirteenth Amendment (1865), became U.S. citizens. In this war, railroads first played a vital role, great naval battles were fought with iron ships, a submarine sank a warship, photographers preserved its images, communications were enhanced by telegraph, and repeating rifles were introduced. The grim combat experiences gained in this war, and the enormous industrial expansion that fueled it, made the United States a power to be reckoned with.

In the view of some historians, the importance of the **Spanish-American War** is underrated. This conflict had its roots in decades of oppression of Cuba by Spain. Beginning in 1895, the yellow press kept the American public fully apprised of Spain's brutality—including its concentration camps—so that public opinion sided decisively with the Cuban revolutionaries. Big business also sided with them, since it had at least $50 million invested in Cuba. And American diplomats appreciated the strategic importance of the large island only ninety miles from their shores.

In October 1897, the Spanish announced that the concentration camps would be closed. The situation appeared resolved, but on February 15, 1898, the U.S. battleship *Maine* exploded in Havana Harbor, ostensibly as the result of an external mine, with the loss of 266 American lives. Accusations were heaped on Spain, though its responsibility was never proved (a Navy board of inquiry in 1976 concluding that the cause was an internal explosion). Washington was alerted via diplomatic channels that Spain was prepared to grant Cuba limited independence, such as Great Britain had accorded Canada, but President William McKinley capitulated to Wall Street, Congress, public opinion, and the press—"Remember the *Maine,* to hell with Spain!" Rather than accept Spain's proffered olive branch, he rattled so many sabers that Spain declared war on April 24, 1898.

On May 1, Commodore George Dewey obliterated the Spanish fleet in Manila Bay in the Philippines. Ten weeks later, Manila was occupied by the Americans. Lieutenant Colonel Theodore Roosevelt made a name for himself in the famous charge with his Rough Riders up San Juan Hill in Cuba. On July 17, the tattered remnants of the Spanish Caribbean fleet surrendered at Santiago, Cuba, and the war was over by the end of the month. Spain signed a treaty on December 10, 1898, by which it relinquished control of Cuba and transferred Guam, Puerto Rico, and—for $20 million—the Philippines to the United States, which emerged with a strong military force and far-flung influence in the Caribbean and Pacific. Along with the annexation of Hawaii in 1898, the Spanish-American War made the United States a country with vital stakes in a Pacific world that Japan would seek to dominate four decades later.

During the early years of **World War I,** which had ravaged Europe since 1914, President Woodrow Wilson made herculean efforts to maintain the neutrality of the United States despite reports of starvation and German atrocities in Belgium and France. After 128 Americans were killed when a German submarine sank the British luxury liner *Lusitania* on May 7, 1915, Wilson denounced the barbarous act so stridently that weak-kneed Secretary of State William Jennings Bryan resigned.

The German submarine campaign abated for several months, and Wilson won reelection in 1916 mainly because "He kept us out of war!" But on January 9, 1917, Kaiser William (Wilhelm) II sanctioned a policy of unrestricted submarine warfare, to go into effect on

February 1, to cripple England's war effort. Fear of U-boat attacks impaired traffic in and out of U.S. ports.

American public opinion was further galvanized by newspaper publication on March 1 of the intercepted Zimmermann telegram to the Mexican President. In this message, the German Foreign Minister proposed a German-Mexican military alliance that, with Germany's financial support, would enable Mexico to reconquer much of the territory it had lost to the United States—Texas, New Mexico, and Arizona.

Meanwhile more ships were sunk and American lives lost. Congress declared war on Germany on April 6, 1917, and the first 243 American soldiers arrived in England on May 18. The timing was fortunate for France and Great Britain, who could no longer pay for the supplies the Americans had been sending for several years. In addition, French troops were beginning to mutiny, and the Bolshevik Revolution would take Russia out of the war by the end of the year.

America's intervention ensured Germany's defeat: Its vast wealth, industrial might, and huge population inspired nightmares of proliferating Allied troops, ships, planes, and weapons in the German High Command. U.S. forces, commanded by General John J. ("Black Jack") Pershing, poured into Europe—more than 1.2 million were in France by September 1918. On October 10, after nearly two months of fighting, the Americans drove the Germans out of the Argonne Forest and later launched a successful offensive on the Meuse. Germany saw the handwriting on the wall and decided that asking for an armistice under the terms of President Wilson's Fourteen Points was the best chance it had to avoid invasion, destruction of its army, territorial dismemberment, and continuing starvation from the British blockade of its seaports (see Question 96).

The armistice was signed on November 11, 1918, and the Treaty of Versailles, signed on June 28, 1919, officially ended the war. But peace did not lead to reconciliation (see Question 30). The horrendous death toll exacted by the war included at least 8.6 million soldiers and 13 million civilians. The United States emerged comparatively unscathed with 49,000 combat deaths. The 1918 influenza pandemic was deadlier for U.S. troops, killing more than 62,000.

In the years after World War I, most Americans accepted the view that the United States had been unnecessarily dragged into that conflict by powerful financiers with interests in an Allied victory. As a result, isolationism and, to a lesser extent, pacifism characterized the 1930s, even as Adolf Hitler rose to power in Germany and Japan proceeded to carve up China. The economic hardships of the Great Depression kept Americans sharply focused on domestic concerns during this decade. Congress passed several Neutrality Acts, which prevented the President from providing aid to either side in the event of another war.

President Franklin D. Roosevelt's confidence in isolationism began to falter in 1938 after the disastrous Munich accords, by which British Prime Minister Neville Chamberlain's policy of appeasement allowed Hitler to snap up Czechoslovakia. In 1939, when Germany's invasion of Poland detonated **World War II,** Roosevelt asked Congress to amend the Neutrality Acts so that Great Britain and France could purchase weapons. After the Germans defeated France in June 1940, Roosevelt resupplied weapons for the British troops evacuated from Dunkirk and traded fifty old destroyers for the right to maintain U.S. military bases in Newfoundland, the Bermudas, and the British Caribbean islands—without the assent of Congress. Late that summer, however, Congress passed the nation's first military draft law during peacetime.

But even as Roosevelt ran for an unprecedented third term in 1940, he continued to claim he would keep the United States out of direct involvement in the conflict. This was a wise public pronouncement, since Gallup polls showed that about 80 percent of Americans wanted the country to stay out of war, although they supported Great Britain's struggle against Hitler. Shortly after his inauguration in 1941, Roosevelt signed the Lend-Lease Act, which made it possible for the British and, shortly afterward, the Soviets, to obtain many billions of dollars in military supplies on credit. The U.S. Navy aided British ships in North Atlantic convoys, and by the fall of 1941 Germany and the United States were involved in an undeclared naval war. Neither Roosevelt nor Hitler was eager to make it official.

Events were no less complicated in the Pacific, where the United States backed China in its war with Japan, yet continued to supply Japan with oil and scrap metal. When the United States finally imposed a scrap-metal embargo in September 1940, Japan quickly joined the alliance of Germany and Italy, forming the Tripartite Pact, or the Rome-Berlin-Tokyo Axis (see Question 50). As late as the summer of 1941, the United States was supplying Japan with oil. When that well ran dry, the Japanese, led by General Tojo, made war on the United States. The plan was to destroy the U.S. Pacific Fleet and grab all of southeast Asia—and its oil—before America could recover from the blow.

Having intercepted and decoded Axis messages, the Americans knew a Japanese attack was forthcoming, but they expected it in the Philippines. On the morning of December 7, 1941, Japanese carrier-based planes began their assault against the U.S. Fleet and airfields at Pearl Harbor, Hawaii. Six battleships were sunk or seriously damaged, 188 aircraft were destroyed, and more than 2,400 Americans were killed and almost 1,200 wounded. On the next day, Japanese war-planes bombed American air bases on the island of Luzon in the Philippines, destroying more than half the aircraft stationed there. Congress immediately declared war on Japan, and Germany and Italy declared war on the United States on December 11, causing British Prime Minister Winston Churchill to exclaim, "So we have won after all!"

But not quite yet. In the winter and spring of 1942, the Japanese took Singapore, the Dutch East Indies, and the Philippines, along with the U.S. island stronghold on Corregidor. General Douglas MacArthur, forced to retreat from the Philippines to Australia, vowed to return. On May 7–8, however, American Navy carrier planes stopped the Japanese push through the Solomon Islands at the Battle of the Coral Sea, quite probably saving Australia from Japanese con-quest. The Japanese offensive through the central Pacific was halted on June 3–6 at the Battle of Midway, in which Japan lost four aircraft carriers, a cruiser, 332 warplanes, and 3,500 men. By February 1943, the Japanese were finally driven from Guadalcanal in the Solomon Islands.

The Germans dominated the North Atlantic through 1942, sinking six million tons of Allied shipping. But by mid-1943, the Allies had gained the upper hand, thanks in part to a titanic American industrial buildup. And although Hitler's conquests stretched from France to Russia and from North Africa to the Arctic Ocean, their very vastness made them difficult to defend and provided the Allies with many targets. The British and Americans, working together as the Combined Chiefs of Staff, determined that Hitler posed a greater threat than Emperor Hirohito and adopted a "Europe First" policy. Forces under the command of General Dwight D. Eisenhower spent most of 1942 and 1943 driving German forces from North Africa, Sicily, and southern Italy.

Then, on D-Day, June 6, 1944, 155,000 British, American, and Canadian troops—the first wave in the invasion of Hitler's "Fortress Europe"—landed on the beaches of Normandy. Paris was liberated on August 25. After a series of major battles in Europe, including the fierce Battle of the Bulge, the Western Allies and the Soviet Army closed in for the kill on a Germany whose cities, like Dresden and Berlin itself, were undergoing devastating bombardment. The advancing Allies found camp after camp bristling with evidence of Nazi barbarities that claimed the lives of six million Jews and nine to ten million Poles, Ukrainians, Belorussians, Gypsies, political dissidents, and homosexuals. On April 30, 1945, Hitler committed suicide in his fortified bunker beneath Berlin just hours before a Soviet soldier planted the Hammer and Sickle on the roof of the Reichstag. What was left of Germany surrendered unconditionally a week later on May 7 in Rheims and May 8 in Berlin.

In the Pacific, the Japanese could not withstand the astounding output of ships, warplanes, submarines, tanks, and weaponry that America threw against them. The United States won the battles of the Bismarck Sea in March 1943, the Philippine Sea in June 1944 (the greatest carrier battle of the war), and Leyte Gulf in October 1944, where Japan's loss of thirty-six warships, including four carriers and three battleships in the greatest sea fight in history, meant the virtual end of its naval capacity. From November 1943 through the following summer, American troops had struck at the Gilbert Islands, the Marshalls, the Carolines, and the Marianas, which included Guam. U.S. Marines landed on Iwo Jima on February 19, 1945, in an effort to convert the tiny volcanic island into an air base for fighter planes escorting B-29 bombers in raids against Japan. A month later, this objective was achieved at a cost of 6,800 American dead.

A ferocious war of its own was fought in Okinawa, only 360 miles southwest of Kyushu, the southernmost Japanese home island. On Easter Sunday, April 1, 1945, about 50,000 Army and Marine troops went ashore, part of the 183,000 combat and 362,000 support personnel deployed by the United States in the last and greatest battle of the Pacific war. Possession of Okinawa was critical for both sides because it was to be the staging area for the American invasion of Japan. The U.S. Navy sustained heavy losses (36 ships sunk and 368 others damaged), especially from 1,900 kamikaze attacks. By the time the island was finally conquered on June 21, more than 100,000 Okinawan civilians and 12,500 American and 110,000 Japanese troops were dead—about one sixth of these being incinerated or sealed in caves by U.S. forces using flamethrowers and explosives. Meanwhile American warplanes were pummeling Japan from the sky, destroying its major cities with firebombs and killing more than 83,000 in Tokyo alone in an incendiary raid on the night of March 9.

The invasion of Japan was set for November 1945 (Kyushu) and March 1946 (Honshu). After Roosevelt died early in his fourth term, President Harry S. Truman ultimately decided on another course he believed would spare the estimated 1 million American lives that a fight to the death on the Japanese home islands would exact. On August 6, 1945, a B-29 bomber, the *Enola Gay,* dropped an atomic weapon on Hiroshima, a city in southern Honshu, killing 80,000 people instantly and wounding the same number. On August 9, a second bomb was dropped on Nagasaki, killing at least another 40,000. The Japanese surrendered on August 14. General MacArthur received the formal surrender aboard the USS *Missouri* in Tokyo Bay on September 2, 1945, ending a war whose human cost remains incalculable and imponderable.

World War II sowed the seeds of the **Korean War,** which has not yet officially ended. Japanese troops stationed above the 38th parallel in Korea (long a Japanese colony) had surrendered to the Soviets, those south of it to the Americans. Attempts by the United Nations to reunite Korea failed, and Soviet and American troops bequeathed the peninsula a Communist government in the North and a non-Communist one in the South.

The North Koreans attacked the South on June 25, 1950. President Truman did not consult with Congress before sending American troops, commanded by General Douglas MacArthur (fighting in his third major war), to join United Nations forces in defense of the beleaguered South Koreans. MacArthur rescued South Korea brilliantly with his daring assault at Inchon and subsequent capture of Pyongyang, the North Korean capital.

But he didn't stop there. Despite warnings from the Chinese, UN and American forces pressed toward the Korea-China border, aiming at total reunification of the peninsula. The Chinese poured 200,000 troops into the widening conflict, pushing the Americans back to the 38th parallel. Only intense bombing thwarted another

Communist invasion of the South. In an extraordinary move, MacArthur appealed to the American people for a broader war effort—that is, knocking out Communist China—instead of making his case privately with the President. In April 1951, Commander-in-Chief Truman fired his insubordinate. After continued fighting, unproductive peace talks, and increased resistance in the United States, newly elected President Dwight D. Eisenhower used diplomatic channels to warn China of the risk of nuclear strikes if a peace settlement remained elusive. A cease-fire was signed in July 1953 with the borders of the North and South where they started—and have remained. About 34,000 Americans died in the conflict.

The bitterly divisive **Vietnam War** had its roots in the French struggle to retain control of its colony of Indochina after the end of World War II. Ho Chi Minh, who had not been allowed to present a petition against the French to President Woodrow Wilson at the Paris Peace Conference in 1919, headed the Vietnamese independence movement, known as the Vietminh. (He lived to lead his nation against the armies of Presidents John Kennedy, Lyndon Johnson, and Richard Nixon until his death in 1969.) The war against the French lasted from 1946 until the disastrous French defeat at Dien Bien Phu and cease-fire of 1954, which divided the country in two at the 17th parallel, with the Communists in the North and the non-Communists in the South—Korea all over again.

Free elections scheduled for 1956 with the aim of reuniting the country were opposed by the leader of the South, Ngo Dinh Diem. Supported by the United States, which feared the spread of communism in southeast Asia, Diem was the recipient of growing military and nonmilitary aid from Presidents Eisenhower and Kennedy. Fighting escalated between Communists in South Vietnam—the Vietcong—and Diem's Army of the Republic of Vietnam (ARVN). More than 10,000 American military so-called advisers were in South Vietnam by the end of 1962.

In August 1964, after President Johnson announced that North Vietnamese gunboats had fired on two American destroyers in the Gulf of Tonkin, Congress authorized full intervention in what many Americans came to view as someone else's civil war. The American air assault began in earnest in 1965 with bombings of the North. By the end of the year, General William C. Westmoreland commanded nearly 200,000 American troops in South Vietnam—and nearly 400,000 by 1967. Although the Americans were vastly superior in firepower and air operations, the Vietcong excelled at guerrilla warfare, which gnawed away at U.S. troop morale.

The Tet offensive, launched by the North Vietnamese and Vietcong at the lunar New Year, January 30, 1968, was a turning point in the war. More than thirty cities were attacked in the South, including the capital, Saigon. Although at least 30,000 Communist troops were killed during the offensive and U.S. forces drove the enemy back from all sites, the American public—sickened by the images of blood and rubble that the evening news shot into their living rooms—began to wonder whether the Vietnamese quagmire would suck the United States down into its first military defeat. The peace movement rocketed into prominence, and President Johnson declined to run for reelection in 1968.

His successor, President Nixon, began troop withdrawals in 1969 in conjunction with a policy of Vietnamization, a means of returning responsibility for their own defense to the South Vietnamese. In 1970, however, the war widened when the Americans entered Cambodia and bombed Laos in pursuit of North Vietnamese troops—a policy vigorously opposed by many at home. The U.S. pullout continued even as the Paris peace talks floundered and American bombs pounded North Vietnamese ports in early 1972.

A peace agreement was signed on January 27, 1973, with continued division at the 17th parallel, and most remaining American military personnel were withdrawn within two months. The North, however, continued to prosecute the war against the South, and on April 30, 1975, the government of South Vietnam surrendered unconditionally. After a bloodbath in the South, the unified country became known as the Socialist Republic of Vietnam. The United States, which had not been so polarized into hostile camps since its own Civil War, reaped the bitter harvest of its foolishly indecisive military and political policies.

Years later, Iraqi President Saddam Hussein's decision to have his army spend their 1990 summer vacation in Kuwait led to America's participation in the antithesis of the Vietnam conflict, the **Persian Gulf War.** Iraqi troops invaded their oil-saturated neighbor on August 2, 1990, claiming it as their nineteenth province. On August 6, the United Nations Security Council banned all trade with Iraq. Undeterred, Hussein poured hundreds of thousands of troops into Kuwait. Iraq's perceived threat to Saudi Arabia led the United States, its NATO allies, Egypt, and Syria to initiate a massive troop buildup in

Arabia known as Operation Desert Shield, which was orchestrated by the Chairman of the U.S. Joint Chiefs of Staff, General Colin Powell, and implemented by General Norman Schwarzkopf. Allied forces numbered more than 700,000, including 540,000 American troops. On November 29, the UN Security Council delivered an ultimatum to Hussein: Get out of Kuwait by January 15, 1991, or face a UN-sanctioned eviction.

When Iraqi forces stayed put in Kuwait, the Allied attack began on January 16 with a terrifying aerial bombardment—Operation Desert Storm—that continued for the duration of the war and was directed against Iraqi air defenses, roads, bridges, military installations, government buildings, communications networks, and oil refineries. Iraq retaliated with SCUD missile strikes against Israel, which failed to do much damage but caused considerable panic.

In February, the Allies used their overwhelming air power to neutralize Iraqi troops in Kuwait. On February 24, they launched the largest ground offensive since World War II, Operation Desert Saber, moving troops rapidly from northern Saudi Arabia into Kuwait and Iraq. Within three days, Iraqi defenses in Kuwait City crumbled. U.S. President George Bush declared a cease-fire on February 28, 1991. Saddam Hussein clung to power in Iraq despite much popular opposition to his government. The Allies lost about 300 troops, and as many as 100,000 Iraqi soldiers may have died. Yet, after presiding over the most lopsided U.S. military victory, President Bush managed to lose the 1992 election to Bill Clinton.

✳ QUESTION 84

What were the 10 Plagues of Egypt?

1. The Nile and other waters of Egypt were turned to blood
2. Frogs
3. Lice (or maggots or mosquitoes or gnats)
4. Flies (or gadflies)
5. Death of livestock by pestilence
6. Boils
7. Hail

8. Locusts   10. **Egyptian firstborn were**
9. Palpable darkness   **slain**

In his *Philosophical Dictionary,* skeptical Voltaire claims that if Moses had really produced prodigies such as the plagues, he would have earned at least a passing mention in ancient Egyptian or Greek writings. Nonetheless, for several thousand years, at the seder meal inaugurating Passover, Jews all over the world have remembered the story of their ancestors' exodus from captivity in Egypt—and the ten plagues that afflicted the Egyptians before the Israelites were allowed to depart on their circuitous, forty-year trek back to a land "flowing with milk and honey."

The story of the plagues that led to the emancipation of the Jews is told in Exodus 7–12. With the aid of his brother, Aaron, the eighty-year-old Moses attempts to persuade Pharaoh to let the people go on a three-days' journey into the wilderness to perform sacrifices—a request that masks the ultimate goal of escape from an increasingly tyrannical "house of bondage." Why were ten plagues required to convince Pharaoh? God himself hardens Pharaoh's heart so that, after all the tribulations visited on them, "the Egyptians may learn that I am the Lord" (Exodus 7:5).

At first, as proof of supernatural sanction, Aaron merely throws down his staff, which becomes a serpent, but Pharaoh's magicians match his feat. Although Aaron's serpent gobbles up all of theirs, Pharaoh is not impressed, so it's time for stronger medicine. When **the Nile and all the other waters of Egypt are turned to blood,** once again the crafty magicians are able to do as much. The Egyptians have to resort to digging for their drinking water, but Pharaoh sees no reason to change his mind. A week later, **a swarm of frogs** is made to emerge from the Nile and invade the Egyptians' houses, beds, ovens, and kneading bowls. But the magicians cause even more frogs to swarm! Pharaoh promises to comply with Yahweh's resolutions but develops amnesia after Moses gets rid of the frogs. When **the lice**—or some other vexing insects—are formed of the dust of Egypt, the magicians are stymied and advise Pharaoh to relent.

But Pharaoh just doesn't get it. He subjects himself and his people to successive plagues of **swarming flies; a pestilence that kills all the Egyptian livestock** (but spares the beasts of the Israelites); **an epidemic of boils** that torments man, animal, and magician, caused by a handful of furnace soot that Moses flings into the air; **a fierce**

hailstorm that destroys farmhands, trees, the flax and barley crop, and whatever livestock had survived the pestilence; and **a horde of locusts** that consumes the new shoots on the crops and infests the Egyptians' houses. The ninth plague is **palpable darkness lasting three days,** during which visibility is zero for the Egyptians (but not where the Israelites resided). Finally, on a grim midnight, **the Lord slays the firstborn of all the Egyptians,** from the firstborn of Pharaoh to those of the Egyptians and even their animals. This devastating plague compels Pharaoh to let the people go. When he later pursues and tries to slaughter them, his armies meet with ignominious destruction at the Red Sea (or Sea of Reeds).

Most of the ten plagues have been interpreted as intensified forms of natural phenomena that did indeed plague Egypt. The changing of the water into blood, for example, has been associated with the periodic flow of red silt down the Nile from its headwaters. Locusts, described as winging in on the east wind, are sometimes swept over Egypt by the hot sirocco from the Arabian Desert. The darkness so thick it can be felt has been linked with the khamsin, a hot southerly wind that blackens the skies of Egypt with dense sand and dust blown up from the Sahara.

An unknown editor has conflated three separate narrative strands in the account of the plagues in Exodus: that of J (the Yahwist, who calls God "Yahweh"), E (the Elohist, who refers to God as "Elohim"), and P (the Priestly narrative). The J text is the main source for the plagues, mentioning six of them. In J, Moses speaks to Pharaoh directly and demands that the Israelites be allowed to depart. Pharaoh refuses, and Moses predicts the next plague. After each plague begins at the preannounced time, Pharaoh begs Moses to intervene with God to end it. Moses does so, but slippery Pharaoh fails to keep his end of the bargain. J claims the plagues do not affect the Israelites because they dwell in the province of Goshen, apart from the Egyptians.

The E strand of Exodus mentions four of the plagues, which are here caused by more directly miraculous intervention than in J, that is, by the actions of Moses, through whom God manifests his power. In E, the Israelites live together with the Egyptians and are spared the plague of darkness, but not of the water turning to blood, the hail, or the locusts. In this text, the Israelites have time to despoil the Egyptians of gold and silver before they depart, whereas in J their hasty exodus—indeed, angry ejection by Pharaoh—is emphasized by their not having time to leaven their bread before baking it.

In P's text, four of the plagues become a kind of contest between the power of Aaron, acting for Moses, and Pharaoh's magicians, who reproduce some of them (the bloody Nile and the frogs) but can't quite manage the lice and are themselves covered with the boils.

The seder (Hebrew, "order") is a reenactment of the meal on the night of the first Passover—in Hebrew, *pesach,* from a verb meaning "to pass over, to spare." The Aramaic form, *pascha,* gave rise to the Greek-derived English adjective, *paschal,* which also gathered associations from the similar-sounding Greek verb *paschein,* "to suffer." Thus, when God struck down the firstborn of Egypt, he "passed over" the houses of the Jews, whose doorposts and lintels had been sprinkled with the blood of the slaughtered paschal lamb.

The ritual text used at the seder is the Haggadah, a story of the bondage in and flight from Egypt, recited by the head of the household. The text is interspersed with hymns, prayers, psalms, and the youngest child's "Four Questions." As each of the ten plagues of Egypt is mentioned, a drop of wine is spilled from everyone's cup to avoid gloating over the misery of others, expressly forbidden in Proverbs 24:17: "Rejoice not when your enemy falls, and when he stumbles, let not your heart exult."

Which were the 11 states of the Confederacy?

South Carolina	Texas
Mississippi	Virginia
Florida	Arkansas
Alabama	North Carolina
Georgia	Tennessee
Louisiana	

The seeds of the Confederacy were sown long before the bitter conflicts over states' rights and slavery tore through the United States in the mid-nineteenth century. They were present from the beginning, arising from geography, climate, culture, and major historical forces of the time such as the Industrial Revolution and the rise of the urban classes. The warm South's economy was agrarian and relied primarily on cotton. The less temperate Northern states rapidly became urbanized and industrialized as factories sprang up to manufacture goods ranging from hydraulic turbines to sewing machines, and their population swelled with the influx of European immigrants. What had seemed like a noble experiment—*E pluribus unum*—at the time the Union was formed gradually came to resemble two separate, and increasingly hostile, societies divided by the Mason-Dixon line.

Political tensions increased through the early decades of the nineteenth century as the country expanded westward and more states were admitted to the Union. North and South each wanted to maintain parity in the number of new slave and free states to avoid being outvoted in Congress. During those years inimitable orators and sectional leaders such as Daniel Webster of Massachusetts, Henry Clay of Kentucky, and John C. Calhoun of South Carolina steered an increasingly acrimonious Congress and nation through a series of crises on tariffs, the extension of slavery, and nullification (on whether individual states had a constitutional right to nullify federal laws). The era was rife with attempts to keep a lid on the seething, conflicting demands of North and South, as evidenced by the very names of the Missouri Compromise (1820–21), the Compromise Tariff of 1833, and the Compromise of 1850 ("the Great Compromise"). Efforts at achieving a consensus grew steadily more futile until the boiling point was reached with the national elections of 1860.

The presidential election was a four-way contest among Democrats Stephen A. Douglas and John Breckinridge, Constitutional Union Party candidate John Bell, and Republican Abraham Lincoln. State elections in Pennsylvania and Indiana held shortly before the national elections were swept by the Republicans—the first intimation of a Lincoln victory, which many Southerners believed would sound a death knell for their way of life. Before midnight of November 6, Election Day, telegraphed returns confirmed that Lincoln had won.

Charleston, **South Carolina,** had been the epicenter of secession fever in the decades leading up to the Civil War. As soon as Lincoln's presidency was assured, the South Carolina legislature called for a secession convention, which assembled in December. At 1:15 P.M., on December 20, 1860, the 169 delegates voted unanimously to adopt the Ordinance of Secession:

We, the people of the State of South Carolina, in Convention assembled, do declare and ordain . . . that the union now subsisting between South Carolina and other States under the name of "The United States of America" is hereby dissolved.

South Carolina was soon followed by **Mississippi, Florida, Alabama, Georgia, Louisiana,** and **Texas.** On February 8, 1861, the Confederate States of America was officially organized with a constitution similar to that of the United States, except that it ensured and protected "the institution of Negro slavery," known among Southerners as "our peculiar domestic institution." Delegates from the seven states of the new polity convened in Montgomery, Alabama, and, on March 11, unanimously ratified the new constitution and chose Mississippian Jefferson Davis as provisional President and Alexander Hamilton Stephens of Georgia as Vice President. Notice was posted that the federal forts and Navy installations in South Carolina and elsewhere were slated for takeover by the state authorities. President James Buchanan, a timid man at the end of a weak presidency, did not contest the secessions.

Lincoln was inaugurated on March 4, and the two nations waited anxiously to see what response he would make to the gauntlet thrown down by the Southern states. Lincoln refused to order the evacuation of Union soldiers holed up in Fort Sumter, located in the harbor of Charleston, South Carolina. In the early morning of April 12, 1861, Confederate cannons began firing on the Union flag over the fort—an act of treason—and war between the Northern and Southern states began.

The seven original states of the Confederacy were joined by **Virginia** in April and **Arkansas, North Carolina,** and **Tennessee** shortly thereafter. (Four other slave states remained in the Union—Delaware, Kentucky, Maryland, and Missouri—and the state now known as West Virginia seceded from Virginia and later joined the Union in 1863.) In May 1861, the capital, originally Montgomery, Alabama, was moved to Richmond, Virginia. In November, when general elections were held, Jefferson Davis was reconfirmed as President. He was inaugurated in February 1862 for a six-year term.

During its brief existence the primary political activity of the Confederate government was planning for and prosecuting the war. The first Congress held four sessions and the second only two. Major concerns that plagued the fledgling Confederacy were shortages of goods, dependence on Europe, and escalating inflation that nearly destroyed what was left of the war-ravaged economy. Further disabled by internal controversies and dwindling morale, the Confederate Congress in Richmond adjourned for the last time on March 18, 1865.

The Confederate states considered the Civil War—the War between the States, as they called it—the second American Revolution, fought against the new tyranny of the North. The story of that war, summarized in Question 83, will not be repeated. But when the fashionable society of Charleston flocked to the waterfront to watch the thrilling display of the war's opening salvos on that April morning in 1861, few expected that during the next four years 620,000 American brothers, husbands, fathers, and sons, both Northern and Southern, would die in the struggle between the Union and Dixie.

A footnote to the brief, bloody existence of the Confederate States of America was the Supreme Court decision in *Texas* v. *White* (1869) declaring secession to be an unconstitutional act.

12

What were the Latin names of the 12 months—and what did they mean?

Januarius: from Janus, the two-faced god of gates and doorways

Februarius: from *februare*, "to purify," because of a Roman purification feast celebrated on February 15

Martius: named for Mars, the Roman god of agriculture and, later, war

Aprilis: from Latin *aperire* ("to open," as in the buds of spring), or perhaps "the month of Venus," from the Etruscan *apru*, from Aphro, an abbreviated form of the Greek Aphrodite

Maius: from Maia, the Italic goddess of spring, daughter of Faunus and wife of Vulcan

Junius: from the name of the Roman Junius clan, related to the name of the goddess Juno, wife of Jupiter and protector of women

Julius: from Julius Caesar, born in this month

Augustus: from Augustus Caesar

September: from *septem*, "seven" (when the Roman year began in March)

October: from *octo*, "eight"

November: from *novem*, "nine"

December: from *decem*, "ten"

Our word *calendar* derives ultimately from Latin *kalendae*, the Romans' term for the day of the new moon and, thus, the first day of their months. The earliest Latin calendar, traditionally attributed to Romulus, had only ten months and 304 days—six months of 30 days and four of 31. Apparently, the time after the end of December—

what later became January and February—was not officially reckoned in this calendar because all agricultural activity came to a standstill with the gathering and storing of the last crops and did not resume until the first preparation of the ground for the next season's crop at the beginning of March.

A more rational calendar may have been introduced to the early Romans by their highly civilized overlords in Etruria in the person of Rome's fifth King, the Etruscan Tarquin the Elder (Tarquinius Priscus). It was also often attributed to their semilegendary second King, the all-purpose savant and religious lawgiver Numa Pompilius.

In this lunar calendar of twelve months and 355 days, four months had 31 days, the new month of February had 28, and the other seven months, including the new month of January, had 29 days. The Romans, who considered even numbers unlucky, thus made all their months contain an odd number of days, except February, which, since it featured a prominent festival in honor of the dead, was considered unlucky anyway. In an attempt to rectify the discrepancy between this lunar 355-day year and the solar year, an intercalary month called Mercedonius (or Mercedinus or Intercalaris) of 22 or 23 days was, perhaps later, inserted into the calendar between February 23 and 24 every two years.

The accumulating errors of this system, which was poorly worked out in practice, caused the year to be about three months out of sync with the true solar year by the time of Julius Caesar. During his dictatorship, Caesar decided to revamp the Roman calendar with the aid of the Alexandrian Greek astronomer Sosigenes. This involved making 46 B.C. a huge year of 445 days before embarking on a solar year, modeled on the Egyptian. The new Julian calendar of 365 days, which was instituted on January 1, 45 B.C., lengthened the shorter months and inserted an intercalary day every four years between February 23 and 24 as a "leap day," whereas we have tacked it to the end of the month as the 29th. This extra day was needed because the solar year is actually about six hours longer than 365 days.

This calendar served well enough until its small lack of precision—eleven minutes and forty seconds—added up over the centuries. In 1582 Pope Gregory XIII promulgated the adoption of a more accurate calendar (which Protestant England and its American colonies did not adopt until 1752, and which Russia only accepted in 1918). To square the calendar with the sun again, the Pope decreed that the day after October 4, 1582, should be October 15. With some further fine-tuning—for example, century years such as 1600, 1700, and so forth, should not be leap years unless evenly divisible by 400—this Gregorian calendar is the one we use today.

January, affixed to the most ancient Roman calendar as the eleventh month, became the first month of the year only in 153 B.C. A *janus* was an arch or gate in Latin, and *janua* was the word for "door." (Compare our word *janitor.*) Janus (JAY-nus), the god with two faces, guardian of all gates and doorways, was later considered to be the god of beginnings, especially of the year, but that was a derivative meaning.

His two-facedness probably arose from the fact that his role required him to be vigilant for thieves, evil spirits, and other forms of intruders. He was subsequently thought to be looking back to the old year and forward to the new—as indicated by his image, which had an old face and a young one, in his small shrine in Rome's Forum, in front of the Senate House. The bronze doors of his shrine were thrown open in times of war and shut in peacetime. During the first seven hundred years of Rome's existence, they were closed on only three occasions. The feast of Janus that occurred during the ninth day of his month was presumably called Ianuar.

February was named for the appurtenances of a purification feast for the atonement for sins celebrated on February 15. This Lupercalia was also a fertility festival that aimed to ensure abundant crops, flocks, and human offspring during the following year. (Remember that February started out as the last Roman month.) Priests called Lupercals ran semi-naked around the bounds of the old city with thongs cut from the hides of sacrificed goats, using them to strike women who stepped forward in the hope that the ritual would prevent sterility or guarantee a good delivery in those who were pregnant. The thongs were called *februa,* from *februare,* "to purify." In Shakespeare's *Julius Caesar,* based on Plutarch's *Lives,* the consul Mark Antony, a member of the Lupercal priesthood, is one of the runners. He makes use of the public spectacle to offer Caesar a royal diadem three times, which the dictator very reluctantly refuses.

March was named for Mars, originally a springtime deity of sprouting vegetation, who had several feasts during this month, including his birthday on March 1. Later, Mars became god of war, probably since the war campaigns broken off during the cold winter months were resumed in March.

Because this month was named for Mars, Ovid (in his *Fasti,* an

367

unfinished long poem, c. A.D. 8, on the Roman calendar) presumed that **April** was named for Venus—war followed by its opposite, love—especially since their counterparts in Greek mythology, Ares and Aphrodite, were lovers (see Question 88). In addition, Mars, as the father of the twins Romulus and Remus, was regarded as the progenitor of the Roman race. Venus, as the divine mother of the Trojan hero Aeneas (who came to Italy after the Trojan War and sired a line of proto-Roman kings), was also a remote ancestress of the Romans. In fact, some have thought the name of the month derives from an Etruscan form of the Greek goddess Aphrodite's name, but it may just come from Latin *aperire,* "to open."

May appears to have taken its name from Maia, an Italic goddess of growing plants. As daughter of Faunus—grandson of the great god Saturn—and wife of Vulcan, the god of volcanic fire, Maia was well connected.

In the *Fasti,* Ovid thought May took its name from *maiores,* the elders of the state, whereas he saw **June** as having been named for the young men, the *juvenes.* The latter month's name, however, is usually assumed to have been borrowed from the Etruscan form of Juno's name, Uni. Some say the name of the Junius clan, which no doubt traced its lineage back to the goddess, was the intermediate link between Juno and the month.

By order of Mark Antony immediately after Julius Caesar's assassination on March 15, 44 B.C., the Senate decreed that Quintilis (the old-time "fifth month"), the month of Caesar's birth, should assume his name, *Julius,* our **July.** Given Caesar's role in revising the calendar—not to speak of his titanic achievements in war, politics, statecraft, oratory, the writing of history, and amatory matters—this was only fair.

August, originally called Sextilis ("sixth month"), was renamed by a decree of the Senate in 27 B.C. to honor the first Roman Emperor Augustus Caesar, who formally accepted the honor only in 8 B.C. This, too, was only fair, since his great-uncle and adoptive father, Julius Caesar, had lent his name to July. The Senate urged Augustus to choose September, his birth month, but Augustus preferred Sextilis, during which he had first become consul, celebrated his three greatest triumphs, and secured the conquest of Egypt. The story goes that, because Sextilis had only thirty days, Augustus filched a day from February so that his month would be no less august in length than Uncle Julius's. Some scholars say Sextilis already had thirty-one days.

Although **September, October, November,** and **December** haven't been the seventh, eighth, ninth, and tenth months in more than twenty-one hundred years, those numbers are still fossilized in their names. The highly conservative and traditional Romans would have liked that very much.

 QUESTION 87

What were the 12 Tribes of Israel?

Reuben	Asher
Simeon	Issachar
Levi	Zebulun
Judah	Joseph (divided into Ephraim
Dan	and Manasseh)
Naphtali	Benjamin
Gad	

The twelve sons of Abraham's grandson Jacob (who was renamed Israel) were born to his two wives—his cousins Leah and Rachel—and to their handmaidens Zilpah and Bilhah. The sons, listed above by birth order, gave their names to the tribes that conquered Canaan between about 1300 and 1200 B.C. Moses led these tribes out of Egyptian captivity and died after gazing on Palestine from Mount Nebo (Pisgah), east of Jericho. The warrior Joshua then brought the people of Israel across the Jordan into the Holy Land (see Question 78).

The sons of Jacob by Laban's daughter Leah were Reuben, Simeon, Levi, Judah, Issachar, and Zebulun. The tribe of **Reuben** settled east of the Jordan and the Dead Sea but was later absorbed by Gad and the Moabites. In the Blessing of Jacob (Genesis 49; late eleventh century B.C.), the patriarch deprives firstborn Reuben of his birthright because of a sexual escapade with one of Jacob's concubines. In the same text, **Simeon** and **Levi** are cursed for their ruthlessness in slaughtering all the male Canaanites of Shechem in reprisal for the rape of their sister Dinah, Leah's youngest child. In fact, the tribe of

The Tribes of Israel
c. 1200 – 1020 B.C.

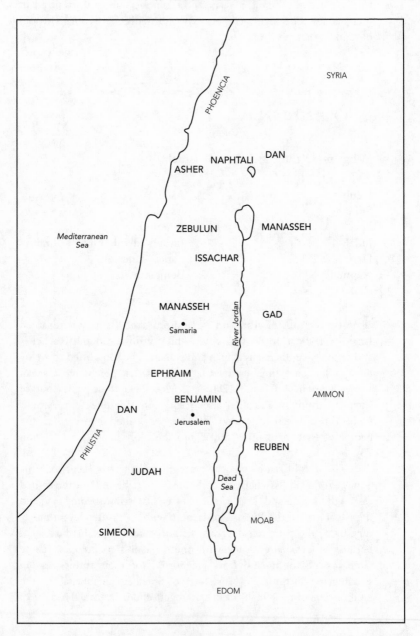

Simeon was absorbed by Judah in early times, and the Levites—the priests and temple servants—received no territory of their own, since their portion was Yahweh himself. The other tribes, however, were required to grant the Levites forty-eight cities within their territories and tithes for their sustenance. Moses, Aaron, and Miriam belonged to this tribe. Jacob likens **Judah** to a lion cub and claims "the scepter shall not pass from Judah." This prophecy was presumably written after David of Judah had become King, c. 1010 B.C. The Evangelists later claimed that Christ was descended from David and Judah (see Questions 32 and 78). Jacob calls **Issachar** "a gelded ass" in service to the Canaanites, who long retained power in Issachar's territory, but **Zebulun** was warlike.

Leah's handmaiden Zilpah bore Gad and Asher to Jacob. The tribe of **Gad** settled east of the Jordan in Gilead, of whose medicinal resin Jeremiah sorely felt the need: "Is there no balm in Gilead?" Gideon smote the Midianites in Gilead; here David fought against his rebellious son Absalom; here Elijah was born, and King Ahab died in battle. In contrast, the tribe of **Asher** was so close to Phoenician territory that it was barely a part of Israel.

Jacob labored a total of fourteen long years to win Laban's other daughter Rachel as his wife. She gave birth to his best-loved sons Joseph and Benjamin. **Joseph,** sold into slavery by his brothers after Jacob favored him with a "coat of many colors," rose to power in Egypt because of his skill in oneiromancy (divination by dreams). He was responsible for Jacob's moving his extended family to Egypt during a famine in the Holy Land. Jacob's youngest son was **Benjamin.** In his Blessing, Jacob cites Benjamin's wolflike fierceness in war. The Benjaminites, famed as ambidextrous archers, were the tribe of King Saul and St. Paul.

Joseph's tribal allotment went to the "half tribes" named after his sons Ephraim and Manasseh by his Egyptian wife Asenath. The half tribe of **Ephraim** lost forty-two thousand of its men—and gave us a word—because of their inability to make a *sh-* sound. The Ephraimites had treacherously attacked the Gileadites. After being routed, they tried to escape back to Ephraim by crossing the Jordan. At each ford, Gileadite soldiers ordered the fleeing men to say "shibboleth," the word for "stream." Those who pronounced it with an Ephraimite lisp as "sibboleth" were unmasked as enemies and butchered (Judges 12:1–6). Mighty Joshua himself was an Ephraimite. The most famous native son of the half tribe of **Manasseh,** which settled both east and west of the Jordan, was the warrior Gideon, who inspired a civilized hotel custom.

Rachel's handmaiden Bilhah bore Dan and Naphtali to Jacob. Most of the tribe of **Dan** wearied of fighting against the Philistines (Samson was the most famous Danite) and migrated from the western central region to the extreme north of the Holy Land. But Dan became the center of bull-calf worship and was regarded as so wicked that Jacob's characterization of it—"a serpent on the road, a viper on the path"—was much later taken to mean that the Antichrist would be a Danite. The book of Revelation (7:5–8) even omits it from the twelve redeemed tribes. Some scholars have suggested that the tribe may have been of Greek origin. There is an analogue of the story of Samson and Delilah in Greek mythology: Scylla—not Odysseus' monster—cuts off a lock of hair and thus debilitates her father Nisus, allowing him to be defeated and killed by King Minos of Crete. And a common name for the Greeks in Homer is *Danaoi*. As for **Naphtali** (NAF-tuh-lye), Jacob calls the tribe either "a spreading terebinth putting forth lovely boughs" *(The New English Bible)* or "a swift hind, dropping beautiful fawns" *(The Jerusalem Bible)*.

After the period of the united kingdom of Israel under Saul, David, and Solomon (c. 1020–922 B.C.), the undiplomatic son of Solomon, Rehoboam, inherited the throne, but only the tribes of Judah and Benjamin (and some of the Levites) adhered to him. His territory then became known as the southern kingdom of Judah. The other ten tribes seceded in a massive tax revolt. When Rehoboam was asked to decrease Solomon's heavy burden of labor-gangs and other levies, he promised instead to greatly increase it: "My father used the whip on you; but I will use the lash" (1 Kings 12:11).

The northern kingdom of Israel broke away under King Jeroboam I. This rival monarchy, with its capital at Samaria, produced ninth-century-B.C. luminaries such as King Ahab, his Baal-worshiping Phoenician Queen, Jezebel, and Elijah, who fulminated against their idolatry. In the late eighth century B.C., the fierce Assyrian King Tiglath-Pileser III took some of the northern tribes of Israel into captivity. The final conquest occurred in 721 B.C., when many of its people were deported to Assyria by King Sargon II.

What became of these ten lost tribes? A Jewish traveler of the ninth century A.D. thought he had found them scattered in Persia, as well as near Mecca and beyond Abyssinia. Some claim they became the Khazars of southern Russia, progenitors of all later Jews. The

Mormons say these tribes were the progenitors of the American Indians, while others say the English.

The southern kingdom of Judah produced Isaiah, Jeremiah, and the strong King Josiah. It was defeated when its capital Jerusalem and Solomon's Temple were destroyed and its people transported to Babylon in 586 B.C. by the Chaldean King of Babylon, Nebuchadrezzar II. The Babylonian captivity ended when King Cyrus of Persia crushed the Babylonians and allowed the Jews to return to Jerusalem in 538 B.C. The second Temple was completed in 515 B.C. and, in the next century, the religious reforms of Ezra ushered in the epoch of normative, Torah-based Judaism.

 QUESTION 88

Who were the 12 Olympian gods and their Roman equivalents?

Zeus (Jupiter or Jove)
Hera (Juno)
Poseidon (Neptune)
Hades (Pluto)
Pallas Athene (Minerva)
Phoebus Apollo
Artemis (Diana)
Aphrodite (Venus)

Hermes (Mercury)
Ares (Mars)
Hephaestus (Vulcan or Mulciber)
Hestia (Vesta), later supplanted by Dionysus or Bacchus (Liber)

The story of the twelve Olympian gods of Greece—epitomes of radiance, beauty, and power—begins at a decidedly primitive state of affairs. At the beginning of time, Earth, or Gaea, who emerged out of Chaos, fell in love with the Sky (Uranus), who, according to very ancient sources, was her own son by the North Wind. She soon bore Uranus six sons, the Titans, who towered above the mountains, and six daughters, the Titanesses, who became their brothers' wives. Although Uranus took great pride in these twelve children (who included Hyperion the sun god, Phoebe the moon goddess, and Oceanus the god of the world-encircling waters), he was revolted by the other offspring Gaea bore him—the three one-eyed Cyclopes and three fifty-headed, hundred-armed sons, the Hecatoncheires. These six monsters Uranus hurled into Tartarus, in the very bowels of the underworld.

Deeply resentful, Gaea begged the Titans to kill their father and free their brothers from Tartarus, producing a flint sickle she had made for the occasion. Only Cronus, the youngest and strongest Titan, accepted the challenge, boldly seizing Uranus by the genitals and castrating him. When the blood spurting from the wound fell to earth, the three Furies sprang up from this sodden ground (see Question 14).

Cronus, who became Lord of the Universe after overthrowing his father, flung his monstrous brothers back into Tartarus almost immediately after he had freed them, enraging his mother. But Gaea knew of a prophecy that one of Cronus's children would be more powerful than his father. Cronus knew it, too, so he promptly gulped down each of the children whom his wife, the Titaness Rhea, bore him: Hestia, Demeter, Hera, Hades, and Poseidon. Naturally, Rhea disapproved of her husband's eating habits. When expecting her sixth child, she conspired with Gaea to save it. Instead of an infant, she handed Cronus a rock wrapped in swaddling clothes, which he scarfed down without suspecting any deceit.

The baby, named **Zeus,** was spirited away to a cave on a mountain in Crete to be raised in secret by the Goat-nymph Amalthea, who nursed him with her milk and fed him the nectar and ambrosia that flowed from her horns. His playmate was his foster brother, the Goat-Pan. Outside the cave, Gaea had placed the armed Curetes to clash their swords against their shields so that Cronus couldn't hear the baby cry. Zeus later expressed his gratitude to Amalthea by placing her in the heavens as the constellation Capricorn (see Question 93).

Zeus attained adulthood in one year and took the Titaness Metis as his first wife. Clever Metis counseled Zeus against trying to defeat his father Cronus on his own. Instead, she and Rhea (who still mourned her first five children) prepared the ancient equivalent of ipecac, which they mixed with Cronus's favorite beverage. He vomited, and returned Hestia, Demeter, Hera, Hades, Poseidon, and the rock-baby—all safe and sound—to their mother. Zeus later placed the rock at Delphi, where it was revered.

With his newly restored brothers and sisters, Zeus now warred on the Titans, who were led by mighty Atlas (for Cronus was getting on in years). Zeus killed Campe, the jaileress of Tartarus, and set free his uncles, the Cyclopes and Hecatoncheires, once again. The Cyclopes, enlisted in the war against the Titans, forged a thunderbolt for Zeus, a trident for Poseidon, and a helmet of invisibility for Hades.

The three brothers made their move against Cronus, and Zeus struck him with his thunderbolt. At that, the Hecatoncheires barraged the rest of the Titans with rocks. When a loud cry from the Goat-Pan struck even further terror into the Titans (hence our word *panic),* they fled either to Tartarus or a British island, with the Hundred-Handed Ones as guards. No harm came to the Titanesses because their number included Zeus's mother Rhea and his wife Metis. Cronus fled to Italy, where, as the Latin god Saturn, he ushered in the Golden Age, when war was unknown, people fed on acorns and drank only water, and no one eviscerated the earth by planting crops or digging for gold, or furrowed the sea with ships in quest of riches.

After Zeus blasted the monster Typhon with his thunderbolt, he moved to form a government. When the three sons of Cronus drew lots, Poseidon became the god of the seas, Hades of the dead and the underworld, and Zeus of the heavens. The earth remained common to all three. Zeus now settled the gods in an otherworldly paradise on the summit of Mount Olympus in the northern Greek region of Thessaly.

This King of the newly established Olympian gods apparently ravished his own mother Rhea in the form of a serpent: He wasn't called "Father Zeus" for nothing. He then went on to sire the Nine Muses on the Titaness Mnemosyne (see Question 75) and the Seasons and three Fates (see Question 19) on Themis, the Titaness goddess of justice. Hermes was his son by Atlas's daughter Maia. Zeus and Leto, also a daughter of Titans, assumed the form of quails to make love when Apollo and Artemis were engendered.

Zeus was also the father of Dionysus. When Semele, daughter of King Cadmus of Thebes, was pregnant with this child, she was convinced by jealous Hera to ask Zeus to reveal himself to her in his true glory. Zeus, who had given Semele any wish—and was angry because she refused him her bed unless he manifested his deity to her—complied with her foolish request. The mortal woman was immediately burned to a cinder amid thunder and lightning. Nonetheless, Hermes managed to save the six-months child by sewing him for an additional three months inside a curious incubator, Zeus's thigh. Dionysus, also known as Bacchus, went on to become the god of wine, intoxication, orgies, and savage revelry, but also of Greek tragedy. He is sometimes called *digonos* ("twice-born").

The innumerable amours of Zeus resulted in the birth of heroes such as Perseus, Minos, Heracles (see Question 90), and many others, not to mention all the Olympian gods who weren't his siblings. The theme of Hera's jealousy over Zeus's philanderings is one of the great comic leitmotifs in Greek mythology, though things often ended tragically for his lovers.

Zeus and his sister **Hera** were reunited after Cronus was banished. He seduced her by taking the form of a cuckoo bird; when she cuddled it, he resumed his own shape and took her by force. Gaea presented them with a tree filled with golden apples, and their wedding night lasted three hundred years. The children of Zeus and Hera included Ares, Hephaestus, and Hebe, though some accounts claim Hephaestus was the offspring of Hera alone. Hebe, the goddess of youth, was cupbearer to the Olympians (until taking a revealing pratfall) and eventually married the deified Heracles.

Hera could renew her virginity each year by bathing in a sacred spring near her favorite city, Argos. Married women turned to this long-suffering First Lady of Olympus for help, and Eileithyia, goddess of childbirth, was sometimes thought to be her daughter (or Hera herself). Capricious and vengeful, Hera became a fierce enemy of Troy mainly because Trojan Paris had offended her pride by awarding the golden apple of beauty to Aphrodite.

The changeable face of the sea mirrors the changing moods of **Poseidon,** who became god of the sea at the same time his brothers Zeus and Hades took possession of the sky and the underworld, respectively. Poseidon lives in a gold palace at the bottom of the sea, and storms abate at the approach of his chariot, which is drawn by brass-hoofed, golden-maned horses. With his trident he can stab the ground to create earthquakes, thus earning the epithet "Earthshaker." He invented horses, whose gallop is like the movement of waves.

Perhaps Poseidon's violent, mercurial nature made it difficult to find a mate. He decided on Amphitrite, a daughter of the old sea god, Nereus, but she fled. Only Delphinus ("dolphin") was able to persuade her to return to Poseidon. Thereafter, dolphins were Poseidon's favorite sea creatures, and in gratitude he placed Delphinus in the night sky as a constellation.

Once, after Poseidon and Apollo had offended Zeus, he compelled them to serve haughty Laomedon, King of Troy, for a year.

Apollo tended Laomedon's flocks on Mount Ida, and Poseidon (with or without Apollo's help) built the walls of the city. But when the King refused to pay them for their work, Poseidon sent a sea monster to ravage Troy. Eventually, the King was forced to offer his daughter Hesione to the monster as a sacrifice to appease Poseidon, but she was rescued at the last minute by Heracles. Poseidon thus bore a grudge against Troy and enthusiastically helped the Greek Army in the Trojan War.

After the war, the wily Greek hero Odysseus escaped death at the hands of the one-eyed Cyclops Polyphemus, a gigantic son of Poseidon, by blinding the monster with a heated stake. For this, the implacable god of the sea delayed Odysseus' return to his homeland of Ithaca by ten years and drowned the rest of his men.

Poseidon's sexual appetite was nearly as impressive as that of his brother Zeus, but some genetic defect caused him to sire mainly horses, monsters, or blue-green sea gods like Triton. (The great hunter, handsome Orion, was an exception.) In the form of a stallion, Poseidon impregnated his sister Demeter, who was unsuccessfully disguised as a mare. The result was the sacred wild horse, Arion. The winged horse Pegasus was said to be his son by the Gorgon Medusa. This loose behavior infuriated Amphitrite, who turned one of her rivals, Scylla, into a voracious six-headed creature with twelve feet. (Odysseus encounters her, too, across from the whirlpool Charybdis.)

Apparently not content with lordship over the sea, Poseidon vied with other gods for the possession of several cities. His most famous dispute was with Athene for Athens. He staked his claim by flinging his trident into the ground near the Acropolis; she planted an olive tree there. The arbitration held on Mount Olympus decided in favor of Athene, for whom the city was named.

With his brothers Zeus and Poseidon, **Hades** ("the unseen one") formed a triad of chief Greek gods. Although grim Hades spent almost no time aboveground, he was, strictly speaking, an Olympian. He was also called Pluto, "the rich one," because all the earth's mineral treasures belonged to him. Since his underworld realm was always ready for new residents, he was sometimes known as "the hospitable one."

Like his brothers, Hades had a troubled marital history. He pursued his niece Koré, "the maiden," who was the daughter of Zeus and Demeter, goddess of agriculture. Perhaps sensing that the girl would not willingly go off to live in such a dead town as the under-

world, Hades kidnapped her in his black chariot. In retaliation, Demeter ruined the harvest, causing mass starvation. Zeus finally told
Hades he had to relinquish his bride, now called Persephone ("she
who brings destruction"). This would be possible, however, only if
she had eaten no food in the underworld, but she had already snacked
on four pomegranate seeds. In a compromise between her husband
and her distraught mother, Persephone spent six (or four) months of
each year with Hades and the rest of the time on earth with Demeter
during the growing season.

The strange birth of **Pallas Athene** brings us back to Zeus's first
wife, Metis. Despite her help in defeating Cronus, Zeus ate her when
she announced her first pregnancy. Like his father, he feared progeny
more powerful than himself. After his meal, however, he got a terrible
headache, and either Hephaestus or the Titan Prometheus was summoned to help him on the banks of Lake Tritonis in Libya. When his
emergency medical technician relieved the pressure in Zeus's head
with a blow of an ax blade, out popped Athene, a full-grown female
warrior in battle regalia.

Gray-eyed Athene became her father's favorite. He soon let her
brandish his thunderbolt and aegis, the shield or breastplate made of
the goatskin of Amalthea embossed with Medusa's petrific head,
which never failed to strike terror into the knees and hearts of all
opponents in battle. Yet Athene's childhood was clouded by a tragic
accident. While engaging in war-play with a human girl, she accidentally killed her. In tribute, she took the girl's name, Pallas, as her own
first name.

As a battle goddess, Athene was a tireless defender of home and
state from enemies and was inevitably accompanied by Nike, the spirit
of victory. She was a fanatical partisan of the Greeks in the Trojan
War, suggested to Odysseus the stratagem of the wooden horse, and
protected that ever-resourceful hero on his long, dangerous odyssey
home from Troy, delighting in his roguish lies and tall tales. Athene
was also the goddess of wisdom and of the wise city of Athens, which
erected the spectacular Parthenon ("temple of the virgin") on its
Acropolis. A hopeless prude, Athene looked askance on any attempts
on her chastity, such as a very clumsy one that Hephaestus once
made.

Athene also had a domestic side, priding herself on the skill of
her weaving and other womanly handicrafts. Usually mild-mannered,
she lost her temper when a young princess, Arachne, challenged her

to a weaving contest. After the angry goddess destroyed the girl's work, Arachne hanged herself, but Athene changed her into that greatest of weavers, the spider.

Apollo was often called Phoebus ("bright" or "pure"). The birth of Apollo and his twin, Artemis, involved considerable travel because Hera, jealous of Zeus's union with Leto, set the serpent Python to pursue her until she was finally able to deliver on the island of Delos after a nine-day labor. Artemis, born first, served as midwife for Apollo. Both were devoted to their mother Leto—so much so that they killed all fourteen sons and daughters of Niobe and King Amphion of Thebes when Niobe boasted that she had seven times as many children as Leto.

His brother Hephaestus presented Apollo with a bow and arrows when he was four days old. His first task was to slay Python, which had fled to Mother Earth's oracle at Delphi on Mount Parnassus. Apollo killed the serpent within the sacred precincts, and when Zeus heard of this sacrilege he ordered his son to purify himself at Tempe and, as further penance, preside over the athletic contests instituted in honor of Python, the Pythian Games. Apollo ignored Zeus and was purified elsewhere. Returning to Delphi, he seized the oracle there for himself. Delphi became the most sacred shrine of prophecy in the ancient world, though Apollo's oracular priestess was still known as the Pythoness.

A splendid musician, as well as a prophet and healer, Apollo taught the Muses to sing, accompanying them on his lyre. His art sometimes turned bloody, as in the case of the flute-playing satyr Marsyas, who challenged him to a musical contest. When the Muses, who were sitting as judges, decided in favor of Apollo, the god flayed Marsyas alive. He also once beat Pan in a musical contest. When King Midas, who had overheard the competition, spoke out in favor of Pan, Apollo conferred on him the insignia of all tone-deaf music critics—a pair of asses' ears.

Although Apollo never married, he fathered quite a few children, including the rowdy Corybantes on the Muse Thalia (see Question 75), and Asclepius, who was the first physician. He loved the nymph Daphne, but while in pursuit of her, he saw her take root and metamorphose into a laurel tree. Ever afterward, the laurel remained his emblem and the symbol of the divine verse he inspired. Apollo also fell in love with a beautiful boy, Hyacinthus, with whom the West Wind Zephyrus was also smitten (see Question 25). One day, while Apollo showed the young man how to throw a discus or quoit, jealous Zephyrus gusted and blew it toward Hyacinthus, splitting his skull open. Sentimental Apollo caused the hyacinth flower to bloom from the dead boy's blood.

Apollo's twin, **Artemis,** was also called Cynthia and Delia in reference to Mount Cynthus on her native island of Delos. According to the Alexandrian poet Callimachus, three-year-old Artemis asked her father Zeus for these things: eternal virginity, as many names as Apollo, a bow and arrows, the ability to light the world, a city of her own, all the world's mountains, sixty ocean nymphs as her maids of honor, twenty more nymphs to care for her hounds, and a stylish hunting outfit. Zeus granted everything.

Artemis was a devoted huntress, aided by ten hounds given her by Pan and a silver bow and arrows forged for her by the Cyclopes. She held a pine torch aloft as she drove her chariot, which was pulled by horned does. Artemis is also goddess of the moon, perhaps in answer to her wish to bring light to the world.

Contradictions abound in the characters of the Greek gods, not least because their attributes and associated myths are an amalgam of numerous minor and foreign deities and a palimpsest of literary or cultic traditions. Artemis is no exception.

She is a virgin but also the goddess of childbirth. She visits the earth with plagues and kills impertinent humans instantly but is also the protector of children and wildlife. Agamemnon was constrained to sacrifice his daughter Iphigenia to Artemis before the Greek fleet could sail for Troy, a penalty for killing one of her stags. When King Oeneus of Calydon forgot to make a ritual sacrifice to Artemis, she sent a boar to ravage his kingdom. When the unlucky hunter Actaeon caught a glimpse of Artemis in the nude as she bathed in a stream, she turned him into a stag and watched him get ripped apart by his own dogs.

Aphrodite ("foam-born"), the goddess of love and desire, was said to have arisen from the foam surrounding the genitals of Uranus when Cronus severed them and flung them into the sea. After her birth, Aphrodite rode a large seashell to Cythera, a small island off the Peloponnesian coast, but then moved on to Paphos on Cyprus, which became a great center of her worship. Hence her names of Cytherea or the Cyprian. In other accounts, she was the daughter of Zeus and Dione, the Titaness goddess of oak trees, where lusty doves nested.

Indeed, Aphrodite was always accompanied by doves and lecherous sparrows. The story of her sea birth may be associated with Mediterranean beliefs about the aphrodisiac powers of seafood.

After Zeus arranged Aphrodite's marriage to the lame blacksmith god Hephaestus, she continued to wear an enchanted girdle that caused men and gods to fall in love with whoever wore it—though she hardly had need of beauty aids. She bore three children, Phobos, Deimos, and Harmonia, who were ostensibly Hephaestus's but actually the fruit of her liaison with the scoundrelly war god Ares.

Informed of his wife's affair, Hephaestus trapped the lovers in his own bed with an invisible, unbreakable web. After summoning the gods to witness Aphrodite's infidelity (the goddesses modestly declined), he asked for a divorce and the return of the gifts he had given Zeus in return for her hand. An amusing scene developed, with Hermes, Apollo, and Poseidon making facetious remarks while practically drooling at the sight of the naked "golden Aphrodite." After being released, the goddess restored her virginity by bathing in the sea near Paphos.

Her renewed virginity didn't last long. She bore the male/female Hermaphroditus to Hermes and a pair of boys to Poseidon. She presented randy Dionysus with a son, Priapus, whom disapproving Hera endowed with a comically outsized phallus.

Not content to mismanage her own love life, Aphrodite wreaked havoc on that of others. When the wife of the first King of Cyprus claimed that the beauty of her daughter Smyrna exceeded Aphrodite's, the miffed goddess arranged for the girl to fall in love with her father, Cinyras, and to trick him into lying with her. The product of this unholy union was the irresistibly beautiful Adonis, who was born when Aphrodite turned Smyrna into a myrrh tree to help her escape her father's wrath. By Adonis, Aphrodite later had two children, but he himself was gored to death by a wild boar. By Butes, one of the Argonauts, she became the mother of Eryx, a future King of Sicily. By the mortal Anchises, she became the mother of the Trojan hero Aeneas, who sailed to Italy after the destruction of Troy and established a dynasty that ultimately led to Romulus and Remus and the founding of Rome.

The rascal **Hermes** was son of Zeus and Maia. He began to look out for his own interests—and his mother's—the day he was born in a cave on Mount Cyllene in Arcadia. While Maia recuperated, Hermes made his way to the pasture where Apollo kept his prized white cows. He stole fifty of them, tying leaves or bark on their hooves and his own feet, to muddle any tracks, and a broom to each one's tail to brush them away. Some say Hermes also made the beasts walk backward to confuse Apollo further while leading them to pasture near his mother's cave. Alerted by an oracle to the theft, its perpetrator, and his whereabouts, Apollo entered the cave and, despite Maia's protests that he was only a newborn, took the cattle rustler to Mount Olympus for arbitration. On the way, Hermes explained that Apollo could have all the cows back except for the two he had sacrificed to the twelve Olympian gods. "Who is the twelfth?" asked Apollo. "*I* am," replied the cocksure Hermes (who had also just been the first to offer animals in sacrifice).

When Apollo heard Hermes play the lyre he had invented out of a tortoise shell strung with seven sheep-gut strings, he offered his cows for it. When he heard the infant play on the reed pipes he also had devised, Apollo traded his golden herding staff for them and made Hermes god of shepherds.

Zeus was impressed with his tiny son's abilities. After gently reprimanding him about lying and stealing, he made Hermes his herald with the responsibility to safeguard treaties, commerce, and unimpeded travel. Healer, Apollo's staff, later known as the caduceus and entwined with two snakes, became an emblem of Hermes' role as messenger, though it now serves as a symbol of physicians.

Thereafter, Hermes traveled with his staff, a winged helmet, and winged sandals, and Zeus admitted him to the Olympian family—a place he had already arrogated to himself. Furthermore, he made sure that his dear mother Maia moved to Olympus with him. Hermes rarely told the whole truth, but he never again lied outright. His ability to think on his feet qualified him as the god of messengers, orators, travelers, and thieves.

Exemplifying Juvenal's dictum of *mens sana in corpore sano* ("a sound mind in a sound body"), Hermes learned how to tell the future and invented astronomy, the musical scale, numbers, weights and measures, and the alphabet (though some say that Cadmus introduced it into Greece—see Question 101), as well as boxing and gymnastics. When someone died, kindly Hermes escorted the soul to the banks of the infernal River Styx, where it embarked on a skiff that Charon ferried across to the realm of Hades (see Question 42). A common epithet of Hermes is Argeiphontes ("slayer of Argus"), referring to the hundred-eyed servant of Hera ordered to keep strict watch on Zeus's paramour Io, disguised as a heifer, to make sure Zeus couldn't get at her. Working for his father, Hermes started playing the flute so soporifically that all of Argus's eyes gradually closed. At that, Hermes cut off his head, but Hera enshrined all those eyes in the tail of her favorite bird, the peacock.

The name *Hermes* may mean "pillar." The earliest images of the god appear to have been the long, square marble or wooden pillars called *hermae,* or herms, that consisted of the god's head at the top and a phallus at the midsection. These were often set up in squares and main roads or as milestones, sometimes with travel directions or other inscriptions.

Ares, a war god and son of Zeus and Hera, was universally hated, even by his parents. He hailed from Thrace, a barely Greek region in the north inhabited by brutish, belligerent primitives. In contrast to Athene, a goddess of "just wars," Ares was a brawler and bully, always on the prowl for armed conflict and bloodshed for their own sake. Much of this turmoil was instigated by his sister and constant companion Eris ("discord"). Other members of his battlefield entourage were the war goddess Enyo and his sons by Aphrodite, Phobos ("fear") and Deimos ("terror"). Whenever Athene opposed him on the battlefield, she trounced and humiliated him, as on the ringing plains of windy Troy, where Ares sided with the Trojans.

Always eager for battle in Homer's *Iliad,* but less than stoical when wounded, Ares tended to flee to Olympus in search of pharmaceutical cures. His relationship with Aphrodite was complex, since she loathed all his deeds except those conducted between the sheets. Their children included Eros (Cupid), the mischievous god of love. Ares was also the progenitor of the Amazons, the tribe of fierce female warriors.

Hephaestus, the god of fire and metalworking, was the son of Zeus and Hera (or, in some versions, of Hera alone by parthenogenesis). Because he was ugly and born with weak, spindly legs, Hera, in an access of unmotherly rage, flung him from Mount Olympus. Fortunately, he landed in the ocean and was raised by the sea nymphs Thetis and Eurynome, who decided that because of his disabilities he might be suited to life as a smith.

In this vocation, he excelled. The jewelry he crafted attracted the attention of none other than Hera, who greatly admired the brooch he had fashioned for Thetis. On visiting his forge, Hera was so taken with his other work that she had his shop moved to Mount Olympus and greatly expanded. There, Hephaestus branched out into general contracting, building the upscale mansions of the gods. He also cast Zeus's shield and scepter, and the armor and shield of Achilles in the *Iliad;* of Heracles in the Hesiod-like poem *The Shield of Herakles;* and, as Vulcan, of Aeneas in the *Aeneid.* After a shaky start, Hephaestus became Hera's favorite, and it was she who arranged his ruinous marriage to Aphrodite—a Greek version of Beauty and the Beast.

Hephaestus was not, however, a favorite of Zeus. When Zeus punished Hera for her cheekiness by suspending her by the wrists, with anvils hanging from her ankles, Hephaestus remonstrated with him. His reward was yet another forcible ejection from Olympus. As John Milton tells it in *Paradise Lost* (1.741–46), he was

> . . . *thrown by angry Jove*
> *Sheer o'er the Crystal Battlements: from Morn*
> *To Noon he fell, from Noon to dewy Eve,*
> *A Summer's day; and with the setting Sun*
> *Dropt from the Zenith like a falling Star,*
> *On Lemnos th' Aegæan Isle.* . . .

Hephaestus landed hard, breaking both his legs. After that, he always wore gold leg braces. Perhaps because of his estrangement from two-timing Aphrodite, Hephaestus created a pair of golden, silver-tongued, and intelligent mechanical women to serve as his helpers in the forge.

Hestia, goddess of the hearth, eldest child of Cronus and Rhea, and sister of Zeus, was a genuine virgin, unlike the retread varieties so common on Olympus. Priapus of the megaphallus once tried to rape her as she slept, but when the braying of an ass (itself an emblem of lust) awoke her in time, she drove Priapus away howling.

Hestia's symbol, the hearth, was revered as the focus of a Greek family's food preparation, warmth, illumination, and spirituality. Prayers were dedicated to her at the beginning and end of every meal. Hestia was regarded as uniformly protective, kind, and charitable. To mistreat a suppliant or guest was an offense against her (and Zeus, too). As a goddess of domesticity, she also invented the art of house-building.

Her public shrines consisted of large hearths with perpetual fires. When locals went on the road, they often took coals from these fires with them. Solemn oaths were sworn in Hestia's name. Yet the virtuous but staid Hestia was gradually supplanted as one of the twelve Olympian gods in post-Homeric myth by **Dionysus,** the divine inspirer of ecstatic frenzies. In religion, the appeal to emotion often outweighs that of simple piety. In Rome, however, the cult and perpetual flame of Hestia's counterpart, Vesta, were tended by the city's most prestigious priestesses, the vestal virgins.

 QUESTION 89

What are the 12 main branches of the Indo-European language family?

Indic	Slavic
Iranian	Baltic
Germanic	Anatolian
Italic	Armenian
Hellenic	Albanian
Celtic	Tocharian

Bhratar, brathair, broeder, Bruder, frater, brat—it's not much of a stretch to understand that these words all mean "brother" (in Sanskrit, Irish, Dutch, German, Latin, and Russian). Or that the English words *rotary* and *rotation* are related to the German word for "wheel," *Rad,* and the Sanskrit for chariot, *ratha.*

Similarities among European languages had been noted for centuries. It wasn't always clear, however, whether they were due to borrowing, influence, or derivation from a common ancestor. We now know that almost all the current languages of Europe, and many of those in India and Iran, have one source: proto-Indo-European. The sounds, vocabulary, and other features of this ancient tongue have been reconstructed by linguists based on the study of living languages and the surviving evidence of many dead ones.

The first big breakthrough came when Sir William Jones, a British judge in India in the late eighteenth century, systematically studied the correspondences between European languages and the ancient

The Indo-European Language Family

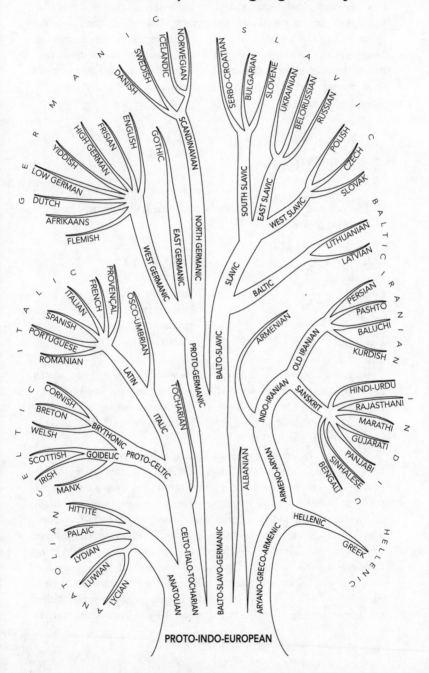

PROTO-INDO-EUROPEAN

Sanskrit of India. What began as an attempt to learn Sanskrit to better understand the Indian judicial process culminated in a presentation of his linguistic findings to the Asiatick Society of Calcutta in 1786. Jones demonstrated so many similarities among Sanskrit, Greek, and Latin that even the most skeptical were eventually convinced that all three languages must have had their roots in a common source.

The trail was picked up by Jacob Grimm (1785–1863) of fairy-tale fame. Grimm demonstrated that certain sound correspondences among languages like Latin, Greek, and Sanskrit, on the one hand, and English and German, on the other, tend to be regular. For example, the initial consonant of Latin *piscis* ("fish") corresponds to the initial *f* of English *fish*—but both words ultimately and independently derive from the Indo-European root *peisk-* or *pisk-*. (An asterisk before a word indicates that it is a scholarly reconstruction, rather than a surviving written form.) Or consider the Latin stem *ped-,* the ancient Greek stem *pod-,* and English *foot,* all three ultimately deriving from Indo-European *ped-*.

Other regular phonetic correspondences demonstrating kinship among Indo-European languages include

- ✦ The *d* in the Latin stem *dent-* and the ancient Greek stem *odont-,* which is related to the initial *t* in English *tooth* (Indo-European *dent-)*
- ✦ The *t* in Latin *tenuis* ("thin") and the *th* in English *thin* (Indo-European *ten-)*
- ✦ The hard *g* in Latin *genu* ("knee") and ancient Greek *gonia* ("angle"), which is related to the initial *k* sound of Old English *cneo* ("knee"). All these forms ultimately derive from Indo-European *genu-*.

Because Grimm systematized these relationships among Indo-European consonants, they are collectively subsumed under "Grimm's Law." Note that these correspondences are *not* the result of word-borrowing but reflect development from a common source, proto-Indo-European, the Ur-language from which well over a hundred tongues are descended, including Greek, Sanskrit, Persian, English, German, Russian, and Latin (with its own numerous offspring, the Romance languages).

But where was the Indo-European proto-language born? Clues have been assembled from assiduous study of ancient texts; peculiarities of grammar, syntax, vocabulary, and phonology; archaeological studies; and even botanical evidence. Some scholars claim the speakers of proto-Indo-European inhabited eastern Anatolia (modern Turkey); others opt for the south Russian steppe, north of the Caucasus, west of the Urals, and far from the sea, for which the original speakers had no general term. Beginning about 3000–2500 B.C., successive waves of Indo-European speakers, with their patriarchal sky god in tow, settled Anatolia and migrated west and north toward Europe, and east and south toward Iran and India. As the various groups parted ways, their original language began its slow evolution into tongues as diverse as Icelandic and Urdu. Today, an Indo-European language is the native speech of almost half the human race.

The easternmost living Indo-European language family is the Indo-Iranian, subdivided into the Indic and Iranian branches. The modern **Indic** languages, spoken by hundreds of millions, are ultimately derived from relatives of Sanskrit, the language of the thousand hymns of the *Rig-Veda* and of the *Upanishads*. The Indic languages include many spoken in India, Sri Lanka, Bangladesh, and Pakistan, such as Hindi-Urdu, Gujarati, Marathi, Panjabi, Rajasthani, Sinhalese, and Bengali (but not the Dravidian languages, non-Indo-European tongues that survive in the extreme south of the subcontinent). Another Indic language, Romany, spoken by Gypsies everywhere, was apparently brought to Europe from northern India more than a thousand years ago. Modern Indo-European **Iranian** languages, spoken in Iran and neighboring areas, include Persian, Tajiki, Baluchi, Kurdish, Pashto, and Ossetic. Ancient Zoroastrian texts such as the *Avesta* were written in the extinct sacred language Avestan.

The **Germanic** branch of Indo-European has its roots in proto-Germanic, spoken in 1000–750 B.C. in Scandinavia and from the Vistula to the Baltic. Three distinct subgroups eventually emerged, fueled by the massive migrations of Germanic tribes to the British Isles, Switzerland, and Austria.

Modern German, a member of the West Germanic subgroup, is the national language of Germany and Austria and one of the four national languages of Switzerland. Its affinities with English, another West Germanic language, are evident. Compare *Fuss* and *foot, Nacht* and *night, Fett* and *fat, Blut* and *blood, stehlen* and *steal*. German loves to form compound words, such as *Krankenwagen,* from *krank* ("sick") and *Wagen* ("wagon") for "ambulance"; *Seehund* ("sea-dog") for "seal"; and *Wasserstoff* ("water stuff") for "hydrogen." Old English poetry, as in the *Beowulf* epic, relished similar compounds, called kennings, which included "whale-road" for the sea, "sword-storm" for battle, "the foamy-necked" for a ship, "sky-candle" for the sun, and "lone-flier" for a wandering mind.

Despite its Germanic syntax and a core of Germanic vocabulary, modern English has vast reserves of non-Germanic words. About half of the English vocabulary—the richest in the world—is Latin-based, either directly or through the Romance languages. Every major language has left its imprint on that greedy borrower, so that many Old English words have died out for lack of anything to do. The language itself is thriving mightily, however, with a half billion native and nonnative speakers throughout the world.

The Germanic-speaking Angles from Schleswig in southern Denmark occupied most of northern England and parts of Scotland by A.D. 500, after the Roman troops were withdrawn. In Old English, the Angles became *Engle* and gave their name to *Englisc*. The possessive form of *Engle, Engla,* gave rise to *Engla land,* the country that the Angles occupied with other invading Germanic peoples, the Saxons and Jutes.

Like modern German, Old English nouns had masculine, feminine, and neuter genders. Speakers were thus obliged to remember that *love* was feminine and required a feminine definite article *(seo lufu)*, whereas the word for *lust* was masculine *(se lust)*. Also as in modern German, verbs often came at the end of clauses. Middle English, the language Chaucer wrote in the fourteenth century, began to evolve shortly after the Norman conquest of England in 1066 (see Questions 74 and 97). By that time, the use of grammatical genders was fading, and the vast influx of Norman French into our language began. Borrowings from other languages, especially Latin, Greek, and Italian, accelerated during the Renaissance, helping shape Modern English (from c. 1500). The language of Shakespeare, to the disbelief of many high school students, is early Modern English.

West Germanic Dutch and Flemish are, in fact, dialects of the same language. It's Dutch when spoken in Holland and Flemish when spoken in Belgium, where it shares official language honors with French. Afrikaans, which developed from Dutch, is now a separate language. Yiddish, another Germanic language, has a considerable Hebrew and Slavic vocabulary, and the written language uses the Hebrew script. (Like Arabic, Hebrew is a Semitic language and thus non-Indo-European.) Frisian, spoken by fewer than a half million people, primarily in remote Netherlandic areas and a few islands in the North Sea, is the living language that bears the closest resemblance to English.

Danish, Norwegian, Swedish, Icelandic, and Faeroese all stem from extinct Old Norse and constitute the North Germanic branch of Indo-European languages. Old Icelandic preserves a rich hoard of Germanic heroic literature and Norse mythology, including the *Elder* (or *Poetic*) *Edda,* the *Younger* (or *Prose*) *Edda,* and dozens of sagas in verse or prose.

The only member of East Germanic is long-dead Gothic, which the barbarian Ostrogoths brought to Italy and the barbarian Visigoths to Spain, where, in both cases, Latin survived and evolved into Italian and Spanish. We possess almost no documents in Gothic besides an early translation of the Gospels and other parts of the New Testament.

The early **Italic** languages developed among the Indo-Europeans who crossed the Alps and settled in Italy. Extinct members of the family include Oscan, Umbrian, and Faliscan. Latin, though dead in the sense that it is no longer anyone's native tongue, lives vibrantly in the languages it sired, such as Italian, French, Spanish, Portuguese, and Romanian. Another Romance language, Old Provençal, was embellished by the exquisite lyrics of love, war, and virtue of the medieval troubadours.

The Romance languages, derived from the language of Rome, stem from Vulgar Latin, the speech of the common people. Italian *cavallo,* Spanish *caballo,* and French *cheval* all share a source in Vulgar Latin *caballus* ("horse"). In Classical Latin, however, a horse was an *equus* (from which English derives *equine, equestrian,* and *equitation)*. The numerous colonial adventures of Romance-language speakers resulted in Spanish, Portuguese, and French being spoken in the Western hemisphere; Spanish in the Philippines; French in many African nations; and Portuguese in Angola and Mozambique.

The **Hellenic** branch of Indo-European includes ancient, Byzantine, and modern Greek. The incomparable heritage of its written texts—such as the works of Homer, the Athenian dramatists, Thucydides, Plato, and Aristotle—originates nearly three millennia ago. Greek-speaking Indo-Europeans settled not only in the Greek mainland but also in the Aegean islands and on the west coast of Asia Minor. Greek colonies were later established on the Black Sea coast, in Sicily and southern Italy, and the Mediterranean coasts of France and Spain. By the fourth century B.C., the various dialects of ancient

Greek—Doric, Aeolic, Ionic, Attic—were subsumed under Koine ("common") or Hellenistic Greek, the lingua franca of Alexander the Great's vast empire in Greece, Egypt, and western Asia. Koine was thus the language in which the New Testament was written and its doctrines widely diffused. Modern Greek began to emerge from Koine during the late Byzantine period.

Considering that the **Celtic** languages have so few native speakers today, it's difficult to imagine a time when these tongues were dominant or prominent in what are now France, Spain, Britain, northern Italy, Eastern Europe, and even a part of Turkey (Galatia). It didn't last. Overwhelmed by Italic and Germanic speakers, Celtic was eventually limited to a few enclaves in northern France, Britain, and Ireland. Celtic is divided into the Goidelic subgroup, which includes Irish and Scottish Gaelic, and the Brythonic subgroup, of which Welsh and Breton (spoken in Brittany) survive.

Slavic languages are subdivided into West Slavic (Polish, Sorbian, Czech, and Slovak), East Slavic (Russian, Ukrainian, and Belorussian), and South Slavic (Bulgarian, Macedonian, Serbo-Croatian, and Slovene). The West and South Slavic languages use the Roman alphabet, while the East Slavic tongues use the Cyrillic, based on the Greek alphabet (see Question 101). Serbo-Croatian uses both—the Cyrillic for Serbian and the Roman for Croatian.

The only living **Baltic** languages are Lithuanian and Latvian, and both bear strong resemblances to Slavic tongues. Linguists suspect both these branches of Indo-European had a common ancestor, Balto-Slavic. Lithuanian is a highly conservative language, which has made it a linchpin of Indo-European studies. In fact, Lithuanian is thought to be the living language that most closely resembles classical Sanskrit. But what about close neighbor Estonian? Like Hungarian and Finnish, Estonian is one of very few major European languages that are not of Indo-European origin. Along with them, it is a member of the Finno-Ugric language family. Basque, another anomalous European tongue, has no known relation to *any* other language on earth.

Anatolian is one of two major Indo-European branches whose members are all extinct—languages like Hittite (the speech of a mighty empire of the ancient Near East, centered in Anatolia), Luwian, Lycian, Lydian, and Palaic. In 1907, clay tablets with cuneiform writing were unearthed from a site near Ankara, Turkey. These finds provided the evidence for classifying Hittite and its siblings as

Indo-European languages, based largely on their verbal conjugation patterns. Anatolian languages were spoken during the second and first millennia B.C. in what is now Turkey.

About six million people worldwide speak **Armenian,** the only member of this separate Indo-European branch. In the early twentieth century, there were about fifty Armenian dialects, not always mutually intelligible. That number is much smaller today. Modern spoken Armenian includes many words borrowed over the centuries from Greek and Persian, as well as from Semitic languages and Turkish.

Albanian, spoken by roughly five million people, is also the only living member of its family. Its two dialects, Gheg and Tosk, have borrowed words from Latin, Italian, Turkish, and Macedonian.

Tocharian, a puzzling extinct language that forms its own branch of Indo-European, was unknown until about a hundred years ago, when manuscripts began to be discovered. Two dialects—Tocharian A and B—were spoken in Chinese Turkestan until about A.D. 1000. Although Tocharian was the easternmost of the Indo-European languages, in certain respects it bore more resemblance to Western languages like Latin than to neighboring Indic and Iranian tongues. In contrast to other Indo-European languages, Tocharian had no sounds for *b, d,* and *g.* So how did speakers of Tocharian A and B say *brother?* They did just fine with *pracar* and *procer.*

❧ QUESTION 90

What were the 12 Labors of Heracles?

1. Kill and flay the Nemean lion
2. Kill the Lernaean Hydra
3. Capture the Arcadian stag
4. Capture the Erymanthian boar
5. Cleanse the Augean stables
6. Kill the Stymphalian birds
7. Capture the Cretan bull
8. Capture the man-eating mares of Diomedes
9. Fetch the Amazon queen Hippolyte's girdle

10. Fetch the oxen of the three-bodied monster Geryon
11. Bring back the golden apples of the Hesperides
12. Bring the three-headed dog Cerberus up from the underworld

The ancient Greeks blamed on feminine wiles all the daunting Labors that Heracles (Latin, Hercules) had to perform. It was the goddess Hera who duped her husband Zeus into taking an oath that made him subordinate his soon-to-be-born son Heracles to Eurystheus, who was also waiting to be born.

Zeus had impregnated Heracles' mother-to-be, Alcmene of Thebes, while her husband Amphitryon was away at war, disguising himself as her homecoming spouse and causing the night they spent together to last the length of three. Hera, ever resentful of Zeus's philanderings, decided to exact revenge by frustrating his grand designs for Heracles.

Zeus had boasted to Hera that his son would rule the royal House of Perseus, the great Greek hero, now dead, who was his son by yet another mortal woman, Danaë. Hera tricked him into swearing that the first prince born of the House of Perseus before nightfall would be the Greek King of Kings. When Zeus readily consented—knowing Heracles' birth was imminent and that of any other contender months away—Hera hastened the birth of Eurystheus, grandson of Perseus, so that this seven-months child was born an hour before Heracles, great-grandson of Perseus, whose birth she delayed. Thus Eurystheus (you-RISS-thoos) grew up to become King of Mycenae, the Greek High King—and Zeus's son Heracles didn't.

Of course, Zeus flew into a rage when he discovered Hera's deceit, but he couldn't renege on his promise. He did, however, exact a compromise by which, although Eurystheus would reign, Heracles would be made a god after he had successfully completed his twelve Labors.

Heracles, whose name means "glory of Hera," was born for adventure, beginning with his strangling two huge snakes Hera sent against him while he was still in his cradle. He became the strongest and greatest Greek hero, delighting in using his wild-olive club and his bow and arrows to deal swift death to fierce animals, monsters, ogres, villains, centaurs, bandits, would-be rapists, bullies, and other offenders against human decency. He had a bad temper, though, and drank far too much wine for the good of those around him. Once, when his music teacher Linus chewed him out for not knowing his lesson, Heracles killed him with a single blow of the master's own lyre. But he had a good heart (and great appetites), often repenting of the manslaughters, homicides, and other indiscretions he committed while enraged or drunk.

One time he went way too far, murdering his wife Megara and their three sons. Although this was the result of a fit of insanity that his implacable foe Hera had visited on him, Heracles was determined to be purified of the heinous deed. When he consulted the oracle of Apollo at Delphi, the priestess advised him to present himself to his kinsman—that's right, King Eurystheus of Mycenae in the Peloponnese, just the kind of guy for dishing out penances—and serve him for twelve years, after which he would become an immortal god. This arrangement was in keeping with the terms of the Zeus-Hera pact.

The Labors *(athloi,* related to our word *athletics)* were all beauts, beginning with the first task Eurystheus imposed on Heracles—**to kill and flay the Nemean lion,** a huge beast with an impermeable pelt. Some traditions say the lion fell from the moon, whereas others claim Hera vomited it up. Nemea, northwest of Mycenae, was being depopulated by the monster. After Heracles failed to kill it with his arrows, sword, and club, he trapped the animal in its cave and strangled it to death, losing a finger in the process. He started back for Mycenae, carrying the dead lion on his shoulders, but not before rededicating the Nemean (nuh-MEE-un) Games to Zeus. These games, along with the Olympian, Pythian, and Isthmian, were the most famous athletic contests of ancient Greece. On shakier authority, Heracles is also said to have founded the Olympian Games (see Question 37).

But how was he going to skin the Nemean lion? It occurred to him that the beast's own deadly claws might have the best chance of piercing its pelt. From that time, Heracles wore the lion's skin as armor and its head as a helmet. Also from that time, whenever Heracles returned with one of his monsters, dead or alive—like something the cat brings home—Eurystheus would cower underground in a brazen urn.

Eurystheus now dispatched Heracles **to kill the Lernaean Hydra.** Lerna, on the east coast of the Peloponnese, southwest of Mycenae, was being devastated by the Hydra, a gigantic venomous water snake with nine serpent heads, of which the middle one was immortal. The Hydra lived near the bottomless Lernaean (lurr-NEE-un) swamp. When Heracles encountered it, he tried to club its heads, but as soon as he smashed one off, two new ones sprouted up to take its place—hence the expression "a hydra-headed problem." Heracles' nephew and charioteer Iolaus now ran up and cauterized the root of each smashed head with a fiery brand. Once the flow of blood was thus stanched, the heads could not regenerate themselves. But the remaining immortal head Heracles cut off and buried under a massive rock. After eviscerating the monster, he dipped his arrows in its gall, which rendered the slightest wound from them lethal.

To capture the Arcadian stag (sometimes called the Ceryneian hind) was the next Labor. The stag, sacred to Artemis, had brass hooves and golden horns and roamed wild in Arcadia, at the heart of the Peloponnese. Heracles hunted it for a full year before capturing it with a precisely aimed bowshot that pinned its forelegs together. The arrow passed between bone and sinew so that it drew no blood—remember, these arrows are poisoned. He then hoisted the beast onto his shoulders and carried it alive all the way back to Eurystheus.

The fourth Labor was **to capture the Erymanthian boar,** a savage beast that ran amok on the slopes of Mount Erymanthus in Achaia, the district north of Arcadia. Killing it would have been far easier than capturing it. Nonetheless, Heracles shouted so loud that he drove it out of its covert and into a snowbank, pounced on its back, and chained it up or trapped it in a net. But after carrying it alive on his shoulders to Eurystheus, he decided to treat himself to a cruise—the first ever—by joining Jason's Argonaut expedition.

Refreshed from his sea voyage, Heracles was now sent by a snickering Eurystheus **to cleanse the Augean stables,** by no means the easiest of his Labors, since King Augeas of Elis in the western Peloponnese hadn't had the job done in thirty years and had three thousand head of cattle. Besides, Heracles had to do it all in one day. No wonder an Augean (aw-JEE-un) task is a formidably difficult and, often, distasteful one. The hero accomplished it, without so much as coming near any dung, by diverting the rivers Alpheus and Peneus through the stables and blasting the filth away. Because of a misunderstanding about the terms of his service, however, Heracles later found it necessary to slay Augeas and all his sons.

Heracles was afterward sent off **to kill the Stymphalian birds**—not cute little feathered friends, but crane-sized man-eaters with brass wings, claws, and beaks. These birds, sacred to the war god Ares, flocked around a marsh in Stymphalus, northwest of Mycenae, often taking to the air and killing their human and animal prey by strafing them with their brazen feathers. They also posed an environmental hazard by discharging their poisonous excrement over cultivated fields. Heracles realized there were too many of them to kill with his arrows, so he made a terrifying noise with a rattle that Athene gave him. When the birds all flocked into the air, he shot as many as he could, while the rest escaped to the Isle of Ares in the Black Sea.

Heracles' seventh Labor was **to capture the Cretan bull,** a fire-breathing monster that was making life tough on the island of Crete. No one is quite sure whether this bull was the one that had fathered the Minotaur on the wife of King Minos, naughty Queen Pasiphaë, or the bull that bore Zeus's love Europa on its back from Tyre to Crete. Be that as it may, Heracles sailed to Crete and took care of business. Eurystheus must have remained hidden in his urn for quite a while after the bull arrived, but he eventually ordered it to be set free as a gift to Hera. Some say it was later slain by "the Athenian Heracles," Theseus, near Marathon.

Next came the order **to capture the man-eating mares of Diomedes.** These four mares of the son of Ares, King Diomedes (die-oh-MEE-deez) of Thrace, in the wild northeast of the Greek world, were bound to their bronze mangers with chains and fed on the flesh of the King's unpleasantly surprised guests. Heracles arrived with some followers, untethered the mares, and drove them toward the sea. When the King and his men pursued, Heracles flooded the plain by cutting a channel. The men turned and ran while Heracles clubbed Diomedes to death and fed him to his own mares. After finishing their meal, the horses were easier to handle, so Heracles yoked them to Diomedes' chariot and drove them all the way back to Mycenae, where Eurystheus set them free.

To fetch the Amazon queen Hippolyte's girdle was the ninth Labor. This was originally the golden girdle of Ares, and Eurystheus wanted it as a gift for his daughter Admete. The Amazons, descendants of the war god, lived near the Black Sea coast. The women, who were the warriors and rulers, broke their infant males' arms and legs to make them unfit for war or travel but still capable of housework. Amazonian women, the first soldiers to use cavalry in war, were fierce fighters who captured Troy and conquered an empire for themselves. But the Amazon queen Hippolyte (hip-OL-i-tee) took a liking to Heracles, who had arrived with a shipful of men, and offered him her girdle as a love gift. Hera had meanwhile spread the rumor that Heracles planned to abduct the Queen, so her followers attacked the Greek force. Heracles thereupon killed Hippolyte, took her girdle, and slaughtered huge numbers of Amazonian warriors.

Geryon (JER-ee-un) was King of Tartessus in Spain, at the limits of the known world. Heracles was now sent **to fetch the oxen of Geryon,** who was supposed to be the strongest man alive, and no wonder, since "he" was really Siamese triplets joined at the waist—with wings, no less. His beautiful red cattle were kept on the island of Erytheia in the western ocean and guarded by a huge herdsman and his two-headed dog. When Heracles got to Tartessus, he set up the so-called Pillars of Heracles on either side of the straits of Gibraltar. (The Romans later thought that *"Ne plus ultra"*—"No farther!"—had been posted on them.) After sailing to the island, Heracles quickly dispatched the herdsman and dog and drove off the cattle. When the King heard the news, he confronted Heracles, but the thrifty hero jumped to Geryon's flank and shot an arrow clean through all three of him. Hera, who had come to the King's assistance, was shot by Heracles through the right breast and sent howling to Olympus. His journey back across Europe with the cattle was jam-packed with adventures in Gaul, Liguria, Italy (including the future site of Rome, after he had taken a wrong right turn down into the peninsula), Sicily, etc. These "side-Labors" (called *parerga*) were sometimes more interesting than the main event.

Now Eurystheus started getting creative. A really difficult assignment was the eleventh Labor, **to bring back the golden apples of the Hesperides.** The precious tree that grew such fruits had been the wedding gift of Gaea, Mother Earth, to Hera, who had planted it in a garden on the slopes of Mount Atlas in Africa (or in the country of the Hyperboreans). Hera asked the three daughters of Atlas, the Hesperides, to guard the tree, but when she realized they were pilfering the fruit themselves, she made the hundred-headed dragon Ladon coil around the tree and remain on the lookout. Now, Heracles had been warned by a reliable source not to pick the apples himself but to let the Titan Atlas do it. The only problem was that Atlas had been sentenced by the victorious Olympian gods to hold up the encircling globe of the heavens on his shoulders. This task Heracles decided to take over while Atlas (actually, his daughters, who were good at it) picked three golden apples. After killing Ladon with a bowshot, Heracles shouldered the skies. But when Atlas regained his freedom, he was reluctant to surrender it, saying he would take the apples to Eurystheus himself. Heracles now employed the ruse of asking the dimwitted giant to hold up the sky again, just for a second, while Heracles put a pad on his head. So long, Atlas. Catch you later.

On his way back with the golden apples, Heracles was confronted by Antaeus, King of Libya, a lion-eating giant who forced all strangers to wrestle with him to the death. As a son of Mother Earth, Antaeus increased in strength as long as his feet or any other part of him remained in contact with her. When Heracles threw him, Antaeus just got stronger, so he did the only thing he could—heaving the giant off the ground, he bear-hugged him to death.

Heracles also stopped off in Egypt, where he killed King Busiris, brother of Antaeus, who wanted to make a human sacrifice of the Greek hero. After that, Heracles unshackled Prometheus from a mountainside in the Caucasus and shot the vulture that ate the Titan's liver, which grew back each day for the bird's next repast. It's clear that the *parerga* are distinctly in danger of stealing the eleventh Labor's thunder.

Last, but certainly not least: **to bring the three-headed dog Cerberus up from the underworld.** Once Heracles had made his way into the nether regions, descending near Taenarum in Laconia in the southern Peloponnese, he was able to intimidate Charon, the ferryman of the infernal River Styx, to convey him across that waterway into Tartarus (see Question 42). This is where Heracles freed his friend Theseus from confinement in a magical chair, to which he had been sentenced for trying to carry off Persephone, wife of Hades, king of the underworld. But when Heracles ripped the Athenian hero from his Super-Glue seat, Theseus left half his butt on it. That is why Athenian men have such trim buns.

When Heracles demanded Cerberus from Hades, the gloomy god replied that he could have him if he was able to subdue him without using his club or arrows. Heracles gripped the monstrous dog by the throat and squeezed hard, just beneath the spot where the three heads, with their manes of hissing serpents, branched off. Cerberus went limp and let Heracles drag him off to the upper world, with the foam that slavered from his mouths turning into the poisonous herb aconite (wolfsbane or monkshood). When they got to Mycenae, Eurystheus was offering a sacrifice and had the temerity to give Heracles a slave's portion of the flesh. By this time totally fed up with Eurystheus, and having paid his full measure of penance, Heracles killed three of his cruel overlord's sons. He then took Cerberus back down to the underworld.

The earliest appearance of the Labors as a group of twelve was probably in the metope carvings of the temple of Zeus at Olympia (c. 560 B.C.). But besides the Labors, Heracles had so many other adventures that to relate them all would take a night as long as the one in which he was conceived. Here are some highlights. He served as a slave and henpecked lover (spinning wool while dressed in women's clothes) to Queen Omphale of Lydia in Asia Minor. He sacked the city of Troy. He helped the gods fight off the Giants on the fields of Phlegra. He wrestled with Death to bring back Alcestis, who had willingly died in place of her husband, King Admetus. A full life by any standards.

He died as he had lived. When his new wife, Deianira, was on the brink of being raped by Nessus the centaur, who was carrying her on his back across the river Evenus, Heracles unleashed one of his poisoned arrows at long range and pierced the brute through the heart. The dying centaur told Deianira that if she mixed his blood into the wool that she used to weave a garment for Heracles, she would never again have to worry about his unfaithfulness to her. Of course, the shirt Deianira wove for her husband, after he had taken a mistress, was poisoned with the gall of the Hydra (see Labor 2) via the blood of vengeful Nessus.

Heracles roared in excruciating pain, tried to rip off the shirt but only succeeded in tearing off his own flesh, plunged into a stream, which only exacerbated the searing torment, and uprooted trees in his agony. This was in fulfillment of a prophecy stating that no living man could ever kill Heracles but that a dead foe would. Heracles now bade his son Hyllus build a lofty funeral pyre for him. As soon as it was kindled, and Heracles lay down on its summit, Zeus struck the pyre with a thunderbolt and consumed his beloved son's mortal part while bringing his soul up to Olympus in a four-horse chariot. Hera now received him as a son and gave him her daughter Hebe, goddess of youth, in marriage.

It's said that after he sired Heracles, Zeus refrained from sex with mortal women because he could never hope to beget another such hero—and we'd have to agree. His first mortal love had been Niobe, whose fourteen children were slain by Apollo and Artemis when she boasted that *their* mother Leto had only two splendid children, whereas *she* had so many. (That's exactly the kind of hubris Greek gods hated.) Alcmene, the mother of Heracles, was sixteenth in descent from Niobe, so Zeus didn't exactly restrain himself unduly, with so many generations of beautiful women from which to choose his lovers.

QUESTION 91

Who were the 12 Apostles?

Peter	Thomas
Andrew	Simon the Zealot
James the Greater	Jude (or Thaddeus)
John	James the Less
Matthew	Judas Iscariot (replaced by
Philip	Matthias)
Bartholomew (or Nathanael)	

In Greek an *apostolos* is "a person sent." Christ sent the twelve Apostles he had chosen on several missions of preaching and teaching and also enjoined them to spread the Gospel after he had ascended into heaven. The selection of twelve Apostles was an allusion to the twelve tribes of Israel (see Question 87), and the Apostles themselves appreciated the importance of maintaining a cadre of twelve when they replaced the traitorous suicide Judas Iscariot with Matthias. Except for Matthew the tax collector—and apparently Judas—they were all men who worked with their hands.

Peter, James the Greater, and John constituted an inner circle within the Twelve. They were with Christ during his Transfiguration on Mount Tabor, at his raising from the dead of Jairus's daughter, and during the Agony in the Garden of Gethsemane.

Simon bar Jonah (son of John) was renamed **Peter,** the Greek name *(Petros)* that corresponds to the Aramaic Kepha, "rock." Simon Peter and his brother Andrew were fishermen and business partners of the brothers James and John in the coastal town of Capernaum on the

Sea of Galilee. According to the Gospel of John, Christ identified Peter as "the rock" at their first meeting, and, from the start, Peter—a bluff, gruff, impulsive man—emerged as the natural leader of the Twelve. He was the first Apostle to affirm the divinity of Christ and to witness the Resurrection. Christ says to him, "You are Petros and on this petra [rock] I will build my Church" (Matthew 16:18). The papacy assumes its authority from this punning Petrine verse, which is emblazoned in huge, gold capital letters, in both Greek and Latin, in the interior of St. Peter's Basilica in Rome. Other Christian denominations, however, do not interpret this verse as instituting a successive high priesthood.

Peter is a central figure in some of the more memorable stories in the Gospels. When he sees Christ walking on the surface of a lake toward his boat, he says, "Lord, if it is you, command me to come to you on the water." At Christ's bidding, Peter steps out of the boat and walks on the water toward his master. Suddenly realizing what he is doing, and noticing the lashing of the winds and waves, he becomes frightened, begins to sink, and cries out, "Lord, save me!" Christ stretches his hand out to him but says, "O you of little faith, why did you doubt?" (Matthew 14:22–33).

The Gospel of John identifies Peter as the disciple who draws his sword and strikes off the ear of the high priest's servant Malchus during Christ's arrest in the Garden of Gethsemane (John 18:10). Yet, by dawn, Peter has three times denied even knowing Christ. This was precisely what he vowed never to do when Christ predicted his renunciation only hours earlier at the Last Supper.

After the Resurrection, Peter was the acknowledged leader of the Christians in Jerusalem for about fifteen years. According to tradition, he was martyred in Rome, where he had reportedly served as its first bishop, during the persecutions of Nero in 64 or 67. Legend says he asked to be crucified upside down because he felt unworthy to die in the same manner as Christ. Despite extensive excavations, the remains of Peter, said to rest in the catacombs of San Sebastiano on the Appian Way or beneath the high altar of St. Peter's Basilica, have never been identified.

Peter's brother **Andrew** (Greek, "manly") was referred to as protokletos, "the first called," in Byzantine tradition, since he is the first Apostle named in John 1:40. According to fourth-century writings, Andrew was crucified on an X-shaped cross, or Andrew's cross. His supposed remains were removed from Pátrai, Greece, to Constantinople in 357. More than a millennium later, his skull was sent to Rome to function as a prop for whipping up enthusiasm for one final Crusade against the Turks. The concocter of this abortive scheme, Pope Pius II (reigned 1458–64), displayed the sacred skull before a crowd of the faithful from the steps of St. Peter's. In 1964, Pope Paul VI was gracious enough to return Andrew's head to Pátrai. Andrew is the patron saint of Scotland (whose flag bears the X-cross) and Russia.

Boanerges, or "sons of thunder" (Grecianized Hebrew), is what Christ called the sons of Zebedee, **James** and **John,** presumably because of their enthusiastic reception of his ministry. At one point, the brothers make the presumptuous request (denied) to sit on either side of Christ's heavenly throne (Mark 10:35–40). The fourth Gospel is credited to John, who is called John the Evangelist (see Question 32) or John the Divine. Tradition also ascribes to him three New Testament epistles and the Book of Revelation (see Question 29). In depictions of the Last Supper, John is usually represented as the youngest Apostle, beardless, and with his head resting on Christ's shoulder as "the disciple that Jesus loved." He was the only Apostle not martyred and supposedly died at a very advanced age at Ephesus.

His brother James, in contrast, is the only Apostle whose martyrdom is described in the New Testament. To appease the Pharisaic Jews in their contention with Christian Jews, King Herod Agrippa I of Judea (A.D. 41–44) had James killed "by the sword" (Acts 12:1–2). (Peter was arrested at about the same time, but an angel appeared in his prison cell and freed him from his chains.) Since medieval times, a legend has maintained that after James was beheaded in Jerusalem, his body was miraculously transported to northwestern Spain, where he had supposedly conducted a mission. Even today, pilgrims travel as much as a thousand miles by foot to the cathedral of Santiago ("St. James") de Compostela, where his remains allegedly rest.

Matthew, also called Levi, was a tax collector, an occupation greatly scorned by the Jews. Christ, who was passing by as Matthew sat at his work table, said "Follow me" (Matthew 9:9). He did, and shortly afterward Christ dined at Matthew's house, much to the surprise of the Pharisees. Christ replied that he had come to save sinners, not the righteous. Matthew was reputed to be the author of the first Gospel. After Christ's Resurrection, Matthew is reported to have traveled to Ethiopia and Persia, although his remains are claimed by Salerno, Italy.

Philip, like Simon Peter and Andrew, came from Bethsaida, and, like Andrew, had been a follower of John the Baptist. It was Philip to whom Christ, surrounded by a teeming crowd at the Sea of Galilee, addressed the question, "Where can we buy enough food for them to eat?" When Philip suggested that even two hundred days' wages would be insufficient, Christ multiplied the few available loaves and fishes. Little else is known of Philip, and various works attributed to him were probably written in the third or fourth century. He may have been crucified.

Bartholomew (Hebrew, "son of Tolmai"), mentioned in the Gospels of Matthew, Mark, and Luke, and a resident of Cana in Galilee, was probably the same person called Nathanael in the Gospel of John. Bartholomew is a family name, and Nathanael may have been his given name. When his friend Philip told him about Jesus, Nathanael asked, "Can anything good come from Nazareth?" Philip brought him to Christ, who said upon seeing him: "Here is a true Israelite. There is no duplicity in him" (John 1:46–47). Perhaps the best-traveled of the Apostles, Bartholomew is said to have preached in southwest Asia, India, Ethiopia, Persia, and Turkey, and to have been skinned alive and beheaded in Armenia. His remains, like those of most of the Apostles, are said to be in Italy (in Rome). In Michelangelo's epic fresco in the Sistine Chapel, *The Last Judgment,* St. Bartholomew holds in his hands his flayed skin—with the artist's doleful self-portrait for a face.

Thomas, called the Twin (Greek, *Didymos)* in John 21:2, is best known as "Doubting Thomas." He was not present with the other disciples at Christ's first few post-Resurrection appearances and, refusing to take these reports on faith, insisted on having more tangible proof. When at last Christ appeared to him and insisted that he put his fingers into the wounds of the crucifixion, Thomas exclaimed, "My Lord and my God!" Christ responded, "Blessed are those who have not yet seen and have believed" (John 20:29). Thomas subsequently preached in northwestern Persia and is said to have been martyred in Madras, India. Several apocryphal writings, including a once-influential Gospel of Thomas, were attributed to him. His remains are of course reputed to be in Italy.

Simon and **Jude** may have been Zealots, members of a nationalistic Jewish group dedicated to violent overthrow of the Roman government in Judea, though whether this movement existed in the time of Christ is controversial. Little is known of them, and they apparently traveled and preached together in Persia after Christ's Ascension. Jude, mentioned in Luke 6 and Acts 1, was probably the same man as the Apostle called Thaddeus in Matthew 10 and Mark 3. Jude is the patron saint of desperate causes.

James the Less, identified as the son of Alphaeus in Matthew, Mark, and Luke, was supposedly martyred in Persia. We don't know whether his remains made their way to Italy.

No one really knows what the second name of **Judas Iscariot** meant. Improbable is the derivation from Latin *sicarius,* "assassin"; a more mundane but plausible explanation is "the man from Kerioth" in the territory of Judah. Medieval legend endows Judas with red hair, an evil portent in the Mediterranean world. He was probably the treasurer of the Apostles. His knack for monetary affairs destroyed his ministry, however, when he sold Christ to the chief priests and elders for thirty pieces of silver after the Last Supper, at which Christ predicted that one of the Twelve would betray him. That night, in the Garden of Gethsemane, Judas identified Christ for his captors with a kiss. Accounts of Judas's suicide vary (hanging or a gut-bursting fall), and Dante places him in the very deepest pit of his *Inferno* (see Question 81).

Two men were nominated to replace Judas: Joseph Barsabbas, whose surname was Justus, and Matthias (Acts 1:23–26). The Apostles prayed and drew lots, deciding on **Matthias,** who is said to have evangelized parts of Turkey. He, too, was martyred and, yes, his remains ended up in Rome.

✣ QUESTION 92

Who were the 12 Knights of the Round Table?

Lancelot	Lamorack
Galahad	Torre
Bors	Kay
Perceval	Gareth
Gawain	Bedivere
Tristan	Mordred

No story of British origin has inspired as much imaginative literature through the ages—in English, French, German, and even medieval Hebrew—as that of King Arthur and his Knights of the Round Table. Yet little is known of the historical Arthur, and the Round Table knights (with one possible exception) are purely fictional characters.

Ancient Latin documents in the British Museum relate that at the Battle of Badon (A.D. 490 or 518), a military leader named Arthur "carried the cross of Our Lord Jesus Christ on his shoulders for three days and three nights, and the Britons were victorious." Scholars believe Arthur may have led the successful defense of southwest Britain, and its Romanized Celtic Britons, against advancing Saxon invaders from the Continent. He may have been an accomplished horseman trained in Roman cavalry techniques, and this may explain his success against the undisciplined hordes of Teutonic barbarians. The victory at Mount Badon was so decisive that it halted the Saxon advance for a half century. But not a shred of evidence suggests that Arthur was a King, held court in Camelot, or presided over a Round Table.

Large-scale embellishment of Arthur's story began, about six centuries after he lived, in the *History of the Kings of Britain* (c. 1136), written in Latin by the chronicler Geoffrey of Monmouth. In the interim, the tale was embroidered by the Welsh, who rallied to fight the Saxons and embraced the Arthurian legend, and by the Britons, some of whom migrated in the sixth and seventh centuries to what is today Brittany in France to escape the Saxons.

Over the ages, Arthur's reputation as a military commander who defended the Christian Britons from the Saxon invaders was inflated into that of Arthur, King of Britain, who conquered much of Europe and whose heroic reign incorporated magic, chivalry, British nationalism, Christian mysticism, courtly love, and boundless romance (see Question 78, where Arthur appears as one of the Nine Worthies of medieval Christendom).

In addition to his association with the Round Table and Camelot (sometimes identified with Caerleon, Monmouthshire, in south Wales), this Arthur of pure legend was said to be the son of the British King Uther Pendragon ("chief dragon"), who begot him on Igraine after the sorcerer Merlin changed the King's form into that of the lady's husband, the Duke of Tintagil in Cornwall. Merlin, son of the devil and a nun, became the boy's mentor. In some versions, Arthur extracted the magical sword Excalibur from a rock, thereby confirming his claim to the British throne at age fifteen; in others, he received it from the Lady of the Lake.

The first surviving mention of the Round Table occurs in the *Roman de Brut* (1155), a fanciful verse history of the Britons written by the Anglo-Norman poet Wace, probably on commission from Henry II of England. Wace tells how Arthur used a round banquet table so that none of his barons could claim precedence over the others—a notion that may have been borrowed from Celtic tradition.

Later writers elaborated the Round Table into the central organizing symbol of Arthurian literature and the medieval chivalric code. To win a place at this table was the most any storybook knight could hope for, and the code of Christian knighthood it exemplified had a profound impact on the princely houses of Europe in the Middle Ages, in which the legend of Arthur was widely known. Fixed to the wall of a thirteenth-century hall in Winchester is a table eighteen feet in diameter reputed to be the Round Table itself. Like the hall, however, it dates from about seven centuries after Arthur supposedly lived.

The motif of the Round Table was powerfully energized when it merged with that of the quest for the Holy Grail (Medieval Latin, *cratella*, "bowl"), the silver cup or platter Christ was said to have used at the Last Supper. Because only the purest knight could approach the Grail, the quest for this ineffably sacred vessel became the ultimate trial of Arthur's Round Table paladins.

The notion of a table vessel imbued with magical powers to produce whatever food one desired stemmed from Celtic legend, but the hollow vessel was also an ancient fertility symbol. In Chrétien de Troyes's unfinished Arthurian French romance, *Perceval, ou le conte du Graal* (c. 1175), the Grail is a mystical hollow platter, now usually interpreted as a female sex symbol, which appears in connection with a phallic bleeding lance or spear (identified with the one used to wound Christ on the cross).

The first unequivocal association of the Grail cup with the one Christ used at the Last Supper occurs in Robert de Boron's French poem *Joseph d'Arimathie, ou le Roman de l'estoire dou Graal* (c. 1202). According to this story, Joseph of Arimathea, mentioned in the Gospels, constructed a table to commemorate the Last Supper, leaving one place empty, the Siege Perilous ("perilous seat"), to mark the betrayal of Judas. By this time, the French *Sangreal* ("Holy Grail") had been thoroughly confused with *Sang Real,* the "royal blood" of Christ, some of which Joseph of Arimathea was supposed to have preserved in the Grail and brought to Wales.

Not only did Arthur come into possession of Joseph's table, but only the Round Table knight destined to succeed in the Grail quest could occupy the Siege Perilous. Other legends say Merlin constructed the Round Table for Uther Pendragon and that Arthur received it as part of his wife Guinevere's dowry from her father, King Leodegrance, who had received it from Arthur's father.

But who were the twelve Knights of the Round Table? No easy answer suggests itself because, in the countless versions of the stories about Arthur, many dozens of knights are assigned a place at his table. Depending on the source, the Round Table seated anywhere from twelve (in remembrance of Christ's Apostles) to a hundred fifty. The most comprehensive listing appears in Sir Thomas Malory's *Morte Darthur* (1470), edited and printed by the first English printer William Caxton in 1485, an epic recounting of nearly all the Arthurian tales. In this first book of magnificent English prose, well over a hundred Round Table knights are named. Although the twelve discussed here are among the most significant, they are by no means canonical.

Foremost is **Lancelot,** the greatest and most tragic of the Round Table knights. He first appears as an Arthurian knight in the twelfth-century poetic romances of Chrétien de Troyes, who narrates the story of his adulterous affair with Guinevere, King Arthur's Queen. He was the son of King Ban of Benwick (in Brittany) but was raised by the enchantress Vivien, the Lady of the Lake, who introduced him to Arthur's court (hence his name Lancelot du Lac). Although most writers considered Lancelot the apotheosis of chivalry, torn between his love for Guinevere and his loyalty to Arthur, he never succeeds in the Grail quest because of his adultery. Moreover, his illicit relationship ultimately causes the death of Arthur and the destruction of the brotherhood of the Round Table. In the end, Guinevere becomes a nun, and Lancelot dies a hermit.

Success in the mystical quest is reserved for Lancelot's son, **Galahad,** "the Grail Knight." Galahad first figures in thirteenth-century French stories about the Grail as the son of Lancelot and Elaine, daughter of King Pelles. When Galahad appears at Arthur's court, a mysterious old man declares him the only one pure enough to sit in the Siege Perilous. Arthur immediately knights the young man, who has inherited his father's fighting mettle but is chaste, pure-hearted, and piously austere. Galahad sees the Grail in the castle of King Pelles, where he also has a vision of Christ.

At the time, Galahad is accompanied by Perceval and **Bors,** who also see the Grail. These three knights of the Round Table are the only ones to accomplish the great quest. Bors later becomes a hermit at Glastonbury and buries the other two Grail knights at the Spiritual Palace at Sarras.

But before the invention of Galahad, **Perceval** was the only knight to win the Grail, the best-known account being in Chrétien de Troyes's *Perceval.* Most versions agree that he was a simple but immensely strong boy raised in the woods by his mother. He encounters knights riding—"glittering hauberks, their bright helmets, lances, and shields"—and thinks they must be angels. When he learns they are Arthur's knights, he leaves his protesting mother to reveal his strength and join the fellowship of the Round Table, in due course transforming himself from country bumpkin into Grail hero.

In the castle of the wounded Fisher King, Perceval sees the Grail and is awed by the vessel's gold and precious stones, "richer and more varied than might be found in earth or sea; no gem could compare with those in the Grail." By remaining speechless before it, however, he misses the opportunity to heal the Fisher King, who is, unbeknownst to Perceval, his uncle. The most celebrated version of Perceval's story is *Parzival* (c. 1210), an epic poem by Wolfram von Eschenbach, a masterpiece of medieval German literature. This poem inspired Richard Wagner's final opera, the mystical *Parsifal* (1882) that Nietzsche so heartily loathed.

Gawain failed in the Grail quest because of placing his trust in the knightly code rather than in the spiritual realm. He is known as Arthur's loyal nephew (or cousin). Scholars trace his literary heritage back to Celtic mythology, in particular the solar god Gwalchmei, whose strength, like Gawain's in some accounts, increased and decreased with the daily waxing and waning of the sun.

Gawain is the hero of a Middle English poetic gem of unknown authorship, *Sir Gawayne and the Grene Knight* (c. 1370). In this narrative poem of superb craftsmanship, Gawain is an honorable and courteous Christian knight who faces a terrifying supernatural challenge. He must withstand the return ax-blow, in one year's time, of a brawny green knight whom he has already beheaded—but to no avail.

He must also fend off an apparent seduction by the beautiful wife of his host, Sir Bercilak. It all ends happily, though the young hero learns that his former exalted opinion of his chivalric honor was a tad overblown.

In the romances of Chrétien de Troyes, Gawain was a notch below the likes of Lancelot and Galahad, with a tendency to womanize and to fight for the sake of fighting. In Malory's *Morte Darthur,* Lancelot unwittingly kills two of Gawain's brothers—Gareth and Gaheris—while rescuing Guinevere from being burned at the stake for her adultery. Gawain swears revenge and, with Arthur and his army, pursues Lancelot to France, where he is fatally wounded by that hero. He dies on his return to Britain.

The tragic love story of **Tristan** (or Tristram) and Iseult the Fair, grafted onto the Arthurian cycle in the early thirteenth century, parallels the adulterous tale of Lancelot and Guinevere, both involving treason to liege lords. Tristan's uncle, King Mark of Cornwall, is to marry Iseult, a young Irish princess. Tristan—irresistibly handsome, valiant, and a wonderful harpist and poet—fetches the bride-to-be, who falls in love with him. Aboard ship on the way to Cornwall, Tristan and Iseult unknowingly drink a love potion, and an overwhelming passion grips them, sweeping aside every other consideration. Iseult is married to Mark, but the two lovers continue their affair, are discovered, and die.

Gottfried von Strassburg's long German poem *Tristan* (c. 1210) inspired Wagner's opera *Tristan und Isolde* (1865), which extolled passionate love as the highest human value. Its heart-wrenching "Liebestod" ("love death") is sung in farewell by Isolde to the dead Tristan in her arms, begging for death as a release just before falling lifeless over his body.

In Malory's account, **Lamorack** of Wales was the son of King Pellinore and the brother of Perceval and Torre. He was the bravest Round Table knight, after the incomparable Lancelot and Tristan. Because of a grudge, he revealed the adulterous relationship of Tristan and Iseult. He himself (like Arthur) was the adulterous lover of Queen Morgawse, who was beheaded by her son Gaheris after he caught them in bed. Another son, Gawain, sent Lamorack to his eternal reward for debauching his mother.

Torre, whom King Pellinore fathered on a milkmaid, was the first to be made a Round Table knight. The fact that he was knighted before Gawain caused consternation in Arthur's court because his father had killed Gawain's father, King Lot.

Arthur's royal seneschal, or steward, **Kay,** was raised with Arthur because Merlin had presented the royal infant to Kay's father, Sir Ector, and his mother. Kay became a churlish, sarcastic name-caller, a rude and boastful but lousy warrior in some accounts. Yet Arthur never set him straight, perhaps because of their early bond. His rough speech was said to have resulted from being raised by a crude wet nurse, since Arthur had usurped Kay's place at his mother's breast.

Gareth of Orkney was the youngest son of King Lot and Queen Morgawse and the brother of Gawain. He agreed to serve as a scullion for a year under Kay, who dubbed him "Beaumains" because of his big hands. Gareth was then knighted and became Lancelot's favorite. After rescuing Lady Lyonesse from Sir Ironsyde in the Castle Perilous, he married her. While Lancelot rescued Guinevere from a fiery death at the stake, he unwittingly killed Gareth, thus earning Gawain's enmity.

At Arthur's bidding, **Bedivere** (or Bedevere), called the Bold, flung Excalibur out over the water so that the Lady of the Lake could retrieve it, raising only her white-robed arm above the surface. One of the few to survive Arthur's last apocalyptic battle against Mordred, Bedivere was with the King on the occasion of his strange removal from the world.

Some sources say **Mordred** was Arthur's bastard son, and others his nephew. The confusion probably arises from Mordred's parentage: He is the product of Arthur's unwitting sexual escapade with his half-sister Morgawse (his aunt, according to Malory), and this would make Mordred both Arthur's son and nephew. In any event, he is the darkest figure in Arthurian lore, the embodiment of Arthur's sin, a kind of Freudian "return of the repressed" who ends up destroying the King and the Round Table knights.

In Malory's account, Mordred reveals to Arthur the affair between Lancelot and Guinevere, forces a conflict between the two men, and then seizes the throne and tries to marry Guinevere while Arthur is fighting Lancelot in France. Arthur and his army rush back to England to face the usurper, but in the ensuing battles almost all the Round Table knights meet their death. In a final conflict on Salisbury Plain, amid countless dead, Arthur runs Mordred through with a spear, just as Mordred deals him a savage blow to the head. So massive was the wound Arthur inflicted on the traitor that the sunlight shone clear through Mordred's body before he fell dead. The wounded Arthur was borne away on a barge by lovely ladies in mourning to the Isle of Avalon, presided over by the enchantress Queen Morgan le Fay, his half-sister.

Some evidence suggests Mordred, too, may have been a historical figure. The same documents in the British Museum that contain the first mention of Arthur and his victory at Badon also note that (in 511 or 539) there occurred "the Battle of Camlann, in which Arthur and Mordred perished."

Fascination with Arthur and his Round Table knights survived well into the nineteenth and twentieth centuries. Here are only a few of many examples: William Morris's "The Defence of Guenevere" (1858); Alfred, Lord Tennyson's series of long poems, *Idylls of the King* (1859–85), a sanitized, bowdlerized, Protestantized version of Malory's uninhibited tales; Mark Twain's irreverent *A Connecticut Yankee in King Arthur's Court* (1889); T. H. White's tetralogy, *The Once and Future King* (1939–58); Lerner and Loewe's musical, *Camelot* (1960), which became a leitmotif of President John F. Kennedy's administration (1961–63); and Marion Zimmer Bradley's bestseller, *The Mists of Avalon* (1982).

Legend says King Arthur, magically healed of his wounds, lies asleep in a cave and will return to defend his beloved England when it is next invaded. This may help explain why the English royal family avoids naming any foreseeable heir to the throne "Arthur"—Henry VIII's elder brother may have been the last—besides the sheer presumptuousness of the gesture. But although Malory assures us Arthur is really dead and buried in Glastonbury, he cannot resist reporting the prophetic epitaph: HIC IACET ARTHURUS, REX QUONDAM REXQUE FUTURUS—"Here lies Arthur, the once and future King."

What are the 12 signs of the zodiac and the sources of their names?

Aries: the Ram whose golden fleece was sought by Jason and the Argonauts

Taurus: the Bull whose shape Zeus assumed to carry off Europa

Gemini: the Twins, usually identified with Castor and Polydeuces

Cancer: the Crab that attacked Heracles while he fought with the Nemean Lion

Leo: the Nemean Lion killed by Heracles

Virgo: the Virgin goddess of justice, Astraea, daughter of Zeus

Libra: the Balance (scales of justice) of Astraea

Scorpio: a Scorpion sent to kill Orion the hunter

Sagittarius: the Archer, usually thought of as the bow-wielding centaur Chiron

Capricorn: the Goat that nurtured the infant Zeus

Aquarius: the Water Bearer Ganymede, cupbearer of the gods

Pisces: the two Fishes that helped Aphrodite and her son Eros escape from the monster Typhon

Early skywatchers in Babylonia are thought to have first proposed that the movements of certain celestial bodies might be used to forecast earthly events. Similar astrological beliefs sprang up in ancient peoples as disparate as the Chinese and the Mayans, but they acquired particular sophistication in Ptolemaic Egypt (305–30 B.C.). There, in line with the Aristotelian principle that earth, the center of the universe, was orbited at regular intervals by the sun, moon, planets, and stars, Greek mathematicians mapped the sun's apparent yearly path.

They divided this celestial circle, the ecliptic, into twelve sections, each thirty degrees wide. Each division was considered to be the residence, or house, of a "planet" known to the ancients (Mercury, Venus, Mars, Jupiter, and Saturn, each assigned to two houses, and the sun and moon to one each). The twelve divisions were each also associated with a zodiacal sign, or constellation.

The constellations were simple groupings of bright stars that suggested to fertile ancient imaginations the outlines of various mythological characters. More important, the complex interplay of the celestial bodies in the macrocosm—their changing relative positions as they rose and set throughout the night and moved across the sky throughout the year—was used to predict events affecting the individual human being (the microcosm). For this purpose, a person was said to have been born under the sign of the constellation that the sun occupied at the time of his or her birth.

The precepts of astrology exerted a significant influence well beyond the Middle Ages, with many Renaissance courts featuring professional astrologers, until the rise of modern astronomy discredited the geocentric worldview and much of its associated baggage. Yet, despite the outdated claims of astrology, fascination with the mysterious zodiac persists, as attested by the horoscope columns of many daily newspapers (not to mention the short-lived "Age of Aquarius" in the sixties).

The constellations still have powerful tales to tell. The remainder of this essay deals with the Greek mythological sources of the zodiacal signs (whose names are all from Latin, though), rather than with their supposed astrological characteristics, which are best left to the noted philosophers and raconteurs of the "So, what's your sign?" school.

The story of **Aries** ("the Ram") begins with Phrixus, a young Aeolian man in a bind. When he failed to respond to his aunt's sexual advances, she accused him of rape. This coincided with a plot against him by his evil stepmother, and he was doomed to be sacrificed to Zeus. As his weeping father was about to cut the young man's throat, Heracles, who was just passing by, wrenched the blade from him and told him that Zeus abhorred human sacrifice. At the same time, one of the gods sent a ram with a golden fleece to rescue Phrixus and his sister Helle.

The two climbed aboard, and the magical ram flew. Helle fell off, splashing down into the strait between Europe and Asia, thereafter called the Hellespont ("Helle's sea"). Phrixus and the ram touched down safely in Colchis on the Black Sea coast. There, the ram instructed Phrixus to sacrifice him to Zeus and take his fleece to the King, Aeëtes, who would become foster father to Phrixus. Many years later, Jason and the Argonauts sailed on the famous expedition to retrieve the golden fleece. To commemorate the ram's accomplishments and self-effacement, Zeus placed him in the sky as a constellation.

The story of **Taurus** ("the Bull") concerns, as do innumerable Greek myths, the amorous adventures of Zeus. This time, he fell in love with gentle Europa. Since she spent her time with friends walking among the herds in Tyre, a city on the Phoenician coast, Zeus assumed the form of a white bull. Europa was enchanted with the lovely creature, who let her drape him with flowers. She trusted him so much that one day she climbed on his back and rode him along the beach. When he suddenly jumped in the water and started swimming out rapidly, she had no choice but to cling to his neck.

Zeus swam to the island of Crete, transformed himself into an eagle, and had his way with her. The result was three sons: Minos (later King of Crete), Rhadamanthys, and Sarpedon. Zeus was so fond of Europa that he named Europe after her, since he had brought her from the shores of Asia to Crete. To remind himself of his dalliance, he made a constellation of his alter-ego bull.

Like many stories about the liaisons of Zeus, that of **Gemini** ("the Twins") is complicated. Zeus impregnated Leda, wife of King Tyndareus of Sparta, in the form of a swan. Since she had also slept with her husband that same night, she conceived his children, too. According to one version, Leda eventually laid two eggs. One contained her immortal children by Zeus: Polydeuces (or Pollux) and his sister Helen, whose face later launched a thousand ships against Troy (actually 1,186). The other egg held Leda's mortal children by Tyndareus: Castor and his sister Clytemnestra, who became the wife and murderer of Agamemnon (see Question 14).

Castor and Polydeuces, often called the Dioscuri ("sons of Zeus"), were a fine team with complementary skills. Castor the equestrian and Polydeuces the boxer were noted victors at the Olympian Games (see Question 37). They rescued their prepubescent sister Helen from the lecherous hands of middle-aged Theseus, sailed with the Argonauts, and participated in the Calydonian Boar Hunt. When mortal Castor was killed in a dispute over women with two other brothers, Polydeuces begged Zeus to let him remain with his beloved

Castor. Zeus arranged matters so that the twins could spend alternate days together in the underworld and on Mount Olympus. He also set them in the heavens as the constellation Gemini because of their brotherly devotion. They are the patrons of sailors and are said to manifest themselves as the bright electrical discharges that sometimes appear on the masts and rigging of ships during storms—usually called Saint Elmo's fire.

The constellation of **Cancer** ("the Crab") is the handiwork of Hera. The area southwest of Mycenae called Lerna was held hostage by the Hydra, a water snake with nine heads, one of which was immortal. As one of his twelve Labors, Heracles was dispatched to kill it (see Question 90). With the help of his nephew, Iolaus, Heracles vanquished the hideous thing, but not before the Hydra's ally, Hera, sent a gigantic crab. When it pinched Heracles on the heel, he smashed its shell with his foot. In appreciation of the crab's valiant effort, Hera immortalized the pathetic creature in the heavens.

Another feat of Heracles is commemorated in the constellation **Leo** ("the Lion"). As the first of his twelve Labors, Heracles was ordered to kill a supernatural lion that was ravaging the countryside on the outskirts of Nemea. Because the creature had an impenetrable hide, Heracles had to strangle it and use its own claws to skin it. Zeus, rightly proud of his awesome son, made a constellation of the vanquished lion.

The constellation **Virgo** represents Astraea, virgin goddess of justice, innocence, and purity. She was the last deity to leave the earth during the Iron Age, which was characterized by crime, war, and depravity. But this daughter of Zeus and Themis will come back when a brighter tomorrow dawns, as Virgil (70–19 B.C.) claimed in his Fourth Eclogue: "Now the Virgin returns, too; now Saturn's Golden Age returns." In the Middle Ages, this was seen as a prophecy of Christ's birth.

Libra ("the Balance"), usually thought of as the figure of a woman holding the scales of justice, or as the scales alone, is often said to refer to Astraea again. This is a boring constellation.

The legend of **Scorpio** is closely connected with that of the gigantic hunter Orion, son of the sea god Poseidon. Several stories associate the Scorpion with Orion's death via the agency of Artemis, goddess of the hunt. In one, Orion boasted that he had killed every beast in Crete—unaware that Artemis was also a wildlife conservationist. In retaliation, she raised a giant scorpion from the earth, which stung Orion to death. The two of them, Orion and the scorpion, were set in heaven as a warning against hubris.

A variant of this story has Artemis discovering that Orion had been lustfully hunting her girlfriends, the seven Pleiades. She conjured up the scorpion to take him out, but then also set Orion and the Pleiades in heaven. In yet another version, Artemis' brother Apollo feared gorgeous Orion might prove irresistible to his virgin sister. He thus tricked her into shooting Orion dead with an arrow while the latter tried to elude the huge scorpion Apollo had sicced on him. On realizing what she had done, Artemis summoned Apollo's son, the physician Asclepius, to restore Orion to life. Before he could do so, however, Zeus zapped Asclepius with a thunderbolt. Artemis then set Orion in the sky as a constellation, forever pursued by the Scorpion.

Sagittarius ("the Archer") is generally assumed to represent Chiron, chief of the centaurs, who taught Asclepius everything he knew about medicine. His demise is linked to the fourth Labor of Heracles, who, during his pursuit of the Erymanthian boar, had a violent confrontation with several centaurs. As they fled to his friend, the archer Chiron, for safety, one of his poisoned arrows accidently struck Chiron in the knee. Although in agony from his wound, immortal Chiron was denied the relief of death. Some stories claim Prometheus accepted the transfer of Chiron's perpetuity to himself so that the learned and kindly old centaur could die. Others say Zeus placed Chiron in the heavens as a constellation, thereby putting him out of his misery.

Capricorn ("the Goat," literally "goat horn") is a stellar representation of the Goat-nymph Amalthea ("tender"), who breast-fed infant Zeus in Crete and gave him nutritional snacks of nectar and ambrosia from her horns while he was hidden from his father, the neonate-eating Cronus (see Question 88). She is associated with the cornucopia, or horn of plenty, either as presenting it to Zeus or receiving it from him. As a full-fledged Olympian, Zeus expressed his gratitude to his wet nurse by placing her in the sky as the constellation Capricorn.

Aquarius ("the Water Bearer") represents Ganymede, the son of Tros, King of Troy. Ganymede, who became cupbearer to the gods on Olympus, was wildly attractive to women everywhere—and to Zeus, too. It's said that the first Olympian cupbearer, Hebe, Zeus's daughter by Hera, slipped and fell while serving at table and was disgraced when her disheveled clothing revealed her finer assets. Zeus capitalized on this mishap to dismiss Hebe. He then assumed the shape of an eagle to abduct young Ganymede from a field near Troy, take him up to Olympus, and make him his catamite (a word derived from Ganymede's name). The cupbearer job was a cover, a stratagem since employed in executive mansions worldwide. Hermes later made a condolence visit to King Tros to assure him that his son was happy and well and that Zeus had conferred on him the gift of immortality—and a constellation in his likeness.

The story of **Pisces** ("the Fishes") involves Aphrodite, goddess of love, and her son Eros (Latin, Cupid). They were being pursued by Typhon (or Typhoeus), the most wicked and formidable monster that ever lived, who had a hundred serpent heads and quantities of serpent hands and feet to match. While trying to confiscate Mount Olympus from the gods, Typhon cornered Aphrodite and Eros on a beach, where they expected the worst. Just in the nick of time, two dolphins arrived, and the erotic pair stepped on their backs and were wafted to safety. Apparently, Typhon was chicken of the sea. He was ultimately blasted by Zeus's thunderbolt and buried in Tartarus beneath Sicily's Mount Etna, whose volcanic eruptions are Typhon's fiery eructations. The helpful dolphins—who were not fish at all—were rewarded with quite a misnomer of a constellation, Pisces.

Which were the 13 original U.S. states, and what do
  their names mean?

1. Delaware: from the Delaware River and Bay, named
   for Lord De La Warr, first governor of Virginia colony
2. Pennsylvania: Latin, "the woodland of Penn" (for
   William Penn's father)
3. New Jersey: from the English Channel island of Jersey
4. Georgia: for King George II of England (reigned
   1727–60)
5. Connecticut: from Mohican Quinnehtukqut, "beside
   the long tidal river"
6. Massachusetts: for Massachuset Indians (Algonquian,
   "at the big hill")
7. Maryland: for Queen Henrietta Maria, wife of
   Charles I (1625–49)
8. South Carolina: for King Charles I (Latin, Carolus)
9. New Hampshire: from the English county of
   Hampshire
10. Virginia: for Elizabeth I (1558–1603), the "Virgin
    Queen"
11. New York: for the Duke of York, later King James II
12. North Carolina: for King Charles I
13. Rhode Island: probably for the Mediterranean island of
    Rhodes

No, Vermont wasn't one of the lucky thirteen—it was the fourteenth. The original states are listed here in the order in which they
ratified the U.S. Constitution after it was signed on September 17,
1787. Delaware was the first, on December 7, 1787. Rhode Island
was the last, with a close 34–32 vote of the legislature on May 29,

1790. Vermont, which had been claimed by both New Hampshire and New York, joined the Union on March 4, 1791. Although we sometimes think of the thirteen colonies as a cohesive national entity, they had decidedly distinct origins, cultures, histories, and attitudes toward personal and religious freedom. The fact that representatives of these often-feuding thirteen colonies attended the Second Continental Congress in May 1775 and managed to cooperate in a six-year war of independence underscores the unity and singularity of purpose that fueled the American Revolution (see Question 83).

In the 1580s, several attempts to establish a permanent settlement in **Virginia,** organized by Sir Walter Raleigh under the aegis of Elizabeth I, ended in failure. When "Virginia" was subsequently chartered by James I in 1606, it stretched from Newfoundland to the Hudson (North Virginia) and from the Potomac to Cape Fear (South Virginia). Jamestown, the first permanent English colony in the New World, was finally established on May 14, 1607, with Captain John Smith as one of the leaders. The bane of slavery arrived in 1619.

British forces under Lord Cornwallis surrendered to General Washington at Yorktown, Virginia, to end the Revolutionary War on October 19, 1781. Virginia is sometimes called "Mother of the Presidents," since eight of them were born there, including four of the first five: Washington, Jefferson, Madison, and Monroe. The long tenure of these last three is sometimes referred to as "The Virginia Dynasty" of 1801–25.

The Pilgrims, fleeing religious persecution, founded the second English outpost, Plymouth Colony, in **Massachusetts** in 1620. A sibling, Massachusetts Bay Colony, was founded in Salem in 1628. This establishment soon grew larger and wealthier than the Plymouth Colony, and its capital was moved to Boston. In 1691, the governments at Plymouth and Boston merged, and Massachusetts assumed approximately the shape we recognize today. The War of Independence may have ended in Virginia, but it started in and around Boston. The Boston Tea Party was celebrated in 1773, and the first battles of the Revolution were fought at Lexington and Concord on April 19, 1775. The third Monday in April is still celebrated as Patriots' Day in Massachusetts. Businesses and schools are closed, and world-class runners compete in the Boston Marathon.

Southwest of Massachusetts, Nieuw-Nederlandt and the surrounding area—Nieuw-Amsterdam (Manhattan), Breukelen (Brooklyn), Boswyck (Bushwick), Vlissingen (Flushing), Bronck's (Bronx),

Oostdorp (Westchester), and Lange Eylant (Long Island)—were settled by Dutch fur traders, based on reports by Henry Hudson, an Englishman working for Dutch exploration. The first vessel from the Netherlands arrived for trading in 1610, and the first trading post was established fourteen years afterward at Willemstadt (Fort Orange), later Albany. In 1626 Peter Minuit, the new governor of Nieuw-Amsterdam, bought Manhattan from the Indians in the infamous $24 deal. But the English, who had long disputed the ownership of Nieuw-Nederlandt, put increasing pressure on the Dutch to relinquish the territory. The Duke of York was presented with Nieuw-Nederlandt by his brother, King Charles II, and in late summer 1664, English warships entered New Amsterdam's harbor and claimed it for the English Crown. The residents failed to rally to their despotic governor, Peter Stuyvesant, and in September the Dutch ceded to the British the territory that was redubbed **New York**. After New York changed hands once again, George Washington was inaugurated as President in Manhattan on April 30, 1789, and New York City was briefly the infant nation's capital.

New Hampshire was part of Massachusetts for thirty-eight years, until it was granted its own royal charter by England in 1679. The first settlers, largely fishermen, were sent there by Captain John Smith in 1623. New Hampshire delegates were the first to vote in favor of the Declaration of Independence, and the state was the ninth to ratify the Constitution (nine states were the minimum required for its adoption).

Delaware was discovered by Henry Hudson, sailing for the Dutch, in 1609, but Peter Minuit, the purchaser of Manhattan, established Fort Christina (now Wilmington) for the New Sweden Company in 1638. From that point on, the Dutch and Swedes jockeyed for control of the tiny territory. Peter Stuyvesant annexed it in 1655, but lost it to the English when he lost Nieuw-Nederlandt. In 1682, when William Penn, governor of Pennsylvania, was granted the charter, Delaware became the Three Lower Counties of Pennsylvania. It became a semiautonomous colony in 1704.

The colony of **Maryland** was established when Charles I granted the territory from Delaware Bay to Cape Charles to Sir George Calvert, a former member of the Privy Council who had converted to Catholicism at a time when Catholics were officially persecuted in England. He had also become an Irish peer as Baron Baltimore. The King nonetheless remained personally friendly toward

Calvert, but the latter died the same year (1632) he was awarded the charter. The King then granted it to Calvert's son Cecil, second Lord Baltimore, whose brother Leonard, with other English Roman Catholics and many Protestants, arrived at what is now Blakistone Island, Maryland, in 1634. The Toleration Act of 1649, which opened the colony to members of all Christian denominations seeking refuge, was quashed by a Puritan revolt in 1654–58. Maryland's boundary disputes with Pennsylvania weren't settled until the English mathematicians and astronomers Charles Mason and Jeremiah Dixon established the Mason-Dixon Line (1763–67), which is still sometimes thought to separate the North from the South.

New Jersey was first settled by Dutch farming families from Nieuw-Nederlandt, who established communities on the Delaware River near what is now Gloucester City and on the Hudson at Hoboken. The Swedes also had outposts, part of New Sweden, in southern New Jersey on the banks of the Delaware. All of these came under English control in 1664. The territory became a Crown colony in 1702, under the jurisdiction of New York, and established its own government in 1738. The state was named after Jersey, the largest island in the English Channel and, more remotely, after Julius and the other Caesars. *Jers-* is derived from the Latin *Caesarea,* and *-ey* meant "island."

Bickering and intolerance in Massachusetts Bay Colony spurred about a hundred Puritans to move in the 1630s to settlements at Wethersfield, Hartford, and Windsor, **Connecticut,** where they edged out Dutch colonials. These early settlers wrote *The Fundamental Orders,* believed to be the first written constitution in the world, which, among other provisions, declared that religious affiliation did not affect citizenship status. Settlers of New Haven Colony, who began arriving from London in 1638, were not so tolerant, establishing a strict Puritan theocracy. Connecticut was granted a royal charter in 1662 and was united with New Haven in 1664. Yale College was founded in 1701 by a group of lofty-minded men who, dissatisfied with Harvard, wanted a truer "school of the prophets."

Charles II granted **Rhode Island** a charter in 1663, nearly thirty years after religious persecution at the hands of Massachusetts Bay Colony Puritans caused Roger Williams to flee and establish Providence Colony. There he was free to expound his belief that civil authorities have no sovereignty over the individual conscience.

North Carolina and **South Carolina** were granted as "Carolina" to Sir Robert Heath in 1629 by King Charles I. In 1663, Charles II granted Carolina to eight lord proprietors, but these men, and the governors they appointed, were harsh and incompetent rulers, though religious toleration was adopted. Pirates haunted the coastline, and the inland areas were often in the throes of rebellions and Indian wars. The later proprietors finally gave up and asked the Crown to buy back the grants. In 1729 the territory was divided into North and South Carolina. The Mecklenburg Resolutions, passed by a committee in Mecklenburg County, North Carolina, on May 31, 1775, urged independence for America, though the so-called Mecklenburg Declaration of Independence is often considered spurious. Since these Southern colonies had been victims of unfair taxation by the proprietors, they were quick to take the part of New Englanders resentful of taxes levied by the Crown, and they proved to be committed revolutionaries.

Like several other American colonies, **Pennsylvania** was claimed for the Dutch by Henry Hudson, partly settled by the Swedes, and grabbed by the English in 1664. But the colony didn't come into its own until 1682 with the arrival of William Penn, a wealthy Englishman seeking refuge for persecuted English Quakers. Charles II owed Penn's family thousands of pounds, and he settled the debt by giving William the area that now includes all of Pennsylvania and Delaware. As a beacon of religious and cultural tolerance, Pennsylvania succeeded where Maryland had failed. Oaths were not required in court. Treason and murder were the only capital crimes. The British referred to the territory as "the insane colony" when they learned that Pennsylvanians had no military defenses and refused to develop them. Penn was deposed for two years until he agreed to organize a kind of border patrol. Much later, when the French and Indian War (1755–63) got under way, the King insisted that Pennsylvania become a Crown colony.

Pennsylvania is sometimes called "The Nation's Birthstate" because the Declaration of Independence was signed in Philadelphia, the U.S. Constitution was drafted there, and the city was the seat of the federal government for most of the time between 1776 and 1800.

Georgia, first claimed by the Spanish and home to the pirate Blackbeard (killed in 1718), was conceived by the British as an enormous buffer zone when it was founded in 1773. The vast area was to act as a land moat between South Carolina and Florida, which was held by the Spanish, and it also was to bear the brunt of French and Indian attacks from the west. The trustees of the colony hoped that the debtors and religious dissidents who ended up in Georgia would cultivate silk, wine grapes, and hemp, but these plans went awry when many settlers discovered the difficulty and precariousness of life there. Georgia floundered economically until 1752, when it became the 13th and last Crown colony, by which time the restrictions on slavery, the amount of land that individuals could own, and the ban on importing rum had been eased. The Spanish had remained troublesome until 1742, when General James Oglethorpe, chief of the original trustees, drove them out at the Battle of Bloody Marsh. Some historians consider this one of the most momentous battles in world history (but compare Question 97) because if Oglethorpe had failed, the Spanish would have continued their northward progress, *con consecuencias desconocidas*.

✳ QUESTION 95

What are the 13 Articles of Faith of Judaism?

1. The existence of God
2. God's unity
3. God's incorporeality
4. God's eternity
5. God's exclusive right to be worshiped
6. The fact of prophecy
7. The superiority of Moses' prophecy to that of all other prophets
8. The divine origin of the Torah
9. The eternity of the Torah
10. The omniscience of God
11. Divine rewards and punishments
12. The coming of the Messiah
13. Resurrection

These basic tenets, principles, or beliefs of Judaism were formulated in the twelfth century by the Jewish philosopher Moses Maimonides (1135–1204). Rabbi Moses ben Maimon, also known by the affectionate acronym Rambam, was born in Cordova, Spain, but moved with his family to Egypt, where he became physician to the vizier of the mighty Saladin in Cairo. Among his medical works, written in Arabic, were treatises on diet, poisons, asthma, hypochondria, and sexual intercourse. He also wrote a *Glossary of Drugs,* sort of an early *Physicians' Desk Reference.*

Maimonides' chief work in Hebrew was the multivolume *Mishneh Torah (Repetition of the Law),* which attempts to explain each of the 613 laws of the Torah (the Pentateuch, the first five books of the Bible) and almost all the laws of the Talmud, which comprises the Mishnah (the collection of originally oral laws) and the Gemara (a commentary on the Mishnah). Before him, no one had attempted a codification of the whole of Jewish law.

Maimonides wrote his two other chief theological and philosophical works in Arabic, the language of the Islamic world in which he lived. *Kitab al-Siraj (Book of Illumination)* is a commentary on the Mishnah. His *Dalalat al-Ha'irin (Guide for the Perplexed)* was written in Arabic with Hebrew letters. Soon translated into Hebrew as *Moreh Nebukim,* the book caused a furious schism in the Jewish world, basically between "progressives" like Maimonides, who had imbibed Aristotelian philosophy, and the "old guard," who considered any admixture of Greek philosophical learning with their own divinely revealed scriptures as little better than sacrilege or idolatry. Several decades after his death, Maimonides' Jewish adversaries denounced his books to the Inquisition, which ordered two separate public burnings of Maimonidean texts.

In *Guide for the Perplexed,* Maimonides did for Judaism what his slightly older contemporary and fellow Cordovan Averroës (1126–98) had done for Islam. These two most learned men of their day used the philosophy of Aristotle—in their time, *the* last word in science, fifteen hundred years after the Greek's death—to underpin their expositions of traditional religious beliefs. In the next century, Thomas Aquinas was to surpass both of these thinkers in the massive scope of his reliance on "the Master of those who know" (Dante's phrase for Aristotle) to buttress the sprawling edifice of late medieval Christianity.

In the *Book of Illumination,* Maimonides listed his thirteen principles or Articles of Faith, which were eventually incorporated in the Daily Prayer Book of the Ashkenazi Jews. While Jewish thinkers have not stressed dogma, they have periodically attempted to identify the sine qua non of their religious belief. Two millennia ago, Philo Judaeus set forth his eight essential principles of scriptural religion, and a number of medieval Jewish writers later devised their own lists. Maimonides was prompted to his formulation, which occurs in his commentary on the tenth chapter of the tractate Sanhedrin in the Mishnah, by a statement there that a share in the world to come is denied to Jews who do not accept the resurrection of the dead or the divine origin of the Torah, and to those who are "Epicureans" (skeptics, freethinkers).

The thirteen tenets of Maimonides address the nature of God, prophecy, the Torah, and the future life. One of his goals was to make sure the common man comprehended the spiritual dimension of Jewish belief instead of interpreting Scripture and the life to come in a literal, simplistic way.

His fundamental principle is that **God exists** as a perfect being who needs nothing external to himself and that he is the cause of the existence of all other beings. In effect, God is Aristotle's "unmoved Mover" whose existence is evident from the presence of design in nature and from the logical need for a First Cause of all the effects we observe in the universe.

God's unity is proclaimed daily in Jewish private prayer and synagogue services (and at the hour of death) in the opening words of the Shema: "Hear, O Israel, the Lord our God, the Lord is One" (Deuteronomy 6:4). God's unity may be viewed as his ontic "simplicity"—that is, his uniformity of nature, his pure, unvaried essence. This stress on the absolute unity of God also serves to differentiate Jewish belief from the Christian doctrine of the Trinity (see Question 7).

Maimonides teaches that **God is incorporeal.** As pure spirit, God does not actually have the hands, fingers, face, voice, and other anthropomorphic attributes that Scripture mentions in order to accommodate itself to the limited understanding of humans. As Maimonides says in *Guide for the Perplexed,* "The Torah speaks in the language of the sons of man." **God is eternal** in the sense that he never had a beginning and will never have an end, but also because he exists outside of time. The fifth principle, **God's sole right to be worshiped,** forbids the invocation of any mediating powers in prayer, such as angels or the souls of dead prophets or loved ones. Prayer must be made directly to God.

Maimonides adopted his view of **prophecy** from Aristotle. Prophets were people with supreme imaginative faculties who transformed the spark of divine illumination, usually revealed through dreams or ecstatic visions, into highly figurative and allegorical speech or writing. Thus, prophetic utterances should usually be interpreted for their moral sense rather than believed as literal truth. On the other hand, as the transmitter of the Law (the Torah), **Moses was the greatest of the prophets** and directly inspired by God in every word he wrote. The imaginative faculty, according to Maimonides, played no part in the prophecy of Moses.

As such, **the Torah is the work of God,** through and through, in the form in which it was delivered to Moses. In addition, **the Torah is eternal and immutable:** It was the first—and only—law delivered to the Jews. It is also a "closed book" because it is not susceptible to additions, modifications, "fulfillment," or any of the other means by which Christians and Moslems used Jewish scripture as a groundwork for further revelations.

Maimonides then turns to issues affecting the future life. In his tenth principle, he affirms **God's omniscience,** which includes knowledge of the actions and thoughts of all humans. This knowledge is the basis for the **divine rewards and punishments** that will be meted out to those who obey and flout God's laws, respectively. Maimonides apparently believed the soul is punished only by the knowledge of its failures. **Belief in the coming of the Messiah** (Hebrew, *Mashiach,* "anointed one") is a central tenet of Judaism. The Messiah will be a savior who will cause the entire world to acknowledge God's sovereignty and will then usher in the Day of Judgment. The doctrine of **bodily resurrection,** whether in this world or the next, was a crux for Maimonides. He believed the soul was eternal, but whether the body was conjoined to it for eternity—and whether the soul retained its individual consciousness—was a different story. Nonetheless, he saw fit to uphold the traditional Jewish belief in resurrection, especially since the passage in the Mishnah that he was commenting on emphasized it so strongly.

Maimonides claimed that every Jew had to acknowledge his thirteen "roots" or "fundamentals," as he called them, to retain membership in the community and a share in eternal life. Many later Jewish thinkers, including Baruch Spinoza and Moses Mendelssohn, formulated their own versions of the essential Jewish creed. Yet none had quite the same influence or staying power as that of the beloved sage of whom the Jews said, "From Moses [the prophet] to Moses [Maimonides] there arose none like Moses [Rambam]."

❧ QUESTION 96

What were the 14 Points of Woodrow Wilson?

1. Open covenants of peace, openly arrived at
2. Freedom of the seas in peace and war, except when abrogated by international action
3. Removal of artificial trade barriers among nations
4. Sweeping reductions in national armaments
5. An absolutely impartial adjustment of colonial claims
6. The evacuation of and self-determination for Russia
7. The evacuation and restoration of Belgium
8. The return of Alsace-Lorraine to France
9. Readjustment of Italy's boundaries along the lines of nationality
10. Autonomy for the subject peoples of Austria-Hungary
11. International guarantees for the integrity of Romania, Serbia, and Montenegro
12. Autonomy for the subject peoples of the Ottoman Empire and free passage for all nations through the Dardanelles
13. Establishment of an independent Poland with access to the sea
14. "A general association of nations . . . formed under specific covenants for the purpose of affording mutual guarantees of political independence and territorial integrity to great and small states alike"

The Fourteen Points of President Woodrow Wilson (1856–1924), paraphrased above, were part of his program, during the last year of World War I (1914–18), to bring about a "just and lasting peace." These points, enunciated in an address to Congress on January 8, 1918, envisioned a peace settlement that would eschew revenge in dealing with former enemies, advance the cause of self-determination along lines of nationality, and create the kind of world in which abominations like the Great War would be less likely to occur. Wilson's hand was forced by the new Soviet government's action of releasing the texts of secret wartime treaties Britain and France had made, which exposed the Allies' plans for landgrabbing after the war. The United States had not been involved, and Wilson wanted to set the record straight.

The idealism of the Fourteen Points was evident, not least of all to the Germans, who later in the year realized their military cause was lost. They also understood that hiding behind the American President, now the most powerful voice in the Allied camp, was their best hope of dodging what British Prime Minister David Lloyd George and French Premier Georges Clemenceau wanted to throw at them (see Question 30). They imagined they could thus hold on to at least some of their gains in the war, avoid the assumption of war guilt, and escape severe punitive measures and political dismemberment. On October 4, 1918, the new German liberal government asked for an armistice on the basis of the Fourteen Points. On November 5, Wilson finally granted it, subject only to Britain's interpretation of Point 1 and the issue of payment for war damages. Yet the Germans should have realized the Fourteen Points said precious little, if anything, about Germany itself; there was bound to be *much* more said about it before a final peace was signed.

On the other side, Wilson's Allies didn't think much of his naive approach to the complex problems of European power politics. (Wilson later elaborated on his points with his Four Principles, Four Ends, and Five Particulars.) Clemenceau claimed he was bored by the Fourteen Points, since "even God Almighty has only ten!" (see Question 82).

A week before Wilson agreed to the German request for an armistice, a secret meeting of his adviser, Colonel Edward M. House, with Clemenceau and Lloyd George had revealed their intentions to dismantle the Austro-Hungarian Empire, split Prussia in two for the benefit of Poland, strip Germany of all its colonies, and demand reparations. In the end, at the Paris Peace Conference, Wilson had to make concessions to the Allies in the text of the Treaty of Versailles, which abandoned a number of the guiding principles of the Fourteen Points. Indeed, the behavior of the Allies emphasized "business as usual" rather than the beginning of a new world order. The Germans called the treaty a dictated peace and a betrayal. Here are some comments on the individual points, their fate, and their implications for the treaty.

1: There were to be no more secret treaties like those the British and French had drawn up with Russia, Italy, and Japan during the war, assigning the spoils of Germany, Austria, and the Ottoman Empire after victory. One such document was the Treaty of London (1915), which promised Italy the Dalmatian coast. Another was the Sykes-Picot agreement (1916), by which Britain and France agreed on how to split up the Ottoman Empire between themselves.

2: The British didn't care for this one, especially the provision about "in peace and war," since a mainstay of Britain's ability to project its power around the world was the threat of a naval blockade that would humiliate, bankrupt, and starve any potential enemies. Germany thought this point implied that the British should lift the blockade that was doing exactly those things to its people. This didn't happen until after the peace treaty was signed on June 28, 1919.

3: The United States itself, a protectionist nation, was certainly not going to be part of any universal free-trade agreements.

4: The Treaty of Versailles required that Germany make drastic reductions in armaments and the size of its army. The Germans offered to do so, if the Allies agreed to abolish conscription and reduce their armaments proportionately with their own. This quid pro quo was absolutely rejected.

5: The treaty stripped Germany of all its colonies and distributed them to Allied countries under League of Nations mandates. Britain and France received most of Germany's African colonies, though South Africa was given German Southwest Africa (see Question 58). Germany's possessions in China and the Pacific islands north of the equator went to Japan; Australia and New Zealand got those south of the equator. The Japanese, South African, and Australian mandates turned into virtual annexations. Italy, one of the Big Four nations, received no mandates.

6: The exact language of this point assured Russia "of a sincere welcome into the society of free nations under institutions of her own choosing." This hardly occurred, since later in 1918 Wilson himself sent American troops to aid Britain and France in an invasion of Russia that aimed at quashing Bolshevism (see Question 46).

7: No arguments here; Belgium had been through hell.

8: The region of Alsace-Lorraine, with its great industrial city of Strasbourg, had been seized from France by Germany in the Franco-Prussian War (1870–71). The Germans now requested that a plebiscite be allowed to determine which nation it would join. This was rejected. Alsace-Lorraine went back to France, was annexed by Germany again during World War II, and then went back to France.

9: This one was a can of worms. Italy basically wanted territorial adjustments via two conflicting methods of adjudication. On the one hand, determination by nationality would give it the Italian-speaking city of Fiume, though the Treaty of London had pledged it to Croatia. On the other, determination by harking back to the Treaty of London would give it Slavic-speaking northern Dalmatia. They received neither, though they did get German-speaking Alto Adige (the South Tyrol) so as to bring its northern frontier in this area to the Brenner Pass (see Question 100). Unsatisfied Italian claims fueled the rise of fascism after the war.

10: Just before the armistice, "autonomy" was reinterpreted by Wilson as independence. This meant the dissolution of the Austro-Hungarian Empire into Czechoslovakia, a Yugoslav state, and an independent Hungary, with only a small Austrian republic left over.

11: These nations had been occupied by the Central Powers. Romania almost doubled its territory at the expense of defeated Hungary. Montenegro, uniting with Serbia, became part of the Kingdom of Serbs, Croats, and Slovenes (later called Yugoslavia).

12: The subject peoples of the Ottoman Empire probably did not consider the League of Nations mandates by which France received Syria (which included Lebanon) and Britain received Iraq, Jordan, and Palestine to be the equivalent of "autonomy," since several of them soon rebelled violently against their new political masters.

13: The treaty gave most of West Prussia to the new state of Poland and created the infamous Polish Corridor west of the Vistula, giving Poland access to the Baltic but cutting off East Prussia from the rest of Germany and making Danzig (Gdansk) a free city. Here were tailor-made grievances for another German war. The Allies were eager both to strip Germany of territory and to build up Poland as a buffer state between the West and what was seen as the huge leper colony of Bolshevik Russia.

14: The idea of a world body to maintain peace is at least as old as Immanuel Kant's notion of it in his *Eternal Peace* (1795) and was promulgated by a number of U.S. and British politicians and intellectuals during the Great War. By the time of the peace conference, the creation of an international body to arbitrate among nations and use its collective influence and pressure to discourage military thuggery had become Wilson's obsession. He was mainly responsible for drawing up the Covenant of the League of Nations, which began functioning on January 16, 1920.

In Paris, Wilson compromised on some of his points for the sake of his League. When he returned home, he fought so hard for it that it practically killed him. Isolationists in the Senate abhorred the thought of America's joining an organization that would involve their nation in the headaches of the entire world and commit it to defend the boundaries and independence of all the League's members. This seemed exactly the kind of "entangling alliance" George Washington had warned against in his "Farewell Address."

On his side, Wilson stubbornly refused to cooperate or compromise with the Republican leadership on this issue and made a near-suicidal barnstorming tour to bring his case directly to the American people. The pols and the people gradually grew weary of him, his preachments, and his League. In November 1919, and again in March 1920, the U.S. Senate refused to ratify the Treaty of Versailles, which had the Covenant of the League of Nations written into it. When

Wilson urged that the 1920 presidential election be a referendum on the League, the nation chose anti-League Republican Warren G. Harding over the Democratic candidate, James M. Cox, by a landslide.

But the world got Wilson's League, powerless as it later proved to be in preventing Japanese aggression in China, the Italian takeover of Ethiopia, and Nazi Germany's *Anschluss* with Austria. Immediately after World War II, the League of Nations, headquartered in Geneva, was replaced by its sturdier offspring, the United Nations.

15

Which were the 15 decisive battles of the world according to historian Edward Creasy in 1851?

1. The Battle of Marathon, 490 B.C.
2. The defeat of the Athenians at Syracuse, 413 B.C.
3. The Battle of Arbela, 331 B.C.
4. The Battle of the Metaurus, 207 B.C.
5. The victory of Arminius over the Roman legions under Varus (Teutoburg Forest), A.D. 9
6. The Battle of Châlons, 451
7. The Battle of Tours, 732
8. The Battle of Hastings, 1066
9. Joan of Arc's victory over the English at Orléans, 1429
10. The defeat of the Spanish Armada, 1588
11. The Battle of Blenheim, 1704
12. The Battle of Poltava, 1709
13. The victory of the Americans over Burgoyne at Saratoga, 1777
14. The Battle of Valmy, 1792
15. The Battle of Waterloo, 1815

Sir Edward Shepherd Creasy (1812–78) was an Englishman who wrote *Fifteen Decisive Battles of the World* in 1851, an intriguing examination of the great military engagements that, in his view, had forever changed the course of history. His choices were astute, and his criterion for selection was reasonable: to focus on turning-point battles that had decided which side would win a war with far-reaching—or even global—cultural or sociopolitical implications. Creasy, educated at Eton and Cambridge, worked as a lawyer and assistant judge but left these occupations to become professor of history at the University of

London in 1840. After publishing *Fifteen Decisive Battles,* he served as Chief Justice of Ceylon (Sri Lanka) from 1860 to 1870 and wrote several other books.

In 1964, an American, Lt. Col. Joseph B. Mitchell, author of books on the decisive battles of the American Revolution and the Civil War, revised Creasy's book and updated it by including five major battles that had been fought in the 113 years since Creasy wrote. Mitchell's five battles are briefly discussed at the end of this essay. Since he wrote, a lake of blood has been shed in wars around the world, but no single battle has had the tidal-wave effect of any of those discussed here.

The Battle of Marathon (490 B.C.) pitted 15,000 to 25,000 soldiers of the invading Persian army against 10,000 Athenians and 1,000 Plataeans. This Greek victory is immortalized in the *History of the Persian Wars* of Herodotus, who tells how the "King of Kings," Darius I (the Great), and his son Xerxes after him, failed in their attempts to subjugate Greece.

The Asian force had been mustered to retaliate for the aid given by the Athenians to their fellow Greeks living on the coast of Asia Minor, who had revolted against Persian rule. What rankled most in Darius's mind was the subsequent burning and plundering of his western capital of Sardis. The man who ruled an empire that stretched from the mouth of the Danube to the Indus was not accustomed to that kind of treatment. In fact, he ordered a slave to whisper in his ear each day, "Sire, remember the Athenians!"

In September of 490 B.C., the Persian force was encamped near Marathon, about twenty-five miles northeast of Athens and not far from the sea. The ten Athenian generals sent to deal with the crisis included three of their most distinguished: Miltiades, Themistocles (future victor of the sea battle of Salamis against the Persians in 480 B.C.), and Aristides "the Just" (future victor at the land battle of Plataea in 479 B.C., which finally convinced the Persians to stay out of Greece). Miltiades opted for an attack on the numerically superior enemy forces, which were reembarking to sail against Athens itself.

Caught by surprise, the Persians and their horses floundered in the water as they were cut down by a phalanx of spear-wielding heavy infantrymen (hoplites) advancing against them at double time. About 6,400 Persians were killed, while the Greeks supposedly lost 192. The survivors boarded their ships and set sail for Athens—but the Athenians had marched back and were defending the heights when the

Persians arrived. Discouraged by their humiliating defeat and uneager to grapple with those spearmen again, they sailed back home.

Greek military superiority was demonstrated at Marathon, although it took two more major victories at Salamis and Plataea to finally extinguish Persian ambitions in Greece. Tiny, comparatively free Athens had triumphed over a despotic foe that, if victorious, would have deported any survivors to serve as Darius's slaves. The incomparable political, intellectual, literary, and artistic achievements of an Athenian culture that was soon to experience its Golden Age under Pericles would never have occurred, and Persia might have proceeded to overrun the rest of Western Europe, too. Rome, if it had arisen as a great power at all, would have been able to transmit much less of enduring worth to Europe and the rest of the world.

The defeat of the Athenians at Syracuse (413 B.C.) occurred during the Peloponnesian War they had been waging against Sparta and her many allies, with some intervals, since 431 B.C. The superb historian of this war, Thucydides, was an Athenian exiled for his unsuccessful generalship in it.

Each spring, the Spartans would march into Attica, the region around Athens, and devastate the countryside without, however, being able to take the impregnable city itself. The Athenians, with their powerful Navy, decided to send a squadron to conquer the fabulously wealthy Greek city of Syracuse in Sicily. From there, the conquest of the rest of Sicily—and perhaps southern Italy, Carthage, and other key strategic regions in the western Mediterranean—would allow Athens to mobilize the resources and manpower of its new dominions against the Spartan enemy.

An armada of 134 galleys and other supply ships conveyed 27,000 Athenian soldiers and laborers to Syracuse in the summer of 415 B.C. The Athenian generals were Nicias, a wishy-washy sort who opposed the whole enterprise; Lamachus, a plain, blunt soldier; and the handsome, wealthy, noble, fascinating, and rowdy Alcibiades, who had instigated the expedition. This brilliant general, who would probably have prosecuted the invasion with vigor, was soon recalled to Athens to stand trial for his life. The charge, probably trumped up, was that on the night before setting sail, he and his drinking buddies had indulged in a bit of sacrilegious fun—smashing a large number of herms (outdoor stone busts of the god Hermes).

Alcibiades—nobody's fool—defected to the Spartans and provided them with valuable intelligence about the Syracusan venture.

The Spartans sent a general, Gylippus, to lead a squadron of Corinthians to spoil the Athenians' Sicilian excursion.

After Lamachus was killed in battle, not much went right for feckless Nicias. The arrival of Gylippus heartened the besieged Syracusans; soon the encircling walls the Athenians had built were invested by counterwalls. Athens sent another 73 war galleys to Syracuse with about 15,000 men under their best remaining general, Demosthenes, in the spring of 413 B.C. In a night attack on the enemy, Demosthenes and Nicias managed to get captured and executed. All Athenian ships were destroyed or seized. All surviving Athenian soldiers were sold as slaves or died in the dungeons of Syracuse. Athens eventually surrendered in 404 B.C., leaving numskulled Sparta as the dominant power in Greece.

The Sicilian disaster precluded Athenian westward expansion, thus permitting the future culture of Western Europe to be based largely on the Latin language and Roman models—certainly as influenced by Rome's avid absorption of Greek civilization, but not in a directly Greek form. The legal, administrative, engineering, and martial achievements of the Romans are what the world gained from a botched Athenian military strategy.

The Battle of Arbela (331 B.C.), fought east of the Tigris in modern-day Iraq, was a crucial victory for the invading armies of the young Macedonian King, Alexander the Great (see Question 78), allowing them to proceed with the conquest of the remainder of the Persian Empire. Since Arbela was actually about sixty miles from the battle site, the encounter is often called the Battle of Gaugamela, after a nearby village.

The Persian forces under King Darius III were estimated at about 200,000 infantry, 45,000 cavalry, 200 scythed chariots, and 15 war elephants. Arrian, an ancient historian of Alexander's wars, claims the Macedonian Greeks had 40,000 infantry and 7,000 horsemen. But Alexander also had a powerful tactical weapon—the Macedonian phalanx. In this formation, each infantryman brandished a twenty-one-foot pike or spear called a sarissa, resting it on the shoulder of the man in front of him. The spears of the first four files projected out beyond the front rank, at different angles, for a total distance of fifteen feet. This huge, bristling hedgehog mowed enemy soldiers down before they could even get within striking distance of the Macedonian front lines.

Alexander had already defeated the Persians at the major battles of the Granicus (334 B.C.) and Issus (333 B.C.). At Arbela, on October 1, 331 B.C., the day was saved for the massively outnumbered Macedonians by Alexander's military genius. About 40,000 to 90,000 men were slaughtered in the Persian Army; the Macedonians lost about 500. Effective Persian opposition to Alexander's continued march eastward was crushed. The unstoppable Macedonian soon seized the mighty Persian cities of Babylon, Susa, Persepolis, and Ecbatana, and then marched his armies beyond the Hindu Kush and Indus River, ultimately defeating the Indian King Porus at the battle of the Hydaspes River (326 B.C.). Alexander wanted to forge ahead, but his mutinous men had had enough. The entire Persian Empire, and more, was now Alexander's, but on returning west he died of a fever in Babylon in 323 B.C. at age thirty-two. His generals divided the empire and then fought among themselves for decades.

If Alexander had been defeated, the culture, science, and even religions of Europe and the western Moslem world would have developed quite differently. As it turned out, the Greek language became a lingua franca throughout the eastern Mediterranean and western Asia, facilitating the spread of Christianity—via Greek-speaking Christian converts and the Greek New Testament—through much of the Near East.

In addition, the conquering armies of the Muslims, a millennium after Alexander's time, encountered the Greek language, cultural tradition, law, philosophy, science, and art, especially in Egypt, Syria, and Asia Minor. Later generations of Muslim scholars translated, commented on, and extended the knowledge contained in ancient Greek scientific, mathematical, and philosophical texts. Translated from Greek into Arabic, these books were subsequently brought by the Muslims into Spain, where they were translated from Arabic into Latin. From Spain, they moved into the rest of Western Europe, where knowledge of Greek had died out but Latin was the common language of churchmen, scholars, and students. The so-called Renaissance of the Twelfth Century, the true birth of Europe as an advanced cultural, artistic, and philosophical center, owed much to this increased diffusion of ancient Greek learning, especially the Aristotelian corpus (see Question 54).

The Battle of the Metaurus (207 B.C.) was a turning-point victory for the Romans that broke the power of the Carthaginians who were ravaging Italy under Hannibal in the Second Punic (Carthaginian) War. Carthage, near modern Tunis, was a colony established by the Semitic Phoenicians in the ninth century B.C. Over the centuries, it became a great maritime and mercantile power and thus inevitably clashed with the expansionist Roman Republic.

In the First Punic War (264–241 B.C.) between these Mediterranean powers, the Romans seized Sicily and made it their first province. After the war, the Romans went on to capture Sardinia and Corsica from Carthage. To compensate for these losses, the Carthaginian general Hamilcar Barca decided to acquire Spain, taking his young son Hannibal with him. Carthaginian military actions in Spain triggered the outbreak of the Second Punic War with Rome (218–201 B.C.). After the death of his father, twenty-nine-year-old Hannibal marched his army over the Alps into Italy in 218 B.C. and proceeded to trounce the Romans at the battles of the Ticinus and the Trebia. In the following year, he dealt them a devastating blow at Lake Trasimene in Tuscany and, in 216, at the battle of Cannae in Apulia, his army slaughtered more than 50,000 Roman soldiers.

Rome now adopted the "Fabian tactics" of Quintus Fabius Maximus, called "Cunctator" ("the delayer"), which sought to wear the enemy down while avoiding any major battles. Nonetheless, Rome was short of men, money, food, and military supplies—when another Carthaginian army from Spain, led by Hannibal's brother Hasdrubal, crossed the Alps and threatened to trap Rome in a vise between his army in the north and Hannibal's in the south. Hasdrubal had about 40,000 men—and the River Metaurus in central Italy at his back—whereas the Romans, under the consul Gaius Claudius Nero, faced him with almost 50,000 soldiers. When a Roman flanking maneuver devastated his army, Hasdrubal rode his horse into the midst of the fighting and was killed. The Romans lost about 8,000 men, but almost all the Carthaginians were cut down or captured. Hasdrubal's severed head was flung over the ramparts of his brother Hannibal's camp.

The Battle of the Metaurus dashed Hannibal's hopes of conquering Rome, thus determining that the Latin language and Roman legislation, political institutions, and culture, rather than Carthage's severely deficient counterparts, would dominate the Mediterranean for more than six centuries and then become the basis of medieval and modern European civilization.

In the last battle of the war, fought at Zama (202 B.C.), inland from Carthage, the young and very great Roman general Publius Cornelius Scipio (called Africanus because of this victory) put the exhausted Carthaginians out of their misery. Most of Spain was added to the Roman dominions, and Rome called the tune in much of northern Africa. In the Third Punic War (149–146 B.C.), Rome decided to completely crush any economic competition from Carthage. The city was razed by Scipio the Younger, adopted grandson of the victor of Zama, and its fields were contemptuously sown with salt so that nothing would grow there for years to come.

The victory of Arminius over the Roman legions (A.D. 9) was a long-delayed comeuppance for the arrogant Roman Empire under Caesar Augustus (see Question 16). That first Roman Emperor had pushed the northern boundary in Germany eastward from the Rhine to the Elbe. The German tribal leader Arminius (Hermann) took advantage of the fact that the local Roman governor, Quintilius Varus, who was leading the legions back to their winter quarters, was not a trained soldier. Of the five legions Varus commanded, Arminius hoped to trap three, which, with their cavalry and auxiliaries, amounted to more than 20,000 men.

The Romans stationed on the River Weser started marching west to the Rhine in September of A.D. 9, and Arminius had deceived them into thinking he was a loyal vassal. As the Romans passed through the dense and hilly Teutoburg Forest, they were greeted on either side by salvos of spears and arrows emanating from deep within the woods. The Romans managed to pitch camp for the night, but when they set out the next morning they had to deal with heavy rain and skirmishers. In the German attack that followed, the Roman cavalry was cut down, and Varus, in true Roman fashion, committed suicide. Few Romans escaped, and the Germans sacrificed all prisoners to their gods. When septuagenarian Augustus heard of the catastrophic defeat, he rent his clothes in anguish and sent his adopted son, Tiberius, the next Emperor, to Germany to make the best of an awful situation. Months after the disaster, Augustus would still beat his head against the wall and howl, "Quintilius Varus, give me back my legions!"

This battle secured the independence and prevented the Latinization of the Germans. For good or bad, Rome was not to impose their culture on them. For all practical purposes, the Rhine, rather than the Elbe, became the boundary between Rome and Germany. Eventually, the descendants of these Germans would be among those to overthrow Rome in A.D. 476 and establish the nuclei of later European kingdoms that enshrined feudalism and a certain fierce, indomitable spirit of aristocratic independence at the core of their political entities.

The Battle of Châlons (451) just barely prevented the savage Huns, who originally hailed from north of the Great Wall of China, from overrunning Western Europe and destroying everything worthwhile and preserving everything abominable. By 441, the Huns under their military genius Attila, "the Scourge of God," were dominant in central Europe from the Caspian almost to the Rhine. They defeated the Eastern Roman Emperor Theodosius II, and the terrified Goths in their path believed the Huns were the offspring of the witches of Scythia who had copulated with the demons of hell.

In 451, the Huns crossed the Rhine, slaughtering, burning, plundering, and raping their way into France. In that same year, however, the legions of the Roman general Aëtius, with the aid of the Christian Visigoths under King Theodoric, in a last valiant effort of Roman arms, triumphed over the invading hordes and their subject allies in Châlons, France. Both sides suffered horrible losses, and Attila was allowed to retreat east with the remnant of his army.

In 452, Attila invaded Italy, but the ravages suffered by his armies at Châlons prevented him from advancing beyond the Po. In the following year, Attila got so drunk on his wedding night that he died of a cerebral hemorrhage. His empire soon disintegrated as a result of the strife between his sons and successful revolts by subject peoples.

The Battle of Tours (732) checked the thrust of Islam into Western Europe and saved Western Christianity from succumbing to it. Masters of Spain, the Saracens (or Moors) next planned to conquer Gaul (not quite yet France), whose Frankish kingdom was giving them cause for concern. Their army of about 80,000, including a superb cavalry, crossed the Pyrenees under Abd-ar-Rahman, emir of Spain, and found themselves pitted at Tours, in October of 732, against the mail-covered infantry of the Frankish chief Charles (grandfather of Charlemagne), who here earned his sobriquet of Martel ("the hammer"; see Questions 67 and 78). After the Muslim leader was killed, his army retreated. This was the Saracens' last serious attempt to extend their empire beyond the Pyrenees.

The Battle of Hastings (1066) allowed the invading force of William the Bastard, Duke of Normandy, to proceed with the conquest of England (see Question 74). In the impending crisis, Harold II, the last Anglo-Saxon King of England, had to rush north first and defeat the invading army of King Harold Hardrada of Norway at the Battle of Stamford Bridge (September 25, 1066). Meanwhile, Duke William, with the blessing of the Pope, was able to land unopposed at Pevensey Bay on September 28, 1066—the last time an invader managed to grab a foot of English soil. After rushing south to deal with the Norman invasion, Harold, both his brothers, and all the greatest thanes of southern England were killed at Hastings, sometimes called the Battle of Senlac Hill, on October 14. His army of fewer than 5,000, after its ordeal in the north and a too-brief conscription campaign in London, was not able to withstand William's force of about 8,000.

The ramifications of the Battle of Hastings are innumerable. The Anglo-Saxon language became flooded with Norman French words, most of them stemming from Latin, so that English became a curious hybrid (see Question 89). Its Germanic syntax and basic everyday lexicon (*I, you, was, were, eat, live, sleep, laugh, die*) were overlaid with a massive influx of the elegant, refined, legal, religious, cultural, culinary, and haute couture terms of the Normans' higher civilization. As a result, English is the richest, vastest word-hoard in the universe, fully deserving its place as the world language par excellence. After the likes of Chaucer, Shakespeare, and Milton had their way with it, English became the most subtle and supple instrument for expressing every nuance of human thought, experience, emotion, and aspiration. The conquest also provided the vigorous, militaristic Normans with an island kingdom, impregnable "Fortress Britain" with its Channel moat. From there, their descendants dispatched formidable armies to France, first, and later to most of the world.

Joan of Arc's victory over the English at Orléans (1429) was won at the cost of only a few hundred lives but led to the ultimate expulsion of the English from France (see Questions 67 and 74). Although the English did not finally depart until 1453—and hung on to Calais until 1558—Joan's action at Orléans was the turning point of the Hundred Years' War between the two countries (1337–1453).

In 1328, England's Edward III had claimed the French throne through his mother, sister of the recently deceased French King. After he and his son, the Black Prince, conquered vast territories in France, he managed to lose most of them again. (And no, he had *not* said to his soldiers, "Men of the Middle Ages! We are about to embark on the Hundred Years' War!") The English claim to the French throne was again asserted by arms in 1415, when Henry V handed the French a major defeat at Agincourt and proceeded to conquer all of France north of the Loire River, including Paris.

After his death, and that of the French King Charles VI, Henry's infant son, Henry VI of England, was proclaimed King of France. The Dauphin, whom Charles VI had repudiated as illegitimate, also declared himself King and prosecuted the war against the English but was driven south of the Loire.

In 1428, the English began the siege of Orléans (on the north shore of the Loire), one of the mightiest fortresses in France and the last important French stronghold protecting the south, where the Dauphin was recognized as King. The independence of France was clearly at stake.

Jeanne d'Arc of Domrémy (1412–31), a peasant girl, had been experiencing visions and revelations since she was thirteen. At age seventeen, she learned in this way that she had been divinely chosen to save France. She left home and was received by the Dauphin, who went along with the girl's bizarre request to be sent into battle. In a suit of white armor, mounted on a black warhorse, and brandishing a battle-ax and sword, Joan was sent to the besieged city with a small army. English carelessness enabled her to enter Orléans, where she led troops into battle, assumed command of the French forces, and returned to battle after being wounded by an arrow. Once their leader was killed, the English made no further resistance and withdrew. Joan reentered Orléans in triumph on May 7, 1429.

In the next three months, Joan took two towns by siege, defeated the English at Patay, drove them north, and entered Rheims in triumph. The Dauphin was crowned King Charles VII of France in Rheims Cathedral on July 17, 1429, while Joan stood by the high altar holding a banner. The momentum had shifted to the French cause, its people now gradually uniting under the man who had been formally anointed their King under the auspices of the Church and with the apparently celestial aid of Joan.

In 1430, Joan was captured in battle by the Burgundians, who sold her to their English allies. After interrogations by an ecclesiastical court at Rouen, lasting over a year, Joan repented of her wrongdoings—heresy and wearing men's clothes—and was condemned to life imprisonment. But when she starting wearing men's clothes again in prison, a secular court condemned her to death as a relapsed heretic. The English burned Joan of Arc at the stake in Rouen on May 30,

1431. King Charles neglected to help her. The Maid of Orléans was declared a saint of the Catholic Church in 1920.

Joan's victory eventually allowed France to free itself from its English enemy and develop into a strong, unified monarchy instead of becoming an appanage of the English throne. Among other long-term effects, this allowed French civilization—especially the glories of its language, literature, art, and legal codes—to develop in an untrammeled fashion and ultimately become one of the great global cultures.

The defeat of the Spanish Armada (1588) meant that the power of Spain was decisively checked, at least at sea, by the rising might of the English nation under Elizabeth I (see Question 74). Spain under Philip II, the most powerful monarch in Europe, was mistress of unimaginable quantities of New World gold and silver, not to speak of southern Italy, Sicily, the Duchy of Milan, and Portugal and all her colonies. In 1571, in the naval Battle of Lepanto, Philip's admiral and half-brother, Don John of Austria, had already crushed the sea power of the Ottoman Turks in the Mediterranean. But Protestant England was a major thorn in Philip's hyper-Catholic side. Not only were the English lending aid to his Protestant Dutch subjects, who were in fierce revolt, but they had also executed the Catholic Mary, Queen of Scots, in 1587; they were attacking his treasure-laden ships, and his ports, colonies, and arsenals, both in the Old World and the New; and they were competing with Spain for lucrative maritime trade. Philip had also been married to England's Catholic queen, Mary I, from 1554 until her death in 1558 and may thus have felt certain lingering proprietary rights. Most of all, with the hearty backing of the Pope, he wanted to make English Protestantism just a bad memory.

In 1587, Sir Francis Drake destroyed most of the fleet Spain was building at Cádiz for the invasion of England. In the following year, the Spanish assembled another force of 130 ships and about 30,000 men and set them sailing for the English Channel. The English had 197 ships, about half of which were too small for battle, and about 17,000 men. But the English ships were generally faster, and their firepower had a longer range.

The naval battles took place in the Channel in late July and early August at sites off Plymouth, Portland Bill, and the Isle of Wight, as well as off Calais and Gravelines on the Continent, where Drake again dogged the Spanish, who were short on ammunition, provisions, and leadership. After losing about a dozen ships, the Spanish admiral decided to make a run for it with the battered remnant of his armada. The weather allowed no sailing back through the Channel, so he had to take a very long way home indeed—into the North Sea and all around England, Scotland, and Ireland. About half of the original 130 ships made it back to Spain and in very shabby trim.

The Tudor monarchs, culminating in Elizabeth, had the sense to start building strong navies to protect their shores and project their power. Since the earth is 75 percent water, a dominant navy (before the rise of air power) could starve or pauperize its blockaded enemies, prevent them from sending out their own warships and transporting their troops overseas, seize treasure or trading vessels, sink fleets, and bombard coastal sites. British sea power, one of the most significant determinants of the subsequent history of the world, was still in evidence in 1982 in the brief war with Argentina over the Falkland Islands.

The Battle of Blenheim (1704) (BLEN-hime, as opposed to Blenheim palace, pronounced BLEN'm) was the first devastating defeat of France's Louis XIV, who dominated Continental Europe like a witty, cultured behemoth. This great English victory was the turning point in the War of the Spanish Succession (1701–14), called Queen Anne's War in the English New World colonies (see Question 74).

In 1700, the Spanish King died heirless, after naming Louis XIV's grandson, Philip of Anjou, as his successor. This eventuality would unite the French and Spanish crowns and all their overseas possessions, resulting in a megastate comprising France, Spain, part of the Netherlands, Sardinia, Sicily, southern Italy, the Duchy of Milan, the Philippines, Canada, the Louisiana Territories, lower California, Mexico, Florida, Central America, and much of South America—all under the control of Louis XIV. "Sorry," said William III of England, as he formed a Grand Alliance against Louis with Holland, Austria, Denmark, and various German principalities. After William died in 1702, Queen Anne carried on his plans, appointing as commander-in-chief John Churchill, who was created first Duke of Marlborough for his victories over the French. Marlborough, one of the most brilliant generals in history, led the Allies to victory at Blenheim and later at Ramillies (1706), Oudenarde (1708), and Malplaquet (1709).

But back in 1704, Louis's armies were planning to march on Vienna and knock Austria out of the war. Marlborough caught up with the French near the village of Blenheim (now Blindheim) on the Danube in Bavaria, northwest of Augsburg. The French army and that of their ally, the Duke of Bavaria, comprised 60,000 men. Marlborough's Anglo-Dutch Army and that of Prince Eugene of Savoy, who commanded the Austrians, totaled 56,000. On August 13, 1704, the French were defeated and retreated to the village of Blenheim, where they surrendered under heavy bombardment. The Allies lost 4,500 killed and 7,500 wounded, whereas only 20,000 of the French-Bavarian force were ever reassembled. The other 40,000 were killed, wounded, captured, or missing.

After this battle, the Allied cause was in the ascendant, and the French fought only defensively. The treaties ending the war were signed at Utrecht in 1713 and Rastadt in 1714. By these settlements, Spain and its New World possessions did go to Philip of Anjou but were to be kept separate from the French throne. The Austrians picked up southern Italy, Milan, Sardinia, and the former Spanish Netherlands. England got Newfoundland, Acadia, and the Hudson Bay Territories from France and Gibraltar from Spain.

John Churchill got his dukedom of Marlborough, and the English government paid for his phenomenally costly palace of Blenheim, where his descendant, Winston Churchill, was born in 1874. The Battle of Blenheim prevented the French from swallowing up most of Europe. Louis XIV was cut down to size, and England's destiny as a superpower was foreshadowed.

The Battle of Poltava (1709) (pull-TAH-vuh), in the Ukraine, determined that the Russians, rather than the Swedes, were to dominate northeastern Europe and become a major European power in modern times (see Question 46). At the beginning of the eighteenth century, Sweden was the great military power of northern Europe under its mighty warrior-king Charles XII, who also ruled over Finland and points farther east, Estonia, and part of Latvia.

The Great Northern War (1700–21) began when Czar Peter the Great of Russia, Frederick IV of Denmark, and Augustus the Strong, Elector of Saxony and King of Poland, ganged up against the eighteen-year-old Swedish King. After knocking Denmark out of the war, Charles XII turned against Russia. He managed to raise the Russian siege of Narva (in his possession of Estonia) with only 8,000 men against Russia's 40,000. Then he rushed south to raise the Polish siege of Riga, recovered Latvia, captured Warsaw, and entered Cracow. While Charles was fighting in Poland, Peter defiantly founded St. Petersburg in 1703 in the Swedish province of Ingria.

After Charles installed his own puppet on the Polish throne, he again turned against Russia—meaning it this time. On New Year's Day of 1708, he crossed the Vistula with 24,000 cavalry and 20,000 infantry. But after Peter adopted a scorched-earth policy, Charles decided to turn south from his advance on Moscow. He spent a fiercely severe winter in the Ukraine—the worst in memory, with 3,000 Swedes freezing to death and the rest maimed by frostbite—but won the Cossacks, under their hetman Ivan Mazeppa, to his cause. In May of 1709, he laid siege to the town of Poltava, somewhat less than two hundred miles east of Kiev. Czar Peter brought an army to bear on the situation. On June 28, Charles and his 19,000 men attacked the 42,000 Russians, who overwhelmed the Swedes with massive artillery fire. The Swedes died or surrendered, and Charles, who had been wounded before the battle, escaped into Turkish territory with a pathetic remnant of about 1,500 men. Russia, which lost only 1,345 dead and 3,290 wounded, was assured of victory in the Great Northern War.

The Peace of Nystadt (1721) transferred Sweden's choice possessions on the eastern Baltic coast to Russia, which now embarked on an expansionist course as a major power. Had Russia lost, it would have lapsed into chaos, since it was at a far less mature stage than when it was invaded by Napoleon in 1812 (see Question 46). In 1828, the greatest of Russian poets, Aleksandr Pushkin, wrote an epic poem on the Battle of Poltava, but before that, Samuel Johnson had already used that catastrophic defeat of Charles XII as a byword for the mutability of fortune in his best poem, "The Vanity of Human Wishes" (1749):

> He left a name at which the world grew pale,
> To point a moral, or adorn a tale.

The victory of the Americans over Burgoyne at Saratoga (1777) was the turning point of the American Revolution (see Question 83). After it, France, and then Spain, entered the war on the American side, confident that U.S. troops were not just "a ragtag and bobtail army."

The British plan was to split the rebel territories in two by driving a wedge between New England and the rest of the colonies. This involved seizing the entire Hudson Valley by means of a three-pronged attack converging on Albany: "Gentleman Johnny" Burgoyne, British general and playwright, was to march south on Albany from Montreal via Lake Champlain; General William Howe was to move north from New York City; and Brigadier General Barry St. Leger was to move down the St. Lawrence to Lake Ontario and then sweep southeast toward Albany by way of the Mohawk Valley.

In early July of 1777, Burgoyne, with about 8,000 men, defeated the Americans and captured Fort Ticonderoga on Lake Champlain. But on August 3, he learned that General Howe was not on his way up the Hudson but was instead moving against the rebel capital of Philadelphia. Several weeks later, he got more bad news: St. Leger's forces, after fighting a savage battle and vainly besieging Fort Stanwix on the Mohawk, were heading back to Canada. Burgoyne's provisions were dwindling rapidly.

Burgoyne had no choice but attack the American position south of Saratoga, where utterly incompetent Major General Horatio Gates commanded about 7,000 men and quarreled incessantly with the brave and splendid soldier, General Benedict Arnold. There were two battles of Saratoga. The first, the Battle of Freeman's Farm, was fought on September 19. It was a Pyrrhic victory for the British, who suffered 600 casualties out of about 3,000 engaged, twice as many as the Americans, who had fielded a force of about the same size. On October 7, the Americans won the decisive Battle of Bemis Heights, largely by Arnold's spirited efforts, and the British lost another 600 men. Gates's army, swollen with reinforcements, was now twice the size of Burgoyne's. The British surrendered their 5,700 officers and men on October 17, 1777.

Although the Revolutionary War would drag on until 1781, Saratoga had given the colonists the morale boost they desperately needed, dealt a blow to British notions of invincibility, and garnered two powerful allies. Had the infant United States lost the Battle of Saratoga, it may never have survived to adulthood.

The Battle of Valmy (1792) was the first victory of the French Revolutionary forces against the foreign enemies of the new regime. It indicated to all the crowned heads of Europe that Revolutionary France was not an incubus that would vanish with "a whiff of grape-shot," as Napoleon would say of his dispersal of a mob, but was a force to be reckoned with. More important, the French were strengthened in their resolve to abolish the monarchy and establish a republic—which the newly convened National Convention did in

Paris on the day after the battle—and to push for a more radical restructuring of the government, now that they felt the Zeitgeist was with and not against them.

France had declared war against Austria in April 1792, only to discover that the Prussians and other powers had formed an alliance with the Austrians. In late summer, the Allied Army marched toward France, intending to take Paris, squash the Revolution, and restore King Louis XVI. Between September 2 and 7, more than a thousand royalists and suspected traitors were executed in "the September massacres," which only added to Europe's horror of the Revolutionary government.

The actual battle as such never really happened. On September 20, 1792, a combined French army of about 50,000 under Generals Charles François Dumouriez and François Christophe Kellermann faced 45,000 Allied forces of Prussians, Austrians, Hessians, and French émigrés, who had invaded France. The nominal commander of the Allies was the Prussian King, Frederick William II, but the actual general was a German princeling, the Duke of Brunswick. The Duke could have flattened both French armies before they combined—or marched straight through to Paris between them, but instead he futzed around while the King tore his hair out in frustration. Nonetheless, they had already captured Verdun and expected the main French forces to turn tail at their approach. The armies met at Valmy in northeast France, just west of the Argonne Forest.

The Allies unleashed a cannonade that lasted about two hours, and the French artillery replied in kind. The Prussian infantry advanced, but still the French pounded them and refused to cooperate by fleeing in panic. And then the Prussians halted. No one really knows why: Was the terrain too muddy or the enemy artillery fire too discouraging? Or did Brunswick decide there was no reason to risk everything in a massive conflict when he could just retreat and consolidate the areas he had already won? He could always make it to Paris the following year. Except he never did.

After this battle, often disparagingly referred to as "the Cannonade of Valmy," in which only about 300 men fell on each side, the French armies went on the offensive, bringing the war into the German states, Savoy, and the Austrian Netherlands. In the following year, Louis XVI and Marie Antoinette were executed, the Reign of Terror began, and France repulsed a second Allied invasion. If there had actually been a battle at Valmy and the French had lost, the

Revolution would never have unleashed the tremendous social, political, intellectual, and military forces that profoundly changed the face of Europe and the world.

On the evening of the battle, Goethe, who was with the Prussian army as an observer, was asked what he thought of the day's events. He replied, "From this place and from this day forth commences a new era in the world's history, and you can all say that you were present at its birth."

The Battle of Waterloo (1815) put an end to the rule of Emperor Napoleon Bonaparte over much of Europe and allowed the weary Allies—especially the English, Prussians, Austrians, and Russians, who had done the bulk of the fighting—to try to restore the *status quo ante bellum* at the Congress of Vienna (see Questions 46 and 67).

Napoleon had abdicated in April 1814, when the Russians, Austrians, and Prussians took Paris. After spending less than a year in exile on the island of Elba off the coast of Tuscany, Napoleon decided to reenter the workforce. His subsequent escape, return to power, recruitment of an army of 125,000, and other events of his "Hundred Days"—including old Louis XVIII's hobbling off into exile—astonished the world and disgusted the Allies, who had been fighting, on and off, against the French Revolutionary and Napoleonic armies for twenty-two years.

The Allied strategy was to assemble two armies in Belgium for the invasion of France: one, under Field Marshal G. L. von Blücher, comprised 116,000 Prussians; the other, commanded by the Duke of Wellington, consisted of 93,000 British, Belgian, Dutch, and German soldiers. They planned to wait until the arrival of their Austrian and Russian allies would swell their force to more than 600,000 men.

Napoleon knew he couldn't sit around waiting for this to happen. He had no choice but to try to destroy the enemy before the odds turned hopelessly against him. As it was, he was outnumbered by almost two to one.

Advancing into Belgium, he decided to drive his army between the two enemy forces and defeat each in turn. On June 16, Napoleon's forces failed to dislodge Wellington at Quatre Bras, but they resoundingly defeated the Prussians at Ligny, eight miles away, though suffering heavy casualties themselves.

The next day, after the Duke of Wellington realized he had to retreat north (toward Waterloo, south of Brussels), the French under Marshal Ney lost their opportunity to pursue and destroy the English army. On the morning of June 18, Napoleon wanted to force a battle before Blücher could arrive with his forces. Wellington, with his 67,600 men, made a stand against Napoleon's 74,000 troops, knowing that the Prussians were on their way.

Napoleon's soldiers attacked ferociously and repeatedly all day—infantrymen, artillerymen, cavalrymen. To cite just one famous instance, Marshal Ney had five horses shot from under him, and his uniform and hat were riddled with bullet holes. When the Prussians arrived on the field, the French were seriously outnumbered. Although Napoleon could have retreated into France under cover of his Old Guard, he realized a defeat at Waterloo would mean the end of his revived empire. Instead, he used these veteran troops in a do-or-die advance supported by French artillery fire. The British infantrymen facing them at the crest of a ridge had been ordered to lie prone with their guns fixed on the French front column, which was seventy men wide. When the two forces were about 150 feet apart, the British command to rise and fire rang out, and the French, who had not seen the concealed enemy, were cut down by musket fire and a bayonet charge.

After Blücher sent another Prussian detachment into the field and Wellington led a counterattack against the French line, Napoleon's troops were routed. French casualties were about 33,000; the British and Dutch lost a total of about 15,000, while the Prussians suffered 7,000 casualties. Napoleon was sent to end his days on the island of Saint Helena in the south Atlantic, and the world was spared further evidence of his conquering genius.

Here are the five battles with which Joseph B. Mitchell chose to update Creasy's list in 1964 in his *Twenty Decisive Battles of the World:*

+ The Vicksburg campaign (1863), which, by securing the Mississippi for the Union, cut the Confederacy in two during the American Civil War
+ The Battle of Sadowa (1866), the decisive conflict in the Seven Weeks' War between Prussia and Austria; this Prussian victory paved the way for the humiliating defeat of France in the Franco-Prussian War (1870–71) and set the stage for the founding of a unified German nation and empire under Chancellor Otto von Bismarck and Kaiser William I

- The First Battle of the Marne (1914), which repulsed the German assault against Paris during World War I, preventing the conflict from ending with a speedy French defeat—and perhaps with the defeat or surrender of Russia and Britain
- The Battle of Midway (1942), in which the Japanese loss of four aircraft carriers and 332 warplanes marked the beginning of America's going on the offensive in the Pacific theater in World War II (see Question 83)
- The Battle of Stalingrad (1942–43), in which 330,000 German troops were lost, effectively ending Hitler's bid to conquer the Soviet Union and, ultimately, of prevailing in the Second World War (see Question 46).

❧ QUESTION 98

What are the 15 republics of the former Soviet Union and their capitals?

Russia: Moscow	Turkmenistan: Ashkhabad
Ukraine: Kiev	Uzbekistan: Tashkent
Belarus: Minsk	Kyrgyzstan: Bishkek
Moldova: Chisinau	Tajikistan: Dushanbe
Georgia: Tbilisi	Lithuania: Vilnius
Armenia: Yerevan	Latvia: Riga
Azerbaijan: Baku	Estonia: Tallinn
Kazakhstan: Almaty	

The world awoke to unsettling news one morning in August 1991: A group of Communist hard-liners had placed Soviet leader Mikhail Gorbachev under house arrest and were moving to reimpose centralized party control over the disintegrating Communist government. Dissatisfied by several years of Gorbachev's increasingly liberal policies—particularly glasnost ("openness") and perestroika ("restructuring" of the economy and government)—the hard-line Communists were desperately trying, with their ill-fated putsch, to stop the fatal hemorrhaging of an empire that had loomed large in twentieth-century history.

Within three days, however, the President of the Russian Republic, Boris Yeltsin, with the aid of his fellow reformers, had crushed the attempted coup, and the official dismantling of the Union of Soviet Socialist Republics (U.S.S.R.) began. In September, Estonia, Latvia, and Lithuania were granted independence, and on December 21, the remaining republics agreed to formally dissolve their union. When Gorbachev resigned on Christmas Day of 1991, what remained of a nation that had once covered more than 8 million square miles (one sixth of the earth's land surface) was a group of fifteen fractious nations containing at least one hundred ethnic groups or nationalities and a total population of 282 million.

The largest and by far the most powerful of the former states of the U.S.S.R. is **Russia,** whose capital of Moscow dominates the nation's political and cultural affairs. Even without its former appendages, Russia, at 6.6 million square miles, is the world's largest country and almost twice as big as China or the United States. Its population of more than 150 million, the sixth largest in the world, includes people of sixty ethnic groups.

The history of the Russian people begins in pre-Christian times with wandering Slavic tribes in the north and Scythians in the south. Scythia was successively overrun by Ostrogoths, Huns, Avars, Magyars, and Khazars. In A.D. 862, warring tribes of eastern Slavs called in the Scandinavian chief Rurik to unite them and rule over Novgorod. The name *Russia* derives from Rurik's Scandinavians, who were called Varangians, or Rus. In subsequent centuries, the town of Moscow, favorably located on important trade routes, grew prominent. Despite the fierce destruction of the Mongol invasions and the establishment of the khanate known as the Golden Horde in the mid-thirteenth century by Batu Khan, grandson of Genghis Khan, Muscovy had become a powerful grand duchy by the time of the fall of Constantinople in 1453. Three decades later, Mongol domination of Russia came to an end.

Ivan the Terrible (reigned 1533–84), who ruled during a period of chaos, was the first Czar of Russia. In 1613, the first Romanov ascended the throne, founding a dynasty that was to endure until 1917. The late seventeenth century saw the accession of Peter the Great (1682–1725), who initiated Russia's Westernization and its gradual transformation into a major European power. Peter formally

Republics of the Former Soviet Union

proclaimed the Russian Empire in 1721. During the eighteenth century, particularly in the reign of Catherine the Great (1762–96), Russia further expanded south toward the Black Sea, with its strategic ports, and west to Poland. By the time of Alexander II (1855–81), Russia had absorbed the Baltics, the Crimea, Ukraine, the Caucasus region, Kazakhstan, and other parts of Central Asia.

The Czars and the ruling aristocracy were rigidly repressive in their dealings with their far-flung subjects. Efforts at reform were largely unsuccessful and, as the population became more urbanized and industrialized, radical movements—including Marxism—sprang up. Political and social conditions continued to deteriorate during the early years of the twentieth century. After a disastrous war with Japan in 1904–5, ruinous involvement in World War I, and continuing feeble reform attempts, the czardom came to a dismal end in March 1917, when Nicholas II abdicated. He and his family were shot on July 16, 1918. During the "ten days that shook the world" in October of 1917, Vladimir Lenin (1870–1924), Leon Trotsky (1879–1940), and their fellow Bolshevik Communists seized power. Extricating Russia from the horrors of the First World War, via a separate peace with Germany signed at Brest-Litovsk, was a chief priority.

Civil war then broke out between the Communists and their foes. At its conclusion, on December 30, 1922, the territories of the former Russian Empire became the U.S.S.R., a confederation of states theoretically based on Marxist principles of communal property and representation in a central soviet, or council. But Lenin and his associates quickly moved to consolidate their power, and the regime instantly became totalitarian. The succession of Joseph Stalin (1879–1953) to power in 1928 brought a quarter century of repression, ruthless "purges," extermination of political enemies, and mass starvation on a scale the country—and the world—had never seen. His legacy was twofold: enslavement of the Eastern European nations overrun in World War II and cold war against the Western powers.

Second only to Russia in size (more than 233,000 square miles) and population (52 million) is **Ukraine,** a vast, flat plain that today is highly industrialized. Its capital, Kiev, on the Dnieper River, which became the capital of the Scandinavian Rus principality in the ninth century, was razed to the ground in 1240 by Batu Khan and his Mongol Tatars.

The later history of Ukraine is one of conflict and annexation, with certain of its territories being claimed at various times by Lithuania, Poland, and Austria. It was incorporated into the Russian Empire in 1793. Efforts toward independence after the Russian Revolution were crushed by the Bolsheviks.

The grip of Soviet rule was harsh and unwelcome to fiercely nationalistic Ukraine. Its black-soiled fertile plains underwent forced collectivization during the early Stalin years, and its foodstuffs were appropriated to feed distant areas of the Soviet Union. The result was a famine during 1932–33 in which 7 million Ukrainians starved. Much of Ukraine was occupied by Germany during World War II and then retaken by the Soviet Union in 1944 (see Question 46).

Although the country possesses considerable natural wealth, largely in mineral reserves, it remained in debt to and dependent on the other Soviet republics prior to the breakup. Energy shortages prompted officials to permit the continued functioning of five nuclear power plants despite safety problems and faulty equipment. A disastrous meltdown at Chernobyl in 1986 resulted in many radiation-induced deaths and illnesses and contaminated surrounding areas. Since the dissolution of the U.S.S.R., reform has come slowly and painfully to Ukraine.

Belarus lies north of Ukraine, occupying territory that has been claimed by Lithuania, Poland, and Russia over the years. Its capital, Minsk, was originally settled more than nine hundred years ago. Belarus, which means "White Russia," encompasses 80,000 square miles and has a population of more than 10 million. It proclaimed independence in March 1918, but the republic was short-lived. By early 1919, the Bolsheviks had taken over, but the country was then invaded by the Poles, who considered the territory historically theirs. The region was divided between Poland and the U.S.S.R. by the Treaty of Riga in 1921.

Like many of its neighbors, Belarus was occupied—and largely devastated—by the Germans during World War II. After annexation by the U.S.S.R. in 1945, it was transformed from an agrarian to an industrialized nation. Although one of the smaller post-Soviet countries, it has played a significant role in recent years in the disarmament and nuclear nonproliferation movements. In 1996 Belarus and Russia entered into a partnership that created close economic, political, and cultural ties while maintaining separate governing bodies.

South of Ukraine lies **Moldova,** an agricultural country dominated by its neighbors since its fifteenth-century founding, first by Turkey in the sixteenth century, then Austria in the eighteenth. The capital and largest city is Chisinau. Russia occupied the eastern part of the country during the first half of the nineteenth century, until Moldova joined with neighboring Walachia to form the Kingdom of Romania in 1859. It was reannexed by Russia nineteen years later, however, and remained in the Russian Empire, as Bessarabia, until the Revolution. In 1918 it rejoined Romania; this unification was recognized by the United States, Britain, and France in 1920, but not by the Soviet Union, which continued to seek its annexation. This took place after the Molotov-Ribbentrop Pact (1939) divided Eastern Europe between Soviet and German spheres of influence. During the war years, the country was retaken and occupied by Romanian forces until 1944, when it was again captured by the Soviet Army.

Issues of ethnicity and territoriality, broadly repressed during the Soviet years, have dominated the Moldovan political landscape since the breakup of the U.S.S.R. When Romanian was declared the official language, Slavic secessionist movements erupted in the southern and eastern parts of the country. The civil strife has not abated, despite the presence of regional peacekeeping forces. Nonetheless, a constitution has been adopted and free parliamentary elections held.

East of the Black Sea lie the three Transcaucasus republics of Georgia, Armenia, and Azerbaijan, which were taken over by the Soviets and annexed together in 1922 as the Transcaucasian Soviet Federated Socialist Republic. They were granted separate republic status in 1936. Throughout their histories, all three have been plagued by Persian, Turkish, and Russian domination, as well as internal ethnic strife and factional warfare.

Georgia, now a small country of 26,900 square miles and 5.7 million people, was a powerful medieval kingdom until its incorporation into the Ottoman Empire in the thirteenth century. Its most infamous son was Iosif Dzhugashvili, who changed his surname to Stalin ("steel"). Glasnost allowed a Georgian national identity to bloom, and Georgian was proclaimed the official language, although most people continued to speak Russian. The country declared its independence in April 1991, but its leader, Zviad Gamsakhurdia, proved to be a dictator. Quickly deposed, he committed suicide in 1993 as his forces attempted to retake the capital city, Tbilisi. After his demise, former Soviet Foreign Minister Eduard Shevardnadze, a Georgian, was installed as President. Additional trouble loomed when the Abkhazian territory and South Ossetia determined to secede and fighting broke out. The country remains beset with severe economic hardship and political strife.

Armenia is a largely agricultural, landlocked republic of 11,500 square miles and 3.5 million people, one third of whom reside in the capital city, Yerevan. The landscape features steppes and mo.:ntains, and the country is subject to severe earthquakes like the one in December 1988, which killed 25,000. Poor economic conditions spurred about a fifth of the population to emigrate by the mid-1990s.

The Armenian people are descended from ancient settlers on the Ararat plain, which even now is the most populous area of the country and the seat of the nation's culture and economy. In the early nineteenth century, Armenia looked to the Russian Empire for liberation from the Turks and Persians. By the 1830s, Russia held all of Armenia except for the western portion, which remained under harsh Turkish domination. Large-scale forced emigrations and massacres occurred, beginning in the 1890s. Turkish attempts to deport native Armenians to Mesopotamia between 1915 and 1923 resulted in the deaths of more than a million people.

Since independence in 1991, Armenia has been troubled by political tensions, armed confrontations, and an economic blockade by its neighbor **Azerbaijan,** which has strong ties to Turkey. Azerbaijani culture is a unique product of Zoroastrian, Greek, Christian, Muslim, and Russian elements. Azerbaijan's huge natural-gas and oil resources are refined in or near the capital, the ancient city of Baku, a port on the Caspian Sea. The Baku area supplied half the world's oil at the beginning of the twentieth century. The Swedish Nobel family was a major developer there, and oil from the region helped fund the Nobel Prizes. Capturing the Baku oil fields was an obsessive concern of Adolf Hitler, but German armies were stopped six hundred miles north of the city.

Only after the breakup of the U.S.S.R. did it become clear that these oil stores are among the largest in the world. In 1994, the state-owned Azerbaijani oil company signed the so-called contract of the century, a $7.4-billion agreement with a consortium of ten companies from six nations to work these fields. Pipeline routes remain a major source of disagreement, however.

Oil has also been a profound economic and political force in recent years in the five Central Asian republics of the former U.S.S.R. Of these, **Kazakhstan** is the richest oil producer. More than a million square miles in area, it is the largest country in Central Asia and the ninth largest in the world. The capital is Almaty, but the seat of government is expected to move north to Aqmola, where earthquakes are less of a threat. The population of 17 million is widely dispersed, though the country has the highest rate (60 percent) of urbanization among the Central Asian republics. Kazakhstan's mineral resources have been coveted by outsiders for centuries and, like the other Asian post-Soviet republics, its history is one of invasion and foreign domination by Mongols, Arabs, and Russians.

During the nineteenth century the Central Asian territories were swallowed up by Russia. They resisted Bolshevik rule for several years after the Revolution, but by the early 1920s the rebellion had been defeated. Kazakhstan, Turkmenistan, Uzbekistan, Kyrgyzstan, and Tajikistan were subsumed into one Soviet state, the Turkestan Autonomous Soviet Socialist Republic, in 1921. All declared independence in 1991 and are now, at least nominally, democratic republics.

Much of **Turkmenistan** is desert, and it is the least populated of the group. Ashkhabad is the capital and largest city. The country's economy remains state-controlled, and its leaders, though elected, face no opposition and retain absolute power. **Uzbekistan,** whose capital is the much-conquered Tashkent, is the third most populous of the former member states of the U.S.S.R., with more than 23 million inhabitants. It, too, maintains close ties with Russia and has done little to reform its economic policies even in the face of a shrinking, troubled economy. Its ancient city of Samarkand, on the fabled Silk Road, was captured by Alexander the Great in 329 B.C. and destroyed by Genghis Khan in 1220. The world-class conqueror Tamerlane was buried in the rebuilt city, his capital, in 1405.

The native residents of mountainous **Kyrgyzstan** are Turkic-speaking Muslims, and the population is concentrated in the river valleys. **Tajikistan,** too, is largely mountainous, and most of its people are of Iranian stock and Sunni Muslim heritage. The capital cities of the two countries are Bishkek and Dushanbe, respectively. As with other former states of the U.S.S.R., conflicts ranging from ethnic warfare and currency instability to lawsuits between energy-development companies have stalled progress, despite the promise of wealth from oil and natural-gas reserves.

The Baltic states **Lithuania, Latvia,** and **Estonia** were the last pieces added to the Soviet puzzle. Lithuania's capital, Vilnius, was the seat of one of the most powerful European states in medieval times. Like its neighbors Latvia and Estonia, Lithuania today is urbanized and heavily industrialized. Riga, the capital of Latvia, and Tallinn, the capital of Estonia, are important Baltic Sea ports.

Annexed by the U.S.S.R. in 1940, the Baltic republics were subsequently occupied by invading Nazi armies before falling under Soviet rule again. Beginning in the war years, large-scale insurrections broke out in Lithuania, to which the Soviet authorities responded by deporting 350,000 Lithuanians to labor camps in Siberia. The United States never officially recognized Soviet hegemony over the Baltic republics, which were the first states to break away from the U.S.S.R., initiating the dissolution of the vast empire in a dominolike reaction that shook the world once again.

What are the unofficial Homeric titles of the 18 chapters
of James Joyce's *Ulysses*?

1. Telemachus	11. Sirens
2. Nestor	12. Cyclops
3. Proteus	13. Nausicaa
4. Calypso	14. Oxen of the Sun
5. Lotus-Eaters	15. Circe
6. Hades	16. Eumaeus
7. Aeolus	17. Ithaca
8. Lestrygonians	18. Penelope
9. Scylla and Charybdis	
10. Wandering Rocks (or Symplegades)	

> *The repeated, but insignificant, contacts of Joyce's* Ulysses *with
> the Homeric* Odyssey *continue to enjoy . . . the harebrained
> admiration of the critics.*
>
> —Jorge Luis Borges,
> "The Approach to Al-Mu'tasim"

Despite this remark of a Borges narrator, the Homeric parallels in
James Joyce's *Ulysses* (1922) have proved a fertile source for helping
readers understand a book that Anthony Burgess described as "the
most complex fictional structure of all time." But why did Joyce
spend seven years composing an eight-hundred-page epic that can
only loosely be described as a novel, centering on only one day in the
life of lower-middle-class Dubliners—and make each of its untitled
eighteen chapters correspond in hundreds of ways to an episode of
Homer's *Odyssey*?

　　Ezra Pound downplayed the importance of the Homeric parallels, calling them "part of Joyce's mediaevalism . . . , a scaffold, a means of construction." But they must be more than that if even the book's title is *Ulysses,* the Latinized name of Odysseus, rather than something like *Leopold Bloom,* the name of its "hero." And why is Bloom, a meek, thirty-eight-year-old Irish Jew who sells advertising space, the counterpart of a titanic Greek hero who figured in legends three millennia before Bloom's time?

Perhaps T. S. Eliot was wiser to the method behind Joyce's apparent madness when he wrote that the parallel with the *Odyssey* had the importance of a scientific discovery, that it was "a way of controlling, of ordering, of giving a shape and a significance to the immense panorama of futility and anarchy which is contemporary history." This "mythical method" of Joyce allowed him to satirize the paltry shabbiness of modern urban life by implicitly setting it against the backdrop of the adventurous tales of the ancient sagas. But it also allowed him to endow modern Dublin—here, a microcosm for the modern world—with a quiet heroism and endurance in the face of poverty and squalor, and these virtues are seen as democratic counterparts of the self-assertive rapaciousness of Homer's proud warrior kings.

In this view, even the most trivial incidents are epiphanies revealing a luminous inner world of human longings, joys, and regrets. Joyce's comic vision is thus enriched by undertones of pathetic grandeur, especially because we so often get inside the heads of the book's three main characters—Leopold Bloom, his wife Molly, and Stephen Dedalus—via the technique of interior monologue, which presents verbatim the ebb and flow of their thoughts.

Joyce claimed the character of Ulysses had fascinated him even as a boy. He originally envisioned what became *Ulysses* as a short story for his collection *Dubliners* (1914). It was to be about Alfred Hunter, a man who apparently took the battered young Joyce home after a street fight over a girl. Hunter was thought to be a Jew and a cuckold, and the irony of the contrast between him and the epic hero whose wife was a model of chastity may have given Joyce his initial impetus. Hunter's kind deed, transferred to Leopold Bloom, sets in motion the denouement of *Ulysses.* The character of Bloom also has significant traces of the Jewish Italian novelist Italo Svevo, whom Joyce knew well in Trieste, and of the nonartistic, domestic, conventional side of Joyce himself.

Joyce was also powerfully influenced by Victor Bérard's study,

The Phoenicians and the Odyssey, which claims the adventures of Odysseus were sea yarns based on the actual wanderings of Phoenician merchants in the ancient Mediterranean. The Phoenicians were Semites: If the antecedent of Odysseus was Semitic, why shouldn't his modern counterpart be? In addition, Joyce believed the Irish language may have been the tongue of the Phoenicians and that this Semitic people had established a great civilization in ancient Ireland.

Besides having a Homeric correspondence, each chapter of *Ulysses* is also associated with a different time of day or night, a place, a human art, an organ of the body, a color, a symbol, and a distinct style. Joyce uses these apparently capricious mechanisms in each episode as springboards for a narrative meditation on various significant issues: betrayal of friends and country, the meaning of history, the ever-shifting contours of external and internal phenomena, domesticity and ethnicity, self-delusion, death, the uses of rhetoric (to indicate broadly the major concerns of only the first seven chapters). But let's focus on the Homeric parallels, which are drawn from two schemas that Joyce circulated privately among his friends as an aid to understanding the book and were later published with his connivance.

The first three chapters of *Ulysses,* concerned with the morning activities of Stephen Dedalus, are known as the "Telemachiad." Stephen is Joyce's twenty-two-year-old alter ego who has already figured as the protagonist of *A Portrait of the Artist as a Young Man* (1916). Joyce took the name "Telemachiad"—story of Telemachus—from the traditional designation for the first four books of the *Odyssey,* which relate the adventures of Odysseus' young son as he goes off in search of news about his father, who has been absent from his kingdom of Ithaca for twenty years (ten years of fighting at Troy followed by ten years of wanderings).

Because Telemachus's modern counterpart, Stephen, does a lot of thinking about fathers and paternity throughout the day, some critics have thought that he, like his Homeric original, is in search of a father, albeit a spiritual one, whom he later meets in the person of Leopold Bloom. But Stephen, as an aspiring young writer, is seeking to become, in effect, his own father, that is, to attain the personal and intellectual autonomy needed to create enduring art.

In **Telemachus,** we meet Stephen at 8 A.M. on Thursday, June 16, 1904 (a date Joyce chose in order to commemorate the first time he went out walking with his future wife, Nora Barnacle). After his mother's death, for which he feels a measure of guilt, would-be poet

473

Stephen has left his unhappy home—full of poverty, siblings, and the drunken pretensions of his father Simon—to share a residence in an old tower on Dublin Bay, south of the city, with a false friend, Buck Mulligan, an ebulliently sarcastic medical student with sex on the brain. Mulligan's Homeric antecedent is Antinous, a leader of Penelope's suitors who, in Odysseus' absence, batten on the Ithacan King's substance. Before, during, and after breakfast in the tower, themes of betrayal and usurpation, on a personal and national level, color Stephen's thoughts and bitter remarks.

Nestor is set at 10 A.M. in a private school for boys where Stephen teaches. Mr. Deasy, the aged headmaster, speaks to Stephen after class and denounces Jews, spendthrifts, and women. This last prejudice recalls Homer's Nestor telling Telemachus about the treachery of Clytemnestra and of Helen of Troy, who is actually mentioned by Deasy. Whereas Nestor, the oldest of the Greek heroes, is a font of traditional wisdom and a crafty counselor (though something of a windbag), his modern counterpart is just a misogynistic and anti-Semitic old fool proffering false "worldly wisdom." The art of this chapter is history, which Stephen is shown teaching. The dejected young poet, tired of listening to Deasy, remarks that history—his own and his nation's—is "a nightmare from which I am trying to awake."

In **Proteus,** set at 11 A.M., Stephen walks north on the beach toward Dublin, wrestling with philosophical and philological problems involving the protean nature of appearances and much else. This mirrors Telemachus's journey to King Menelaus and Queen Helen in Sparta, during which the Spartan King tells the young man how, in trying to discover how to get home from Troy, he had to wrestle with the protean god Proteus to get him to reveal this knowledge. He also assures Telemachus that Proteus had told him Odysseus was alive but was being kept on Calypso's island by the amorous goddess.

With the fourth episode begins the "Odyssey" proper of Joyce's book, which stretches over a dozen chapters and presents the wanderings of the book's (anti)hero, the Dubliner and nonpracticing Jew, Leopold Bloom, a modern Odysseus but also an Everyman who happens to be middlebrow, fussy, and henpecked. Because of his Jewish background, Bloom is an exile in his own land, mistrusted, kept at a distance, or ridiculed by many of his fellow Dubliners. From this perspective, he, too, becomes a type of the socially isolated artist. In fact, as one of the other characters remarks, "There's a touch of the artist about old Bloom." The first three chapters of the "Odyssey" section take us back in time a few hours so that we can learn what Bloom was doing in the morning at the same times as Stephen.

In **Calypso,** we see Mr. Bloom making breakfast for himself and his wife Molly, a zaftig concert singer who lolls in bed the whole time. In this chapter, set at their Dublin home at 7 Eccles Street at 8 A.M., Molly assumes the aspects of Calypso, the goddess who detains Odysseus on her island as her lover for seven years. Bloom's uxoriousness and subservience to Molly are the modern analogue, but we also discover Molly has a lover, her concert manager Blazes Boylan, who makes an assignation with her for 4 P.M. via a letter that Bloom deferentially delivers to her. The Blooms have a fifteen-year-old daughter, Milly (a little Molly), but their only son, Rudy, died more than ten years earlier, shortly after birth. That was the last time the couple had intercourse, Bloom apparently having developed psychological impotence. When Bloom encounters Stephen later in the book, he sees in him a potential substitute son.

The mood of **Lotus-Eaters** is all inertia, idleness, languor, and torpor, to reflect the adventure of Odysseus' men who, after landing at an island, eat a mysterious flower and forget about their return home, wanting to dream away the rest of their lives under the drugged influence of the lotus. Bloom is shown wandering around Dublin at 10 A.M., the "dead" hour of the morning, and stopping by a druggist's to order some face lotion for his wife. The chapter is packed with herb and flower imagery, and the Eucharist that Bloom sees distributed at a local church is viewed as the ultimate opiate for believers. At the end of the chapter, Bloom goes to a public bath, and his impotent penis in the water is described as "a languid floating flower."

At 11 A.M., we see Bloom and some acquaintances, including Stephen's father, Simon, attending the funeral of a Dublin barfly named Paddy Dignam. In this **Hades** episode, Bloom spots Stephen from the funeral carriage he is riding in, the first in a series of rapprochements between the two that will end with their meeting during the evening. Various characters in this chapter correspond with Hades, Cerberus, Elpenor, Agamemnon, Ajax, and others in Book 11 of the *Odyssey,* which describes Odysseus' journey to the world of the dead.

Aeolus, set at noon, takes place in a newspaper office where the editor Myles Crawford, Stephen, and some local idlers are discussing various specimens of Irish oratory. The Homeric analogue is with the episode in the *Odyssey* in which the wind god Aeolus gives Odysseus a bag of imprisoned winds to ensure that his journey home to Ithaca will not be disrupted by troublesome squalls. While Odysseus naps, his men, thinking the bag contains treasures, open it and let loose a tempest that drives them back out to sea (see Question 25).

In Joyce's book, the "wind" is windy rhetoric—that of newspapers (the editor, blustery Crawford, is "Aeolus"), but also of the patriotic and nationalistic oratory with which Ireland has been so abundantly graced. An interesting device in this chapter is Joyce's use of sixty-three newspaper headlines for his narrative, which evolve in style from the staid to the colloquial and slangy. Another is his use of practically every rhetorical device and figure of speech mentioned by Quintilian in his *Institutes of Oratory* (see Question 54). In this chapter, Bloom and Stephen just miss running into each other.

Lestrygonians is set at 1 P.M.—lunchtime. In the *Odyssey,* the Lestrygonians are gigantic cannibals who eat one of Odysseus' men and shower boulders down on their ships, smashing all but one. This chapter, as expected, is full of references to food and eating, and we watch Bloom have lunch: a Gorgonzola sandwich and a glass of burgundy.

Scylla and Charybdis takes place in the National Library at 2 P.M., where Stephen gives a talk on Shakespeare to a few members of the Dublin intelligentsia. The parallels with Homer are the monster Scylla and the whirlpool Charybdis between which Odysseus must steer his ship. Here Stephen, a would-be Shakespeare, must steer a middle course between the cynical obscenity of Buck Mulligan and the syrupy mysticism and aestheticism of Richard Best, John Eglinton, and George Russell. Stephen's talk interprets Shakespeare's plays from an extremely biographical perspective, which is perhaps Joyce's way of saying that even the most supposedly "impersonal" artist, writing in the most distanced literary medium, the drama, may use his own life and family entanglements to discover the universal in the particular—as Joyce did in all his works. In this chapter, Stephen and Bloom have a slight encounter.

The chapter called **Wandering Rocks** depicts, in nineteen short vignettes (with Bloom's right in the middle), the simultaneous meanderings of a host of Dubliners at 3 P.M. The episode begins with a Jesuit priest taking a walk and ends with the viceroy's carriage driving through the city. Between these, trying to avoid collisions with a powerful Church and the British state, are the everyday Dubliners who go about their humble business. This is the only chapter in which the parallel is not with an episode in the *Odyssey,* but from the myth of Jason and the Argonauts (though Jason's adventure is mentioned in Homer). Jason's ship, the *Argo,* manages to sail between two wandering rocks (sometimes identified with the Symplegades, clashing rocks) that smash together whenever anything—a ship, a bird— passes between them.

In **Sirens,** the enchantresses who lure unwary mariners to death with their irresistible singing become two Dublin barmaid tarts, Miss Lydia Douce and Miss Mina Kennedy. The chapter, set at four o'clock in the Ormond Hotel bar, is packed with sentimental music and song, but Bloom escapes both from the tempting ladies (not that they're interested in him) and from "drowning" in the saccharine inertia of his drink- and song-befuddled fellow Dubliners, especially Stephen's father, the fine old tenor Simon Dedalus. During this chapter, while Bloom listens sadly to the singing and munches on his dinner, Boylan and Molly are vigorously fornicating in Bloom's bed—and he knows it.

In the *Odyssey,* the Greek hero and his men blind the cannibalistic, one-eyed giant, Polyphemus the Cyclops, and manage to sail away safely, although the monster flings a huge boulder after them in response to Odysseus' taunts. In Joyce's **Cyclops** episode, Bloom is in Barney Kiernan's pub between 5 and 6 P.M. when he becomes involved in a verbal altercation with "the Citizen," a burly old former athlete and drink-cadging bore of an Irish Nationalist who corresponds to the savage giant. The style of the chapter is "gigantism," which uses hyperbole and bloated ironic descriptions to celebrate the swaggering, pseudo-Celtic-epic attributes of the Citizen. His anti-Semitism riles the usually mild-mannered Bloom into some uncautious retorts, and the chapter ends with Bloom's being hustled out the door and onto a streetcar by some friends. The enraged Citizen charges after him and, in response to Bloom's Parthian shot—"Christ was a jew like me"—hurls an ill-aimed biscuit tin at him.

The namby-pamby, romance-magazine style of **Nausicaa** is a parody of Samuel Butler's thesis, in *The Authoress of the Odyssey,* that the Homeric character Nausicaa was the actual writer of the Greek epic. Paralleling the attraction that young Princess Nausicaa feels for Odysseus, flirtatious Gerty MacDowell shows Bloom some leg (from a safe distance) during a fireworks display near the seashore where both are relaxing at twilight, between eight and nine o'clock. Bloom surreptitiously masturbates in response but feels a twinge of guilt when, as Gerty walks away, he notices she has a limp.

At 10 P.M., Stephen and Bloom finally run into each other in the **Oxen of the Sun** chapter. Stephen and his medical-student friends are having quite a few beers in a maternity hospital where Bloom, ever compassionate, has come to inquire about an acquaintance, Mina Purefoy, who has been in labor for days and gives birth during the episode. The chapter is narrated by means of a long series of virtuoso parodies of English prose styles, beginning with pre-English Celtic, Latinate English, and Anglo-Saxon, and stretching to Joyce's somewhat muddled notion of American revivalist lingo, with the major English authors sandwiched between in chronological order—Malory, the Elizabethans, Milton, Swift, Sterne, Goldsmith, Gibbon, Landor, and many more. This verbal display of the growth and development of English literary style mirrors the growth of Mrs. Purefoy's fetus within the womb until its birth, but its main purpose was to give Joyce a chance to show off: "I can do anything I want with words," he once truthfully remarked. The Odyssean parallel refers to the sacrilege his hungry men commit in slaughtering the sacred cattle of the sun god Helios. These beasts, symbols of fertility, are sinned against in Joyce's chapter because the irreverent medical students are drunkenly talking about contraception, onanism, and cheap sex. At the end, they all rush off to another bar, and sober Bloom decides to tag along to make sure blotto Stephen doesn't run into trouble.

Circe takes place at midnight, the witching hour, in a brothel in Dublin's red-light district, which Joyce calls "nighttown." By far the longest chapter (180 pages), it is cast in dramatic form, complete with elaborate stage directions. Here the beautiful Greek enchantress Circe, who turns Odysseus' men into hogs, becomes the ugly old madam Bella Cohen, who figuratively does the same to the patrons of her establishment. Bloom is still keeping an eye on Stephen, whom his false friend Mulligan has callously abandoned.

The hallucinatory phantasmagoria of this chapter (in which Bloom at one point becomes a woman and has eight children, and the end of the world occurs—and speaks) is an exaggerated acting out of Bloom's and Stephen's conscious and unconscious fears and fantasies. The climax of the book occurs when Stephen smashes the brothel's chandelier with his walking stick in a delirium of grief and guilt over his mother's painful death, and in anger against a God who allows such suffering to occur. Outside, a fracas erupts between Stephen and

478

some English soldiers. Bloom saves Stephen from arrest and, after the young man takes a wallop in the face, he does his Good Samaritan deed by bringing him back to his senses, helping him up, and brushing him off.

The final three chapters of *Ulysses* are referred to as the "Nostos" (Greek, "return home"), the word used of Odysseus' homecoming to Ithaca and Penelope, and paralleled by Bloom's returning home to Molly at the end of his long, exhausting day. **Eumaeus** is named for the faithful swineherd who shelters Odysseus on his return to Ithaca. The chapter shows Bloom steering Stephen to a cabman's shelter— run by a much shadier version of Eumaeus—for some coffee after his ordeal. The style is a "tired" one, reflecting the weariness of the two protagonists in its hundreds of clichés, repetitions, mixed metaphors, and awkward, tedious grammatical constructions. It's a beautifully written example of awful writing. At about 2 A.M., the pair head out for Bloom's house.

Ithaca, Joyce's favorite chapter, is in the form of a demented catechism of 309 questions and 308 answers that convey (and obscure) the plot. The style, however, is not that of religion but of the impersonal, polysyllabic, periphrastic language of science and technology, and most of the questions are answered in mind-numbing detail. The two men are sitting in Bloom's kitchen—his "Ithaca"—having some cocoa.

As in the previous chapter, they are talking at cross purposes. The artist and intellectual Stephen has very little to say to the garrulous Bloom, who has notions of Stephen's moving in with him and Molly, coaching his wife in Italian for her operatic singing, and perhaps distracting her from the awful Blazes Boylan. It's certainly the last thing Stephen has in mind. But perhaps his encounter with the decent man who helped him when his fortunes were at their nadir may have inspired him with just that scintilla of hope for humanity's future that artists need if they are to devote their entire lives to their vocation. Was the meeting decisive for Stephen's maturity as a man and a writer—or was it a total nonstarter? We don't find out whether he goes on to write *Ulysses*.

In any event, Stephen goes off, and Bloom potters around before going to bed. There he lovingly and lingeringly kisses Molly's buttocks (a little ritual of his), talks with her awhile, and falls asleep.

The last chapter, **Penelope,** comprises eight long, unpunctuated sentences that go on for forty-six pages. It is the interior monologue of Molly Bloom—largely based on Joyce's wife Nora—who, before drifting off to sleep at dawn, reviews her life as a woman so unabashedly that the Irish writer Mary Colum called her randy soliloquy "an exhibition of the mind of a female gorilla."

At the end of the *Odyssey,* after the hero has slaughtered all the suitors, he and his faithful wife are reunited in bed. So are Leopold Bloom and his adulterous wife in *Ulysses.* Bloom, too, has annihilated his unfaithful Penelope's suitors, not by violence, but by acquiescence in what must be. After Molly mentally surveys her past and current lovers and admirers, she dwells on her husband's fine, responsible qualities, which set him apart from the other men in their circle. And her famous last thoughts before sleep are of the first intimate moment she shared with Bloom, when she got him to propose and then answered "yes I said yes I will Yes."

20

What are the 20 regions of Italy?

Sicily (Sicilia)	The Marches (Le Marche)
Sardinia (Sardegna)	Tuscany (Toscana)
Calabria	Emilia-Romagna
Basilicata (formerly Lucania)	Liguria
Apulia (Puglia or Le Puglie)	Piedmont (Piemonte)
Campania	Valle d'Aosta
Molise	Lombardy (Lombardia)
Abruzzi	Trentino-Alto Adige
Latium (Lazio)	Friuli-Venezia Giulia
Umbria	Veneto

> *Italians . . . consider themselves the finest people in the world and, because of the excellent qualities no one can deny them, they can maintain this view with impunity.*
>
> —Goethe, *Italian Journey*

> *Italians . . . above all nations are endowed with a sense of the beautiful.*
>
> —Schopenhauer, *The World as Will and Representation*

> *The Italian [national genius] has made by far the freest and finest use of what it has borrowed, and contributed a hundred times more to it than it took: as the richest genius, which had the most to give.*
>
> —Nietzsche, *The Will to Power*

Taking a cue from these hard-to-impress Teutonic geniuses, let's examine the twenty Italian regions from the perspective of their *own* "richest genius," whether for "excellent qualities," "a sense of the beautiful," or, in a case or two, the greatest infamy. Instead of a typical guidebook approach, this survey paints individual portraits of Italy's regions via just a very few of their most famous sons or daughters.

The island of **Sicily** (capital: Palermo; other major cities: Messina, Catania, Syracuse, Agrigento) was the birthplace of three of modern Italy's greatest authors. Giovanni Verga (1840–1922) was the foremost Italian novelist of the late-nineteenth century and the leading exemplar of *verismo* (realism). His chief themes are the mores and miseries of Sicilian peasants and fishermen. Verga's best novels are *I Malavoglia (The House by the Medlar Tree)* and *Mastro-Don Gesualdo,* and he is also known for his short stories, packed with gritty Sicilian dialogue and details. D. H. Lawrence translated many of Verga's works into English. Sicilian-born Luigi Pirandello (1867–1936), Italy's greatest dramatist, was awarded the Nobel Prize in Literature in 1934 for probing the boundaries between illusion and reality in plays such as *Six Characters in Search of an Author* and *Henry IV.* Firmly grounded in reality is the sole novel of a Sicilian prince, Giuseppe Tomasi di Lampedusa (1896–1957). *The Leopard* is a beautifully nuanced study of the effects of Italian unification in the mid-nineteenth century on the old Sicilian aristocracy—a Sicilian *Gone with the Wind,* written by a master stylist and penetrating psychologist.

The island of **Sardinia** (Cagliari), famed today for its Emerald Coast, has produced an honorary son, Giuseppe Garibaldi (1807–82), the greatest military leader and conqueror during Italy's unification movement, the Risorgimento. This "Hero of Two Continents," who also fought in various liberation movements in South America, was the epitome of Italian patriotism, lionized in Italy and abroad as the legendary leader of the guerrilla troops known as the Red Shirts. Although Garibaldi wasn't born in Italy, but in Nice, this city became part of the Kingdom of Sardinia when he was seven years old. Garibaldi made his home and was buried on the island of Caprera, off the Sardinian coast.

The Holy Roman Emperor Frederick II (1194–1250) was born in Jesi in the Marches, but his castles and legend still loom over the three poor, largely mountainous regions of **Calabria** (Reggio di Calabria), **Basilicata** (Potenza), and **Apulia** (Bari; Taranto, Brindisi). Called Frederick the Great and *Stupor Mundi*—"wonder of the world"—this Hohenstaufen King of Germany, southern Italy and

The Regions of Italy

Sicily (with a magnificent court at Palermo), and even of Jerusalem, was a cultured forerunner of the Renaissance, patron of arts and sciences, founder of the University of Naples (1224), friend of Islamic and Jewish scholars, a poet himself and a patron of the earliest Italian poets, author of a remarkable treatise on falconry, keeper of a harem in Lucera (Apulia), and inveterate enemy of the Church, which hounded him and his immediate successors to death. One of them, his son Manfred, was born in Venosa (Basilicata). From Melfi, also in this region, Frederick promulgated the *Constitutions of Melfi* (1231), often considered the finest law code in the West since the time of Charlemagne, more than four centuries earlier (see Questions 67 and 78).

Long before Frederick, these three regions had been the site of the thriving ancient Greek coastline settlements of Magna Graecia, as well as the wars of Goths, Lombards, Byzantines, Saracens, and Normans. The area had the misfortune subsequently to fall under the sway of Angevins, Spaniards, and Bourbons, who kept these domains backward to prevent any challenge to their sleepy tyrannies.

Also within the wide orbit of Magna Graecia and Frederick II was **Campania** (Naples; Salerno). Much later, it was the birthplace of Torquato Tasso (1544–95), the last great poet of the Italian Renaissance. His epic *Jerusalem Delivered,* which deals with the capture of Jerusalem under Godfrey of Bouillon in the First Crusade (see Question 78), influenced Edmund Spenser and John Milton, and his tormented life moved Goethe to write a play about him. Tasso's contemporary Giordano Bruno (1548–1600) was a philosopher, poet, and defrocked Dominican who led a wandering, anguished existence that was capped off by his being burned at the stake by the Inquisition. His defense of Copernican astronomy, denial of absolute verities, notion that opposites coalesce, and belief in an infinity of worlds clashed with received wisdom but made him a forerunner of modern philosophy and recommended him to James Joyce, who made use of Bruno's theories in *Finnegans Wake* (1939). Another Campanian philosopher, Giambattista Vico (1668–1744), author of *The New Science* (see Question 10), provided Joyce with another main structural underpinning for his epic.

Campanians have been prominent in art and music, too. Gian Lorenzo Bernini (1598–1680), the greatest sculptor and architect of the Italian Baroque, is famed for his work in St. Peter's Church in Rome (the throne of St. Peter, the swirling-columned baldachino over the high altar, and the colonnade of St. Peter's Square); his statues of *Apollo and Daphne, David,* and *The Ecstasy of St. Teresa;* and his *Fountain of the Four Rivers* in Rome's glorious Piazza Navona. He remained the chief influence on European sculpture and architecture for almost two centuries. The Neapolitan Baroque composer Domenico Scarlatti (1685–1757) left more than five hundred harpsichord sonatas and a noted *Stabat Mater.* Enrico Caruso (1873–1921), often considered the finest operatic tenor of all time, also hailed from Naples.

The small region of **Molise** (Campobasso), which was severed from Abruzzi in 1963, was the home of what might be by far the earliest Italian genius—and European human genus. *Homo aeserniensis* (c. 1,000,000–800,000 B.C.), whose remains were discovered in Isernia in 1979, is the oldest human yet found in all of Europe. The serendipitous unearthing of this oldest and most extensive European Paleolithic settlement occurred while a highway was being built. Since a fireplace was found at the site and, nearby, the bones of elephants, rhinos, hippos, bison, and bears, *Homo aeserniensis* might well be dubbed "the Italian Prometheus," who brought fire into the peninsula, as well as "the founder of Italian cuisine" (or barbecuing).

The neighboring region of **Abruzzi** was the homeland of Gabriele D'Annunzio (1863–1938), a passionate and decadent master stylist who wrote novels, plays, and reams of poems, and fought heroically in World War I (see Question 30). Another Abruzzese, Benedetto Croce (1866–1952), Italy's greatest twentieth-century philosopher, was also a noted historian and literary critic. A philosophical disciple of Hegel (see Question 5), Croce wrote penetrating works on aesthetics and on history as the story of ever-expanding human liberty. If D'Annunzio was Italy's leading proto-Fascist, Croce was the Fascist era's most influential liberal opponent, whose worldwide reputation precluded any attempts to silence him.

Latium (Rome), site of the Eternal City, has given birth to its share of saints and sinners. St. Bonaventure (1221–74), called by the Church "The Seraphic Doctor," was a general of the Franciscan order who was embroiled in lifelong theological controversies about the relation of St. Francis of Assisi's spiritual and emotional approach to belief versus that of the learned Aristotelians and Averroists of his day. As such, he had cause to be concerned about some of the Aristotelian exuberances of his fellow Latian, St. Thomas Aquinas (1225–74), "The Angelic Doctor" and Dominican scholar who penned the *Summa Theologica,* the *Summa contra Gentiles,* and a library of other works in his relatively short life. He was the greatest medieval theologian, and his meticulously elaborated philosophical system is still a repository of Roman Catholic belief.

All this meant little to Cesare Borgia (1476–1507), although he was for a time a cardinal. He and his sister Lucrezia Borgia (1480–1519) were the Roman-born illegitimate children of the notorious Pope Alexander VI. The warrior Cesare fully deserves his reputation as the ruthless and treacherous model for Machiavelli's "Prince," whereas Lucrezia has been much maligned. Her supposed poisonings and incestuous relationships were fabrications, though she was used as a beautiful marriage pawn by her father and brother. Her third marriage made her Duchess of Ferrara, where she presided over a splendid court, earning the praises of the learned Pietro Bembo and Lodovico Ariosto, and supposedly writing verse in Italian, French, Spanish, Latin, and Greek.

Music and science also receive their due in our survey of Latian notables. Giovanni Pierluigi da Palestrina (c. 1525–94) took his name from his natal village southeast of Rome. Composer of a treasure trove of liturgical music, Palestrina wrote about a hundred Masses, such as the *Mass for Pope Marcellus,* for unaccompanied voice. A master of polyphony and creator of secular works, too—including well over a hundred madrigals—Palestrina is one of the greatest Renaissance composers. Our last Latian, the physicist Enrico Fermi (1901–54), moved to the United States in 1938. He studied beta decay (see Question 28) and the neutrino, which he named; won the Nobel Prize in Physics in 1938 for his work on radioactivity; achieved in 1942 the first self-sustaining nuclear chain reaction; worked in Los Alamos on the Manhattan Project to develop the atomic bomb; helped develop the hydrogen bomb; and had an element, fermium (atomic number 100) named after him, as well as the Fermilab for nuclear research in Batavia, Illinois.

Umbria (Perugia) was the home of St. Francis of Assisi (1182?–1226), the Christ-like founder of the Franciscan order of mendicants who also wrote the earliest notable poem in Italian, "The Canticle of the Sun" (or "of the Creatures"). St. Francis was the greatest Christian exponent of reverence for all things, both animate and inanimate, which he called his brothers and sisters. Care of the sick, the poor, and the outcast was his life's mission, and he enjoined the most abject poverty on himself and his followers. Two years before his death, he was said to have received the wounds of Christ, the stigmata. A great fellow Umbrian, the Renaissance painter born near Perugia and thus known as Perugino (1446–1523), studied under Verrocchio along with Leonardo da Vinci and later became the teacher of Raphael. Perugino embellished the Sistine Chapel, where he painted his fresco of *Christ Giving the Keys to St. Peter.*

The Marches (Ancona; Urbino), rich in genius, saw the birth of Bramante (1444–1514), the High Renaissance architect whose most important work was done in Rome: the graceful, circular Tempietto; the Belvedere courtyard in the Vatican; and the original plan for the rebuilding of St. Peter's Basilica. Urbino was the birthplace of Raphael (1483–1520), who painted lovely, flesh-and-blood Madonnas; superb portraits, including those of Pope Julius II, Pope Leo X, Castiglione, and himself; and sublime frescoes in the Vatican, such as *The School of Athens* and *Parnassus.* The art historian Vasari chides Raphael for his amorousness, however, claiming "he was always indulging his sexual appetites" with his mistress, whom he painted many times. Vasari even asserts that the consummate artist's death at age thirty-seven stemmed from this propensity: "On one occasion he really overdid it, returning home afterward with a violent fever."

Even more short-lived was the consumptive Marchigiano composer Giovanni Battista Pergolesi (1710–36), creator of oratorios, instrumental music, a masterly *Stabat Mater,* and operas, including *La serva padrona (The Servant Mistress),* the earliest noteworthy opera buffa. A later student of Pergolesi's operatic technique was Gioacchino Rossini (1792–1868), composer of *The Barber of Seville, La cenerentola (Cinderella), La gazza ladra (The Thieving Magpie), Semiramide, The Siege of Corinth,* and his masterpiece, *William Tell,* as well as a curiously operatic *Stabat Mater.* Rossini's contemporary, Count Giacomo Leopardi (1798–1837), famed for his pessimistic verse and essays, in which humankind finds itself the victim of an implacably hostile universe, was one of the greatest European poets of the Romantic era.

An important Marchigiana is Maria Montessori (1870–1952), the first woman to receive an M.D. degree in Italy (1896) and founder of the "Montessori Method" of education for young children. Relying on self-motivation and self-pacing, her method emphasizes the fun-and-games aspect of learning as discovery and the crucial role of encouraging and enhancing each child's spontaneity and originality.

And now we come to **Tuscany** (Florence; Siena, Pisa, Arezzo,

Lucca), the incontestable genius capital of Italy, perhaps of the world. Here's a necessarily brief *assaggio* ("tasting or sampling, as of foods"):

+ *Fourteenth century:* The pioneering painters Duccio and Giotto; the supreme poets Dante Alighieri (see Questions 13 and 81) and Francesco Petrarca (Petrarch); the author of the *Decameron,* Giovanni Boccaccio (born in Paris to a Florentine merchant); and the great mystic, St. Catherine of Siena.

+ *Fifteenth century:* The architect who built the enormous dome of Florence's cathedral, Filippo Brunelleschi; the sculptors Lorenzo Ghiberti, Donatello, and Andrea del Verrocchio; the painters Fra Angelico, Luca della Robbia, Masaccio, Fra Filippo Lippi, Piero della Francesca, Sandro Botticelli, and Domenico Ghirlandaio; the politician, poet, and patron of the arts Lorenzo de' Medici ("the Magnificent"); and the explorer who gave his name to America, Amerigo Vespucci.

+ *Sixteenth century:* The universal geniuses Leonardo da Vinci and Michelangelo Buonarroti; the historians and political theorists Niccolò Machiavelli and Francesco Guicciardini; the New World explorer Giovanni da Verrazano; the "Faultless Painter" Andrea del Sarto; the satiric and pornographic writer, Pietro Aretino, "The Scourge of Princes"; the architect, painter, and unsurpassed biographer of artists Giorgio Vasari; and the sculptor, metalsmith, and boastful autobiographer Benvenuto Cellini.

+ *Seventeenth century:* The astronomer, mathematician, and physicist Galileo Galilei; and Jean-Baptiste Lully (Giovanni Battista Lulli), the Florence-born operatic composer for Louis XIV of France.

+ *Nineteenth and twentieth centuries:* The operatic composer Giacomo Puccini; and the painter Amedeo Modigliani.

Emilia-Romagna (Bologna; Parma, Ferrara, Ravenna, Rimini) is another region saturated with genius. The Ferrara-born Dominican, Girolamo Savonarola (1452–98), was a puritanical religious reformer whose electrifying sermons led to his becoming de facto ruler of Florence in 1494, after the Medici were exiled. Although his "Bonfire of the Vanities" consigned to the flames many paintings we would like to have today, he himself was burned at the stake in Piazza della Signoria when the Florentines (and the Pope) wearied of his stuffed-shirt jeremiads. Light-years away from the spirit of Savonarola was that of Lodovico Ariosto (1474–1533). The masterpiece of this greatest poet of the Italian Renaissance was the sprawling, romantic, comic, chivalrous, and often bawdy epic, *Orlando Furioso,* based on legends of Charlemagne and his nephew and paladin Roland (Orlando).

Two noted painters from Emilia-Romagna are Correggio (1494–1534) and Parmigianino (1503–40). Correggio's most famous mural, the daringly foreshortened, proto-Baroque *Assumption of the Virgin,* adorns the dome of the cathedral of Parma. Among his best-loved works are his captivatingly sensuous treatments of mythological subjects: the fresco *Diana Returning from the Chase, Jupiter and Antiope, Danaë, The Rape of Ganymede, Leda,* and the stunning *Jupiter and Io,* in which the god, in the form of an amorous storm cloud, embraces his recumbent and gratified lover. Parmigianino, a follower of Correggio, is famous for an early masterpiece, a self-portrait done on a convex panel from his reflection in a convex mirror. The elongated dimensions of the figures in *The Madonna of the Long Neck* are textbook definitions of the exaggerated Mannerist style. Parmigianino ended his short life as a bearded, poverty-stricken alchemist.

Emilia-Romagna also produced musical geniuses. Arcangelo Corelli (1653–1713) was a Baroque composer and violin virtuoso who eventually settled in Rome. He is famed for his sonatas and for establishing the form of the concerto grosso, thereby inspiring Vivaldi, Bach, and Handel. What can be said about Giuseppe Verdi (1813–1901)? That he was the greatest Italian operatic composer (which is saying quite a bit), that he was an ardent patriot inextricably linked with the struggle for Italian independence and unification, that he composed his most magnificent works at ages seventy-three *(Otello)* and seventy-nine *(Falstaff).* The best of Verdi's operas are the lyrical and dramatic jewels of many a repertoire around the world: *Rigoletto, Il trovatore, La traviata, I vespri siciliani, Un ballo in maschera, La forza del destino, Don Carlos, Aïda.* Verdi's *Requiem* for the novelist and patriot Alessandro Manzoni is a revered example of its genre.

When Verdi died, a quarter of a million mourners paid their respects, while another musical genius, Arturo Toscanini (1867–1957), led a chorus from the dead master's *Nabucco.* Toscanini, born in Parma, was one of the most remarkable conductors in history. At age nineteen, he was in the audience at a performance of *Aïda* in Rio de Janeiro, when the conductor resigned before the opera began. Toscanini ascended the podium and brilliantly conducted the entire opera without consulting the score. After being hired by the ensemble, he went on to conduct another eighteen operas for them, all from memory. Toscanini later became the dictatorial principal conductor and artistic director of Milan's La Scala and, after moving to the United States, conductor of New York's Metropolitan Opera and musical director of the New York Philharmonic and the NBC Symphony Orchestra, which was founded for him. He also conducted at the Bayreuth Wagner Festivals of 1930 and 1931 and at the Salzburg Festival. He led his last concert—an all-Wagner program—with the NBC Orchestra in 1954 at age eighty-seven.

Also from Emilia-Romagna were a famous scientist, dictator, and film director. Guglielmo Marconi (1874–1937), born in Bologna of an Italian father and an Irish mother, developed wireless telegraphy, the predecessor of the radio, and shared the Nobel Prize in Physics in 1909. In 1895, at age twenty-one, he transmitted long-wave signals for more than a mile. He received and transmitted the first transatlantic wireless signals between Cornwall and Newfoundland in 1901 and sent the first radio message from England to Australia in 1918. The stark, windswept remains of his dismantled seaside transmitting station in South Wellfleet, Massachusetts, is well worth getting off the main road for, the next time you're in Cape Cod.

Marconi was made a marchese (marquis) in 1929 by the government of the Romagnole Benito Mussolini (1883–1945). This inventor of fascism was not quite the stage-Italian cliché or clownish blockhead of contemporary historical thought, nor was he in the same moral league as his monstrous contemporaries, Hitler and Stalin. Known as Il Duce ("the leader"), Mussolini was fairly moderate during the early years of his rule in Italy (1922–28), but he became increasingly dictatorial after dissolving the Italian Parliament and trying to vie with Hitler, who came to power in Germany in 1933. In 1935–36, Mussolini conquered Ethiopia, defying the ineffectual League of Nations, and he sent Italian troops and armaments to assist Franco during the Spanish Civil War. He conquered and annexed Albania early in 1939, but Italy was not prepared, militarily or psychologically, to fight in World War II. In 1943, Mussolini was deposed by his Fascist Grand Council and the King, and then liberated by German paratroopers and installed as a puppet ruler in northern Italy (see Question 50). His capture and summary execution by Italian partisans ended the career of the man who had tried to revive the

Roman Empire without the requisite wealth, power, military and political leaders, and national will.

From Mussolini to Fellini, both Romagnoles, is a shorter step than may at first appear. Mussolini was a master of illusion, until disillusion caught up with him, while Federico Fellini (1920–93) was a master of both. From comic evocations of his misspent youth and feckless friends in *I Vitelloni* and *Amarcord* to the pathos of *La Strada* and *La Dolce Vita;* from the lyrical fantasia of *Juliet of the Spirits* to the escapist fantasy of *8 1/2* and the obscene fantasies of *Satyricon,* Fellini flooded the screen with unconventional characters, bizarre sets, and exteriorized inner worlds of human longings confronted by an uncooperative universe.

The tiny coastal strip of **Liguria** (Genoa; Savona) has contributed a large and varied group of luminaries. All except Julius II were born in the seaport of Genoa, capital of a vast mercantile empire in the Middle Ages. Liguria's most brilliant native was Leon Battista Alberti (1404–72), a truer "Renaissance Man" than even Leonardo da Vinci. Besides being a painter, Alberti was an outstanding architect who refurbished the Gothic church of San Francesco in Rimini (also known as the Tempio Malatestiano) into what is practically an ancient Roman temple. Other striking works include the Palazzo Rucellai and the marble facade of Santa Maria Novella in Florence, and the churches of San Sebastiano and Sant'Andrea in Mantua. He wrote an extremely influential book in this field, *The Ten Books of Architecture,* as well as seminal treatises on painting and sculpture.

Two self-portraits in bronze relief and an autobiography attest that Alberti was handsome, strong, and athletic, especially enjoying horse-taming and mountain-climbing. He hobnobbed with Popes and potentates and was a learned poet in Italian and Latin, an essayist, and a humanist. At age twenty, he wrote a comedy in Latin that fooled the professors of his time (and long afterward) into considering it a rediscovered ancient work. He also wrote and worked learnedly in the fields of mathematics, philosophy and ethics, civil and canon law, and cryptography. As if that weren't enough, he also sang well and was a noted organist. To Alberti, it all seemed to come naturally: "Men can do anything they set their minds to."

The only fields Alberti seemed to avoid were government and warfare—and here his fellow Ligurian, Pope Julius II, excelled. Born near Savona, Giuliano della Rovere (1443–1513) was elected Pontiff in 1503, after the death of the scheming Borgia, Alexander VI (and the month-long reign of Pius III). Preferring the field of battle to theological disputes, he led armies out to reconquer the Papal States from the usurpations of the Venetians and local tyrants, and he formed the Holy League coalition to expel the French armies of Louis XII from Italy. The martial occupations of Pope Julius's Rome—and the need to raise money to finance them—are graphically described at the beginning of a sonnet by Michelangelo:

> *Here they turn chalices into swords and helmets*
> *and sell the blood of Christ by the bucketful;*
> *here Cross and Thorns are exchanged for shields and lances,*
> *and even Christ himself is losing patience.*
> *But if he ever dared to show his face,*
> *they'd send his blood spurting up to the stars,*
> *since here at Rome they sell his very hide,*
> *and all the paths of righteousness are barred.*

But it is as the greatest papal patron of art that Julius's fame still shines brightly. He sat for a majestic portrait by Raphael and set that graceful painter to adorn various rooms of the Vatican with some of the most renowned personages of classical, Jewish, and Christian history and fable. He alternately cajoled and bullied Michelangelo into painting the Sistine Chapel and working on his tomb, which resulted in the *Moses,* carved after the Pope's death. Julius chose Bramante's design for the new St. Peter's Basilica and laid the foundation stone on April 11, 1506 (though the huge church was completed, after many changes of design, only in 1626).

Genoa has given birth to scores of famous navigators, most notably the renowned hero and villain Christopher Columbus (1451–1506). Giovanni Caboto (aka John Cabot; c. 1450–c. 1499), probably born in Genoa, sailed for the English in the time of Henry VII. He set foot in North America on June 24, 1497, either on the Labrador coast of Newfoundland or on Cape Breton Island. Cabot dutifully claimed the land for the English King, convinced he had landed in the country of the Great Khan in northeast Asia. On his second voyage the next year, this time in quest of Cipangu (Japan), Cabot explored the eastern coast of Greenland and may have then turned west and cruised along the North American coast from Baffin Island down to Chesapeake Bay—or the expedition may have perished. England's later claims in the New World were founded on Cabot's discoveries.

The Genoese composer and virtuoso Niccolò Paganini (1782–1840) was thought by some to have traded his soul to the devil for the pyrotechnics of his violin playing. A child prodigy, he later toured Europe, mesmerizing audiences with his diabolic appearance and striking musical effects, some of which he achieved by devices such as abnormal tuning (scordatura). Paganini is especially noted for his six violin concertos and twenty-four caprices for solo violin.

Only a bit more low-key was Paganini's younger contemporary Giuseppe Mazzini (1805–72), the Genoese patriot and revolutionary who fought for Italian unification. Mazzini lived most of his life in exile in Switzerland, France, and England, returning to Italy only to sponsor various abortive uprisings in Rome, Milan, and the south. Starting at age sixteen, he always dressed in black, claiming to be in mourning for his beloved Italia, and he wrote incessant propaganda to further the cause he regarded as sacred, God-appointed, mystical. Representing the radical wing of the Risorgimento, Mazzini, an anti-clerical republican, was deeply disillusioned by the finally united Italy's decision to establish a monarchy.

Piedmont (Turin) scores big with Count Camillo Benso di Cavour (1810–61), the canny premier of the kingdom of Piedmont-Sardinia who made his sovereign, Victor Emmanuel II of the ancient house of Savoy, the first King of a united Italy in February 1861. If Mazzini was the soul and Garibaldi the muscle of the Risorgimento, Cavour was the brains. He liberalized and modernized the government of Piedmont-Sardinia and then cynically involved his tiny country in the Crimean War against Russia (see Question 46) just to gain a hearing for Italian-independence issues at the peace conference to follow.

Aside from Bismarck, no other contemporary European statesman was Cavour's equal in the realpolitik of ends justifying means. He conspired with Napoleon III to eject the Austrians from Lombardy in return for ceding Nice and Savoy to France. This Italian nucleus of Piedmont-Sardinia and Lombardy soon attracted to itself the states of Tuscany, Modena, Parma, Bologna, and Romagna, which all voted for union in 1860. Using Garibaldi for all he was worth, Cavour and his King reaped the fruits of that indefatigable general's liberation of Sicily and southern Italy from the Bourbons. The Kingdom of Italy was duly proclaimed and, after Cavour's early death, the Veneto was recovered from the Austrians in 1866 and Rome seized from Pope Pius IX in 1870.

The miniature region of **Valle d'Aosta** (Aosta), set in the shadow of Mont Blanc and the Matterhorn among Alpine passes into France and Switzerland, was the birthplace of St. Anselm (1033–1109), the great theologian who, much against his will, was made Archbishop of Canterbury in 1093. He is vaguely remembered today for his "ontological proof" for the existence of God, elaborated in his *Proslogion*. The argument begins with the assumption that God is the being than whom nothing greater can be conceived. If that is accepted, then the conclusion that he exists must follow, too. The reason? If that being did not exist, except in our minds, then we *can* imagine a greater being—one who exists in actuality. This sophistical and circular argument never really convinced anyone, but its sheer paradoxicality made it a favorite late-night chestnut for university students from Anselm's time until the death of learning in about 1972.

The historic region of **Lombardy** (Milan; Cremona, Mantua, Pavia) has contributed a fairly variegated group of notables. Count Baldassare Castiglione (1478–1529) is famed for his treatise on the comportment and accomplishments of the ideal gentleman, *Il libro del cortegiano (The Book of the Courtier)*. This work, published in 1528, was loosely based on actual discussions of the courtier's education, bearing, social graces, martial exercises, witty discourse, and duties to his prince, as well as of Platonic love and the ideal court lady. Castiglione gained his experience in these matters at the hypercivilized court of Urbino, and his book set the standard of polite behavior for aristocratic Europe in the Renaissance and afterward. Translated into English as early as 1561, it established the pattern for phenomena like Sir Philip Sidney and countless lesser luminaries of gentlemanly sophistication.

The masterpiece of a much later Lombard author, the Milanese Alessandro Manzoni (1785–1873), is traditionally considered "the great Italian novel." *I promessi sposi (The Betrothed)* is an epic tale of love and intrigue set in seventeenth-century Milan during the Thirty Years' War. Its main plot describes the struggle of two peasants, Renzo and Lucia, to marry despite the enmity of Don Rodrigo.

The foremost painter of Lombardy was Caravaggio (1573–1610), a bohemian hothead who once stabbed a friend to death in a brawl. His paintings were marked by a naturalism that was unusual in his day and by a dramatic use of light and dark areas (chiaroscuro), as in *The Calling of St. Matthew,* that influenced artists such as Rembrandt. An eminent Lombard from the musical world was Claudio Monteverdi

(1567–1643), the first great operatic composer whose works in this genre began with *Orfeo* in 1607 and culminated in his masterpiece at age seventy-five, *The Coronation of Poppaea,* in 1642 (see Question 23). He also wrote three Masses and nine collections of madrigals. Another beloved operatic composer from Lombardy was Caetano Donizetti (1797–1848) whose corpus of sixty-seven operas includes a core of repertoire staples: the opera buffa *L'elisir d'amore, Lucrezia Borgia,* the tragic *Lucia di Lammermoor,* the comic opera *The Daughter of the Regiment,* and the opera buffa *Don Pasquale,* sometimes considered his finest work.

An influential physicist and a superb actress round out our Lombard survey. Alessandro Volta (1745–1827) invented the electric battery in 1800 and was made a count by Napoleon after he demonstrated how it generated an electric current. The volt was named after Count Alessandro in 1881. Eleonora Duse (1858–1924), greatest of Italian actresses, was born while her family was on an acting tour in Lombardy. At fourteen, she played Juliet in Verona. The only serious contemporary rival of Sarah Bernhardt, Duse was famed for her complex portrayals of Émile Zola's Thérèse Raquin, La Dame aux Camélias of Dumas *fils,* Santuzza in Verga's *Cavalleria rusticana (Rustic Chivalry),* Hedda Gabler, Ellida in Ibsen's *The Lady from the Sea,* Nora in his *A Doll's House,* and Gabriele D'Annunzio's Francesca da Rimini. Duse had an affair with D'Annunzio, who felt obliged to describe it in his novel *Il fuoco (The Flame of Life).* Most of his plays were written for her, and he dedicated one of them to "Eleonora Duse of the beautiful hands."

Probably the greatest genius to emerge from the Alpine, semi-German region of **Trentino–Alto Adige** (Trent and Bolzano, co-capitals) was that of the Catholic Church, whose leading prelates and theologians met in three sessions between 1545 and 1563 in an ecumenical council held at Trent. Still reeling from the Protestant challenge to its unity, integrity, and dogma, the Church set about reforming itself and charting a new course for a new era. Convoked by Pope Paul III, the Council of Trent precisely defined Catholic belief regarding the sacraments (see Question 59), the need to interpret Scripture within the context of Church tradition, and the duties of the lower clergy and bishops. The decrees of the council were confirmed by Pope Pius IV in 1564, paving the way two years later for the promulgation of the *Tridentine Catechism* (Tridentum being the Latin name for Trent).

The Catholic Counter-Reformation inaugurated by the council is often criticized (along with stultifying foreign political domination) as the main stumbling block to Italian creative and intellectual energies during the seventeenth and eighteenth centuries—recall the Church opposition Galileo had to face. Be that as it may, the cohesiveness and internal reforms fostered by the council helped prevent the Church from fragmenting. The council's decisions remained the chief arbiters of Roman Catholic belief and liturgical practice until the Second Vatican Council (1962–65).

Friuli-Venezia Giulia (Trieste), at the northeastern border of Italy with Austria and Slovenia, claims a major writer as a son, Italo Svevo (1861–1928), but he was born in Trieste when it was actually still part of the Austrian Empire. An Italian Jew of Hungarian descent whose real name was Ettore Schmitz, Svevo created, in the novels *A Life, As a Man Grows Older,* and especially *The Confessions of Zeno,* modern Italian classics of profound psychological insight that depict various losing battles with external realities.

Some of the world's foremost painters and other visual artists were born in our last region, the **Veneto** (Venice; Padua, Verona). In the fifteenth and sixteenth centuries, their ranks included Giovanni Bellini, Andrea Mantegna, Giorgione, Titian, the architect Andrea Palladio, Tintoretto, and Paolo Veronese. Outstanding in the eighteenth century were Giovanni Battista Tiepolo, Canaletto, and the engraver Giovanni Battista Piranesi.

The Veneto was also the birthplace of the famed early traveler to the Orient and author of his *Travels,* Marco Polo (1254–1324), and the greatest Italian Baroque composer, Antonio Vivaldi (c. 1675–1741), known for his half a thousand concertos, especially his ubiquitous *The Four Seasons.* Last, and perhaps least in this august company, is the Venetian memoirist, gambler, spy, and incomparable sexual athlete, Giacomo Casanova (1725–98), who wrote that his chief business in life was "to cultivate the pleasures of the senses." How strange that the great lover spent his last fourteen years as the librarian in a Bohemian castle.

24

What are the 24 letters of the ancient Greek alphabet?

Alpha	Nu
Beta	Xi
Gamma	Omicron
Delta	Pi
Epsilon	Rho
Zeta	Sigma
Eta	Tau
Theta	Upsilon
Iota	Phi
Kappa	Chi
Lambda	Psi
Mu	Omega

Although the Greeks were by no means the first people to develop writing, they were the earliest to devise a true alphabet, from which all other ancient and modern European ones are directly or indirectly derived. Named for the first two Greek letters, the alphabet was in use in the Greek world by 800 B.C., though it comprised only twenty-one letters at the time. It was adapted from the writing system of the Phoenicians, a Semitic people from the area of modern-day Lebanon who had extensive seafaring, mercantile, and colonial interests throughout the ancient Mediterranean. This is why in Greek myth Cadmus, who brought the alphabet to Greece, was said to be a native of Phoenicia. The Phoenician writing system was similar to those of other Semites living in Syria and Palestine, including the Hebrews. To the Hebrew and Greek alphabets we owe the preservation of the twin underpinnings of Western civilization—the Jewish and Christian religions and the unsurpassed literary, philosophical, and scientific culture of the Greeks. The New Testament, originally composed in

Greek, transmitted the Christian legacy via the language of the Hellenes.

The alphabet was the culmination of varied efforts since prehistoric times to represent ideas or events in a permanent, visual form. Early attempts to make records of fleeting thoughts, primitive reckonings, or awe in the face of nature resulted in notches on sticks, geometric symbols, and paintings on cave walls. From pictographs—pictures of things themselves—some peoples developed writing systems that allowed a comprehensive registering of ideas via stylized pictures. These eventually became complex symbols, as in Egyptian hieroglyphics ("sacred carvings") and Chinese ideograms.

A further improvement in efficiency was attained by syllabic writing systems, or syllabaries, which used written symbols to represent specific syllables instead of whole words. The economy consists in needing fewer graphic symbols in the overall system (though not in the words themselves). For example, the syllable we pronounce "floo" might be conveyed by one character in a syllabary, thus allowing the first syllable in *fluent, fluid,* and *floozy* to be represented uniformly instead of requiring three separate ideograms for the words. Syllabaries may be seen as intermediate stages between ideographic systems and true alphabets. The Phoenician, ancient Hebrew, and other related Semitic scripts, as well as the Sanskrit graphic system, had features of syllabaries. Moreover, the Semitic systems did not have separate characters for representing their vowels.

An ancient writing system developed by the Greeks was Linear B, a syllabary of about ninety characters originating in the fifteenth century B.C. but deciphered only in 1952 by Michael Ventris and John Chadwick. Linear B was used by the advanced Mycenaean civilization of Crete and the mainland. After the invading Dorians destroyed this culture in the twelfth century B.C., Greece was plunged into its Dark Age. During this period of almost four hundred years, Linear B was forgotten, and illiteracy apparently engulfed the Greek world.

But by about 800 B.C., the Greeks had adapted Phoenician and other Semitic letters for their own use. Like the Semitic languages, early Greek was often written from right to left until the sixth-century B.C. ascendancy of the boustrophedon style—"as the ox turns" (in plowing furrows)—in which alternate lines were written right to left and left to right. After about 500 B.C., left–right writing became the norm. From their original capital letters, ideal for monu-

Evolution of the Greek Alphabet

Phoenician (1100 B.C.)*	Modern Hebrew*	Hebrew Name	Classical Greek	Greek Name	Modern Roman**
✗	א	Aleph (Ox)	A α	Alpha	A
9	ב	Beth (House)	B β	Beta	B
٦	ג	Gimel (Camel)	Γ γ	Gamma	C/G
◁	ד	Daleth (Door)	Δ δ	Delta	D
⅄	ה	He (?)	E ε	Epsilon	E
Ɪ	ז	Zayin (Balance?)	Z ζ	Zeta	Z
日	ח	Heth (Fence)	H η	Eta	H
⊗	ט	Teth (Ball of Yarn?)	Θ θ	Theta	TH sound
Z	י	Yod (Hand)	I ι	Iota	I/J
Ψ	כ	Kaph (Palm of Hand)	K κ	Kappa	K
ι	ל	Lamed (Staff)	Λ λ	Lambda	L
ϡ	מ	Mem (Water)	M μ	Mu	M
ч	נ	Nun (Fish)	N ν	Nu	N
‡	ס	Samekh (Support?)	Ξ ξ	Xi	X sound
O	ע	Ayin (Eye)	O o	Omicron	O
ʔ	פ	Pe (Mouth)	Π π	Pi	P
◁	ר	Resh (Head)	P ρ	Rho	R
W	שׁ	Shin (Tooth)	Σ σ,ς	Sigma	S
+	ת	Taw (Mark)	T τ	Tau	T
Ⴤ	ו	Waw (Nail)	Y υ	Upsilon	U/V/W/Y
			Φ φ	Phi	PH sound
			X χ	Chi	X
			Ψ ψ	Psi	PS sound
			Ω ω	Omega	Long O sound

*Letters that did not influence Greek letters have been omitted. The order has also been modified.

**Each Roman letter is matched with a Greek letter whose *shape* influenced its development. In the absence of such a correspondence, the approximate *sound* of the Greek letter is indicated.

ments or inscriptions, the Greeks later developed a script of lowercase letters that were easier to write by hand.

The Greek alphabet had two main, quite similar branches—the eastern or Ionic branch and the western or Chalcidian branch. In 403 B.C., the Ionic form was officially adopted by Athens and thus became what we know as the classical Greek alphabet. In contrast, it was probably the Chalcidian branch that gave rise to the Etruscan alphabet (c. eighth century B.C.). The Latin or Roman alphabet, which we use today, was derived from the Etruscan.

When the Greeks first began adapting Semitic letters, they broke down the syllables of their spoken language into single, distinct sounds (phonemes) and assigned a character to each. In the process, they often reversed the orientation of Phoenician letters to make them more symmetric (see illustration). Because Semitic languages had sounds that Greek did not have, the thrifty Greeks appropriated some superfluous Semitic consonants to represent vowel sounds. Thus, the Semitic letters *aleph, he, yod, ayin,* and *waw* gradually became the Greek vowels alpha, epsilon, iota, omicron, and upsilon, which correspond to our five vowels. This marked a crucial innovation in the precision with which the sounds of words could be transcribed.

Although alphabetic letters represent sounds, most letters in the Greek alphabet had their ultimate origin in Hebrew and Phoenician pictographs. The first letter, **alpha,** took its name from *aleph,* "ox." The second, **beta,** was derived from *beth* ("house"). **Gamma,** with its hard *g* sound, corresponds to *gimel* ("camel") and ultimately gave rise to two of our letters, C and G. The Greek **delta** is from Semitic *daleth* ("door"). The Greeks made this letter triangular, and the Etruscans gave it the curved shape we recognize as a D.

Epsilon started life as the Phoenician letter *he,* which had an *h* sound. The Greeks reversed its orientation and used it for their short *e* sound *(epsilon* meaning "simple *e").* Their separate letter for the sound of long *e,* which they called **eta** and wrote like our capital *H,* was taken from the Semitic letter *heth,* which meant—and looked like—a fence. The Greek vowel **iota,** adapted from the Semitic letter *yod* ("hand"), has passed directly to us as our *I* (and its later development, *J).* Two English words for a tiny amount—*iota* and *jot*—come from this diminutive Greek letter.

In Phoenician times, the letter *kaph* ("palm of the hand") represented a *k* sound and provided Greek with its **kappa. Lambda,** which the Greeks used for their *l* sound, was adapted from the Semitic letter called *lamed* ("staff"). **Mu** and **nu,** with their *m* and *n* sounds, respectively, had long tails in the Phoenician alphabet. Mu was derived from *mem* ("water") and nu from *nun* ("fish"). Water and fish—this may account for the visual similarities and alphabetic contiguity of these two letters.

Omicron, meaning "little *o"* in Greek, stood for a short *o* sound in that language. The letter's round shape was already present in Phoenician, in which its name *ayin* meant "eye," but it had a consonantal rather than a vocalic sound. **Pi,** which gave rise to our *p* sound, was taken from Semitic *pe* ("mouth"). The Greek letter **rho,** written like our capital *P* but pronounced like *r,* came from the Semitic letter *resh* ("head"). After the Romans added the leg to differentiate it from *P,* it became our letter *R.* **Sigma,** of course, is the modern *S,* and **tau** is *T.* These letters were derived from the Semitic consonants *shin* ("tooth") and *taw* ("mark").

A few letters the Greeks lifted from the Phoenicians came to Latin-based alphabets by a circuitous route—or didn't make it at all. *Zayin* represented the *z* sound in Semitic writing systems, and the Greeks named it **zeta.** The Romans stuck the *z* at the very end of their alphabet since it was apparently the last letter they borrowed from Greek, and they used it exclusively to spell Greek loanwords. **Theta** has no corresponding letter in the Latin alphabet. When the Romans needed this sound for Greek loanwords, they used the combination *th.* **Xi,** pronounced like our *x,* was represented in the Etruscan alphabet but not in the Latin.

A few letters dropped out of the Greek alphabet fairly early. The most noted of these is the digamma, which was written roughly like our *F* but had a *w* sound. Its importance for correctly reading Homeric and other early Greek verse was first discovered by the great English classical scholar Richard Bentley (1662–1742). From apparent irregularities in many of Homer's dactylic hexameter lines, Bentley realized that some words beginning with vowels in our Greek texts of Homer, as edited by the Athenians in classical times, must originally have begun with a digamma in Homer's day, hundreds of years earlier. Thus, the classical Athenian word for wine, *oinos,* must once have been pronounced "woinos." The Athenians had just edited out a letter—and a sound—they no longer used.

The tail end of the ancient Greek alphabet remains to be mentioned. **Upsilon,** pronounced like French *u* or German *ü* and meaning "simple *u* sound" to distinguish it from the diphthong *ou,* was already discussed as a vowel derived from Semitic *waw*. Though written like our capital *Y*, upsilon gave form to our capital *V*, which, through various permutations, became our letters *U, W,* and *Y*. Phi, chi, psi, and omega were all purely Greek inventions. Neither **phi** nor **psi** has an equivalent letter in Latin-based alphabets. The Greeks pronounced the first like the *ph* sound in *uphill* (an aspirated *p)* rather than as the two *f* sounds in our word *philosophy*. Psi was pronounced like the *ps* sounds in *collapsed synapses*. **Chi,** which the Greeks pronounced like an aspirated *k (kh),* became our *X*. The Romans, instead of using their own letter *X*, which already had an *x* sound in native words like *pax* ("peace"), spelled Greek loanwords like *XPISTOS* (pronounced *christos)* with *ch*. Hence our spelling of *Christ*—and our abbreviation Xmas for Christmas.

The twenty-fourth and last letter of the Greek alphabet, **omega,** means "big *o,*" which was differentiated from the short *o*, omicron. In the book of Revelation (1:8), Christ says, "I am the Alpha and the Omega." In this usage, omega has come to designate the last in a series, or just

THE END.

Ω

SUGGESTED READING

The authors recommend these materials for further exploration of the topics covered in the 101 questions and essays.

The Ancient World

Aeschylus. *Aeschylus I. Oresteia: Agamemnon, the Libation Bearers, the Eumenides.* Translated by Richmond Lattimore. Chicago: University of Chicago Press, 1983.

——. *Aeschylus II. Four Tragedies: Prometheus Bound, Seven Against Thebes, the Persians, the Suppliant Maidens.* 2nd ed. Chicago: University of Chicago Press, 1992.

Archilochus, Sappho, Alkman: Three Lyric Poets of the Seventh Century B.C. Translated by Guy Davenport. Berkeley: University of California Press, 1984.

Aristotle. *The Politics.* Translated by T. A. Sinclair. New York: Viking Press, 1992.

——. *The Rhetoric and the Poetics.* Translated by W. Rhys Roberts and Ingram Bywater. New York: Modern Library, 1954.

Arrian. *The Campaigns of Alexander.* Translated by Aubrey de Sélincourt. Revised by J. R. Hamilton. New York: Viking Penguin, 1987.

Bulfinch, Thomas. *Bulfinch's Mythology: The Age of Fable.* Edited by Norma L. Goodrich. New York: New American Library/Dutton, 1995.

Caesar, Gaius Julius. *The Civil War.* Translated by Jane F. Gardner. New York: Viking Penguin, 1976.

——. *The Gallic War.* Translated by Carolyn Hammond. New York: Oxford University Press, 1996.

Catullus. *The Poems of Catullus.* Translated by Guy Lee. New York: Oxford University Press, 1991.

The Chinese Classics: The Confucian Analects, the Great Learning, the

Doctrine of the Mean, the Works of Mencius. Translated by James Legge. Pasadena, Calif.: Oriental Book Store, 1983.

Clayton, Peter A., and Martin J. Price, eds. *The Seven Wonders of the Ancient World.* New York: Dorset Press, 1988.

The Confucian Odes: The Classic Anthology Defined by Confucius. Translated by Ezra Pound. New York: New Directions, 1954.

Confucius. *The Great Digest, the Unwobbling Pivot, the Analects.* Translated by Ezra Pound. New York: W. W. Norton and Company, 1969.

Diogenes Laertius. *Lives of the Philosophers.* Edited and translated by A. Robert Caponigri. Chicago: Henry Regnery Company, 1969.

The Egyptian Book of the Dead. Translated by E. A. Wallis Budge. New York: Dover Publications, 1967.

The Epic of Gilgamesh. Translated by N. K. Sandars. New York: Penguin USA, 1987.

Euripides. *Euripides I: Alcestis, the Medea, the Heracleidae, Hippolytus.* Chicago: University of Chicago Press, 1983.

———. *Euripides V: Electra, the Phoenician Women, the Bacchae.* Chicago: University of Chicago Press, 1969.

Graves, Robert. *The Greek Myths.* 2 vols. New York: Viking Penguin, 1990.

The Greek Anthology and Other Ancient Epigrams: A Selection in Modern Verse Translations. Edited by Peter Jay. New York: Penguin USA, 1982.

Greek Lyrics. Translated by Richmond Lattimore. 2nd ed. Chicago: University of Chicago Press, 1960.

Hadas, Moses. *A History of Greek Literature.* New York: Columbia University Press, 1950.

———. *A History of Latin Literature.* New York: Columbia University Press, 1952.

Hamilton, Edith. *Mythology.* New York: New American Library, 1991.

Herodotus. *The Histories.* Translated by Aubrey de Sélincourt. New York: Penguin USA, 1996.

Hesiod and Theognis. *Theogony, Works and Days, and [Theognis'] Elegies.* Translated by Dorothea Wender. New York: Viking Press, 1976.

Homer. *The Iliad.* Translated by Robert Fagles. New York: Penguin USA, 1991.

———. *The Iliad.* Translated by Richmond Lattimore. Chicago: University of Chicago Press, 1951.

———. *The Odyssey.* Translated by Robert Fitzgerald. New York: Doubleday Anchor, 1975.

———. *The Odyssey of Homer.* Translated by Richmond Lattimore. New York: Harper & Row, 1965.

The Homeric Hymns. Translated by Charles Boer. Woodstock, Conn.: Spring Publications, 1979.

Horace. *The Complete Odes and Epodes with the Centennial Hymn.* Translated by W. G. Shepherd. New York: Penguin USA, 1983.

I Ching: The Book of Changes. Translated by James Legge. New York: Random House, 1996.

Jaeger, Werner. *Paideia: The Ideals of Greek Culture. I: Archaic Greece—The Mind of Athens.* 2nd ed. Translated by Gilbert Highet. New York: Oxford University Press, 1986.

Kramer, Samuel Noah, ed. *Mythologies of the Ancient World.* New York: Doubleday Anchor, 1961.

Kyle, Donald G. "Winning at Olympia." *Archaeology.* 49 (July/August 1996): 26–37.

The Mahabharata. Abridged and translated by William Buck. New York: New American Library, 1979.

Mencius. *The Works of Mencius.* Translated by James Legge. New York: Dover Publications, 1990.

Ovid. *Heroides.* Translated by Harold Isbell. New York: Penguin USA, 1990.

———. *The Metamorphoses.* Translated by Horace Gregory. New York: New American Library, 1960.

———. *Metamorphoses.* Translated by Rolfe Humphries. Bloomington, Ind.: Indiana University Press, 1955.

Pindar. *The Odes of Pindar.* Translated by C. M. Bowra. New York: Viking Press, 1982.

———. *The Odes of Pindar.* Translated by Richmond Lattimore. Chicago: University of Chicago Press, 1947.

Plato. *The Collected Dialogues of Plato Including the Letters.* Edited by Edith Hamilton and Huntington Cairns. Princeton: Princeton University Press, 1963.

———. *The Republic of Plato.* Translated by Allan Bloom. 2nd ed. New York: Basic Books, 1991.

Plutarch. *The Lives of the Noble Grecians and Romans.* 2 vols. Translated by John Dryden. Revised by Arthur Hugh Clough. New York: Modern Library, 1992.

The Ramayana. Abridged and translated by William Buck. Berkeley: University of California Press, 1981.

Sappho. *Sappho: A New Translation.* Translated by Mary Barnard. Berkeley: University of California Press, 1988.

Syme, Ronald. *The Roman Revolution.* New York: Oxford University Press, 1960.

Thucydides. *History of the Peloponnesian War.* Translated by Rex Warner. New York: Penguin USA, 1986.

Virgil. *The Aeneid.* Translated by Robert Fitzgerald. New York: Vintage Books, 1990.

Wheelwright, Philip, ed. *The Presocratics.* New York: Odyssey Press, 1966.

Web site:
The Perseus Project (Classics Department, Tufts University)
http://www.perseus.tufts.edu/

Art/Architecture

Alberti, Leon Battista. *The Ten Books of Architecture.* New York: Dover Publications, 1987.

Cellini, Benvenuto. *The Autobiography of Benvenuto Cellini.* Translated by George Bull. New York: Viking Press, 1956.

Clark, Kenneth. *The Nude: A Study in Ideal Form.* Princeton: Princeton University Press, 1972.

Gardner, Helen, Fred S. Kleiner, Mariann Lee (ed.), and Richard G. Tansey. *Gardner's Art Through the Ages.* 10th ed. New York: Harcourt Brace, 1996.

Henri, Robert. *The Art Spirit.* New York: HarperCollins, 1984.

Janson, H. W., and Anthony F. Janson. *History of Art.* 5th rev. ed. New York: Harry N. Abrams, 1997.

Levey, Michael. *Florence: A Portrait.* Cambridge, Mass.: Harvard University Press, 1996.

Palladio, Andrea. *Four Books of Architecture.* New York: Dover Publications, 1976.

Perlman, Bennard B. *Painters of the Ashcan School: The Immortal Eight.* New York: Dover Publications, 1988.

Piranesi, Giovanni Battista. *The Prisons (Le Carceri)*. New York: Dover Publications, 1974.

Richter, Gisela M. A. *A Handbook of Greek Art*. 9th ed. New York: Da Capo Press, 1987.

Sloan, John, and Robert Henri. *Revolutionaries of Realism: The Letters of John Sloan and Robert Henri*. Edited by Bennard B. Perlman. Princeton: Princeton University Press, 1997.

Vasari, Giorgio. *Lives of the Artists*. 2 vols. Translated by George Bull. New York: Viking Press, 1988.

Vitruvius. *Ten Books on Architecture*. Translated by Morris H. Morgan. New York: Dover Publications, 1960.

History (Postclassical)

Allen, Thomas B. "Remember the *Maine*?" *National Geographic*. 193 (February 1998): 92–111.

Ambrose, Stephen E., and C. L. Sulzberger. *American Heritage New History of World War II*. New York: Viking Press, 1997.

Barzini, Luigi. *The Italians*. New York: Atheneum, 1996.

Boorstin, Daniel J. *The Discoverers: A History of Man's Search to Know His World and Himself*. New York: Random House, 1985.

Brogan, Hugh. *The Penguin History of the United States of America*. New York: Viking Press, 1991.

Creasy, Edward Shepherd. *Fifteen Decisive Battles of the World: From Marathon to Waterloo*. New York: Da Capo Press, 1994.

Daniloff, Ruth. "Waiting for the Oil Boom [in Azerbaijan]." *Smithsonian*. 28 (January 1998): 24–35.

Davidson, Basil. *Africa in History: Themes and Outlines*. New York: Scribner, 1995.

Einhard and Notker the Stammerer. *Two Lives of Charlemagne*. New York: Viking Press, 1969.

Fraser, Antonia. *The Wives of Henry VIII*. New York: Vintage Books, 1994.

Froissart, Jean. *Chronicles*. Translated by Geoffrey Brereton. New York: Viking Press, 1978.

Geoffrey of Monmouth. *History of the Kings of Britain*. Translated by Lewis Thorpe. New York: Penguin USA, 1981.

Gilbert, Martin. *The First World War: A Complete History*. New York: Henry Holt and Company, 1996.

————. *The Second World War: A Complete History*. New York: Henry Holt and Company, 1989.

Haskins, Charles Homer. *The Renaissance of the Twelfth Century*. Cambridge, Mass.: Harvard University Press, 1979.

Johnson, Paul. *Modern Times: The World from the Twenties to the Nineties*. Rev. ed. New York: HarperPerennial, 1992.

Joinville, Jean de, and Geoffrey de Villehardouin. *Chronicles of the Crusades*. Translated by M. R. B. Shaw. New York: Viking Press, 1963.

Leckie, Robert. *Okinawa: The Last Battle of World War II*. New York: Penguin USA, 1996.

Mailer, Norman. *Oswald's Tale: An American Mystery*. New York: Ballantine Books, 1996.

Massie, Robert K. *Peter the Great: His Life and World*. New York: Ballantine Books, 1996.

Mitchell, Joseph B. *Twenty Decisive Battles of the World*. New York: Macmillan, 1964.

Morison, Samuel Eliot. *The Oxford History of the American People: Prehistory to 1789*. New York: Penguin USA, 1994.

————. *The Oxford History of the American People: 1789 Through Reconstruction*. New York: Penguin USA, 1994.

————. *The Oxford History of the American People: 1869 Through the Death of John F. Kennedy, 1963*. New York: Penguin USA, 1994.

Palmer, R. R., and Joel Colton. *A History of the Modern World*. 8th ed. New York: McGraw Hill, 1994.

Polo, Marco. *The Travels*. Translated by Ronald Latham. New York: Viking Press, 1982.

Schama, Simon. *Citizens: A Chronicle of the French Revolution*. New York: Random House, 1990.

Shirer, William L. *The Rise and Fall of the Third Reich: A History of Nazi Germany*. New York: Simon & Schuster, 1990.

Smith, Denis Mack. *Modern Italy: A Political History*. Ann Arbor: University of Michigan Press, 1998.

Weir, Alison. *The Six Wives of Henry VIII*. New York: Ballantine Books, 1993.

Language/Linguistics

Baugh, Albert C., and Thomas Cable. *A History of the English Language*. 4th ed. Paramus, N.J.: Prentice Hall, 1993.

Gamkrelidze, Thomas V., and V. V. Ivanov. "The Early History of Indo-European Languages." *Scientific American*. 264 (March 1990): 110–16.

McCrum, Robert, William Cran, and Robert MacNeil. *The Story of English*. Rev. ed. New York: Penguin USA, 1993.

Literature (Postclassical)

Ackroyd, Peter. *T. S. Eliot: A Life*. New York: Simon & Schuster, 1984.

Aretino, Pietro. *Aretino's Dialogues*. Translated by Raymond Rosenthal. Nyack, N.Y.: Marsilio Publications, 1995.

Beckett, Samuel. *Waiting for Godot*. New York: Grove Press, 1987.

Blasco Ibáñez, Vicente. *The Four Horsemen of the Apocalypse*. New York: Carroll and Graf, 1983.

Bradley, A. C. *Shakespearean Tragedy*. 3rd ed. New York: St. Martin's Press, 1992.

Brontë, Anne. *Agnes Grey*. Edited by Angeline Goreau. New York: Penguin USA, 1989.

———. *The Tenant of Wildfell Hall*. Edited by Stevie Davies. New York: Penguin USA, 1996.

Brontë, Charlotte. *Jane Eyre*. Edited by Michael Mason. New York: Penguin USA, 1996.

———. *The Professor*. Edited by Heather Glen. New York: Penguin USA, 1989.

———. *Shirley*. New York: Viking Press, 1974.

———. *Villette*. Edited by Jerome Beaty. New York: New American Library, 1990.

Brontë, Emily. *Wuthering Heights*. Edited by Pauline Nestor. New York: Penguin USA, 1996.

Burgess, Anthony. *ReJoyce*. New York: W. W. Norton and Company, 1968.

Castiglione, Baldesar. *The Book of the Courtier*. Translated by Charles S. Singleton. New York: Anchor Books, 1959.

Chaucer, Geoffrey. *The Canterbury Tales*. Abridged and translated into modern English by Nevill Coghill. New York: Penguin USA, 1989.

Chrétien de Troyes. *Arthurian Romances*. Translated by William W. Kibler. New York: Penguin USA, 1991.

Dante. *The Divine Comedy of Dante Alighieri: 1. Inferno*. Translated by John D. Sinclair. New York: Oxford University Press, 1983.

———. *The Divine Comedy of Dante Alighieri: 2. Purgatorio*. Translated by John D. Sinclair. New York: Oxford University Press, 1961.

———. *The Divine Comedy of Dante Alighieri: 3. Paradiso*. Translated by John D. Sinclair. New York: Oxford University Press, 1971.

Dostoyevsky, Fyodor. *The Brothers Karamazov*. Translated by David McDuff. New York: Viking Penguin, 1993.

Dumas, Alexandre. *The Three Musketeers*. New York: New American Library/Dutton, 1993.

Eliot, T. S. *Four Quartets*. New York: Harcourt Brace, 1974.

Ellmann, Richard. *James Joyce*. New York: Oxford University Press, 1959.

———. *Ulysses on the Liffey*. New York: Oxford University Press, 1973.

Fraser, Rebecca. *The Brontës: Charlotte Brontë and Her Family*. New York: Fawcett Books, 1990.

Gardiner, Juliet. *The Brontës at Haworth: The World Within*. New York: Clarkson Potter, 1992.

Gaskell, Elizabeth. *The Life of Charlotte Brontë*. Edited by Elisabeth Jay. New York: Penguin USA, 1998.

Gibbons, Stella. *Cold Comfort Farm*. New York: Penguin USA, 1996.

Gilbert, Stuart. *James Joyce's Ulysses*. New York: Vintage Books, 1958.

Gottfried von Strassburg. *Tristan*. Translated by A. T. Hatto. New York: Penguin USA, 1967.

Joyce, James. *Dubliners*. New York: Modern Library, 1993.

———. *Finnegans Wake*. New York: Penguin USA, 1982.

———. *A Portrait of the Artist as a Young Man: Text, Criticism, and Notes*. Edited by Chester G. Anderson. New York: Viking Press, 1977.

———. *Ulysses: The Corrected Text*. New York: Random House, 1986.

Kazantzakis, Nikos. *The Last Temptation of Christ*. New York: Touchstone Books, 1998.

Lampedusa, Giuseppe Tomasi di. *The Leopard*. Translated by Archibald Colquhoun. New York: Pantheon Books, 1991.

Mailer, Norman. *The Gospel According to the Son*. New York: Ballantine Books, 1998.

Malory, Sir Thomas. *Le Morte d'Arthur*. New York: Random House, 1994.

Manzoni, Alessandro. *The Betrothed*. Translated by Bruce Penman. New York: Penguin USA, 1984.

Milton, John. *Paradise Lost and Other Poems*. New York: New American Library, 1996.

———. *Paradise Lost and Paradise Regained*. New York: New American Library, 1989.

Pirandello, Luigi. *Naked Masks: Five Plays*. Edited by Eric Bentley. New York: E. P. Dutton, 1991.

Pound, Ezra. *The Cantos of Ezra Pound*. New York: New Directions Paperbook, 1996.

Shakespeare, William. *As You Like It*. Edited by Albert Gilman. New York: Signet Classic Shakespeare, New American Library, 1998.

———. *The Complete Works: The Oxford Shakespeare: Compact Edition*. Edited by Stanley Wells and Gary Taylor. New York: Oxford University Press, 1988.

———. *The Tragedy of King Lear*. Edited by Russell Fraser. New York: Signet Classic Shakespeare, New American Library, 1989.

Sir Gawain and the Green Knight. Translated into modern English by Marie Borroff. New York: W. W. Norton and Company, 1967.

The Song of Roland. Translated by Dorothy L. Sayers. New York: Viking Press, 1957.

Svevo, Italo. *The Confessions of Zeno*. Translated by Beryl De Zoete. New York: Vintage Books, 1989.

Swift, Jonathan. *Gulliver's Travels*. New York: Modern Library, 1996.

Tales from the Thousand and One Nights. Translated by N. J. Dawood. New York: Viking Press, 1973.

Tillyard, E. M. W. *The Elizabethan World Picture*. New York: Random House, 1959.

Tindall, William York. *A Reader's Guide to Finnegans Wake*. Syracuse, N.Y.: Syracuse University Press, 1996.

Verga, Giovanni. *The House by the Medlar Tree*. Translated by Raymond Rosenthal. Berkeley: University of California Press, 1984.

———. *Mastro-Don Gesualdo*. New York: Hippocrene Books, 1985.

White, Richard, ed. *King Arthur in Legend and History*. London: Routledge, 1998.

Wolfram von Eschenbach. *Parzival*. Translated by A. T. Hatto. New York: Penguin USA, 1980.

Web site:
Great Books of the Western World
http://www.mirror.org/books/gb.home.html

Music/Dance

Carse, Adam. *History of Orchestration*. New York: Dover Publications, 1935.

Copland, Aaron. *What to Listen for in Music*. New York: Mentor Books, 1989.

Greskovic, Robert. *Ballet 101: A Complete Guide to Learning and Loving the Ballet*. New York: Hyperion, 1998.

Jenkins, J. S. "The voice of the castrato." *Lancet*. 351 (June 20, 1998): 1877–80.

Machlis, Joseph, and Kristine Forney, eds. *The Enjoyment of Music: An Introduction to Perceptive Listening—Chronological*. 7th ed. New York: W. W. Norton and Company, 1995.

Vaganova, Agrippina. *Basic Principles of Classical Ballet: Russian Ballet Technique*. Rev. ed. New York: Dover Publications, 1975.

Compact discs

The Mighty Five

Balakirev: *Symphony No. 2, Tamara*/Hyperion.
  Yevgeny Svetlanov/Philharmonia Orchestra.

Borodin: *Symphonies Nos. 1–3, Prince Igor Overture and Dances, In the Steppes of Central Asia, etc.*/Deutsche Grammophon (2 CDs).
  Neeme Järvi/Gothenburg Symphony Orchestra.

Mussorgsky, Borodin: *Pictures at an Exhibition, Polovtsian Dances, etc.*/BMG Classics.
  Eugene Ormandy/Philadelphia Orchestra.

Mussorgsky, Borodin, Rimsky-Korsakov, Balakirev, etc.: *Orchestral Pictures from Russia*/Melodiya.
  Yevgeny Svetlanov/USSR Symphony Orchestra.

Rimsky-Korsakov: *Great Orchestral Works*/Philips Duo.
  David Zinman/Rotterdam Philharmonic Orchestra (2 CDs).

Rimsky-Korsakoff, Borodin, Cui, Mussorgsky, Balakirev: *Russian Piano Music of "The Mighty Handful"*/Chandos.
  Margaret Fingerhut (piano).

Rimsky-Korsakov, Rachmaninov, Mussorgsky, Balakirev: *Russian Masterpieces*/IMP Masters.
　Djong Yu/Philharmonia Orchestra.

Les Six
Honegger: *Le Roi David*/Erato Hommage.
　Charles Dutoit/French Instrumental Ensemble.
Milhaud: *Chamber Music for Winds and Piano*/Orfeo.
　Aurele Nicolet (flute), Oleg Maisenberg (piano), etc.
Milhaud, Poulenc, Ibert: *la création du monde, Le boeuf sur le toit, Les biches, etc.*/Chandos.
　Yan Pascal Tortelier/Ulster Orchestra.
Poulenc: *Complete a capella Sacred Choral Music*/Conifer.
　Richard Marlow/The Choir of Trinity College, Cambridge.
Poulenc, Auric, Tailleferre, Honegger, Durey, Milhaud: *Le Groupe des Six Play Poulenc, Auric, Tailleferre, etc.*/ADDA.
　Loic Poulain (flute), Daria Hovora (piano)/Le Groupe des Six.
Poulenc, Milhaud, Saint-Saëns: *French Chamber Music*/RCA Victor.
　André Previn (piano), Ani Kavafian (violin), etc.

Philosophy (Postclassical)

Descartes, René. *The Essential Descartes*. Edited by Margaret D. Wilson. New York: New American Library, 1969.
Freud, Sigmund. *The Ego and the Id*. Translated by James Strachey. New York: W. W. Norton and Company, 1962.
―――. *The Interpretation of Dreams*. Translated by James Strachey. New York: Avon, 1983.
―――. *An Outline of Psycho-Analysis*. Translated by James Strachey. New York: W. W. Norton and Company, 1989.
Hegel, Georg Wilhelm Friedrich. *Phenomenology of Spirit*. New York: Oxford University Press, 1979.
Hyman, Arthur, and James J. Walsh, eds. *Philosophy in the Middle Ages: The Christian, Islamic, and Jewish Traditions*. 2nd ed. Indianapolis: Hackett Publishing Company, 1983.
Machiavelli, Niccolò. *The Prince*. Translated by George Bull. New York: Penguin USA, 1979.
Marx, Karl, and Friedrich Engels. *The Communist Manifesto*. New York: Viking Press, 1985.

Nietzsche, Friedrich. *Twilight of the Idols and the Anti-Christ.* Translated by R. J. Hollingdale. New York: Viking Press, 1990.

Vico, Giambattista. *The Autobiography of Giambattista Vico.* Translated by Max Harold Fisch and Thomas Goddard Bergin. Ithaca, N.Y.: Cornell University Press, 1963.

————. *The New Science of Giambattista Vico.* Translated by Thomas Goddard Bergin and Max Harold Fisch. Ithaca, N.Y.: Cornell University Press, 1984.

Voltaire. *Philosophical Dictionary.* Translated by Theodore Besterman. New York: Viking Press, 1984.

Religion

Allen, Charlotte. "Q: The Search for a No-Frills Jesus." *Atlantic Monthly.* 280 (December 1996): 51–68.

Aquinas, Saint Thomas. *Summa Theologiae: A Concise Translation.* Allen, Tex.: Christian Classics, 1997.

Augustine, Saint. *The City of God: An Abridged Version.* Translated by Gerald G. Walsh, et al. New York: Image Books, 1958.

————. *The Confessions of St. Augustine.* Translated by John K. Ryan. New York: Image Books, 1960.

The Bhagavad Gita. Translated by Juan Mascaró. New York: Viking Penguin, 1962.

The Bible. *Authorized King James Version.* New York: Oxford University Press, 1997.

————. *The New American Bible for Catholics: Standard Edition.* Collegeville, Minn.: Liturgical Press, 1988.

————. *The New Jerusalem Bible: Reader's Edition.* New York: Doubleday, 1990.

Bloom, Harold. *The American Religion: The Emergence of the Post-Christian Nation.* New York: Touchstone Books, 1993.

Buddha (Siddhartha Gautama). *Teachings of the Compassionate Buddha.* Edited by Edwin A. Burtt. New York: New American Library/Dutton, 1990.

Gould, Stephen Jay. *Questioning the Millennium: A Rationalist's Guide to a Precisely Arbitrary Countdown.* New York: Harmony Books, 1997.

Maimonides, Moses. *Guide for the Perplexed.* Translated by M. Friedlander. New York: Dover Publications, 1950.

Mohammed. *Al-Qur'an [The Koran]: A Contemporary Translation.*

Translated by Ahmed Ali. 2nd rev. ed. Princeton: Princeton University Press, 1988.

Roberts, Paul William. *In Search of the Birth of Jesus: The Real Journey of the Magi.* New York: Riverhead Books, 1996.

The Upanishads. Translated by Juan Mascaró. New York: Viking Press, 1965.

Web site:

New Advent (works of Catholic content including full text of *The Catholic Encyclopedia* and Thomas Aquinas' *Summa Theologica)*
http://www.sni.net/advent/

Science

Feynman, Richard P. *QED: The Strange Theory of Light and Matter.* Princeton: Princeton University Press, 1988.

————. *Six Easy Pieces: Essentials of Physics Explained by Its Most Brilliant Teacher.* Reading, Mass.: Addison-Wesley Publishing Company, 1996.

Hawking, Stephen W. *A Brief History of Time: From the Big Bang to Black Holes.* New York: Bantam Books, 1990.

Kuhn, Thomas S. *The Structure of Scientific Revolutions.* 3rd ed. Chicago: University of Chicago Press, 1996.

Liss, Tony M., and Paul L. Tipton. "The Discovery of the Top Quark." *Scientific American.* 277 (September 1997): 54–59.

Pauling, Linus. *General Chemistry.* New York: Dover Publications, 1989.

Rothman, Tony. *Instant Physics: From Aristotle to Einstein, and Beyond.* New York: Fawcett Books, 1995.

Web sites:

Astronomy
The Nine Planets (University of Arizona)
http://seds.lpl.arizona.edu/nineplanets/nineplanets/nineplanets.html
Planetary Sciences at the National Space Science Data Center (NASA's archive)
http://nssdc.gsfc.nasa.gov/planetary/
Welcome to the Planets (California Institute of Technology/NASA)
http://pds.jpl.nasa.gov/planets

General Science
Martindale's: The Reference Desk
http://www-sci.lib.uci.edu/~martindale/Ref.html

Taxonomy
University of Michigan Museum of Zoology's Animal Diversity Web
http://www.oit.itd.umich.edu/bio108/

INDEX

534

About the Authors

Peter D'Epiro has published a book and several articles on Ezra Pound's *Cantos,* a book of translations of African-American poetry into Italian, and rhymed verse translations of parts of Dante's *Inferno.* After receiving his B.A. and M.A. from Queens College (CUNY), he earned a Ph.D. in English from Yale University. He works as an editor for the medical journal *Patient Care,* for which he has written more than seventy feature articles. He has a grown son and lives with his wife in Ridgewood, New Jersey.

Mary Desmond Pinkowish also works as an editor for *Patient Care,* for which she has written numerous feature articles over the last decade. After obtaining a B.A. from Trinity College in Hartford, Connecticut, where she studied biology and art history, she received a master's degree from Yale University. Ms. Pinkowish lives in Larchmont, New York, with her husband and two children.